With Ever Joyful Hearts

Essays on Liturgy and Music Honoring Marion J. Hatchett

J. Neil Alexander
Editor

 CHURCH

Church Publishing Incorporated, New York

Library of Congress Cataloging-in-Publication Data

With ever joyful hearts : essays on liturgy and music : honoring
    Marion J. Hatchett / J. Neil Alexander, editor.
        p.   cm.
    Includes bibliographical references (p.   ).
    ISBN 0-89869-321-7 (pbk.)
    1. Episcopal Church–Liturgy. 2. Church music–Episcopal Church.
    I. Alexander, J. Neil, 1954–   . II. Hatchett, Marion J.
BX5940.W58   1999
264'.03–dc21   99-17532
                                                            CIP

Church Publishing Incorporated
445 Fifth Avenue
New York NY 10016

5 4 3 2 1

Contents

With Ever
Joyful Hearts

Introduction

THE ESSAYS IN THIS VOLUME celebrate the distinguished life and ministry of Marion Josiah Hatchett–a tireless scholar, a devoted teacher of liturgy and music, a faithful presbyter of the Episcopal Church. Those who have contributed to this book include those with whom he has studied, his own students, and a variety of colleagues in Episcopal seminaries and various ecumenical centers of theological education. Two are doctoral students who offer their contribution to this work, representing all those whose study of the liturgical tradition, particularly as the Episcopal Church has received it, would have been quite different without Dr. Hatchett's careful work to guide their way.

Marion Hatchett is a scholar of wide-ranging interests. Because of his substantial commentary of the American Book of Common Prayer 1979, his history of the making of the first Prayer Book in America, and his large number of essays related to various aspects of the prayer book tradition, many have come to think of Hatchett as "Mr. Prayer Book." He would, of course, find such an accolade highly embarrassing. Hatchett has taught us by his example that collegial and collaborative effort is required of all of us in service to the church's worship. He is a naturally unselfish man who is as free with his scholarly insights and pastoral wisdom as anyone I know. To limit our conception of Hatchett's work to the study of the Prayer Book, as important as that is, would be to miss the quite important contributions he has made to the study of hymnody and church music, Christian initiation, Eucharist, church architecture, and liturgical-pastoral theology to mention only the most obvious.

The students of the School of Theology of the University of the South have enjoyed Professor Hatchett for thirty years. In classroom lectures, liturgics practica, music rehearsals, rota groups, advanced degree seminars, and tutorials, the students have encountered a man who is passionate about his subject, faithful to the tradition, in love with the church, and genuinely devoted to them—the future deacons, presbyters, and bishops of the Episcopal Church. He has offered them not the dying vision of choral evensong in a tired cathedral of another time and place, but of faithful liturgical prayer and durable music that is vital to the life and health of the sorts of parish churches most of his students will serve in their ministries.

But Dr. Hatchett's influence reaches far beyond Sewanee. His writings have instructed more than a generation of parish clergy. Church musicians and liturgical animateurs depend upon his planning guides, liturgical and scriptural indices, and other resources. Many unsuspecting parishioners, marveling at what wonderful hymns were sung at the Sunday Eucharist, might be surprised to discover that the little professor, tucked away in the hills of East Tennessee, almost surely inspired the choices!

When speaking of Marion Hatchett it is easy to focus on his contributions to liturgical studies and the church's worship and too easily overlook his disciplined devotion as a presbyter of the Episcopal Church. As one gets to know Marion personally, one begins to understand that his scholarship is not for the sake of itself, nor is his professorship simply a job to be done. At the heart of it all is Marion's personal and spiritual formation as a presbyter in Christ's church. Underneath the rubrics there is a pastor unceasingly amazed by grace—*in his own life and in the lives of all*—a servant devoted before all else to the Gospel of Jesus.

At the time this volume was conceived, it was decided not to organize the essays around a common theme, but simply to ask the writers, all familiar with Dr. Hatchett's work, to contribute an essay—academic, pastoral, or reflective—that would be a fitting tribute to a colleague who has served us well in so wide a variety of ways. Not surprisingly, each essay makes a vital connection to the work of Marion Hatchett, some by drawing directly upon his work, others by contributing to conversations in which he participates. One group of essays centers around Christian initiation, particularly confirmation. (The fact that several essayists, independent of each other, chose to write on confirmation may signal, at the very least, that there is more work to come for liturgical scholars, sacramental theologians, ritual specialists, and pastoral theologians.) Another group of essays concerns hymnology, another of Dr. Hatchett's research interests. Essays on aspects the American prayer book tradition, liturgical evangelism, preaching, and sacramental theology broaden the scope of the volume, but only begin to capture the breadth of Dr. Hatchett's own work and interests.

A work such as this requires significant support from a variety of sources. Without the efforts of Mr. Frank Hemlin, Publisher, and Mr. Frank

J. Neil Alexander

Tedeschi, Managing Editor, a book of this scope would have been impossible. The essayists took time from other projects, many during an already busy summer, and not only created fine contributions to the book, but also endured my frequent cajoling about deadlines. Mr. John Runkle, a senior in the School of Theology, with characteristic good humor, double-checked all manner of details and kept the project moving forward. Ms. Shawn Horton, faculty secretary of the School of Theology, gave her computer expertise, her editorial skills, and her willingness to go the extra distance. To all of them I am grateful and in their debt.

Pulling together such a variety of writing styles—variant spellings, forms of documentation, organizational formats—is no easy task. An effort has been made to conform these details for a uniform presentation throughout the book. At certain points, however, particular usages seem to have an internal logic of their own and to force them into the overall style of the book would have a negative impact on a particular author's work. I trust that I have been faithful in bringing the style of the book under control without unduly tampering with the distinguished voices of the essayists.

Finally, I want to pay personal tribute to Marion Hatchett. For almost two decades I have known him as teacher, mentor, colleague, fellow presbyter, and cherished friend. My first teaching position was to cover his liturgics classes and chapel music duties while he was on a well-deserved sabbatical leave in the early 1980s. What an awesome task! But more valuable than anything else that term were the late-into-the-night conversations on the Hatchetts' back porch with Carolyn and Marion: talking liturgics and church music, sipping Tennessee whiskey, and being regaled with a sort of oral presentation of the "Sewanee tradition" of Anglican and Episcopal history. I am not sure that I have ever learned so much in so short a period while having such a good time doing it! The memories of those days help me to remember that no matter what happens in my classroom or in my study, the most important work might well be what happens on my back porch. Thanks, Marion!

J. Neil Alexander
Sewanee, Tennessee
The Feast of St. Luke 1998

Odium Politicum
Odium Liturgicum:
Sectionalism and the First
American Prayer Book

Paul V. Marshall

M ARION HATCHETT'S STUDY of the American church's first Book of Common Prayer alludes in several places to sectional differences in the church's post-revolutionary years. My own investigations of Bishop Samuel Seabury's career as bishop and liturgist confirm the importance of these differences, which were even more profound when viewed from the North. They seem naturally to group them under three heads: life before the Revolution, revolutionary experience, and the common view of southern clergy. Each topic will be explored primarily from Seabury's point of view.

Pre-Revolutionary Experience

Seabury's differences from principal figures in the post-revolutionary church are pronounced. They are so in part because Anglican experience in New England, and particularly in Connecticut, was very little like that of members of the Church of England living in the "southern" colonies. Outside of New England, Anglicans had the upper hand to one degree or another, and Maryland, Virginia and South Carolina had even transplanted the system of English parish life to the colonial setting.[1] Although political rights granted to dissenters varied among the southern colonies, most Anglicans lived in colonies where there was at least some toleration in matters of worship, and in many of those places they had preeminence. Only in Virginia was the

Church of England the sole legally recognized religious body, but even there *de facto* toleration of other Protestants was of long-standing, and was certainly unremarkable by the third quarter of the eighteenth century.[2]

If south of Connecticut Anglicans had at least a level playing field, and often enjoyed considerable advantage, the case was quite different in New England. There life was sometimes made quite difficult for Churchmen, as Congregationalists and Anglicans alike termed those loyal to the English establishment.[3] Non-Congregationalists were to suffer some civil disabilities in Connecticut until 1818, when the federal government forced that state to adopt a formal constitution in place of the Standing Order.[4] In that year a non–Congregationalist for the first time delivered the Election Day sermon. Harry Crosswell, rector of Trinity Church in New Haven, was by no means unwilling to highlight the radical cleavage between church and state that had taken place. He used on that occasion prayers from the Book of Common Prayer and from Seabury's state prayers, and took as his text, "Render unto Caesar the things that are Caesar's and to God the things that are God's." Puritan antidisestablishmentarianism died hard, however, and it was only some years later that Connecticut and Massachusetts abandoned state support of Congregationalist churches.

Those days were to come long after Seabury's death, however. The notion that the "Pilgrims" and their successors had a commitment to religious liberty for anyone other than themselves is an American myth that seems incapable of dying. Generally speaking, their view of religious liberty for others was "free liberty to keep away from us."[5] Connecticut's laws imposing religious taxation and strictly regulating Sabbath observance were considered extremist by the Congregationalists of other New England colonies.[6] In the matter of maintaining orthodoxy, New Haven, during its time as a free-standing colony, was somewhat tolerant, however, and would let a Quaker preacher go with a warning after a first offense. A second offense, however, meant branding on the face with an H (for heretic), and imprisonment until the preacher had worked off the cost of expulsion from the colony. The truly persistent were to have their tongues bored through with red-hot pokers.[7]

Toleration of Anglicanism had been imposed by the Crown in Massachusetts. As more and more of Connecticut's citizens chose to follow non-Congregationalist ways, it adopted in 1708 an Act of Toleration that excused them from Sabbath attendance in Congregationalist churches, but at first Anglicans were still required to pay the taxes levied to support the Puritan establishment. In the early days of this uneasy peace, a good deal of sniping at Anglicans took place, a favorite assault being the state imposition of days of fasting to coincide with major feasts of the Anglican liturgical calendar, a practice that was still complained of late in the century. It is to be remembered that not even Christmas was observed in Connecticut. Failure to observe the fasts was punished by fines or imprisonment.[8]

That lay people loyal to the Church of England would want to come to Connecticut was thinkable to Congregationalists, and they did come, from England and from other colonies. That members of their own fold should leave it for Anglicanism was not as easy to understand, and such defections provoked very strong feeling. There is no more striking example of this reaction than that of the sister of Richard Mansfield of Derby: when he went to England for Anglican ordination, she prayed that he might be lost at sea.[9]

That such a charged atmosphere, together with the use of corporal punishment, taxation, and imprisonment in religious matters, was not unprecedented in the Anglican mother country is not the point here, nor is our burden the discrediting of the Puritan societies erected in New England. These details are important only in beginning to explain why the New England participants in the formation of the Episcopal Church were usually so much more conservative than their southern counterparts. That explanation begins with the suggestion that those who suffer attack or disabilities because of their religious affiliation would have a conservative attitude towards, and strong allegiance to, their religion's distinguishing principles. Those distinguishing principles were to be in New England exactly what had been the center of debate in England since Elizabeth's time: episcopacy and liturgy. The debate came to a head in a way that has kept Anglican-Congregationalist tensions in Connecticut alive in many memories to the present day.

Yale College had been founded in 1701, and began operation in 1702 to provide the colony with clergy, physicians, and jurists. Together with Harvard it produced most of the clergy working in Connecticut in Seabury's day, Congregationalist or Anglican. In 1722 its rector (president) was Timothy Cutler, who had been brought from Massachusetts to Stratford, Connecticut, because he was one of the best preachers in New England. Connecticut church leaders hoped that his eloquence would counter the attractiveness of Anglicanism to increasing numbers of Congregationalist lay people. At Yale, Cutler and the college tutor, Daniel Browne, read and discussed theology with local Congregationalist clergy, including Samuel Johnson, later president of King's (Columbia) College. Johnson had been studying the Book of Common Prayer since at least 1716, and was using selections from it in his worship services in West Haven. The practices of the other members of the group are not known, but on the "Dark Day," September 12, 1722, Cutler ended his prayers at Yale with a phrase from Psalm 106:48 that signaled his own departure from the passivity of public prayer in Congregationalism: "and let all the people say, Amen." Anglican congregations said their Amens to liturgical prayers aloud; Congregationalist assemblies did not audibly join the minister's prayer. There could have been few clearer signals that Cutler had changed loyalties.[10] On the next day the college trustees met with Cutler, Brown, Johnson, John Hart (East Guilford, now Madison), Samuel Whittlesey (Wallingford), Jared Eliot (Killingworth), and James Wetmore (North Haven). Sometime later the seven "Yale Apostates" gave in to the relentless pressure to communicate their sentiments in writing:

> Having represented to you the difficulties which we labour under, in relation to our continuance out of the visible communion of an Episcopal Church, and a state of seeming opposition thereto, either as private Christians, or as officers, and so being insisted on by some of you (after our repeated declinings of it) that we should sum up our case in writing, we do (though with great reluctance, fearing the consequence of it) submit to and comply with it, and signify to you that some of us doubt the validity, and the rest are more persuaded of the invalidity of the Presbyterian ordination, in opposition to the Episcopal; and should be heartily thankful to God and man, if we may receive from them satisfaction therein, and shall be willing to embrace your good councils and instructions in relation to this important affair, as far as God shall direct and dispose us to it.[11]

There was not to be any dialog on the nature of apostolic ministry, however. The trustees instead voted "to excuse the Rev. Mr. Cutler from all further service as Rector of Yale College."[12] It may be an overstatement to say that "this event shook Congregationalism throughout New England like an earthquake, and filled its friends with terror and apprehension,"[13] but it is not much of one, and ink was to be spilled for decades in the effort to pick up the pieces. At least one young man decided that, in the wake of the tumult, Yale could not be depended on for an orthodox education, and left to study divinity at Harvard. He was Samuel Seabury, the father of our subject. Cambridge was not to prove a safer haven for him, however, for Seabury was ultimately to follow the Yale Apostates into Anglican orders.

The Apostates, like the many Anglican clergy who subsequently experienced conversion to Anglicanism during or after their Yale years, were to be committed to conservative or high church principles regarding liturgy and episcopacy in the days of the Episcopal Church's formation; those principles were, after all, what they had converted for. By and large they had become missionaries of the conservative Society for the Propagation of the Gospel in Foreign Parts (SPG). The SPG, founded in 1701, was to follow the British flag around the globe, but its first efforts were in the Americas.[14] Some of the missionaries of the "Venerable Society" gave a good deal of energy to polemical writing, particularly in New England.[15]

While a system of resident "commissaries" was attempted to provide quasi-episcopal oversight in some of the southern states, the New England clergy received direction in a general way from the SPG, and ultimately from the

8

Bishop of London, who had charge of all colonial clergy. Both before 1776 and to the end of the Revolution, SPG missionaries were at the front of the movement for a resident bishop in the New World.[16] The request for a bishop was not just theoretical or sentimental. Besides the obvious inconvenience and mortal danger involved in sailing to England for ordination,[17] lack of immediate episcopal presence or ecclesiastical courts left priests and lay people in suspended animation upon occasion, as the following letter from Jeremiah Leaming to the secretary of the SPG so well illustrates:

> I desire to lay the following before the Lord Bishop of London, and His Grace the Archbishop of Canterbury, and beg you to acquaint me with their determination. The case is this: There was a sailor married a woman, and soon after went to sea, in the last war, [vs. the French] was taken by the enemy and put in prison. Soon after his captain was released, and supposed the sailor to be dying, as he was very sick when he left him. When the captain came home, he reported the sailor was dead: the wife, supposing she was a widow, married three years after. Six years after she was married, and ten years after the sailor leaving her, she received a letter from him, being the first notice she had of his being alive, though he had been nine years in Jamaica, and neglected to write. Three years after she received this letter, the sailor came here; but he would not live with her, as she had children by the last man, and none by him. It is now four years since he went from hence, and has not been heard of. Now the man and woman who live here, desire to be admitted to the Lord's Supper, and are very worthy people, except the affair above mentioned. I beg the advice of my spiritual rulers, that I may know whether I ought to admit them or not. If you can send it soon, you will greatly oblige.[18]

Did these missionaries understand themselves to be subversives? They could hardly have done so, for they were never injected into a locale to start a church by wooing members away from the Congregationalist establishment, but were sent in response to a request from an already-gathered congregation of Anglicans. Part of the umbrage taken at their presence comes from the title "missionary." When Anglicans responded to Puritan outrage at the presence of missionaries by pointing out that their mission was to congregations already in place, the reply came that this could not be the case because only a bigot would have scruples over attending the worship services of the Congregationalists.[19] Many settlers who had come to New England in the 1630s were non-separatist Puritans, continuing what they considered to be the best parts of England's established religion. The sentiment that the colonial Puritan establishment continued the Church of England did not survive to be employed in the eighteenth century debates, but the idea that it was the true church did, although this claim was also made by American colonists of many other persuasions as well. Despite this competition, more than once has it been observed that among a wide range of colonial Protestants a rudimentary kind of ecumenical consensus existed, namely that the Church of England was second best.

Nonetheless, the Anglican presence grew. It grew in part because it provided an alternative to what some considered the excesses of the Great Awakening. Perhaps surprisingly, it grew during the Revolution, particularly in Connecticut. Charles Inglis attributed this growth to the Connecticut clergy's loyalty and integrity:

> Their adherence to the dictates of conscience by persevering in loyalty and preaching the gospel unadulterated with politics, raised the esteem and respect even of their enemies, whilst the pulpits of dissenters resounded with scarcely anything else than the furious politics of the times, which occasioned disgust in the more serious and thinking. The consequence is that many serious dissenters have actually joined the Church of England.[20]

Almost a century before, however, as Anglican presence had begun to grow in Boston, the Congregationalist establishment tightened its myth of origins. Cotton Mather uttered what has become the classic statement of this position in 1690, hitting out at bishops, the Prayer Book, and the surplice:

> We came into the wilderness because we would worship God without episcopacy, that Common Prayer, and those unwarrantable ceremonies, which the land of our Fathers' sepulchers has been defiled with . . . . Let us not so much as touch the unclean thing, or hide so much as a rag or pin of a Babylonish garment with us.[21]

What was worship without Prayer Book, bishop and surplice like? Was there in fact a liturgical or sacramental consensus shared by all New Englanders that would have shaped young Seabury's mind and necessitated his rethinking those subjects entirely when he met his Scottish consecrators?[22] The answer is a nuanced no.

One point of agreement is perhaps unexpected: laity in both Anglican and Congregationalist assemblies knew what the service would be like, although the Anglicans knew both structure and text, while the Congregationalists could anticipate structure only. This foreknowledge came from the fact that, although the Congregationalist establishment worshiped without a Prayer Book, there was little liturgical anarchy among his New England neighbors in Seabury's youth. That is, the shape of the Congregationalist service was not of the minister's design, as it might well be today, but followed the "form and order"[23] with enough rigidity that William Blacktree is remembered as complaining that he "had left England to escape the power of the Lord's Bishops, but found himself in the hands of the Lord's Brethren."[24] New England produced more than forms of worship: the Ainsworth psalter and the Sternhold and Hopkins psalter had been replaced with one of America's first important literary works, the *Bay Psalm Book*.

However, the fact of predictable form does not make for consensus, when the contents of the form were significantly different. Where an Anglican would know the words of each prayer ahead of time, and could participate in them through that knowledge, a Congregationalist neighbor had to go wherever the minister's extemporaneous prayer went, and the prayer could cover significant ground, as extemporaneous prayer was known to go on for more than two hours.[25] To the Congregationalist used to such a prayer, the collects, General Thanksgiving, and even the Prayer for the Whole State of Christ's Church in the Prayer Book services must have seemed a sparse and dilettantish stab at praying, while to the Anglicans the minister's prayer in their neighbors' churches must have seemed something of a rant or a display of ego.

For Horton Davies, the fundamental difference between Puritans and Anglicans can be detected in the refusal of the former to observe a liturgical calendar. He locates this refusal not in a simple disagreement over whether such observances were superstitious, but in the core issues of spiritual formation. For him, the refusal to commemorate the past, even events in the life of Christ, let alone events in the lives of the saints, puts all the emphasis on present day sanctification. "Puritans, in their type of spirituality did not, like Roman Catholics or Anglicans, aim directly at the imitation of Christ. Rather they recapitulated the story of Everyman Adam, from temptation and fall, through reconciliation, restoration, and renewal."[26] Davies believes that basic understanding of the sacraments themselves was also quite different in the two communities. At first glance, what they had in common obscures their difference, and that common terminology is the use of the word covenant. Covenant terminology is used differently with regard to sacramental worship, however. When it came to attendance at the Lord's Supper, Anglicans found in holy communion the repair of breached covenant, and it is arguable that the 1552 rite on which 1662 was based was in fact a structured experience of justification by grace. For the Congregationalists, the sacrament is God's seal on the covenant, and also the sign that as communicants we belong to it and are living its terms.[27] Accordingly, "visible sainthood" was required both for church membership and for admission to holy communion.[28] Fear of attendance at the Lord's Supper in an unregenerate state brought terror to many Congregationalists.[29] This had the result of producing a fairly small group of communicants in each congregation, who often became the identified elite.

Puritan worship had done away with sponsors at Baptism; parents brought their own children to the font, relying on the scriptural assurance that "the promise is to you and your children." (Acts 2:39) The precondition for baptism that parents be regenerate led to a crisis: what was to become of the children of parents who could not report an experience of regeneration? Were they to grow up as heathen? The Ministerial Conventions of 1657 and 1662 produced the "Half-Way Covenant," by which parents who were believers, even if not regenerate and communicants, could bring their children to baptism and pass church membership on to them.

The great sacrament of unity was another point of division. Congregationalist discussion of the Lord's Supper came to fall chiefly under three heads. Some held it to be entirely a memorial in the psychological sense, of benefit only if the recipient's attitude were right. Others, led by Solomon Stoddard, believed (as Wesley would) that attendance at the supper was in itself a "converting ordinance," participation in which could help bring about regeneration. A third view implied some mystical presence of Christ, but like the "converting ordinance" view, it implied no presence of Christ's body or blood.[30]

Davies doubts that there was a general "sacramental renaissance" between 1680 and 1720 among New England Congregationalists. He supports this contention by appeal first to all the literature of the time that laments poor attendance at the sacrament, but also notes that the "converting ordinance" theory reduced holy communion to a sermon. Time was not kind to Stoddard's theory, and his grandson, Jonathan Edwards, was one of the clergy who were to repudiate his views, returning to a strict requirement of regeneration before communion.

Davies's evaluation of the developed Congregationalist eucharistic theology in New England is balanced, and helps to show how different it was from that of Anglicans:

> In the case of the Lord's Supper, the memorial aspect is never forgotten, nor that of deep thanksgiving, which is true eucharist. The aspect of mystery is often overshadowed by excessive pedagogical explanation . . . but it is never wholly lost. Increasingly, as the seventeenth century ends, the sense of the banquet shared with Christ is dominant, though rarely is there any adumbration of the eschatological banquet in eternity. The sense of the communion of saints is weak . . . . The renewal of Christian hope in life after death is not strongly stressed in the rite (the Crucifixion overshadows the Resurrection . . .) nor is there any sense of the sacrifice of the Church as linked with the Sacrifice of Christ . . . . The Communion never ceased to be a spur to Christian ethics and a stimulus to sanctification.[31]

Converts to Anglicanism cannot be said to have brought much of the Congregationalist view of the sacraments with them. Regarding baptism, regeneration, and church membership, they celebrated a rite redolent of the language of sacramental regeneration. Nothing could be clearer than the priest's declaration after the actual baptism, "seeing then that this child is regenerate . . . " The Prayer Book view was that God acted in baptism and grafted the newly baptized into the church; membership depended on God's gift rather than individual experience of regeneration.

More to the point that is critical for anyone assessing Seabury's eucharistic theology, and particularly his behavior from 1785 through 1789, it is to be noted that Anglicans spoke of holy communion in very different terms than did other New Englanders. Where their neighbors may have been terrified to receive the sacrament because of uncertainty as to their regeneration, the Prayer Book invited Anglicans to "Draw near with faith, and take this sacrament to your comfort." This invitation was followed by a confession of sins, the absolution, and the recitation of the "Comfortable Words" (scriptural passages of assurance about forgiveness). Then the eucharistic dialog continued, "lift up your hearts." Receiving communion was the sealing of the breached covenant's repair. It was precisely for what may be considered the "unregenerate" aspect of each life that the 1552–1662 communion service was designed.

This contrast in the theology of worship may be seen in the acknowledged leader of the Connecticut clergy, Samuel Johnson. He oversaw the training of so many seeking Anglican orders, including young Samuel Seabury, that one historian has termed him a "one-man seminary."[32] There are several studies of Johnson, the most persuasive of which is that of Louis Weil.[33] Weil saw the Connecticut converts in particular as part of the "Arminian threat to Puritan orthodoxy" because they give due place to reason and placed emphasis "upon the importance of the sacraments for the spiritual growth of the believer." In him, and in the students he prepared, we can see not only the differences between Anglicans and Puritans writ large, but also the high church principles that set off the New England clergy from many of their "southern" counterparts.

For Johnson, liturgy itself was part of the process by which people are sanctified, and this emphasis on the process of "nurturing virtue" rather than instantaneous conversion is an important part of what was different about Anglicanism. Besides taking the common Anglican position that knowledge of what will be said in the service aids devotion, Johnson understands the assembly itself to be of theological importance, both in terms of the experience of union, and in engagement of the senses in stirring up and recreating the heart:

> For not only the eye, as I observed before, but also the ear would affect the heart, and it would not only animate a spirit of devotion towards God, but a spirit of charity towards one another, to find ourselves surrounded with our Christian neighbors and brethren, all joining together, and according to the pattern of the holy Apostles (Acts 4:24), lift up our voices with one accord in the prayers and praises offered up to Almighty God. My neighbor's voice will be so far from interrupting that it will rather animate my devotion, and give it the more life and spirit.[34]

Johnson goes on to say that this union with other worshipers transcends the bounds of the local assembly, connecting us with other believers in other places. Johnson further insisted that the senses were to be used in worship, and accordingly insisted that aesthetics had a place in considerations of worship. In "The Beauty of Holiness," he argues that the "perfection in form" of the liturgy is an experience of beauty that brings us into contact with the Holy, to which we respond in adoration. Because beauty participates in the Holy, it gives access to the Holy.[35]

In addition to Johnson's development of a liturgical aesthetic, Weil finds him to have "synthesized Caroline theology," passing on to his students what may be considered the classic high church position on worship and the sacraments. Like most writers of his time, Johnson employed the notion of covenant freely, but he understands the sacraments to "convey . . . benefits of Covenant grace," rather than seeing them as signs of already-accomplished conversion. In terms of the eucharist, "convey" implies that faith receives, but does not create, the benefits of communion.[36] In "The Oeconomy of the Redemption of Man by Jesus Christ" (1727), Johnson sees the eucharist as renewing and ratifying the covenant, language which could be bent to the Puritan approach, had he not also moved on to speak of the growing soul that "partakes of the Body and Blood" of Christ.[37] For Johnson the eucharist is a constant commemoration "so that the transaction may be represented on earth while it is performed in heaven."[38] Here the high church notion of Christ eternally presenting his sacrifice to the Father while the church below re-presents it, is unmistakable, and separates Johnson's students from any Congregationalist theories. It also could distinguish them from some Anglicans of the time, but not many: even for the "central" churchmanship of Waterland, "commemoration" implies the present link between the earthly eucharist and the sacrifice "which our Lord himself commemorates above."

The Anglicans in Connecticut could be distinguished from many of their southern counterparts by their relationship to the state and by their fairly uniformly high church views. Those views of the church and its ministry meant that they, along with SPG missionaries in New York and New Jersey, were the principal source of requests to England for a resident episcopate, while southern churches experimented with other means of governance, including commissaries and direct control by the colonial government. Did Anglicans seeking an episcopate for New England imagine themselves as a fifth column, intent on overthrowing egalitarian Puritan democracies and planting government by prince-bishops in their place?

The first response to such a question must be another question: were New England colonies in fact egalitarian societies? Carl Bridenbaugh thought they were, and thought that Anglicans looked down on the inhabitants of those colonies as "republican boors."[39] Bridenbaugh dismisses all Anglican proposals for a "purely spiritual" episcopate as "clerical double-talk" meant to disguise the real intentions of those he repeatedly describes as the "invaders" of New

England, whether or not they were born there.[40] Bridenbaugh apparently wrote in liturgical and theological innocence, and thus could not understand what led the Yale Apostates to their position, or evaluate on their own ground the writings of those interested in an American episcopate.

Furthermore, it does not seem that pre-Revolutionary America was a society that enjoyed any great equality among persons, as Bridenbaugh suggests. The burden of Gordon Wood's study is that it is impossible to appreciate the American Revolution if one cannot appreciate the deep chasm that virtually everyone believed to exist between gentry and ordinary folk in the order of things: the Revolution changed not just the government; it changed how people related to each other. The notion that "all men are created equal" was very radical thinking.[41]

Wood's example-in-chief of how far the Revolution was to take American society is not the Anglican south, but Congregationalist New England. For New Englanders, as for virtually everyone at the time, society was hierarchical; their society, particularly in its religious dimension, was accordingly an example of "pure patriarchal rule."[42] Congregational churches seated their members according to their social place, and both Harvard and Yale clearly ranked students according to the respectability of their families. Inside its own fence, Yale severely punished students who did not show their betters proper respect.[43] "Massachusetts courts debated endlessly over whether or not particular plaintiffs were properly identified as gentlemen."[44] In an age when a civil suit could fail if the right form of words was not employed and the alleged wrong not properly spelled out, New England courts would reject pleadings if the social rank of a disputant was misstated.[45] Wood rounds out his survey of colonial social attitudes with an exploration of John Adams's contempt for non-gentry, and then exposes Benjamin Franklin's devotion to that foundation of middle class morality, the "work ethic," as a sham. As soon as Franklin could afford it, at age forty-two, he retired from work to live the life of a gentleman.[46]

The principal basis for social standing was wealth; one was a member of the gentry precisely because there was no need to devote time and energy to earning one's bread. If they practiced a profession, the true gentry did not live off their work, and John Locke himself had observed that "trade is wholly inconsistent with a Gentleman's calling."[47] Certain learned professions, such as the law and medicine, gave the honorary status, if not the means, of a gentleman.[48] In the case of clergy, the accolade was given cautiously, and clergy without private means, or at least a university education, were not counted, and some uneducated clergy could be dismissed as "pettifoggers, charlatans, quacks."[49]

Without the glebes or state support that many of their southern counterparts enjoyed, northern SPG clergy were at best members of the second tier, the honorary gentry, living on about £50, while young Samuel Provoost was to have a £200 beginning wage as an entry-level assistant at Trinity Church in New York.[50] Many of the SPG clergy kept school to make ends meet; a smaller number practiced medicine or other professions; Seabury did both while a presbyter. The New England world they inhabited was not an egalitarian one, and there is room to suspect that at least to some degree the presence of a bishop would provide a threat to the Congregationalist clerical caste, whose social status was already in some ways granted as a sufferance. The often-repeated story of Ezra Stiles peevish reply, "We are all bishops here, but if there be room for another, he can occupy it," when asked to provide a seat for Seabury at Yale commencement certainly reflects some such feeling at least as much as it does a theology of holy orders. Of course, it also reflects a change of tactics: before Seabury's arrival as a bishop, Puritans had avoided use of the term bishop entirely.

Nor were New England Anglicans the party of elitists in the secular aspects of their society. While the southern Anglicans numbered quite a few wealthy people in their folds, in New England those people tended to be Congregationalists, Presbyterians, or even Quakers. New England Anglicanism's attraction was primarily for the middle ranks and the poor in the colonial period, and their SPG missionaries were truly involved with "all sorts and conditions."[51]

But were they perceived as a dangerous fifth column as Bridenbaugh claims? Another study of statistical data indicates a steady increase in the numbers of Anglicans elected to office in pre-revolutionary Connecticut from 1730 on. Lay people didn't perceive them as a threat, and were increasingly to share political power until the Revolution. The ever-growing body of Anglican officeholders infuriated Ezra Stiles and other Congregationalist ideologues. They could not fathom that in some towns Anglicans were elected to the Assembly in numbers beyond their proportion of the population. Anglicans became militia officers and justices of the peace. They were not elected high court judges, however. The election of Anglicans in increasing numbers seems to reflect three factors. First, some Anglicans were beginning to enjoy economic success. Second, some political alliances were forged with the Old Lights after the Great Awakening. Finally, and perhaps most important, Anglicans could be elected because most of them were adult converts who had come over in reaction to the Great Awakening, or because of the liturgy, or because of a belief in the necessity for apostolic ministry as Anglicanism understood it. They still had Congregationalist family and friends who were not willing to shun them, despite the urgings of their ministers. As much as Stiles and others tried to stir up popular enmity, people were by and large trying to get along with each other, particularly with their kinfolk, on a daily basis.[52]

Congregationalist objection to the presence of bishops was certainly based on principle. It was also based on practicalities: sufficiently large numbers of their people had already converted to Anglicanism and accepted its account of the doctrines of the church and of apostolic ministry; the presence of a bishop would only lead to the loss of more people.[53] Notwithstanding those concerns, was the possible arrival of a bishop a cause for declaring independence? The theory that the possibility of bishops being sent was a cause of the Revolution goes back to Mellen Chamberlain in 1898.[54] However, given the fact that the writers of the Declaration of Independence listed their grievances against the Crown in detail, and nowhere mention religious issues, it is extremely likely that the threat of episcopacy was not a cause of rebellion in their minds.

Nonetheless, the proposals of Samuel Johnson and others for a purely ecclesiastical episcopate did not quell fears of temporal lordship. This was because neither the English bishops nor the Connecticut Congregationalists could entirely imagine bishops with purely "spiritual" powers.[55] Arguably, they could have been able to do so, because there was an American model of a church without civil power already in place in the southern colonies. Besides their sitting in Parliament, English bishops performed a number of civil (not secular) functions, including jurisdiction over the probate of wills and the issuing of marriage licenses. In the southern colonies where the church was established, these episcopal functions had been taken over by the governor, or else the legislature substituted alternative officials, and no provision was made for an ecclesiastical presence in the legislature.[56] When pressed, Ezra Stiles would admit that his fears of episcopacy were really of "futurity"–his imaginings of what it might become.[57] This did not stop him from mounting a propaganda campaign and crying disingenuously, "For us in New England to be harassed with even the moderate episcopacy, at least to have it imposed on us, whose fathers fled here for asylum, is perfectly cruel."[58] No one had ever suggested that Congregationalists should be subject to the Anglicans' bishop or bishops, but the Congregationalists found allies in some colonial political authorities, some southern Anglicans, the Calvinist clergy, and in the Whig government, sufficient to prevent any bishops being appointed for the American colonies. Thus the SPG clergy in New England, New York, and northeastern New Jersey were virtually alone in their determination to have an American episcopate, but there is no convincing evidence that their neighbors took up arms against the king over the issue.

New England in the Revolution and its Aftermath

The Connecticut high churchmen suffered several kinds of shock during the war. They endured some persecution and also found their theology tested. There were economic consequences as well, and they also found themselves at cross purposes with many of their co-religionists to the south.

A simple equating of Anglicans with Tories would be a mistake; not all Tories were Anglican, and not all Anglicans were Tories. David Holmes studied the positions taken by Anglicans of every stripe during the war.[59] His findings help explain the position in which the Connecticut clergy found themselves after the war. In his research, he found only four clergy north of Pennsylvania who supported the Revolution, and two of them were in fact mild Tories. Only Samuel Provoost of New York and Robert Blackwell of New Jersey were active supporters of the revolution. Samuel Parker and Edward Bass of Massachusetts were "nominal patriots."[60] On the other hand, of the more than one hundred clergy in Virginia, at least seventy-four were known to be supporters of independence.[61] William Smith the elder, "the intellectual and somewhat vulgar Provost of the College of Philadelphia," with whom we will have a great deal to do below, changed loyalties often enough to be trusted by neither side.[62] Holmes's summary of key findings is memorable:

> Roughly speaking, Anglican clergy were loyalists in direct proportion to the weakness of Anglicanism in their colony, to the degree of their earlier support of an episcopate for the American colonies, to the 'highness' of their churchmanship, to the degree of their support by the S.P.G., and to the numbers of converts and recent immigrants from Britain and Scotland among them. In lesser percentages, Anglican laity tended to be loyalists for the same reasons.
>
> Conversely, with the exception of the clergy of Maryland, Anglican clergy were patriots in rough proportion to the strength of Anglicanism in their colony, to the degree of their earlier coolness towards an American episcopate, to the extent to which they were low or latitudinarian churchmen, and to the degree to which their parishes were self-supporting. In greater percentages, Anglican laity tended to be patriots for the same reasons.
>
> Where the Anglican church was established at the time of the Revolution, both laity and clergy tended to support the position on the war held by the American members of that establishment; where another denomination was established, almost all of the Anglican clergy and a significant number of the laity tended to be anti-establishment and to support the position on the war opposite to that taken by the religious establishment. With the exception of the clergy in Maryland and the possible exception of the laity in Connecticut, most Anglicans, like most colonists of all backgrounds, seemed to follow their leaders in the Revolution—the missionaries following the English-based S.P.G., the locally-supported clergy following their patriotic vestries and parishes, and the laity following the public will. Although Anglicanism supplied more loyalists during the Revolution than any other denomination in the colonies, the majority of all Anglicans were patriots.[63]

Holmes's findings, especially his conclusion that the majority of the patriotic clergy seem to have belonged either to the latitudinarian or to the Low Church schools of churchmanship[64] are predictive of the early history of the Episcopal Church. Northern, high church, bishop-seeking, SPG-supported clergy tended to be loyalist and royalist. Southern, locally-supported, low-church, bishop-resistant clergy tended to support the Revolution and principles of democracy and "the rights of man." Looked at from Holmes's point of view, the idea that the existence of so consistently packaged a complex of emotionally charged issues would make ecclesiastical and liturgical union a problem, should surprise no one. We will see that old disagreements on the political issue would pollute later discussion of other questions with some frequency.

Anglican reaction to the war varied greatly. The vestry of Christ Church, Philadelphia, met with William White, their rector, on the night of July 4, 1776, and together with him altered the state prayers. This act was probably the first acknowledgement by a public body of the claims of the Declaration of Independence. Later in the war, White would be the only Anglican cleric active in Pennsylvania.[65] Trinity Church, Boston, omitted all reference to the King in its liturgy from July 18, 1776, and its rector, Samuel Parker, was to be the only Anglican cleric active in Boston.[66] Edward Bass, later to be Massachusetts's first bishop, omitted the state prayers at the request of his vestry.[67] In 1777, Massachusetts was to enact legislation forbidding any preaching or prayer that undermined the revolutionary cause.[68] This was, of course, aimed at the Prayer Book, and the fine, £50, was the customary annual wage of an SPG missionary.

On the other hand, many loyalist clergy shut their churches rather than omit prayers for the King and royal family. Charles Inglis read the state prayers in the presence of George Washington and the Continental Militia.[69] Jonathan Beach of Redding and Newto[w]n swore that he would "pray for the King till the rebels cut out his tongue," and appears to have been shot at during at least one service.[70] Many of the Connecticut clergy met on July 23–25, 1776 to consider adjustments necessitated by the war. Their conclusion was at first to abandon use of the Book of Common Prayer, rather than alter it. They adopted a substitute form, consisting of singing, scripture, psalms, sermon, "and lastly, Part of the 6th chapter of St. Matthew, ending with the Lord's Prayer, all kneeling.–The Blessing."[71] A few parishes used this form; others seem to have closed for a while. Another New England practice was to allow lay readers to lead Morning Prayer, as they were not bound by any ordination oaths, and could alter the service without breaking any promises.[72]

These solutions were not satisfactory, of course. At their meeting on September 14–15, 1779, the clergy wrote to England for permission to use the

Prayer Book liturgy without any state prayers.[73] The reply came to do whatever they thought "prudent" under the circumstances, provided that they did not insert prayers for the Congress. By the end of the war, Connecticut churches were using the Prayer Book without the prayers in it that named any political entity.[74] In a curious way, their strategy for survival was not unlike that of the Scottish Nonjurors, who prayed for the sovereign without mentioning any names.

The (perhaps clumsy) subterfuge of having lay readers lead the services because they were not bound by ordination oaths, gives us some introduction to the theological state of the loyalist mind. Holmes, with tongue planted firmly in cheek—or at least one hopes so—reminds his readers that there was a time when people took their oaths very seriously, and adds that they thought that breaking their word was a grave offense that could bring divine retribution.[75] The oath in question, that of the King's Sovereignty, was taken at ordination to both diaconate and presbyterate, and was unambiguous:

> That the Kings Highness is the only Supreme Governor of this Realm, and of all other His Highnesses Dominions and Countries. And that no foreign Prince, Person, Prelate, State, or Potentate hath, or ought to have any jurisdiction, power, superiority, preeminence of authority Ecclesiastical or Spiritual within this Realm.

Clergy serving overseas further swore to "assist and defend all jurisdictions, privileges, preeminences and authorities granted or belonging to the King's Highness, His Heirs and Successors, or united and annexed to the Imperial Crown of this Realm." Clergy were bound by this oath to be more than neutral: they were bound to take up the King's side, whatever their private opinions. Clearly the way that clergy were to serve the Crown was by their prayers, so the decision to omit them had to have given many a priest second thought. Clergy who supported the rebellion again remind us of the crisis that produced the Nonjuror movement: like the vast majority of English clergy who opted to swear allegiance to William and Mary, most of the American priests said that since July 4, 1776, Congress was the *de facto* ruler, and was the proper object of supportive prayer.[76]

A good deal of the theological shock endured by the loyalist clergy came from the attack that the Revolution unleashed on their idea of divine order. Their position was that the governing order in the world was of divine origin, and was tampered with at great peril.[77] Both sides of the question were bolstered by appeals to theories of providential intervention in American history, and were doing so randomly, Anglicans having no central organization for discussing issues.[78] While clergy who supported independence saw the war as the working of God's will for that cause, Thomas Bradbury Chandler thought them "hair-brained fanatics" and considered that "the present rebellious disposition of the Colonies" was "intended by Providence as Punishment" for Britain's failure to promote Anglicanism in its overseas possessions.[79] Loyalists, in short, saw the rebellion as civil war, rebellion against the King and against the God who ordered creation. A loyalist sermon of 1777, possibly by Seabury, warned of the results of rebellion:

> How great must be their Crime, how atrocious their Wickedness, who, in Contempt of every Obligation, have excited, and still support and carry on, the present Rebellion against the legal Government of the British Empire to which they belonged!–breaking through all the Bonds of civil Society, effacing the Principles of Morality from among Men, treading under Foot the Dictates of Humanity and the Rights of their Fellow Subjects, subverting the most mild and equitable System of Laws, introducing the most horrid Oppression and Tyranny, and filling the Country with confusion, Rapine, Destruction, Slaughter and Blood!–How happily, how securely, we once lived under the mild Government of *Great-Britain* you all know. How we have been oppressed and harassed by Congresses, Committees and Banditties [sic] of armed Men, none of you can be ignorant. The cruel Effects of their lawless Tyranny many of you yet feel in the Distress of your Families, the Destruction of your Property, the Imprisonment of your Friends, and the Banishment of your Persons from your formerly peaceful and quiet Dwellings–These are the *proper*, the *genuine* Fruits of Rebellion.[80]

Seabury certainly knew what it meant to have been "oppressed and harassed" for his views and actions, although there is no record of his ever uttering a reproachful word concerning his sufferings after the war. This is not to say that those sufferings were unprovoked: Seabury was the author of *Letters of a Westchester Farmer*, witty and well-aimed attacks on the revolutionary establishment. Presaging a good deal of later American thought, Seabury argues, among other things, that the rebellion is good for the cities, and very bad news for farmers. The letters were answered by Alexander Hamilton, then nineteen years of age; the answers were not very good, but they gained Hamilton a place among the revolutionary elite. On January 5, 1775, the Sons of Liberty, the colonists' most important terrorist organization, produced an elaborate public burning of the Westchester Farmer's work.[81]

It needs to be said in the Farmer's defense, that he did not think the relationship of the colonies to the mother country was problem-free. What he proposed instead of bloodshed was a written constitution and something like the commonwealth relationship that Canada now has with Britain. As he would be in the new church, Seabury was an advocate of conservative solutions to freely admitted problems.

On November 22, 1775, the Sons of Liberty kidnapped Seabury from his grammar school in Westchester. Paraded as a captive through New Haven, Seabury was then kept incommunicado for seven weeks. His freedom was obtained early in 1776 by the efforts of Samuel Johnson's son, William, and the New York officials. Although the New Yorkers' position was largely in favor of independence, they objected strongly to having been invaded by a force from Connecticut. Seabury returned to Westchester and enjoyed some peace until the British left Boston. Returning colonial forces went out of their way to trouble him, and threatened to roast the Westchester Farmer alive if they should find him. Seabury fled to Long Island, and later became a chaplain and guide in the Loyal American Regiment, for which service he received a small pension after the war.

It is commonly said that friends come and go, but that an enemy is forever. One can begin to understand Seabury's later treatment by the General Convention if one remembers that John Jay and James Duane (later mayor of New York) were deputies at the conventions of 1785 and 1789. However, in 1776 they were members of the New York Committee for Safety. At the committee's September 11 meeting, they were among those voting to send an expedition to arrest Seabury on Long Island, so that he could not give the British further assistance as guide. As the later actions of their protégé and family connection, Bishop Provoost, made clear, they never forgot or forgave Seabury.

While it could possibly be argued that Seabury, as a prominent opponent of revolution, was a fair target for the terrorists, certainly gentle Jeremiah Leaming was not. The Sons of Liberty picked him up on a raid, and imprisoned him without even a bed from late winter until late summer of 1776, never charging him with any offense. Already in his fifties, Leaming's six months on bare stone left him crippled for life. "Tory hunting" mobs repeated this story many times. Samuel Peters, perhaps not the most attractive of personalities, barely escaped with his life. Samuel Andrews was imprisoned and his Wallingford church closed. Matthew Graves was pulled from the pulpit by the mob, which then closed his church. James Scovil was a frequent victim of terror raids. Ebenezer Dibblee, lived in continual fear of mob violence.[82] By 1781 eight Anglican clergy had been killed in the war.

In Massachusetts, the Rev. William Clark was arrested on suspicion of giving directions to fleeing Tories. When arrested, contemporary records tell us, he was "carried to a public house and shut up in a separate room for _ hour to view the picture of Oliver Cromwell."[83] His subsequent fate is less amusing to relate. He was banished, but was not actually sent away; instead he was interned in a prison ship, where his health broke.

Like many other colonies, Connecticut passed laws aimed at Tories. The Act of May, 1778 confiscated all real and personal sproperty, "as recommended by the Continental Congress, of those who aided, joined, or accepted protection" from the English.[84] The probate judge could, if he thought it warranted, leave something for the survival of the wife and children of the accused, but this was not guaranteed. Another Connecticut statute condemned to the mines anyone who even uttered a loyalist sentiment, and prescribed death for putting such sentiments in writing. Another act denied prisoner-of-war status to those who put themselves under the protection of British troops, and ordered death or thirty-lashes plus prison, and in either case, the confiscation of estates.[85]

In the minds of New England loyalists, there was no greater symbol of their suffering under their rebel neighbors than the Mines of Simsbury, Connecticut. A contemporary account is quite sobering:

> Symsbury, with its meadows and surrounding hills, forms beautiful landscape, much like Maidstone in Kent. The township is 20 miles square, and consists of nine parishes, four of which are episcopal. Here are copper mines. In working one many years ago, the miners bored half a mile through a mountain, making large cells forty yards below the surface, which now serve as a prison, by order of the General Assembly, for such offenders as they chuse not to hang. The prisoners are let down on a windlass into this dismal cavern, through an hole, which answers the triple purpose of conveying them food, air, and—I was going to say light, but it scarcely reaches them. In a few months the prisoners are released by death . . . . The General Assembly have never allowed any prisoners in the whole province a Chaplain.[86]

In actuality, the situation appears to have been a bit worse, as the plans show the main shaft to be ordinarily covered by a shack. The only airway constantly open was 1.5 inches wide.[87] Other colonies considered the mines the perfect prison for loyalists, and George Washington himself was impressed. Nineteenth-century historian, Noah Phelps, whose writing minimizes the horrors of the place, still had to give some details of life in Connecticut's *Niebelheim*, including its slave labor force.[88] The claim that prisoners were not allowed a chaplain must be taken to mean that they were not allowed an Anglican chaplain, for they did receive the comforts of religion from such preachers as the author of "Tyrranicide proved Lawful."[89]

It is customary to compare the aftermath of the American Revolution with the "excesses" of the French Revolution, noting that America saw no Reign of Terror.[90] This is largely but not entirely true, however. Some states passed retaliatory laws against Tories, some banishing them and confiscating their estates, with the result that many fled the country.[91] New York even passed a bill of attainder, to which Bishop Provoost appealed more than once in his campaign against Seabury, whose "life was forfeit," and whom he would apparently have gladly seen dead.

It is difficult to number the refugees, but conservative estimates place the total at eighty thousand, with twenty thousand going to Nova Scotia and Cape Breton.[92] These numbers were hardly insignificant in those days, when the national population was under four million. Losing eighty thousand people was a loss of more than two percent of the population. At the time, it was like a city with a population more than 2.5 times that of New York City simply disappearing. Seabury was involved, from the summer of 1782 on, in organizing and dispatching from Manhattan refugees from New York, New Jersey, Connecticut and Rhode Island, to Nova Scotia, where the King had given each loyalist two hundred acres of land.[93] Seabury had planned to load the refugees and then take the last ship out himself. The New York clergy, including himself, had written on March 21, 1783 asking for the American episcopate to be located in Nova Scotia. Three days later the Connecticut clergy elected Seabury. It was in April, during his evacuation work, that news of his election reached him in New York.

Suspicion of the Southern Clergy

We have already noted that New England clergy were more likely to have a high view of church, ministry, and sacraments when compared to their southern colleagues. The difference in religion was matched by a difference in politics: there was much more clergy support for independence in the southern colonies than there was in New England. The adversarial relationship to a hostile state church in New England gave Anglicans a different outlook as well. There were grounds for additional suspicion in the not entirely uncommon perception that the southern colonies harbored immoral or unfit clergy among their many faithful and hard-working priests. For instance, Seabury's predecessor in Westchester, John Milner, had been run out of town for persistent drunkenness and sexual assault on a warden's son. What was particularly galling to the SPG clergy was that the man fled to Virginia and became rector of Newport parish in Isle of Wight County.[94] Bishop White's adoring nineteenth-century biographer had to admit that "the church had suffered, too, in general estimation, by the bad conduct of many of her clergy in Maryland and Virginia, and the states south of them." He suspected a variety of reasons for the development of this situation, including the sending of unsuitable candidates for ordination and the general leaving of clergy unsupervised.[95] The personal conduct of Provost William Smith scandalized Episcopalians and Congregationalists alike in more than one way. Attempts earlier in the present century to rehabilitate the reputations of the rotten apples among southern clergy have been unsuccessful.[96] The north had its own colorful clergy, of course, but by and large, their excesses were such as patrician Samuel Provoost's reputation for extraordinarily lavish entertainment, and the baronial pretentions of Samuel Peters of Connecticut, who returned to England during the Revolution, just ahead of a mob. There may well have been more serious offenders who remained in office, but our point here is that it was the south that had the reputation for employing rogue clergy. The resulting mistrust was real, and may well have inspired the gratuitous venom New York printer James Rivington added to his advice to Seabury, "As to the *Southern Bastards* I hope yourself, and every [one] of your Clergy will always keep aloof from them. You can never associate with absurdity & inconsistency."[97] It should be noted that Seabury himself is not known to have engaged in such talk, and was quite restrained in his very few criticisms.

New England clergy viewed the "south" with distrust based on differences of experience, theology, and politics. The first efforts to organize the Episcopal Church on principles much like those guiding the new nation served to widen the gap between New England and the southern states to something more of the proportions of a chasm. That there would be suspicion of liturgy and theology of Seabury and the New England churches seems so natural that it has become a commonplace to observe that it is a miracle that one Episcopal Church emerged in 1789.

Notes

1. David L. Holmes, "The Episcopal Church and the American Revolution," *Historical Magazine of the Protestant Episcopal Church* 47 (1978) 2. [Hereinafter, the *Magazine* is *HMPEC.*]

2. Elizabeth Davidson, *The Establishment of the English Church in Continental American Colonies* (Durham: Duke U. Press, 1936) 87.

3. "Episcopalians" was also in use well before 1776. The more polemical expression "Churchmanship," however, belongs to the next century.

4. See John J. Reardon, "Religious and Other Factors in the Defeat of the 'Standing Order' in Connecticut, 1800–1818," *HMPEC XXX* (June 1961) 93–110.

5. Nathaniel Ward, quoted in Glenn Weaver, "Anglican-Congregationalist Tensions in Pre-Revolutionary Connecticut," *HMPEC XXVI* (1957) 267.

6. Maud O'Neil, "A Struggle for Religious Liberty: An Analysis of the Work of the S. P. G. in Connecticut," *HMPEC XX* (June 1951) 173ff.

7. Weaver, 269, citing *New England Colonial Records,* 239.

8. Weaver, passim, and esp. 280.

9. Charles Mampoteng, "The New England Clergy in the American Revolution," *HMPEC IX* (1940) 285.

10. It is of some interest that Cutler's bidding of the Amen later became quite common among Congregationalists, and may still be heard today.

11. Text in Louis Weil, "Worship and Sacraments in the Teaching of Samuel Johnson of Connecticut: A Study of the Sources and Development of the High Church Tradition in America, 1722–1789," (Th. D. thesis, Institute Catholique de Paris, 1972) 41ff.

12. William Sprague, *Annals of the American Pulpit.* Vol. V. *Episcopalian* (New York: Robert Carter and Brothers, 1859) 51.

13. O. E. Winslow, Johnathan Edwards, in Weaver, 278.

14. O'Neil, op. cit., provides a general introduction.

15. For example, Jeremiah Leaming (1717–1804), who was to be the first choice

of the Connecticut clergy for bishop, was in many ways a stereotype of the adult convert who became an SPG missionary: converted after Yale graduation, he went to England for orders and then served parishes as an SPC missionary. He published *A Defence of the Episcopal Government of the Church* (1766) and *A Second Defence of the Episcopal Government of the Church* (1770), as well as the sermon he preached at the funeral of Samuel Johnson.

16. Samuel Jarvis's last letter to the SPG requesting continued financial support and above all a bishop, but not naming a candidate, was written on May 5, 1783 (after Seabury's acceptance of election), reminding the Society that the SPG missionaries did not cause or support the Revolution. Text in Kenneth Walter Cameron, ed. *Abraham Jarvis, Connecticut's Second Episcopal Bishop. Materials for a Biography* (Hartford: Transcendental Books, 1983) 25ff.

17. Samuel Seabury wrote to the SPG that "it is evident from experience that not more than 4 out of 5 who have gone from the Northern Colonies have returned; this is an unanswerable argument for the absolute necessity of Bishops in the Colonies. The Poor Church of England in America is the only instance that ever happened of an Episcopal Church without a Bishop and in which no Orders could be obtained without crossing an ocean of 3000 miles in extent." Samuel Seabury to Secretary, SPG, 17 April 1766, in Herbert Thoms, *Samuel Seabury: Priest and Physician* (Hamden Conn.: Shoestring Press, 1963) 33.

18. Jeremiah Leaming to Secretary, SPG, 10 June 1761, in Francis L. Hawks and William Stevens Perry, *Documentary History of the Protestant Episcopal Church in the United States of America. Connecticut.* 2 Vols. (New York, 1863, 1864) Vol. II, 23. [Hereinafter *H&PII*] There is no record of a reply.

19. William Hogue, "The Religious Conspiracy Theory of the American Revolution: Anglican Motive," *Church History* 45 No. 3 (September 1976) 286 and 288.

20. Charles Inglis to SPG, 5/20/1780. Thoms, 21.

21. Weil, 40.

22. The "consensus" theory is proposed in Bruce Steiner, *Samuel Seabury 1729–1796: A Study in the High Church Tradition.* (Athens, Ohio: The Ohio University Press, 1971) 342ff., and requires a study of its own.

23. Horton Davies, *The Worship of the American Puritans, 1629-1730* (New York: Peter Lang, 1990) 145.

24. On the extent to which Puritan religion filled the ritual gap created by abandoning the Prayer Book with rites of their own creation, and for an appreciation of the extent to which ritual created social cohesion for them, see E. Brooks Holifield, "Peace, Conflict, and Ritual in Puritan Congregations," *The Journal of Interdisciplinary History* 23, 3 (Winter, 1993) 551–570.

25. Davies, 17.

26. Davies, 41.

27. Davies, 156.

28. Davies, 13.

29. Davies, 170ff.

30. Davies, 169.

31. Davies, 31.

32. George E. DeMille, "One Man Seminary," *HMPEC* XXXVII (1969) 373–379.

33. Weil, 40, but see also, Donald F. M Gerardi, "Samuel Johnson and the Yale 'Apostasy' of 1722: The Challenge of Anglican Sacramentalism to the New England Way" *HMPEC* XLVII (1968) 153–175.

34. Samuel Johnson, "The Beauty of Holiness," *Works,* Vol. 3, 530, in Weil, 70.
35. Weil, 71.
36. Weil, 123.
37. Weil, 128ff.
38. Weil, 148.
39. Carl Bridenbaugh, *Mitre and Sceptre: Transatlantic Faiths, Ideas, Personalities and Politics.* (New York: Oxford University Press, 1962) xiii.
40. On republican boors, Bridenbaugh, xii; on Anglicans as invaders, 26, 65ff., 69, for just a few examples. In his view, all Congregationalists were sincere and high-minded, while all Anglicans were deceitful and arrogant hypocrites. 218, 223, and passim.
41. Gordon S. Wood, *The Radicalism of the American Revolution* (NY: Alfred A. Knopf, 1992.) 5, 6, 27ff.
42. Wood, 44.
43. Wood, 20ff.
44. Wood, 25.
45. Wood, 21.
46. Wood, 31, 38.
47. Wood, 36ff.
48. Wood, 21ff., where we also read, "On the eve of the Revolution the colonists squabbled over the proper seating order at the governors' tables to the point where Joseph Edmunson, the Mowbray herald extraordinary of the English College of Arms, had to be called in to prepare "rules of Precedency" to lay down the precise social position of the various colonial officials."
49. Wood, 3.
50. E. Charles Chorley, "Samuel Provoost, First Bishop of New York," *HMPEC* II no. 2 (June 1933) 3.
51. For the data, see Bruce E. Steiner, "New England Anglicanism: A Genteel Faith?" *William and Mary Quarterly* XXVIII (1970) 122–135.
52. Bruce E. Steiner, "Anglican Officeholding in Pre-Revolutionary Connecticut: The Parameters of New England Community," *William and Mary Quarterly* XXXI (1974) 369–384.
53. This Hogue's reasoning, at 288. He also notes, 282, that "the colonials' fear of Anglicanism was quite simply their apprehension of defections from their own churches should there be acceptance on a wide scale of Anglican arguments denying the spiritual authority of non-Anglican orders . . . and they accused the Anglicans of being at odds with the English government, not in collusion with it."
54. Arthur Lyon Cross, *The Anglican Episcopate and the American Colonies* (New York: Longmans, Green, and Co., 1902) 269.
55. Weaver, 284.
56. Davidson, 79ff.
57. Bridenbaugh, 228.
58. Charles Mampoteng, "The New England Clergy in the American Revolution," *HMPEC* IX (1930) 268.
59. Holmes, David L. "The Episcopal Church and the American Revolution," *HMPEC* 47 (1978) 261–291.
60. Holmes, 266,280.
61. Holmes, 267.
62. Holmes, 282.
63. Holmes, 265.

64. Holmes, 278.

65. Holmes, 291.

66. Marion Hatchett, "The Making of the First American Prayer Book," (Th.D. thesis, New York: The General Theological Seminary, 1972) 88. [This passage does not appear in the published form.]

67. Sprague, 143.

68. Mampoteng, 270.

69. Holmes, 275.

70. Hatchett, 89. The Redding church keeps on display in its narthex a lead ball with an explanatory note about its being dug out of the wall behind the pulpit during the Revolution. If pressed, a warden will explain that the ball and its successors have been stolen many times in two centuries, and that a supply of lead balls must be kept on hand in the church as replacement relics continue to be needed.

71. Original documents are reproduced in Kenneth Walter Cameron, ed. *Anglican Experience in Revolutionary Connecticut and Areas Adjacent* (Hartford: Transcendental Books, 1987) 70.

72. Holmes, 271.

73. Cameron, *Anglican Experience, 72.*

74. O'Neil, 187; Holmes, 272; Hatchett, 90.

75. Holmes, 269.

76. Holmes, 279.

77. See John F. Berens, "A God of Order and Not of Confusion: The American Loyalists and Divine Providence, 1774–1783," *HMPEC 47* (1978) 207–219.

78. See Glenn T. Miller, "Fear God and Honour the King: The Failure of Loyalist Civil Theology in the Revolutionary Crisis," *HMPEC 47* (1978) 221–242.

79. Berens, p. 215. Chandler was later to suggest that the danger of bishops coming to America provoked the Revolution, but there is no evidence for such a theory, which certainly takes Anglicanism more seriously than did many of Chandler's contemporaries.

80. Anon., *St. Peter's Exhortation to Fear GOD and Honor the KING, Explained and Inculcated (New York, 1977)* 19.

81. The Seabury-Hamilton logomachy and its aftermath are reported in some detail in Steiner, 127-154.

82. More stories in this vein are reported by O'Neil, 185.

83. Mampoteng, 280, quoting Worthington's *History of Dedham*. The indentification of the revolutionary cause with the Roundheads of the previous century was by no means uncommon.

84. Cameron, *Anglican Experience, 290.*

85. Cameron, *Anglican Experience, 6.* Thirty lashes could itself be a death sentence.

86. Cameron, *Anglican Experience, 6.*

87. The plan is reproduced in Cameron, *Anglican Experience, 7.*

88. Noah Phelps, *History of Simsbury, Granby, and Canton* (Hartford: Case, Tiffany & Burnham, 1845) 120-135. On prisons in general during the Revolution, see Larry G. Bowman, *Captive Americans* (Athens, Ohio: Ohio University Press, 1976). More on the Simsbury prison mine can be found in Richard H. Phelps, *Newgate of Connecticut and Other Antiquities* (Copper Hill, CT: S. D. Viets, 1895) and Charles E. Stow, *Simsbury's Part in the War of the American Revolution* (Hartford: Lockwood and Brainard, 1896). "Old Newgate" as the mines at Simsbury, later East Granby were called, is operated as a tourist attraction today.

89. Simeon Baxter, *Tyrannicide proved Lawful, from the Practice and Writings of Jews, Heathens, and Christians.* A discourse delivered in the Mines at Symsbury. In the Colony of Connecticut, to the Loyalists confined there (London, 1782).

90. E.g., Wood, 3.

91. Thoms, 83; Mampoteng, 270; *Anglican Experience,* 76.

92. Holmes, 285.

93. Cameron, *Anglican Experience,* 86.

94. Steiner, 82.

95. Bird Wilson, *Memoir of the Life of the Right Reverend William White, D.D., Bishop of the Protestant Episcopal Church in the State of Pennsylvania* (Philadelphia: James Kay, 1839) 94.

96. See David C. Skaggs & Gerald E. Hardagen, "Sinners and Saints: Anglican Clerical Conduct in Colonial Maryland," *HMPEC XLVII* (1978) 177–195. The authors review the attempts at rehabilitation and return to the documentary evidence to find that most indictments are merited.

97. James Rivington to Seabury, July 25, 1785, in Steiner, 232.

The Fourth Order: General Convention's Proposed Ordination Liturgies for Deaconesses, 1919–1965

Jill Burnett

IN 1889, THE GENERAL CONVENTION of the Protestant Episcopal Church in the United States of America enacted a canon recognizing and regularizing the Office of Deaconess.[1] Article VIII of the canon as finally adopted stated, "No woman shall act as a Deaconess until she has been set apart for that office by an appropriate religious service, to be prescribed by the General Convention, or, in the absence of such prescription, by the Bishop."[2] During the following eight decades, subsequent General Conventions debated the status of deaconesses, and as David Sumner points out, "[t]he church never really resolved whether or not 'deaconess' was an order of the ministry, but finally abolished the office when it voted to allow women into the diaconate in 1970."[3] From the beginning, much of the debate turned on one central question: were these women in *holy* orders or in a *religious* order?

A concern to differentiate deaconesses from female religious, on the one hand, and from male deacons, on the other, pervaded the General Convention's discussions, illustrating the office's liminality with respect to both kinds of orders. This concern surfaced in continued conflict over whether deaconesses should be celibate and in repeated calls for clarification of the office and function of deaconesses. The conflict also surfaced liturgically. During the course of those eighty years, General Conventions considered a series of proposed rites by which women would be admitted to the office, in an attempt to prescribe the "appropriate religious service" referred to in 1889. Perhaps because the Houses of Bishops and Deputies were never able to define the status of deaconesses, they never approved any of these rites for inclusion in the Prayer Book as the common ordination service for Episcopal deaconesses. This essay considers the liturgical prehistory, construction and legislative fortunes of each of these proposed rites, in an attempt to show how the process—unsuccessful in the end—reflected the General Convention's inability to resolve the issue of the status of deaconesses with regard to holy orders.

Background: The Revival of the Order

The revival of the Order of Deaconess in the nineteenth century was one of the ways in which the various churches responded to the challenges of a changing society. The industrial revolution was transforming life in Western Europe and America, not always in positive ways. In an attempt to address the needs of the poor and sick in Germany, Lutheran pastor Theodore Fliedner and his wife founded the Deaconess Training Institute at Kaiserswerth in 1836. The success of the Kaiserswerth sisterhood inspired imitation in English and American churches as they attempted to respond to similar societal needs.[4]

In America, forces other than the industrial revolution also played a part in the revival of the office. According to Mary Sudman Donovan, one of the forces at work was a society-wide "professionalization" of medical, legal, educational and social occupations, a trend "characterized by an increasing identification of the individual on the basis of occupation, by the formation of national organizations that limited entry into each occupational field on the basis of specific educational requirements, and by the development of a process of examination to determine the applicant's professional competency." This trend toward professionalism was felt in the churches as well, "producing a demand for an authentic profession through which church women might minister to the sick, the downtrodden, and the dispossessed."[5] To meet the demand in New York City, Anne Ayres and William Augustus Muhlenberg founded the first Episcopal sisterhood in 1845, when Sister Anne made her profession privately "in an empty Church, with only Muhlenberg and the sexton 'waiting to put out the lights' as witnesses."[6]

Another contributing factor to the revival of the diaconate of women was the Civil War and its aftermath. The high number of casualties meant an increased number of widows, orphans and disabled veterans requiring care. Opening orphanages and hospitals and staffing them with deaconesses was the way bishops in several dioceses attempted to meet two post-war challenges—caring for those left ill or destitute while at the same time providing a respectable profession for women.[7]

In each of these dioceses, the women chosen to minister in the church's name to the poor, sick and orphaned were liturgically set apart to that ministry in a rite chosen by the bishop. These setting apart liturgies shared some common elements, although the configuration of those elements varied from service to service. The rites usually contained prayers, an address to the congregation and candidates concerning the history and duties of the office, an examination of each candidate to determine her ability and willingness to discharge those duties, and some visible sign of admission to the office. This sign was usually a hand clasp, accompanied by words of reception, as opposed to the laying on of hands in ordination, as in ancient practice.[8] In 1858, Bishop William Rollinson Whittingham of Maryland performed the earliest known formal service of setting apart in the Episcopal Church in the United States, organizing the women who administered the Infirmary of the Diocese of Maryland into a community of deaconesses.[9] According to George Hodges, these women "were formally admitted to be 'servants of the Church of God as deaconesses.' The bishop in a public service received them with counsels and prayers and the giving of the right hand of fellowship."[10] In December of 1864 Bishop Richard Hooker Wilmer of Alabama set apart "by prayer, but without the imposition of hands" three deaconesses to run the diocesan orphanage.[11] In 1872, Bishop Abram Newkirk Littlejohn of Long Island admitted seven women to the Order of Deaconesses of the Diocese of Long Island.[12] His "Form of Admitting Deaconesses to Their Office" did not call for him to lay on hands but rather to take each candidate's right hand and to "*give her his blessing.*"[13] In 1887, Bishop Henry Codman Potter set apart Julia Forneret at St. George's, New York City, by taking her hand and receiving her: "For the service of our Lord we receive thee, to be henceforth known and called by the name and title of a Deaconess in the Church of God."[14] Mary Truesdell maintains that Potter *did* lay on hands in this service,[15] but there is no indication of this in the liturgy as published.

Ayres and Muhlenberg had consciously modeled the Sisterhood of the Holy Communion on the Kaiserswerth community, and many of the later communities were also organized after this pattern. As Truesdell points out, the members of these early "experiments" were not "true deaconesses" in the ancient sense, an assessment she bases on the rites used to set them apart. She writes, "Conceptions of the terms 'deaconess' and 'sister' were hazy; these devoted women were neither 'religious' sisters nor were they true deaconesses in the technical meaning of the term. They were admitted to their communities by giving the right hand as pledge, whereas the *sine qua non* of the historic office of deaconess is the imposition of episcopal hands."[16]

A shift in practice regarding the sign of admission began even before the deaconess canon was passed in 1889. Truesdell attributes this in part to the influence of developments in the Church of England. She writes:

Under the wise leadership and careful study of antiquities by such men as Dean Howson, Bishop Lightfoot, Bishop Thorold, Canon Body, and others, when the office of deaconess was finally restored in the Church of England, it was done in accordance with primitive Catholic tradition, which differed quite essentially from the Lutheran pattern. In 1862, Bishop Tait of London admitted Elizabeth Ferard to the office of deaconess with the imposition of hands. She thus became the first woman to hold this historic office in England after the lapse of several centuries.[17]

Truesdell maintains that in restoring the office in their dioceses, Bishops Wilmer and Potter followed the Bishop of London in taking care that the setting apart liturgies they used contained three "*essential* parts": prayer, imposition of hands, and the giving of authority of office.[18] As noted above, Bishop Potter, "still sensitive to the negative attitude toward women's orders,"[19] did not, in fact, follow this pattern. However, in 1885, Bishop Wilmer set apart two more deaconesses in Alabama, Mary W. Johnson and Mary Caroline Frigell, in a service that did include the laying on of hands.[20]

An observation made by Barbara Brandon Schnorrenberg about Bishop Wilmer's setting apart of deaconesses in Alabama in 1864 can be applied to all such services prior to 1892, whether or not they included the laying on of hands. She writes, "Wilmer was acting without canonical authority; his deaconesses had no standing outside his diocese."[21] However, according to Walter Whitaker, Wilmer and other bishops like him did not feel compelled to wait for canonical authority. He writes:

The institution of the order of deaconesses proved that Bishop Wilmer's conception of the inherent powers of the Episcopate was not fettered by the shackles of canonical provision. This primitive order, with Phoebe of Cenchrea as its best known representative, had no place in the polity of the American Church. But men of a catholic grasp of mind could not wait for a slow-moving General Convention to give its imprimatur to an inalienable right and the supplying of an immediate necessity.[22]

The growth of the movement soon attracted the attention of the General Convention. Twelve years after Bishop Whittingham had encountered an apathetic and fearful House of Bishops,[23] the General Convention of 1871 asked the Committee on the State of the Church to develop a training and deployment plan for deaconesses. The Committee advised against the development of such a national plan at that time, on the grounds that the "prejudice which identifies every such movement with the false and pernicious system of the Church of Rome" would cause opposition to any recommendations that General Convention might make, rendering it unworkable. The Committee felt that this issue was better addressed at the diocesan level.[24] Nevertheless, the Convention established the Joint Committee on Reviewing the Primitive Order of Deaconesses to study the matter of regularizing the status of deaconesses;

among the committee members were some of the "staunchest advocates of women's ministries in the national Church"–Bishops Littlejohn and Wilmer, Bishop Horatio Potter of New York, as well as clergymen William Reed Huntington and John F. Spalding and layman William Welsh, founder of the Bishop Potter Memorial House, a training school for church workers in Philadelphia.[25] From 1874 to 1883 drafts of a canon were proposed, debated, amended, even passed by one of the houses, but none ever achieved bicameral adoption, and the matter was always referred back to the Committee. The General Convention of 1886 did not even address the issue. However, despite General Convention's inability to pass legislation on deaconesses and religious orders, the number of orders continued to increase.[26] The deaconesses themselves were not of one mind on the issue of canonical regulation. As Pamela Darling writes, "Some believed they were better off without the regulation that would come with canonical status, but more thought their ministries would be enhanced and their positions made more secure through official recognition, so legislative efforts continued."[27]

Mary Abbot Emery Twing, founder of the Women's Auxiliary to the Episcopal Church's Board of Missions, believed that national recognition of deaconesses and the addition of an admission service to the proposed *Book of Offices* would remove the uncertainty she thought was keeping many women from serving in this way. In the October 1889 issue of her publication, *Church Work*, she wrote:

> If a canon of Deaconesses similar to that presented during the General Convention of 1880, could be cordially approved and adopted by both Houses, and, more important still, if an "Office for the Reception of Deaconesses," similar to that already in use in the dioceses of Alabama, Long Island and New York, could be added to the "Book of Offices" to be proposed in the General Convention of 1889, no doubt many women would offer themselves for service, under a rule thus clearly set forth, who now hesitate, uncertain what the Church really wishes of them, or in what way she desires them to work for her.[28]

No such service was included in the *Book of Offices* proposed by the Committee on Liturgical Revision to the 1889 Convention.

This Convention did, however, finally pass the canon recognizing and regulating the Office of Deaconesses. It was introduced to the House of Bishops by Henry Codman Potter and to the House of Deputies by William Reed Huntington, but much of the credit for its final success in 1889 belongs to Twing, who not only campaigned heavily among influential clergy and laymen, but also drafted the Resolution that Bishop Potter presented to the bishops.[29] The adoption of the deaconess canon was significant in that it was the first official recognition at the national level of the ministry of women in the Episcopal Church. As Donovan observes, "Although the canon made no mention of the relationship of deaconess to the three traditional orders of ministry—bishop, priest, and deacon—and made no provision for including her in the Church's organizational structure, it did at least suggest that the ministry was not an exclusively masculine domain."[30]

The deaconesses now enjoyed canonical status in the national church, but the rite by which they were admitted to the office remained a matter for each individual bishop's discretion.

Ordaining Deaconesses: The First Attempts at a Uniform Liturgy

The canon was amended in 1901[31] and 1904, but no action was taken on a common setting apart rite until 1919. However, it is interesting to note that an informal and unofficial process of standardization seems to have taken place. Deaconess Caroline H. Sanford was able to report to the Archbishop of Canterbury's Committee on the Ministry of Women, appointed in 1917, that "'The Form of Service for the setting apart of Deaconesses,' adopted first by the New York school, is now in general use throughout the American Church, with slight local changes."[32] This form, taken from the 1916–1917 *Year-Book of the New York Training School for Deaconesses*, is also appended to the report.[33] This means that, by the time Sanford wrote, most Episcopal deaconesses in America were set apart in a service that followed this outline:

> Presentation
> Declaration of office and work of a deaconess
> Bidding of objections
> Versicles and responses
> Prayer for the candidates
> Versicles and responses
> *Magnificat*
> Examination
> Imposition of hands with formula granting authority
> Blessing
> Dialogue
> Prayers for newly set apart deaconesses, those in need, and
>   final blessedness
> Benediction

No Propers were provided, indicating that this rite did not normally take place in a eucharistic context. Although this form contains the same basic elements as did the various nineteenth-century forms, there is one major difference: the imposition of hands and authority-granting formula have replaced the hand clasp and words of reception.

A similar but not identical service was set forth for the American church in *A Book of Offices: Services for Occasions Not Provided for in The Book of Common Prayer*, published in 1917 "by authority of the House of Bishops." The preface states that ". . . while there is considerable new matter in the Book, the offices are mainly taken from those in use for many years in dioceses in England and Canada, with some help from American diocesan forms."[34] The deaconess service must be from this last source, because structurally it more closely resembles the form used in New York and Pennsylvania than any of the various English forms in use in this period.[35] There are, however, a few important differences. First, the *Book of Offices* form assumes that the setting apart will take place in a eucharistic context and, therefore, provides Propers. The declaration of the office and work of a deaconess is abbreviated by omitting the references to the women who ministered to Jesus during his earthly ministry and to the women who went to the tomb to prepare his body for burial. Only the reference to Phoebe and the listing of canonical duties remain. The reading of Rom. 12 and the singing of the *Jubilate Deo* or the *Magnificat* precede the Versicles and Responses. The material derived from the deaconess ordination prayer in the *Apostolic Constitutions* is omitted from the prayer for the candidates. The examination questions are fewer and bear more resemblance to the questions contained in the nineteenth-century forms, particularly that used by Bishop Littlejohn in Long Island. The post-examination prayers are also completely different. Finally, the words accompanying the laying on of hands do not confer authority of office; first the bishop blesses the candidate and then admits her to the office of deaconess.

At the 1919 General Convention, the Joint Commission on the Revision and Enrichment of the Book of Common Prayer, which had been created in 1913, included among its recommendations just one new service for inclusion in the Book of Common Prayer, the "Office for the Admission of Deaconesses,"[36] which it suggested be "inserted immediately after the Office of Institution of Ministers."[37]

In constructing its proposed rite, the Commission drew material from the *Book of Offices* service, but its model was clearly the diocesan form used in New York and Pennsylvania. This is not particularly surprising, given the fact that Bishop Philip Rhinelander of Pennsylvania was a member of the Commission; this service had been authorized in his diocese in 1895 and, therefore, had been in use there for twenty-five years. The service proposed in 1919 follows its model almost exactly from the presentation through the examination. There are, however, a few differences. First, the title has been changed to "A Form of Admission to the Office of Deaconess," and all occurrences of the phrase "set apart" have, therefore, been changed to "admitted" through-out. Second, the *Magnificat* and its accompanying Versicles and Responses have been moved to the end of the service. Finally, the examination questions are slightly revised, and one has been added:

> Will you be diligent in prayer and in reading of the Holy Scripture, and in such studies as help to the knowledge and teaching of the same?

After the examination, the 1919 service departs from its model entirely. The prayers following the admission are new and now include the Lord's Prayer. In the rest of its departures from the diocesan model, the 1919 service follows the *Book of Offices* service instead. First, the imposition of hands is accompa-nied by an admission formula, rather than by the authority-granting formula and blessing as in the diocesan form. Second, it provides Propers, although they differ from those in the *Book of Offices* service; the Collect is new, the Epistle is the reading about Phoebe from Rom. 16, and the Gospel appointed is Mt. 25:34–45, the parable of the sheep and the goats. Finally, the pre-examination prayer for the candidates lacks the section derived from the deaconess ordination prayer of the *Apostolic Constitutions*: "O Eternal God, Father of our Lord Jesus Christ, Creator of man and woman; who didst anoint with the Spirit Miriam and Deborah and Anna and Huldah; who didst not disdain that Thine only-begotten Son should be born of a woman; who also in the tabernacle of the testimony and in the temple didst ordain women to be keepers of Thy holy gates . . . . "

The Commission was confident that its recommendation would be approved; the report reads, "It is believed that the inclusion of this Office will commend itself, and that it is the mind of the Church that the work of women in the Church should be recognized by giving this Office a place in the Book of Common Prayer."[38] However, instead of adopting the service, the General Convention referred it to the newly-appointed Joint Commission On Adapting the Office of Deaconess to the Present Tasks of the Church,[39] weakening its chances of being given a place in the Prayer Book. We know from the Third Report of the Joint Commission on the Revision and Enrichment of the Book of Common Prayer, prepared for the General Convention of 1922, that the service they had proposed in 1919 was "remitted to that new Commission for consideration."[40] As we shall see, however, the new Deaconess Commission chose not to base its service on that or any other previous setting apart service; it looked elsewhere for its model, boldly following the forward-looking work of the Lambeth Conference of 1920.

The Deaconess Commission gave its first report in 1922. The report states that the Commission had unanimously passed two resolutions that guided its subsequent work. It adopted as its first principle a statement contained in the report of the Bishop of Ely's Committee of the Lambeth Conference of 1920. The report, entitled "The Position of Women in the Councils and Ministrations of the Church," stated that "the ordination of a Deaconess confers on her Holy Orders. In ordination she received the 'character' of a Deaconess in the Church of God; and therefore, the status of a woman ordained to the Diaconate has the permanence which belongs to Holy Orders."[41] The Deaconess Commission made this statement its own, despite the fact that Lambeth had failed to include it in its final resolutions concerning deaconesses. The Deaconess Commission's second resolution was to follow Lambeth's Resolution 49 in drafting a new Canon:

> The office of a Deaconess is primarily a ministry of succour, bodily and spiritual, especially to women, and should follow the lines of the primitive rather than of the modern Diaconate of men. It should be understood that the Deaconess dedicates herself to a lifelong service, but that no vow or implied promise of celibacy should be required as necessary for admission to the Order. Nevertheless, Deaconesses who desire to do so may legitimately pledge themselves either as members of a Community, or as individuals, to a celibate life.[42]

The Deaconess Commission's sub-committee "On a Service of Ordination," chaired by Edward Lambe Parsons, Bishop Coadjutor of California, drafted a rite that clearly embodies both of these principles. On the one hand, the proposed rite is presented as a conferring of holy orders. The report refers to it as the "service of ordination" and proposes that it be incorporated into the Book of Common Prayer, being "inserted in the Ordinal, after the Communion Service."[43] Perhaps more significantly, "The Form and Manner of Making Deaconesses" was clearly modeled after "The Form and Manner of Making Deacons." On the other hand, the sub-committee's *departures* from that model embody the Deaconess Commission's second resolution—that the revived diaconate of women is to be different from the diaconate of men.

A closer look at the rite shows the interplay of these two dynamics. The service is almost identical in structure to the 1892 service for making deacons, including its placement of the laying on of hands by the bishop in its traditional location for deacons, immediately before the reading of the Gospel. Parallel placement of outlines of the two services shows this structural correspondence:

"The Form and Manner of Making Deacons" (1892 Book of Common Prayer)	"The Form and Manner of Making Deaconesses" (Proposed, 1922)
[Morning Prayer]	[Morning Prayer]
Sermon or Exhortation on duties and office of deacons	Sermon or Exhortation on duties and office of deaconesses
Presentation of Candidate(s) Bidding of Objections Litany with special suffrage for candidates	Presentation of Candidate(s) Bidding of Objections Silent Prayer

Communion Service
  [Lord's Prayer]
  Collect for Purity
  [Decalogue]
  [Summary of Law]
  [Kyrie]
  Decalogue Collect
  Collect of the Day
    (Proper for Deacons)
  Epistle–1 Tim.3:8–13 or Acts 6:2–7
	Communion Service
	  [Lord's Prayer]
	  Collect for Purity
	  [Decalogue]
	  [Summary of Law]
	  [Kyrie]
	  Decalogue Collect
	  Collect of the Day
	    (Proper for Deaconesses)
	  Epistle–Phil. 2:1–11

Examination of Candidate(s)	Examination of Candidate(s) [*Veni, Creator Spiritus*]
Imposition of hands with formula Delivery of New Testament with formula	Imposition of hands with formula
Gospel, read by one of the newly ordained–Luke 12:35–38	Gospel–Luke 12:32–40

Communion Service continues as
  usual through the singing of *Gloria
  in excelsis* or some other hymn
	Communion Service continues as
	  usual through the singing of *Gloria
	  in excelsis* or some other hymn

Closing Collect (Proper)	Closing Collect (Proper)
Blessing	Blessing

This synopsis also reveals some significant differences. For example, instead of the Litany, there was space for silent prayer. There was no delivery of the New Testament, despite Lambeth's recommendation that this be included.[44]

39

The singing of *Veni, Creator Spiritus* was a specified option just prior to the imposition of hands; this was not sung in the ordination of deacons. Finally, an extra prayer for power to fulfill this service acceptably was provided immediately after the examination.

The most significant differences between the two services occur in terms of *content*, and here Lambeth's vision for the restored order of deaconesses is clearly borne out. There are differences in wording; these are sometimes incidental, sometimes significant. The Propers are also different. The Collect appointed for the making of deaconesses, though clearly modeled after that for making deacons, omits the reference to St. Stephen and to the work of administration. Surprisingly, the reference to apostolic origin has also been omitted, although Lambeth Resolution 48 had referred to "the stamp of apostolic approval"[45] enjoyed by the order of deaconess:

Deacons (1892)

ALMIGHTY God, who by thy divine providence hast appointed divers Orders of Ministers in thy Church, and didst inspire thine Apostles to choose into the Order of Deacons the first Martyr Saint Stephen, with others; Mercifully behold these thy servants now called to the like Office and Administration: so replenish them with the truth of thy Doctrine, and adorn them with innocency of life, that, both by word and good example, they may faithfully serve thee in this Office, to the glory of thy Name, and the edification of thy Church; through the merits of our Saviour Jesus Christ, who liveth and reigneth with thee and the Holy Ghost now and for ever. *Amen.*

Deaconesses (1922)

Almighty God, who by thy divine providence hast appointed divers Orders of Ministers in thy Church;

Mercifully behold these thy servants now called to the Office of Deaconesses: so replenish them with

innocency of life, that, both by word and good example, they may faithfully serve thee in this Office, to the glory of thy Name, and the benefit of thy Church; through our Saviour Jesus Christ, who liveth and reigneth with thee and the Holy Ghost, now and for ever. *Amen.*

The Epistle appointed for the ordination of deaconesses is Phil. 2:1–11, hymning the humble obedience of Christ in taking the form of a servant. The service for deacons gives a choice of Epistles: 1 Tim. 3:8–13, specifying the desired qualities of deacons and their families, or Acts 6:2–7, narrating the appointment of and imposition of hands upon Stephen and the others chosen as the first deacons. The Gospel appointed for the deaconess service is the same as that for deacons, Jesus' admonition to the disciples to be ever watchful until his return, though the reading is expanded from Lk. 12:35–38 to include verses 32–34 and 39–40.

The sub-committee's treatment of the examination section is significant, both in how it followed its model and in how it departed from that model. The first two questions are identical in both services:

> Do you trust that you are inwardly moved by the Holy Ghost to take upon you this Office and Ministration, to serve God for the promoting of his glory, and the edification of his people?
> *Answer.* I trust so.

> Do you think that you are truly called, according to the will of our Lord Jesus Christ, and according to the Canons of this Church, to the Ministry of the same?
> *Answer.* I think so.

The third question is quite different:

Deacons (1892)
Do you unfeignedly believe all the Canonical Scriptures of the Old and New Testament?
Answer. I do believe them.

Deaconesses (1922)
Are you persuaded that the Holy Scriptures contain all doctrine required as necessary for eternal salvation?
Answer. I am so persuaded.

However, this is only an *apparent* difference. The question in the deaconess service merely incorporates the revision to the deacon service proposed in 1919 to bring it into conformity with the question asked of candidates for the priesthood.[46] The fourth question reflects the fact that deacons and deaconesses had different duties with regard to scripture:

Deacons (1892)
Will you diligently read the same unto the people assembled in the Church where you shall be appointed to serve?
Answer. I will.

Deaconesses (1922)
Will you be diligent in prayer and in reading of the Holy Scriptures, and in such studies as help to the knowledge and teaching of the same?
Answer. I will.

The fifth question reflects the different duties of the two offices, again illustrating that leadership in public worship[47] was the main area of difference between the diaconate of men and that of women:

Deacons (1892)
It appertaineth to the Office of Deacon, in the church where he shall be appointed to serve, to assist the Priest in Divine Service, and specially when he ministereth the Holy

Deaconesses (1922)
It appertaineth to the Office of Deaconess to care for the sick, to comfort the afflicted, to supply the wants of the poor and needy, to teach the ignorant, and to labour in all ways

Communion, and to help him in the distribution thereof; and to read Holy Scriptures and Homilies in the Church; and to instruct the youth in the Catechism; in the absence of the Priest to baptize infants; and to preach, if he be admitted thereto by the Bishop. And furthermore, it is his Office, where provision is so made, to search for the sick, poor, and impotent people of the Parish, to intimate their estates, names, and places where they dwell to the Curate, that by his exhortation they may be relieved with the alms of the Parishioners, or others. Will you do this gladly and willingly?
Answer. I will so do, by the help of God.

for the extension of the Church of Christ. Will you do this gladly and willingly?
Answer. I will do so, by the help of God.

The sixth and seventh questions are essentially identical in the two services:

> Will you apply all your diligence to frame and fashion your own lives, and the lives of your families, according to the Doctrine of Christ; and to make both yourselves and them, as much as in you lieth, wholesome examples of the flock of Christ?
> *Answer.* I will so do, the Lord being my helper.

> Will you reverently obey your Bishop,[48] and other chief Ministers, who, according to the Canons of the Church, may have the charge and government over you; following with a glad mind and will their godly admonitions?
> *Answer.* I will endeavor so to do, the Lord being my helper.

The closing Collects in the two services are completely different, the deaconess collect being modeled after the ordination prayer from the *Apostolic Constitutions*:

Deacons (1892)

ALMIGHTY God, giver of all good things, who of thy great goodness hast vouchsafed to accept and take these thy servants unto the Office of Deacons in thy Church; Make them, we beseech thee, O Lord, to be modest, humble, and constant in their Ministration, to have a ready will to observe all spiritual Discipline; that they, having always the testimony of a good conscience, and continuing ever stable and

Deaconesses (1922)

O eternal God, Creator of man and woman; who did not disdain that thine only begotten Son should be born of a virgin; Look mercifully we beseech thee, upon these thy handmaids now appointed to the Office and work of Deaconesses, and give them thy Holy Spirit that they may worthily accomplish the work committed unto them, to thy glory and the praise of thy Christ, to whom with thee, O Father, and thee O

strong in thy Son Christ, may so well
behave themselves in this inferior Office,
that they may be found worthy to be called
unto the higher Ministries in thy Church;
through the same thy Son our Saviour
Jesus Christ, to whom be glory and honour, world without end. *Amen.*

Holy Spirit, be glory and worship, world
without end. *Amen.*

The House of Bishops adopted Lambeth's resolutions on deaconesses but did not adopt the Deaconess Commission's report. A Special Committee appointed to consider the report recommended that the Deaconess Commission be continued and directed it to report to the 1925 General Convention;[49] the ordination service was once again referred back for additional consideration.

Trying Again: A "Service of Admission"

The Commission's 1925 report reflects a continued concern to differentiate deaconesses from both female religious and male deacons, as well as a growing frustration with the church's delay in taking action on the matter of the ministry of deaconesses. It states:

> One conviction has dominated the deliberation of your Commission and has put a note of urgency in its findings and recommendations; namely that, at the present time, there is offered to the women of the Church through the ministry of Deaconesses a unique opportunity for varied and far-reaching service, and that the Church will greatly suffer if this opportunity is not adequately met.[50]

Obviously, the issue was not the *creation* of the Office of Deaconess; despite the failure of the General Convention to take action on the issues of pensions, a revised canon and a uniform admission service, women continued to be trained and set apart for this ministry and to execute its duties. However, since their numbers were apparently dwindling, the issue was *recruitment.* The 1925 report goes on to point out that ". . . if necessary additions to their number are to be secured, something must be done, and that without delay, to give our Deaconesses a new standing and a fuller recognition by the Church."[51]

Achieving this enhanced status for deaconesses was the Deaconess Commission's chief concern in formulating its proposals to the 1925 General Convention. The report states that the Commission continued to adhere to its 1922 principles while modifying "in some important details" its earlier recommendations. However, the principles as stated in the 1925 are only loosely based on those stated in the 1922 report; in 1925, there is no mention of conferral of holy orders, and the Commission's current concerns about support and recruitment have become integral.

First, that the ministry of Deaconesses must be taken by the whole Church very seriously, and as a matter which vitally concerns its welfare and efficiency, so that a full measure of sympathy, interest and support may be forthcoming.

Second, that in order to secure for our Deaconesses the respect and esteem which are so justly due them, and in order to draw into the order the right type of candidates, our Deaconesses must be given a more definite and authoritative commission in the name of the Church; a more uniform and complete training for their work; and more adequate support both during active service and after retirement or disability.

Third, that the true goal to be aimed at is not at all to approximate the office and work of a Deaconess to that of a Deacon, which latter, as is well known, has ceased to have significance save as a short probationary period before admission to the priesthood. On the contrary, our aim should be to give to the office of Deaconess a distinctive place of its own in the official ministry of the Church such as it had in ancient days.[52]

This concern to differentiate between deacon and deaconess is clearly evident in the proposed setting apart service appended to the Deaconess Commission's report. It is significantly different both in content and in structure from its predecessor of 1922, in some ways more closely resembling the service proposed in 1919. Parallel outlines make the differences among the three services apparent.

A Form of Admission to the Office of Deaconess (Proposed 1919)	The Form and Manner of Making Deaconesses (Proposed 1922)	The Office for the Making of Deaconesses (Proposed 1925)
Presentation	Presentation and declaration of suitability	Presentation
Address to People		Address to People
Bidding of Objections	Bidding of Objections	Bidding of Objections
Versicles and Responses	Silent Prayer	Versicles and Responses
Prayer Examination		Prayer
Imposition of hands with formula of admission		
Lord's Prayer		
Prayer		
Versicle and Response		
Magnificat		[*Magnificat* or other hymn]
[Communion	Communion	Communion
Proper Collect	Proper Collect	Proper Collect
Epistle–Rom. 16:1–5	Epistle–Phil. 2:1–11	Epistle–1 Cor.12:4–11
Gospel–Matt. 25:34–40]		Gospel–Lk. 12:32–38
		Creed

	Sermon on duties and office
Examination	Examination
	Silent Prayer
[*Veni, Creator Spiritus*]	[*Veni, Creator Spiritus* or other hymn]
Imposition of hands with formula granting authority Gospel–Lk. 12:32–40	Imposition of hands with authority formula and blessing
Communion continues; Special Closing Collect	Communion continues; Special closing Collect
Blessing	Blessing

First, it has a new name. "The Form and Manner of Making Deaconesses" has become "The Office for the Making of Deaconesses," and the report refers to it as the "service of admission," not the "service of ordination" as in 1922.

Second, it has a new structure. Although it follows 1919 almost *verbatim* through the presentation, address and bidding of objections, it differs from all of its predecessors in the placement of the ordination unit. This unit now takes place between the Liturgy of the Word and the Holy Communion, that is, after the Creed and the Sermon and before the reception of alms, as in the rite for consecrating bishops.[53] The construction of the ordination unit itself is more like that of 1922 than that of 1919 in that the formula accompanying the laying on of hands grants authority of office instead of admission to the office, and the permissive use of *Veni, Creator Spiritus* is retained.

Third, it has new content. The service for deacons and the 1922 service for deaconesses began after Morning Prayer with a sermon or exhortation explaining the office and duty of the deacon or deaconess. In the service proposed in 1925, the content of that explanation is specified, the material being taken from the service proposed in 1919. The Liturgy of the Word is also heavily revised. The 1922 collect, which so closely followed the collect for the making of deacons, has been replaced by one continuing the emphasis on the ministry of women in scripture:

> Almighty and most merciful Father, whose blessed Son was ministered unto by devout and holy women; Grant that these thy servants now to be admitted to a like ministry of mercy may so faithfully serve thee in this office that they may attain thy manifold rewards in the world to come; through the same thy Son Jesus Christ our Saviour, who liveth and reigneth with thee and the Holy Ghost, one God, world without end. Amen.

The Epistle appointed is 1 Cor. 12:4–11 on the diversity of spiritual gifts, replacing Phil. 2:1–11. The Gospel reading is the same, though shortened slightly.

Most of the questions in the examination are from the service proposed in 1919, although the question concerning diligence in prayer and scripture reading has been retained from 1922. The vow of obedience has been revised along the lines of the 1917 *Book of Offices* service:

> Will you be obedient to them that are over you in the Lord, cheerfully and faithfully performing the service that shall be appointed to you?
> *Answer.* I will, by the help of God.

The closing Collect is also new:

> Almighty God, Who art the source of all power and strength; Look mercifully, we beseech thee, upon *these* thy *servants*, now admitted to the office and work of Deaconess. Protect *them* in the way wherein *they* go, and grant that in singleness of purpose, and with a ready mind *they* may fulfill thy holy will, and finally by thy mercy obtain everlasting life; through Jesus Christ our Lord. Amen.

The report states the Deaconess Commission's belief that these proposals are "restrained and conservative," as well as its "great confidence that the Convention will acknowledge their reasonableness and necessity."[54] If such an acknowledgment was made, it did not translate into definitive action. On the fifth day of the Convention, the House of Bishops referred the proposed service to its Committee on the Prayer Book,[55] which made a number of suggested changes. These included changing the title to "The Form and Manner of Admitting Deaconesses," omitting the reference to Jesus' birth from the Virgin in the pre-*Magnificat* prayer, changing the word "Order" to "Office," omitting the rubric permitting the singing of *Veni, Creator Spiritus*, and changing the authority-granting formula to an admission formula.[56] On the thirteenth day, the House of Bishops adopted the amendments, as well as a resolution to authorize the amended service for use during the following three years. Message 171 was sent to the House of Deputies, informing them of the bishops' actions on the service. On the fifteenth day, the House of Deputies informed the House of Bishops that it had also adopted an amended service, but the deputies' amendments were much more extensive.[57] Because the bishops had already taken action on the service and had already notified the deputies of this action, the bishops requested a Committee on Conference.[58] The deputies also referred to this Committee the bishops' message about authorizing the service for three-year use. The next day, the Committee on Conference presented its report on this matter, stating, "The Committee does not see how, at this late hour in the Session, it is possible to adjust the differences between the Houses in any satisfactory way. They are convinced that further study of the proposed service for the admission of Deaconesses, in light of the action of both Houses, is desirable . . . . " The Convention adopted the Committee's resolutions to continue the Deaconess Commission but referred the service back to the Commission on the Revision of the Book of Common Prayer for report to the 1928 General Convention.[59] Because final action on the revision of the Prayer Book was taken in 1928, the failure to act on the deaconess service in 1925 insured that it would not have a place in the new Book of Common Prayer.

That the question of a service for making deaconesses continued to be troublesome to the General Convention members is evident in the disillusioned words of the Deaconess Commission's report to the 1928 General Convention:

> Your Commission has the hardihood to believe that, if General Convention were more alive to, and more familiar with, the need and opportunity for the work of trained women in the Church, and for adapting the office of Deaconess to this need, our reports to previous Conventions would have met with a more interested and more favorable reception. We can not but feel that the debates and discussions on this subject in recent General Conventions have been largely abstract and academic; concerned rather with difficult and debatable questions and theories of Church order than with an actual situation in our Church life, recognized as critical and as demanding adequate and effective treatment.[60]

The report goes on to blame the church for the fact that many women were looking elsewhere for opportunities to serve, because it "has not understood their minds and motives, and has been unwilling, or at least unready, to mark the signs of the times and to open the doors at which her children knock, and through which they are prepared to pass to loyal service, under the Church's authority and guidance."[61] The report also describes the fate of the Service for Admission:

> . . . although amendments to the Service as presented by your Commission to the last General Convention were adopted by *each* of the two Houses separately, there was no *concurrent* action, save by a final and somewhat hasty vote referring the whole matter to the Commission on the Prayer Book . . . . After much discussion, we have decided to stand by the Service of Admission as we prepared it in 1925. It represents much careful thought and study by those of us who were most familiar with the subject matter and most competent to deal with it. We are not now asking that any Service be included in the Prayer Book. We are only asking that there be set forth for general use in the Church . . . a Service which, at least for the time, shall serve as a norm or standard, and shall have the approval of competent authority. If the Prayer Book Commission shall see fit, with this in mind, to present our Service of 1925, as an appendix to its own report, we shall be satisfied and grateful. Failing this, it is our purpose to refer it to the House of Bishops, with the request that they give it such approval and authorization as they have given to similar services in the past.[62]

The Joint Commission on the Revision and Enrichment of the Book of Common Prayer had been discharged on the second day of the 1928 Convention from further consideration of a liturgical form for admission of deaconesses, so the matter was referred to the House of Bishops' Committee on the Prayer Book. This Committee recommended several changes to the service. For example, the reference to the Son's birth from the Virgin was dropped from the prayer for the Holy Spirit's help and guidance that precedes the singing of the *Magnificat*, as had been suggested by the House of Bishops in 1925. The ordination unit was moved back to its 1922 position immediately before the reading of the Gospel. Also in compliance with the bishops' amendments in 1925, the rubric specifying that *Veni, Creator Spiritus* or some other hymn may be sung immediately before the imposition of hands was changed to "*Here may be sung a hymn.*" The phrase "in the Church of God committed unto thee" was stricken from the formula granting authority to execute the office. The Bishops adopted these changes along with a resolution to set forth this amended form for general use in the church at the discretion of each bishop in his diocese.[63] It is unclear whether this happened, but when the *Book of Offices* was revised in 1940, this was *not* the service included. On the twelfth day of the 1928 session, "[o]n motion of Bishop Rhinelander, the report of the Committee on the adoption of a Form for Making of Deaconesses was withdrawn."[64] The Deaconess Commission was continued, as it had requested, "for the special purpose of carrying forward the study and discussion of the Survey of Women Workers in the Church prepared for the Woman's Auxiliary in 1923."[65]

The Enthusiasm Cools

With the 1928 General Convention, the period of Prayer Book revision came to a close, and although the quest for a uniform admission service remained on the Deaconess Commission's agenda, it was overshadowed by other concerns. Throughout the next three decades, the Deaconess Commission repeatedly brought before the General Convention issues such as the need for adequate wages and pensions, better training and recruitment strategies and clarification of the status and purpose of deaconesses, but no service of admission was proposed.

Several dioceses and one province petitioned the 1931 General Convention to "take action . . . designating the status of Deaconesses in accordance with the declaration of the Lambeth Conference . . .,"[66] which in 1930 had clarified its resolutions of 1920. The Deaconess Commission's[67] report to the General Convention of 1931 identified three practical problems concerning the deaconess matter: pensions, recruitment and the setting apart service. The report reveals the ongoing discomfort with ordaining deaconesses, but it also states firmly that the content and publication of the service should bear out the apostolic authority of the Office of Deaconess, despite Lambeth's omission of this statement from its final resolutions :

> It has been definitely agreed by the Bishops at Lambeth that this should include the laying on of hands with prayer for the gift of the Holy Spirit, a definite commission for the Church's work and also the delivery of the New Testament. There is a strong feeling on the part of many well informed persons in the Anglican Communion against the equation of the Office of Deaconess with the Office of Deacon. With this your Commission is in agreement. The Deacon is preparing, in most cases, for the priesthood and has opportunity to exercise his office for a comparatively short time. The Deaconess, on the other hand, has a lifelong vocation. She can find within the Office an unlimited opportunity for service, and your Commission would again emphasize the fact that no ministry to the needs of humanity can be complete that does not call for both men and women, each exercising special gifts, faculties and powers with which God as endowed them. They are not alike and never can be alike. One is not superior to the other but their functions differ. It is the conviction of your Commission that the Office for the setting apart of a deaconess should occupy the same position in the Ordinal as the Office for the ordination of a Deacon. In no other way can the principle be maintained that the Church has a ministry of women apostolic in its authority and supported by the deliberate intention of the whole Church acting through the Bishop as its instrument.[68]

In 1937, the Deaconess Commission reported that it " . . . continues to consider the preparation of one, uniform Service for the Making of Deaconesses to the intent that it may be presented to the House of Bishops for their approval."[69] However, no such service appeared or was mentioned again for the duration of the tenure of the Deaconess Commission and its successor, the Advisory Commission on the Work of Deaconesses, appointed in 1937 and dissolved in 1952.

One reason for its disappearance from the agenda may have been that an "Office for the Setting Apart of Deaconesses" was included in two new editions of the *Book of Offices*, published in 1940 and 1949. This liturgy was a minor revision of the service published in 1917. However, this still did not achieve the goal of a single uniform service, because the *Book of Offices* service was just a suggested form, one choice among several, as is evidenced in the report of the Advisory Commission on the Work of Deaconesses to the 1949 General Convention: "According to the several forms of service used, the candidate publicly declares her conviction as to her vocation as Deaconess, and makes certain vows."[70] According to the report, these various forms all share a common core: the Bishop lays his hands upon each candidate, saying, "Take thou authority to exercise the office of a Deaconess in the Church of God, whereupon thou art now set apart," and then blesses her, saying,

"Blessed be thou of the Lord, my daughter. The Lord recompense thy work, and a full reward be given thee of the Lord God of Israel, under whose wings thou art come to trust."[71]

The Advisory Commission's report also made one thing absolutely clear: the admission services did not constitute ordination to the diaconate. The report states, "The setting apart of a Deaconess is not an ordination in the sense of the ordination of a man to the Diaconate; but it is the recognition on the part of the Church, acting through a Bishop, of a sense of vocation, and the acceptance of vocation and consecration for work in the Church of God." In support of this view, the report reiterates the statement of Lambeth 1931, which had been reaffirmed by Lambeth 1948, that "'The Order of Deaconess is an Order *sui generis* not to be regarded as the female equivalent of Deacon, but as a distinct Order marked by the solemnity of its ordination and the importance of its functions.'"[72]

Renewed Calls for a Common Ordination Service

A new Joint Commission on the Work of Deaconesses was created in 1955; it reported to the General Convention of 1958 that not all bishops shared Lambeth's view, and that there were once again stirrings to include a service in the Book of Common Prayer. In preparation for its report, the Deaconess Commission had surveyed the bishops for their opinions about the Order of Deaconesses. Some bishops objected to the use of the word "Order," since the Ordinal referred only to three orders–bishop, priest and deacon–and since neither the canon nor the *Book of Offices* used the words "order" or "ordained." On the other hand, the report states that

> . . . some American bishops and others feel that deaconesses are and should definitely be recognized as being ordained persons, as they are at present in the Church of England, that the Canon should so state, and that a Service of Ordination of Deaconesses should be included in the Prayer Book.[73]

At a Special Meeting of the House of Bishops in 1959, the Standing Liturgical Commission presented proposals for another revision of the *Book of Offices*. The Commission recommended either omitting the Deaconess service altogether or amending it along the lines of "Bishop Parsons' report," by which they meant the service proposed in 1919 by the Joint Commission on the Revision and Enrichment of the Book of Common Prayer, not the service proposed in 1922.[74] The bishops chose to keep the service in the *Book of Offices*, despite a motion to transfer it to a new book of services generally restricted to the use of bishops, and they adopted all of the Standing Liturgical Commission's proposed revisions. The revised service, published in a new edition of the *Book of Offices* in 1960, was structurally similar to its predecessors of 1917, 1940 and 1949. The influence of the 1919 proposed service can be seen mainly in the expansion of the examination; although the first and last questions are slight revisions of the first two (of three) questions in the *Book of Offices* service as it stood, three others from the 1919 service have been added. The post-examination prayers and subsequent Versicles and Responses are also from the 1919 service.

Two significant changes in the deaconess canon at the General Convention of 1964 in St. Louis brought the century-long confusion over the status of deaconesses to a crisis point. At that Convention, the requirement that deaconesses be unmarried or widowed was dropped, and the phrase "appoint" was replaced by the word "ordered."[75] The change in requirement concerning marriage was designed to help recruitment efforts. The change in terminology sparked a crisis that marked "the beginning of the end of the ambiguous treatment of women in the ministry."[76] However, some confusion remained, as William Stringfellow and Anthony Towne observe:

> The underlying issue, which the St. Louis vote had apparently only succeeded in confusing, was whether deaconesses are merely specialized laywomen or in holy orders, and, if in holy orders, whether in the diaconate, the so-called third order of ministry, with the same status as male deacons with access to the other two orders of priest and bishop, or in a fourth order reserved to deaconesses or female deacons excluded from succession through the other orders.[77]

Bishop James E. Pike of California interpreted the change in the wording of the canon as a removal of the distinction between the diaconate of women and that of men. He announced that he would comply with the General Convention's change in canon law by recognizing the orders of Deaconess Phyllis Edwards and vesting her in the garb of the perpetual diaconate. Bishop Pike's plan evoked nationwide opposition.[78] At the request of Bishop Francis Lickfield of Quincy, President of the American Church Union, he agreed to postpone Deaconess Edwards's ordination until the House of Bishops could clarify the issue at its Special Meeting in Glacier Park, Montana, in early September of 1965.

The bishops' decisions at Glacier Park indicate that they considered the order of deaconesses to be a fourth order;[79] at their ordinations, deaconesses received the "indelible character" of holy orders but not eligibility for the presbyterate or episcopacy. Resolutions adopted declared that "the Order of Deaconesses is *at present recognized as* the one and only Order of the Ministry for women in our branch of the Anglican Communion," and that "when a Deaconess is 'ordered' by the Bishop with prayer and the laying on of hands, together with a formula giving authority to execute the Office of Deaconess in the Church of God, she receives an indelible character for this specialized ministry in the Church of God."[80] However, in clarifying the canon's description of the chief functions of deaconesses, the bishops maintained a major distinction between the male and female diaconates: "Resolved, That we declare that Canon 50, Section 2(b) describes the chief functions which presently shall be entrusted to Deaconesses. It is the judgment of this House that Deaconesses may not be permitted to administer the Elements of Holy Communion."[81]

The bishops also considered another proposed admission service, "The Form and Manner of Making Deaconesses According to the Order of the Protestant Episcopal Church in the United States of America." It is clearly modeled on "The Form and Manner of Making Deacons"; the collects are similar, although the collect of the day lacks the reference to Stephen, and the closing collect lacks the reference to moving on to the "higher Ministries" in the church. However, it differs from its model in significant ways, even more so than did the service proposed in 1922. The great liturgical divide between deacon and deaconess is illustrated in a number of ways in the construction of this service, particularly regarding the proclamation of scripture in public worship. This is borne out structurally in the placement of the ordination unit of examination, imposition of hands and formula conferring authority, and delivery of New Testament and cross. This unit is placed before the liturgy of the word, removing it from close proximity to the reading of the gospel, the primary liturgical role of the diaconate. The distinction is also borne out in the omission from the examination of the question put to male candidates concerning scripture: "Will you diligently read the same unto the people assembled in the Church where you shall be appointed to serve?" The difference is made even more explicit in the words accompanying the delivery of the New Testament:

Deacons (1928)	*Deaconesses (1965)*
Take thou Authority to read the Gospel in the Church of God, and to preach the same, if thou be thereto licensed by the Bishop himself.	Be diligent to study the things which are written in this Book; that, as much as in thee lieth, thou mayest teach the gospel of the grace of God and be an example of faith and of holy living.

Bishop Pike suggested three amendments, the adoption of which would make the deaconess service more closely resemble its model. Two of these amendments were adopted. First, an initial rubric was added: "*Before he ordains a woman as Deaconess, the Bishop shall require that she take the Oath of Conformity stated in Article VIII of the Constitution of the Church.*" This refers to the declaration required of candidates for ordination or consecration to the other three orders: "I do believe the Holy Scriptures of the Old and New Testaments to be the Word of God, and to contain all things necessary to salvation, and do solemnly engage to conform to the Doctrine, Discipline, and Worship of the Episcopal Church." Second, after the laying on of hands and conferral of authority to execute the office, the bishop was to deliver the New Testament to the new deaconess, although the accompanying words differed from those said to a new deacon, as noted above. Bishop Pike also proposed that "the Litany be used, in the same place as in the Service of Ordering of Deacons and Priests, with the word 'deaconess' used in the appropriate suffrage," but this amendment was defeated.[82]

Conclusion: From Liminality to Elimination

The service as amended was adopted by the bishops on September 8, and the bishops apparently felt that they had at long last clarified the deaconess issue, although they maintained that their actions did not represent a departure from earlier practice and intention. They adopted this statement at the end of their session:

> It is the judgment of this House that, in "setting apart" Deaconesses through the years, it has been the intention of our branch of the Church to give the Deaconesses the gifts and powers traditionally associated with their office. We regard the action of the General Convention of 1964, in amending the Canon on Deaconesses, not as giving Deaconesses a new status with regard to their Ministry, but as clarifying a status that was already theirs.[83]

However, shifts were already underway in the Anglican Communion that would challenge the bishops' statement and render their deaconess ordination service unnecessary within five years. These challenges began almost immediately. Bishop Pike interpreted the action taken at Glacier Park somewhat differently than did his brother bishops. On September 13, 1965 in Grace Cathedral, San Francisco, he used an adapted form of the newly-adopted service to recognize Phyllis Edwards's diaconal orders, vesting her in a deacon's stole, delivering a gospel book to her, and adding her name to diocesan records as a full member of the clergy.[84]

Continued calls for additional consideration of the matter indicate that others in the church also thought that the bishops' actions at Glacier Park were insufficient. At the 1967 General Convention, the Diocese of Bethlehem presented a memorial asking the Committee on Deaconesses to consider "the status of Deaconesses in relation to the Orders of the Ministry." The Committee asked to be–and was–discharged from this duty, "because the House had expressed its mind on the matter in its Special Meeting of 1965."[85] In its report, the committee presented results of a survey conducted in 1966 by a committee of nine deaconesses, which found that there was still a "need for clarification of the role of the Deaconess in the Episcopal Church today."

The Committee presented a resolution that a new Joint Commission be appointed to report to the next Convention, "describing the role of the Deaconess in her ministry of service to the Church today . . . ."[86]

At their meeting at Glacier Park, the bishops had also asked the presiding bishop to appoint a special committee to study "the proper place of women in the Church's Ministry" and to put the "entire question before the Lambeth Conference of 1968, for fresh consideration."[87] Lambeth 1968 helped to resolve the confusion by making several important statements concerning the diaconate. First, it sought to broaden the churches' understanding of the third order by recommending that it be open not only to those seeking ordination to the priesthood, but also to "men and women remaining in secular occupations," and "full-time church workers." Lambeth also recommended that member churches revise their ordinals to reflect the "new role envisaged for the diaconate," to remove any "reference to the diaconate as 'an inferior office,'" and to emphasize the "continuing element of *diakonia* in the ministry of bishops and priests." Lambeth's third recommendation concerned deaconesses specifically; it asked that "those made deaconesses by the laying on of hands with appropriate prayers be declared to be within the diaconate" and that "appropriate canonical legislation be enacted by provinces and regional Churches to provide for those already ordained deaconesses."[88]

In 1970, the General Convention brought the Episcopal Church into compliance with Lambeth's recommendations by repealing the canon "Of Deaconesses" and replacing it with the canon "On Women in the Diaconate," thereby abolishing the office of deaconess and fully opening the diaconate to women.[89] The confusion concerning the status of deaconesses in relation to holy orders had finally been resolved, but at the cost of the order of deaconesses. The action taken in 1970 also eliminated an eighty-year-old liturgical problem. This legislation brought female deacons under the same canonical provisions as male deacons—except for those provisions relating to the priesthood[90]—and qualified them for the same ordination process and liturgy,[91] officially bringing to an end the quest for an authorized, uniform service of admission of deaconesses.

Notes

1. Protestant Episcopal Church in the United States of America, *Journal of the Proceedings of the Bishops, Clergy and Laity of the Protestant Episcopal Church in the United States of America in a General Convention Held in the City of New York, From October Second through October Twenty-fourth, Inclusive, in the Year of Our Lord 1889* (n.p., 1890) 135; subsequent references will be cited as *JGC 1889*. The canon received second and final approval at the General Convention of 1892.

2. *JGC 1889,* 109. The final version of this article was an amended form adopted by the House of Deputies. The House of Bishops concurred, although it had already adopted the original article proposed by the Committee on Canons, which read,

"Until a form of prayer for the setting apart of a Deaconess shall have been prescribed by the General Convention, such form shall suffice as may be set forth by the Ordinary."

3. David E. Sumner, *The Episcopal Church's History: 1945–1985* (Wilton, Conn.: Morehouse Publishing, 1987) 15.

4. Mary P. Truesdell, "The Office of Deaconess," in *The Diaconate Now*, Richard T. Nolan, ed. (Washington: Corpus Books, 1968) 159; Mary Sudman Donovan, *A Different Call: Women's Ministries in the Episcopal Church, 1850–1920* (Wilton, Conn.: Morehouse-Barlow, 1986) 92. The revival of the Order of Deaconess in the Church of England was also greatly influenced by the Oxford Movement. For more information, see Donovan, 24–26.

5. Donovan, 88–89.

6. Donovan, 32, quoting Anne Ayres, *The Life and Work of William Augustus Muhlenberg* (New York: Thomas Whittaker, 1889) 188.

7. Barbara Brandon Schnorrenberg, "Set Apart: Alabama Deaconesses, 1864–1915," *Anglican and Episcopal History* 63 (1994) 472–473.

8. Canon XIX of the First Council of Nicea and Canon XV of the Council of Chalcedon refer to the ordination of deaconesses by the imposition of hands. *Apostolic Constitutions* VIII.19-20 prescribes the prayer to be used at the laying on of hands in ordaining deaconesses.

9. Bishop Whittingham raised the issue of deaconesses at the General Convention of 1859, asking the House of Bishops to consider several questions on the subject. According to William Francis Brand, "The House declined giving what was asked of them; they were not prepared to express any opinion on the subject; although some informally disapproved of any setting apart with ceremony. It was thought better that the Bishop of Maryland should meet the difficulties that might present themselves in his own way, lest, should evil grow out of this action, it might be said that he had appealed to the House and received no contrary opinion" (*Life of William Rollinson Whittingham, Fourth Bishop of Maryland*, Vol. 1 [New York: E. & J. B. Young & Co., 1883] 458).

10. George Hodges, *Henry Codman Potter: Seventh Bishop of New York* (New York: The Macmillan Company, 1915) 77. There is some uncertainty about whether or not Whittingham set apart these deaconesses with the laying on of hands. Donovan maintains that he used the "Service of the Ordination of Deaconesses" from the Kaiserswerth deaconess manual (Donovan, 92). If Hodges is correct about the sign of admission being a handclasp, then Whittingham used an *adapted* form of the Kaiserswerth service, which, in fact, calls for the laying on of hands accompanied by words of blessing (A Lady, *Kaiserswerth Deaconesses. Including A History of the Institution, the Ordination Service and Questions for Self-examination*, 1st American ed. [Baltimore: Joseph Robinson, 1857] 48).

11. Walter C. Whitaker, *History of the Protestant Episcopal Church in Alabama 1763–1891* (Birmingham: Roberts & Son, 1898) 170.

12. Donovan, 95.

13. The Diocese of Long Island, *The Form of Admitting Deaconesses to Their Office, According to the Use of the Diocese of Long Island* (Brooklyn: Orphan's Press–Church Charity Foundation, 1872) 9.

14. "Service for the Admission of the Deaconesses," *Church Work* 2:10 (August 1887) 277–278.

15. Truesdell, 160.

16. Truesdell, 159.
17. Truesdell, 159.
18. Truesdell, 160–161.
19. Donovan, 103.
20. Truesdell, 160.
21. Schnorrenberg, 475.
22. Whitaker, 170.
23. See note 9.
24. Protestant Episcopal Church in the United States of America, *Journal of the Proceedings of the Bishops, Clergy and Laity of the Protestant Episcopal Church in the United States of America in a General Convention Held in the City of Baltimore, Md., From October Fourth through October Twenty-sixth, Inclusive, in the Year of Our Lord 1871* (n.p., 1872) 148–149.
25. Donovan, 95.
26. Donovan, 97.
27. Pamela W. Darling, *New Wine: The Story of Women Transforming Leadership and Power in the Episcopal Church* (Cambridge, Mass.: Cowley Publications, 1994)106.
28. Mary Abbot Twing, "Legislation on Woman's Work in the American Church: Conclusion," *Church Work* 4:12 (October 1889) 356.
29. Donovan, 102–103; Darling, 106. The canon passed only after sisterhoods were excluded from its provisions.
30. Donovan, 105.
31. The General Convention of 1901 opened the Office of Deaconess to widows.
32. Caroline H. Sanford, "The Deaconess Order in the American Church," appendix 12 of *The Ministry of Women: A Report by a Committee Appointed by His Grace the Lord Archbishop of Canterbury* (London: Society for Promoting Christian Knowledge; New York: The Macmillan Company, 1919) 213.
33. "Some Other Modern Liturgical Forms," appendix 15 of *The Ministry of Women*, 288–292. The New York and Pennsylvania forms are almost identical; New York omitted one of the questions in the examination.
34. [Protestant Episcopal Church in the United States of America] preface to *A Book of Offices: Services For Occasions Not Provided For in the Book of Common Prayer* (Milwaukee: The Young Churchman Co., 1917) v–vi.
35. For a synopsis of English forms from this period, see "Forms for the Ordination of Deaconesses," appendix 14 of *The Ministry of Women*, 240–277.
36. The text of the service was not published with the Commission's Report in the Journal of General Convention, but it may be found in the separately-published *Second Report of the Joint Commission on The Book of Common Prayer Appointed by the General Convention of 1913* (New York: Macmillan Company, 1919) 210–218.
37. *Second Report*, 210.
38. Protestant Episcopal Church in the United States of America, *Journal of the General Convention of the Protestant Episcopal Church in the United States of America, Held in the City of Detroit From October Eighth through October Twenty-fourth, Inclusive, in the Year of Our Lord 1919* (n.p., 1920) 607.
39. *JGC 1919*, 404–405. The General Convention of 1919 also created a Commission on Women's Work in the Church but failed to appoint any women to it. However, the resolution creating the Joint Commission on Adapting the Office of Deaconess to the Present Tasks of the Church directed that its membership include three deaconesses and three other women, giving women a voice in the debate about

deaconesses. Deaconesses Ruth Byllesby, Clara Carter, Romola Dahlgren, Helen Fuller, Jane Gillespy, Anna Newell and Edith Smith, along with laywomen Mary Van Kleek, Mrs. Augustus Hand and Elizabeth Matthews, became the first women to be *appointed* by the General Convention to one of its commissions, although women had *served* on commissions before. In 1910, at the very end of its session, the General Convention had expanded the Joint Commission on the Relations of Capital and Labor and renamed it the Joint Commission on Social Service. Because it did not have time to make the appointments needed to fill the vacancies, the Convention authorized the Commission to do so between Conventions. Vida Scudder, Deaconess Susan Knapp and Mary Simkhovitch were appointed by the Commission, making them the first women to *serve* on a Commission of the General Convention. However, they were not appointed by the Convention, and their appearance on the Commission later caused a tightening of the appointment rules. More information is in Darling, 37–38.

This Commission will hereafter be referred to as the Deaconess Commission.

40. Protestant Episcopal Church in the United States of America, *Journal of the General Convention of the Protestant Episcopal Church in the United States of America, Held in the City of Portland From September Sixth through September Twenty-third, Inclusive, in the Year of Our Lord 1922* (n.p., 1923) 731; subsequent references will be cited as *JGC 1922*.

41. *JGC 1922*, 674, quoting *Report of Lambeth Conference 1920*, 102.

42. *JGC 1922*, 677.

43. *JGC 1922*, 682.

44. Resolution 50 of Lambeth 1920 read: "In every branch of the Anglican Communion there should be adopted a Form and Manner of Making Deaconesses such as might fitly find a place in the Book of Common Prayer, containing in all cases provision for: (a) Prayer by the Bishop and the laying on of his hands; (b) A formula giving authority to execute the Office of a Deaconess in the Church of God; (c) The delivery of the New Testament by the Bishop to each candidate. The Forms for the Making and Ordering of Deaconesses should be of the same general character, and as far as possible similar in their most significant parts, though varying in less important details in accordance with local needs." (*JGC 1922*, 677–678.)

45. *JGC 1922*, 677.

46. *Second Report*, 199. This proposed amendment was adopted in 1922 and received final approval in 1925.

47. Canonically, a deaconess's duties in this period were non-liturgical: care of the poor and sick, religious training of the young and others, and the work of moral reformation. At this General Convention, the Deaconess Commission proposed an amendment that would have expanded the duties to include preparing candidates for baptism and confirmation, as well as officiating in public worship "as her office allows, and when licensed thereto by the Bishop" (*JGC 1922*, 678). This proposed amendment aroused opposition, because such provision might lead clergy to allow a Deaconess "to read or preach in ordinary services, greatly to the displeasure and distress of many devout worshippers." Like the proposed liturgy, this amendment was referred back to the Deaconess Commission for further consideration and report (*JGC 1922*, 155).

48. The 1892 service for making deacons uses "Ordinary" here; this was changed to "Bishop" in 1928.

49. *JGC 1922*, 90–91, 123.

50. Protestant Episcopal Church in the United States of America, *Journal of the*

General Convention of the Protestant Episcopal Church in the United States of America, Held in the City of New Orleans From October Seventh through October Twenty-fourth, Inclusive, in the Year of Our Lord 1925 (n.p., 1926) 599; subsequent references will be cited as *JGC 1925.*

51. *JGC 1925,* 599–600.

52. *JGC 1925,* 600.

53. Paul F. Bradshaw, *The Anglican Ordinal: Its History and Development From the Reformation to the Present Day,* Alcuin Club Collections, no. 53 (London: S.P.C.K., 1971) 109.

54. *JGC 1925,* 600.

55. *JGC 1925,* 45.

56. *JGC 1925,* 124.

57. *JGC 1925,* 148–149.

58. *JGC 1925,* 327.

59. *JGC 1925,* 155.

60. Protestant Episcopal Church in the United States of America, *Journal of the General Convention of the Protestant Episcopal Church in the United States of America, Held in the City of Washington, D.C. From October Tenth through October Twenty-fifth, Inclusive, in the Year of Our Lord 1928* (n.p., 1929) 449.

61. *JGC 1928,* 450.

62. *JGC 1928,* 450–451.

63. *JGC 1928,* 77.

64. *JGC 1928,* 105.

65. *JGC 1928,* 451.

66. Protestant Episcopal Church in the United States of America, *Journal of the General Convention of the Protestant Episcopal Church in the United States of America, Held in the City of Denver, Colorado From September Sixteenth through September Thirtieth, Inclusive, in the Year of Our Lord 1931* (n.p., 1932) 227–228; subsequent references will be cited as *JGC 1931.*

67. At this Convention, the Commission on Adapting the Office of Deaconess to the Present Tasks of the Church requested that its name be changed to the Commission on the Work of the Deaconesses (*JGC 1931,* 470). It will continue to be referred to as the Deaconess Commission.

68. *JGC 1931,* 469–470.

69. Protestant Episcopal Church in the United States of America, *Journal of the General Convention of the Protestant Episcopal Church in the United States of America, Held in the City of Cincinnati, Ohio From October Fourth through October Twenty-sixth, Inclusive, in the Year of Our Lord 1937* (n.p., 1937) 424.

70. Protestant Episcopal Church in the United States of America, *Journal of the General Convention of the Protestant Episcopal Church in the United States of America, Held in the City of San Francisco, California From September Twenty-sixth through October Seventh, Inclusive, in the Year of Our Lord 1949* (n.p., 1949) 390; subsequent references will be cited as *JGC 1949.*

71. *JGC 1949.* 390.

72. *JGC 1949,* 390.

73. Protestant Episcopal Church in the United States of America, *Journal of the General Convention of the Protestant Episcopal Church in the United States of America, Held in the City of Miami Beach, Florida From October Sixth through October Seventeenth, Inclusive, in the Year of Our Lord 1958* (n.p., 1958) 408.

74. Protestant Episcopal Church in the United States of America, *Journal of the General Convention of the Protestant Episcopal Church in the United States of America, Held in the City of Detroit, Michigan From September Eighteenth through Twenty-ninth, inclusive, in the Year of Our Lord 1961* (n.p., 1961) 61.

75. Protestant Episcopal Church in the United States of America, *Journal of the General Convention of the Protestant Episcopal Church in the United States of America, Held in the City of St. Louis, Missouri From October Twelfth through October Twenty-third, inclusive, in the Year of Our Lord 1964* (n.p., 1964) 247–48, 833.

76. Darling, 110.

77. William Stringfellow and Anthony Towne, *The Death and Life of Bishop Pike* (Garden City, NY: Doubleday & Company, Inc., 1976) 316–317.

78. Bishop Pike's intentions regarding Deaconess Edwards also gave some of his opponents an excuse to bring heresy charges against him. A petition from the diocese of Arizona came before the bishops at Glacier Park, listing accusations concerning Pike's views on the Virgin Birth, Trinity, Incarnation, Resurrection and Ascension. Bishop Pike was not allowed to answer the accusations, but he was given the opportunity to make a statement, in which he reaffirmed his ordination vow of "loyalty to the Doctrine, Discipline, and Worship of the Episcopal Church." The charges were dropped (William Stringfellow and Anthony Towne, *The Bishop Pike Affair: Scandals of Conscience and Heresy, Relevance and Solemnity in the Contemporary Church* [New York: Harper & Row, 1967] 32–37).

79. Stringfellow and Towne, *Death and Life*, 317.

80. Protestant Episcopal Church in the United States of America, *Journal of the General Convention of the Protestant Episcopal Church in the United States of America, Otherwise Known as The Episcopal Church, Held in the City of Seattle From September Seventeenth through Twenty-seventh, inclusive, in the Year of Our Lord 1967* (n.p., 1967) B7–8; subsequent references will be cited as *JGC 1967*. On motion of Bishop Pike, the word "specialized" was subsequently stricken.

81. *JGC 1967*, B8.

82. *JGC 1967*, B25.

83. *JGC 1967*, B24.

84. Darling, 111.

85. *JGC 1967*, 58.

86. *JGC 1967*, 407.

87. *JGC 1967*, B30.

88. *Report of Lambeth Conference 1968*, quoted in V. Nelle Bellamy, "Participation of Women in the Public Life of the Church from Lambeth Conference 1867–1978," *Historical Magazine of the Protestant Episcopal Church* 51 (1982) 94–95.

89. Protestant Episcopal Church in the United States of America, *Journal of the General Convention of the Protestant Episcopal Church in the United States of America, Otherwise Known as The Episcopal Church, Held in the City of Houston, Texas From October Eleventh through October Twenty-second, inclusive, in the Year of Our Lord 1970* (n.p., 1970) 249.

90. See Sections 4 and 5 of the new Canon 50.

91. Darling, 113.

New Perspectives on
Christian Initiation From
the Byzantine Tradition

Byron D. Stuhlman

MEMBERSHIP IN THE CHURCH is bestowed not by birth, but by the rites of Christian initiation. These rites developed as the primary means of Christian formation–as the way in which the Christian is shaped in the likeness of Christ and begins to grow into the full stature of Christ. In recent decades an enormous amount of research has been devoted to Christian initiation and the fruits of this research are evident in the revised rites of most Western liturgical traditions.

Initiation has come to be understood more as a process (a kind of apprenticeship) culminating in baptism than as a single rite: perhaps the most impressive fruit of the research on initiatory rites is the set of guidelines and services known as the RCIA (the Rite of Christian Initiation of Adults)–which embraces a period of initial inquiry, the catechumenate, the period of candidacy during Lent, the rites of initiation themselves at the paschal vigil, and a period of post-baptismal catechesis.[1] This has been a model for similar processes in other traditions as well.[2] In the RCIA, the initiatory process has been restored to the context of the church year: Lent regains its function as a time of intensive catechesis on the meaning of the Christian faith and the Easter Vigil is restored as the principal occasion for the baptismal liturgy.

But impressive as these gains have been, the almost exclusive focus on the initiation of adult converts and the tendency to set initiation only in the context of the church's celebration of Christ's death and resurrection present theological and pastoral problems and fail to take account of the full range of initiatory theology and practice which are part of the church's tradition. Initiatory theology and practice would both be immeasurably enriched by drawing on a wider range of sources and taking the experience of the Byzantine tradition into account.

The explanatory literature which has grown up around the RCIA often gives the impression that it represents a contemporary adaptation of the standard initiatory process of late Christian antiquity (from the time of Justin Martyr until the disintegration of the process in the early Middle Ages) and that this process is the norm for initiation in the church.[3] This is a highly misleading impression and it does real disservice to contemporary Christians who try to devise an appropriate initiatory strategy for the church today. The problem is not so much with these new rites of initiation themselves as it is with the claim that there is a single *normative* path for the journey to baptism—what Miguel Arranz calls the initiatory *iter*—and with a theology of initiation based on this one particular path for that journey.

The impression is often given that there was a single, stable course everywhere in the church throughout this period for the initiatory journey—a process of preparation for initiation that can be taken as a norm. A careful examination of the relevant literature from the period dispels this illusion, however, and suggests that, since people come to baptism in many ways, no one pattern for the initiatory journey can be taken as the norm. In particular, it makes problematic both the long-standing claim by most major Western traditions that baptism as soon as possible after birth is the norm and the claim set out at the Reformation by advocates of believers' baptism and more recently by proponents of the RCIA and similar programs in other churches that the baptism of adult converts is the norm. Neither side of this debate takes adequate account of the fact that some come to Christ by a process of conversion while others grow into Christ by a process of nurture within the Christian community.

Initiation in the Early Church

The initiatory journey in the early centuries was very sensitive to context.[4] In the Jewish milieu of much of the early Syrian and Armenian traditions, the Christian faith may have been seen more as a fulfillment of Judaism than as conversion to a worship of different God. Jews or Gentiles attracted to Judaism who turned to Jesus as Israel's Messiah had to learn the doctrinal and ethical implications of Christianity as Messianic Judaism, but they were already grounded in the basic presuppositions of Christianity and had come to understand the God of Abraham, Isaac, and Jacob as the God and Father of our Lord Jesus the Messiah. Their initiatory journey would be a relatively brief one, therefore, and the lapse of time between their acceptance of Jesus as Messiah and their baptism would be relatively short. This is borne out by the witness of the New Testament (where baptism followed immediately on profession of faith), the Jewish-Christian catechism on the two ways found in several early documents (which presupposes a short period of preparation),[5] and the witness of the early Armenian tradition.[6] There was a single stage of preparation, exorcism was not called for, and, in the earliest stratum of this tradition, the dominant paradigm for our baptism is the messianic anointing of Jesus at his baptism in the Jordan.

Near the Mediterranean, littoral Christian traditions developed in a predominantly pagan milieu. Christian converts had to be renounce the pagan gods that they once served and to be taught the basic presuppositions of Christian ethics and doctrine. For the first three centuries, they had to do this in a predominantly pagan and often hostile society.[7] Initial instruction might be given by Christian philosophers such as Justin Martyr, or it might be more directly under the control of the authorities of the local church. In the process described in the *Apostolic Tradition*, this initial stage of preparation (the catechumenate)[8] concerned itself primarily with the appropriate manner of life—what we would call ethics. It was adjusted to the circumstances of the convert, and might last several years. Enrollment in the final stage of preparation for baptism (candidacy)[9] was dependent, the *Apostolic Tradition* tells us, primarily upon testimony to the catechumen's manner of life (*tropos*). The decision to seek admission as a candidate for baptism involved risk—of ostracism in the arena of the public life of the society, of sporadic persecution by pagans or Jews, and sometimes of death. The risks involved and the preparation required meant that only the seriously committed sought baptism. Even Christian parents were inclined to postpone the baptism of their children, although in the third century bishops in North Africa attempted to establish the baptism of such children soon after birth as the policy of the church in that region. The final stage of preparation, with its focus on doctrine, was relatively brief. No indication of its duration is given in the *Apostolic Tradition*; in many traditions, it appears to have been about three weeks in length. The curriculum was no doubt the baptismal formula itself—what Irenaeus called the rule of faith and what would later develop into the creed. Because candidates had to be freed from their ties to pagan gods (often understood by Christians as demons rather than as simply non-existent), a part of the preparation was frequent exorcism to cast out such alien powers. Often a renunciation of such powers was a component of the baptismal rite. The primary paradigm for baptism in this strand of the Christian tradition was our participation in Christ's death and resurrection (Rom. 6) and from the end of the second century the Easter Vigil was the primary occasion for baptism in many regions, with the day of Pentecost (which concluded the paschal season) as a secondary baptismal occasions."[10]

By the late fourth century the context had shifted dramatically within the Roman empire. The conversion of Constantine early in the century had brought, first, toleration, then imperial favor, and finally (after the abortive pagan restoration of Julian the Apostate in mid-century) legal establishment for the church during the final decades of the century. Even after the cessation of persecution many postponed baptism, treating admission to the catechumenate as a nominal commitment to the church which did not require the moral rigor of full membership—a custom which is well-attested in the fourth century. As Herman Wegman writes,

> Originally a time of personal conversion toward a Christian style of life, now [the catechumenate] became the step that was compulsory for a person if he or she wanted to count in society. People took this step as far as it was necessary: they became catechumens, but for the most part a deeper engagement or authentic conversion did not follow. As a catechumen, a person was officially a member of the church, but at the same time he or she was free of the burdens that were borne by baptized Christians. The catechumenate was no longer a time of testing but a half-Christian state of life.[11]

By the end of the century, bishops had begun to succeed in ending this abuse of the catechumenate. Those who sought baptism, however, were no longer a select band of the seriously committed; the baptized now had a privileged position in society, and a flood of applicants of untested commitment sought baptism. Bishops of the great sees and their presbyters (Cyril in Jerusalem, the presbyters Theodore of Mopsuestia and John Chrysostom in Antioch, Ambrose in Milan)[12] devoted the best of the church's resources to turning these half-converted pagans into serious Christians. The first stage of the catechumenate (the period before enrollment for baptism) had, for all intents and purposes, disappeared by this time: the rites for making a catechumen in the sacramentaries and euchologies that have come down to us are, in fact, used to enroll candidates for baptism, not to admit them to the catechumenate as the *Apostolic Tradition* uses that term.[13] In the course of the century the period of candidacy had been expanded to a forty-day season, which we know as Lent, and it appears that all formal catechesis was given during this season.[14] In the impressive setting of splendid churches erected through imperial largesse, an expanded repertoire of dramatic ritual (highly dramatic exorcisms, handing over and returning the creed, rites of renunciation and allegiance, the heightened drama of the baptismal rite itself) and the skillful rhetoric of the Lenten catecheses on doctrine and the Easter-week catecheses on the rites themselves were deployed to full advantage in an effort to secure the serious commitment of those who came to the font. Nevertheless, the standards of Christian conduct and the level of doctrinal comprehension began to fall precipitously.

The question of how children of Christian families were initiated has been largely ignored in the standard histories of Christian initiation. The historical record is silent on this question until the end of the second century. Early Christianity was a missionary movement, and the primary interest of both early Christian authors and contemporary historians is focused on the story of the growth of the church through conversion. By the time the question of how such children were initiated was addressed in early Christian literature, many treated the baptism of children as unremarkable (the baptism of children, even those too young to speak for themselves, is noted without comment in the *Apostolic Tradition*, and Origen treats the practice as apostolic in origin),[15] while at least one author (Tertullian) acknowledged the custom but regarded it as ill-advised.[16] By the mid-third century North African bishops at a council of Carthage were insisting on the baptism of infants shortly after birth.[17] By the fifth century most candidates for initiation were children, and the challenge which the church now faced was to devise appropriate initiatory journeys to fit the situation. The response, as we shall see, would be very different in the Latin-speaking West and the Greek-speaking East.

Initiation in the Middle Ages in the West

By early in the fifth century, the population in most areas of the empire was nominally Christian, and children of Christian families were being baptized in infancy or early childhood. The carefully crafted initiatory journey for adults was becoming dysfunctional or redundant for the majority of candidates for baptism. In the West the great majority of such adult candidates for baptism as there were came from tribes to the North of the Mediterranean centers of the Latin Christianity. Conversion was usually by tribe at the initiative of their leaders. The Latin rites used for the initiation of such converts were in a language foreign to them and consequently could not function as originally intended in their formation, such catechesis as was given was usually rudimentary at best, and mass conversion and initiation resulted in incomplete evangelization.

At first infants and children within the Western empire were initiated in a process originally designed for adults and only minimally adapted for younger candidates. Sufficient liturgical creativity did not exist in the declining culture of the Western empire to design a process geared to children. In the rites set out in the Ordo Romanus XI and the latest stratum of the Gelasian Sacramentary (seventh or eighth century)[18] the catechumenate appears to have been fused with candidacy;[19] the major rites of candidacy (the scrutinies) were shifted from Sundays to weekdays. Catechesis was impossible since the candidates were in most cases too young to be instructed, and in the rites themselves candidates replied by proxy (a cleric or a sponsor answering for them).[20] In an increasingly mechanical way all the emphasis was put on the efficacy of the ritual actions themselves.[21] It was not long before the catechetical elements were entirely eliminated from the rites for candidates, and candidacy was soon telescoped into a single rite ("for making a catechumen"),[22] celebrated shortly before baptism or immediately prefaced to the baptismal rite. Fear of death before baptism led to the gradual abandonment of Easter and Pentecost as the primary occasions for baptism, and the requirement (originally peculiar to Rome) that the bishop conclude the rite with the laying on of hands and anointing led to the accidental creation of a separate rite of "confirmation," eventually postponed to "the age of discretion" and in many times and places never administered at all. In the later Middle Ages, baptism no longer admitted to communion, as it had in Ordo Romanus XI; this too was postponed until "the age of discretion," before or after confirmation. By the end of the Middle Ages, sponsors and parents were often charged with responsibility for seeing that children learned key Christian texts, so that a minimum of catechesis was restored between baptism and admission to communion or confirmation.[23] These texts were the basis of the sixteenth century catechisms of both the Catholic Church and the churches of the Reformation. But both Roman Catholics and adherents of the major Reformation confessions in the sixteenth century used rites of initiation that were ill-adapted for either infants or adult converts. In the process, the very function of baptism changed. It had been the culmination of the initiatory journey and admitted candidates to full participation as in the life of the church. Now it had become the first step in an initiatory journey which reached its goal at confirmation and/or admission to communion. Of necessity, such catechesis as was given came after baptism rather than before. By the end of the Middle Ages the baptismal rite no longer served to admit candidates to communion. Baptism had become the functional equivalent of the rite for the admission of catechumens in the early church. The churches of the Reformation that practiced infant baptism increased the emphasis on post-baptismal catechesis but did not introduce any fundamental change in the initiatory journey (though they tended to treat confirmation or a similar rite as the service which marked the conclusion of catechesis and marked admission to communion, rather than as a sacrament that bestowed grace).

Developments in the Byzantine Tradition

The East showed considerably more liturgical creativity than the West, and the documents of the Byzantine rite include initiatory journeys tailored to the circumstances of children of Christian families, to heretical or schismatic Christians who wished to unite with Catholic Christianity, and to pagans, Jews, and eventually Muslims.[24] The initiatory journey of children is documented in the euchologies and in the rubrics of what is known as typikon of the Great Church (that is, the synaxarion and kanonarion of the Hagia Sophia of Constantinople). Provisions for the initiatory journey of adult converts can be also be found in the euchologies of the Byzantine tradition. The early provisions for such converts are based on canons attributed to the council of Laodicea and to the first council of Constantinople. Supplementary provisions were made as need arose: after the Council of Chalcedon, provision needed to be made for the reconciliation of non-Chalcedonian Christians, and the rise of Islam necessitated provisions for Muslim converts. Whereas the Western church continued to worship in Latin, even in regions when that was an alien tongue to most people, the churches of the Byzantine tradition outside the boundaries of the empire developed their own liturgical languages, rather than retaining Greek for their worship, so that liturgy retained its catechetical function in the formation of both children and adults in their initiation.

Our first witness to Byzantine initiatory usages is Gregory of Nazianzus, who restored Nicene orthodoxy to the capital of the Eastern Empire during his brief tenure as patriarch before the first Council of Constantinople.[25] One of his homilies for Epiphany (celebrated as the Feast of Christ's Baptism) reveals two important facts about baptism at the end of the fourth century in what was to become the Byzantine rite. First, the church kept three baptismal feasts: Easter, Pentecost, and Epiphany. Second, parents were encouraged to postpone the baptism of their children until they were old enough to take some part in their own initiation.

Let us first examine the baptismal feasts. In course of his homily Gregory sets out arguments of those who postpone baptism: "I am waiting for Epiphany; I prefer Easter; I will wait for Pentecost. It is better to be baptized with Christ, to rise with Christ on the day of his resurrection, to honor the manifestation of the Spirit."[26] Their argument signals to us the three baptismal feasts observed in Constantinople at that time. The addition of Epiphany (observed as the Feast of Christ's Baptism) to the list of baptismal feasts allowed the Byzantine tradition to articulate a fuller baptismal theology than prevailed in the West, where the strongly paschal focus of baptismal theology reflects the restriction of baptism to Easter and Pentecost. The celebration of baptism at Epiphany gave expression to the strand of baptismal theology which took the baptism of Christ as its paradigm for the meaning of the sacrament.

Let us turn now to the age at which children of Christian families were to be baptized. Except in emergencies, Gregory encouraged parents in Christian families to postpone their children's baptism until the children were old enough to take some part in their own initiation:

> [W]hat have you to say about those who are still children, and conscious neither of the loss nor of the grace? Are we to baptize them too? Certainly, if any danger presses. For it is better that they should be unconsciously sanctified than that they should depart unsealed and uninitiated. A proof of this is found in the circumcision on the eighth day, which was a sort of typical seal and was conferred on children before they had the use of reason . . . . But in respect of others [who are not in danger] I give my advice to wait till the end of the third year, or a little more or less, when they may be able to listen and to answer something about the sacrament, even though they do not perfectly understand it, yet at any rate they may know the outlines; and then to sanctify them in soul and body with the great sacrament of our consecration. For this is how the matter stands; at that time they begin to be responsible for their lives, when reason is matured, and they learn the mystery of life (for sins of ignorance owing to their tender years they have no account to give), and it is far more profitable on all accounts to be fortified by the font, because of the sudden assaults of danger that befall us stronger than our helpers.[27]

This is a quite different pattern than the one recommended to parents in the West at this time. The North African understanding of original sin led to the pressure in Western traditions for immediate baptism (or baptism at the next baptismal feast after birth).[28] But a different practice originally prevailed in the East.

Let us examine the initiatory journey of the children of Christian families more closely. Miguel Arranz provides a close study of the process in the commentary to his critical edition of Byzantine initiatory rites.[29] The key documents here are the early euchologies and the typikon of the Great Church. The earliest euchology is that of Barberini Manuscript 336, which is customarily dated to the late eighth century and is of Italian provenance. Another key manuscript euchology (which Arranz uses as the basis of his text) is the Codex Bessarion, which dates from the late eleventh or early twelfth century and reflects the usage of Constantinople rather than Byzantine usage in Italy and which was the basis of the earliest printed euchology. The dating of the documents from which the so-called typikon has been reconstructed is less certain: they probably date from the tenth and eleventh centuries.[30]

The early euchologies provide two prayers, to be used on the eighth and fortieth days after the birth of a child. The model for these observances is obviously the accounts in Luke's infancy narratives of the naming of Jesus at his circumcision eight days after his birth and his presentation in the temple forty days after his birth.[31] The text of these prayers is as follows:

On the eighth day after birth:

> O Lord our God, we pray unto thee and we beseech thee: let the light of thy countenance be marked upon thy servant N., and let the cross of thine only-begotten Son also be marked upon his heart and upon his thoughts, that he may avoid the vanities of the world and every evil device of the adversary and that he may follow thy precepts. And grant, O Lord, that thy name may abide in him, never repudiated, that he may be united in due season to thy holy church and attain perfection through the awesome mysteries of thy Christ: so that, having walked according to thy commandments and kept intact the seal, he may attain to the blessedness of thine elect in thy kingdom: through the grace and mercy and loving-kindness of thine only begotten Son, with whom thou art blessed, together with thine all-holy and good and life-giving Spirit, now and forever, and unto the ages of ages. Amen.

On the fortieth day after birth:

> O Lord our God, who in accordance with the law didst go up on the fortieth day to the temple with Mary thy holy mother and wert received in the arms of the righteous Simeon: Let thy servant N. grow through thy power so that, coming to the bath of incorruption, he may become a child of the light and of the day and, having attained a share in the heritage of thine elect, may become a partaker of the precious body and blood of thy Christ, protected by the grace of the holy, consubstantial, and indivisible Trinity: For thy glory and that of thine only-begotten Son and of thine all-holy and life-giving Spirit, now and forever, and unto the ages of ages. Amen.

The references in both prayers to future baptism are unmistakable. The prayers serve to give the status of a catechumen, as we see in the rubrics for the initiation of converts from other religions, who are described after admission as catechumens as "unbaptized Christians, as in the case of children of Christian parents awaiting baptism."[32]

We have little evidence of what catechesis was given to children in this first, informal stage of their catechumenate. On the basis of provisions for adult converts (see below), we might suppose that their families were expected to teach them the Lord's Prayer, the creed, and certain psalms (perhaps the oldest of the fixed psalms of the morning and evening office, Psalms 51 and 148–150 for the morning and Psalm 141 for the evening). They would have perhaps been exposed to the readings assigned to the eucharist and to the readings of the Daily Office during Lent, whose original purpose was the instruction of catechumens.

Enrollment in the second stage of the catechumenate (candidacy for baptism) according to the witness of the euchologies and the typikon of the Great Church took place during the fourth week of Lent. This is still the time when intercessions for "those to be enlightened" (baptized) are added to intercessions for catechumens at the offices of terce-sext and vespers in the Byzantine rite. Two rubrics in the typikon confirm the witness of the rubrics in the Daily Office. They prescribe that on the Sundays before the second and third weeks in Lent notice be given that families should bring any of their members whom they wish to present for baptism to church in the fourth week of Lent, so that they can be enrolled and duly instructed before baptism. In his analysis of the rubrics Arranz concludes:

> As regards the candidates for baptism, it seems to us that the texts of [the notices,] the [symbols here] and the prosfwnetikov and the prokhruktikos are eloquent enough to give us an indication of the age of these candidates: young enough to need to be brought to church by their parents, but old enough to be able to follow the catechesis offered to them and to understand something at the baptism itself.[33]

The rationale which underlies this practice is quite different from what we find in the West, particularly North Africa, where the church inculcated in its members the fear that children who died before baptism had no hope of salvation and mandated baptism as soon as possible after birth. What is suggested by the Byzantine tradition is that a different initiatory journey is appropriate for the children of Christian families from the journey(s) set forth for adult converts. The journey of children is a journey *of growth* into Christ in the context of the life of the Christian community; the journeys of the adults who turn to Christ are journeys of *conversion* from another faith. The different journeys converge at the time candidates are enrolled for baptism.

From the time of enrollment as a candidate the initiatory journey of both children and adults, candidates in the Byzantine tradition takes a path that is much the same as that found throughout the church in the earlier period.[34] The form used to enroll candidates for baptism is entitled "a prayer for making a catechumen." Although the diaconal litanies and dismissals at terce-sext and vespers in the latter part of Lent distinguish between catechumens and "those preparing for enlightenment" (candidates for baptism), the rubrics in the initiatory rites of the euchologies appear to equate catechumens with candidates for baptism (as did Western sacramentaries of the same period). The euchology also provides exorcisms to be used during candidacy and a prayer for use as the day of baptism approaches. On Maundy Thursday, chrism was consecrated for use at baptism, and on Good Friday the candidates made their renunciations and gave their allegiance to the triune God. Baptism was then administered on the morning of Holy Saturday and at the Vigil of Easter Eve.[35] Presumably those to be baptized on Lazarus Saturday or Pentecost were also prepared during the catechesis given during the second half of Lent. We have no witness in our liturgical texts to when catechesis was given to those baptized at Epiphany (and Christmas).

Arranz summarizes his conclusions on the initiatory journey of children during the first stage of their catechumenate as follows:

> The prayers of the eight and fortieth days after birth . . . in truth recorded the spiritual life of a newborn child of a Christian family. We can say that these two prayers, particularly the first, made the newborn a true Christian, to whom adults coming from heretical groups whose baptism was not recognized could be compared, as well as Jews, Moslems, and others after their renunciation of their original faith . . .
>
> This first stage of the catechumenate for young children could be extended until they acquired the use of reason . . . .
>
> Since the child was already "Christian," people did not fear for his eternal destiny in case of death . . .; they waited until the age of "first communion," we might say, so that the rites of renunciation of Satan and allegiance to Christ which preceded baptism were followed by the candidate himself and not just by his godparent—a usage which, nevertheless, already began to make its appearance in our patriarchal euchologies . . .[36]

This is a markedly different initiatory journey than the one followed by children in the Western church.

Unlike the Western sacramentaries of the same period, Byzantine euchologies set out specific requirements for adult candidates for baptism. While the first stage of the catechumenate had disappeared, provision was made for an analogous period of preparation. The euchologies set out the following requirements for such converts:

a preliminary fast of fifteen days,
the discipline of regular morning and evening prayer,
study of certain psalms, the Lord's Prayer, and the Creed,
a formal renunciation of error,
admission to the catechumenate with prayer.

Since candidates for baptism were enrolled during the fourth week of Lent, it appears that the preliminary stage of preparation and fasting took place during the first three weeks of Lent. Notice that this preliminary stage does not begin with admission as a catechumen, but concludes with it. In actual fact, the term used here is "unbaptized Christian, as in the case of children of Christian parents awaiting baptism," the term "catechumen" being reserved by the time of the euchology for candidates (that is, catechumens "who are preparing for enlightenment"). The following day adult catechumens and the children of Christian families are enrolled for baptism. As in the Western sacarmentaries, the prayer of the rite is designated as a prayer "for making a catechumen."

The provisions for the period of candidacy are not given in any detail. The euchology contains three exorcisms and a prayer when the day of baptism is approaching, the rite of renunciation and allegiance (in two forms, the longer of which includes a homily and is assigned to terce-sext of Good Friday).

Forgotten Perspectives:
The Wisdom of the Byzantine Tradition

Western churches immeasurably enriched their baptismal theology when they came to understand baptism from a paschal perspective and crafted contemporary adaptations of the rites for the baptismal journey and initiation of adult converts that were part of the classical Western liturgical tradition. But the classical liturgical traditions of the East, particularly the Byzantine liturgical tradition, also have contributions to make as contemporary Christians seek to work out appropriate initiatory rites for the situation of today's church—contributions which can open up the narrowly paschal focus of the theology of the new initiatory rites of the Western churches and can also assist contemporary Christians in rethinking the baptismal journey of the children of Christian families.

Baptismal Feasts and Baptismal Paradigms

The classic baptismal feast since the end of the second century has been Easter. In the fourth century churches of almost all traditions made the Easter Vigil the primary occasion of baptism and developed Lent as the primary season for the catechetical formation of candidates for baptism. Many traditions also made the day of Pentecost a baptismal feast—a kind of back-up for those candidates who for one reason or another could not be baptized at Easter. While today we think of the day of Pentecost as the Feast of the Holy Spirit, it was apparently chosen as a baptismal day because it was the closing feast of the paschal season rather than because of its association with the gift of the Spirit. Papal correspondence, cited above, insisted that baptisms be reserved to these two feasts except in emergencies and selected the Lord's Day as the alternative in case of such emergencies because it was the weekly analogue of the annual feasts of Easter and Pentecost.

So deeply rooted was the custom of baptism on these two feasts that provisions for baptism at their vigils remained in the Roman missal until the reforms of Vatican II, even though few if any were baptized at these services in recent centuries. This choice of baptismal occasions gives an almost exclusively paschal context for baptismal theology, taking as the dominant paradigm the Pauline theme of participation in Christ's death and resurrection. Although the theme of rebirth (a Johannine emphasis) was also important in Western baptismal theology; in that tradition rebirth was subordinated to the paschal paradigm. This was a theology which was perfectly adapted to the situation of the Christian convert in the midst of a hostile pagan society in the early centuries: baptismal death to the world that the convert had been part of was a deeply felt reality. In the pagan society of the Roman Empire, converts had to break their ties with their pagan past in order to become Christian, and so the catechumenate came to be understood as a struggle to break free from the service of pagan gods—gods that the church generally understood as demonic powers, defeated by Christ on the cross,[37] whose continuing hold had to be broken by repeated exorcisms.[38]

The understanding of baptism as entailing renunciation of ties to the pagan past and a contract of allegiance to Christ in his service—an understanding dramatically enacted in the rite of renunciation and profession of allegiance on Good Friday—grew out of this way of understanding paganism and was linked to the paschal paradigm. For adult converts in American society today, however, this use of exorcism may be less suitable. Neither converts from Judaism and Islam nor those adult candidates who have no distinctive religious commitments are under the power of pagan gods which we might understand as demons. And for the same reason it is problematic to include exorcism in the preparation of candidates who are children of Christian parents.

The Byzantine tradition had three major baptismal feasts in the fourth century, as we have seen in the homily of Gregory Nazianzus—adding Epiphany as the Feast of Christ's Baptism to the feasts of Easter and Pentecost.[39] Epiphany was particularly important as a baptismal feast, for it gave expression to the other major strand of baptismal theology in the early church—the strand that took the baptism of Christ as the paradigm for Christian baptism. This strand was dominant in the early Syrian tradition. Working with Jewish themes, it saw Jesus at the moment of his baptism as invested with the role which Adam was created to fill in paradise, but had forfeited by his sin—the royal priesthood of God's son. It is the anointing of Jesus by the Spirit at his baptism which makes him the Messiah (Christ in Greek, Anointed One in English)[40]—an anointing which was prefigured by the anointing of Israel's kings,[41] priests,[42] and (sometimes) prophets.[43]

Our baptism into Christ invests us with the same roles.[44] The church understood Christ as God's Son by birthright; in baptism we through the same Spirit become God's sons and daughters by adoption.[45] This adoption brings us into Christ's relation to God, so that we too can approach the Father with the boldness or free access of children[46] and call God Father. What Paul speaks of as adoption, John spoke of as new birth (regeneration)[47]—a major motif in many prayers of the rite. Through it Christ the light enlightens our minds with the true knowledge of God—and enlightenment (symbols here)[48] is a frequent name for baptism in the Byzantine rite.

Syrian Christians (both Syriac-speaking and Greek-speaking), were in close contact with Judaism, and also understood Christian initiation as akin to the rites for Jewish proselytes.[49] Baptism could be understood as the "circumcision not made with hands,"[50] by which we put off the old, sinful humanity of Adam and put on the new humanity of Christ.[51] It is in this sense a "new creation," since the redemption which we make our own in baptism can be understood as a new creation,[52] and for Syrian authors we reenter paradise through baptism.[53] This theme was eventually used to interpret the undressing before the baptismal immersion and the new clothing put on when emerging from the font. Earlier, however, the robe of glory or garment of incorruption or immortality[54] put on through baptism was understood as the Spirit or as Christ himself.[55]

The mark of circumcision was now understood to be fulfilled in the "mark" of the Spirit[56] given to the Christian in baptism. This was like the brand which identified the baptized as sheep of Christ's flock[57] or members of Christ's army.[58] It was also a mark which protected them against the forces of evil and death. It was like the imprint of the Christ on their souls (and so also associated with the sign of the cross). The mark was generally understood to be given by the prebaptismal anointing which imparted the Spirit to the candidate for baptism. A postbaptismal anointing, which was not an original part of the rites of Syria, was sometimes spoken of as the "seal" of the Spirit,[59] which brought the initiation to its completion. In Greek sfragis word usually used for both "mark" or "seal;" but two quite distinct Syriac words are used for these two meanings.

Another cluster of themes associated with baptism at Epiphany focuses on the baptismal waters themselves. They are assimilated to the waters of creation, the waters of the Red Sea over which Moses led the people of Israel, and especially the waters of Jordan over which Joshua (Greek, "Jesus") led the people of Israel and in which Jesus was baptized, as well as other waters. These are the themes which come to the fore in the texts associated with the blessing of waters and with baptism at Epiphany. Much of this rich tapestry of themes is reflected in the liturgical texts for baptism in the Byzantine tradition, especially the blessings of water, the oil of gladness, and the myrrh or chrism. In the Byzantine tradition the two strands

73

of baptismal theology which we have picked out (that which took the death and resurrection of Christ as its dominant paradigm and that which took the baptism of Christ as its paradigm) were joined in a fruitful dialectic and understood as complementary to each other rather than as in conflict.

In the reforms of Vatican II, the Roman Catholic Church reduced its baptismal feasts from two (Easter and Pentecost) to one–Easter. Many other Western churches, however, not only retained Pentecost as a baptismal feast in addition to Easter, but also restored the Feast of Christ's Baptism (observed on the Sunday after Epiphany) as a third baptismal occasion. American Lutherans and Episcopalians have also added All Saints' Day or Sunday to the list of baptismal feasts. These four feasts present a rich tapestry of baptismal themes and are material for a fuller baptismal theology than one which is almost exclusively paschal in focus. In fact, the themes associated with Christ's baptism provide a better way to interpret the baptism of the children of Christian parents than those associated with the paschal paradigm.

The Baptismal Journey for Children of Christian Families

As we have just seen, one problem with recent Western initiatory rites (particularly the RCIA) is that they take the paschal paradigm for baptism as the basis for their baptismal theology and neglect the alternative paradigm based on Christ's baptism. Another problem is the failure to think through the problem of the initiation of children of Christian families at sufficient depth. Some Roman Catholics have suggested that the baptism of young children is a departure from the norm, but resign themselves to continuing the late medieval pattern of infant baptism, subsequent catechesis, and a delayed culmination of "confirmation" and admission to communion after this catechesis. Most other Western churches now use a baptismal rite reintegrated with the texts and gestures associated with initiatory "confirmation" for children as well as adults. In growing numbers, they treat even infants baptized by such a rite as communicants. Most have rethought confirmation as a non-initiatory (and repeatable) affirmation of baptismal vows associated with a strengthening by the Holy Spirit. But while this avoids the anomalies of present Roman Catholic practice for the children of Christian parents, it continues to separate any process of Christian formation and apprenticeship in the faith from the initiatory process itself and to make children purely passive participants in their own initiation. Catechesis in such cases is part of the process of formation for a non-initiatory "confirmation" rather than for baptism.

Those who are uneasy with the baptism of infants generally hold up the baptism of adults as the norm. They treat the process of catechetical formation as a process of conversion.[60] But children who grow up in

Christian families are not converts in the ordinary sense of the word; they do not turn to Jesus from some other faith. The issue of formation here is not a matter of putting off some other identity and assuming a Christian identity, but a matter of growing into a Christian identity. Such a journey is not a journey of conversion, but one of nurture, and so a norm based on conversion is inappropriate.

The baptismal journey for children of Christian parents which we find in the early Byzantine tradition provides a good starting point in working out an effective strategy for the initiation of children today. In the early Byzantine tradition, as we have seen, children were made catechumens at birth and underwent preliminary formation under the guidance of their parents. When they were old enough to take some part in worship, they were enrolled for baptism and underwent final catechesis before baptism at a baptismal feast. The advantages here are that children were active rather than passive participants in their own initiation and that baptism was the culmination of an appropriate process of formation. Baptism was understood as full initiation into the church and was sealed with communion. We might note that this is the pattern suggested by the RCIA for unbaptized children of catechetical ages and the pattern suggested by the Episcopal Church if parents and sponsors decide to defer the baptism of an infant. What the experience of the Byzantine tradition suggests is that the exceptional provisions for children of Christian families in the RCIA and the Episcopal *Book of Occasional Services* should become the norm in these two churches for such children.[61] Because we all stand in need of continuing conversion, however, baptism should not be the end of the formation of such children. Catechesis and formation subsequent to their baptism appropriately leads to reaffirmation of the baptismal covenant at some future time.

Moving Beyond Nominal Christianity

Since the fourth century the church has faced the problem of nominal commitment to Christ in a "Christian world." In the last two centuries, Christian faith has eroded in this world to such an extent that many do not even become nominal Christians. The supposedly Christian world needs to be effectively evangelized. Effective formation of adult converts and of the children of Christian families in a catechumenate that shapes Christian identity through a practical apprenticeship in Christianity before baptism is a strategic necessity in this situation. Provisions for the adult catechumenate are in place in many churches; provisions for a similar catechumenate for children are urgently needed, and we have seen what a model for such a catechumenate might be.

A final component of the church's initiatory strategy must take account of both the fact that there are many under-evangelized but baptized nominal Christians who need to be brought to the fullness of the faith and that in a divided Christendom those baptized in one denomination may find in another a home where they bring their faith to fuller expression. Neither of these groups are catechumens in the ordinary sense of the word and they should not be assimilated to unbaptized converts in the catechumenate. Nevertheless a parallel journey or process is appropriate for them. Provisions for such processes are made by both the RCIA (in the form approved for use in the United States and by the Episcopal *Book of Occasional Services*. They culminate in most cases in an affirmation of the baptismal covenant–an appropriate culmination for such a journey. But the theological evaluation of such an affirmation in many cases presents anomalies. Understanding the Episcopal rites of "confirmation" and reception as rites that impart strengthening by the Spirit on such occasions as times of intensified commitment makes theological sense, but the unconditional reservation of administering these rites to bishops is problematic. The Roman Catholic theology which understands the "confirmation" associated with such an affirmation (except for those received from Eastern churches) to impart an indelible character distinct from baptism and the similar Orthodox understanding of the chrismation of converts is rooted in a very problematic theology of baptism. The processes in both cases are appropriate strategies for apprenticeship, but the theology of the rite in which they culminate needs re-examination.

Notes

1. A convenient English edition of the current rites can be found in *Rite of Christian Initiation for Adults,* study edition (Collegeville, MN: Liturgical Press, 1988). The Latin title, *Ordo initiationis Christianae Adultorum,* is more accurate. The document is an order, not a single rite, but a series of rites. The order (in the current version authorized for American Catholics) also embraces similar processes for the baptism of children of catechetical age, for baptized but uncatechized Catholics, and for Christians from other denominations seeking reception into the Catholic Church. For a commentary on the RCIA, see Aidan Kavanagh, *The Shape of Baptism* (New York: Pueblo, 1978).

2. See, for example, the baptismal rite in the Book of Common Prayer 1979 of the Episcopal Church and the preparatory rites for baptism in that church's *Book of Occasional Services* (4th edition, New York: Church Hymnal Corporation, 1995), known as the Preparation of Adults for Holy Baptism and the Preparation of Parents and Godparents for the Baptism of Infants and Young Children. A process which in some ways parallels the process for baptized but uncatechized adults in the RCIA is a Preparation of Baptized Persons for Reaffirmation of the Baptismal Covenant. It leads to the laying on of hands by the bishop upon mature reaffirmation of the baptismal covenant at a time of intensified commitment ("confirmation"), when a person comes from another tradition ("reception"), or returns to the practice of the faith after a lapse

("reaffirmation"). For a commentary, see Daniel Stevick, *Baptismal Moments, Baptismal Meanings* (New York: Church Hymnal Corporation, 1987).

3. See the treatment by Aidan Kavanagh in *The Shape of Baptism*, especially his description of infant baptism on page 108 as an abnormality, even if it is a "benign abnormality." The Episcopal liturgist Louis Weil echoes him in his article, "Reclaiming the Larger Trinitarian Framework of Baptism," in Ralph McMichael, ed., *Creation and Liturgy* (Washington, DC: Pastoral Press, 1993) 129–143, especially 138.

4. For documents discussed below, see E. C. Whitaker, *Documents of the Baptismal Liturgy* (London: SPCK, 1960). A fuller selection of materials from various traditions in the early centuries may be found in the two volumes of Thomas M. Finn, *Early Christian Baptism and the Catechumenate: West and East Syria and Italy, North Africa, and Egypt* (Collegeville, MN: Liturgical Press, 1992). A fuller bibliography for the Roman and Byzantine rites will be given below.

5. For our purposes, the most important is the *Didache*: see the excerpt in Finn, *Early Christian Baptism and the Catechumenate: West and East Syria.*

6. See Gabriele Winkler, *Das Armenische Initiationsrituale: Entwicklungsgeschichtliche und liturgievergleichend:. Untersuchung der Quellen des 3. bis. 10, Jahrhunderts. Orientalia Christiana Analecta 217.* (Rome: Pont. Institutum Studiorum Orientalium, 1982).

7. For key texts here, see the excerpts from Justin Martyr and the reconstructed church order attributed to Hippolytus and known as the *Apostolic Tradition* in Finn, *Early Christian Baptism and the Catechumenate: Italy, North Africa, and Egypt.*

8. "Catechumen" (one under instruction) is the Greek term, but is frequently used in Latin as well, which also uses the terms *auditores* and *audientes* (hearers).

9. "Candidates" is the standard English term for someone in this second stage of preparation for baptism. At Rome candidates were known as the "elect"; elsewhere in Italy they were known as *competentes* (applicants); the Greek term was *photizomenoi* (those being enlightened).

10. See the late second-century treatise of Tertullian on baptism and, in a later period, the letters of Popes Siricius and Leo the Great. The texts of Tertullian and Leo may be found in Finn, *Early Christian Baptism and the Catechumenate: Italy, North Africa, and Egypt.* For the text from Sircius, see Gordon P. Jeanes, *The Origins of the Roman Rite* (Bramcote, Nottingham, UK: Grove Books, 1991) 8. Note that in Tertullian the reference to Pentecost appears to be a reference to the fifty-day paschal season, not to the day of Pentecost. Egypt stands outside this consensus, with its tradition of baptism after a forty day fast following Epiphany, observed as the Feast of Christ's Baptism.

11. Herman Wegman, *Christian Worship in East and West: A Study Guide to Liturgical History* (New York: Pueblo, 1985) 107–108.

12. The catecheses of these bishops on the sacraments are conveniently collected in E. Yarnold, *The Awe-Inspiring Rites of Initiation* (Slough, UK: St. Paul Publications, 1972).

13. In the Byzantine euchologies, as we shall see below, the prayer for enrolling candidates was entitled the "prayer for making a catechumen." The Gelasian Sacramentary in the Roman tradition entitles the rite of enrollment "prayers over the elect [candidate] for making a catechumen," thus conflating the two stages.

14. In some places (such as Antioch in the days of John Chrysostom) there were two simultaneous series of catechesis during Lent—one the general catechesis intended for catechumens and the other the catechesis intended for candidates for baptism. Elsewhere the first part of Lent might be given over to general catechesis and the final part devoted to catechesis on the creed.

15. The *Apostolic Tradition* simply says "And they shall baptize the little children first. And if they can answer for themselves, let them answer. But if they cannot, let their parents answer or someone from their family" (see Whitaker, *Documents of the Baptismal Liturgy*, 5). Origen in *In Epistulam ad Romanos Commentarium 5:9* (PG 14:1057) says: "The church has received from the apostles the tradition of baptizing even very young children." He addresses himself to the rationale for infant baptism in Homily 14 on St. Luke (see Finn, *Early Christian Baptism and the Catechumenate: Italy, North Africa, and Egypt*, 202–205).

16. See Finn, *Early Christian Baptism and the Catechumenate: Italy, North Africa, and Egypt*, 127.

17. See Epistles 64 and 74 in his correspondence (CSEL numeration =PL 3:1047ff. and 3:1173ff.).

18. See the excerpts from these given in Whitaker, *Documents of the Baptismal Liturgy*.

19. To sort out what belongs to each rite, see A. Chavasse, *"Les deux rituels romain et gaulois de l'admission au catéchuménat que renferme le Sacramentaire gélasien"* in *Etudes de critique et d'historie religiouse* (Lyons: Vitte, 1948) 79–98.

20. Prayers for making a pagan a catechumen are found in additional materials elsewhere in the sacramentary. It has become an occasional office: the formation of pagan converts is no longer the principal focus of the Lenten liturgy.

21. For the history of the disintegration of the ancient Roman initiatory rite, see J. D. C. Fischer, *Christian Initiation: Baptism in the Medieval West. A Study in the Disintegration of the Primitive Rite of Initiation* (London: SPCK, 1965).

22. In the Roman tradition such a rite first appears in the supplement to the Gregorian Sacramentary. By the end of the Middle Ages it was the standard rite in most rituals. It was used immediately before baptism, except when baptism was administered in the context of the vigils of Easter and Pentecost.

23. In the Sarum manual we find the following rubrics at the end of the baptismal rite: "Men and women who receive children at baptism [their godparents] are appointed their sureties before God, and therefore must frequently admonish them when they are grown or capable of discipline, that they are bound to teach them that they guard their chastity, love justice, hold to charity, and above all things are bound to teach them the Lord's Prayer and angelic salutation [the Hail Mary], the symbol of the faith [the creed] and how to sign themselves with the sign of the cross . . . . And also no one must be admitted to the sacrament of the body and blood of Christ, save in danger of death, unless he has been confirmed or reasonably prevented from receiving the sacrament of confirmation." Earlier in the rite we find a vernacular version of these rubrics that has been inserted as an address to godparents: "Godfaders and god moders of thys chylde whe charge you that ye charge the fader and moder to kepe it from fyer and water and other perels to the age of vii yere, and that he lerne or se yt be lerned the Our Father, Hail Mary, and I believe, after the lawe of all holy churche and in all goodly haste to be confermed of my lorde of the dyocise or of hys depute . . . ." For these texts, see the translation of the rite in Fischer, *Christian Initiation: Baptism in the Medieval West*, Appendix 3. Similarly, the exhortation to godparents in the English Book of Common Prayer 1662 instructs godparents "chiefly you shall provide, that he may learn the creed, the Lord's Prayer, and the Ten Commandments, in the vulgar tongue" and a rubric at the end of the confirmation rite provides that "there shall none be admitted to the holy Communion, until such time as he be confirmed, or be ready and desirous to be confirmed."

24. See the critical edition of the Byzantine rites of initiation with commentary published by Miguel Arranz under the title *"Les sacrements de l'ancien euchologe constantinopolitain"* in *Orientalia Christiana Periodica* (*OCP*) 48 (1982)–55 (1989). For a very brief consideration of the rites for children, see Kenneth Stevenson, "The Byzantine Liturgy of Baptism," *Studia Liturgica* 17 (1987) 176–190.

25. Before this time we really cannot speak of a Byzantine rite, for various regions simply followed the liturgies of their patriarchates and Constantinople had not risen to any particular prominence among the Eastern sees.

26. Oration 40:24: "On Holy Baptism," PG 36:397–398 (translation from NPNF, 2nd series, Vol. 7, 368). The editors generally date the sermon to Epiphany in 381 in Constantinople, immediately after a sermon the previous day "On the Holy Lights." Paul Bradshaw in *"Diem baptismo sollemniorem,"* 49, understands this to be an argument for baptism at any time; from the context, I would conclude that it is an argument against those who on one baptismal feast (in this case, Epiphany) find an excuse to put baptism off to another. In later usage baptism was celebrated twice at Easter—on the morning of Holy Saturday and again at the vigil; Lazarus Saturday was also a baptismal occasion, and Christmas may also have been observed as a baptismal feast in some areas.

27. Gregory Nazianzus, Oration 40:28, "On Holy Baptism," PG 36:399–400 (translation from NPNF, series 2, Vol. 7, page 370).

28. Roman bishops certainly encouraged that baptisms be reserved for Easter and Pentecost except when the child was in danger of death. It is not clear that the same held true in the North African church.

29. The material specifically related to the first stage of the catechumenate for children is found in *"Les sacrements de l'ancien euchologe constantinopolitain"* 3, *OCP* 49 (1983) 284–302.

30. For the Greek text of the Barberini Manuscript, see F. C. Conybeare, ed., *Rituale Armenorum* (Reprint edition, Ann Arbor, MI: University Microfilms, 1990; original Oxford: Clarendon Press, 1905). This is the basis for the most convenient edition of the euchology, Jacobus Goar, ed., *Euchologion sive Rituale Graecorum* (Venice: Ex Typographia Bartholomaei Jovarina, 1730; reprint, Graz: Akademische Druck- und Verlagsanstalt, 1960). In his critical edition Arranz uses Bessarion as his basic text and collates its with other early manuscripts. The standard edition of the so-called typikon (which Arranz incorporates into his text as appropriate) is Juan Mateos. *Le typicon de la grande e'glise. Ms. Saint Croix 40 Xe siecle: Introduction, texte critique, traduction et notes.* 2 vols. *OCA 165–166.* (Rome: Pont. Institutum Orientalium Studiorum, 1962–1963.)

31. The reference to naming is found in the introductory rubric of the appropriate prayer (there is no explicit reference to the naming of Jesus); reference to the presentation of Jesus is found in the prayer for the churching of the child. Provisions for both occasions are elaborated somewhat in later euchologies; those for the fortieth day include a prayer for the purification of the mother not found in early manuscripts.

32. The phrase is taken from the rubrics in rites for receiving heretics, Jews, and pagans as catechumens. See Arranz, *"Les sacrements"* 2, *OCP 49* (1983) 63, 67, 71.

33. Arranz, *"Les sacrements"* 4, *OCP 50* (1984) 48 (my translation).

34. Arranz gives a critical edition of this material in *"Les sacrements de l'ancien euchologe constantinopolitain"* 4–10, appearing in *OCP* 50–55 (1984–1989).

35. It would appear that children were baptized in the morning, for this was the service celebrated in the small baptistry, which had baptismal basins. At the

vigil the rite was celebrated in the great baptistry, which had a large baptismal pool.

36. Arranz, *"Les sacrements"* 3, *OCP 49*, pages 301–302 (my translation).

37. Eph. 4:22; Col. 3:15.

38. The New Testament makes no reference to exorcism in preparation for baptism, and its later use seems directly connected to the understanding of pagan gods as demons from whose control converts from paganism had to be freed. See Henry Anskar Kelley, *The Devil at Baptism: Ritual, Theology, and Drama* (Ithaca, NY, and London: Cornell University Press, 1985).

39. The later tradition of Constantinople made Lazarus Saturday (the day before Palm Sunday) a baptismal feast, but this is an something of an historical accident (see the discussion by Thomas Talley in *The Origins of the Liturgical Year* [New York: Pueblo, 1986], Part III, especially section 8). In some churches in this tradition, Christmas also seems to have been a baptismal feast. On these five feasts, the baptismal troparion (Gal. 3:27) replaces the trisagion as an entrance chant at the eucharist, even though provisions for baptism on these days disappeared when monastic typica displaced the synaxarion of the Great Church as the directory for parish worship.

40. See Mk. 1:9–11 and parallels in Mt. and Lk.

41. Cf. I Sam. 10:1.

42. Cf. Ex. 29:7.

43. Cf. Elijah's commission to anoint Elisha prophet in 1 Kings 19:16.

44. 1 Pet. 2:5, 9; Rev. 1:6; cf. Ex. 19:6.

45. Rom. 8:15; Gal. 4:4–5.

46. Heb. 4:16. The words "boldness," "free access," or "confidence" translate the Greek term [symbols here] which is important in both the biblical texts and patristic literature.

47. Jn. 3:5; cf. 1 Tim. 2:4 in Pauline literature.

48. Cf. Heb. 6:4; Jn. 1 :9; Eph. 5:8 ("children of light"); 1 Pet. 2:9.

49. On the themes of Syrian initiatory theology, see especially Sebastian Brock, "The Transition to a Postbaptismal Anointing in the Antiochene Rite," in Brian Spinks, *The Sacrifice of Praise* (Rome, 1982) 215–225, and *The Holy Spirit in the Syrian Tradition* (Poona, India: Anita, 1979), and Gabriele Winkler, "The Original Meaning of the Prebaptismal Anointing and Its Implications," *Worship 52* (1978) 24–45.

50. Cf. Col. 2:11.

51. Cf. Col. 3:9–10, Gal. 3:27.

52. See 2 Cor. 5:17.

53. Rev. 21:1–22:5 presents the new heaven and new earth as paradise regained (with the water of life and the tree of life, as well as the new Jerusalem.)

54. Cf. Isa. 61:10; Bar. 5: 1–2; I Cor. 15:53–54. Patristic authors often argued that Adam put off his robe of glory when he sinned and was given a "garment of skins," which is what is put off again in baptism. See Sebastian Brock, *St. Ephrem the Syrian: Hymns of Praise* (Crestwood, NY: St. Vladimir's Seminary Press, 1990) 66–72, for the robe of glory in the Syrian tradition.

55. Gal. 3:27.

56. Cf. Rev. 7:2–3, Ezek. 9:6

57. Cf. Jn. 10; Ps. 23, 100.

58. Cf. the military imagery of Eph. 6:13–17. John Chrysostom and Theodore develop these themes in their baptismal homilies.

59. Cf.2 Cor. 1:22, Eph. 1:13.

60. See, for example Aidan Kavanagh, *The Shape of Baptism* (New York: Pueblo, 1978).

61. Such children might be baptized earlier if they are in danger of death, as Gregory of Nazianzus suggests. But according to the provisions of both the RCIA and the Episcopal *Book of Occasional Services*, catechumens are entitled to a Christian burial, so fear of their damnation (or relegation to "limbo") if they die unbaptized is unwarranted.

The Fifteenth Century Bohemian Origins of the Reformation Understanding of Confirmation

David R. Holeton

ONE OF THE AREAS OF ONGOING confusion in the churches today is the question of the theology and meaning of confirmation. While the academic debate over confirmation's origin and significance is centuries old, its importance has perhaps never been greater, as its consequences affect the contemporary reforms of the churches' patterns of initiation which are of even greater magnitude than those of the sixteenth century. Some clarity about confirmation's origins and development is essential to this contemporary process of reform of rites and the renewal of their theology.

It is generally acknowledged by liturgists today that confirmation, as it exists in the churches, has two distinct origins. Confirmation, as found in the Roman Catholic Church,[1] has its origins in the second postbaptismal anointing of the ancient Roman use to which the *Apostolic Tradition* of Hippolytus is the earliest witness.[2] This anointing, reserved to the bishop alone, (as was made clear in the famous letter of Innocent I to Decentius of Gubbio)[3] became separated from the rite of baptism as the Roman rite was imposed upon the dioceses in Gaul, and by the sixth century had begun to live a life of its own. Subsequently, it drew to itself various theological rationales of which the sermon *De Pentecosten*,[4] often attributed to Faustus of Rietz, is among the earliest and best known.[5] Of these various theologies, the primary one which has dominated catholic theology over the centuries is that, in confirmation, the fullness of the Holy Spirit is gifted upon the candidate. While the age at which confirmation has been administered has varied tremendously over the centuries, the fundamental theology of the rite is that it is a sacrament of initiation and can take place at the time of baptism regardless of the age of the candidate—that is to say, in order to receive the sacrament licitly, no active cognitive response is required of the candidate. Within the rite itself, the relative importance of the imposition of the hand and of the chrismation has been debated, but both are held to play a fundamental role in the celebration of the rite.

Confirmation as practiced by the churches issuing from the Reformation of the sixteenth century, however, is quite different from confirmation as practiced in the Roman Catholic Church. While theologies of reformed confirmation have varied, the rite has not been understood as a sacrament of initiation but, rather, as one of maturity in which the cognitive response of the candidate is essential. While, again, the age at which Reformed churches have confirmed candidates has also varied somewhat, it has generally not been before early adolescence. After candidates have "confirmed" the promises made on their behalf when they were baptized as infants, the presiding minister "confirms" them by the imposition of hands and prayer. In some churches this may also be understood as a formal admission into the (eucharistic) fellowship of the church itself. While reformed confirmation is sometimes understood as a strengthening by the Holy Spirit, it is not understood as a gifting of the Spirit in the same unique manner as is Roman Catholic confirmation.

The distinction between Roman and reformed confirmation can be kept clear (at least theoretically) in languages where the rites bear distinctive names (e.g. *Firmung* vs. *Konfirmation* in German). Unfortunately, in most western languages, there is no linguistic distinction between the two and, as a result, there is considerable confusion as to the theology of, and role played by, confirmation. This is particularly true in this more ecumenical age when there is a more widespread circulation of literature between the churches. As a result, theologies appropriate to one type of confirmation are imposed on the other where they sit ill. Moreover, a clearer delineation of the two distinct origins of confirmation is particularly important today as churches continue in the reform of their present practice of Christian initiation as a whole and act on the theological consequences of baptism, restoring the communion of all the baptized, regardless of age.

While the origins of Roman confirmation have been well studied and there is a general consensus among liturgists about its development, this is not true of the origins of reformed confirmation. Too often they are assumed to be the same as those of Roman confirmation, which leads only to theological and ritual confusion. In order to clarify the differences between the two types of confirmation, it would be helpful to trace the later, reformed, understanding of confirmation back to its historical roots which lie in the Bohemian Reformation of the fifteenth century. While a few liturgists have acknowledged this distinction between Roman and reformed confirmation in general terms, the genealogy of reformed confirmation has yet to be traced to its beginnings. It is the purpose of this paper to undertake that task.

Fourteenth Century Challenges to Confirmation

Since its inclusion by Peter Lombard among his enumeration of the seven sacraments in his *Sentences*, confirmation has been a frequent object of historical and theological challenge. None, perhaps, was as vitriolic or fundamental as that of the fourteenth-century English theologian John Wyclif. And, because of this, he has often been given credit for the creation of "reformed" confirmation.

In his *Dialogus, De quattuor sectis novellis,* and *De Antichristo* Wyclif invoked confirmation among a catalogue of alleged abuses which he used as a basis for his attack on the episcopacy.[6] In particular Wyclif maintained that the bishops had reserved to themselves certain clerical functions so that they could be turned to fiscal profit. While, in *De quattuor sectis novellis*, Wyclif claimed that, in the early church, presbyters could confirm (as well as ordain deacons), his writing remained at the level of polemic and advanced no suggestions for the actual reform of confirmation.

In his *Trialogus*, Wyclif treated confirmation much more extensively in the context of a dialogue which he created between Alethia and Phronesis.[7] Through this conceit, Wyclif examined the biblical basis claimed for confirmation and found it wanting. He then dismissed, as without biblical foundation, the bishops' claim to be able to gift (or confirm the gift of) the Spirit and, as such, suggested that they were making a claim greater than that made by the apostles themselves. The Holy Spirit, argued Wyclif, is given in baptism and without this gift there is no valid baptism. If confirmation were to be counted as a sacrament, it was such only in the loosest of senses for in no way is it necessary for salvation. Thus, if there were to be any sort of episcopal hand-laying it should take place at baptism and not separated from it in time.[8]

However, what is more significant for our purposes than this broadside attack against contemporary confirmation practice is that Wyclif offered no positive suggestions for the reform of confirmation. While (anachronistically) accepting the separation of baptism and confirmation as antedating Constantine (when he claimed presbyters could confirm), Wyclif made no suggestion that this separation in time was such that it allowed either for catechesis or for a cognitive response of faith from the candidate, both of which were to play an essential role in the "myth of primitive confirmation" as it was to develop as a justification for the "reformed" understanding of confirmation. Thus, Wyclif's historical observations on confirmation miss the fundamental element in "reformed" confirmation from which any reformation-style program for the renewal of the rite could be derived. On these grounds, alone, it is difficult to attribute to Wyclif the role of inspiring confirmation as it was to appear in Bohemia in the century following his death.

Among those looking for the origins of reformed confirmation, however, there has been a general tendency, to attribute what happened in Bohemia to Wyclifite inspiration. This comes chiefly from those who are disposed to see the Bohemian Reformation simply as an implementation of the Wyclifite program in the Czech lands.[9] Such an accusation, in the case of confirmation at least, cannot be sustained.

The Bohemian Liturgical Revival

When Wyclif's writings arrived in Bohemia, they were read in a context quite different from that in which they were written. While there is much to say for the reforming ideas of Wyclif, it can hardly be claimed that a principal target of his reforms was the sacramental and liturgical life of the church. On the other hand, late fourteenth century Bohemia was the setting of an indigenous liturgical movement focused initially on the frequent reception of the eucharist but which, in time, widened its scope to include such matters as the restoration of the lay chalice, the communion of all the baptized, vernacular liturgy and popular hymnody.[10]

At first, Wyclif's ideas on confirmation appear to have fallen on deaf ears in Bohemia. Hus, for example, knew Wyclif's *Trialogus* when he produced his *Super IV Sententiarum* between 1407 and 1409. And while Hus was certainly not above criticizing the church's practice of his own day, and while he had much sympathy for some aspects of Wyclif's thought[11], his own reading of confirmation in the *Sentences* was very much in keeping with that of his Bohemian contemporaries, and not with Wyclif. While referring to Wyclif elsewhere in his commentary, he makes no reference of any sort to Wyclif's ideas on confirmation, and certainly did not advocate the implementation of the Wyclifite "program" on the matter, whatever that may have been.[12]

If, in his exposition of the *Sentences,* Hus did something new on the subject of confirmation, it was his creation of a contextual distance between himself and Peter Lombard. Lombard, like most of his contemporaries in the twelfth century, assumed that the interval between baptism and confirmation would be relatively short (a matter of days or weeks rather than months or years) and that confirmation would be received by infants regularly so that the reception of confirmation by older children would be the exception rather than the norm. Hus, on the other hand, was the product of an ecclesiastical culture in which, because of the size of the archdiocese of Prague and the general disinterest in confirmation among the faithful, the interval between baptism and confirmation was usually one of years rather than weeks. Thus, Hus, in his brief commentary on confirmation in the context of his general observations on the sacraments,[13] could interpret it as a sacrament for those of intellectual understanding, founding it upon a curious citation from Rom. 10:10: "he who believes through the faith of baptism [rather than Paul's "belief with the heart"] to justification will confess with the mouth [at confirmation] and be saved."[14]

If an opening to the reform of confirmation in Hus's writings is to be found, it is here. Later, in his more extensive commentary on confirmation, Hus affirms only the commonplace: confirmation is confected through the traditional formula using chrism and the sign of the cross; it is a sacrament of character; which may, in the absence of a bishop, be performed by a presbyter.[15]

Hus's acknowledgement of the extended lapse in time that would ordinarily pass between baptism and confirmation appears, however, to have been a commonplace in his Bohemian context. Tomáš of Štítný, a layman who wrote in Czech on both religious and secular matters during the late fourteenth century, was of the same opinion. In his "Chapters Concerning the Seven Sacraments"[16] Tomáš devoted a very short chapter to confirmation.[17] In language that draws heavily on medieval images of chivalry derived from Faustus's De Pentecosten, Tomáš begins his chapter by saying that confirmation "is given by a bishop to a person who is baptized and is able to think for himself," and concludes by observing that "the one who is confirmed acknowledges those responsibilities which his baptismal sponsor acknowledged for him, namely that he will always keep his true faith."[18]

Thus, in a rather matter of fact way, Tomáš has articulated an understanding of confirmation that is consonant with the kernel of what "reformed" confirmation was to become: it is for those who are of age (can think for themselves) and involves a personal acknowledgement of the vows made on their behalf at baptism. There is no mention of the Spirit nor, even more surprisingly, given the importance placed on it by medieval theologians, of chrism. What Tomáš says of the rite actually sounds more like something he derived from his reading of Augustine on the catechumenal rites:–"The bishop places a cross on the person's forehead, making the cross in the name of the Holy Trinity so that the person being confirmed is never afraid nor ashamed of his God,"–than it does of medieval confirmation.[19]

While Tomáš, in his insouciance, may have articulated something approaching "reformed" confirmation, there is no evidence that anyone made anything of it at the time. If one were to speculate why, the most reasonable answer would seem to be that, on the one hand, theologians were certainly not reading Tomáš (they mocked his use of the Czech language, which they thought to be unworthy when writing about theological matters, and certainly would not have looked to him for theological originality) and, on the other, the laity seem to have been indifferent to the matter of confirmation, largely because they rarely, if ever, saw a bishop, and thus never had the opportunity to have themselves or their children confirmed. Given the widespread use of Tomáš's writings for popular catechetical purposes, however, it would not be incautious to suggest that his affirmation of confirmation as a sacrament for those "of age" which demanded a personal response became a seed sown that would germinate in its own time when confirmation was once again to become a pastoral issue.

Radical Sacramental Debate

A serious challenge to confirmation did not arise in Bohemia until after 1419 when the Hussite revolution was well underway.[20] Not surprisingly, its source was radical Tábor. While, in the early days of the Táborites, Laurence of Brežová tells us in his *Historia Hussitica* that, among the many acts of Táborite sacrilege, chrism was used to oil boots, it is unlikely that this was related to a rejection of confirmation in any conscious sense.[21]

Later, however, in the 1431 debate between the Prague university masters and the priests of Tábor, confirmation was included among the matters under discussion. Jan Rokycana, leader of the university side (and later Utraquist Archbishop of Prague) drew up a list of seven Táborite "errors."[22] First among these was that the Táborites did not observe all the sacraments—here naming unction and confirmation. The latter, Rokycana claims, they called "frivolous" and a "work of the devil," while the chrism they called "corrupt and fetid,"[23] language which has a particular Wyclifite ring to it.[24]

In the debate, Rokycana justified the church's "traditional" practice of confirmation on scriptural, sub-apostolic, patristic and scholastic grounds, presenting a dossier that was impeccible by both late medieval scholastic and Utraquist standards.[25] The Táborites, however, would have nothing to do with the traditional medieval justifications for the sacrament. Having argued for a radically simplified baptismal rite which eliminated almost all the traditional ceremonies, the Táborites proceeded to suggest that the "corrupt" medieval rites of confirmation be allowed to pass away and, in their stead, proposed the restoration of what they called "the sacrament of the imposition of hands."[26]

Their justification of this sacrament is based first on the need for spiritual strengthening after baptism,[27] and is linked to the passage Hus had also invoked from Rom.10:10 (cited accurately in this instance) "as the heart believes for righteousness, so the lips utter confession for salvation." The act of hand-laying itself was said to have as its basis Jesus laying his hands upon children in Mk. 10:16 and the apostolic hand-layings in Acts 2 and 19.

While, as we shall soon see, the Táborites drew heavily on Wyclif in their attack on the contemporary practice of confirmation, their proposed "sacrament of hand-laying" was hardly Wyclfite in inspiration, accepting, as it did, a separation in time between baptism and hand-laying, and claiming for it sacramental status, for which both Jesus's own ministry as recorded in the gospels and apostolic practice as recorded in Acts were invoked as biblical proof-texts for the "restored" rite.

When, in the course of the university debate, the Táborites turned their attention to confirmation as practiced in the contemporary church,[28] their focus was the attendant ceremonies (chrism, chrysom, and buffet) and their lack of scriptural foundation. In making their case, they first of all invoked Wyclif, then scripture and scholastic witnesses, and finally returned to Wyclif and his dialogue between Alethia and Phronesis from the *Trialogus.*

In assessing both Rokycana's presentation on behalf of mainline Utraquism and Milulás of Pelhřimov's case for the Táborite position, it must be said that Rokycana presents an impeccable case for one working in the scholastic tradition, and thus for accepting the role played by post-biblical development in the liturgical life of the church. Mikuláš, on the other hand, has the advantage if biblical witness is the only criterion by which the liturgical use of the church can be judged. There is, of course, no biblical foundation for the chrysom or the buffet, nor for the use of chrism apart from baptism itself.[29] It is significant, however, that the bulk of Mikuláš's case was based on his historical claims. He invoked S. Thomas[30] and Pierre de Tarentaise (Innocent V)[31] both of whom cite the opinion held by some scholastics that confirmation was of conciliar or ecclesiastical institution and not instituted by Christ. Mikuláš final historical argument came from the chronicle *Flores Temporum* which, like the much earlier *Liber Pontificalis*, attributes various liturgical innovations (often erroneously) to particular popes. The use of chrism with confirmation, says Mikuláš, was decreed by Callixtus in the year 218.[32] The essential point Mikuláš is making is summarized in a gloss on Pierre de Tarentaise's *Commentary of the Sentences*: "Confirmation, in so far as the imposition of hands goes, has its origins in the apostles; but in so far as the chrismation goes, it has its origins in the church."[33]

The significant advance towards some sort of "reformed" confirmation made by the Táborites in this 1431 debate is the propagation of the position that there was an apostolic post-baptismal hand-laying, separated in time from baptism itself, whose character was sacramental, and which was a means of grace and spiritual strengthening. Moreover, this "primitive sacrament" was ritually independent of the later chrism, chrysom and buffet which had come to play such an important visual (and theological) role in medieval confirmation.

While the Táborite proposition is interesting, we do not know how this "sacrament of hand-laying" was practiced. There are no extant Táborite liturgical texts and, while Táborites were quite explicit about their baptismal practice,[34] I know of no accounts of Táborite liturgical practice which describe this aspect of their liturgical life.[35] The defeat of the Táborite armies at the Battle of Lipany in 1434 and the subsequent repression of their radical liturgical uses makes it plausible that the practice of this "sacrament" was very short-lived. Our first record of the pastoral practice of "reformed" confirmation does not appear until almost forty years after the concept was articulated by Mikuláš in the University debate.

Utraquists present at those debates, however, were not at all convinced by the Táborite theories of "the sacrament of hand-laying" and continued to enumerate confirmation (with chrism, chrysom and buffet) among the seven sacraments.[36] Utraquist failure to secure the historic episcopate, however, meant that their theological position on confirmation could never progress beyond the theoretical for their pastoral experience of the sacrament very limited.[37]

Petr Chelčický and the "Apostolic" Model of Confirmation

Watching the 1431 debates (either from close at hand or from a distance) was Petr Chelčický, an Utraquist "monastic" of radical theological and social opinions whose effect on the church in Bohemia was to be far-reaching.[38] His *Instruction on the Sacraments*[39] was a response to the university debate. In it, Chelčický challenged both Rokycana and Mikuláš on their acceptance of the normative character of infant baptism. For Chelčický, this practice simply perpetuated the error of traditional "Constantinian" Christianity. Baptism, according to Chelčický, is normatively for those who have believed in the gospel, have attested to that belief, and who then can be baptized "in truth." A reform of the fundamental principles on which baptism was to take place was necessary, argued Chelčický, if the life of the church as a whole were to a practical ecclesiological weight. Scholastic theologians, Utraquists and Táborites alike had all assumed the inherited model of a church in which all those born of baptized parents would be baptized without question.

Having cast the debate in an entirely new context, Chelčický made provision for infant baptism on what he considered an apostolic basis. Citing Pseudo-Dionysius as an authority, Chelčický allowed that the infants of believing parents could be baptized on the condition that those children would then be entrusted to a good teacher who would assure their education in the faith.

Chelčický describes this practice in his chapter on confirmation, which he calls the sixth sacrament.[40] First, following a line of exegesis and reasoning very close to that of Wyclif's *Trialogus*, Chelčický searches in vain for a dominical or apostolic foundation for confirmation as practiced in the contemporary church, and then for an apology for the sacrament that credibly makes it consonant with the "Law of God."[41]

Failing in his task, Chelčický relates that he has only once encountered a satisfactory account of confirmation's beginnings, and that was from a university master called Stanislav whose teaching "is quite respected in Prague." (This could only be Hus's teacher Stanislav of Znojmo.)[42] According to Chelčický, Stanislav recounted the time in the apostolic church when (believing) parents had their children baptized, raised them as best they could according to God's will, and when they were old enough, brought them to the bishop who taught them all things necessary for salvation. Having undertaken to follow these teachings and walk in the way of Christ, the bishop confirmed the adolescent giving him/her a light buffet to show that Christians must be prepared to turn the other cheek. Those unwilling to make the required promises were expelled from the community so that the devil would not have a means of access to it. All this is said to be witnessed to by Pseudo-Dionysius the Areopagite, whose writings, it must be remembered, were still regarded as those of Paul's convert from Athens.[43]

The passage in question comes from Pseudo-Dionysius's *De Ecclesiastica Hierarchia* (VII,iii,11) in which the author replied to a question from "Timothy" (allegedly the companion of Paul). Timothy's concern was that it seemed ridiculous to many to initiate into the church through the sacraments of baptism and communion infants who cannot understand their meaning. In his reply, Dionysius suggests that the custom of baptizing infants is of the earliest tradition[44] and takes place on the assumption that the parent or sponsor will bring the child up in faith and teach him the faith when he or she can understand it. This is stated even more strongly in the paraphrase of Dionysius by Peter of Spain which circulated widely in Bohemia and which was used interchangeably with the more accurate translation of John Saracen.[45] In Peter's paraphrase, the parents turn the child over to a good teacher who, in turn, teaches the child all things necessary for salvation, and then presents the child to the bishop.[46]

Thus, in Chelčický, we find a significant advance in the emergence of "reformed" confirmation. First, Chelčický provides us with a witness whose authenticity was beyond question for the "apostolic" practice of confirmation.[47] The "myth"of confirmation's origins in what was to become its "reformed" form had begun, for according to Dionysius, not only was there a lapse in time between the baptism of the children of believing parents and their presentation to the bishop, but furthermore those intervening years were filled with both parental nurture in the "way of Christ" and episcopal catechesis. While we are not told at what age this "apostolic" confirmation took place, we do know that it was at an age at which those who were unwilling to make the required promises could be expelled from the community and still make a life for themselves. It is safe to presume that this was not before adolescence.

There is no evidence to suggest that Chelčický ever put his ideas about "apostolic" confirmation into pastoral practice. As he lived a monastic life with his confrères in the isolated community of Chelčice, and as we have no evidence of any "missionary" activity by the Brethren of Chelčice, there is no reason to believe that he had any candidates for the rite. It was necessary to wait for the appearance of a later group for whom Chelčický's teaching played an important role: the Jednota Bratrská—usually known outside the Czech lands as the *Unitas Fratrum* or Unity of Brethren.

The Jednota Bratrská and the Birth of Reformed Confirmation

Before the ordinations of 1467, which mark the beginning of the formal separation of the Jednota from the Utraquist Church, Brother Řehoř, the leader of the (then) devotional fraternity within Utraquism had spent time with the Chelčice community and its leader, Petr, during his religious quest. For some (unknown) reason, Řehoř and his religious brothers chose not to remain at Chelčice but to begin their common life in the more isolated village of Vilemov in Northern Bohemia. All the same, Chelčický's hand can be seen clearly in the theology of the Jednota as it distinguished itself from that of Utraquism. The Jednota's theology and practice of Christian Initiation show clear signs of his influence both in its restriction of paedo-baptism to the infants of believers and in the institution of confirmation on a fundamentally Chelčickian model.

As early as 1468, in an apology for their faith and practice presented to Archbishop Rokycana, the Jednota reported that they required three sponsors for each infant to be baptized. Then, "when the child is grown up and can answer for himself, [the sponsors] bring him to the pastor and give testimony concerning how he has been preserved in the strength of his baptism and has received instruction."[48] The pastor is then to question the candidate as to his intention to persevere in the way of Christ and the faith of the apostles. Having been assured both by the sponsors and the candidate himself of this resolve, and determined that the candidate is of age, "he shall receive him into the congregation and by the imposition of hands confirm him, and pray that God will give him strength."[49]

While this does not incorporate Chelčický's ideas on confirmation in every detail (we are not told if those who are of age but are unwilling to make the promises are expelled from the community), it is our first witness to the pastoral implementation of "reformed" confirmation. Those baptized as infants, once of age, affirm the promises made on their behalf at baptism (to follow Christ and to profess of the apostolic faith) and then receive the imposition of hands with prayer for strengthening–an act called confirmation.

In an extended apology for the Jednota's faith and practice written in the summer of 1503,[50] the sections devoted to confirmation reveal a considerably developed rationale for the new pastoral practice of confirmation, a practice which is claimed to be apostolic. The biblical foundation for the rite is said to be found both in the Acts of the Apostles (Peter and John in Samaria and at the baptism of Cornelius) as well as in Jesus's blessing of children in Mark.[51] More interesting, perhaps, is the citation of Pseudo-Dionysius's apology for the baptism of infants[52] which has clearly become a fundamental "apostolic" model for the Jenotá's own pastoral practice.

At about the same time (1503/4), in an apology for the Jednota sent to King Vladislav,[53] the Brethren begin with the assertion that, because their faith is taken from the sacred scriptures, confirmation as they practice it is of apostolic origin. (No proof texts are offered for this claim.) As in their earlier apologies, the emphasis is on the candidates' having come to a living faith and their willingness to promise their intention to persevere in the same:

> Such a person should be confirmed in the hope of the truth he has attained, and also aided by the prayers of the church, so that there he may receive an increase of the gifts of the Holy Spirit for steadfastness and the warfare of faith. Finally, by the imposition of hands to confirm the promises of God and the truth held in virtue of the name of the Father and of his Word and the kindly Spirit, let him be received into the fellowship of the church.[54]

It is interesting to note that, while in their first apology to Rokycana, the Jednota made the point "that in the old church . . . this was called strengthening (*potvrzování*), but today in the Roman church it is called confirmation (*biřmování*),"[55] in their two apologies of 1503/4 the appropriate sections are titled "*O biřmování*" and "*De confirmatione.*" While this may simply be a device through which the Jednota tried to assert its continuity with the historic practice of the church as reformed on a "primitive" model, it may also be an intentional distancing from Wyclif's attacks on confirmation and the Táborites' "sacrament of hand-laying." In either case, the apologies themselves use both the language of strengthening and confirmation, something which could already suggest a confusion between the two distinct rites. The introduction of the idea that "there may come to [the confirmand] an increase of the gifts of the Holy Spirit for steadfastness and the warfare of the faith"[56] walks a very narrow theological line. While it avoids suggesting that the spirit is "gifted" in confirmation as it was in Roman confirmation, it comes very close by speaking of an "increase of the gifts" of the Spirit, particularly when used in the context of the language of "warfare" which could not but evoke Faustus's "later [in confirmation] we are confirmed to fight."

In confirmation, as the Jednota had begun to practice it, we can see not only "reformed" confirmation as it was to be adopted in the churches of the Second Reformation of the sixteenth century, but also the latent theological problems that were to arise in the practice of this new rite. In the two apologies, the candidate is said to be received either "into the congregation" or "into the fellowship of the church." This does serious violence to the biblical (and catholic) understanding of baptism as incorporation into the Church—something that was fiercely maintained by Utraquism's insistance that all those baptized (regardless of age) were to receive the eucharist as the weekly ongoing sign of their membership in the Body of Christ, the church. The Jednota were surely conscious of this, for they ceased to communicate infants and young children from the time of their break with Utraquism.[57] There is also a certain sectarian ring to the strong emphasis placed on the examination of the character of the candidate and his resolve to remain unsullied in his walk in the Christian way. While this reflects the rigor of the early Jednota, as has been noted, there is no evidence that it included that part of Chelčický's model which called for the expulsion of those adolescents who refused to make the required promises.[58]

After over a century of gestation, "reformed" confirmation had come to birth and with it the "myth" of its apostolic roots. While what emerged owed its greatest debt to the inspiration of Petr Chelčický and his transmission of Stanislav of Znojmo's version of Pseudo-Dionysius's *De Ecclesiastica Hierarchia*, the actual practice and its interpretation was a mixture of a variety of sources.

The medieval language "in baptism we are born to life, in confirmation we are strengthened to fight," inherited from Faustus of Rietz' *De Pentecosten*, remains a part of the theological rationale for confirmation, as well as for the prayer at the imposition of hands.[59] The relatively low level of popular attachment to confirmation in the late middle ages and the assumed lapse in time between baptism and confirmation also played in the Jednota's favour. Had there been a strong attachment to medieval confirmation, or had there been as short a lapse in time between baptism and confirmation as there had been in Lombard's day, the Jednota would likely have had as little success in undoing that popular attachment or ritual practice as they had in their attempt to reject paedo-baptism.

The Czech writings of Tomáš of Štítný can also be attributed a role in the genesis of reformed confirmation. The Jednota, most of whom had relatively simple educations, were, on the whole, much more at home in Czech than in Latin. That Štítný's works were widely read, is well known. His affirmation that confirmation was a rite for those "of age," in which candidates made a personal response and acknowledged their own baptismal responsibilities, were features that were reflected in the Jednota's reformed confirmation.

It is difficult to estimate what contribution, if any, was played by the Táborite position at the 1431 university debate. While much of the Jednota's liturgical use was marked by a simplicity like that of the Táborites before them, and while they are known to have been influenced by Táborite thought and practice, we do not know enough about the actual use of "the sacrament of hand-laying" to be able to say how directly it influenced the Jednota. Certainly, the Jednota's continued use of the word "confirmation" (*biřmování*), so strongly rejected by the Táborites, would lead us to conclude that, at the very least, the Jednota wished to distance themselves from Táborite belief (and practice?) on this issue.

It is remarkable, however, how little influence Wyclif's position seems to have had on the Jednota's reformed confirmation. Admittedly the chrism, chrysom and buffet are all gone, but their elimination was a common theme and could equally derive from scholastic distinctions on what was and was not dominical in the rite (e.g. Pierre de Tarentaise), from the Táborite's own historical research, or from Dionysius. That either bishop or priest could confirm, probably derives from the Jednota's adherence to the late medieval opinion that there was no essential difference between the two orders, rather than from Wyclif.[60] What certainly is not the result of Wyclifite influence on the Jednota's practice, however, is the continued separation in time of confirmation from baptism, and the claim that such a practice is of apostolic origin.

Confirmation and the Second Reformation

When news of the sixteenth century Reformation began to spread through the Czech lands, it was greeted by the Jednota with interest and even some enthusiasm. While it is important to acknowledge the mutual independence of the two reformations, it is also important to realize that "they met and for a short while and went hand in hand."[61] During this meeting, ideas were exchanged which influenced the development of both the Jednota and the churches of the second reformation. Among these was the Jednota's practice of confirmation, an idea that appears to have been transferred through Erasmus, and soon found favor in the churches of the second reformation.

Towards the end of the second decade of the sixteenth century, Erasmus had contact with members of the Bohemian churches (both Utraquist and the Jednota) during which he made inquiry into their faith and practice. In his *Paraphrase on St. Matthew* of 1522, Erasmus recommends a catechetical practice that appears to be based on the Jednota's practice of confirmation. At puberty, boys should be required to be attend discourses in which it is made clear to them what the baptismal profession involves. Having been examined privately to see whether they have retained sufficiently what has been taught them, they would be asked whether they will ratify what their godparents have promised on their behalf. If they do, then "that profession would be renewed at public gathering of their peers with solemn ceremonies, fitting, pure, serious, and magnificent, and such things as become that profession of which there is none more sacred." Erasmus then adds that "these things indeed will have greater authority if they are performed by the bishops themselves and not by parish priests or hired suffragans."[62] Without using the word confirmation, which would have been problematic if he wished to retain his claim to developed western catholic tradition, Erasmus proposes the introduction of the essence (both theologically and ritually) of the Jednota's practice of confirmation.

Bucer claimed to have been practising something similar to the Jednota's confirmation from the beginning of his time in Strasbourg (1520). While this appears to have been some form of preparation for First Communion, it is not clear whether he thought it was confirmation or not. In 1530 we find him in correspondence with the Jednota on the subject of the imposition of hands, at which time he attributes the mandate to the act of Jesus blessing the children, rather than to the hand-laying of the apostles.[63]

Luther's first contact with the Jednota was in May 1522 when he was visited by Brother Jan Horn. Later that same year he was visited by two other delegations from the Jednota.[64] In a sermon preached in 1523, Luther advocates a practice similar to the one practiced by the Jednota and proposed by Erasmus. While confirmation "as the bishops would have it" is not to be observed, each pastor may examine children as to their faith and, if he find it to be good and real, should lay his hands on them and confirm them.[65] It is impossible to know if Luther's ideas for reformed confirmation emerged from his conversations with members of the Jednota or if he drew it from his reading of Erasmus. Whatever the case, there is little doubt that the inspiration for Luther's confirmation lies in the Jednota.

Confirmation, as it appeared in England, also has its roots in the practice of the Jednota. William Tyndale, who was at Cambridge while Erasmus was lecturing there, proposed a reform of confirmation very much on the Jednota's model, in which we also find clear traces of Pseudo-Dionysius.[66] The first Book of Common Prayer contained a rubric after the Catechism which is very reminiscent of the Jednota's apology. The English rite itself is ingenious for, while it retains the name confirmation, it has placed all that was thought essential to medieval confirmation into the baptismal rite[67] and made of confirmation something that is a profession of baptismal faith followed by an episcopal imposition of hands, in which the accompanying prayer asks for an increase in the gifts of the Spirit: in other words, Jednota's confirmation.

Again and again, the reformers of the sixteenth century saw themselves as restoring an ancient use in which the baptized, having come of age, are examined on the baptismal profession made on their behalf.[68] There is no empirical evidence of any sort for this "ancient use."[69] I suggest that we have seen how this myth was born in Bohemia, and propose that it made its way into the thought of sixteenth century reformers through their contact with the Jednota Bratrská rather than through their reading of any patristic text.

Conclusion

Confirmation, as it is found in the churches issuing from the reformation of the sixteenth century, is a complex amalgam. In its inception, it had little to do either with Roman confirmation or the early church. The fathers of Trent recognized this and anathematized advocates of the idea that those baptized as infants must be questioned as to whether they wished to ratify what their godparents had promised in their name at the time of their baptism.[70] In a single act, Trent made clear that what had begun in Bohemia and come to fruition in the Jednota as well in as the churches of the Second Reformation[71] was irreconcilable with confirmation as known in the Roman tradition.

In just short of a century, a series of Bohemian writers had managed to give the cachet of antiquity to something that was, in fact, a novelty.[72] The practice as it came to be used in the Jednota had little difficulty in commending itself to the reformers of the sixteenth century who were, no doubt, beguiled in part by how well it sat with the renaissance emphasis on the importance of being able to articulate the faith. How, in a world in which the Areopagite's authorship of the Dionysian corpus had been definitively exploded, there could be such a willing acceptance of the apostolic character of what was, in effect, a novelty, remains a mystery that has yet to be unravelled.

What I hope has been demonstrated, however, is that a reformation that is little studied and often forgotten in the West, made a contribution to the life of the churches of the Second Reformation of the sixteenth century that has had an immeasurable effect on the piety of the faithful. While those who presently work on the renewal of initiation practices within those churches may rue the day that the Jednota began to practice what has become, perhaps, the biggest stumbling block in their work, I suggest that knowing the cause of a headache is often the beginning of its relief.

Notes

1. This would also apply to the Old Catholic Churches of the Union of Utrecht.

2. *Apostolic Tradition* 21. See among others: J.D.C. Fisher, *Christian Initiation in the Medieval West* [Alcuin Club Collections No. 47] (London, 1965); Leonel Mitchell, *Baptismal Anointing* [Alcuin Club Collections No. 48] (London, 1966); and Gabriele Winkler, "Confirmation or Chrismation? A Study in Comparative Liturgy" in *Worship* 58 (1984) 2–17. One of the most prolific contemporary Roman Catholic authors on the question of confirmation, Paul Turner, writes "the earliest ancestor among liturgical texts for confirmation is the Apostolic Tradition of Hippolytus . . ." *Confirmation: The Baby in Solomon's Court* (New York, 1993) 29. The authorship and composite nature of the *Apostolic Tradition* are beyond the scope of (and not fundamentally germane to) this paper. See Paul F. Bradshaw, *The Search for the Origins of Christian Worship* (New York: Oxford University Press, 1992) 89–92.

3. Robert Cabié, *La Lettre du Pape Innocent Iᵉʳ à Décentius de Gubbio (19 mars 416)* [*Bibliothèque de la Revue d'Histoire Ecclésiastique 58*] (Louvain, 1973) 22–24.

4. *Homilia* 29, *De Pentecosten* 1–2, *Corpus Christianorum – Series Latina* 101:337ff. The *CC* edition attributes the sermon to the anonymous Eusebius Gallicanus.

5. L.A. Van Buchem, *L'homélie pseudo-Eusébienne de Pentecôte. L'origine de la confirmatio en Gaule Méridionale et l'interprétation de ce rite par Fauste de Riez* (Nijmegen, 1967).

6. *Dialogus,* 24; 35, Alfred W. Pollard ed., *Iohannis Wycliffe: Dialogus sive Speculum Ecclesie Militentis* (London, 1886) 50, 83; *De Quattuor Sectis Novellis,* VI, Rudolf Buddenseig ed., *John Wiclif's Polemical Works* (London, 1883) I, 260; *De Antichristo* I,13, Johann Loserth, ed., *Iohannis Wyclif: Operis Evangelici . . . sive de Antichrito* (London, 1896) 49.

7. *Trialogus,*iv.14, Gotthard Lechler ed., *Joannis Wyclif: Trialogus cum Supplemento Trialogi* (Oxford, 1869) 292–295.

8. If this had this been acted on, "Roman" confirmation would have been reintegrated into the baptismal rite from which it had long been separated. Had Wyclif

paid more attention to contemporary pontificals, he would have seen that this was still the rubrical norm at baptisms presided over by a bishop at the Easter vigil and, hence, at any baptism. This possibility was, in fact, followed at the baptism of the future Elizabeth I well over a century after Wyclif's death, and appears as well to have been the case at royal baptisms in Bohemia during Wyclif's own time. See Charles Wriothesley, *A Chronicle of England during the reigns of the Tudors, from A.D. 1485 to 1559,* [Camden Society n.s. 11] (Westminster,1875) I:22–3.

9. The extent of Wyclif's influence in the Bohemian Reformation is an ongoing debate often colored by nationalist questions. German scholars, particularly those of the nineteenth century, have been unwilling to impute any indigenous character to the reform movement in Bohemia. This position has often been adopted uncritically by English scholars. See my "Wyclif's Bohemian Fate: A Reflection on the Contextualization of Wyclif in Bohemia," *Communio Viatorum* 32,4 (1989) 209–222 and Vilém Herold, "How Wyclifite Was the Bohemian Reformation?" *The Bohemian Reformation and Religious Practice* [BRRP] 2 (1998) 25ff.

10. See my "The Evolution of Utraquist Liturgy: A Precursor of Western Liturgical Reform" *Studia Liturgica* 25,1 (1995) 51–67; "The Bohemian Eucharistic Movement in its European Context," *The Bohemian Reformation and Religious Practice* [BRRP]1 (1996) 23–47; "The Evolution of Utraquist Eucharistic Liturgy: a textual study," BRRP 2 (1998) 97–126 and "The Czech Utraquist Eucharist: An Independent Path of Liturgical Reform," BRRP 3 (in press) . There is yet no study of Czech Hymnody in an easily accessible language. The classic study remains Zdeněk Nejedlý, *Dějiny zpěvu předhusitského* [The History of Pre-hussite Song] (Prague, 1904); *Počátky husitského zpěvu* [The Beginning of Hussite Song] (Prague, 1907) and *Dějiny zpěvu za válek husutských* [The History of Song During the Hussite Wars] (Prague, 1913) republished in 6vv. as *Dějiny husitského zpěvu* [History of Hussite Song] (Prague, 1954–56).

11. In his commentary, for example, Hus took issue with the common judgement that Wyclif was damned (*Super IV Sent.* IV., dist. xx, 3, Václav Flajšhans ed., *Mag. Joannis Hus: Super IV. Sententiarum* [Spisy M. Jana Husa 4–6][Prague, 1904] 621*)* and, at the same time, distanced himself from some of the English theologian's ideas by avowing his loyalty to clerical celibacy in the face of Wyclif's opposition to it. *Super IV Sent.* IV., dist. xxxviii, 6, (Flajšans, 682).

12. If Hus were to have followed a Wyclifite "position" on confirmation, this would have been the appropriate time. When, in May 1409, Hus began his exposition of the Fourth Book of the *Sentences,* the Czech party at the University held the hegemony of power, Wencelaus IV having just abrogated the privileges of the three foreign (German) "nations." The foreign masters left Prague in May of that year, leaving the University a safer place in which to advocate Wyclif's ideas without the risk of a German denunciation to Rome, as had happened the previous year with Hus's friend and teacher Stanislav of Znojomo.

13. It is his shortest commentary on any of the sacraments (*Super IV Sent.,* IV., dist. vii, 1–5 Flajšhans 550–53) followed closely by that on the unction of the sick *Super IV Sent.,* IV., dist. xxiii Flajšhans 630–33. It is these two sacraments that were to be the most contested by the radical wing of the Bohemian reformation. First the Táborites and, later, the *Jednota Bratrská* (Bohemian Brethren) denied both the dominical institution and sacramental nature of these rites.

14. *Super IV Sent.,* IV., A. Incepto I,5 (Flajšhans 504).

15. Ibid., IV., dist. vii,3–5 (Flajšhans 551–2).

16. *O sedmeře kostelní svátosti* [About the Seven Church Sacraments] in Jaroslav

Vrťátko ed., *Thómy z Štítného knihy naučení křesťanského* [Tomáš of Štítný: Books on Christian Discipline] (Prague, 1873) 306–340.

17. "O biřmováni" [About Confirmation] ibid., 314–15.

18. "O biřmováni," 315.

19. See, Augustine's Commentary on Psalms 30 and 141 in Eligius Dekkers and Iohannes Fraipont edd. *Sancti Aurelii Augustini Enarrationes in Psalmos* CC 38,218–19 and 40,2052. Curiously, this image was to figure prominently in the negotiations with the Armenians at the Council of Florence *Concilium Florentinum documenta et scriptores* 1:2, 129.

20. The best study of the Hussite Revolution remains Howard A. Kaminsky, *A History of the Hussite Revolution* (Berkeley and Los Angeles, 1967) see also Thomas A. Fudge, *The Magnificent Ride: The First Reformation in Hussite Bohemia* (Aldershot, Hants and Brookfield VA, 1998).

21. There was a long litany of offences imputed to the Táborites. These ranged from the merely iconoclastic (destruction of images of the Lord, the Blessed Virgin Mary and the saints), to acts of vandalism (smashing chalices and monstrances, destroying liturgical books and vestments), to the sacrilegious (trampling consecrated hosts into the ground, oiling boots with chrism, defecating in baptismal fonts). Only with great difficulty could one suggest that those who participated in these mob actions were of such theological sophistication as to be conscious of which sacramental actions of the church were being rejected. Rather, these acts of lawlessness were directed at everything for which the medieval church stood. Laurence of Březová, *Historia Hussitica* in Jaroslav Goll ed., *Fontes rerum Bohemicarum* V (Prague,1893) 398, 400, 403ff.

22. *De septem culpis taboritarum* MS Prague Bib. Cap. D.88ff.190–266.

23. Ibid.,ff.200ᵃ–204ᵇ.

24. This is hardly surprising as the Táborites were quite open about their espousal of much of Wyclif's teaching and had in their midst Peter Paine, an English student of the "*Doctor Ewangelicus*" (as Wyclif came to be known by many in Bohemia) himself.

25. *De septem culpis, loc. cit.*

26. "*De sacramento manus imposicionis in fide scripture habente fundamentum*" in Amedeo Molnár and Romolo Cegna edd. *Confessio Taboritarum* [Fonti per la Storia d'Italia 105] (Rome, 1983) 74–75.

27. It is interesting to note how profoundly Faustus's *De Pentecosten* had affected medieval language on the subject, for there is nothing essentially biblical in relating strengthening and confirmation.

28. "*De crismacione, quam nunc vocant sacramentum confirmacionis, carente ut scripture fundamento*" in *Confessio Taboritarum* 76–77.

29. Whether or not chrism was used at the "sphragis" (seal) of New Testament baptism is still moot. It was, however, in use by the second century.

30. *Summa* III, q.72, a.1.

31. *In IV. Librum Sententiarum Commentaria* Dist. VII, q.1, a. I,3 (Toulouse, 1651) IV, 80 col a.

32. The *Flores* is a late fourteenth century chronicle of Franciscan provenance. Mikuláš has probably misread the text as both MSS Prague NK IV.H.18 f.11ᵇ and Bib. Cap. C 41 f.217ᵃ attribute chrism at confirmation to Callistus's successor Urban.

33. "*De crismacione*," *Confessio Taboritarum* 77. I have been unable to locate a manuscript of Pierre de Tarentaise's commentary on the *Sentences* containing this gloss.

34. The 1434 Synod of the clergy of Bohemia made explicit that the traditional

rites and ceremonies were to be observed in the celebration of baptism. The Táborite clergy declined to conform to any of the traditional ceremonies, including the threefold immersion. The Articles of the Synod relating to baptism are reprinted in *Confessio Taboritarum* 354 and the Táborite rebuttal in *"De sacramento baptismatis,"* ibid.363. That there was no mention of the practice of "hand-laying" in their response to the Praguers probably indicates that the practice was a dead issue in Tábor.

35. In their reaction to the 1432 Articles of the Masters and Priests of Prague, the Priests of Tábor accepted that there were seven sacraments of which "the imposition of hands," rather than confirmation, was accepted as the second. *"Articuli sacerdotum Taboriensium supra dictis articulis magistrorum in pluribus contrarii,"* *Confessio Taboritarum* 347.

36. The eleventh chapter of Jan Rokycana's *De septem sacramentis ecclesiæ,* for example, presents a rationale for the sacrament and its medieval rites and ceremonies drawing on the usual citations from the Acts of the Apostles, Melchiades (Faustus) and S. Thomas. Rokycana's tractatus was edited by Ioannes Cochlaeus, *Historiae Hussitarum libri duodecim* (Moguntia, 1549) 466–472. This Utraquist position on confirmation did not change even after Utraquism had lost its access to bishops in the historic succession. A list of Utraquist articles on the sacraments dating from 1525 limits the administration of the sacrament to regularly ordained bishops, thereby excluding the validity of confirmation administered by the bishops of the Jednota Bratrská. Klement Borový, *Jednání a dopisy konsistoře katolické i utrakvistické* [Acts and Letters of the Catholic and Utraquist Consistories] (Prague, 1868) I,10.

37. Neither Rokycana nor his suffragans had been consecrated and could not(or would not) confirm and Utraquist access to "episcopal mercenaries" from abroad ceased with the deaths of the Italian bishops Augustine Sancturien, Bishop of Mirandola, and Philip of Villa Nova, Titular Bishop of Sidon and Auxiliary Bishop of Modena, who exercised their episcopal ministry in Bohemia on behalf of the Utraquists between 1482–1493 and 1504–1507 respectively. In fact, there is no known reference to a confirmation within Utraquism after the death of Philip of Villa Nova. [This latter information I owe to my colleague Zdeněk David.]

38. The only monograph in English on Chelčický is Murray Wagner, *Petr Chelčický: A radical reparatist in Hussite Bohemia* (Scottdale PA,1983).

39. *Zprávy o svátostech,* Milan Opočenský ed., [Acta Reformationem Bohemicam Illustrantia I] (Prague, 1980) 17–94.

40. "Šestá svatost," ibid. 66–75.

41. For the development of this concept during the Bohemian Reformation see Thomas A. Fudge, "The 'Law of God': Reform and Religious Practice in Late Medieval Bohemia," BRRP I (1996) 49–72.

42. Chelčický must have heard this in the first decade of the century, as Stanislav renounced his radical position after being accused of heresy in 1408 by the German university masters and subsequently tried in Rome.

43. "*Šestá svatost,*" 73f.

44. Hereby giving away his claim to be Paul's convert.

45. *"Expositio In Librum: De Ecclesiastica Hierarchia,"* in *Pedro Hispano: Exposição sobre os livros de beato Dionisio Areopagita,* P.Manuel Alonso ed. (Lisbon, 1957) 125–242. Peter's paraphrase was a fundamental text in the Bohemian sacramental debates. His introduction to the third chapter of *Eccl. Hier.,* in which he stated that no sacrament was complete unless consummated in the eucharist, was a pivotal text in the restoration of the communion of all the baptized.

46. Ibid. 241.

47. It was not until later in the fifteenth century that it was first suggested that the author of the works of Pseudo-Dionysius the Areopagite and the convert of S. Paul were not one and the same person.

48. "*Čtvrtý list k Mistru Rokycanovi*" [Fourth letter to Master Rokycana] in Ivan Palmov, *Cheshskie bratya v svoikh konfessiyah* [The Czech Bretheren and their Confessions] (Prague,1904) II, 15.

49. Loc. cit.

50. "*Apologia nebo konfesi vydaná leta 1503*" [Apology or confession edited in the summer of 1503] Palmov II, 157–246.

51. "*O biřmování*," Ibid. 175.

52. "*Apologia*," 225.

53. '*De confirmatione*' in "*Oratio excusatoria atque satisfactiva fratrum Waldensium Regi Wladislao ad Hungariam missa*," Palmov, II, 146–57.

54. Ibid., 151.

55. "*Čtvrtý list*," Palmov II, 15.

56. "*De confirmatione*," Palmov II, 151.

57. In so doing, they did a complete *volte face* with a practice that had been fundamental to Utraquism since 1417. [See my *La communion des tout petits enfants: Une étude mouvement eucharistique en Boheme vers la fin du Moyen-Age.* [*Bibliotheca Ephemerides Liturgicae Subsidia*, No. 50] (Rome, 1988).] At first, the Jednota merely discontinued the practice. Later, they threw their lot in with Lutheranism, which had attracted the Bohemian nobility and denounced it vociferously. Utraquism, on the other hand, held tenaciously to the practice until its suppression by the Counter Reformation after the defeat at Bilá Hora (the White Mountain) in 1620. In a polemical attack on the Jednota, the Jesuit Václav Šturm complained that the Jednota's emphasis on baptism and confirmation (*potvrzování*)had led them to neglect the importance of the eucharist. *Srownanij wijry a učenij bratřij* [*A Comparison of the Faith and Doctrine of the Brethren*] (Litomyšl, 1582) II, 366–67.

58. From a sociological point of view, such a practice was probably not necessary for early adolescents who had been nurtured in a close community. Expulsion or "shunning" would likely be necessary only later in life after more serious contact with the wider world and its allure.

59. It is important to note that this language, while in itself biblical, has no actual relationship with any of the biblical proof-texts used for the justification of confirmation.

60. The Jednota's acceptance of the historic "apostolic" episcopate and their myth around how they received it clearly has more to do with their need to be accepted as a church with apostolic roots than it does with a theology of the historic threefold ministry. See my "Church or Sect? The Jednota Bratrská and the Growth of Dissent from Mainline Utraquism," *Communio Viatorum* 38,1 (1996) 24ff.

61. Ludek Broz, "A New Evaluation of the Theology of the *Unitas Fratrum*," *Communio Viatorum* I, 2–3 (1958) 125.

62. Disiderius Erasmus, *In Euangelium Matthaei paraphrasis* (Basel, 1522) Pio Lectori, n.p. [= 5ff.]. A facsimile edition of the collected prefaces can be found in *Desiderius Erasmus: Prefaces to the Fathers, the New Testament, on Study*, Robert Peters ed., (Menston, 1970).

63. D. Herzog, "*Ein wichtiges Document, betreffend die Einführung der Reformation bei den Waldenser*," *Zeitschrift für die historische Theologie* 36 (1866) 311–338.

64. See Joseph T. Müller, *Geschichte der böhmischen Brüder* (Herrnhut, 1922) I, 401ff. and "*Luthers Stellung zu den Böhmischen Brüdern*" in Erhard Peschke, *Die Böhmischen Brüder im Urteil ihrer Zeit* (Stuttgart, 1964) 109 -120.

65. "*Predigt am Sonntag Lätare Nachmittags* [15 March 1523]" Weimar ed., XI,66.

66. William Tyndale, *An Answer to Sir Thomas More's Dialogue, The Supper of the Lord,* Henry Walter ed. [The Parker Society] (London, 1850) 71–2.

67. In particular, the signation on the candidate on the forehead rather than the crown of the head while using a prayer that incorporated Faustus's language of warfare. It was Marion Hatchett's unpublished S.T.M. thesis *Thomas Cranmer and the Rites of Christian Initiation* [The General Theological Seminary, (New York, 1967) 186–190] that demonstrated the importance of this neglected aspect of Cranmer's liturgical work.

68. This "myth of apostolic confirmation" was widespread and was believed by a variety of contemporary theologians. See, for example, Thomas Cranmer *Cathechismus* (London, 1548) iii; James Calfhill, *An Answer to John Martiall's Treatise of the Cross,* Richard Gibbons ed. [The Parker Society] (London, 1846) 215; John Calvin, *Institutes* IV,xix,4.

69. In writing of "the anciente and laudable ceremonie of Confirmation . . . in the olde state" loc. cit. Cranmer does not cite any ancient witness to the practice. Calfhill cites Augustine *De Baptismo* III,16 which is an anachronism as Calfhill supposes the existence of an imposition of hands separated from the baptismal rite and Calvin cites a text from Leo the Great (*Ep.* 156) which has to do with the imposition of hands for the reconciliation of heretics and not at all with confirmation as a rite of affirmation of baptismal faith.

70. Session VII, *De Baptismo*, Canon xiv.

71. It should be pointed out that all churches of the second reformation did not feel the need for "reformed" confirmation. The Church of Sweden, for example, had no such thing as confirmation until the nineteenth century when it was introduced as a rite of admission to communion.

72. We still know so little about Pseudo-Dionysius's actual providence and about the liturgical use he is reflecting, that it is very difficult to make a comment on the addendum to his last chapter of the *Ecclesiastical Hierarchy* for which we have no corroboration from the period in which he wrote. His description of baptism (with communion) in the second chapter certainly resonates with what we know of the west Syrian rite of his time, his "response to Timothy" remains an anomaly for which we have no explanation.

Mitchell on Hatchett
on Cranmer

Leonel L. Mitchell

W HEN THE LATE DEAN URBAN T. HOLMES wrote that, in spite of
the declarations of the Standing Liturgical Commission to the contrary, the
1979 Prayer Book did make theological changes,[1] I am sure that he had the
revision of the baptismal rite in mind. Not only was Holmes a member of that
drafting committee from 1973 to 1976, but the changes made in the rites of
Christian initiation are the most radical of any in the book. Whether the Book
of Common Prayer 1979 is responsible for the changes, or if they simply
reflect changes in the thinking of Anglicans is a more difficult question. But it
is clear that the understanding of baptism, not only by the Episcopal Church,
but by the Anglican Communion has changed. The International Anglican
Liturgical Consultation meeting in Toronto in 1991 affirmed:

> Baptism affirms the royal dignity of every Christian and their call and
> empowering for active ministry within the mission of the church. The renewal
> of baptismal practice, with a consequent awareness of the standing of the
> baptized in the sight of God, therefore has an important part to play in
> renewing the church's respect for all the people of God. [2]

This was followed up by the statement of their interim conference in Finland
in 1997:

> We affirm a baptismal ecclesiology as the proper context for understanding the
> nature of Christian ministry, as expressed in the ecumenical document, *Baptism,
> Eucharist, and Ministry.* [3]

It is quite unlikely that either of these statements would have been made in 1967 when work on the revision of the initiation rites of the American Prayer Book began. The revisers certainly did not concoct a new doctrine of baptism and attempt to impose it on the church. Their work reflected both the pastoral situation in the American Episcopal Church at the time and the extensive study of Christian initiation that had been going on in the Church of England and the Roman Catholic Church. They had before them resolutions of the Lambeth Conference of 1968 [4] recommending the trying out of new patterns to replace the faltering Anglican pattern of infant baptism followed by adolescent confirmation and First Communion, and the text of a critique of contemporary confirmation practice by the Rt. Rev. Frederick J. Warneke, then Bishop of Bethlehem.[5]

The so-called "Mason-Dix line," set forth by Dom Gregory Dix in his pamphlets *Confirmation, or the Laying on of Hands?*[6] and *The Theology of Confirmation in Relation to Baptism,*[7] was widely accepted in the Episcopal Church, and by some members of the drafting committee. His position was that confirmation constituted the essential second part of Christian initiation, water baptism being the first, that confirmation was originally the anointing with chrism on the forehead of the baptized (called the seal), that it was the rite in which the Holy Spirit was given, and that it had nothing at all to do with coming of age. This enabled Dix to say that those who had been baptized but not confirmed (e.g., English dissenters) were not fully initiated Christians. The principal alternative view held by theologically minded Anglicans was that of Geoffrey W. H. Lampe.[8] He argued that Christian initiation was complete in water baptism, in which the Holy Spirit was given. He argued that the seal of the Spirit was not a separate rite, but the inward and spiritual grace of baptism, of which immersion in water was the outward and visible sign. Such actions as anointing, Lampe argued, were explanatory ceremonies, like the signing with the cross in Anglican baptism, which did not themselves convey grace, but did make clear the meaning of some particular aspect of baptism.

The majority of Episcopalians had probably never heard either of these views, but, as the senior warden of the parish of which I was then rector explained to me, considered baptism an ecumenical rite which made you a sort of generic Christian, while confirmation made you an Episcopalian. However unpalatable this view may be to the theologically sophisticated, it certainly conforms to the way the Episcopal Church acted, requiring confirmation before communion and counting only confirmed persons as communicant members in good standing, and labeling all others mere "baptized members."

Somewhat illogically, Dix did not argue for the reintegration of baptism and confirmation. It seemed to the committee, however, that this was the way to go and the rite which was published as *Prayer Book Studies 18*[9] included signing with the cross, prayer for the sevenfold gifts of the Spirit, and, optionally, the anointing with chrism (the sealing) as a part of the baptism rite. The hope was that this would be acceptable both to the followers of Lampe, who considered the signing and sealing unnecessary explanatory ceremonies, and to the disciples of Dix, who considered them the essential second half of Christian initiation. We hoped that everyone would be able to use the rite and continue to discuss its meaning.

Hatchett's Thesis

It was as the committee began its consideration of how to do this that Marion Hatchett, then a doctoral student at General Theological Seminary where the committee was meeting, showed the text of his unpublished S.T.M. thesis[10] to Bonnell Spencer, O.H.C, the committee chair. He brought Hatchett and his manuscript to the committee meeting, and we began to look at what Cranmer had intended Anglican confirmation to be, and what he intended the post-baptismal consignation which replaced the anointing in his 1552 baptismal rite to mean.[11]

In his thesis Hatchett examines both the 1549 and 1552 versions of the rites. The Sarum rites, like the classic Roman sacramentaries which were their source, contained three anointings, before and after baptism and at confirmation. Cranmer eliminated two in 1549 and all three in 1552. In 1549, as Hatchett points out, Cranmer substituted a signation (a signing with the cross) for the anointing associated with the pre-baptismal exorcism. The formula accompanying this signation contained the phrase which was to become a part of the post-baptismal signing in 1552 and succeeding Prayer Books through 1928:

> . . . in token that thou shalt not be ashamed to confesse thy fayth in Christe crucifyed, and manfully to fyght under his banner against synne, the worlde, and the devill, and to continewe his faythfull soldiour and servaunt unto thy lyfes ende.[12]

He also quotes the prayer accompanying the post-baptismal chrismation, the one anointing which Cranmer retained. The prayer is translated from the Sarum rite and is a variant of a common Western form found in the *de Sacramentis* of St. Ambrose and in the classic Roman Sacramentaries.[13] Cranmer, however, made a significant alteration in the Sarum prayer, the concluding phrase "[God] anoints thee with the chrism of salvation," was changed to "he vouchsafe to anoynte thee with the unccion of his holy spirite." Hatchett quotes my statement that this is theological interpretation and cites the explanation of the chrismation from *The Rationale of Ceremonial*:

Then after his baptism, he is anointed with holy chrism, on the head as the supreme and principal part of man, signifying thereby that he is made an Christian man by Christ the head of his congregation; and that he is anointed with the spiritual unction of the Holy Ghost that by his assistance and grace he may attain everlasting life.

He comments:

The fact of this significant change in the prayer which accompanies the anointing, the fact that the anointing comes after rather than before the giving of the vesture, and the fact that there is no anointing in the 1549 Confirmation Rite have caused the question to be raised as to whether this anointing that was retained was an anointing traditionally associated with baptism or the anointing associated with confirmation.[14]

I had mentioned in *Baptismal Anointing* that the phrase *unctio spiritus sancti* was common among medieval theologians, but was usually applied to the second post-baptismal anointing which was unique to the Roman rite and had come to be called "confirmation."[15] Hatchett carried the investigation much farther, examining both Cranmer's understanding of confirmation and the post-baptismal rites. Hatchett's conclusion is "that if there was any intention of perpetuating that peculiar second post-baptismal anointing which was a peculiarity of the Roman rite and which was thought by many to be the matter of the medieval rite called 'confirmation,' that it was at this point in the baptismal rite that it was perpetuated."[16] He also cites the opinion of Charles Wheatley to the same effect.[17]

Hatchett concludes his examination of Cranmer's confirmation rite by saying:

The order of the rite has remained very close to that of the Sarum Manuale, but the rationale has been drastically changed. It has been remodeled to give liturgical expression to Cranmer's theology of Confirmation. For Cranmer, Confirmation is not the infusion of the Holy Ghost, nor is it the completion of baptism, but an examination in the profession which was made for the child at Baptism, with prayer that the Holy Ghost might give "strength and constancy, with other spiritual gifts" to those who have come to "The yeres of discrecion" and have learned their Catechism. The structure of the rite is that of Sarum, but the but the rationale is that of Hermann [von Wied].[18]

Cranmer followed the same pattern in dealing with confirmation that he did in dealing with other rites. To the extent that he could, he followed the Sarum structure and translated, or more frequently paraphrased the Sarum text. The theology which the new rite expressed was often unclear. Cranmer often made room for his own theological views, as he clearly did in his reworking of the eucharistic prayer, but crafted the prayers so as not to exclude the more traditional theology. This rationale to which Hatchett refers is in this case the Reformed understanding of confirmation, expressed by Calvin in the *Institutes,* and put into practice by Martin Bucer and Hermann von Wied of Cologne.[19] Calvin wrote:

> Those who had been baptized as infants, because they had not then made confession of faith before the Church, were at the beginning of adolescence again presented by their parents, and were examined by the bishops according to the form of the catechism, which was then in definite form and in common use. But in order that this act, which ought by itself to have been weighty and holy, might have more reverence and dignity, the ceremony of the laying on of hands was also added.[20]

Calvin was, of course, mistaken about the existence of such a rite in the early Church, but his view was commonly held. Martin Bucer, for example, wrote in Hermann's *Consultation* concerning confirmation:

> When they solemnly profess their faith and obedience before the congregation the very nature of faith requireth again that the congregation pray for them solemnly and desire for them the increase of the Holy Ghost that he will confirm and preserve them in the faith of Christ and obedience of the congregation . . . Therefore our elders following the example of Christ and the apostles, did use the laying on of hands as a sign of this confirmation.[21]

Hatchett appears to have proved that Cranmer believed much the same thing as Calvin and Bucer, and that his rite of confirmation in 1949 and 1552 were attempts to provide a rite such as they describe. He quotes a letter from Cranmer to Edward VI:

> Or yf the aunciente and laudable ceremonie of Confirmation hadde continued in the olde state, and bene duely used of the ministers in time convenient, where an exacte and strayghte examination was had of all suche as were of ful age, both of theyr profession that they made in baptisme touching their beliefe and keepyng of goddes commandmentes and of all tharticles of theyr fayth.[22]

This was powerful ammunition for the drafting committee, since we wished to alter the traditional Anglican structure of infant baptism, followed by adolescent confirmation and admission to communion. The structure, we learned from Hatchett, is from the Reformation, not the patristic church!

Hatchett provided one further string to our bow, his examination of the consignation which replaced the anointing in 1552. Although this was not a chrismation, it was a signing on the forehead with a cross. The signing of the forehead with a cross was considered in the late middle ages to be the outward sign of confirmation. The signing which accompanied the post-baptismal anointing was on the top of the head, and that which accompanied the pre-baptismal exorcism was not with chrism and was on the forehead and breast. The language which Cranmer used in the formula accompanying the consignation is clearly shown by Hatchett to correspond more closely to the 1549 formula accompanying the signing with the cross in confirmation than to the baptismal anointing. "We do signe him with the sign of the crosse" is modeled after "I signe thee with the signe of the crosse," from 1549 confirmation, rather than, "Receive the sign of the holy Crosse," which began the formula when it was used for the pre-baptismal anointing in 1549. The language in common to the two formulae Hatchet shows to be parallel to language used of confirmation by Thomas Aquinas, the fifteenth Council of Florence, and, perhaps most tellingly, The Bishops' Book and The King's Book:

> ...To confess boldly and manfully their faith before all the persecutors of the same, and to resist and fight against their ghostly enemies, the world, the Devil, and the flesh, as also to bear the cross of Christ....[23]

Hatchett's Influence on Prayer Book Studies 18

Hatchett made the portions of his thesis detailing these points available to the drafting committee working on *Prayer Book Studies 18* in the triennium between the 1967 and 1970 General Conventions. I worked from his original copies in writing this essay. His position was accepted by the committee as a working principle and used to defend the actions taken including what was clearly intended to be the confirmation signing with the cross in our baptismal rite. In a real sense it is possible to claim that Marion Hatchett, although not a member of either the Standing Liturgical Commission or the Christian Initiation Drafting Committee at that time, was a principal influence on the resulting rite.

The drafting Committee, however, did not produce the rite simply on the basis of Hatchett's view. It was our conviction that, in Holmes's words, "the old understanding of Confirmation was theologically, historically, and psychologically untenable,"[24] which moved us to the conclusion that the gift of the Spirit was properly a part of baptism, and that to the extent that it was symbolized by the signing of the cross on the forehead, laying on of a hand, and anointing with chrism, they should be a part of the baptismal liturgy, along with the prayer for the sevenfold gifts of the Spirit.

Holmes's claim, "It was written by a subcommittee of the SLC with E. C. Whitaker's Documents of the Baptismal Liturgy (London, SPCK, 1960) in one hand and Marion Hatchett's STM thesis. . . in the other,"[25] is certainly overstated, but it gets the essential point right. We had studied the Mozarabic and Ambrosian baptismal liturgies, studies of which I had already published in, *Studia Liturgica*,[26] as well as the Byzantine and other Eastern liturgies. Among the factors influencing the production of the rite of *Prayer Book Studies 18* were our study of the historical rites, the pastoral situation in the Episcopal Church at that time, and Hatchett's interpretation of Cranmer. The primary importance we saw in Hatchett's work was that it provided a solidly Anglican grounding for what we were trying to do, which we felt (or at least Bonnell Spencer and I felt) would be more generally acceptable to Episcopalians than any amount of evidence from Eastern and non-Roman Western medieval rites.

The Mozarabic Baptismal Rite

The chief model before us was the Mozarabic *Liber Ordinum*,[27] in which following the baptism, the priest anoints the newly baptized with chrism, signs their forehead with the cross, and lays on hands with prayer for the sevenfold gifts of the Spirit. There was no separate rite of confirmation. I wrote of the Mozarabic baptismal rite in 1964:

> In Spain the integrity of the baptismal rite was retained, and the officiating presbyter, acting in the bishop's name and with his permission, baptized and anointed (with episcopally consecrated chrism), and laid on hands. The impositio manuum was neither deferred until the bishop might personally "confirm" the neophytes, as in the Roman rite, nor omitted, as in the Eastern and Gallican rites. Similarly, the administration of first Communion remained a part of the baptismal rite, even for children.[28]

I went on to state what I believed to be the proper understanding, not only of the Mozarabic rite, but of Christian initiation generally. I believe it to be true both of the rite of *Prayer Book Studies 18* and that which is now in the Book of Common Prayer:

> Although the Spanish Church recognized that the washing with water was the essential act which would suffice *in periculo mortis*, it did not forget that baptism consisted of washing, anointing, and the laying on of hands, and that it was as a result of the complete rite that we were crucified and raised up with Christ, made members of his royal and priestly Body, the Church, and received the indwelling grace of the Holy Spirit.[29]

If I were writing that today, I would put consignation, or signing with the cross, in a prominent place along with the chrismation which accompanied it, but otherwise I believe it still. I understand Hatchett to believe that that was also Cranmer's intention, although he did not expect infant neophytes to be communicated.

We know that Cranmer was familiar with the *Mozarabic Missale Mixtum*,[30] since he used its prayer for the blessing of the font as a basis for that in the 1549 Prayer Book. It tends to make one suspicious that he was also familiar with the traditional Mozarabic baptismal rite, and used that for his source, but, as far as I know, that would be difficult to prove.

Other Sources of Prayer Book Studies 18

The other Western sources were the Ambrosian and Gallican liturgies, which both assigned a single chrismation and consignation following the water baptism to the presiding priest, whether bishop or presbyter. It was not until the time of Charlemagne that the non-Roman Western rites came to be pressured into adopting the Roman service of confirmation.

It was widely assumed in the 1960s that the Drafting Committee had the Byzantine baptismal liturgy in mind as a model. We were, of course, aware that the rite of Constantinople included a post-baptismal chrismation and had no episcopal confirmation, but it was not a principal model. Attempts to equate the Eastern chrismation with the Western confirmation are somewhat problematical. It would probably be better to say that they do not have any rite corresponding to Western confirmation, but consider both the baptism with water and the chrismation to be a part of a single rite.

The Lambeth resolutions of 1968 suggested two possible lines of experimental change in the traditional Anglican pattern: (A) the admission of baptized children to communion, followed by admission to communion at "an appropriate age," with confirmation deferred "to an age when a young man or woman shows adult responsibility and wishes to be commissioned and confirmed for his or her task of being a Christian in society," or (B) infant baptism and confirmation administered together, admission to communion "at an early age," and, finally, "in due course the bishop would commission the person for service when he or she is capable of making a responsible commitment."[31]

Prayer Book Studies 26 *and Confirmation*

Clearly *Prayer Book Studies 18* followed suggestion (B), although it went farther in asserting the right of baptized children to receive communion,[32] a position which is increasingly becoming the practice of the Episcopal Church. In any event, the rite of *Prayer Book Studies 18* was not adopted, and was severely limited in trial use. The rite which was adopted, that of *Prayer Book Studies 26*,[33] with some revision, might be assumed to be an adaptation of the Lambeth suggestion (A), but in fact, the differences are simply linguistic. Is the post-baptismal anointing of the American Book of Common Prayer 1979 confirmation, or simply a post-baptismal ceremony? I believe that depends on how you define confirmation. If you define confirmation as

Gregory Dix and Pope Paul VI (in his papal constitution *Divinae Consortium Naturae*) did, as "the seal of the Holy Spirit," of which the external sign is the signing of the forehead with a cross, this is a part of Anglican baptismal practice, and has been since 1552. If, on the other hand, you define confirmation as the Reformers did, as "an examination in the profession which was made for the child at Baptism, with prayer that the Holy Ghost might give 'strength and constancy, with other spiritual gifts' to those who have come to 'the yeres of discrecion'"[34] to which is added the laying on of hands as a sign of "the confirmation of the Holy Ghost,"[35] then this is the rite of confirmation in the present Prayer Book. In other words, we are doing what Hatchett tells us Cranmer was doing, including the theological core of medieval confirmation in the baptismal rite, and providing a separate rite of confirmation, which is not the bestowal of the seal of the Spirit, but "the rite in which we express a mature commitment to Christ, and receive strength from the Holy Spirit through prayer and the laying on of hands by a bishop."[36] Confirmation in the Book of Common Prayer is not the completion of Christian initiation, which is declared to be complete in baptism,[37] but is a renewal of the baptismal covenant, accompanied by the imposition of a hand.

Even though the Reformers, apparently including Cranmer, were mistaken about the existence of such a rite of confirmation in the early church, the importance of providing an opportunity for those who did not personally assume the baptismal covenant at their baptisms to do so as mature adults should not be overlooked, especially in a secular society such as ours in which neither Christian education nor Christian nurture can be assumed. As I have indicated elsewhere,[38] confirmation is one of the problems left unresolved in the Book of Common Prayer 1979. Holmes says that, being unable to educate the bishops as to the true meaning of confirmation,

> . . . the alternative was to make the Confirmation rite as ambiguous as possible in the hope that eventually greater theological clarity would emerge and the rite would be a source—not a resource—for understanding the meaning of the sacrament.[39]

Holmes is correct, but the root of the confusion goes back to Cranmer and his dealing with Sarum confirmation. I think that there can be little doubt that Hatchett is correct as to what Cranmer intended confirmation to be, but it is certainly true that the Anglican Church has not unanimously agreed with his theology of confirmation, any more than it has his eucharistic theology. Richard Hooker, the Puritans, the Caroline divines, the Evangelicals, the Tractarians, Gregory Dix and G.W.H. Lampe all have contributed, often contradictorily, to the contemporary theological understanding of confirmation. In a real sense the Reformed understanding of confirmation as an act of the candidate ratifying and confirming allegiance to the baptismal covenant has co-existed with the traditional Catholic view that confirmation is the bestowal of the sevenfold gifts of the Spirit, and the medieval view that it is a sort of Christian bar mitzvah in which the adolescent receives the appropriate strengthening gifts of the Spirit needed to fight against the temptations of the world, the flesh and the devil. All of these are read out of, or perhaps into, Cranmer's rite. Like the revisers of 1979, Cranmer was attempting to produce rites that could be used by those who held widely differing theological views. The ambiguity has not gone away, and it causes practical difficulties. Daniel Stevick has pointed out some of these in his essay "To Confirm or to Receive?"[40] I have pointed out others in "What Shall We Do about Confirmation?"[41] These, however, are another set of issues.

Conclusion

I believe that the rites of the Book of Common Prayer 1979 are liturgically better than either of Cranmer's versions. The theology of baptism is more clearly stated, the rite is fuller, and the connection between baptism and the eucharist is restored. It also clearly claims to be "full initiation by water and the Holy Spirit,"[42] a position with which the Reformers would certainly have agreed. Confirmation is more ambiguous, and the addition of a rubric concerning the confirmation of those baptized as adults which was not in The Draft Proposed Book of Common Prayer presented to the 1976 General Convention has made it even more so,[43] but this is nothing new. Bishops like Gardiner certainly read Cranmer's confirmation rite in the light of traditional medieval Catholic theology and saw it as a revision of the Sarum form. Those like Hooper, Latimer, and Ridley undoubtedly read it as an attempt to recreate the mythical pure confirmation rite of the early church.

It is still unclear, at least to me, to what extent Cranmer knew or understood the patristic theology of baptism, but he certainly rejected the late medieval understanding of confirmation in which, in Calvin's strong words, "a half of the efficacy of baptism is lopt off."[44] It is tempting to read Cranmer's views on confirmation in the light of Luther's statement, "I allow that confirmation be administered provided that it is known that God has said nothing about it, and knows nothing of it, and that what the bishop's allege about it is false."[45] In 1549 Cranmer called the post-baptismal chrismation "the anointing of the Holy Spirit," a description usually applied to the anointing of confirmation, and in 1552 he restored the consignation of the forehead to baptism and applied to it terminology which identified it with medieval confirmation. Baptism in the 1979 Prayer Book follows this lead. The Drafting Committee actually came to this through looking at pre-Reformation rites, but once Hatchett pointed out Cranmer's intentions to us, we recognized the importance of that element of continuity in our work.

This is true also of confirmation, as it appeared first in *Prayer Book Studies 26* and is now (in somewhat revised form) in the Book of Common Prayer. This is Cranmer's confirmation theologically, if not liturgically his rite. It is clearly not the "seal of the Spirit" of the middle ages, but a solemn blessing by the bishop with prayer for the increase of the Holy Spirit accompanying the personal ratification of the baptismal covenant. I believe, as Hatchett has shown, this is what Cranmer believed confirmation to be. This does not make it true, however, and some Episcopalians cling to the medieval view that confirmation is a necessary part of Christian initiation, a view which Holmes called "theologically, historically, and psychologically untenable."[46]

I believe that it is difficult to get a clear historical reading of confirmation. If any such rite existed in the early church, it was clearly a part of baptism. The Reformers were quite correct in saying that late medieval confirmation was unscriptural, and that its theology had been carved out of baptism by assigning some of its effects to confirmation. They were also right in seeing the utility of a rite in which those coming of age could take on the baptismal promises for themselves, and that is what they made confirmation into. Anglicans have, of course, tried to have it both ways, and still do. This is clearly possible, as long as we recognize what we are doing. We need more clarity, but not necessarily univocity. We can even continue confirmation, while, like Luther, allowing that it is not a divine ordinance. We are, after all, as Hatchett has so well reminded us, following in the steps of Thomas Cranmer.

Notes

1. "Education for Liturgy: An Unfinished Symphony in Four Movements," in Malcolm C. Burson, *Worship Points the Way: Celebration of the Life and Work of Massey H. Shepherd, Jr.* (New York: Seabury Press, 1981) 134.

2. *Growing in Newness of Life: Christian Initiation Today*, edited by David R. Holeton (Toronto: Anglican Book Centre, 1993) 236.

3. *Anglican Orders and Ordinations*, edited by David R. Holeton, *Joint Liturgical Studies* 39 (Cambridge, England: Grove Books, 1997) 50.

4. *The Lambeth Conference 1968. Resolutions and Reports* (London and New York: S.P.C.K. and Seabury, 1968) 99.

5. This was later published as "A Bishop Proposes" in the Executive Council book *Confirmation Crisis* (New York: Seabury Press, 1968) an American version of the English publication *Crisis for Confirmation.* Michael Perry, editor (London: SCM Press, 1967).

6. London: S.P.C.K., 1936.

7. London: Dacre, 1946.

8. *The Seal of the Spirit.* (London: S.P.C.K. 1951) (2nd edition, 1967).

9. *Holy Baptism with the Laying-on-of-Hands: Prayer Book Studies 18 On Baptism and Confirmation* (New York: Church Pension Fund, 1970).

10. Marion J. Hatchett, "Thomas Cranmer and the Rites of Christian Initiation," (S.T.M. Thesis, General Theological Seminary, 1967).

11. Hatchett summarized many of his conclusions in his article "The Rite of 'Confirmation' in the Book of Common Prayer and in Authorized Services 1973," *Anglican Theological Review 56* (1974) 292–310.

12. Quoted from the First Prayer Book of Edward VI in Hatchett, "Cranmer," 107.

13. There is a table showing the various forms in which the prayer has appeared in Leonel L. Mitchell, *Baptismal Anointing* (London: S.P.C.K., 1966) 122.

14. Hatchett, "Cranmer," 123–124.

15. Mitchell, *Baptismal Anointing,* 179.

16. Hatchett, "Confirmation," 200.

17. *A Rational Illustration of the Book of Common Prayer of the Church of England* (first ed., 1718; reprinted into the last half of the nineteenth century). Quote in Hatchett, "Cranmer," 124, cited in Hatchett, "Confirmation," 200, n. 21.

18. Hatchett, "Cranmer," 146.

19. cf. Hatchett, "Confirmation," 296–297.

20. John Calvin, *Institutes of the Christian Religion,* 4.19.4 ed. J.T. McNeil, trans., F.L. Battles, Library of Christian Classics, vol. 21 (Philadelphia: Westminster 1960) 145ff.

21. John Daye's 1548 translation of *Einfältigs Bedenken* ("A simple and religious consultation of us, Hermann by the grace of God Archbishop of Cologne . . . ," quoted in J. D. C. Fisher, *Christian Initiation: The Reformation Period,* Alcuin Club Collections 31 (London: S.P.C.K., 1970) 195.

22. The letter forms an introduction to the catechism of Justus Jonas, and is quoted by Hatchett, "Confirmation," 298–299.

23. Hatchett, "Cranmer," 287–289.

24. Holmes, "Education for Liturgy," 137.

25. Holmes, "Education for Liturgy," 133.

26. "Ambrosian Baptismal Rites," *Studia Liturgica 1* (1962) 241–253; "Mozarabic Baptismal Rites," *Studia Liturgica 3* (1964). 78–87; "The Order of Baptism (Ambrosian Rite)," (text and translation) *Studia Liturgica 4* (1965) 1a, 1–10. I also prepared an English translation of the Mozarabic rite for *Studia Liturgica* which was not published., as they abandoned their plan to print texts.

27. *Le Liber Ordinum en usage dans l'église Wisigothique et Mozarabe d'Espagne du Cinquiäme au Onziäme Siäcle,* D. Marius Ferotin, ed. (Paris: 1904, reprint Westmead, England: Gregg International Publishers, 1969) 32–35.

28. Mitchell, "Mozarabic Baptismal Rites," *Studia Liturgica 3* (1964) 87.

29. Mitchell, "Mozarabic Baptismal Rites," 87.

30. The *Missale Mixtum secundam Regulum Sancti Isidori, dictum Mozarabes* (Toledo, 1500) was produced through the efforts of the famous Cardinal Francisco Ximenez de Cisneros for use in the Mozarabic chapel which he endowed in the Cathedral of Toledo. It was compiled from Mozarabic material, but organized like the Roman Missal. It does not contain baptismal rites, but the blessing of the font which Cranmer copied is included in the Great Vigil of Easter. The text is most readily available as volume lxxxv of J.P. Migne, *Patrologia Latina.*

31. *The Lambeth Conference 1968. Resolutions and Reports,* 99.

32. "Those who have been christened may receive Holy Communion." *Holy*

Baptism with the Laying-on-of-Hands: Prayer Book Studies 18 On Baptism and Confirmation (New York: Church Pension Fund, 1970) 40.

33. New York: Church Hymnal Corporation, 1973.

34. Hatchett, "Cranmer," 146.

35. The phrase is Bucer's, from Hermann's of Cologne's *Consultation,* see note 21 above.

36. The Book of Common Prayer, (Catechism) 860.

37. The Book of Common Prayer, 298.

38. e.g. "What Shall We Do about Confirmation?" in *A Prayer Book for the 21st Century: Liturgical Studies 3,* ed. Ruth A. Meyers for the Standing Liturgical Commission (New York: Church Hymnal Corporation, 1996) 104–109.

39. Holmes, "Education for Liturgy," 138.

40. In *Baptism and Ministry, Liturgical Studies 1,* ed. Ruth A. Meyers (New York: Church Hymnal Corporation, 1994) 55–85.

41. In *A Prayer Book for the 21st Century, Liturgical Studies 3,* ed. Ruth A. Meyers for the Standing Liturgical Commission (New York: Church Hymnal Corporation, 1996) 104–109.

42. BCP, 298.

43. "Those baptized as adults, unless baptized with the laying on of hands by a bishop, are also expected to make a public affirmation of their faith and commitment to the responsibilities of their Baptism in the presence of a bishop and receive the laying on of hands." BCP, 412.

44. *Antidote to the Canons on Confirmation III,* quoted in Fisher, *Christian Initiation,* 255. *Von ehelichen lebeni,* quoted in Fisher, *Christian Initiation,* 172. Holmes, "Education for Liturgy," 137.

45. *Von ehelichen lebeni,* quoted in Fisher, *Christian Initiation,* 172.

46. Holmes, "Education for Liturgy," 137.

Scholarship Shaping Liturgical Reform: Massey Shepherd's Influence on Rites of Christian Initiation

Ruth A. Meyers

ALTHOUGH THE PROCESS OF REVISION leading to the 1979 Book of Common Prayer was formally authorized by the General Convention of the Episcopal Church in 1967, the origins of that process can be found at least two decades earlier in the deliberations and proposals of the Standing Liturgical Commission. In 1943, the commission proposed to the General Convention a systematic revision that would be presented to the church for study not later than 1949, the four-hundredth anniversary of the first English Prayer Book. The convention took no notice of the proposal and neglected even to fund the commission for the next triennium. However, the commission continued its work, in accord with its canonical charge to consider matters relating to revision of the Book of Common Prayer. At its June 1945 meeting, the offices of the Prayer Book were assigned to different commission members for study with an eye toward needs for revision. Baptism was assigned to Henry Ogilby, who invited Massey Shepherd to assist him in his study.

The commission then proposed to the 1946 General Convention a more modest series of "Prayer Book studies," each focused on a different office, to be published for the purpose of study. Noting a lack of explicit Convention authorization for the project, the 1946 Convention declined to grant additional funds specifically for the commission to continue work on the studies. Undaunted, the commission proceeded to develop the Prayer Book studies. The next Convention, in 1949, finally voted funds to subsidize the commission's plan, and the series of Prayer Book studies was launched.

The first study, prepared by Massey Shepherd (who was appointed to the commission after the 1946 convention) along with Henry Ogilby and Charles Hill, considered baptism and confirmation together as rites of Christian initiation.[1] As revisions of the 1928 rites rather than wholly new rites, the proposals were in many respects quite modest. The pamphlet was sold throughout the Episcopal Church, and the Standing Liturgical Commission received a number of comments from individual clergy and laity as well as groups that studied the document.

While the commission continued to receive comments, it took no further action on the initiatory rites until 1959, when it began to discuss which of the several Prayer Book studies then in print needed further revision. Massey Shepherd commented that not only had the earlier proposal for baptism been a compromise, he had changed his mind about confirmation.[2]

The minutes of the Standing Liturgical Commission do not record the nature of Shepherd's revised opinion about confirmation. Nor did Shepherd continue to contribute directly to the revision of the Episcopal Church's initiatory rites. By the 1960s, his energies were devoted to work on the calendar. But his writings offer clear evidence of the changing trajectory of his thought and suggest as well some ways in which he influenced not only the rites presented in the 1950 Prayer Book study but also the shape of the 1979 rites.

Confirmation as "Ordination of the Laity:" Shepherd's Early Writing

Shepherd's earliest published writing on Christian initiation appeared in his regular column, "The Living Liturgy," in the popular periodical *The Witness*. The column followed the pattern of his mentor William Palmer Ladd, whose column "Prayer Book Interleaves" appeared in *The Witness* in the late 1930s. Like Ladd's columns, Shepherd's early columns were published together in a single volume.[3]

The Living Liturgy included just two articles on baptism and one on confirmation, and only the article on confirmation discussed the overall pattern of Christian initiation. Describing the American rite of confirmation as a "masterpiece," Shepherd called attention to the two "principal actions of the rite": the renewal of baptismal vows by the candidates, and prayer and imposition of hands, a sacramental action signifying God's grace. Continuing, Shepherd noted the popular designation of confirmation as "ordination of the laity." He cautioned against pressing that analogy too far, since in baptism individuals "become fully members of Christ's body and sharers in his eternal priesthood."[4]

While Shepherd thus asserted that baptism makes one a full member of the body of Christ, he nonetheless suggested that the analogy of ordination could be applied to the practice of confirmation. Just as ordination was integrated with the service of Holy Communion, so too might confirmation include communion, thus allowing confirmands to receive their first communion from the bishop. In addition, the sacramental portion of confirmation could incorporate ceremonial from the ordination rite: silent prayer by the congregation for the candidates after they had renewed their baptismal promises; singing a hymn comparable to *Veni, Creator Spiritus* just before the prayer and laying on of hands. Shepherd limited the analogy, however, reminding his readers that during the imposition of hands the bishop offered prayer rather than conferring authority as in ordination.[5]

The ceremonial proposed by Shepherd would underscore an interpretation of confirmation as a sacramental bestowal of the Holy Spirit. His essay did not address the theological issues, but a subsequent column in *The Witness* did. On the one hand, Shepherd said, the Prayer Book viewed baptism as full initiation into Christ, asking God not only for the gifts of forgiveness of sin and spiritual rebirth, but also for the gift of the Holy Spirit. Yet the 1928 rite of confirmation, prefaced by a reading from Acts 8:14–17, implied that the confirmands had not received the Spirit. Furthermore, the prayer immediately preceding the imposition of hands asked for the gifts of the Spirit, although Cranmer had revised the original Latin petition "send into them thy Holy Spirit" to read instead "strengthen them with the Holy Ghost." Suggesting that confirmation is the sacramental completion of baptism, Shepherd argued that confirmation should be understood as "complementary" to baptism and "not merely supplementary," although he did not deny that the Spirit "comes into a personal, effectual relationship with those who are baptized." To clarify the relationship between baptism and confirmation, he called for a thorough reconsideration of the historical, theological, and practical aspects of Christian initiation. As a first step, he proposed that baptism and confirmation be administered at the same time, in a single rite, at the bishop's visitation, although he offered no specific recommendations for the structure of such a rite.[6]

This second column on confirmation marks a significant shift in Shepherd's perspective. His first column, acknowledging the various historical layers underlying the American rite of confirmation, had characterized the resulting rite as a "masterpiece." Yet just a few years later, in view of the same historical developments, Shepherd asserted that the teaching of the Prayer Book was confusing and ambiguous. What led to such a markedly different interpretation? Although Shepherd did not identify a change in his position, the interval between the two columns coincided with new developments in the Anglican debate about the relation between baptism and confirmation.

The Meaning of Confirmation in Relation to Baptism

The issues were first staked out in the late nineteenth century by F. W. Puller and A. J. Mason, who asserted that the indwelling gift of the Spirit is bestowed at confirmation and not at baptism, and by A. Theodore Wirgman and Darwell Stone, who countered that the Holy Spirit is bestowed at baptism.[7] The debate received little attention in the Episcopal Church. In what became the standard textbook on the 1928 Book of Common Prayer, Edward Lambe Parsons and Bayard Hale Jones suggested that the Spirit is bestowed both at baptism and at confirmation, in the latter rite as a particular gift to enable or strengthen the laity in their vocation and ministry, that is, as a kind of ordination.[8]

In England, the debate received renewed attention beginning in the 1940s in response to pastoral concerns about a large discrepancy between the number of children baptized and the number subsequently confirmed. A preliminary report, *Confirmation Today*, presented in 1944 by Joint Committees of the Convocations of Canterbury and York, argued that at baptism the Holy Spirit effects redemption and incorporation into the Body of Christ, while confirmation, the ordination of the laity, provides an increase of gifts of the Spirit to commission and strengthen Christians for their ministry.[9]

Disputing the interpretation given in the report, Gregory Dix, in a 1946 lecture given at Oxford, distinguished between baptism of water and baptism of the Spirit. He argued that these were distinct elements of a single baptismal rite in the early church, baptism of water serving only as a preliminary to baptism of the Spirit. During the Middle Ages, when the two elements became separate rites, the original theological content of the postbaptismal seal shifted to water-baptism. Confirmation then came to be understood as an increase of grace. Dix called for a restoration of an understanding of confirmation as a sealing of the Holy Spirit which completes initiation. For those baptized as infants, it was essential to associate this gift of the Spirit with the conscious response of faith.[10]

With the renewed controversy came awareness of a need for thorough consideration of the theology of Christian initiation. To that end, the Archbishops of Canterbury and York appointed a theological commission, separate from the Joint Committees on Confirmation. Dix was a member of the new commission, but the commission did not adopt the extremes of his position. Thus when reviewing the evidence for initiation in the apostolic church, the report rejected Dix's distinction between baptism in water and baptism in the Spirit: "It seems clear to the majority of us that within the life and practice of the church there is no trace of any such distinction." The report then described a post-apostolic pattern of initiation in which immersion signified cleansing from sin, death, and rebirth, while chrismation and imposition of hands were associated with sealing with the Spirit. The report claimed that the gift of the Spirit was particularly associated with those portions of the rite later known as confirmation (the "seal of the Spirit," signified by the chrism), but it also asserted that the action of the Holy Spirit was assumed in every part of the rite.[11]

While in the latter claim the theological commission thus parted company with Dix, its view of the medieval developments followed Dix more closely in arguing that the gift of the Spirit came to be associated with water-baptism, and confirmation was then interpreted as an increase of grace. Anglican reforms restored an important dimension of the primitive practice by including in confirmation the dimension of conscious faith. Although recognizing that the Prayer Book unequivocally teaches that baptism makes us members of the church, the commission argued that full Christian initiation should be understood as beginning with a request for baptism and concluding with first communion.[12]

Turning to the question of the contemporary church's teaching about confirmation, the report described confirmation as the "seal" that includes both strengthening for Christian service in this world and, using a phrase repeatedly employed by Dix, an eschatological "sealing unto the day of redemption" (Eph. 4.30). The report noted that it did not wish to make "any negative inferences about the relation to the Holy Spirit of baptized but unconfirmed persons," although it did not make any positive statements about the work of the Spirit in baptism. In addition, while affirming an association of confirmation with the acceptance of Christian responsibility, the report criticized the popular designation of confirmation as "ordination of the laity." There is no individual office of lay priesthood, the report argued, but rather all Christians share in the common priesthood of the entire church by virtue of their Christian initiation.[13]

The report of the theological commission was available at the 1948 Lambeth Conference, at which a separate committee considered baptism and confirmation. The Lambeth committee agreed with the theological commission that Christian initiation comprises baptism, confirmation and first communion and that personal response of faith is an essential complement to the operation of God's grace in the initiatory process. Turning to the question of the role of the Holy Spirit in baptism and in confirmation, the

Lambeth committee insisted that "the dissociation of the Holy Spirit's operation from any part of the Initiation is strongly to be deprecated, as is also the attempt to measure His operation quantitatively." Nonetheless, because the Spirit's activity is "conditioned by human capacity to respond," Christians are endowed with more abundant grace as they are able to offer themselves for fuller responsibility and service.[14]

Shepherd's 1948 column, published prior to the Lambeth Conference, took note of the renewed debate in the Church of England. But his first substantial discussion of the historical issues is found in his Prayer Book commentary, published in 1950. Here he prefaced specific comments on the texts and rubrics of the rites of baptism and confirmation with a survey of the historical development of initiatory rites. Although he did not use Dix's terms "baptism of water" and "baptism of the Spirit," he followed the same line of argument as Dix: the primitive pattern of initiation, seen most fully in the third-century document *Apostolic Tradition*, included baptism, conferring forgiveness of sin, regeneration, and adoption by God, and confirmation, the imposition of a hand and chrismation, bestowing the "indwelling and strengthening Spirit as earnest of eternal redemption." Shepherd's view of the medieval developments accorded with that of Dix and of the Church of England theological commission, that is, that confirmation came to be seen as an increase of grace, the strengthening gift of the Spirit. Shepherd noted that the medieval view had been retained to a certain extent in Anglican Prayer Books, leading to Anglican ambiguity about the necessity and significance of confirmation. Viewing baptism as full initiation and confirmation as the strengthening of grace already received could result in confirmation being seen as superfluous, but understanding confirmation as the completion and sealing of initiation begun at baptism could eliminate a sense of a personal gift of the Spirit operative in baptism. Shepherd concluded by citing Oscar Hardman's pamphlet "Bishoping": the Spirit is active throughout a child's life, from the moment of birth; the church "initiates the child into the Christian relationship with the Spirit at the earliest possible moment"; and the process of initiation is then completed when the child is able to enter consciously and responsibly into association with the Spirit and the church.[15]

In his interpretation of the rites, Shepherd sought to apply this broader view of the work of the Spirit. Wanting to avoid the absurdity of denying the Spirit's activity in baptism, Shepherd identified references in the baptismal rite to the work of the Spirit: the opening exhortation referred to baptism as "spiritual birth," given "by the operation of the Holy Spirit"; the blessing of the font set apart water to signify the cleansing effected by God through the Holy Spirit.[16] Moreover, he cautioned that the lesson from Acts at confirmation "should not be interpreted strictly to imply that the Holy Spirit has not been imparted to those who have been baptized in His Name."[17]

Yet, though acknowledging the work of the Spirit at baptism, Shepherd asserted that confirmation, the seal of the Spirit, completes Christian initiation. This distinction in the operation of the Spirit, said Shepherd, is summarized in the confirmation prayer for the gifts of the Spirit:

> The preamble sums up the gifts of grace just received in Baptism, regeneration and "forgiveness of all their sins," and the petition proceeds to invoke the completion of initiation by requesting the indwelling Spirit in all His several virtues.

Shepherd pointed out that the original Latin form of the prayer as well as the 1549 form were clearer in their intent, since they asked God to "send" the Holy Spirit. He attributed the 1552 change in phrase, "strengthen them . . . with the Holy Ghost," to Cranmer's adherence to the medieval theology of confirmation.[18]

Shepherd's Prayer Book commentary makes clear that he was persuaded by Dix's reading of the historical evidence. Like Dix, Shepherd argued that the apostolic pattern of Christian initiation was a two-stage process, normally administered in a single rite, with the first part conveying forgiveness of sin and rebirth and the second, "the seal of the Spirit," bestowing the gifts of the indwelling Spirit. In his interpretation of the contemporary Anglican pattern, however, Shepherd on the one hand was apparently in agreement with Dix that confirmation should be seen as the completion of Christian initiation, but on the other hand departed from Dix by pointing out the theological absurdity of denying any role for the Spirit in the baptismal rite.

Prayer Book Studies I: *A Dixian Proposal*

Both the rites and the introductory essay in *Prayer Book Studies I* reflect the Mason/Dix line: confirmation is the sealing with the Holy Spirit that completes Christian initiation. It is likely that Shepherd had a major role not only in producing the rites of baptism and confirmation but also in articulating the historical and theological basis for the proposals, since he along with Henry Ogilby and Charles Hill constituted the "Committee on the Orders of Baptism and Confirmation."

The introduction to *Prayer Book Studies I* identified three concerns underlying the proposed revision of baptism: "the length of the service, the clarification of rubrics to meet modern needs and demands, and the simplification of the ritual text."[19] However, there appears to be an additional, unstated principle: the elimination of references to the bestowal of the Holy Spirit at baptism. For example, the opening exhortation in both the 1928 rite and *Prayer Book Studies I* stated: "None can enter into the Kingdom of God, except he be regenerate and born anew of Water and of the Holy Ghost." The 1928 exhortation then directed the congregation to call upon God to grant that the child "may be baptized with Water and the Holy Ghost, and received into Christ's holy Church," but in *Prayer Book Studies I* the phrase was reworded: "that he, being baptized, may be received into Christ's holy Church."[20] Likewise, the 1928 prayer immediately preceding the promises specifically asked God to "give thy Holy Spirit to this child." This prayer was omitted in *Prayer Book Studies I,* and although the introduction explained that the content of the petitions had been incorporated into the thanksgiving at the end of the baptismal rite, no petition for the bestowal of the Holy Spirit appeared in the latter prayer.[21]

Shepherd's Prayer Book commentary had argued that the sanctification of the water was intended to set it apart as a sign of the cleansing effected by God through the Holy Spirit. In the 1928 rite, the prayer over the water asked God that the child might "receive the fullness of thy grace," but in *Prayer Book Studies I* it asked instead that the child might "grow in thy grace and favour."[22] The introduction explained that the 1928 phrase raised the question of the nature of the gifts of grace bestowed at baptism and at confirmation. Acknowledging the ambiguity in Anglican theology and citing the work of Oscar Hardman in his pamphlet "Bishoping" (including the same paragraph cited by Shepherd in his Prayer Book commentary), *Prayer Book Studies I* was equivocal. On the one hand, it stated that it would be "an intolerable doctrine" that denied that the Spirit is given in baptism or that the Spirit acts upon the baptized only externally. Yet, while admitting that the Spirit must be "capable of influencing the growth in grace of a child after baptism," it did not state definitively how the Spirit is operative in baptism. Describing this as a great mystery, it maintained that the goal of the revision was to give confirmation its proper weight:

> All that the present revision claims for itself is that it has sought to avoid any phraseology which would foster an interpretation of Baptism with Water in such a way that it usurps or makes superfluous the normative and necessary place of Confirmation in the perfecting of the Christian, or would reduce the meaning of Confirmation to a mere strengthening of what has been received in Baptism.[23]

Desire to underscore the significance of confirmation is evident in both the proposed revision of confirmation and the rationale presented in *Prayer Book Studies I.* The introduction explained that the revisions were "designed to restore the primitive view of Confirmation as the gift of the indwelling Spirit in all His fullness to the baptized, and not merely as an added, strengthening grace."[24] The rite was divided by subheadings: Introduction, The Presentation of the Candidates, The Renewal of the Vows of Baptism, and The

Confirmation, thus distinguishing renewal of baptism from "confirmation" proper. "The Confirmation" included the prayer for the sevenfold gifts of the Spirit, revised to ask God to "send" the Holy Spirit (rather than "strengthen" the confirmands with the Spirit), and the imposition of a hand by the bishop, who prayed that God would "confirm" (rather than "defend") the confirmand with heavenly grace.[25]

In light of Shepherd's stance that the original form of confirmation was the imposition of a hand and chrismation by the bishop, bestowing the indwelling and strengthening Spirit and thus completing Christian initiation, it is tempting to attribute to him the revisions proposed in *Prayer Book Studies I.* He may indeed have played a significant role in the revisions made to underscore confirmation as the second half of a two-stage process. But his influence on the baptismal rite is less certain. Not only did he remind the Standing Liturgical Commission in 1959 that the baptismal rite in *Prayer Book Studies I* was a compromise, his book *The Living Liturgy* included as an appendix a proposed revision of baptism which differed in two significant ways from *Prayer Book Studies I.*

Shepherd's suggested baptismal rite did not go to the same extremes as *Prayer Book Studies I* in removing references to the Spirit. The opening exhortation continues, like the 1928 Prayer Book, to ask the congregation to pray that the baptizand "may be sanctified with the Holy Ghost," and the thanksgiving after baptism (like *Prayer Book Studies I*, this prayer incorporates petitions from the 1928 prayer before the promises) stated explicitly that the individual is "now sanctified by Baptism with thy Holy Spirit." The blessing of the font moved away from the 1928 petition for the "fullness of thy grace," but nonetheless asked that the baptizand "may receive the benediction of thy heavenly grace." Moreover, in the invocation immediately following the opening exhortation, Shepherd added a petition that the baptizand "may be born anew of the Holy Ghost."[26]

It is possible that Shepherd's thought on baptism had developed after the 1946 publication of *The Living Liturgy.* A change in his assessment of confirmation was certainly evident in his subsequent column in *The Witness.* Yet although in his Prayer Book commentary Shepherd followed Dix closely in interpreting the historical evidence, Shepherd refused to go to the extreme of denying any role for the Spirit in baptism. Instead, he specified that the Spirit is operative at baptism to effect regeneration and forgiveness of sin. Perhaps the compromise Shepherd alluded to a decade later centered on the key phrases about the activity of the Spirit at baptism. It may be that the elimination of those phrases was not at Shepherd's initiative, but rather proposed by another member of the Standing Liturgical Commission.

It is also possible that this compromise was made in respect to another aspect of the baptismal rite. In *The Living Liturgy*, Shepherd commented on the difficulty of understanding the phrase "remission of sin" when the baptismal candidates were infants: "It is hard to think that anyone nowadays believes that God holds little infants accountable for original *sin*, who have not yet committed actual *sins*." He pointed out that a reference to forgiveness of sin included in the opening invocation of the 1928 rite was not found in the original Latin text of that prayer.[27] Not only did his proposed rite excise the phrase in that prayer, he also removed references to forgiveness of sin from other places in the rite. While the rite continued to acknowledge the power of sin, for example, in the renunciations, it no longer included phrases which implied that the baptizand had sinned. This seems to be not an outright denial of the reality of sin but rather an effort to make the rite more intelligible to twentieth-century Christians. Yet none of these omissions regarding sin are evident in *Prayer Book Studies I*, nor does the introduction include any substantial discussion of this aspect of baptism. Hence it is possible that Shepherd was forced to compromise in this area.

While Shepherd may have made a compromise in the baptismal rite in *Prayer Book Studies I*, regarding the inclusion of references to sin and/or the omission of references to the work of the Spirit, the basic components of his essentially Dixian position on Christian initiation are evident: confirmation completes initiation by the bestowal of the indwelling and strengthening gifts of the Spirit. Shepherd's hand is also apparent in the provisions made in *Prayer Book Studies I* for baptism and confirmation to be celebrated as a single continuous service when there were adults prepared to receive full Christian initiation. The Prayer Book study provided the ritual form to implement the proposal he had made in his 1948 column in *The Witness*, although the Prayer Book study was intended for study and discussion and not for actual practice.

New Perspectives: The Seal of the Spirit

Shepherd's understanding of confirmation as the completion of Christian initiation is evident in *The Worship of the Church*, published just two years after his Prayer Book commentary. While the new book had the same primary purpose, that is, the interpretation of the American Book of Common Prayer, it had the added weight of being part of *The Church's Teaching Series*, giving it a quasi-official status.

Yet although Shepherd continued to describe confirmation as the completion of initiation, there are some significant differences. Rather than asserting that chrismation dates back to apostolic times, Shepherd argued that laying on of hands was more likely the apostolic custom. He acknowledged that the New Testament does not offer clear or consistent evidence of the bestowal of the Spirit in initiation. However, while admitting the possibility that imposition of hands did not always accompany baptism, he claimed that it was highly likely and that the imposition of hands was the means of bestowing the Spirit.[28]

Not only did Shepherd modify his view of the apostolic practice of Christian initiation, there is also indication of a shift in his view of the contemporary practice of confirmation. He offered a different interpretation of the two dimensions, renewal of baptism and bestowal of grace:

> In Baptism we are made members of [God's family] indeed; but in Confirmation we become responsible for our membership. Yet even in Confirmation we are recipients of God's gifts of grace, by the imparting of His Holy Spirit to strengthen us and help us in our responsibilities.[29]

There is no mention of confirmation as a bestowal of the "indwelling" Spirit, and greater emphasis is given to confirmation as a renewal of baptism.

This is a remarkable change. Confirmation did not originate, as Shepherd had maintained only two years earlier, in an apostolic practice of chrismation. The contemporary rite of confirmation completed Christian initiation not by a bestowal of the indwelling Spirit but by a Christian's individual response to God's redemptive action, accompanied by the strengthening gift of the Spirit.

Shepherd's revised interpretation can readily be explained if we consider the 1951 publication of Geoffrey Lampe's *The Seal of the Spirit*, described in the bibliography of *The Worship of the Church* as "a most important work of careful scholarship."[30] Although Shepherd did not fully adopt Lampe's position, the influence is clear.

The Seal of the Spirit directly challenged Dix's assertion that baptism in the Spirit, distinct from water-baptism, is the necessary completion of Christian initiation. Where Dix had described initiation during the apostolic period as a two-stage rite, Lampe argued that the "seal of the Spirit" was one aspect of baptism in water. While Acts includes various reference to the imposition of hands, Lampe claimed that this action was best understood as a means of association with the apostolic and missionary task of the church and not as a component of baptism. Furthermore, New Testament texts do not provide firm evidence for a practice of anointing in connection with baptism. It was only during the patristic period that anointing and imposition of hands came to be included in the baptismal rite, and as the rite became increasingly complex, the gift of the Spirit came to be associated variously with the water-baptism, pre- or postbaptismal anointing, and/or the imposition of hands.[31]

According to Lampe, the New Testament offers little evidence to establish imposition of hands as a universal practice in the apostolic church, either as a rite distinct from baptism or as an integral part of initiation. Shepherd read the evidence differently, although he admitted that it was not certain that "the laying on of hands always accompanied Baptism as the means of giving the Spirit."[32] But Shepherd seems to have been convinced by Lampe's reading of the New Testament evidence (or lack thereof) for anointing as part of baptism. Lampe acknowledged that it was possible to read *Apostolic Tradition* as evidence of "a continuous liturgical tradition from the primitive Church," but he cautioned, "such an assumption would be dangerous in the extreme."[33]

Shepherd also seems to have followed Lampe in his assessment of the contemporary practice of confirmation. Lampe lauded the Anglican reformers for including in confirmation a means to supply the response of faith not possible for those baptized as infants. Confirmation thus completes baptism by providing for this response of faith, and after the individual's confirmation of the promises made at baptism, the individual receives "a new and fuller apprehension of the Spirit" in response to prayer. For those baptized as adults, confirmation provides both a blessing and a commissioning for service, although Lampe lamented that confirmation loses much of its force when separated from the baptism of an adult.[34] While Shepherd, in *The Worship of the Church*, did not discuss adult baptism and confirmation, he described the catechetical emphasis of confirmation as "a very significant addition to the Confirmation rite" made by the Reformers.[35]

Shepherd's abandonment of Dix's position is explicit in *The Liturgy and the Christian Faith*, a published version of lectures delivered to clergy in Tokyo and Hong Kong in summer 1954. In a brief summary of the New Testament and patristic evidence for rites of Christian initiation, he covered much of the same ground as he had in his earlier writing, but he specifically repudiated Dix:

> It is not possible, as some scholars have attempted (notably Dom Gregory Dix), to separate the various gifts of grace in this initiation, and assign them to the several parts of the liturgy. The fathers speak very loosely, sometimes referring to Baptism, sometimes to Confirmation . . . They did not distinguish the gifts in Baptism from those imparted in Confirmation. And the Eucharist also was considered as conferring forgiveness, new life, and the Spirit.

After discussing the medieval separation of baptism and confirmation, Shepherd claimed that the Anglican Reformers understood baptism as full initiation and confirmation as a strengthening gift of the Spirit. However, said Shepherd, Anglicans who studied patristic writers came to realize that baptism and confirmation were both necessary elements of Christian initiation, thus precipitating considerable confusion. But Shepherd refrained from proposing any new patterns or practices. Instead, as he had in his Prayer Book commentary, he acknowledged conflicting positions and the weaknesses of each position: if baptism is viewed as full initiation and confirmation as an added gift of the Spirit, then the importance of confirmation, particularly the ministry of the bishop, is depreciated; if confirmation is seen as the gift of the Spirit and thus as the completion of initiation, then baptized persons have no personal relation with the Holy Spirit until their confirmation, and those baptized but not confirmed have no real part in the church.[36]

The Seal of the Spirit thus had a significant impact on Shepherd. It challenged him to reconsider a method of scholarship that extrapolated from *Apostolic Tradition*, presumed to describe third-century Roman practice, to speak with certainty about initiatory practices during the apostolic period nearly two centuries earlier. And it encouraged him to give greater weight to the catechetical dimension of confirmation as it had emerged in the Reformation. But his 1954 lectures indicate that he was still unwilling to diminish the significance of confirmation.

A New Understanding of Christian Initiation

A few years after his lectures in Hong Kong and Tokyo, Shepherd remarked to the Standing Liturgical Commission that he had changed his mind about confirmation. An indication of his reassessment of the historical evidence is found in *The Paschal Liturgy and the Apocalypse*, published in 1960.

As he had in his earlier writing, Shepherd relied heavily on the account of baptism in *Apostolic Tradition* to describe the annual paschal liturgy at the beginning of the third century. His account used the division common to mid-twentieth-century scholarship, that is, baptism, confirmation, eucharist. In a footnote, however, he maintained that he did not use the term "confirmation" to imply a sacrament distinct from baptism, but rather had adopted the "later terminology of the Church solely as a convenience for analysis." Shepherd's analysis noted that "the Fathers did not think of the Paschal mystery as a series of distinct sacraments, but took the whole complex of rites and ceremonies as a whole." Declining to address questions about the relation between baptism and confirmation or the moment of the gift of the Spirit, Shepherd continued with a brief discussion of New Testament evidence for the laying on of hands and of patristic evidence for the laying on of hands, chrismation and consignation. Nowhere did he make a definitive claim about bestowal or sealing with the Spirit in relation to any of these actions as practiced in the apostolic or post-apostolic period, instead noting varying practices and interpretations.[37]

Shepherd's thesis in *The Paschal Liturgy and the Apocalypse* was that the ancient paschal liturgy provided the outline of the book of Revelation. Applying this outline to Revelation, he identified not "baptism" and "confirmation" but "initiation," which included both "washing" and "sealing with the Name." By the latter he seems to have meant signing with the cross on the forehead, since he commented that the seal might also recall chrismation and imposition of hands in "confirmation," but "this cannot be so definitely read out of the text."[38]

Behind Shepherd's revised interpretation of the historical evidence lies Lampe's *The Seal of the Spirit.* Shepherd not only acknowledged the lack of definitive New Testament evidence for chrismation as part of Christian initiation, he also recognized that the laying on of hands was capable of multiple meanings, not all of them initiatory. Yet contrary to Lampe, Shepherd insisted, "That the rite of laying on of hands in close proximity to Baptism was practised in the apostolic age cannot be disputed."[39] Moreover, in *The Paschal Liturgy and the Apocalypse,* it is apparent that Shepherd continued to view initiation in the apostolic and post-apostolic periods as a two-stage process, albeit an integral "complex of rites and ceremonies" rather than distinct sacraments.

Shepherd's new understanding of the essential unity of the paschal liturgy eventually led him to propose a new approach to Christian initiation in the contemporary church. In the Bradner lectures delivered at the General Theological Seminary in February 1964, Shepherd declared:

> There is no good reason why we should not reintegrate in one single rite Baptism, Confirmation, and admission to the Eucharist—whether this is done for infants or for adults, depending upon the pastoral needs in these respective cases. A Christian should be fully initiated once for all, for at whatever age he undergoes this experience, whether in infancy, childhood, adolescence, or adulthood, he will need Christian nurture for the rest of his life.[40]

This goes far beyond Shepherd's proposal, years earlier, that baptism and confirmation be administered in a single rite for adults at the bishop's visitation. What is most innovative is his recommendation that the same rite suffice for initiates of any age, including infants.

A footnote in the published version of the lectures cites *Baptism and Confirmation,* the 1959 report of the Church of England Liturgical Commission. This report proposed a unified service comprising baptism, confirmation and communion, but only for adults. For infants, the commission offered separate rites for infant baptism and for adult confirmation, the latter described "as a corollary of infant baptism."[41]

The Church of England proposal for a single integral rite may well have encouraged Shepherd to recommend that Christian initiation be administered in one unified rite. But Shepherd's proposal was far more radical, making no distinction in the ritual pattern for infants and adults. This was unprecedented in Anglican tradition.

Yet it is also a logical conclusion from a study of the initiatory patterns of the early church. *Apostolic Tradition* referred to the baptism of the "little ones," including those who could not speak for themselves. Here was patristic, if not apostolic, evidence for including infants in the full initiatory liturgy. Moreover, Shepherd's study *The Paschal Liturgy and the Apocalypse* reflected his profound appreciation for the importance of the paschal mystery celebrated in the rich ceremonial of an initiatory rite integral to the annual paschal vigil liturgy. While he did not recommend limiting the contemporary celebration of initiation to Easter, he did comment:

> Whatever the day or hour, whether Sunday or a holy day or some other day, this fullness of the liturgy of the people of God with their chief apostolic pastor would point to and manifest the Easter-Pentecost reality . . . there are advantages of witness, and certainly of edification, in exhibiting the wholeness of the Mystery.[42]

A significant dimension of this proposal is the presidency of the bishop. Episcopacy is a hallmark of Anglicanism, and Shepherd described episcopacy as "one of God's great gifts to his Church," manifesting "the Church's temporal and visible unity." The bishop's presidency, however, did not arise solely from this symbolic value of the episcopacy. Shepherd noted that the bishop is the minister of orders in the church, and the laity "is the fundamental Holy Order in the Church." Contrary to earlier assertions that confirmation is the ordination of the laity, Shepherd was adamant that baptism conferred ordination of the laity. Confirmation, according to Shepherd, "strengthens what is given in Baptism, our personal relationship to God the Holy Spirit and the church in which he indwells, that we may be responsible witnesses to the faith that is in us."[43]

Shepherd did not specify in his lecture what he understood to be the ritual aspects of confirmation. In his earlier writings he had pointed out that Anglican confirmation included both reaffirmation of baptism and imposition of hands with prayer for the gifts of the indwelling or strengthening Spirit. Since his proposed unified initiatory rite could be administered to infants as well as adults, Shepherd seems to have opted for the latter ritual action alone. Thus Shepherd's reintegrated rite would replicate in some ways the patristic pattern of initiation as he understood it. Baptism in water would be followed immediately by confirmation, that is, imposition of a hand, and the rite would culminate with the eucharist, with a bishop presiding over the entire rite.

Yet Shepherd's proposal was more than an exercise in nostalgia or a liturgical fundamentalism that attempted to recover the supposed pristine purity of the church's earliest initiatory practices. He was also concerned to foster the development of responsible Christian faith and witness in the context of twentieth-century post-Christendom society. The Bradner lectures hint at this concern: "The Church today is a mixed lot of committed, half-committed, and only formally committed persons and families."[44] This issue would be much more sharply focused in later lectures. In a 1971 address to a (Roman Catholic) diocesan liturgical commissions meeting and his 1978 response to the Berakah Award given by the North American Academy of Liturgy, Shepherd maintained that the emergence of post-Christendom meant that the church could no longer assume that society would provide an environment for the Christian nurture of baptized children. Thus "the restructuring of initiation rites is a pastoral necessity."[45]

The restructuring proposed by Shepherd was intended to permit ongoing nurture of children in the household of faith, in particular their regular nourishment at the eucharistic table. Here Shepherd drew upon contemporary pedagogical theory, which stressed that children learn by doing, as well as the fourth-century catechetical practice of withholding commentary on sacraments until the candidates had been initiated. According to Shepherd, children would learn about the significance of eucharist first and foremost by their experience of it. He suggested that incorporating children into the fullness of Christian life, beginning at an early age, could cultivate responsible, committed Christian witness at least as well if not better than the then current practice of infant baptism and adolescent confirmation leading to admission to communion.

In addition to addressing contemporary pastoral concerns, Shepherd's proposal allowed him to resolve the dilemma he had acknowledged in his Prayer Book commentary and again in his 1954 lectures in Hong Kong and Tokyo. He could describe baptism as full initiation and confirmation as an added gift of the Spirit without depreciating the importance of confirmation and the ministry of the bishop, since confirmation was administered immediately following baptism and the bishop presided. This is still, however, a two-stage rite, albeit a unified rite. Baptism in water is followed by confirmation, that is, prayer with imposition of a hand. The gift of the Spirit is identified with baptism, although confirmation is understood to strengthen this gift.

"Full Initiation by Water and the Holy Spirit:" The 1979 Book of Common Prayer

Although Shepherd did not serve on the Drafting Committee on Christian Initiation, his vision of a unified initiatory rite was realized in the 1979 Prayer Book. No doubt in his role as a member of the Standing Liturgical

Commission he supported the overall shape of the rites developed by the drafting committee. There are also at least two points of more direct impact by Shepherd.

First, one who heard Shepherd's 1964 Bradner lectures was Leonel Mitchell, who at the time was completing his doctoral studies at the General Theological Seminary, and who served on the Drafting Committee on Christian Initiation throughout the revision process leading to the 1979 Prayer Book. The subject of Mitchell's dissertation was baptismal anointing in the liturgies of the church up to the tenth century. Based upon the historical evidence, Mitchell advocated the restoration of the postbaptismal anointing to the Anglican baptismal rite, a stance he set forth in a 1965 article in *Anglican Theological Review.*

In his article, Mitchell called for a rite conforming to the classical "shape" of Christian initiation. This rite would include water baptism, anointing accompanied by consignation, presentation to the bishop with laying on of hands preceded by the traditional prayer for the gifts of the Spirit, and celebration of the eucharist with reception of communion by the newly baptized. While recommending this rite as the only permissible method of adult baptism, Mitchell suggested two possibilities for the baptism of infants. First, the rite for adult initiation could be used and infants thereby admitted to communion, a pattern that Mitchell noted had been advocated by Massey Shepherd in his lecture. But Mitchell was not optimistic that Anglicans would readily abandon the traditional practice of adolescent confirmation and admission to communion, and so he proposed a modified rite for infant initiation, a rite that would include anointing and consignation but would postpone to the traditional age laying on of hands by the bishop and admission to communion.[46]

While Mitchell was not prepared to take the radical step Shepherd had advocated by proposing to admit infants to communion, his hesitation arose from his sense of the readiness of Episcopalians to accept such a major revision of the traditional initiatory pattern. However, just a few years later the drafting committee proposed precisely such a dramatic revision. *Prayer Book Studies 18: Baptism and Confirmation* offered to the Episcopal Church a rite entitled "Holy Baptism with the Laying-on-of-Hands."[47] This rite included water baptism, prayer for the gifts of the Spirit, imposition of a hand with consignation and optional chrismation, and communion, and it permitted a priest to preside in the absence of a bishop. It was the product of lengthy deliberation by the drafting committee, considering historical and theological issues as well as contemporary pastoral concerns.[48] Although Shepherd did not directly determine the shape of this rite, his vision was probably one of many factors influencing the committee's deliberations. Not only had Mitchell heard Shepherd's 1964 lecture, but it is likely that Bonnell Spencer, who chaired the drafting committee, was also present, since the lecture coincided with a meeting of the Standing Liturgical Commission held at the General Theological Seminary and Spencer had become a member of the commission by that time.

The rite presented in *Prayer Book Studies 18* was rejected by the 1970 General Convention, and the drafting committee spent the next several years wrestling with the meaning and necessity of "confirmation." The end result was a baptismal rite whose structure is markedly similar to that of the Prayer Book study: water baptism, prayer for the gift of the Spirit, and imposition of a hand with consignation and optional chrismation. But there was considerable debate about the sequence and the wording of the postbaptismal sequence.

Some clergy found it awkward to administer the water rite, return the child to a parent or sponsor for the prayer for the gifts of the Spirit, then go back to each baptizand for the consignation. Why not perform the series of ceremonial actions, water bath followed by consignation/ [chrismation]/ imposition of a hand, then conclude with prayer for gifts of the Spirit? Shepherd was adamantly opposed: "Either they are just ceremonies like the present signing with the cross in the Prayer Book baptismal rite, or they are a true laying on of hands in the ancient sense."[49] Eventually a compromise was reached, maintaining in the text of the rite the sequence of post-baptismal prayer followed by action, but adding a rubric that allows the action to be done prior to the prayer. That rubric makes it more difficult to argue that the laying on of hands is a sacramental action distinct from the water bath, but it does not entirely preclude such an interpretation.

The formula at the imposition of a hand was also fiercely debated. Various wordings were adopted at different stages of the revision process: "you are sealed by the Holy Spirit"; "you have been sealed by the Holy Spirit"; "by the water of baptism you have been sealed by the Holy Spirit"; "you are sealed by the Holy Spirit in baptism." The underlying issue is whether the gift of the Holy Spirit is identified with the water (Lampe's view) or with the imposition of a hand (Dix's view) or not identified with any particular action. A related question is whether laying on of hands is a distinct sacramental action or rather an explicatory action unfolding the theological richness of baptism. Shepherd clearly viewed it as a separate sacramental action, though an integral component of the initiatory rite, but he did not necessarily limit the initial bestowal of the Spirit to the post-baptismal action.

The formula finally accepted, "you are sealed by the Holy Spirit in baptism," is ambiguous. For the Roman Catholic liturgical scholar Gerard

Austin, it is possible to see in the 1979 rite the reunification of the fragmented initiatory rite. Nevertheless, the phrase "in baptism" "might cause difficulty by implying that this act of sealing is not a distinct sacramental rite, separate from the water-bath itself."[50] In contrast, the English Evangelical bishop Colin Buchanan, who speaks disparagingly of "two-stagers," acknowledges that "the rite goes as far as it can, whilst retaining both water and the laying on of hands, not to allow a theological divide between them."[51]

Although a compromise, the 1979 baptismal rite is clearly a single rite of Christian initiation that includes the ancient (if not apostolic) ceremonies of imposition of a hand, chrismation (albeit optional), and consignation. Difficulties in interpretation and implementation arise not so much from questions about whether the postbaptismal prayer and handlaying/ [chrismation]/ consignation constitute a distinct sacramental action, but how the initiatory rite relates to the separate rite entitled "Confirmation with forms for Reception and for the Reaffirmation of Baptismal Vows." The best indication of Shepherd's position appears in his 1971 talk to a diocesan liturgical commissions meeting, at which he acknowledged the desire for personal commitment that had been a component of the traditional Anglican confirmation rite, but concluded:

> We should . . . not confuse the rites of sacramental initiation—the paschal mystery—with other desirable and edifying rites [i.e., rites of reaffirmation of Christian commitment] which may follow upon a Christian's full and complete incorporation into the mystical body of Christ and participation in the continuing mysteries of the holy eucharist.[52]

Unfortunately, such clarity is lacking in the rites as finally adopted in the 1979 Book of Common Prayer.

Scholarship Shaping Liturgical Reform

Over the course of two decades, Massey Shepherd made significant shifts in his appraisal of Christian initiatory rites. Not only did he modify his interpretation of the extant evidence for apostolic and post-apostolic practices of Christian initiation, he also revised considerably his recommendations for the optimal pattern for the contemporary church as it adjusted to its post-Christendom context. His stance was influenced by the continuing Anglican debate over the meaning of confirmation and the seal of the Spirit, a debate which Shepherd seems to have followed closely.

One change came in the area of methodology. In earlier decades of the twentieth century, it was common in liturgical scholarship to assume that one could determine practices during the first century by reading backward from sources dating several centuries later. Thus Shepherd, following Dix, argued in his Prayer Book commentary that the apostolic practice of confirmation consisted of a bishop laying on hands and anointing candidates, effecting the bestowal of the indwelling and strengthening Spirit. His reading of Lampe apparently caused him to abandon the idea that chrismation dated to apostolic times, although he seems never to have relinquished entirely his conviction that laying on of hands was closely associated with baptism and that it constituted a distinct sacramental action.

While Shepherd thus provides an example of a scholar open to new interpretations and willing to modify his position, of perhaps greater interest is the interaction of scholarship and contemporary pastoral concerns evident in his work. Most of his writing on Christian initiation applies the most recent scholarship to the contemporary liturgical forms of the Episcopal Church. This is true of the column that he wrote during the 1940s and of his Prayer Book commentary and the volume he contributed to *The Church's Teaching Series*. These writings show him grappling with the confusing and conflicting layers of tradition and viewing that material from different perspectives as he followed the developments in England.

Recognition of the theological and historical complexities of the church's initiatory practice made Shepherd cautious for several years. Both his 1950 Prayer Book commentary and the lectures he gave in 1954 in Hong Kong and Tokyo show him struggling to maintain the significance of confirmation while not accepting the theologically dubious concept that the gift of the Holy Spirit is bestowed only at confirmation and not at baptism.

It took Shepherd several years to make the bold suggestion that the bishop should administer baptism, confirmation, and first communion at the same time to individuals of any age. This proposal reflected a number of concerns and interests. Since it was based upon Shepherd's reconstruction of the initiatory liturgy of the early church, it enabled Shepherd to implement the Anglican liturgical principle that recovery of the worship of the early church should be a primary aim of Prayer Book revision.[53] By describing the celebration of the full initiatory rites as a manifestation of the paschal mystery, the proposal drew upon twentieth-century liturgical theology that emphasized the paschal mystery as the heart of Christian worship. In addition, Shepherd called for new patterns of incorporation and Christian nurture as an important response to pastoral concerns emerging as the church began to deal with the shift to post-Christendom.

As the Episcopal Church begins yet again to consider revision of the Prayer Book (and even the place of a Book of Common Prayer in our contemporary computer age), the same willingness to address contemporary pastoral issues in light of current historical and theological scholarship is needed. The rites and patterns adopted in the 1979 Prayer Book—practices such as public baptism at a designated baptismal feast or the principal Sunday service, communion of all the baptized, reaffirmation of the baptismal covenant by the entire congregation–are reshaping the Episcopal Church's understanding of initiation. Scholarship continues to develop. Contemporary liturgical scholars are far more reticent to speak of a single, normative apostolic liturgical pattern, from which all subsequent liturgies evolved, and much more likely both to suggest a variety of liturgical practice during the apostolic period and to point out how little can be determined from the extant evidence.[54] The 1991 International Anglican Liturgical Consultation, moving away from the two-stage theology of initiation that dominated Anglicanism for at least a century, adopted principles of Christian initiation specifying that "baptism is complete sacramental initiation," while "confirmation and other rites of affirmation . . . are in no way to be seen as a completion of baptism."[55] Insights such as these must inform the continuing renewal of patterns of Christian initiation and nurture and must as well help shape the next revision of the Prayer Book.

Notes

1. *Prayer Book Studies: I. Baptism and Confirmation; II. The Liturgical Lectionary* (New York: Church Pension Fund, 1950). The two studies were published together in a single pamphlet.

2. Minutes of the Standing Liturgical Commission of the Episcopal Church, Aug. 4–5, 1959, 17 (Record Group 122, Archives of the Episcopal Church, Austin, Texas). My research at the Archives of the Episcopal Church was supported in 1990 by a grant from the Zahm Research Travel Fund of the University of Notre Dame, and in 1991 by a Visiting Fellowship from the Episcopal Theological Seminary of the Southwest in Austin.

3. Massey Hamilton Shepherd, Jr., *The Living Liturgy* (New York: Oxford University Press, 1946); William Palmer Ladd, *Prayer Book Interleaves* (New York: Oxford University Press, 1942).

4. Shepherd, *Living Liturgy*, 97–98.

5. Shepherd, *Living Liturgy*, 98–100.

6. Massey H. Shepherd, Jr., "The Living Liturgy: One Sacrament or Two?" *The Witness* (March 18, 1948) 12. (Shepherd continued to produce his column after the 1946 publication of his book, but the later columns were never published in a separate collection.)

7. F. W. Puller, *What Is the Distinctive Grace of Confirmation?* (London, 1880); A. J. Mason, *The Relation of Confirmation to Baptism as Taught in Holy Scripture and the Fathers* (New York: E. P. Dutton, 1891); A. Theodore Wirgman, *The Doctrine of Confirmation Considered in Relation to Holy Baptism as a Sacramental Ordinance of the Catholic Church* (London: Longmans, Green, and Co., 1897); Darwell Stone, *Holy Baptism* (London: Longmans, Green, and Co., 1899).

8. Edward Lambe Parsons and Bayard Hale Jones, *The American Prayer Book: Its Origins and Principles* (New York: Charles Scribner's Sons, 1937) 224, 245.

9. Convocations of Canterbury and York, *Confirmation Today* (London: Press and Publications Board of the Church Assembly, 1944) 9–14.

10. Gregory Dix, *The Theology of Confirmation in Relation to Baptism* (London: A. & C. Black, 1946).

11. *The Theology of Christian Initiation* (London: SPCK, 1948) 9–13, quotation on 10.

12. *The Theology of Christian Initiation*, 14–20.

13. *The Theology of Christian Initiation*, 23–24.

14. Lambeth Conference 1948, *The Encyclical Letter from the Bishops; together with Resolutions and Reports* (London: SPCK, 1948) 108–10, quotations on 110.

15. Massey H. Shepherd, Jr., *The Oxford American Prayer Book Commentary* [*OAPBC*](New York: Oxford University Press, 1950) 271.

16. Shepherd, *OAPBC*, 273–74, 279.

17. Shepherd, *OAPBC*, 296–97.

18. Shepherd, *OAPBC*, 296–97.

19. *PBS I*, 12.

20. Prayer Book 1928, 273–74; *PBS I*, 25.

21. Prayer Book 1928, 276; *PBS I*, 14, 29–30.

22. Prayer Book 1928, 279; *PBS I*, 28.

23. *PBS I*, 18–19.

24. *PBS I*, 21.

25. *PBS I*, 31–34.

26. Shepherd, *Living Liturgy*, 129–34.

27. Shepherd, *Living Liturgy*, 94.

28. Massey H. Shepherd, Jr., *The Worship of the Church*, The Church's Teaching Series 4 (Greenwich, CT: Seabury Press, 1952) 167, 170–74.

29. Shepherd, *Worship*, 177.

30. Shepherd, *Worship*, 233.

31. G. W. H. Lampe, *The Seal of the Spirit* (London: Longmans, Green, and Co., 1951) 3–93.

32. Shepherd, *Worship*, 172.

33. Lampe, *Seal*, 82.

34. Lampe, *Seal*, 310–22; quotation on 319.

35. Shepherd, *Worship*, 178.

36. Massey H. Shepherd, Jr., *The Liturgy and the Christian Faith* (Greenwich, CT: Seabury Press, 1957) 25–32; quotation on 30.

37. Massey H. Shepherd, Jr., *The Paschal Liturgy and the Apocalypse*, Ecumenical Studies in Worship 6 (Richmond, VA: John Knox Press, 1960) 61–63; quotations on 61.

38. Shepherd, *Paschal Liturgy* 89–91; quotation on 91.

39. Shepherd, *Paschal Liturgy*, 61.

40. Massey H. Shepherd, Jr., *Liturgy and Education* (New York: Seabury Press, 1965) 106.

41. *Baptism and Confirmation: A Report submitted by the Church of England Liturgical Commission to the Archbishops of Canterbury and York in November 1958* (London: SPCK, 1959) x.

42. Shepherd, *Liturgy and Education*, 107.

43. Shepherd, *Liturgy and Education*, 105–6.

44. Shepherd, *Liturgy and Education*, 105.

45. Massey H. Shepherd, Jr., "The Berakah Award: Response," *Worship* 52 (1978) 309; see also idem, "Confirmation: The Early Church," *Worship* 46 (1972) 19–20.

46. Leonel L. Mitchell, "The 'Shape' of the Baptismal Liturgy," *Anglican Theological Review* 47 (1965) 416–19.

47. New York: Church Pension Fund, 1970.

48. For a thorough study of the development of the 1979 rites, see Ruth A. Meyers, *Continuing the Reformation: Re-Visioning Baptism in the Episcopal Church* (New York: Church Publishing Inc., 1997).

49. Massey Shepherd to Leo Malania, Oct. 30, 1974 (Record Group 122, Archives of the Episcopal Church, Austin, Texas).

50. Gerard Austin, *Anointing with the Spirit: The Rite of Confirmation* (New York: Pueblo, 1985) 76.

51. Colin Buchanan, *Anglican Confirmation*, Grove Liturgical Study 48 (Bramcote, Nottingham: Grove Books, 1986) 42.

52. Shepherd, "Confirmation: The Early Church," 21.

53. The 1958 Lambeth Conference had adopted a resolution urging "that a chief aim of Prayer Book Revision should be to further that recovery of the worship of the Primitive Church which was the aim of the compilers of the first Prayer Books of the Church of England": Lambeth Conference 1958, *The Encyclical Letter from the Bishops together with the Resolutions and Reports* (London: SPCK, New York: Seabury Press, 1958) 1.47.

54. See Paul F. Bradshaw, *The Search for the Origins of Christian Worship* (New York and Oxford: Oxford University Press, 1992).

55. "Walk in Newness of Life: The Findings of the International Anglican Liturgical Consultation, Toronto 1991," in David R. Holeton, ed., *Growing in Newness of Life: Christian Initiation in Anglicanism Today* (Toronto: Anglican Book Centre, 1993) 229.

Confirmation: Sacramental Rite or Rite of Discipline and Politics?

Linda L. B. Moeller

IN 1974 MARION HATCHETT wrote an article that was published in the *Anglican Theological Review*, entitled "The Rite of 'Confirmation' in The Book of Common Prayer and in *Authorized Services 1973*." The concluding sentence of that article stated:

> . . . this author feels that he can give a hearty endorsement to the rites of Christian Initiation of *Authorized Services 1973*, and he hopes that in 1979 it will be basically these rites which will become the official rites of the Episcopal Church in the United States of America.[1]

His hopes were not to be realized.

Confirmation has sometimes been called a "sacrament in search of a theology" or a "sacrament with too many theologies." Within all such witticisms there is usually a grain of truth. What remains clear is that the Episcopal Church has not been able to reach consensus regarding confirmation. There is general agreement that the roots of confirmation are found in the unitive rites of the primitive church. After the fourth century, however, the dissolution of those rites becomes complex territory and the sources of what will become confirmation become all the more unclear. Volumes have been written that dissect the ancient texts and analyze the descriptions of the rites of initiation. *The Apostolic Tradition* of Hippolytus, the *Apostolic Constitutions*, the diary of Egeria, catechetical lectures, sermons, and papal letters—all present part of the great puzzle, but none provide the clarity for which we might hope.

Ritual studies and theological discourse are both foundational components for the conversation surrounding confirmation. That conversation, however, lacks a critical element when the socio-political influences on the church are not considered. This is perhaps nowhere more evident than in the American church. In a country whose birth is relatively recent on the global time line it is far easier to document the labor pains that attended that birth as well as the birth of the church that we know today as the Episcopal Church in the United States of America.[2]

"In Saint Paul's Chapel, there were about five hundred and fifty who were confirmed, and among these, many of the most respectable members of congregation. And such too, we apprehend, should be the conduct of the communicants among us who have not been confirmed."[3] With these words from a sermon preached in 1788 at the first confirmation rite ever to be held at St. Paul's Chapel, New York, the Reverend Uzal Ogden spoke volumes about the attitudes in the Protestant Episcopal Church in the United States concerning confirmation. The most obvious conclusion to be drawn from the text is that neither membership nor communicant status, as would later be the case, was based on having received confirmation since it was "many of the most respectable members" who were confirmed and the remaining "communicants" were urged to participate in the rite at its next offering.

Another point to be noted in the sermon concerns the essential role a bishop played in the rite. Confirmation had not been available to the church in United States because there were no bishops, hence the startling number of confirmands that morning at St. Paul's. The close association of the rite with the bishop derives from our patristic picture of a unitive rite of initiation. Confirmation, in time, was separated from baptism for reasons that were at least as practical as they were ecclesiological. For better or worse, at that separation, confirmation became inextricably linked with the office of the bishop, part of that ministry's *raison d'être*. Years became centuries and the connections between confirmation and the sacrament of baptism became more and more obscure and the necessity more and more questionable. After time, about all that was certain was that a bishop was required for the rite.

As previously noted, during the colonial period and in the early years of the new republic, the Church of England in the colonies had no bishops to preside over what was an episcopal rite. In *Continuing the Reformation* Ruth Meyers reminds us that "until the nineteenth century, confirmation was of little significance in the life of the Church. This was true . . . in the United States, where the absence of bishops precluded confirmation . . . "[4] It is interesting, however, that ordination was not precluded for the want of an episcopal presence, nor was ecclesiastical governance, the other two foci of episcopal jurisdiction. The young Episcopal Church found, as did its predecessor the Church of England in the colonies, ways to provide for the other vital dimensions of episcopal ministry, despite the exorbitant cost of both life and money. It would seem that confirmation was not deemed important enough for either the procurement of a bishop or of an alternate means to provide for the rite in question.

Political and social history and the continuing struggle over questions of episcopal identity have played a larger part in the development of the rite than the purely theological arguments that began in the nineteenth century and that have continued through the publication of the 1979 Prayer Book. It is not unreasonable to propose that the difficulty we have in determining a theology for confirmation is born of ignoring its less theological character-istics. If the liturgy of our church is to be a living, authentic expression of faith, then we are challenged to fully explore all aspects of the rite. *Scripture*, of course, provides us with no dominical warrant for confirmation, and *reason* suggests little basis to continue confirmation as we know it. *Tradition*, seems to suggest that confirmation has been a valuable ritual moment for many in the church, and therein lies the need to revisit the development and the future of confirmation. Is it finally a *pastoral* question?

A full examination of the rite and its future in the church must begin by taking into account the political milieu of the radically independent, newly formed nation of which the church and its rites were now a part; the association of confirmation with the privileged episcopacy in a now disestablished church; and all against the background of the theological and ecclesiastical dimensions of the history of the rite. Much was written in the nineteenth century about confirmation. More recent scholarship has centered around ritual studies and the historic disintegration of the rite of initiation. Nothing, aside from the rubrical direction of our liturgical books, explores confirmation's place in the history of the American church or the effect of American political and social history upon it development and pastoral use in the Episcopal Church. Our Prayer Books provide us with the rubrics and the prayers–a place to start–but a fuller documentation of parallel theological understandings and the "popular piety" attached to confirmation will need to be explored in further depth.

Where Did We Go Wrong?

Our first mistake in dealing with confirmation probably came when we took what we were already familiar with and worked back in time. We have tried to interpret our current practice using modern, post-Enlightenment rationale for a ritual that at best was a part of a whole, integrated rite. More realistically, though, confirmation has evolved through the centuries and become something that the early church would never recognize. Instead of praxis developing from theology and ecclesiology we have imposed theology and ecclesiology on established praxis. Each successive generation has then added their own layer to the interpretation, resulting in what Nathan Mitchell calls "accumulated symbolism." Mitchell goes on to say that the law of accumulated symbolism maintains that "there is a limit to the amount of symbolic ambiguity a rite can sustain . . . [before] the basic architecture of the rite will begin to crumble."[5]

Our next blunder occurs when we attempt to divorce the rite from its historical and political setting. To assume that population growth and its inherent effect on the hierarchy of the church would not result in a further alteration of the rite that first became fragmented because of population growth is to close our eyes to reality. Specifically within both the Church of England and the Episcopal Church there are issues of "establishment" and "power" that also must be considered. It is hard to imagine that the acceptance or rejection of an episcopal rite would not be directly affected by the popular perception that the bishop is associated with and indeed a member of the privileged class of an oppressive government.

The last error that this paper will suggest is our desire to perpetuate the familiar even if it means re-inventing its purpose. As our society has changed there is a strong desire to restore values that seem threatened by an evolving culture. The family unit and all that implies about the maturation process of individuals appears to be under attack from outside influences over which we have no control. Using the rite of confirmation as either the carrot or the stick will not insure a return to "the good old days" when children grew up enjoying the benefits of an extended family in which the church played a vital role. Confirmation will not supply the glue to hold our families together in a post-Christian world.

The Ritual Beginnings of Confirmation

Scripture has long been the starting place when looking for dominical warrant for any of the church's doctrines or rituals. Confirmation is no different in that respect. As noted above, there is no clear-cut warrant to be found in Scripture. Instead we have taken discreet passages and constructed what often turns out to be a foundation built on sand. Acts 8, for example, has been a favorite text for proponents of confirmation as a necessity—as a completion of baptism—and for its reservation to the bishop. The story of Peter and John, traveling from Jerusalem to give the Holy Spirit to those in Samaria who had been baptized, would seem to establish the need for a completion of baptism by additional prayers and laying on of hands by an apostle, a bishop, if you will. It suggests a pneumatic character for confirmation that further fractures baptism: a pneumatic character that seems to be the possession of only certain ministers and therefore, theirs to dispense. Does the Spirit "hold back" in baptism only to be fully present after confirmation? Is the Christian who is "merely" baptized of another class than the super elite Christian who has been baptized and confirmed?

But when the Acts 8 citation is examined alongside Acts 10:44–48 and 11:14–18 a different picture emerges. In these passages, the Spirit comes to rest on individuals *before* their baptism by hearing the Word in Peter's preaching. Evidently, there was no need of a "completing action," or a more senior minister to coax the Holy Spirit into being present.

Earlier it was noted that we are quick to use phrases such as "the disintegration of the rite" and "the unitive rite of the early church" when discussing confirmation. Both phrases tend to carry judgmental baggage that alludes to a golden age when the church knew exactly what it was about; an age that existed only in the minds of the generations that would follow. A more honest reading of the sources might suggest we say something like this: We find a group of people who are trying to discern and be faithful to what Jesus intended for them. Recalling what Jesus had said, reading first-hand accounts and reacting to the world around them, the first Christians created a rite that would make new Christians while protecting themselves in a hostile world.

The Politics of Confirmation

All too often we seem to forget that forces outside of the church affect the way that those inside the church view our world and behave in it sacramentally. This is made very clear when we examine the letters and other documents authored by both clergy and laymen of the Church of England that discussed the need for a bishop in the colonies that would one day become the United States. The lack of episcopal authority on American soil was seen as a great injustice to the clergy, many of whom were Loyalists, and as a boon to those who had chafed under the authority of the established church in England. For the latter group, bishops were seen not as descendants of the apostles but as long-reaching arms of the Crown. The loss of confirmation was not seen to be great enough to risk the possibility of a reduction in their freedoms. It is also interesting that the Loyalist clergy were not as much concerned with the episcopal administration of ordination and confirmation as they were for the episcopal oversight of ecclesiastical behavior of the colonial clergy. Even then, there was "much disturbance, great anxiety, and apprehension"[6] predicted should there be any interference by a bishop in the way Anglicans had come to order their lives. The fear of a monarchical episcopal power base being loosed on the colonists is obvious in one of the plans for securing a bishop for America. It said in part "that no coercive Power is desired over the Laity in any case; but only a power to regulate the Behavior of the Clergy who are in Episcopal Orders; and to correct and punish them according to the Law of the Church of England, in case of misbehavior or neglect of duty . . . "[7]

It would seem that we have looked back in time and imposed our concern for the administration of confirmation on a church that had little of its own. This is one of the cases in which, despite our possession of the liturgical texts, i.e. the Prayer Book with its rubrics, we have little knowledge of attitudes and practical experience. We can deduce from the absence of bishops in this country that confirmation was not available to American Anglicans. What we can not be sure of is how keenly that loss was felt. From the texts of sermons preached at confirmations when, at last, the episcopacy was established in America, we know that neither church membership or communicant status was called into question due to the lack of confirmation. In a letter written to Edmund, Lord Bishop of London in 1731, Samuel Johnson wrote " . . . relating to the Exhortation after Baptism to the Godfathers to bring the child to the Bishop to be confirmed. Some [clergy] wholly omit this exhortation because it is impracticable others insert the words "if there be opportunity" because it is mere jest to order the Godfathers to bring the child to the bishop, when there is none within a 1000 leagues of us . . . ."[8]

Archbishop Peckham's thirteenth century canon which would eventually become the basis for a Prayer Book rubric appears, despite its good intentions, to have created much of the distress over confirmation that we live with today. In an effort to encourage confirmation and to provide impetus to the bishops to make their visitations, the canon created a "confirmational quarantine" of the eucharist: no confirmation, no communion. Implied by the very need for such a canon was the decline in the use of the rite. Time and circumstances would expand the then known world of Archbishop Peckham and a church without bishops would find the flaw in the canon and, with action born of necessity, ignore the rubric.

In Alexis De Tocqueville's *Democracy in America* a French visitor looks at America and the American people and sees things that from an insider's (i.e. American citizen's) vantage point are often missed. His understanding of the link between religion and republic, while not speaking of confirmation or any rite of the church directly, does speak implicitly to the relationship between an episcopally governed church and a free society. As he looks at the relationship between religion and politics De Tocqueville writes that by the side of every religion is to be found a political opinion, which is connected with it by affinity . . . The greatest part of British America was peopled by men who, after having shaken off the authority of the Pope, acknowledged no other religious supremacy: they brought with them into the New World a form of Christianity which I cannot better describe than by styling it a democratic and republican religion . . . and from the beginning, politics and religion contracted an alliance which has never been dissolved.[9]

The Discipline and Pastoral Character of Confirmation

In the days immediately following the sack of Rome by the Visigoths, Pope Innocent I (d. 417) used confirmation as a tool to further the restoration and expansion of Roman Christianity. A part of the ongoing effort to make Roman Christianity paradigmatic for the West was the "latinizing, stabilizing and commending of Roman liturgical procedures to churches outside the City."[10] In that vein, Pope Innocent I wrote a letter to Bishop Decentius of Gubbio detailing Roman practice concerning what happens liturgically following baptism and chrismation. Of all the details covered the only aspect about which he was adamant was that only bishops were to be the completing ministers.

> It belongs solely to the episcopal office that bishops consign and give the Paraclete Spirit. This is proved not only by ecclesiastical custom but also by that reading of the Acts of the Apostles which recounts how Peter and John were directed to give the Holy Spirit to the already baptized.[11]

Innocent is using the example of Peter and John to enact an episcopal hegemony upon confirmation to strengthen the position of the bishop as unique and indispensable. He is attempting to provide some degree of stabilization through hierarchy at a time when it was sorely needed. As the Roman Church tried to regain its equilibrium following the sack of Rome and to counteract the church's alienation from society[12] that was a result of the violence, the bishop as a central and irreplaceable focus of authority and symbol of unity was of paramount importance.

As numbers in the church increased over the centuries, the episcopal hegemony of confirmation provided a pastoral link between the bishop and the people. As dioceses became large and unwieldy and the tenuous link between the people and their bishop was being stretched, individuals could be assured that at least one time in their faith journeys they would pass under the hand of their bishop–at the time of their confirmation. Yet even this justification is called into question when the bishop's visitation is limited to one Sunday service every year or so. While the people may pass under his/her hand, there is no time for a pastoral relationship to develop.

Confirmation has at different times and in different places taken on the guise of a rite of passage and become a foundation for Christian education. Evangelical Episcopalians have used confirmation to encourage the baptized to examine their spiritual lives and, if necessary, to repent and be born again.[13] In the nineteenth century in the evangelical wing of the Episcopal Church, admission to full membership came only after confirmation and confirmation came after giving sound spiritual evidence of an experience of grace. In essence, the evangelicals combined the rite of passage aspect with the educational requirements and then added a spiritual dimension, a reportable experience of God's grace. Bishop McIlvaine wrote that "knowledge[14] is a small part of the qualifications required for Confirmation. There is a preparation of the heart as well as the answer of the tongue."[15]

In the twentieth century a movement arising from the revision process that gave us the Prayer Book of 1979 favored the reunification of confirmation and the baptismal rite. The rite offered in *Proposed Services 1973* attempted to remove some of the layers of accumulated symbolism. After its publication the House of Bishops met and ultimately issued what has become known as the "Pocono Statement." In that statement the bishops cast their vote with tradition. Siding with the experience of confirmation that is "greatly to be cherished in the historic practice of Anglicanism" the bishops acquiesced to the comfort of the familiar and declined to do the hard work of restoring the integrity of the initiation rite.

There are kernels of value in the Pocono Statement. Unfortunately those gems are attached to layers of accumulated symbolism and wishful thinking. The bishops wrote that "confirmation, as Anglicans have practiced it, is liturgically and sacramentally a significant occasion" of particular intervention of God the Holy Spirit. The actual experience of confirmation in the parish differs greatly from this grand and sweeping statement. Liturgically we usually find confirmation dropped into an already too busy Sunday morning eucharist when the bishop makes his/her annual visit. The confirmands are generally teenagers who have finally decided to be confirmed not as "a public, mature decision for Christ" but to stop their parents' harangue. Sacramentally the theologians no longer claim consensus regarding just what we are about and what does happen at confirmation. The "significant occasion" of the Pocono Statement is just as likely to be the visit of the bishop as it is confirmation. O.C. Edwards may have summed up the reality behind the Pocono Statement with this comment:

> I wonder if the Pocono Statement really isn't to be understood as a statement of the desire on the part of the bishops to retain the old practices while they are admitting tacitly that the theory on which they had grounded the old practice

had now been sawed from under them . . . . [T]hey still say, "Well it was a good thing even if [the reception of the Spirit in a unique way isn't] the reason to do it and so let's keep doing it and try to figure out some justification for it.[16]

Where Do We Go From Here: The Next Prayer Book

Confirmation, the rite that continues to struggle with its identity, must be a high priority agenda item as we begin the work that will produce a Prayer Book to carry us into the twenty-first century. If we allow the most recent scholarship to guide us and partner that scholarship with the practical experience of living faith communities we may indeed know the "significant occasion of particular intervention of God the Holy Spirit" that the bishops were writing about in the Pocono Statement. Before we begin our journey to that experience we must decide what it is that we require from this rite. Do we want to understand it as it was? Can we even determine what it was? If we determine what it was originally, does the time we live in still invest the rite with meaning? And then finally, what do we want it to be?

Our first step toward that grace-filled experience is to acknowledge the limitlessness of the Spirit. Not a demi-god to be parceled out in bits and pieces, the fullness of the Spirit comes in Holy Baptism. Confirmation is not required to complete that gift of the Spirit. Jesus promised us that he would send the Spirit, not a part of the Spirit. Then we must let go of the theologies and symbols we have layered upon the rite. No matter what we would like it to be, confirmation is not about church membership, it is not about "completing" a semi-Spirit filled baptism, it is not a ritual of puberty, it is not the tool of an educational program. *Tradition* tells us that there is value in confirmation. *Reason* tells us that to continue a practice that has become separated from its meaning empties a valuable tradition of its meaning. Similarly, layering symbolism onto the rite, even to achieve a good end, demeans the action.

The full resolution of this question is not the intent of this paper. To imply that the "answer" is so easily supplied would be arrogance of the highest order. It is possible, however, to suggest some preliminary steps that would, perhaps, bring us closer to our goal. First, it is imperative that we reclaim the fullness of our baptismal identity. Recognizing that fullness would lead to a restoration of the integrity of the initiation rite, understanding that God holds nothing back when we are called by name. An additional rite is not required to complete that which is already finished. In a rite that reunited baptism with the liturgical action we now call confirmation, the minister of baptism would be the minister of the entire rite. The reunification of the rite would lead us directly into the second level of our journey. The second task required of us is to realign our expectations of the rite and acknowledge that the desired pastoral connection between the bishop and the members of the diocese will not be achieved by one liturgical coming together. Through the years, the office of bishop has changed from the one who presided over or shepherded a particular community to one who shepherds the shepherds. We have seen the responsibility of the office develop from oversight of one church, to one city, to one diocese, yet we expect one rite to restore the intimacy, now lost, that the bishop once knew in pastoring a vastly smaller community.

Today we find ourselves living as Christians in a decidedly post-Christian world. Things such as living in Christian community that once could be assumed can no longer be taken for granted. That there is an ever increasing hunger for things of the Spirit cannot be denied. A trip to the bookstore's "religion" section shows shelf upon shelf of books about angels and New Age spirituality; watching television it is hard not to be "touched by an angel." Yet we have become accustomed to relying on fast food to thwart starvation instead of supplying more nutritious fare. Confirmation cannot supply all that is missing in twentieth century life, despite all of the explanations that we heap upon it.

It takes time and effort to establish a pastoral relationship. It takes time and investment to educate our young people. It takes time and love to shepherd teenagers through life's passages. Do we really believe all this can be accomplished in one rite? The time has come for us to re-evaluate not only our expectations of confirmation, but also our commitment to living the life of the baptized.

Notes

1. Marion J. Hatchett, "The Rite of 'Confirmation' in The Book of Common Prayer and in *Authorized Services 1973*," *Anglican Theological Review 56* (July 1974) 292–310.

2. Hereafter known as the Episcopal Church.

3. Uzal Ogden, Sermon preached in St. Paul's Chapel, New York City, 1788.

4. Ruth A. Meyers, *Continuing the Reformation: Revisioning Baptism in the Episcopal Church* (New York: Church Publishing Incorporated, 1997) 67.

5. Nathan D. Mitchell, "Dissolution of the Rite of Christian Initiation," in *Made, Not Born*, from The Murphy Center for Liturgical Research, (Notre Dame: University of Notre Dame Press, 1976) 70.

6. Myles Cooper, *An Address from the Clergy of New York and New Jersey to the Episcopalians in Virginia Occasioned by some late transactions in that Colony relative to an American Episcopate* (New York: Hugh Gaine, 1771) 8.

7. Myles Cooper, 21–22.

8. Letter from Samuel Johnson to Edmund, Lord Bishop of London. June 4, 1731. *Fulham Papers* (Vol. I) 245.

9. Alexis De Tocqueville, *Democracy in America* (1835)(New York: Alfred A. Knopf, Inc.,1972) 301.

10. Aidan Kavanagh, *Confirmation: Origins and Reform* (New York: Pueblo Publishing Company, 1988) 56.

11. Epistle 25.3, J.P. Migne, *Patrologia Latina* (PL 56.515).

12. Popular opinion placed much of the blame for the fall of Rome at the doorstep of the church. The people believed that Rome had fallen because the old gods had been forsaken for the Christ and were angered. It was in response to this outcry that Augustine wrote *De Civitate Dei.*

13. Diana Hochstedt Butler, *Standing Against the Whirlwind: Evangelical Episcopalians in Nineteenth-Century America* (New York: Oxford UP, 1995) 43.

14. The Episcopal Church required that the confirmand know the Apostles' Creed, the Lord's Prayer, the Ten Commandments and the Catechism.

15. Charles P. McIlvaine, *Bishop McIlvaine on Confirmation* (n.p. 1840) 13.

16. O. C. Edwards, "Documentation and Reflection: Confirmation Today," *Anglican Theological Review* 54(1972) 112.

"By Water and the Spirit": An Essay in Understanding References to Water and Baptism in the Fourth Gospel

Charles P. Price

IT IS AN HONOR AND A PLEASURE to contribute an essay to this *festschrift* for Marion Hatchett. Professor Hatchett's writings have instructed and inspired a generation of both teachers and students. He has helped to change the way we worship. I gladly count myself among those he has influenced. The entire church is in his debt.

For some years I have wondered about the remarkable interest shown by the author of the Fourth Gospel in water and baptism. It seems particularly appropriate to commit to writing my thoughts on this subject for this collection of essays, for Professor Hatchett's own interest in baptism is well known and has greatly assisted a renewed understanding and a transformed practice of baptism in our church.

I.

The material to be presented as evidence has been variously treated by a wide spectrum of commentators. Rudolf Bultmann in general ignores or downplays baptismal implications in the text.[1] He regards the weight of manuscript evidence at Jn. 3:5, for example, as sufficient to omit the phrase, "water and" from the verse, " . . . no one can enter the kingdom of God without being born of water and the Spirit," thus removing a fairly definite baptismal allusion. Oscar Cullmann, on the other hand, undertakes "to submit the proof that there can be traced in the gospel of John a distinct line of thought connecting with the service of worship" (of the early church).[2] He is able to claim "an astonishingly large number of passages" as supporting his argument.[3] Raymond Brown, insisting on adequate internal evidence before he feels able to recognize baptismal nuance, does acknowledge baptismal overtones in the story of the blind man,[4] but denies it in the case of the lame man,[5] and is uncertain about Nicodemus.[6]

The position taken in this essay is closer to Cullmann than to either Bultmann's or Brown's. My indebtedness to Cullmann's analysis of the pertinent texts will be obvious on nearly every page. Nevertheless my point is considerably different from his. I do not contend that the author of the Fourth Gospel had the services of the church in mind, or the sacraments, or even baptism as such, in the numerous passages where water looms in the background. It is closer to the truth to say that the author of this gospel shaped already existing material for the interest of readers—or, in the first instance, more likely hearers—who brought existing concerns. Perhaps they are hearers coming to faith; perhaps they are already members of a Christian community. But they care, among other things, about water baptism.

II.

The healing of the blind man (Jn. 9) is the most obvious example. That story begins with an account of Jesus' restoring sight to a man blind from birth. It is similar in many respects to synoptic accounts where there is no allusion to water or to baptism (cf. Mk. 8:22ff.; 10:46ff.). In the Johannine version, however, Jesus anoints the eyes of the man with dust from the ground, which he makes into mud with his saliva. The word for *anoint* in Jn. 9:6,11, *epechrisen,* later became the technical word for baptismal chrismation—to mark with the mark of Christ. It is rare in the New Testament, however. Then Jesus tells the blind man to bathe in the pool of Siloam, which the text explicitly interprets as *sent,* a frequent appellation in the Fourth Gospel of Jesus himself. The man does as bidden and his sight is restored. The reference to Christian baptism is deafening. The Epistle to the Hebrews also apparently links "baptisms" and "enlightenment" (Heb. 6:1-5). Baptism was often called "illumination" in the early church.

By way of comparison and contrast, the healing of the lame man who languished beside the pool of Bethesda (Jn. 5:1-15) also begins with a narrative which has synoptic parallels without baptismal overtones (Mk. 2:1ff. et par.). Unlike the synoptic parallels, however, and like the case of the blind man, a pool of water features largely in the story. The name of the pool is variously reported in the manuscripts as Bethesda, Bethsaida and

Bethzatha. Bethesda is the reading of the AV (KJV), and as Brown points out, that reading gains some support from the fact that a Qumran scroll designates with the name *Bet' Esda* an area near the Temple where a pool was to be found.[7] Bethesda, like Siloam, may have a symbolic meaning–House of Flowing or House of Compassion.

Unlike the blind man, however, the lame man did not enter the pool. Water by itself, it is implied, would be of no avail. Jesus' word alone made him well, as in the synoptic analogues. "Stand up; take up your mat and walk" (Jn. 5:11).

The Johannine account of the healing of the lame man makes a point of the presence of water, and indeed of bathing in water. From the beginning of the story the reader anticipates that the man will finally enter the pool. That he does not seems to suggest some tension between washing in water–water baptism–and the healings accomplished by Jesus. In this case Jesus' word sufficed. In the case of the blind man, healing was by water and the word of Jesus. Add word to thing to get a sacrament, said Augustine.

III.

Where, one might ask, might such a tension arise? The answer surely lies near at hand: among the followers of John the Baptist. On one hand the Baptist declares roundly, "I have baptized you with water, but he will baptize you with the Holy Spirit" (Mk. 1:8, cf. Mt. 3:11, Lk. 3:16). The testimony of the Fourth Gospel itself is fuller.

> And John testified, "I saw the Spirit descending from heaven like a dove and it remained on him. I myself did not know him, but the one who sent me to baptize with water said to me, He on whom you see the Spirit descend and remain is the one who baptizes with the Holy Spirit" (Jn. 1:33).

In the gospel view, John the Baptist thought that Messiah would baptize only with Spirit. No room there for water baptism.

On the other hand, it is clear in all four gospels that the Christian movement arose within the circle of John the Baptist. This point is underlined by the enigmatic report, found only in the Fourth Gospel, that in fact Jesus himself, at least at the beginning of his ministry, did baptize in water, concurrently with the Baptist (Jn. 3:26, 4:1). That report is not so subtly corrected at Jn. 4:2: " . . . although it was not Jesus himself but his disciples who baptized." None of the synoptic gospels indicates that Jesus ever baptized with water. It would not have been in keeping with the accepted view of the Spirit-filled Messiah to have baptized with water alongside his forerunner. On the grounds that the Fourth Evangelist would not have represented Jesus as baptizing at all had Jesus in historical fact not done so, one concludes with some degree of probability that Jesus himself did baptize with water at least at the outset of his ministry, and so did his disciples.

If this consideration were true, it would illuminate what otherwise seems to be a nearly inexplicable fact. At the conclusion of Peter's Pentecost sermon as reported in Acts, Peter urges hearers to "[r]epent and be baptized every one of you in the name of Jesus Christ so that your sins may be forgiven and you will receive the Holy Spirit" (Acts 2:38). Whatever the historical value of the sermon itself may be, there seems to be no reason to doubt that from the very beginning of life in the new church, from Pentecost on, baptism *in water and in the name of Jesus* formed the ritual initiation into the new life of the Spirit. In other words, water baptism was introduced into the earliest church without dropping a stitch, so to speak. It seems reasonable to suppose that the primitive community retained a memory that the pre-resurrection Jesus and his disciples had practiced water baptism, perhaps when the preaching of Jesus and John was the same, perhaps before the death of the Baptist provoked Jesus to a deeper understanding of his messianic identity (Mk. 1:4, 15).

We know of at least one place where followers of the Baptist became Christian disciples: in Ephesus. There the disciples had received John the Baptist's baptism and did not even know there was a Holy Spirit. Paul *baptized them in Jesus' name* and laid his lands on them, and they received the Holy Spirit (Acts 19:1–5). John's baptism alone had not conveyed to these believers the fulness of new life.

It is worth noting in this connection that early tradition held Ephesus to be the place where the Fourth Gospel was written. In recent times, questions have been raised about this place of origin, but Brown accepts it without question.[8]

In any case, the origin of the Fourth Gospel must have been in a place like Ephesus, where at least some members of the new community had received the baptism of John and had come to know also that water baptism in the name of Jesus was required if the gift of the Spirit was to be received. Members with only John's baptism would have been baptized with water again, this time in the name of the Lord Jesus, in order to receive that gift. The practice doubtless raised questions.

Thus we might look on the healing of the lame man at the pool of Bethesda without washing as a comment on the adequacy of Jesus' word alone, spoken by him in person during his lifetime. After all, it was so in the synoptic tradition. The healing of the blind man, on the other hand, occurring as it does later in the sequence of events in the Fourth Gospel, might be taken as a commentary on the post-resurrection necessity of the full initiatory formula which the Fourth Evangelist put on the lips of Jesus himself. " . . . no one can enter the kingdom of God without being born of water and the Spirit" (Jn. 3:5). It was a provision, no doubt, for the interim before the consummation of the kingdom.

IV.

This reference brings into view Nicodemus's visit to Jesus by night (Jn. 3:1–21). It occurs early in the gospel, immediately following Jesus' cleansing of the Temple and his proclamation—which, we are told, no one understood until he was raised from the dead—that if this "temple" was destroyed, it would be raised up in three days. He was speaking of the temple of his body (Jn. 2:19–21). One recalls Paul's question to the Corinthians, "[D]o you not know that your body is a temple of the Holy Spirit?" (I Cor. 6:19). In the light of this association, may we not suppose that Jesus in the Fourth Gospel claimed that his body was a temple of the Holy Spirit? He himself was the bearer of the Spirit, though no one else understood that fact until after the resurrection, until after Jesus was glorified and the Spirit then given to the church (Jn 7:39, 20:22–23), spiritual things being spiritually discerned.

Consequently, when Nicodemus, "a leader of the Jews," comes to Jesus in the night of disbelief, the hearers and readers of the gospel would understand that Jesus spoke to Nicodemus in the power of the Spirit in insisting that Nicodemus must be born again of water and the Spirit to enter the kingdom of God (Jn. 3:5). The hearers and readers of the story, we begin to see, were, like Nicodemus, Jews who devoutly wished to enter the kingdom and were concerned about baptism. This story, early in the gospel narrative, is programmatic for the whole. Jews, even disciples of the Baptist, are to be baptized—not only with water, as John's followers were, but also with the Spirit, which Jesus at this point in the Johannine account bears alone and unrecognized, but which Jesus conferred upon the apostolic community after the resurrection, and granted the apostles power to confer it on others (Jn. 20:21–22). The Baptist's baptism alone would not suffice.

As we have already noticed, Bultmann, following Wellhausen, Wendt and others, regards the manuscript evidence for the phrase "water and" as "at least very questionable."[9] It is omitted in Vaticanus and a family of miniscules.[10] The omission, of course, buttresses Bultmann's view of the entire Fourth Gospel as non-sacramental. On the other hand, Hoskyns[11] and Barrett[12] read the evidence for the omission to be so weak as to constitute no textual support. Brown[13] accepts the phrase without argument, although he explains at length why a baptismal interpretation of the story should be regarded with suspicion.[14]

V.

During the time that John the Baptist and Jesus were working concurrently, the ministry of Jesus apparently raised for John the possible messianic identity of Jesus. "Are you the one who is to come, or are we to wait for another?" (Mt. 11:3, Lk. 7:20). Jesus answered, *"The blind receive their sight, the lame walk,* the lepers are cleansed, the deaf hear, *the dead are raised,* and the poor have the good news preached to them" (Mt. 11:5, Lk. 7:22).

In the Fourth Gospel, both the first and second of these messianic works are dealt with in the manner we have now examined, in a way which seems to be addressed to a community interested in baptism, perhaps some of the disciples of the Baptist himself. Although the Fourth Gospel is silent about lepers and the deaf, there is also, at a climactic place, the story of the raising of Lazarus from the dead.

Like the accounts of the lame man and the blind man, the raising of Lazarus has an analogue in the synoptic tradition—the raising of the widow of Nain's son (Lk. 7:11–17; cf. Mk. 9:14ff., esp. v.26; *vide* 10, 193ff.). Probably in each of the three Johannine narratives, the original healing story was drawn not directly from synoptic texts, but "from the still-flowing stream of tradition"[15] common to all the gospels. There is no need to stipulate in this case (or in the earlier ones for that matter) a direct dependence on the synoptics.

As with the lame man and the blind man, the original narrative of the raising of the dead man is elaborated in a way which can only be described as characteristic of Johannine theology. This story is peopled with friends of Jesus—Lazarus, Martha and Mary—and a company of disbelieving Jews. It ends with a lengthy discussion of the resurrection, leading many Jews as well as Martha to confess their faith in Jesus as Messiah, and others to plot his death. Somewhat similar discussions involving resurrection and messianic faith appear in the stories of the lame man and the blind man also. Those motifs are by no means out of place in a consideration of baptism.

Yet is there any internal evidence to connect the raising of Lazarus with those earlier accounts? Is there anything to suggest a connection with baptism? In the context which this essay seeks to establish, one sentence stands out sharply. Some of the Jews said, "Could not he who opened the eyes of the blind man have kept this man from dying?" (Jn. 11:37). Schnackenburg remarks, " . . . the reader is meant to draw a line from the healing of blind man to the raising of the dead one. The two great miracles belong together because they reveal Jesus as the light and life of man."[16] One may conclude also that they belong together because it is *by baptism in water and the Spirit* that one comes to participate in both that light and that life. If the healing of the blind man is about baptism, the raising of Lazarus is about baptism. "Do you not know that as many of us as were baptized into Jesus were baptized into his death?" (Rom. 6:3). Nor need one appeal to St. Paul to establish the connection between baptism and resurrection. A discourse about death and resurrection forms the conclusion of the lame man's healing (Jn. 5:19–29), and a discussion of eternal life ends the dialogue with Nicodemus (Jn. 3:11–16).

If one were to think that the hearers or readers of the Fourth Gospel were approaching their own baptism at Easter, or the baptism of new members into their community, one might remark on the dramatic sequence of baptismal references, from the lame man, who found water alone to be not adequate, to the blind man, restored to sight by baptism in both water and the Spirit, to Lazarus, who was raised from the dead. The Fourth Evangelist recounts the events of Holy Week immediately after Lazarus comes forth from his tomb.

VI.

Brown points out that the story of Nicodemus, the healing of the lame man, and the restoring of sight to the blind man were "three great Johannine readings used in the preparation of catechumens for baptism."[17] He allows baptismal reference only to the cure of the blind man however, arguing that internal evidence is lacking in the other cases.[18]

Hoskyns, on the other hand, whom Brown cites with general approval in this connection, reports a slightly different list of Johannine readings used in early lectionaries during Lent: the Samaritan woman, the lame man and the blind man. "There is, therefore," he concludes (after A. Baumstark in *Festbrevier und Kirchenjahr der Syrischen Jacobiten*), "a fairly general agreement about the importance of these three sections of Saint John's gospel in the lectionaries of the early church and about their liturgical use. This agreement points to a traditional usage reaching back behind the fourth century. Since the Woman of Samaria, the Paralytic, and the Blind Man appear in the second-century frescoes in the catacombs at Rome as baptismal symbols, the liturgical baptismal use of these chapters may perhaps have its roots in the second century."[19] Such a date comes within a generation or two of the Fourth Gospel itself.

On the basis of internal evidence, what can be said about the story of the Samaritan woman (Jn. 4:7–42)? This passage comes on the heels of the verses which inform us that Jesus was "making and baptizing more disciples than John" (Jn. 4:1ff.). Thereupon Jesus passed through Samaria on the way back to Galilee and found himself, tired out, at Jacob's well. By this introduction our attention has already been pointed to baptism.

The encounter between Jesus and the Samaritan woman has no precise analogue in the synoptic gospels. Jesus, of course, did have dealings with Samaritans on his way through the region between Samaria and Galilee (Lk. 17:11–19), and he had a conversation with a Syro-Phoenician (or Canaanite) woman (Mk. 7:24, cf. Mt. 15:21–28). The Johannine incident as such would not be inconceivable in that "still-flowing stream of tradition."

As we have found on the other occasions which began with a simple narrative, this story is followed by a lengthy dialogue characteristic of Johannine theology, culminating in Jesus' declaration of himself as Messiah (Jn. 4:26), an indirect indication of the woman's own belief (Jn. 4:29), and the direct assertion of belief on the part of other Samaritans (Jn. 4:39–42).

What initiates the dialogue is the water of the well, which Jesus contrasts to the water which he can give, "gushing up to eternal life" (Jn. 4:14). Washing in that water is never in question. The water is to be drunk. Is there a connection between drinking and baptism? In fact it lies close at hand, for we read, a few chapters later, that Jesus went up to the Festival of Booths (Jn. 7:2), where we know that water was drawn from the fountain of Gihon on each of the first seven days.[20] On the last day of the festival, Jesus stood and cried out,

> "Let anyone who is thirsty come to me, and let the one who believes drink. Out of the believer's heart shall flow rivers of living water." Now he said this about the Spirit which believers in him were to receive; for as yet there was no Spirit, because Jesus was not yet glorified." (Jn. 7:37–39)
> (The alternative reading of the text is an apt commentary: "for as yet the Spirit had not been given . . . " (*NTG*, 254).

For the first hearers and readers of the Fourth Gospel, Jesus himself embodied the Spirit, as we have seen. To drink the water that he gives is to drink the Spirit and so to receive the Spirit. In the post-resurrection community, one does so by baptism. Paul makes the point: "For in one Spirit we were all baptized into one body . . . and we were all made to drink of one Spirit" (I Cor. 12:13, cf. I Cor. 10:4)

VII.

The report of Jesus and his disciples baptizing at the same time as the Baptist has pointed in one direction, forward, toward the woman of Samaria. There is also an allusion, admittedly tenuous, which points backward, toward the miracle at Cana of Galilee (Jn. 2:1–11).

In the Cana story we read that Jesus ordered six stone jars to be filled with water. The jars were used "for the Jewish rites of purification" (Jn. 2:6, cf. Mk. 7:3). In the presence of Jesus, who is the bearer of the Spirit throughout the Fourth Gospel, the water (for ritual washing?) was transformed into good wine. Washing and drinking are again joined. Jesus turns the water of ritual purification into the wine of eternal life.

In the account of Jesus and John the Baptist baptizing together, we find that "a discussion about *purification* arose between John's disciples and a Jew (or some Jews)" (Jn. 3:26). This reference to purification and the one in the Cana story are the only instances of the word *katharismos* in the Fourth Gospel. The Baptist's discussion with the Jews was abruptly terminated and, therefore, inconclusive, for John's disciples interrupted to tell John that Jesus was baptizing "and all are going to him" (Jn. 3:26). Jesus, the carrier of the Spirit, was found to bestow in his baptism what John did not. John was then moved to disclaim his own messianic identity. His baptism did not convey the Spirit, who must be received "from heaven" (Jn. 3:27).

It would be at least possible to argue then that whereas John's discussion with the Jews over their respective rites of purification was inconclusive, Jesus' presence turns the water of baptism (Ch. 3) or of ritual washing of any kind (Ch. 2) into the drink of eternal life.

If we suppose that the hearers and readers of the Fourth Gospel were interested in the relation between the Baptist's water baptism and Christian baptism by water and the Spirit, would they not easily recognize that neither the washings of the Jews nor the purification of the Baptist brought new life, but that the Christian baptism "by water and the Spirit" was like the wine of the messianic banquet?

VIII.

Our exploration of the baptismal significance of a number of passages of the Fourth Gospel has so far proceeded inductively. We began where the reference was most obvious, in the story of the blind man, and worked backwards and forwards in the text as clues emerged to move us in one direction or the other. It will now be helpful to recapitulate this material in the order provided by the Fourth Gospel itself. We find a subtle and dramatic sequence.

Ch. 1: The Baptist acknowledges that he baptizes with water, but one is to come who will baptize with the Spirit.
Ch. 2:1–11: In the presence of Jesus, the water of Jewish purification becomes the good wine of eternal life, life in the Spirit.
Ch. 2:13–25: Jesus claims that his body is the bearer of the Spirit.
Ch. 3:1–16: Jesus tells Nicodemus, a leader of the Jews and an inquirer into the gospel, that he must be born again "by water and the Spirit."
Ch. 3:22–4:6: Jesus and John the Baptist baptize simultaneously. The crowd

goes to Jesus, however, suggesting that both Jewish and Baptist purifications are of no avail.

Ch. 4:1–53: Jesus offers the Samaritan woman the water of eternal life to drink. She and other Samaritans come to faith in Jesus as Messiah.

Ch. 5:1–47: Jesus heals the lame man at the pool of Bethesda by his word alone. Water without the Spirit is not effective (Cf. "The Lord is the Spirit" II Cor. 3:17).

Ch. 7:37–39: Those who believe drink the living water of the Spirit, arguably by baptism.

Ch. 9:1–41. The blind man, blinded to God by the sin of the world, is restored to sight by the anointing of Jesus and by bathing in the pool of Siloam.

Ch. 11:1–57. Jesus raised Lazarus from a tomb described in terms very much like Jesus' own. He who restored sight to the blind will restore life to the dead, by baptism.

The argument of this essay, that the Fourth Gospel was written, at least in part, for persons interested in water and baptism, possibly for followers of John the Baptist, who were baptized by him in water and who now face or who recently have faced Christian baptism by water and the Spirit, is given considerable weight by this cumulative evidence.

IX.

Chapter 11, with all its overtones of baptism and resurrection, comes almost at the end of the first part of the Fourth Gospel, the "Book of Signs."[21] Before we go further, mention must now be made of the feeding of the five thousand in Chapter 6, with its accompanying discourse regarding the bread of life. It is the one place in the Fourth Gospel with an unmistakably eucharistic sense.

It is a characteristic Johannine composition, beginning with an incident well-known in the tradition and ending with a far-reaching discussion of the meaning of Jesus' sacrificial life and death for the world. At its conclusion, some come to faith and others turn away. The structure is parallel to that of the stories of the Samaritan woman, the lame man and the blind man. We have argued that those narratives were shaped for the interest of persons concerned about baptism. The feeding narrative, then, might have been shaped for those particularly concerned about the common meal. If so, perhaps Cullmann's contention is correct after all: the thought of the Fourth Gospel is connected with the services of the church and not with baptism only.

In that case, however, would not the question of balance arise, since there are so many references to baptism and only one to the eucharist? Even if one were to understand the changing of water into wine as eucharistic (ignoring the mention of the use of jars intended for ritual purification and taking the wine to be eucharistic) and were to understand the discourse on the true vine as an allusion to the wine of the eucharist (for which there is no compelling internal evidence), it would bring the number of eucharistic allusions to only three as opposed to the nine we have found for baptism. The eucharist was celebrated much more frequently than baptism. Should it not be given at least equal time?

This essay has no answer to that question except to suggest that the hearers and readers we have in view would also have had an interest in the eucharist, that the Fourth Evangelist addressed that concern in his character-istic way, but that, knowing his audience, he did not emphasize eucharist as much as he did baptism. Barnabas Lindars's contention that the whole sixth chapter was added by the Evangelist to a "second edition" of the gospel may go too far, but it draws attention to a problem.[22]

X.

The last chapters of the Fourth Gospel, (Jn. 12–21), comprise Dodd's "Book of the Passion." Interest in water and baptism comes into focus on one more critically important occasion—the footwashing (Jn. 13:1–20).

Already baptized or about to be baptized into the death of Jesus (Jn. 11), believers enter into the events of Holy Week. The footwashing is presented as the prelude to the Last Supper. It is the only mention of footwashing in any of the gospels.

"Jesus, knowing that the Father had given all things into his hands, and that he had come from God and was going to God" (Jn. 13:3), washed the feet of his disciples as an example of what they should do for each other. The example of Jesus involved his death, and the death of the Johannine Jesus entailed his resurrection to a new life in the Spirit. Although there is no synoptic analogue to the footwashing, the synoptic Jesus declares, "I am among you as one who serves. I confer on you as my Father has conferred on me, a kingdom, so that you may eat and drink at my table in my kingdom . . . " (Lk. 22:27). In the footwashing of the Fourth Gospel this final act of service is powerfully dramatized.

How are the disciples to share this new life of the kingdom? Brown remarks, "[I]t is clear that the footwashing is something that makes it possible to have eternal life with Jesus."[23] Is it intended to denote baptism however? Critical opinion, of course, varies widely. The following consider-ations seem persuasive:

> 1. If the account of the footwashing is historical, if it took place in actual fact at the Last Supper and included Jesus' explicit command to repeat it (Jn. 13:14), it is difficult to understand why footwashing did not become a major liturgical rite, alongside baptism and eucharist.

2. There is evidence in the synoptics that baptism in the mind of Jesus came to signify his death (Lk. 12:50) and that the word *baptism* could denote the participation of the disciples in Jesus' death (Mk. 10:38). The footwashing is a vivid depiction of Jesus' enabling the disciples to "have a share" with him, to participate, then, in his death and new life in the Spirit. But the cumulative argument of this entire essay is that precisely *baptism* enables such participation. The water of footwashing can best be understood as the water of baptism.

3. If this interpretation is right, it helps to clarify a difficult passage in the footwashing narrative which seems to refer to two acts: a complete bathing (*leloumenos*) and also a *washing* (*nipsasthai*). "One who has bathed (completely) does not need to wash, except for his feet, but is entirely clean" (Jn. 13:10). The thought is obscure. Bultmann calls it "grotesque."[24]

But suppose, as we have been doing all along, that the Evangelist's hearers and readers included disciples of the Baptist who had received John's baptism, as perhaps some of the circle of Jesus' original disciples had, perhaps even Peter. That baptism would have been by full immersion, by "bathing."[25] Do they need further baptism? This text answers that only their feet need to be washed then, and they are entirely clean. They need Christian baptism "by water and the Spirit," baptism into the crucified and risen Lord, which was administered from an early date with candidates standing ankle-deep in running water.[26]

A final notice of baptism is contained in the word about the spear wound which the soldiers at the crucifixion inflicted on Jesus, from which "at once blood and water came out" (Jn. 19:34). There is nearly universal critical agreement that the blood and water symbolize eucharist and baptism.[27] This passage, however, does not seem to be especially illuminated by the hypothesis that hearers or readers had a particular concern about baptism.

XI.

Raymond Brown suggests five stages in the composition of the Fourth Gospel.[28] In the second stage Brown thinks that traditional material was "sifted, selected, thought over, and molded into the form and style of the individual stories that became part of the Fourth Gospel. This process was probably accomplished through oral preaching and teaching."[29]

The conclusion which is suggested by the analysis presented in this essay is that at this second stage, there was a significant number of followers of John the Baptist among the hearers and that the Evangelist pointed this material to their concerns. Even if Brown's five-stage theory should not commend itself, at least one could hold that at some early stage of its composition, the Fourth Gospel went through such a process of sifting and shaping with Christian baptism in mind. Baptism was almost certainly not the only concern of the Evangelist,[30] but it was central enough to have left a remarkable impression on the text which we have sought to decipher. It is hoped that the result will shed a new and revealing light on the meaning of the gospel.

In *Identity and Difference*, in quite another connection, Martin Heidegger remarked, "In this realm one cannot prove anything but one can point out a great deal." So here.

Notes

1. Rudolf Bultmann, *Das Evangelium des Johannes* (Gottingen: Vandenhoek und Ruprecht, 1968) 3ff.

2. Oscar Cullmann, *Early Christian Worship* (Napierville, Ill., Alec R. Allenson, 1953) 37ff.

3. Cullmann, *Early Christian*, 116.

4. Raymond E. Brown, *The Gospel According to John*, 2 vols., The Anchor Bible (New York: Doubleday, 1966–70) II:380.

5. Brown, *John*, II: 211.

6. Brown, *John*, II:143.

7. Brown, *John*, II:206–207.

8. Brown, *John*, II:ciii.

9. Brown, *John*, II:98.

10. *Novum Testamentum Graece*, ed. Eberhardt Nestle, Erwin Nestle, and Kurt Aland, 22 Aufl. (New York: American Bible Society, 1956) 236.

11. E.C. Hoskyns, *The Fourth Gospel*, ed. Francis Noel Davey (London: Faber and Faber, 1947) 214.

12. C.K. Barrett, *The Gospel According to John* (New York: Macmillan, 1956) 174.

13. Brown, *John*, II:131.

14. Brown, *John*, II:141ff.

15. Barrett, *John*, 294.

16. Rudolf Schnackenburg, *The Gospel According to St. John*, tr. Cecily Hastings et al. (London: Burns and Oates, 1979) 337.

17. Brown, *John*, II: 211.

18. Brown, *John*, II: 380–381.

19. Hoskyns, *Fourth Gospel*, 365.

20. Brown, *John*, I: 327.

21. C.H. Dodd, *The Interpretation of the Fourth Gospel* (Cambridge:University Press, 1953).

22. Barnabas Linders, *Essays on John*, ed. C.M. Tuckett (Leuven: University Press, 1992) 64.

23. Brown, *John*, 566.

24. Bultman, *Das Evangelium des Johannes*, 357, n. 5.

25. Bultmann, *Johannes*, 357, n. 5.

26. Bultmann, *Johannes*, 357, n. 5.

27. Cullmann, *Early Christian*, 114, n.5.

28. Brown, *John*, II: xxxiv–xxxvi.

29. Brown, *John*, II: xxxiv–xxxv.

30. R. J. Cassidy, *John's Gospel in New Perspective* (Maryknoll, N.Y.: Orbis Books, 1992) 182ff.

Preaching the Kingdom of God in the Synoptic Gospels

William H. Hethcock

BOTH JOHN THE BAPTIST and Jesus make clear in all three synoptic gospels that Jesus' primary purpose in his ministry is heralding the arrival of the kingdom of God. John the Baptist's announcement warns in Matthew, "Repent, for the kingdom of heaven has come near (3:2)," and later Jesus himself declares the same message (4:17). Each evangelist states early in his gospel Jesus' primary purpose:

> Jesus came to Galilee, proclaiming the good news of God, and saying, "The time is fulfilled, and the kingdom of God has come near; repent, and believe in the good news" (Mk. 1:14b–15).

> From that time Jesus began to proclaim, "Repent, for the kingdom of heaven has come near" (Mt. 4:17).

> [Jesus] said to [the people], "I must proclaim the good news of the kingdom of God to the other cities also; for I was sent for this purpose" (Lk. 4:43).

There is no argument among scholars that all of Jesus' words and deeds—teaching, healing, story and parable telling, table fellowship—are aimed at accomplishing his compelling purpose of announcing the kingdom.

It is noteworthy, however, that preachers tend to forget Jesus' primary purpose in their exegesis of the readings assigned in the lectionary's three-year synoptic cycle. They tend, especially in the Sundays after the Epiphany and in ordinary time, to interpret the Scriptures without reference to Jesus' primary concern, and in so doing, they miss the meaning a given reading strongly presses when the urgency of Jesus' kingdom of God message is taken into account. This is not to say that such preaching is of no effect, but sermons that miss, omit, or sidestep the kingdom of God implication in the reading result in preaching which strains the preacher's imagination in directions scarcely touching Jesus' direct and important intention. All too frequently they miss the point entirely.

This is a good time to look again at Jesus' central concern and to allow it to inform our teaching and preaching. New scholarship, especially that given us by Professor N. T. Wright, is looking with fresh perspective at the kingdom of God context of the scriptures. Wright contends that Jesus was radically redefining the reign of God in new and revolutionary ways and that the kingdom was actually being inaugurated as Jesus spoke. "The old picture of Jesus as the teacher of timeless truths, or even the announcer of the essentially timeless call for decision, will simply have to go," says Wright.[1] Authentic preaching of the synoptic texts requires the preacher's consistent awareness of this either stated or implied kingdom theme and careful and conscientious consideration of how the text for the day is designed to incorporate it, to enlarge on it, and to set it forth. We may summarize briefly the history of contemporary kingdom scholarship as a guide to informing ourselves and our preaching and teaching today.

The Contemporary Study of the Kingdom of God

My purpose is not to examine all of the various interpretations of the kingdom of God in recent scholarship, which would be impossible in this short essay. I intend rather to stress the importance of preachers becoming aware of some of the interpretations which come to us in recent commentaries and other writings. The emphasis here will be on the importance of bringing these interpretations into the study of synoptic lectionary readings for preaching. The message Jesus believed himself compelled to deliver, that "the kingdom of God is near," was the driving force in his ministry. The gospels repeatedly indicate how he was clearly aware that the urgency of his kingdom-preaching was moving him toward conflict with the religious authorities who would seek his arrest and execution. The preacher who recognizes this truth will discover the importance of bringing Jesus' own urgency and challenge into today's sermons.

While Mark and Luke consistently use the term "kingdom of God," Matthew prefers to use "kingdom of heaven" almost exclusively. Most scholars assume that the terms are interchangeable and that, since Matthew is writing for a Jewish audience, he is merely dutifully avoiding a serious religious transgression.

Unlike the Gospels of Mark and Luke, which were written for Gentile believers, Matthew was written for Jewish believers. In the Judaism of the first century, even as in Orthodox Jewish circles today, there was great reverence for the name of God. In order to protect himself from breaking the third commandment ("You shall not take the name of the Lord your God in vain; for the Lord will not hold him guiltless who takes his name in vain" [Ex. 20:7]), the devout Jew scrupulously avoided using the sacred name of God. This practice applied primarily to the tetragrammaton, i.e., the name YHWH. This name was too sacred to be uttered. In its place one would read or state instead the term "Adonai" (Lord) or "Elohim" (God).[2]

While this explanation is generally accepted and seems satisfactory for the most part, there remains the question of why Matthew four times in his gospel does indeed use the term "kingdom of God." John Christopher Thomas writes:

> If the majority of scholars are correct in their view that kingdom of heaven and kingdom of God are synonyms, that heaven serves as a circumlocution for God, and that occasionally Matthew has intentionally used kingdom of God in the place of kingdom of heaven, then the most plausible explanation for the substitution of kingdom of God for kingdom of heaven in 12.28, 19.24, 21.31, and 43 is that for Matthew kingdom of God is a literary device used to draw the reader's attention to passages of special significance. More specifically, if the use of heaven is a means of avoiding the offence caused by use of the divine name, then Matthew's intentional use of the divine name in this formula is no doubt a most graphic means of emphasis.[3]

Thomas points out that each of Matthew's four verses reading "kingdom of God" gives a special word of warning to the community. He goes on to say, "This evidence suggests that the readers of Matthew, who were accustomed to seeing kingdom of heaven, would at the very least pause at the sight of kingdom of God and ponder the content of these passages."

The false idea that the kingdom can be brought into present reality through the devout longing and good works of humankind has been an ongoing misinterpretation of Jesus' proclamation. The kingdom is God's, and the faithful may respond to God's reign, but they may not effect its coming through any human means. Yet, from the time of the liberal movement in the Church, this well intended human effort has persevered, oblivious to a more accurate interpretation of Scripture. The liberal movement and the social gospel are associated with an 1890s notion of the rediscovery of the kingdom of God in terms of rebuilding the society along ethical and moral lines as these ideas are erroneously extrapolated from the synoptic gospels.

> The idea of the kingdom of God became a powerful motif among moderate to liberal Protestants between 1880 and the 1920s. . . . Adapting the thought of European figures such as W. H. Fremantle, Frederick Denison Maurice, and

Albrecht Ritschl, the advocates of the new view regarded the kingdom as a present ethical reality growing to fulfillment in *all* areas of human life.[4]

The movement came to be seen as a God-inspired, Scripture-endorsed, human effort using modern business tools and developing western cultural ideas of progress and aiming them toward molding the future, both religious and secular, into a kind of utopia. Although the decades in which such interpretations predominated have passed, the idea of encouraging the church to "establish," "build up," or "extend" the kingdom unfortunately still crops up in writing, teaching, and preaching. Those concerned with the church's structure, mission, and finance may occasionally be found to rally the people to their cause with such mistaken "kingdom building" language.

Jesus never defined the term "kingdom of God" in a specific and direct way. Instead, he used both the terms "kingdom" and "kingdom of God" as if they would be clearly understood by his listeners, and the synoptic evangelists also recorded their versions of Jesus' teaching and deeds as if their audiences were already aware of what he meant. On the one hand, Jesus could assume that his disciples and the Jewish crowds were conversant with the terms so that on one level no explanation was necessary. On the other hand, as we shall see, his cryptic language may have been required by the danger the very message itself was engendering for his followers and himself.

The reign of God was anticipated before Jesus in many quarters of Judaism as a part of their religious heritage. Indeed, N. T. Wright argues that though the physical exile of Israel had ended, a metaphorical exile had not ended, nor would it end until the reign of God might fully come.

> Many if not most second-Temple Jews . . . hoped for the new exodus seen as the final return from exile. The story would reach its climax; the great battle would be fought; Israel would truly "return" to her land, saved and free; YHWH would return to Zion. This would be in the metaphorical sense, the end of the world, the ushering in at last of YHWH's promised new age. . . . This, I suggest, is the proper and historically appropriate context in which to understand Jesus' sayings about the kingdom, or kingship, of Israel's god [sic].[5]

Eduard Schweizer also explains that Jesus is referring to a concept which was, as he spoke, already in the minds of ardent Jews:

> Judaism in the time of Jesus spoke of the sovereignty of God which one accepted if he submitted obediently to every commandment; in addition, it spoke of the reign of God which comes after the annihilation of every foe and the end of all suffering. In the one instance its coming was entirely dependent upon human decision, and in the other case it was seen as something which happens in the normal course of events.[6]

Of course, this is not to say that Jesus in using the words "kingdom of God" meant precisely the same thing that his hearers may already have been thinking. On the contrary, his purpose was to take what was known, assumed, believed, and expected and to add to it what was to many a troublesome and revolutionary dimension. Dale Patrick argues that Jesus' teachings began with a concept that the people understood and then proceeded to an expanded or changed idea which was new and challenging. Jesus was designing his parables, for example, to take into account what was already familiar to the people. But then the end of the parable would shock, stretch, and challenge his listeners so that they would be brought to a different place from where they had been in the beginning. Jesus used his kingdom of God preaching:

> to arouse in his listeners a complex of ideas, associations, and metaphors. They already have some idea of what he is talking about. Whatever particular twist he wishes to give to his idea, he relates it to the various conceptions his hearers have in their minds. To the degree that their conceptions clash with his, he is endeavoring to get them to reconceptualize, to understand something in a new way.[7]

And this reconceptualizing, this understanding in a new way, was clearly subversive from the point of view of the religious establishment who heard Jesus' teaching as threat, so much so that in Mark Jesus three times predicts his own arrest and execution (8:31, 9:31, 10:33–34; cf. Mt. 17:22–23, Lk. 9:43–45).

Past Interpretations of the Kingdom of God

Interpretations of what Jesus meant by "kingdom of God" have varied through history. The modern discussion of the kingdom started with the publication of Johannes Weiss's *Jesus' Proclamation of the Kingdom of God* (1892), and with the subsequent popularization of Weiss's views in Albert Schweitzer's *The Quest of the Historical Jesus* (1906). They both held an eschatological view of Jesus' kingdom-teaching determining that the kingdom was "an object of imminent expectation, yet still to come."[8] Schweitzer was especially adamant in saying that the whole of Jesus' teaching and work were based on the belief that the *parousia* was to take place immediately.

The work of C. H. Dodd is primary among the opponents of the views of Weiss and Schweitzer. Dodd proposed that the kingdom which others determined was "yet still to come" actually arrived with the coming of Jesus, that it was then and is today a here and now happening. The term "realized eschatology" applies to Dodd's view.

> Jesus declares that this ultimate, the Kingdom of God, has come into history, and He takes upon Himself the "eschatological" role of "Son of Man." The absolute, the "wholly other," has entered into time and space. And as the

Kingdom of God has come and the Son of Man has come, so also judgment and blessedness have come into human experience.[9]

According to Dodd, one enters the kingdom, not on the Day of the Lord or at the end of time, but at the moment of coming to faith in the good news as it is revealed by Jesus. "The Kingdom of God in its full reality is not something which will happen after other things have happened." Rather, "it is that to which men awake when this order of time and space no longer limits their vision."[10]

With these and other opposing interpretations of the reign of God either as actually begun with Jesus' announcement or as yet to come, an enlivened dialogue began. Out of the controversy came popular arguments encompassing opposing views into one; the kingdom is both now and in the future as well. Ron Farmer summarizes the discussion during the mid-years of this century. "As a result of the difficulty in understanding the kingdom as entirely future or entirely present, most interpreters began to view the kingdom as somehow both present and future." In the larger school, which maintained that "the tension between present and future is to be understood temporally," Joachim Jeremias proposed that "Dodd's realized eschatology should be modified to 'eschatology in the process of realization,'" a wording Dodd later endorsed. Werner George Kümmel saw present and future related as "present fulfillment carrying with it the certainty of future promise." An "inaugurated eschatology" advocated by Oscar Cullmann described the Christ event, using World War II slang, as "D-Day" and the *parousia* as "V-Day."[11]

An opposing school identified a "dialectic tension" interpreted "existentially rather than temporally." In this thinking, Günther Bornkamm, and Ernst Fuchs broke with Rudolf Bultmann, their mentor, determining that the kingdom had been fulfilled in part in history. "The decisive event which confronts humanity with the crisis of decision took place in the ministry of Jesus."[12]

Norman Perrin made a notable and persuasive contribution to interpreting the kingdom of God in his book, *Jesus and the Language of the Kingdom: Symbol and Metaphor in New Testament Interpretation* (1976). Actually, Perrin was by the time of this writing nearing the end of a lifetime study in which he had changed his thinking from an opposing point of view in his earlier *The Kingdom of God in the Teaching of Jesus* (1963) and a developing perspective in *Rediscovering the Teaching of Jesus* (1967). He expressed his thanks to Amos N. Wilder whose work on symbols and myths led Perrin to break new ground in his last major work.[13]

Wilder helped Perrin to identify his difficulty with previous scholarship. Perrin observed that Weiss and others constantly spoke of "'the *concept*

Kingdom of God,' of Jesus' '*conception of the Kingdom of God,*' and this kind of language is common parlance in the discussion." Re-reading his own work, he discovered that he had used the same language himself. Previous scholarship, even his own, had made "kingdom" a "steno-symbol," a symbol which has only one referent.

> But I now want to argue that such language is imprecise. "Kingdom of God is not an *idea* or a *conception*, it is a *symbol*. As a symbol it can *represent* or *evoke* a whole range or series of conceptions or ideas, but it only becomes a conception or idea if it constantly represents or evokes that one conception or idea, and we then take the step of creating a kind of verbal shorthand in speaking of the "conception of the Kingdom." . . . We make Kingdom of God a steno-symbol on the lips of Jesus.[14]

Perrin's language regarding symbols is derived from Philip Wheelwright's *Metaphor and Reality* and Paul Ricoeur's *The Symbolism of Evil.* Wheelwright offers terms which become very useful to Perrin in the development of his own interpretation of the kingdom of God. When "kingdom" is perceived as a concept or idea, it becomes a static symbol, a "steno-symbol," with only a one-to-one relationship to that which it represents, such as the mathematical symbol *pi*, and it is therefore a "steno-symbol." But Perrin came to perceive the word kingdom as having "a set of meanings that can neither be exhausted nor adequately expressed by any one referent, in which case it is a 'tensive-symbol.'"[15]

Perrin's new insight opened up for exegetes a broad interpretation of Jesus' kingdom sayings and references, as well as of kingdom-oriented pericopes in which the kingdom is not specifically mentioned. All interpretation must, of course, remain guided by the context of the reading at hand. When meanings "can neither be exhausted nor adequately expressed by any one referent," the preacher is challenged not only by the more apparent interpretations but by layers of subtle and mysterious meaning. Perrin attempted to establish the fact:

> (that) in the proclamation of Jesus "Kingdom of God" was used as a tensive symbol, and that it was used to evoke the myth of God acting as king. The challenge of the message of Jesus was to recognize the reality of the activity of God in the historicality of the hearer's extensive world, and especially in the experience of a "clash of worlds" (an expression of Amos Wilder's) as the hearer came to grips with the reality of everyday human existence.[16]

Perrin then leaves the exegetes to their task asserting that the "literary forms and language" Jesus used were "such as to mediate the reality evoked" by the kingdom of God symbol. "It is of the very nature of such forms of language that they resist translation into another mode of discourse" as well as into "the form of propositional statements." Perrin considers his offering complete when he restates that "Jesus used the Kingdom of God as a tensive symbol."[17]

A more recent scholar, N. T. Wright, presents a convincing argument regarding the kingdom of God. As stated above, Wright begins with the assertion that the reign of God is clearly in the minds of the Jewish people in the time of Jesus. Kingdom of God, he explains, as "historically and theologically considered, is a slogan whose basic meaning is the hope that Israel's god is going to rule Israel (and the whole world), and that Caesar, or Herod, or anyone else of their ilk, is not." The Torah will be fulfilled, the Temple will be rebuilt, and the Land will be cleansed. The God of Israel will rule the nation through divinely appointed persons and means.[18]

> The phrase 'kingdom of god,' therefore, which occurs only sporadically in texts of this period, functions, when it occurs, as a crucial shorthand expression for a concept which could be spoken of in a variety of other ways, such as the impossibility of having rulers other than Israel's god, or the divine necessity of reversing the present political situation and re-establishing Israel, Temple, social, political, cultural and economic aspiration of the Jews of this period, and invests it with the religious and theological dimension which, of course, it always possessed in mainline Jewish thinking.[19]

The term embodied a sense of national hope anticipating a day when this reign of God would be fulfilled and complete.

Conflicts and revolutionary talk smouldered during Jesus' time. Though there was a measure of peace because of the power of the controlling foreigners, there was always talk of revolution because of the discontent of the Jewish citizenry with the domination they suffered. And there was hope and trust that they would be vindicated by their God. Those who were talking about the reign of Israel's God were talking about how "the covenant god would act to reconstitute his people, to end their exile, to forgive their sins." Anyone talking about the reign of Israel's God was assumed to be referring to the fulfilment of Israel's ancient and fervent hope. The time was coming when "Israel would no longer be dominated by the pagans. She would be free. The means of liberation were no doubt open to debate. The goal was not."[20]

Jesus entered into this atmosphere, Wright explains, using the kingdom of God metaphor knowing that it called up in the minds of his disciples and the other people a future time when their life would be restored to what they believed it had been anciently. But Jesus in his teachings, his parables, and sayings consistently, though often cryptically, was constantly redefining the people's notion of God's reign. He was telling everyone what this reign would be like, and his descriptions were markedly and shockingly different from the expectations that existed in their traditions. Wright concludes that

Jesus was doing two things when he spoke of the "reign" or "kingdom of Israel's god": he was "deliberately evoking an entire story line that he and his hearers knew quite well," and he was "retelling this familiar story in such a way as to subvert and redirect its normal plot." Even without going to the parables to support this point, Jesus' "basic announcement carries, by implication, the complete story in its new form."[21]

This interpretation helps us to understand how it becomes urgent for the preacher exegeting the synoptic texts to be aware of their preoccupation with Jesus' primary purpose. As Wright points out, Jesus' announcement of the kingdom was not a benign message from a good teacher who merely meant well. Jesus was instead warning that a new age was being introduced with dramatic, if not catastrophic, implications for all. He was summoning his hearers to a change of heart and a new direction in their lives. He was calling them into a new way of being Israel, and he was calling them into the danger he had created for himself. The day of understanding Jesus as a well intended teacher of a magnificent if unattainable ethic that has the potential of helping us live in the troubled times of our life today, if it was ever appropriate, is well past us now. The urgent message of repenting and receiving the reign of God today is what Jesus' preaching was about. He was preaching about a radical renewal and redirection of our lives. Your preaching and mine must say no less than that.

The Kingdom of God in the Parables of Jesus

The primary means for Jesus' spreading his message is, of course, his parables, which he uses to accomplish his kingdom-teaching vocation. As mentioned before, Jesus never defined the kingdom of God in the kind of language you and I would call a definition. At the same time, his parables are crafted for "those who have ears to hear" to give them a picture of the kingdom along with an experience of what it will be like. That which is unfamiliar, unknown, beyond imagining, even threatening and shocking, is "thrown down beside" (which is what the word "parable" means) that which is familiar and every day. His message is communicated in a startling, confrontational, and sometimes baffling and angering fashion. While Jesus is not clearly defining the kingdom in the direct words we might long for, he seems at times to be struggling to get his teaching across with introductory words such as, "With what can we compare the kingdom of God, or what parable will we use for it?" (Mk. 4:30). We ourselves frequently rediscover in contemporary conversation, in teaching, or persuading how much easier it is to engender an entirely new concept than it is to take an old teaching and give it new shape and new meaning, especially when the listener is culturally and religiously indisposed to receiving a new perspective. Extensive scholarship is available to explain to us the literary and rhetorical patterns of communication and storytelling within Jewish tradition which are precursors of the New Testament parable as a teaching device. The helpfulness of this research is limited by our awareness that Jesus' message gives an unanticipated twist to an old story, the Jewish story, and that, in his hands, the parable does work with his hearers which is different from the work done by his predecessors.

At one time in the church's preaching, parables were always interpreted allegorically with various characters and instances representing ideas, concepts, and morals. We see allegory here as a literary, dramatic, or pictorial device in which characters and events stand for abstract ideas, principles, or forces, so that the literal sense has or suggests a parallel, deeper, symbolic sense. When parables were interpreted in this way, much was left to the ingenuity and imagination, if not to the prejudices, of the preacher. Martin Luther, for example, was committed to interpreting the parables literally and grammatically, but, sound in theory though he was, according to Robert H. Stein, "he tended to allegorize the parables and find everywhere in them examples of the doctrine of justification by faith."[22] John Calvin joined Luther in "failing to follow their more sound hermeneutical principles" so that their perceptions were soon lost. In his 1841 book, *Notes on the Parables of our Lord*, Archbishop R. C. Trench demonstrated the epitome of questionable allegorizing in his discussion of the Good Samaritan parable in a list of interpretations greatly abbreviated for inclusion here:

The man going down to Jericho = Human nature or Adam
Jerusalem from which he was going = Heavenly city
Jericho = Profane city, under a curse
Stripping him = Stripping him of his original robe of righteousness
Priest and Levite = Inability of the Law to save
Good Samaritan = Christ
Wine = Blood of Christ's passion
Inn = Church
Whatever more you spend = Reward for righteous service[23]

The end of this kind of interpretation of the parables was brought about by Adolf Jülicher in his *Die Gleichnisreden Jesu* in 1888. He maintained strongly that parables are not and do not contain allegories.

> Jülicher's main contribution to the investigation of the parables was that he pointed out the difference between parables and allegories and in so doing laid to rest the allegorical method of interpreting the parables which had plagued

the church for centuries. Parables are not allegories, for a parable is an extended simile and thus has only one *tertium comparationis*, or point of comparison, whereas an allegory is a chain of metaphors.[24]

As clean as this was, it was a pendulum swung too far. Jülicher decided that parables included no allegory at all, and in so doing, decided that the presence of allegorical details gave reason to question the text's authenticity. He attributed all allegorical content in a parable to editing by the early church. This fallacy in Jülicher's thinking came about because, according to the custom of the day, he depended upon Aristotle rather than the Old Testament or other scriptural traditions to define what a parable is. Even Stein, in commenting on Jülicher, is conservative on the subject of allegory in the parables. He remarks:

> Whether the parables of Jesus at times contain allegorical details and whether these details are authentic must be demonstrated on exegetical grounds, not on philosophical or *a priori* grounds. It would appear, nevertheless, to be a wise rule not to interpret the parables of Jesus or the details of the parables allegorically unless such an interpretation is absolutely necessary. We should find allegory in the parables of Jesus only when we must, not simply when we can![25]

Because of his view that the term kingdom is a tensive symbol, Perrin also resists allegorical interpretation of parables. On this point, Wright seriously disagrees with Perrin. He believes that "kingdom" may indeed have only one referent allowing at the same time for other "resonances." In addressing Perrin's symbol theory, Wright argues that:

> it is perfectly possible, and within the Jewish context very likely, that a symbol could have one main, overarching referent, while evoking various echoes and allusions. Perrin's all-too-neat scheme seems designed to highlight the symbolic nature of the parables while retaining the scholarly orthodoxy of his day by holding 'allegory' at bay, a task now rendered unnecessary by subsequent scholarship.[26]

Jülicher's second point concerning parables was his view that Jesus always included a general moral truth. Jülicher was a liberal according to the liberal theology of the late nineteenth century, which caused his *tertium comparationis* to be tainted with this theological perspective. Since according to Jülicher the parables are essentially instructional, he saw them as the means for Jesus to give information about the kingdom of God. Perrin sees the result as unfortunate.

> Jesus turns out to be very much a late nineteenth-century German liberal, for this Kingdom of God is "a fellowship in God . . . a fellowship of brothers and sisters under the protection of their father," a fellowship already at work "in seeking and finding the lost . . . already enjoying in full measure the gifts of God, forgiveness, loving kindness, peace, joy, security," a fellowship in which "spiritual effort and endeavor is demanded of all its members. . . ."[27]

In spite of these two limitations of Jülicher's work, he is to be given great credit for having broken the tenacious grip of the allegorical interpretation of parables which had been in practice up to his time.

Dodd, in *Parables of the Kingdom* (1935), required "that the parables must be interpreted in the context of the ministry of Jesus and his message and not in the context of nineteenth-century liberalism or the present situation of the believer." While this may seem obvious to contemporary preachers, Dodd was correcting the fallacious hermeneutical practice he observed. He was asserting that before we may attempt to understand what the parable is saying to us today, we must endeavor to discover what the parable meant and how Jesus intended to apply it for his listeners in the first century. Stated another way, "Dodd demonstrated that the question, What does the parable mean to me today? must be preceded by the question, What did the parable mean to the original audience then?" What was the first *Sitz im Leben* of Jesus' parable?[28] There are two principles:

> (i) The clue must be found, not in ideas which developed only with the experience of the early Church, but in such ideas as may be supposed to have been in the minds of the hearers of Jesus during His ministry. . . . (ii) The meaning which we attribute to the parable must be congruous with the interpretation of His own ministry offered by Jesus in explicit and unambiguous sayings, so far as such sayings are known to us.[29]

Further, Dodd directs, the meaning must be consistent with the "general view" of Jesus' teaching in his non-parabolic sayings.

There is no doubt that Dodd brought new life into the interpretation of parables. In the case of the Good Samaritan, for example, examining the story's *Sitz im Leben* brings about an awareness of the festering hatred Jews sustained for Samaritans and rescues the parable's meaning from a mere admonition about doing good for someone in trouble or need. Instead, we have a confrontational demand that "neighbor" include even those whom we hold in our utmost disdain. The revered Jewish clergy, the priests and Levites, turn out to be villains, and the hero is an odious and disgusting Samaritan. Note that in response to Jesus' call for the true neighbor to be identified the lawyer cannot get the loathsome word "Samaritan" out of his mouth. The angry lawyer admits with great difficulty, "The one who showed him mercy."

Dodd's important thesis regarding "realized eschatology" may have contributed to his "main limitation."

> For Dodd, all such eschatological parables as Mk. 13:28–30 (the parable of the fig tree); Mt. 24:45–51 (the parable of the good and the bad servant); Mt. 25:1–13 (the parable of the wise and the foolish virgins); and Lk. 12:35–38 (the parable of the waiting servants) refer not to a future eschatological judgment but to a situation and crisis in the early ministry of Jesus.[30]

174

He could see Jesus' message only according to this perspective, and he interpreted all the parables from his bias. At the same time, Dodd had introduced the kingdom of God as the subject of the parables, thus rejecting Jülicher's notion that a parable is always a general moral or spiritual instruction. Dodd recognized that the kingdom of God is the central subject and message of Jesus. From Dodd forward, therefore, what one holds to be true about the kingdom of God affects how one interprets the parable, and, further, how one interprets the parable affects how one perceives the kingdom of God.

Joachim Jeremias summed up the work of Jülicher and Dodd. He reworked his *The Parables of Jesus* making significant additions through the sixth edition in 1962, praising the work of Dodd in his introduction: "Professor Dodd's book has opened a new era in the study of the parables," and in spite of differences of opinion, "it is unthinkable that there should ever be any retreat from the essential lines laid down by Dodd for the interpretation of the parables of Jesus."[31] He continued to urge that the original meaning of the parables must be uncovered. His rewording of "revised eschatology" to read "eschatology in the process of realization" indicates that he was insisting further that the parables had to be interpreted with respect to their historical context in the ministry of Jesus.

> Each of his parables has a definite historical setting. Hence to recover this is the task before us. What did Jesus intend to say at this or that particular moment? What must have been the effect of his word upon his hearers? These are the questions we must ask in order, so far as may be possible, to recover the original meaning of the parables of Jesus, to hear again his authentic voice.[32]

Jeremias perceived that the parables have been reinterpreted in the Christian community. He determined that the method of reinterpretation could be reconstructed. For some parables an allegorizing interpretation has been appended, the best example being noted in the Parable of the Sower (Mk. 4:13–20). Some allegories are internal, such as might be the case in The Great Supper (Mt. 22:1–14, cf. 14:16–24) in which the fall of Jerusalem and the fate of Jesus and the prophets are represented by the killing of the servants and the king's dispatch of his army. In some instances an interpretation is formed by the addition of a moral, maxim, or adage. In a parable such as The Good Samaritan, the setting of the story itself, a crowd of listening Jews, gives interpretation to the parable's meaning.

Understanding the value of Jeremias's contribution, Perrin sees one prominent difficulty. Jeremias, he says, is primarily concerned with the message of the historical Jesus and therefore aims his interpretation of the parable to discover this message. In so doing, he fails to see the parables as texts "with an integrity of their own, needing to be interpreted in their own right."

His ultimate concern is the message of Jesus as a whole, and the interpretation of the parables is for Jeremias only a means to the end of reconstructing this message. For all the time and effort he has spent on the interpretation of the parables he is really only interested in them as contributing to an overall understanding of the message of Jesus. He does not respect their integrity as texts. [33]

Dan Otto Via, Jr. in his 1967 book on parables, began to bring some light to the interpretation of parables for preaching. He brought clarity to the question of whether a parable may make only one point, as Jülicher had maintained, or whether this view limits what the parable may be communicating. Further, he reversed the resistence to allegorical interpretation. An allegory, Via contended, "communicates to a person what he already knows, though it communicates it in symbolic and altered fashion."[34] Some familiarity with the story must exist in the minds of the listeners for the allegorical referent to make sense. It will for that reason completely confound the understanding of those who are without this necessary foreknowledge. Via contends that this may be the clue to understanding Jesus' words, "To you has been given the secret of the kingdom of God, but for those outside, everything comes in parables; in order that 'they may indeed look, but not perceive, and may indeed listen, but not understand; so that they may not turn again and be forgiven'" (Mk. 4:10–11 and parallels Mt. 13:10–15 and Lk. 8:9–10). The allegorist, Via pointed out, begins not with an image which suggests a meaning, but with a meaning for which he must find an image. There is a difference between interpreting a story which is allegorical and treating a story that is not an allegory as if it were, the practice which had influenced Jülicher's radical rejection of the parables as containing any allegory at all. Clearly some of the parables are allegorical in nature, and therefore this allegory affects interpretation.

Via's acceptance of allegory as a dimension of parable refutes Jülicher's one-point theory. Via asserts:

A particular parable may have one central point and also have other elements that call for consideration. An allegory corresponds at more points than a parable to the old story or the situation being referred to, but the dividing line is hard to draw; therefore, the difference is one of degree, not of kind.[35]

For Via, the possession of only one point is not a definitive qualification for a parable.

Via also moves away from an exclusively historical approach as primary for understanding parables. While seeking to discover the parable's *Sitz im Leben* is useful on the one hand, on the other, a strictly historical view of the parable fails to recognize its aesthetic dimensions. "Expressed in the broadest possible way," he writes, "the historical approach focuses on the historical context as a clue to the meaning of the parables while a recognition of their aesthetic quality would focus on the parables themselves."[36] Perrin enthusiastically enlarges on Via's insight.

> However important historical criticism may be it is not in and of itself hermeneutics. Even after one has achieved an adequate historical understanding of the parables there still remains the essential hermeneutical step of relating the historically understood text to the present of the interpreter. Having determined what it *said*, we have still to determine what it *says*; insofar, of course, as it *says* anything. We may determine that a text has only a purely historical interest for us, but most interpreters of the parables would strenuously resist that conclusion.[37]

Seen as aesthetic objects, the parables are literary in nature with recognizable deliberate organization within themselves. They have purpose and intent as they occur in the text so that their meaning cannot be separated from their literary integrity. "The goal of historical and literary criticism is to be able to take any text on its own terms," Via writes. Where parables are concerned, this axiom means that parables are better interpreted "by recognizing their aesthetic nature than by first of all deriving their meaning from the historical context or by making them illustrations of ideas."[38]

This understanding of parables as aesthetic objects permits Via to see them also as "language events." In the terms of linguistic analysis, they have a "performative function"—they accomplish something or cause something to take place. They become, as it were, an event, not merely telling listeners about their subject, such as the reign of God, but also involving them in it. They are, in this respect, especially vital to Jesus' kingdom-teaching purposes. They "introduce a new possibility into the situation of his hearers," and they call for them to make a decision. As a result, in the hermeneutical effort not only is the language interpreted and clarified, "but the interpreter and his situation are illuminated."[39]

Like Via, John Dominic Crossan, writing in 1973, is well versed not only as a New Testament scholar, but also as a literary scholar and critic. Their approach to their study of parables is similar, but while Via has no interest in Jesus as the author or speaker of the parables, Crossan is profoundly interested in the historical Jesus. The parables lead him to his understanding of Jesus, but more than that, "they contain the temporality of Jesus' experience of God; they proclaim and they establish the historicity of Jesus' response to the Kingdom." In a sense, for Crossan, the search for the historical Jesus is informed by the discovery of Jesus himself in the parables which reflect Jesus' life and historical situation. Crossan arrived at a view which contradicts interpretations coming to him from others.

There is, of course, more to Jesus' life than the parables which express its ontological ground. He was not crucified for parables but for ways of acting which resulted from the experience of God presented in the parables. In this regard the parables are cause and not effect of Jesus' other words and deeds. They are not what Joachim Jeremais called "weapons of warfare"; they are the cause of the war and the manifesto of its inception. In summary: as against Jülicher, the parables are not timeless moral truths beyond all and above all historical situations; but, as against Jeremias, neither are they to be located *in* Jesus' own historical experience as visual aids to defend a proclamation delivered before them and without them. Jesus' parables are radically constitutive of his own distinctive historicity and all else is located in them. Parable is the house of God.[40]

Moving from this point, Crossan begins to interpret parables by identifying clue or "key" parables which he says give guidance for understanding all others. The parable of the hidden treasure and the pearl of great price (Mt. 13:44–45) are among these. They share three main verbs–"finds, sells, buys"–which emerge for Crossan as the prototype for all parables–"advent, reversal, action." Jesus proclaims that a new age (advent), God's new reign, has come. Humankind is required to respond by turning away from their past (reversal) and moving in a new direction (action). "In their totality, . . . the parables proclaim the Kingdom's temporality and the three simultaneous modes of its presence appear most clearly in the key parables." Jesus is teaching us that "we do not live in firm time but on giant shifting epochs whose transitions and changes are the eschatological advent of God." Jesus is taking the third commandment seriously: "keep time holy!"[41] Not every parable contains all three modes reflected in the prototype, but Crossan can classify parables under headings which show which modes are predominant in each parable.

Through this understanding of the parables Crossan leads us toward a transforming action aimed at changing not only the immediate situation but also the world at large. John Fuellenbach concludes from Crossan's view that:

> what really drives the individual to action is the "joy" over the unexpected treasure, the great blessing of salvation, the experience of God's gracious giving that transforms life. Jesus is telling his listeners to realize God's gracious coming into the present enabling them to reverse their lives and become doers of a new kind of action. The parables of Jesus seek to draw us into the present of the Kingdom. They then challenge us to act and to live in accordance with this gratuitous experience.[42]

Norman Perrin draws heavily upon the work of both Via and Crossan in his approach to parables in *Jesus and the Language of the Kingdom.* He cites two reasons for his fascination with their study. The first is paradox. The parables challenge those who hear them to explore numerous possibilities of experiencing God as king. On the one hand, "God is to be experienced in the historicality of the world of everyday, while, on the other hand, [the parables] claim that God is to be experienced precisely in the shattering of that everyday world." In so doing, like good art and music, they bring us to the dangerous boundaries of human existence in the world where we are able to live only briefly from time to time and not every day. Perrin's second source of continuous fascination is "the sheer complexity of the hermeneutical problems they present."[43] He ends his update of his own interpretation of the word "kingdom" by acknowledging the enormous challenge that confronts the parables' interpreter. Perrin stands in awe of both the text and the hermeneutical task, finally saying that "the texts must be allowed to speak for themselves; all our efforts as interpreters must ultimately be geared to that end. It is as important for the interpreter to know where his work ends as it is for him to know anything else about the theory and practice of hermeneutics."[44]

N. T. Wright emphasizes the Jewishness of the parables. He perceives that they are intimately associated with the Jewish prophetic tradition. They are akin to the messages of Isaiah, Ezekiel, and Jeremiah, and, just as were the words of those ancient prophets, they are aimed at changing the contemporary world view. When properly received, Wright asserts, they are confrontational, subversive, and dangerous. The literary background of the parables is apocalyptic. They convey:

> a message designed to encourage those who 'have ears to hear' to believe that they really are the true Israel of the covenant god, and they soon will be vindicated as such—while the rest of the world, *including particularly the now apostate or impenitent Israel,* is judged. This is how apocalyptic literature works; this is the characteristic message it conveys. I suggest that Jesus' parables worked in much the same way, and conveyed (at this level of generality) much the same message."[45]

But clearly not all had "ears to hear," and so the parables are secretive. Wright reiterates frequently that Jesus is not merely a "universal teacher" giving us "timeless truths." Instead, he is the instigator of a movement, the planter of a seed that will grow into a plant before most are aware of it. The parables are, therefore, "necessarily cryptic." Their "explosive" nature escaped public interpretation, though some could and did hear and follow. Wright admits that our study of the parables is "as yet in its infancy" with much work left to be done. He stresses that the fruit of that work will come forth when "once, and only once, their total context, and setting within the ministry of Jesus is fully understood."[46]

With this perspective, then, the preacher may not commend a view of the parables that merely gives information about the kingdom of God or sketches a benign notion of God's reign as an intangible ideal. Wright maintains that the parables are actually a means of bringing the kingdom to birth. Referring to the work of Ben F. Meyer, he argues, "the parables are not merely *theme*, they are also *performance*. They do not merely talk about the divine offer of mercy; they both make the offer, and defend Jesus' right to make it." Stories in the Jewish idiom are a powerful way to accomplish this feat.[47]

Preaching the Kingdom of God

This brief historical sketch of the study of the kingdom of God in the church's later years leaves the preacher who must elucidate the synoptic message with a variety of somewhat contradictory interpretations. This shouldn't surprise us. When two commentaries consistently agree, one of them is unnecessary. Perrin admits that the task of interpretation is perpetually complex, and Wright assures us that the study is still in its infancy. At the same time, we can discern in these various studies a movement toward a growing awareness of the urgency of speaking the kingdom message and an increasingly practical approach to how it may be preached. The influence of literary and linguistic analysis not only teaches a more fruitful hermeneutic, but perhaps also, if we will allow it, it assists us in seeing what Jesus intended in a way that renders us less encumbered by our own cultural baggage.

We consider the parables to be sacred literature. We assume that they are basically religious in nature, because they are given to us by Jesus. Actually, on closer inspection, we can observe that the parables are secular stories. Some actually do have a religious Jewish setting. "Two men went up into the Temple to pray." "A man bought a vineyard." For the most part, however, parables are simply stories that come from life. The oral tradition of the first century held a place perhaps like our television, family yarns, books and novels, or movies and theater. The stories become sacred only because Jesus used them as vehicles to bring about an awareness of the reign of God. We interpret them with a spiritual eye of our own, which isn't all bad, but we would do well to begin our exegetical look at a given parable by seeing it as a simple secular story whose importance only comes about because of Jesus' use of it. In and of itself, the parable often has nothing of a religious nature to say.

Although the meaning of the parable in its original setting is important to be discerned, the parable as it appears in the scripture before us is also important. This is the reflection of the teaching of gospel as it was being accomplished during the first century, during the years immediately after Jesus' ascension and Paul's letter writing. We believe that the gospels were written to inform specific situations in the church and perhaps also to address specific congregations with specific points of view with the perspective of their authors. Within carefully guarded limits and always informed by the best scholarship we can muster, the text as it appears before us is that on which we will be preaching.

Several years ago I heard a painful lecture given by a seminary professor of New Testament who was refuting a statement he had received from a colleague: "New Testament scholarship has rendered the New Testament unavailable to preachers." The painful part of the lecture for us hearers was that the professor underscored and reinforced rather than refuted this critique of his academic calling. Clearly, such was not his intent, just as it is not the intent of scholars who have carefully studied and variously interpreted Jesus' kingdom of God preaching and parables for the last two centuries. On the contrary, the scholarly work briefly represented here, frequently contradictory though it may be, is a challenge to all preachers to search diligently for the meaning of the synoptic texts and to strive faithfully to interpret lectionary readings from the pulpit.

What will sermons be like from those preachers who take seriously their study of Jesus' central message in the synoptic gospels that "the kingdom of God has come near"? A number of characteristics will prevail in their sermons. Their preaching will have a strong sense of *urgency*. Jesus' kingdom-message is always a demand for immediate awareness and action. The message calls for a change in one's life. The formula Crossan perceives as the prototype of all synoptic parables, advent-reversal-action, endorses this sense of urgency in Jesus' purpose. We are cautiously aware that we do not, through our behavioral compliance, effect the coming of the kingdom, but we do respond to its ethic, its renewed way of life. Jesus is saying that the time for that response is now.

The kingdom-emphasis will call on sermons to be *confrontational.* Jesus' audience was not made up of people who did not believe in God. They were faithful worshiping Jewish believers for whom Torah was central and godlessness an abomination. They were also either complacent in their acceptance of the religious status quo, or they were sincerely entertaining end time expectations that were contrary to Jesus' message. He had to speak with a radical trouble-making effrontery to break through the wall of predisposed certainty that pious religious parlance somehow always allows to develop. The likeness of Jesus' audience fills our pews if not our pulpits as well. People made dangerous by their certainty that they already knew it all and had God's approval surrounded Jesus then just as they surround the church today. Jesus' preaching never insulted or demeaned, but it did confront, pull the rug from under, and find wanting. Today's preaching can be confrontational with the same tough grace.

The preacher must be ready to give a message that is somewhat *paradoxical and mysterious*. The kingdom of God is both here and now, but also not yet. With all our scholarly attempts to understand what we mean by kingdom of God, the message comes to us with some of the same wonder and question Jesus gave his disciples. We are "bold to say" his prayer that implores that the kingdom might come, but there is more faith than certainty in our awareness of what we are asking for, and the mystery makes us appropriately humble. Only the reckless are positive, and those with limited tolerance for ambiguity are doomed to even greater confusion. A part of the beauty of God's reign is its mystery, and proclaiming the kingdom's nearness is always paradoxical in the light of what we experience life to be like in the world today.

But with all of that, the kingdom of God sermon will include a message of *hope*. Jesus proclaims that God reigns even now in spite of appearances to the contrary. In Jesus' only friendly encounter with a scribe, he responded to the man's wise spiritual insight by saying, "You are not far from the kingdom of God" (Mk. 12:28–34). For those with ears to hear, Jesus' message was not abrasive or upsetting; it was reassuring and encouraging. Further, learning that faithfulness brings us near to the kingdom is a message of *peace*. While Jesus calls the world into question with his parables and his preaching, he also makes it a safe place for those whose faith is open to learning and growing. As we attune our ears to hearing, we are nearer to experiencing the reign of God ourselves.

The kingdom-sermon carries a message of *inclusivity* and *unity*. Even though few understood Jesus' parables as he was speaking them and few were with him to the end, clearly his message was to all who would listen or could hear. The divisions that exist among us over polity and doctrine actually have little place in the light of Jesus' universal message, the prayer he gave his disciples, and his challenge to go and tell. A unity exists among us even though we fail to recognize, honor, and celebrate it. Jesus' kingdom-teachings do not imply a discipline or structure for the church so much as they call for commitment and challenge us to repent and renew. The quality of personal life in the inclusive community of believers is stressed by the parables and the sermon on the mount much more strongly than are the structure or discipline of the church. Ironically, the reign of God brings unity to the community of faith in spite of our continuing separations. The metaphor implies only one God and only one kingdom. As Dodd urged us to realize, one begins to experience the kingdom at the point of faithful response.

Finally, kingdom-preaching will emphasize *justice*. As humankind is lifted to the level of equality in the kingdom, everyone becomes responsible for the well-being of others. This is more than all our good programs of missionary zeal, community concern, and local outreach; it is the good news of mutual responsibility. Jesus proclaims this truth the most strongly in the parable of the good Samaritan in which the mind of his listeners is stretched to understand the word "neighbor" as not only extending beyond what was commonly perceived, but extending limitlessly throughout humankind.

Ultimately, the preacher must understand that the kingdom of God is a spiritual concept and that it is central to all Christian spirituality. The image of God as king cannot be dismissed, as some try to do, as irrelevant to Americans in a free society who not only have no king but also have rejected the concept of monarchy in their declaration of freedom. The sermon that begins with "of course, you and I have no king" and continues by trivializing the metaphor simply won't wash. Such an avenue of avoidance is, in our contemporary slang, a "cop-out." In spite of the fact that our cultural orientation influences all our efforts at interpretation, we are obliged as part of the hermeneutical task to move as far as possible beyond that here and now influence to discern meaning and truth where we can. When worshipers pray "thy kingdom come," they are asking for the fulfillment of God's reign as Jesus Christ announced it and described it in his parables. Jesus' prayer anticipates the active and guiding presence of the God of all who reigns as king. While we may seek inclusive language that accommodates our concern about sexism, or we may struggle to find words less archaic for anti-authoritarian post-modernists, or we may question the word "king" and seek language more accommodating to the democratic government of free political states, we must remain aware that we are not at liberty to reject the nature of the reigning God spoken of in the authoritarian kingdom metaphor. It is entirely worthwhile and appropriate for us in our spiritual struggles to look for an intimate relationship with this God, a closeness, a personal familiarity and sense of divine presence. Such a pursuit is urgent. Whatever we may come up with within our private selves and our secret prayers, however, we must not negate the concept of a reigning king and both the already and also the yet to come kingdom in which we are joyful and free subjects of the God of history who even today saves and reigns. The message is one of both God's challenge and grace, and it longs to be preached and taught faithfully by God's courageous, humble, and faithful subjects.

Notes

1. N. T. Wright, *Jesus and the Victory of God* (Minneapolis; Fortress Press, 1996) 172.

2. Robert H. Stein, *The Method and Message of Jesus' Teachings* (Philadelphia: The Westminster Press, 1978) 62–3.

3. John Christopher Thomas, "The Kingdom of God in the Gospel According to Matthew," *New Testament Studies*, vol. 39, 1993, 141.

4. James H. Moorhead, "Engineering the Millennium: Kingdom Building in American Protestantism, 1880–1920," *The Princeton Seminary Bulletin*, supplementary issue, no.3, (1994) 105.

5. N. T. Wright, 209. For Wright's discussion of his use of a lower case "g" for God, xiv–xv.

6. Eduard Schweizer, *The Good News According to Mark*, Donald H. Madvig, trans. (Atlanta: John Knox Press, 1970) 45.

7. Dale Patrick, "The Kingdom of God in the Old Testament," from *The Kingdom of God in 20ᵗʰ-Century Interpretation*, Wendell Willis, ed. (Peabody, Massachusetts: Hendrickson Publishers, 1987) 70.

8. John Fuellenbach, *The Kingdom of God: The Message of Jesus Today* (Maryknoll, New York: Orbis Books, 1995) 188.

9. C. H. Dodd, *The Parables of the Kingdom* (London: Nisbet & Co., Ltd.,1956) 107. The term "realized eschatology" appears in Dodd's *The Apostolic Preaching and Its Developments: Three Lectures* (New York: Harper & Brothers Publishers, ca. 1935 [no date given]) 93.

10. Dodd, 108.

11. Ron Farmer, "The Kingdom of God in the Gospel of Matthew," Wendell Willis, ed., *The Kingdom of God in 20ᵗʰ-Century Interpretation* (Peabody, Massachusetts: Hendrickson Publishers, 1987) 122.

12. Farmer, 123.

13. W. Emory Elmore, "Linguistic Approaches to the Kingdom: Amos Wilder and Norman Perrin," *The Kingdom of God in 20ᵗʰ-Century Interpretation* (Peabody, Massachusetts: Hendrickson Publishers, 1987) 59.

14. Norman Perrin, *Jesus and the Language of the Kingdom: Symbol and Metaphor in New Testament Interpretation* (Philadelphia: Fortress Press, 1976) 33.

15. Perrin, 30.

16. Perrin, 196.

17. Perrin, 56.

18. N. T. Wright, *The New Testament and the People of God* (Minneapolis: Fortress Press, 1992) 302.

19. Wright, *People of God*, 303.

20. Wright, *Victory*, 151.

21. Wright, *Victory,* 199.

22. Robert H. Stein, *The Method and Message of Jesus' Teachings* (Philadelphia: The Westminster Press, 1978) 49.

23. Stein, 50–51.

24. Stein, 52.

25. Stein, 52.

26. Wright, *Victory*, 178, n. 127.

27. Perrin, 96. He is quoting Adolph Jülicher, *Die Gleichnisreden Jesu*, vol. I (1888–1889) 149.

28. Stein, 53.

29. Dodd, 32.

30. Stein, 53–54.

31. Joachim Jeremias, *The Parables of Jesus*, S. H. Hooke, trans. (New York: Charles Scribner's Sons, 1963) 9.

32. Jeremias, 22.

33. Perrin, 107.

34. Dan Otto Via, Jr., *The Parables: Their Literary and Existential Dimension* (Philadelphia: Fortress Press, 1967) 7.

35. Via, 13–14.

36. Via, 24.

37. Perrin, 144.

38. Via, 24.

39. Via, 53–56.

40. John Dominic Crossan, *In Parables: The Challenge of the Historical Jesus* (New York: Harper & Row, Publishers, 1973) 32.

41. Crossan, 34–35.

42. Fuellenbach, 76.

43. Perrin, 199–200.

44. Perrin, 201–202.

45. Wright, *Victory*, 178.

46. Wright, *Victory*, 181–182.

47. Wright, *Victory*, 176.

"From the Rising of the Sun to its Going Down": Times and Themes of Christian Daily Prayer

H. Boone Porter

THE PRESENT ESSAY will offer some reflections on time, especially on the morning and evening, from the perspective of Christian humanism and of respect and admiration for the created universe. Some pertinent biblical material will be briefly surveyed, and then the ancient themes of formal Christian prayer will be examined. With these considerations in mind, the Daily Offices of the Book of Common Prayer will be analyzed, particularly in the present American edition of this book.

The Mystery of Morning and of Evening

Sunrise and sunset are the most striking and unique events occurring frequently and regularly on this earth. They are not merely important points within time, but for us they *are* time, they constitute the framework of daily living both for humans and other warm-blooded creatures, and for plant life. The lives of almost all people are built upon a twenty-four hour cycle. Not only sunrise and sunset, but the intervals of solar movement–mid-morning, midday, and afternoon–have significance within our varying human cultures. It is within this framework and its ramifications that daily Christian worship, like other daily activities, has found its niches, but the exact ways it has done so, and the meanings it has had, have varied and do vary.

We may arise before or after sunrise, and some of us rarely see it. Does this event matter? It matters for more reasons than we can enumerate.

186

Sunrise is astronomically defined as the time that the place where we live, revolving eastward, has reached a certain angle toward the sun. Yet this scarcely suggests what sunrise means. Sometimes a little before or after, we and ten thousands of other creatures begin a new round of life.

Dawn does not come in a moment. First there is only twilight, a vague and apparently directionless light. Then, if we are up early, we can distinguish land and bodies of water. Next the forms of trees and plants appear clearly. Then the sun itself peeps over the horizon and soon climbs into the sky. Animals and birds become active and so too do we, often the late-risers. All of this is the daily reenactment of the story of creation on the first page of the Bible. Every day, this tells us, is God's day, God's creation, and we are invited to recognize it as such, and to be ourselves renewed as God's creatures. Thus it is suggestively expressed in Eleanor Farjeon's (1881–1965) morning hymn (Hymn 8, *Hymnal 1982*):

> Morning has broken,
> like the first morning,
> black-bird has spoken,
> like the first bird.
> . . . fresh from the Word.

Nature awakens, and we do too. How remarkable this is! At night we lie inactive, helpless, unconscious, appearing as if dead, resigned to whatever angelic protection there is. Some nights we are vividly in the land of the dead, seeing and conversing with dead people. Then we somehow resuscitate, a minor daily miracle for which the thoughtful will give thanks. Birds fly forth. Roosters crow. Various animals waken and crawl or step from their resting places. But men and women wake up; we get up.

Upness is of profound significance for us, ever since we struggled as babies to learn to stand and walk upright.[1] It is a pre-verbal perception for us as individuals, and perhaps as a race. To be down is to be helpless, perhaps wounded and defeated, sick, or actually dead. To be up is to be in control, healthy, awake, and alive. Even if we do not like leaving our bed and our minds are groggy, rising up is still an affirmation of our identity, our life, and our vital powers. Our erect posture sets us apart from almost all other mammals, and it is suggestive of the divine image in us.

What is the material expression of all this? Of course it is the sun. Rising from its invisible sleeping place, it moves steadily upward. Its light cheers the mind, and the day calls us to our duties and activities. Thus the morning, unhappy as it sometimes may be, is a minor resurrection, from down in helplessness and near-death, up into life and activity, a transition objectively and unfailingly affirmed by sunrise.

Morning is also for most people most of the time, a return to living in human society and intercourse. To talk in one's sleep is an object of humor. When one is awake, communication reflecting thought and consciousness begins. For the prayerful, it is also a time to speak to God.

Such considerations may evoke varying reflections in the reader, as we recall events in the morning, hopes in the morning, and challenges of different days. In any case, these considerations may provide sufficient substance to the concept we would describe as *the mystery of the morning*. It involves that story of creation which is unfolded at greater length each spring, and which is evoked more briefly in the lighting of the paschal candle and the first portion of the Easter Vigil. In the mystery of the morning, creation and resurrection touch each other as we allow our minds to be illumined by the Holy Spirit, and we may ourselves be lifted up by a sense of renewed creation.

The day unfolds. Mid-morning has its place. At noon, when the sun is at its zenith, there is a sense of plenitude. For centuries, it has been a time that bells are rung and today when whistles are blown. Work desists for the luncheon hour. For some it is again a time to pray, perhaps briefly and silently, or perhaps to attend a midday church service. Subsequently in the afternoon, fatigue sets in and work slows down. The day's end is foreseen.

There is *a mystery of the evening*, but it is not the same as that of the morning. For many, work has ceased and there is a quiet time. Perhaps one attends to some light chores in the garden or elsewhere. Ideally, the Christian humanist may feel, it should be a time of reflection and of prayer. Returning to Genesis, the evening should be the Sabbath of the day. The sunset is often the most beautiful sight of the day. Yet the sun's descent also speaks to us of the brevity of the day and of life itself. Soon it will be time for sleep once more, death's daily sister. In the prayer of the blessed Bishop Lancelot Andrewes (1555–1626):

> The evening draweth nigh: make it bright.
> There is an evening, as of the day
>   so of life withal:
> The evening of life is old age:
> old age hath overtaken me:
>   make it bright.[2]

Yet evening provides other elements. In the setting of artificial light, it is the time of sociability with family and friends. It is when we may eat and drink together. Parties are usually in the evening, and then even today, we prefer candle light. We sometimes enjoy music, dancing, or theatrical performances. It is the time for long conversations and for reading. It is a time for husbands and wives to be together. As opposed to the practical activities of the working day, these evening and nocturnal activities may be distinctly human and cultural.[3]

It is also to be recognized that today this classical and humanistic view of the evening is damaged. A quick supper of frozen food takes the place of a proper dinner. Conversation, music, and so forth are provided artificially by television. The latter may be an eye-opening and enriching experience for some, but on the whole our culture is making us idle, passive, irresponsible spectators of the scenes of life. The older experience of a family gathered by the fireside or with a candle or burning lamp in their midst, enfolded by the surrounding darkness, is a luxury for the few, and scarcely even a memory for the many. Even at churchly gatherings, the cocktail hour may crowd out Vespers from the schedule.

The mystery of sundown as a quiet interval, bringing the working day to a close, drawing us together around the light, and leading on certain occasions to festivity—this is something to be grasped for today. Here are primordial roots of civilized human society, speaking to us of older times, when sociability was something around a fire, when families were close, and the joys and sorrows of life and death were experienced and shared directly.

Another dimension of darkness is danger and the human sense of fear. Even if we lived in a world free of crime and drunken driving, any of us may stumble on an unlighted step and experience a serious fall. Danger is real, and fear may be exacerbated by the imagination, indeed we sometimes enjoy enhancing fear by a murder mystery or a ghost story. In any case, the desire to have the safety of light, to be warm and indoors, or if out-of-doors, to have the company of others, is all part of our perception of evening. Yet, paradoxically, we may find it enjoyable and even inspiring to stand outside alone and contemplate the moon and the stars.

So night comes, the time of slumber. What then is the mystery of evening, this time which comes daily, yet which remains puzzling, elusive, sometimes joyful and sometimes sad, lonely or dangerous? Quiet, peace, and ultimately death are part of it, but also pleasures and the wonder of light, even a little of which banishes darkness and danger. The setting sun gives natural expression to a part of this, as does artificial light, which humans alone have mastered. The evening involves nature, but also the fire we have added to nature. For Christians, there is the paradoxical memorial of the death of the Savior and of him as light come into the dark world.

The Bible and Daily Prayer

As Christians we properly look to the Bible for the roots of our faith and of our response to circumstances of life. There are of course numerous passages about prayer, particularly in Psalms. Appropriately, it is the poets of the psalter who often link prayer with particular time and who speak with admiration of morning and evening. A few examples may suffice. "Wake up, my spirit; awake, lute and harp; I myself will waken the dawn" (Ps. 57:8, 108:2). "In the evening, in the morning, and at noonday" (Ps. 55:18; cf. Dan. 6:10, 13). "The lifting up of my hands as the evening sacrifice" (Ps. 141:3). Worship by those "that stand by night in the house of the Lord" (Ps. 134:1).

As all readers of these ancient poems know, the psalmists speak of praying frequently, and they call on their readers to do likewise. Priests and Levites, all God's people, and, repeatedly, all nations are summoned to worship, as is the natural world. Many of the pertinent psalm verses are of great beauty and have established the spirit and feeling, as well as providing many actual phrases, for later Christian daily prayer.

For a rule of daily Hebrew worship, we look to the temple at Jerusalem. There, every morning and evening, a lamb was to be offered as a burnt sacrifice, together with cereal and a libation of wine. When the high priest tends the lamps morning and evening, incense is also to be burned (Ex. 29:38-42, 30:7-8, Lev. 24:1-4, Num. 28:1-8, Ezra 3:3, Ezek. 46:13-15). The exact spiritual function of the daily sacrifices is not explained.

These two daily sacrifices continued in the temple through the centuries, but the evening sacrifice was moved, apparently for convenience, to the mid-afternoon, the ninth hour. This became known as the hour of prayer and was apparently a popular time for worshipers to visit the temple, and we find the apostles doing so (Acts 3:1). Daily worship in synagogues developed later, and was to have at least a little influence on some Christian usages.[4]

The New Testament, like the Old Testament, strongly encourages frequent prayer. The Lord's Prayer, with its petition for daily bread, plainly implies daily use. The hour of prayer in the temple, however, is our first hint of fixed times of day when Christians prayed. Why was this time popular? It may be suggested that if the Mediterranean custom of a nap following the midday meal was generally observed, it was very suitable to attend worship just afterwards, before the distraction and business of the late afternoon had begun. Elsewhere in the New Testament, St. Peter prays at midday (Acts 10:9). Was this a customary time for prayer, or purely happenstance in this episode? In any case, if Peter's dream is a crucial revelation that Gentiles may be admitted to the church, the event is of some importance.

Early Christian Developments

As we move from the Bible to distinctly Christian developments of daily worship, our first stop is the book known as the *Didache*, or *Teaching of the Twelve Apostles.* Many believe it to have been written soon after the latest books of the New Testament. There is one paragraph on prayer.[5] After an injunction to fast on Wednesdays and Fridays, the text of the Lord's Prayer is given, with the laconic rubric, "Pray thus three times a day." We might assume this means morning, midday, and evening, but we shall see that this is not necessarily so.

The first real ancestor of the Book of Common Prayer is *The Apostolic Tradition,* ascribed to St. Hippolytus, a presbyter or perhaps bishop in Rome in the early third century.[6] Here many rules for operating a Christian community are briefly given, and prayers are suggested for ordination, baptism, and various other occasions—some of Hippolytus's words are still followed. The intended readers seem to have been the clergy or devout lay people.

Here the directions for daily worship are extensive.[7] Christians are to wash their hands and pray when they get up in the morning, and it is desirable to go to the church ("where the Holy Spirit abounds") especially on days when instruction is offered, or when a special teacher comes. Otherwise they should read the Bible at home. Deacons and presbyters are to meet with the bishop every morning.

At the third hour, our nine o'clock, one should pray, at least silently, remembering Christ's crucifixion at this hour (Mk. 15:25). Prayer at this time is also linked with the morning sacrifice in the temple. Would Christian shopkeepers in their little places of business along crowded streets have called for silence for a few minutes at these times of prayer? At noon, the sixth hour, the crucifixion is recalled and the darkness which then occurred. For the ninth hour, "great prayer and great thanksgiving" are called for—it is still an hour of prayer.

The individual is to pray before going to bed, and then rise for prayer again at midnight. At that time, all nature pauses for a moment, and the Lord may come again. At cockcrow Christians are once more to be at prayer, for then "the children of Israel denied Christ," but we look in hope of the resurrection "for his Day." It is in the last verses of Psalm 95, the *Venite,* that Israel's provocation and a warning for the day are spoken of. We can only wonder if this psalm was already in daily use. Although Hippolytus does not mention it, we naturally also think of St. Peter's denial at this time. It is part of the fascination of Hippolytus that, while explaining little, his provisions open the doors to many possible meanings.

What is more properly evening worship is described elsewhere, in the context of a church supper.[8] With the bishop present, a deacon brings in a lamp, and the bishop standing in the midst of his people blesses it first greeting them ("The Lord be with you") and bidding them to give thanks. He then thanks God for inextinguishable light through Jesus Christ, for the blessing of the past day, and the light of evening. A prayer of this sort was destined to become the ancestor of the later beautiful *Exsultet* at the Easter Vigil. After supper, young people sing psalms and specially blessed bread and wine are taken. The author reminds the reader that this is not the eucharist. Such a rite, with the people gathered to eat and drink together as a family around their bishop, illuminated by a light symbolizing Christ, provides a striking liturgical expression of the mystery of evening.[9]

While the events of the crucifixion are recalled, it is the main intervals of the natural and secular day which are observed.[10] Beneath the surface there is the movement of the sun, suggesting Christ raised high on the cross in the third and sixth hours, descending at the ninth, then being buried in the evening, and rising from the dead the next morning. It is this external and phenomenological aspect of the daily cycle which, we suppose, silently imparts its dynamism and which contributes to the power of the daily observance of the paschal mystery. The solar reference is quite explicit in some later formularies.

A contemporary of Hippolytus was the vivacious North African Latin writer, Tertullian (ca. 160–ca. 220). His essay *On Prayer* is helpful.[11] The Lord's Prayer is discussed at some length, as are some customs associated with public prayer, as the lifting of the hands and exchanging the kiss of peace. As to times of prayer, the third hour recalls the coming of the Holy Spirit, an important theme; Peter's prayer on the housetop recalls the sixth; and the apostles at the temple confirm the hour of prayer in the afternoon. As will be noticed, the typology is different from that of Hippolytus. These three occasions of prayer are also taken to symbolize the Trinity. Tertullian correctly observes that the scriptural passages do not command prayer at these three times, but they make it appropriate. Daniel's three times of prayer are taken to be these hours. Meanwhile, he writes, we need no admonition for "our regular prayers" morning and evening.

Three times of prayer honoring the Trinity are also spoken of by the Egyptian, Origen (ca. 185–ca. 254), the great scholar of the early church. He identifies the times as morning, the sixth hour (recalling St. Peter's prayer) and evening–a somewhat different view.[12]

Turning back to North Africa, the next great Latin Christian writer was the bishop St. Cyprian (ca. 205–258). Following Tertullian, he too wrote a treatise on prayer.[13] He similarly regards the three hours of prayer to have been observed by Daniel and his companions and to be symbolic of the Trinity. The third hour again recalls Pentecost, and noon recalls St. Peter's prayer. From the sixth to the ninth hour, Christ suffered for us. Cyprian then fills in the picture by urging morning prayer, "that the Lord's resurrection may be celebrated." Similarly, we must also pray at sunset, when the earthly sun departs, that we may have the light of Christ, our true sun. Cyprian goes on to expound Christ as our sun and our day. Prayer during the night is also urged, but no particular time within the night is specified.

It is thus with Cyprian that we have a rich scheme of daily prayer with a typology which will remain in centuries to come. With him, moreover, morning and evening regain their primacy. We must wait until St. Basil (ca. 330–379) in the fourth century assures us that previous generations were using the *Phos hilaron,* "O gladsome Light," when the lamps or candles were lit in the evening.[14] Here is the full cycle, as the understanding of Christ as our true light, while the material sun sets, is poetically expressed.

The worship of the early church provided a daily Christian response to the physical day and to the mystery of morning and evening, and related them to the paschal mystery of the redeeming works of Christ. It is not to be said that worship in the twentieth or twenty-first centuries should be exactly like that of the third. On the other hand, the physical day remains the framework of earthly life whether we like it or not, and the deeds of Christ remains the basis of our salvation. Thus the daily worship of the early church provides, at the least, a measuring rod and basis of comparison for analyzing and evaluating our own usages.

Later Christian Centuries

The history of daily worship in the middle ages[15] and Reformation era[16] is an interesting field of such scope and complexity that it cannot even be summarized here. Attention is to be given, however, to several points especially pertinent to the present study.

In the Eastern Churches, the greeting of Christ as our light at Vespers remains important, and the midday hours continue, among other things, to commemorate the coming of the Holy Ghost and the passion of Christ.[17] So much poetic, devotional, and prayerful material has been added, that it is difficult to discern single dominant themes in the different offices.

In the West, the offices have consisted mainly of psalms, together with biblical canticles and metrical hymns. The psalms provide extensive praise for creation which becomes the dominant theme in the whole daily cycle. Christological meanings must be read into the psalms by the worshiper. The Christian focus remained in the New Testament canticles in the morning and

193

the evening. Meanwhile, the multiplication of saints' days and other commemorations bring their own themes into the offices. A more massive change was the adoption of eucharist daily. The passion of Christ and our redemption became focused in the eucharistic liturgy.

In the sixteenth century Archbishop Thomas Cranmer (1489–1556) chose for his two morning and evening services the well-known canticles which were recited daily in the so-called "Little Office" provided in the books of hours or primers.[18] The canticles are the fixed acts of worship in Cranmer's offices. The *Venite* and Song of Creation celebrate creation, and the *Te Deum* and Song of Zechariah offer christological content, with some reference to resurrection. The Collect for Purity at the beginning of the eucharistic rite remains as a vestige of the recitation of the Third Hour before eucharist on Sundays and Feasts. The Holy Spirit was not much emphasized either in the medieval books or by Cranmer.

The Songs of Mary and Simeon give an incarnational emphasis in the evening, with brief reference to Christ as the "light to lighten the Gentiles."

Cranmer, like his predecessors, saw the eucharist as the place to celebrate redemption, that rite having virtually no reference to creation. The historic themes of the offices were further mitigated by the lengthy Old and New Testament lessons with their own points of interest from day to day. Yet in Cranmer's offices the few canticles, repeated day after day, acquired a powerful place in the hearts and memories of regular worshipers. These services have proven fully usable for private recitation, stately choral services, and less formal recitation by smaller congregations on weekdays. In the seventeenth and eighteenth centuries, such daily recitation was widespread.[19]

Since antiquity, various prayers of intercession and petition have been recited at the end of various offices, in behalf of the church, the state, those in need, and so forth. There does not appear, however, to have been a consensus for attaching particular prayers of intercession to particular times. It may be mentioned at this point, however, that in the Anglican tradition the Great Litany has provided a comprehensive and eloquent prayer expressing the church's concern for all aspects of earthly life. It was formerly required after Matins on Sundays and also on Wednesdays and Fridays, the ancient weekly fast days. It was certainly so used on Sunday. In churches having Matins daily, we may assume the Litany followed the office on the appointed days. For churches in which the morning office was not said daily, it was not uncommon, in past centuries, for Matins and Litany to be recited on Wednesdays and Fridays. We trust it was a pastoral occasion meeting the prayerful needs of many suffering illness and other misfortunes.[20]

The midday offices and Compline retained some place in private Anglican devotion, as in the greatest of the English Primers, *A Collection of*

Private Devotions, 1628, by John Cosin (1594–1672).[21] Many other devout handbooks have offered devotions at intervals during the day, often based more or less on the historic patterns.

The Present American Prayer Book

In the light of the foregoing considerations, what do we find in the 1979 American Book of Common Prayer? First of all there is a change in balance from earlier editions, a change already adumbrated in 1928. The penitential opening, once an earmark of Anglican worship, may be shortened or omitted. Biblical lessons are usually short, and one is encouraged to have only one lesson at one of the offices—usually Evensong. In this case it may become a highly devotional and a less didactic service.[22] The creed may be omitted at one service, and the prayers proposed at the end of each office are briefer. Thus the whole service may be relatively short, and the acts of worship in the canticles, of which there are now many, stand out more clearly.

Of the traditional themes we have discussed, creation is still prominent in the *Venite* and Song of Creation. It is to be noticed by people today that in the latter the various creatures offer their own worship to God: they are not simply the servants of humans. The Song of the Lamb also honors the Creator. For the resurrection, the Easter invitatory may be said on nearly one seventh of the year. The Song of Moses, the Third Song of Isaiah, and the Song of the Redeemed are all read in the light of the Easter message. So too are the Song of the Lamb, the *Gloria in excelsis*, the *Te Deum*, and less explicitly in the Song of Zechariah (The suggestion that the latter be read after the Old Testament lesson may diminish the christological reference.) In our worship we not only acknowledge the resurrection as a fact, but honor Jesus as our living Lord who has made us his fellow-heirs.

An outstanding expression of the paschal mystery for regular morning use is the prayer, "O God the King eternal . . ." by William Reed Huntington (1838–1909). Here creation, morning, the hope of the resurrection, and the Song of Zechariah are beautifully brought together.

In the evening, a new note is struck with "O gladsome light," from the Eastern Church Vespers. It seems to have been widely welcomed. Any of the morning canticles may be used, but the Song of Mary or of Simeon are generally preferred. These give an incarnational perspective. The Song of Simeon continues to speak of Christ the light. Again there is a fine Huntington prayer, "O God, the life of all who live," which links life, light, death, and Christ's resurrection. Thus the ancient vesperial theme of Christ as our light is fully restored.

With only two offices the events of the passion cannot be assigned to successive hours of the day, but the historic themes are now integrated into the week, with Christ's crucifixion and death spoken of on Friday in the collects and suggested most weeks in the choice of psalms. Saturday is the Sabbath, but it is surprising that our Lord's own rest in the tomb is not spoken of. Sunday is plainly the day of light and of the resurrection. Perhaps the gift of the Holy Spirit is not sufficiently articulated.

The 1979 Prayer Book has three peripheral offices. The Midday Office may be used at approximately the Third, Sixth, or Ninth Hours, and collects appropriate to these Hours, referring to the gift of the Spirit, the prayer and dream of St. Peter, and the passion (not in that order) are given.

The Order of Worship for the Evening focuses on Christ and the gift of light in various ways. As used to introduce Evensong, or as the basis for some other form of evening worship, it is very flexible. The classic concept of the evening is expressed in a prayer adapted from Bishop Andrewes:

> Blessed are you, O Lord, the God
> of our fathers, creator of the
> changes of day and night, giving
> rest to the weary, renewing the
> strength of those who are spent,
> bestowing upon us occasions of
> song in the evening . . . [23]

Compline inevitably echoes some of the material of Evening Prayer, with the Song of Simeon and prayers for protection. One may wonder why Christ's burial was not recalled here, and why there is no petition for the departed.

During recent generations, large numbers of Anglicans have known Morning Prayer or Matins exclusively at eleven o'clock on Sunday. Obviously its link with sunrise became tenuous. In the era of the 1928 edition of the Prayer Book, widespread use of the shorter canticles eviscerated much of the theological content of the office. By evicting Matins from this place on Sundays, the 1979 Prayer Book would appear to have clarified the historic early morning position of the office.

Yet the public use of Sunday Matins, now clearly celebrating creation and the resurrection, has diminished. On weekday mornings, the office competes with the daily eucharist in many places, although the two may be felicitously combined with Matins as the Ministry of the Word. There has also been some interchange of content, with creation now being spoken of in the eucharistic prayer and Christ's passion entering the Daily Office on Friday. One may wonder whether increased attention to the Holy Eucharist on Sunday may lead to some reduction of its use on weekdays in the twenty-first century.

It is evident that the offices of the 1979 Prayer Book offer great variety. The ancient recognition of the mystery of the morning and of the evening is there, in minimal or very full form, depending on the choices made. This is somewhat integrated with the paschal mystery on ordinary days, and more fully on Friday and Sunday. There is a double thrust: the natural day, creation, and its spiritual significance on the one hand, and the story of Christ's redemption of us on the other. It is hoped that an awareness of these themes will assist those performing the offices, in public and in private, to make sensitive choices of material, and to experience the joy of celebrating and of entering into these sublime mysteries.

Notes

1. The author is indebted to the Rt. Rev. Arthur A. Vogel for this helpful insight regarding children.

2. Lancelot Andrewes, *The Private Devotions* (Gloucester, Mass., 1983) 107, and other editions.

3. Sebastian de Grazia, *Of Work, Time, and Leisure* (Garden City, 1964) 108.

4. C. W. Dugmore, *The Influence of the Synagogue Upon the Divine Office* (Westminster, 1964) Chapter 4.

5. C. N. Jefford , ed., *The Didache in Context* (Leiden and New York: Brill, 1995) 5. The footnotes in this essay are mainly to aid English language readers, and several texts we will cite are most easily accessible to such readers in the *Ante-Nicene Fathers,* cited as *ANF,* with volume and page. For n. 5 here, *ANF* VII, 379.

6. The office and commendable position of Hippolytus are discussed at great length by Allen Brent, *Hippolytus and the Roman Church in the Third Century* (Leiden, 1995).

7. Geoffrey J. Cuming, *Hippolytus: A Text for Students* (Bramcote, Notts., 1976) 27, 29–31. *The Apostolic Tradition* is so short that the places can be easily found in other editions.

8. Cuming, *Hippolytus,* 23ff.

9. N. D. Uspensky, *Evening Worship in the Orthodox Church* (Crestwood, N.Y.: St. Vladimir's Seminary Press, 1985) 14–19.

10. Dugmore, *Influence of Synagogue,* 66–7.

11. *On Prayer,* xxv, *ANF* III, 689–90. In another place, Tertullian also speaks of the church supper, but mostly in terms of its dignity and sobriety, Apology, xxxix, *ANF* III, 47.

12. Origen, *On Prayer* xii, 2, quoted by Maxwell E. Johnson, *Liturgy in Early Christian Egypt,* Alcuin Club (Cambridge, UK: Grove Books 1995) 40.

13. Treatise IV (on the Lord's Prayer) 34, 35. *ANF* V, 456–7

14. Quoted, among many others, by Robert Taft, *The Liturgy of the Hours in East and West* (Collegeville, MN.: Liturgical Press, 1986) 78.

15. Taft's account, n. 14 above, is outstanding.

16. An outstanding treatment is G.J. Cuming, *A History of Anglican Liturgy* 2nd edit. (London,UK: Macmillan, 1982). Much unusual information is offered by George Guiver, *Company of Voices: Daily Prayer and the People of God* (New York: Pueblo, 1988).

17. These three classic themes are quite explicit during Lent. Isabel F. Hapgood, *Service Book of the Holy Orthodox-Catholic Apostolic Church* (3rd ed.)(Brooklyn, NY: 1956) 46, 50–1, 55.

18. The contents of the primers of the Tudor era are most accessible in *Private Prayers during the Reign of Queen Elizabeth,* Parker Society (Cambridge, 1851). The contents of the important King's Primer of 1545 can be seen here with the footnotes of the Primer of 1559, 1–114.

19. J. Wickham Legg, *English Church Life from the Restoration to the Tractarian Movement* (London, 1914) 108–10, offers a three page chart with times and occasions of nearly 100 parishes in London and Westminster for six years in the period from 1692–1824. A somewhat different and briefer chart is given by Guiver, *Company of Voices,* 118. The modern reader may be surprised that some of the metropolitan parishes offered one or both offices twice each day, to accommodate the schedules of working people and of the more leisurely.

20. Guiver's chart, n. 19 above, indicates widespread observance of Wednesday and Friday in London churches in eighteenth century.

21. John Cosin, *A Collection of Private Devotions,* P.G. Stanwood edit., (Oxford, 1967) a fine annotated edition; several earlier editions exist.

22. On the other hand, the choice of using three lessons at one office has the opposite effect, making the service very didactic.

23. Andrewes, *Devotions,* 108, 113, 117.

"Established by God in Creation": Were Adam and Eve Really 'Married'?

William Seth Adams

WHAT A JOY IT IS TO WRITE so as to honor Marion Hatchett! While there are other valiant souls who have labored to serve the church as liturgical scholars and teachers, surely no one else in recent times has enhanced so abundantly the life of liturgical study and reflection in the Episcopal Church as has Dr. Hatchett. Nor can anyone match his contribution to the store of resources for liturgical musical learning. We are all beneficiaries of his graces.

Having so said, one must go on to say that in order to do Professor Hatchett honor, one ought to offer a deep and thorough treatment of something significant, something on which much might turn, something of concern to the broader liturgical world. What I have to contribute is rather more modest than all that, but it is offered with no less honor intended. What concerns me in these remarks is a small thing, niggling really, but still deserving of few moments of puzzlement and consideration. The issue goes back to an assortment of assumptions and convictions from very early times, convictions now (and for centuries before) enshrined in the Prayer Book rite for marriage. (This matter attracts no attention in Professor Hatchett's *Commentary on the American Prayer Book* beyond a passing historical reference[1] and Leonel Mitchell, in *Praying Shapes Believing*, gives it no time to speak of, either.[2])

Among the rites contained in the Prayer Book, the marriage rite is the only one to contain an opening declaration, an announcement or description of what we are about.[3] In the current edition of the Prayer Book, in the declaration that begins "The Celebration and Blessing of a Marriage," we read, "The bond and covenant of marriage was established by God in creation . . . " A bit later we are told that marriage is to be entered into "in accordance with the purposes for which it was instituted by God."[4] It is this declaration that draws our attention, the suggestion that "marriage" was instituted by God, that "marriage" was established in creation.

I have been intrigued by this claim for a long time, unsettled by it I would admit, sensing that there was something unstable or not entirely dependable about it. As this concern has risen in me, it has become harder and harder to make this announcement at the beginning of weddings. This declaration, after all, is a liturgical rehearsal of what we want to "teach" people about marriage. Though surely "a didactic monologue," as Jennifer M. Phillips has called it, and not to be treasured beyond that, this declaration is where the church announces publicly its fundamental claims about marriage.[5] What we say in this setting is particularly important since it is at weddings (and funerals) that the Prayer Book has the most significant access to non-Episcopalians. This being so, what we declare in this setting is both catechetical and, in a way, evangelical. Consequently, in this appropriate and necessary catechetical work, we ought to be on solid ground. We ought to be saying what we mean and what we intend to mean.

I think that currently we are not. And this conviction/suspicion has led to assorted musings.[6] What follows is something of a digest of these rather undisciplined wonderings.

Another contributing factor to the teasing of my curiosity is the concern about the blessing of same sex unions, a concern with which I have much sympathy. In Andrew Sullivan's *Virtually Normal*, his suggestion that "marriage" is the right word for what is desired by gays and lesbians seeking the church's blessing on their promises, causes me and others to hope that the whole idea of "marriage" will be re-thought.[7] As I read the draft of the proposed rite for the blessing of such unions that came from the first consultation of Episcopalians on the blessing of same sex unions, I was struck not only by its general beauty, but also by the fact that there was nothing specific to same sex couples about it. Its premise, language, imagery, all these were inclusive of couples in general, whatever the mix of sexes. Indeed, this text came into my possession as I was about to marry, and the proposed text bore rather directly on matters of my heart.[8]

Perhaps, then, in some way, these modest ruminations will contribute to this fundamental "re-thinking." I would be pleased were that so.

I cannot leave these introductory remarks without saying that the form of this essay is likely not a form that Marion Hatchett would choose. It may not even be one he would favor. He (and others no doubt) will find this exercise far too speculative and undocumented ever to associate it with his own careful and commonly well attested scholarship. Frankly, what I offer here, I hope, will be the stimulus for someone else's more detailed consideration of matters I will treat rather breezily. It will also be very clear that my research has been in the service of my own assumptions. I have tried to be obvious about this so the reader will not have to be suspicious of my motives. I have tried to make my concerns obvious and to make it evident that I am searching for sources that will support them. I hope that someone will be moved to take what I suggest and to expand my speculation. I look forward to that more rigorous further development of what may prove, in my hands, to be delightfully loose-jointed.

The Prayer Books and their Companions

First, we should look at the Prayer Books. Through the years, what have we announced to people at the beginning of the marriage rite? What have we taught people about marriage? A search of Prayer Books ancient and modern yields a rather narrow range of language about the matter under review. In the first English Prayer Book (1549), we find "holy matrimonie" described as "an honorable estate instituted by God in paradise, in the time of mannes innocencie . . . "[9] Subsequent English Prayer Books have said essentially the same thing. The companion to the current English Prayer Book (1662), the *Alternative Service Book 1980 (ASB)*, declares that "marriage is a gift of God in creation and a means of his grace . . . "[10] Though not quite the equivalent of a modern turn on the older phrase, this phrasing nonetheless still accounts for marriage by invoking the creative impulse of God, be it gift or institution.

The claim of divine institution has also been current in the American Prayer Books, although the 1979 Book of Common Prayer (BCP) introduced the refinement "bond and covenant" of marriage which had not appeared before so far as I know. Though this addition mildly deflects the concerns driving the current inquiry, in the end, this change continues to invite puzzlement.

A look at Prayer Books and other books in current use across the Anglican Communion yields other evidence. The Canadian *Book of Alternative Services 1985* takes the English *ASB* teaching and refines it to read, "Marriage is a gift of God and a means of grace," making no mention of creation.[11] *A New Zealand Prayer Book 1989* offers three forms for marriage. None of them has a declaration like the one in question. The First Form speaks thusly, "Marriage is a gift of God our creator, whose intention is that husband and wife should be united in heart, body and mind."[12] In use in the

Province of Southern Africa, *An Anglican Prayer Book 1989* makes no connection between marriage and creation in the declaration in the rite itself. However, in the preface, we are told that marriage exists by "divine institution" and that because such is the case, marriage is "a lifelong and exclusive union and partnership between one man and one woman."[13]

Further searching yields similar results and need not take space here. It is simply true to say that, even from this rough sampling, it is clear that for the most part and over the larger span of time, we have and still do claim that "marriage" or "the bond and covenant of marriage" is somehow a product of divine intention and divine institution. This is certainly the "tradition."[14] And it has its obvious source.

Source and Commentary

Charles Wheatley's commentary on the Book of Common Prayer, *A Rational Illustration of the Book of Common Prayer of the Church of England,* was first published in 1710. It was the most widely used commentary in England during the eighteenth and nineteenth centuries. He begins his exposition of the rite of marriage by saying,

> That this holy state was instituted by God, is evident from the two first chapters in the Bible: whence it came to pass, that amongst all the descendants from our first parents, the numerous inhabitants of the different nations in the world, there has been some religious way of entering into this state, in consequence and testimony of this divine institution.[15]

To this beginning, the author appends a footnote citing patristic and conciliar testimony in support of his observation. From Genesis, Wheatley extracts the idea that there is "some religious way of entering into this state [marriage]," and presumably he would place the rite in the Prayer Book in this lineage.

Kenneth Stevenson, whose *Nuptial Blessing: A Study of Christian Marriage Rites* is likely the most common source in current use among Anglicans, writes about the biblical history of marriage by saying, "The Old Testament gives us a varied picture, but hardly a consistently worked out scheme. At root, however, is the conviction that marriage is divinely inspired."[16] Indeed, Stevenson writes in these early pages of his good book from the assumption/conviction that these central passages in Genesis are indeed unquestionably about marriage and could not be construed otherwise. Stevenson also argues, as others have before him, that Gen. 1:26–29, where the "image of God" is described and the charge is made to "be fruitful and multiply," is directed at a monogamous, married couple.[17]

My wanting commentators to lay aside these kinds of assumptions finds little encouragement, even in the texts themselves. That is to say, I cannot "blame" commentators for passing on to countless generations what seems to have been the assumption of the writer/editor of these passages in the first place.

In the New Revised Standard Version of the Bible, the *ur* text reads:

> . . . the rib that the LORD God had taken from the man he made into woman and brought her to the man. Then the man said, "This at last is bone of my bones and flesh of my flesh: this one shall be called Woman, for out of Man this one was taken." Therefore a man leaves his father and mother and clings to his wife, and they become one flesh. [Gen. 2:22–24]

And if we look at Jesus' connection to the Genesis story, we find, for example in Mk. 10:7–9, that the assumptions of the original writer, the assumptions of the tradition of interpretation and the assumptions of Jesus are all alike. Jesus quotes Gen. 2:24, "'For this reason a man shall leave his father and mother and be joined to his wife, and the two shall become one flesh.' So they are no longer two, but one flesh. Therefore what God has joined together, let no one separate." [It seems more than a little ironic, given what I am up to, that this citation to the views of Jesus should occur as he begins a discussion on divorce.]

Granting the dearth of "traditional" commentators willing to say what I hope to find, I have sought some relief in the work of feminist critics. I have discovered that there is only a limited amount of such help to be found.

Why is "marriage" presupposed in the creation story? Even in reading feminist writers, little challenge is raised to the use of the word "wife" to name the woman. In Mary Phil Korsak's new treatment of Genesis, summarized in "Genesis: A New Look,"[18] no challenge is raised to the introduction of the social institution of "marriage" into a story about sexuality and companionship.

Similarly, in *Discovering Eve: Ancient Israelite Woman in Context*, Carol Meyers seems accepting of the language of "wife" and "marriage" in association with Gen. 2. Meyers wants to argue for a kind of mutuality and complementarity in this story. "In the ideal world of Eden, male and female complement each other." She goes on, "The conjugal bond rather than the parental bond is given priority. Only in *marriage* [emphasis mine] are male and female complementary parts of the whole, for the parent-child relationship is an intrinsically hierarchical one in a way that the wife-husband one is not."[19] Aside from reminders of natural law and what is "natural" about the conjugation of male and female bodies, the author's willingness to accept "marriage" as the proper designation for the relationship of proto-man and proto-woman is remarkable. And if "conjugal" is taken to mean "related to marriage" as most dictionaries would suggest, it is a remarkable word to use to describe this sexual union, if "sexual union" be what "one flesh" means. Again, how have we moved from sexuality and companionship to "marriage"?

On the other hand, and happily, sources of genuine aid are those offered by Phyllis Trible and Christopher Webber. Trible's important book *God and the Rhetoric of Sexuality*, written in 1978, treats the creation stories in Gen. 2 and 3 in a chapter called "A Love Story Gone Awry."[20] Here she scrupulously reconstructs the second Genesis account of creation, and does so in a way that sheds good light on the matter of current interest.

Trible does not follow the pattern of most translators when she comes to 2:24–25, the point at which the woman in the story is called "wife." Trible calls her "his woman," referring to her association with the man. "Therefore a man leaves his father and his mother and cleaves to his woman." Trible writes, "The result of this convergence of opposites is a consummation of union: 'and they become one flesh.' No procreative purpose characterizes this sexual union; children are not mentioned. Hence, the man does not leave one family to start another; rather, he abandons . . . familial identity for the flesh of sexuality."[21] It is not "marriage" finding expression here, but rather sexuality. Whatever "marriage" may be, this Genesis story, at the hands of Phyllis Trible, is not ammunition for its endorsement, furtherance or even its existence.

In *Re-Inventing Marriage: A Re-view and Re-vision*, Christopher Webber writes engagingly and with insight about the current and perhaps future state of marriage (though sadly without discussing the possibility of "marriage" between persons of the same sex). In straightforward terms, the author reports, "The Book of Genesis . . . makes no reference to either love or 'marriage' in the story of Adam and Eve. Eve was brought to Adam as a companion and, after the Fall, they 'knew' each other and raised Cain."[22] Exactly! As Webber says a few pages earlier, " . . . the creation of male and female was for companionship, not procreation."[23]

These kinds of insights move us in the new and promising direction, one toward some new language that we might offer in our liturgical teaching about marriage, a direction towards which we shall move eventually. For the moment, we need to entertain the suggestions of Bruce Kaye.

Kaye, an Australian writing in *Colloquium: The Australian and New Zealand Theological Review*, has taken a hard look at the biblical idea of "one flesh," an idea given first voice in Gen. 2.[24] In his exploration, Kaye begins to wonder why the writer/editor of Genesis introduces the idea of "marriage" into the second creation story. In Kaye's view, this move on the author/editor's part means that the story will "sanctify marriage very profoundly." Kaye goes on, "It means, as an aetiological story, that the marriage which is known to the writer and his contemporaries is now said to be, in its social relations and in its internal relationships, something which participates in and derives from an original and foundational intention of God"[25] And the implications of this claim are precisely what the Prayer Book continues to announce to anyone who might be listening.

Kaye goes on to speculate as to what might provoke the writer/editor to such a move. "[T]he comment can be regarded as taking the general picture of the relationship between man and woman in the creation story and drawing it into relationship with a particular social problem with which the institution of marriage was confronted." Kaye's hunch is that what it says in Gen. 2:24–25 "may be addressed to a situation in which marriage was being interfered with by external pressure, perhaps from near relatives."[26] Very interesting! This perhaps suggests more than many would want to say about the work of the writer/editor of the Genesis story, but it continues to point us in the direction chosen by Webber and Trible, and that is the way we want to go.

The surest thing to say about God's intention as recorded in the Genesis material is to say that if we see there the "institution" of anything at all, it is the "institution" of an antidote to loneliness. The story seems to demonstrate God's sympathy with the human situation and God's generosity in overcoming primordial despair.[27]

Speculation

I have never sought to explore the history of marriage before. As a divorced and remarried person, I have had my share of dealings with the realities of marriage but have never before been provoked to ask some rather fundamental questions: How is marriage "accomplished"? Is marriage the product of a wedding or of something else or of nothing else? What is marriage for? Does biology have to do with marriage? For human beings, is sexual expression sufficient to "accomplish" marriage? When one asks, "Where does/did marriage come from?" a variety of answers can be imagined. One answer moves us forward.

Eustace Chesser, writing in the mid–1970's in a book with the tantalizing title, *Is Marriage Necessary?*, observes quite directly, "Marriage . . . is a product of society, not Nature."[28] Further, he writes, "Marriage is not a biological necessity but a means of stabilizing whatever social order exists."[29]

Here I find something like what I have been looking for. And coincident with this discovery is my re-reading of Sharon Welch's *Communities of Resistance and Solidarity: A Feminist Theology of Liberation*.[30] This has stimulated my imagination and given it a certain "flavor," as the following will attest.

Typically, I have discovered that the scholarly study of these questions does not engage the matter the way I wish it did. I have a notion that over time, something called "marriage" evolved; that it evolved from something less "institutional" to something more so. [Related to the views of Bruce Kaye as cited earlier, I suspect that this view of marriage had evolved by the time of the writing or writing down of the Genesis story.] I have the notion that "marriage," as the evolved institution, was something of interest and necessity to certain groups in society and not to others. That is, I imagine that people of property, principally men of property, found "marriage" more necessary and attractive than men and women of more diminished economic standing. To the extent that "marriage" is a socio-political reality, aimed in some measure at least at protecting and conveying money and property, to that same extent it would be of no interest to the poor. Similarly, if matters of "legitimacy" were of interest, it would only be of interest to those who had property to protect from claims of "illegitimacy." Whatever social stigmas might be attached to this category, the taint of "illegitimacy" is surely economic in origin. "Illegitimate" would typically mean "not entitled to inherit." What Chesser describes seems to make sense of this view.

Is it this social institution that the church wants to claim was established by God in creation? I would hope not. Further to this question is the lived experience of people, particularly women, as participants, even "partners," in "marriage," as historically and socially understood.

Without looking too hard at "marriage," and without particular reference to any given culture or age, it seems indisputably true that many good and beautiful things might be said about "marriage." But from these same points of view, it is also possible to say other things. "Marriage" is, for example, the context for submission and domination [with biblical warrant], for spousal abuse and neglect, for sanctified savagery, for political control, for the making of political and military alliances. In certain times and places, while one can imagine that "marriage" might be a means by which women might be empowered or enriched to certain levels, it is more typically the means by which women have been trivialized, demeaned, ravaged and caused to "disappear." Even in our own time, the taking of the husband's name is a reminder of that disappearance.[31]

One wonders if these realities and the tradition they conjure are what the church means to credit with divine institution. Or is divine institution in reality the warrant by which much that is sad and sorrowing has been made tolerable in "marriage."

In an era when "family values" flourish within a vaporous biblical mist and when Anglican bishops are heard to say in public, "What the Bible says is what we do!" voices more in touch with both human experience and the tradition of biblical interpretation are necessary and useful.[32] These voices need to be added to the mix and perhaps challenge the received tradition. And there is the very real fact of divorce to season the conversation!

Moving now in another direction, and going directly back to the Genesis material, one wonders about another way the realities of this story could be construed, much to the frustration of those who would despair at this tactic. [It will not turn out the way critics will want.]

In an article published in the *Anglican Theological Review* entitled "The Church Does Not Make A Marriage," Louis Weil recounts his experience as a priest in Puerto Rico.[33] He reports that in the early 1960s, statistics indicated that perhaps 80% of the "marriages" extant in a specific locale were accomplished by "consensual unions," that is, without any role being played by the church, or the government for that matter. Professor Weil says that Puerto Rican law recognized these unions as legal and counted the children as legitimate.[34] Moving from this experience, Weil argues that it is always the couple who "make" the marriage, whether in rural Puerto Rico or anywhere else. He also declares his distaste for the role the church plays in marriages as the agent of government in many places, as the church's ordained ministers serve as license signers and, by implication, license fee gatherers. (Like many others in my position, I share this distaste.) His point is that it is the action of the couple that "makes" the "marriage" and not the action of the church. It is the church's role and delight to bless such unions, not to accomplish them.

Now, taking this well made point as to the couple's role in accomplishing the "marriage," and laying that side by side with the Genesis account in which generations of critics and commentators seem to find "marriage," one is able to raise an interesting suggestion. If "marriage" is accomplished by the couple, and if the Genesis account is rightly to be treated as attesting to the divine "institution" of same, then the Genesis pattern for the making of a "marriage" is very simple.

In Genesis we read, " . . . a man leaves his father and mother and clings to his wife, and they become one flesh" (2:24) Clearly, then, it is "leaving" and "clinging" that accomplish the "marriage," if that is what this text is about. The making of "one flesh" by the act or art of "clinging" is the necessary kernel, and apparently all that is required, *if* this text is about "marriage."[35] One also must wonder about what the Prayer Book means when, in the prayers for the newly married couple, it speaks directly to God suggesting that it is God who makes the woman and the man "one flesh."[36] Who *is* the "maker" here?

So, now we come to the matter: To what exactly is the church [and the Bible] according divine institution? Is it "marriage" as a politically, socially, economically informed and conditioned historical "institution," or is it something else? Or, to press the matter even further, is there in the Genesis story any "institution" at all? And, whether there is or not, what should we say, if anything, at a gathering that celebrates and blesses the promises of a loving couple?

What to Say, Then?

Does the rite for Christian marriage require a declaration at its outset? Do we need to tell people what we are doing and why? When I began these remarks, I confessed that I had been thinking about the Prayer Book claim for some time, troubled by its apparent misrepresentation. Part of my hesitation in writing anything about this unease had to do with coming to this point in the exercise, the place where something constructive would be needed.

I am clearest about what we ought not to do. That is, we should not continue to say that "marriage" is God's institution, citing Genesis (and Jesus' use of it) as our warrant. We should also recognize "marriage" to be what it has been over time and not imagine it to be otherwise. Truth telling requires that we listen to other voices on the subject which need to be heard, voices that would announce what Sharon Welch (after Michel Foucault) would call "subjugated knowledge."[37] These voices would rightly temper our claims and inform our theological perspective. This is not to say that we would need to rehearse the failings of "marriage" as an overture to the ritualization of promise making. It is just that these "voices" ought to inhibit our eulogizing "marriage" and invite us into quite specific theological categories.

What might these categories be? They would include the following:

- faithfulness modeled on the fidelity of God;
- companionship modeled on the example of Jesus and his command to love as he loves;
- respectful and joyous sexuality tied to the goodness of creation;
- mutuality anchored in a common view of humanity's penchant for both good and evil; and
- the abandonment of both "submission" and "domination" from our theological vocabulary. (This last would require the avoidance of saying "[The bond and covenant of marriage] signifies to us the mystery of the union between Christ and his Church," as the Prayer Book now puts it—following biblical precedent. This image unavoidably leads to the association of Christ's "headship" of the church with the role of the bridegroom in the "marriage." This is very like what the writer of the Epistle to the Ephesians does in Chapter 5:25ff.)

In addition to these, and as we admit that this promise-making rightly expresses itself in and with the body, so also we admit that it expresses itself in and with the Body. As intimate as sexuality and promise making are, their sociality is not private to the promise makers. For Christians, the sociality of "marriage" is part of the life and sociality of the Body of Christ. In several senses, "marriage" is both "corporate" and "corporeal."

If we say anything at the beginning of the rite, these kinds of themes and concerns might serve to inform the text, though it seems quite a lot. At the same time, my real intent is not so much to provide content as it is to test and perhaps challenge what we are saying now. I would not shy away from the constructive work associated with text writing but I am more concerned now with the frustrating work of arguing against what we currently say, and have said for a long time.[38]

Earlier I expressed the hope that someone would be intrigued enough by this exploration to take it further, both backward in details and forward in implications. For the present, I myself can say no more on the matter, other than to wish that someone else will be awakened to do the Marion Hatchett-like hard work that remains to be done, work I have in some measure either neglected or assumed. Should that come to pass, I will be glad.

Notes

1. Marion J. Hatchett, *Commentary on the American Prayer Book* (New York: Seabury, 1980) 432–433.

2. Leonel Mitchell, *Praying Shapes Believing* (Harrisburg, PA: Morehouse, 1985) 187.

3. Burial II invites such a declaration [492] but it is optional and no "script" is provided.

4. The Book of Common Prayer, 423.

5. Jennifer M. Phillips, "A Critique of the Rite of The Celebration and Blessing of a Christian Marriage," in *A Prayer Book for the 21ˢᵗ Century: Liturgical Studies 3*. Ed. Ruth A. Meyers. (New York: Church Hymnal Corporation, 1996) 126.

6. I have gone through this sort of doubting process before, as I have reported in "Given and Shed for Whom? A Study of the Words of Administration," *Anglican Theological Review*. LXVII/1 (January 1985) 31–45.

7. Andrew Sullivan, *Virtually Normal: An Argument About Homosexuality* (New York: Alfred A. Knopf, 1995).

8. The language that struck such a warm chord was contained in the vows, where each promises to love and cherish the other "as my companion, lover and friend." *An Illustration of a Rite for the Celebration of Commitment to a Life Together*. Privately circulated: November 1994, 11.

9. 1549 English Prayer Book, 252.

10. *Alternative Service Book* 1980, 288.

11. *Book of Alternative Services* 1985, 528.

12. *A New Zealand Prayer Book* 1989, 780.

13. *An Anglican Prayer Book* 1989, 457.

14. At the recent Lambeth Conference of Anglican bishops, during the discussion

of the report on human sexuality, the bishop representing the group of bishops from Central and East Africa reminded the assembly that marriage "is ordained of God in creation." This statement was not made so much in support of marriage, but rather as a part of a strategy to blunt any "accommodation" of homosexuality by the assembly. This is reported from the author's own personal experience.

15. Charles Weatley, *A Rational Illustration of the Book of Common Prayer of the Church of England* (London: G.B. Whittaker, 1985) 404.

16. Kenneth Stevenson, *Nuptial Blessing: A Study of Christian Marriage Rites* (New York: Oxford, 1983) 5.

17. Ibid., 4.

18. Mary Phil Korsak, "Genesis: A New Look," In *A Feminist Companion to Genesis,* Athalya Brenner, ed. Sheffield, UK: Sheffield Academic Press, 1993.

19. Carol Meyers, *Discovering Eve: Ancient Woman in Context* (New York and Oxford: Oxford University Press, 1988) 86.

20. Phyllis Trible, *God and the Rhetoric of Sexuality* (Philadelphia: Fortress, 1987) 72–143.

21. Ibid., p. 104.

22. Christopher Webber, *Re-Inventing Marriage: A Re-view and Re-vision* (Harrisburg, PA: Morehouse Publishing, 1994) 191.

23. Ibid., 188.

24. "'One Flesh' and Marriage." *Colloquium.* Volume 22/Number 2 (May, 1990) 46–57.

25. Ibid., 49.

26. Ibid.

27. This interpretation, of course, unintentionally suggests that (1) marriage is God's "preferred" solution to loneliness; and (2) that there is something perhaps "unGodly" about living or being alone.

28. Eustace Chesser, *Is Marriage Necessary?* (London and New York: W.H. Allen, 1974) 9.

29. Ibid., 19.

30. Sharon Welch, *Communities of Resistance and Solidarity: A Feminist Theology of Liberation* (Maryknoll, New York: Orbis Books, 1985).

31. In the midst of writing this essay, I attended a wedding at which the preacher talked about the mutuality of marriage, about the woman and man as equal partners in this new relationship. By the time the couple was introduced to the congregation, however, the woman had "disappeared." She was named in this formula, "Mr. and Mrs. John Jones." Whatever name she bore before, in formal address it was gone, and so was she.

32. This comment was made in the midst of the report from the bishops of West Africa during the human sexuality debate at Lambeth 1998. Author's notes.

33. *Anglican Theological Review* LXXII:2 (1990) 172.

34. Ibid. The author says nothing about the Church's reaction.

35. On this interpretation, though it goes further than she does, Phyllis Trible's insights are interesting. She, too, fixes on "leaving" and "cleaving." *God and the Rhetoric of Sexuality,* 104. Bruce Kaye touches the same matter. "'One Flesh' and Marriage." 48.

36. BCP 429.

37. See Welch, *Communities of Resistance,* 20ff.

38. I have done this before. See note 6 above.

The Entry into Jerusalem in Liturgical Tradition

Thomas J. Talley*

A BROADLY WELCOMED FEATURE of the Book of Common Prayer, given final authorization for use in the Episcopal Church in 1979, is a series of Proper Liturgies for Special Days, providing modern adaptations of some of the older forms of worship for special occasions known to liturgical history and others of somewhat later development. One of these proper liturgies that has found wide acceptance and use is that for what is styled, "Sunday of the Passion: Palm Sunday." It is characterized by an opening "Liturgy of the Palms," celebrating the triumphal entry of Christ into Jerusalem, and the account of that entry is read from one of the synoptic gospels, according to their distribution by the triennial lectionary. In the following eucharist of the Sunday of the Passion, the passion narrative is read from the same gospel. These two liturgical functions are linked by a procession of the congregation, bearing palm branches, from the place of the Liturgy of the Palms to the church where the eucharist is to be celebrated. This dual liturgy presents a unified aspect that casts into high relief the ironic contrast between the shouts of "Hosanna," with which the crowds greeted Jesus at his coming into Jerusalem, and the shouts of, "Crucify him," with which the same crowds rejected him on Good Friday. Worshipers today

---

*The author wishes at the outset to express his gratitude to his learned neighbor and friend, Frederick Platt, without whose intelligent, generous and indefatigable assistance this essay, however flawed, could never have been written.

may well benefit from that dramatic reminder of the peril of inconstancy, but, as we shall see, the juxtaposition of the celebration of the entry into Jerusalem and the liturgy of Passion Sunday is more the result of liturgical evolution than of conscious design.

In his extensive *Commentary on the American Prayer Book,*[1] Professor Marion Hatchett, the respected colleague and friend whose contribution to liturgical studies this volume celebrates, observes that many of the ceremonies that had been associated with particular days in the liturgical year were condemned in the book of homilies issued in 1547 and were prohibited by the Injunctions of Edward VI.[2] Among these was the Palm Sunday procession, with the consequence that the Sunday at the head of Holy Week was called only "the Sunday next before Easter" in the Book of Common Prayer of 1549 and its successors until this century. Although it is likely that the reformers' rejection of the blessing of things was an element in the removal of the palm ceremony, nonetheless, as we shall see, the character of the Palm Sunday procession in English ceremonial, especially as exemplified in the widely followed Sarum Use, struck at the heart of Cranmer's eucharistic theology.

Although it is unlikely that they were motivated by liturgical conservatism, the reformers' rejection of the Palm Sunday procession left the Prayer Book focused entirely on the reading of St. Matthew's Passion on the day at the head of Holy Week, giving the English liturgy precisely the focus of the liturgy of Rome in the time of Leo the Great and still in the time of Gregory the Great. In Roman liturgy, the celebration of Christ's triumphal entry into Jerusalem was a late addition to the Sunday liturgy already characterized by the proclamation of St. Matthew's Passion. Not every church in the West had always observed that Sunday with the reading of the passion, although by the time of the reformation that dual celebration of the entry and the passion had taken deep root in popular piety.

However, as with so many of the more bold initiatives of the Cranmerian program, the radical excision of Palm Sunday failed to extirpate that concept from English memory. The Chronicle of the London Grey Friars reports for 1550, "Item the XXX[ti] day of Marche was Palme sonday," and for the following year, "Item the XXIJ day of Marche was Palme sonday." An entry in the diary of Henry Machyn for 1560 refers to, "The VIJ day of Aprell, the wyche was Palm sonday." A register of St. Peter's, Cornhill, notes that in 1635 one Thomas Hind made provision of six pounds and twenty shillings to the minister for preaching a sermon every year upon the eve of Palm Sunday. While these and other incidental references to Palm Sunday reported by Vernon Staley[3] testify to the persistence of traditional terminology even when it derived no support from the Prayer Book; they do not indicate any attempt to restore to the Sunday next before Easter the commemoration of the Lord's triumphal entry into the Holy City.

Things may have begun to shift by 1821, by which time, it seems, John Keble had written the poem, "The Children in the Temple," which, in 1827, he included in *The Christian Year*, under the title, "Palm Sunday." Based on Lk. 19:40, it is concerned in the first instance to encourage poets to employ their gifts in the praise of God, ". . . to lead / His Hosannas here below."[4] There are allusions to the voices of children and to flowers and stones, but there is still nothing here that would make a hymn in honor of the triumphal entry. But in the same year as the first edition of *The Christian Year*, a collection by Reginald Heber was published in the year after his death in 1826, entitled *Hymns, written and adapted to the Weekly Church Service of the Year*. There the hymn appointed for Palm Sunday is the great text by the Oxford professor of poetry, Henry Hart Milman, "Ride on, ride on in majesty."[5] Here there can be no doubt that the hymn is intended for a liturgy which celebrates the entry into Jerusalem, and sees that as intimately connected to the passion, as revealed in the line, "in lowly pomp ride on to die." It is difficult to doubt that in some form, at least in hymnody, the triumphal entry had regained a place in Anglican liturgical life at the head of Holy Week.

Hymnody in the Episcopal Church was long limited to metrical psalms, a selection of which were frequently bound up with the Prayer Book. But in 1874 the first separate hymnal was issued for the church, and there we find a section of hymns for "Palm Sunday and Passion Week." The first hymn in that section is "All glory, laud and honor," an important element in the medieval Palm Sunday procession. Composed by St. Theodulph of Orleans (ca. 750–821), its very structure suggests the liturgical processions in which, by at least the middle of the tenth century, it became so firmly rooted. Here, again, it is the triumphal entrance into Jerusalem that is celebrated, but as oriented toward the passion that provided the older content of this Sunday before Easter. In that first hymnal of 1874, "All glory laud and honor" is followed immediately by "Ride on, ride on in majesty." Yet, of Christ's entry into Jerusalem on this Sunday at the head of Holy Week, the liturgy of the Book of Common Prayer still said nothing.

Revision of the lectionary for the Daily Office has long required a less complex procedure than revision of the Prayer Book itself. The lectionary for Morning and Evening Prayer was amended in 1883, some six years after that first hymnal, and the Old Testament reading at Morning Prayer was now Zech. 9, including its memorable ninth verse so often associated with Christ's entry into Jerusalem: "Rejoice greatly, O daughter of Zion; shout, O daughter of Jerusalem; behold, thy King cometh unto thee; he is just, and having salvation; lowly, and riding upon an ass, and upon a colt the foal of an ass." Even though this appointment of Zech. 9 suggests a step toward the recovery of Palm Sunday, the New Testament reading was still Mt. 26, the beginning of Matthew's passion narrative. Those appointments for Morning Prayer continued in the first revised Prayer Book of 1892, and a new edition of the hymnal, approved in that same year, changed the section on "Palm Sunday and Passion Week" to "Holy Week," still retaining "All glory, laud and honor"as the first hymn in that section, followed by "Ride on, ride on in majesty."

When I was young in the church, palms were much in evidence as decorations on what we all called "Palm Sunday," as had the Prayer Book itself in the subtitle, "Commonly called Palm Sunday," appended to "The Sunday next before Easter" since the revision of 1928, the first overt mention of Palm Sunday in the Prayer Book since the Reformation. The processional cross, often veiled in violet since the preceding Sunday, would have fronds of palm tied to its shaft, though the procession, with one of the great processional hymns, was simply the usual approach to the sanctuary, itself adorned with palms on the altar. Apart from such decoration, a small wicker basket of crosses fashioned from palm leaves stood by the door so that departing worshipers could take one and, with a straight pin provided, attach it to their clothing. With all this, the Prayer Book text itself said nothing at all of actual palms or the triumphal entry until 1945, when a revision of the lectionary appointed Mk. 11:1–11 as an alternative to Mt. 26 at Morning Prayer.[6] With that development, one might say that the Book of Common Prayer had come once again to celebrate both Christ's triumphal entry into Jerusalem and the passion on the Sunday at the head of Holy Week, although hardly at the same service, since by 1945 the celebration of both Morning Prayer and Holy Communion at a single service would have been extremely rare, if it happened at all. Still, a recovery in which the hymnal seems to have led the way had finally found some slight expression in the Prayer Book. Finally, in 1960, a new edition of a supplemental *Book of Offices* provided forms for a blessing of palms and a Palm Sunday procession in a section devoted to "forms for certain traditional ceremonials of the Christian Year that have had widespread revival throughout the Church in recent times."[7]

The celebration of Palm Sunday, however, had not been so laconic in those Anglo-Catholic parishes that followed one or another of the missals that blended the provisions of the Book of Common Prayer with elements of the *Missale Romanum* of Pius V. There, instead of the relatively brief Palm Liturgy now shared, with but modest variation, by the Episcopal, Lutheran and Roman Catholic churches, the Liturgy of the Palms presented a full word liturgy including an entrance chant, collect, a reading from Exodus, a gradual, and St. Matthew's account of the triumphal entry. A collect in the place of the usual *Secreta*, its concluding "world without end" sung as ekphonesis, led into the eucharistic dialogue, a preface concluded by the singing of *Sanctus*, and a series of prayers for the blessing of the palm branches. The branches, sprinkled and censed, were distributed at the altar rail, and then the procession began, moving around the churchyard, all bearing palm branches and, when the procession turned back toward the church, singing "All glory, laud, and honor" in dialogue with cantors inside the church. The crucifer knocked on the doors with the foot of the cross, and the procession reentered the church to the singing of further anthems regarding the Lord's entrance into the Holy City. Then the eucharistic liturgy began anew with the introit and was completed without further reference to the palms, save that all held their palms in their hands during the Passion according to Saint Matthew.

It was a somewhat different rite that the English reformers knew in the medieval English uses such as were followed at Salisbury and Hereford, known for the magnificence of their ceremonial. Similarities to the use of Rouen, the capital of Normandy, have suggested that this English ceremonial tradition, along with many other aspects of church life, was a consequence of the Norman conquest, though no direct dependency can be found in any cathedral.[8]

At Salisbury, after the customary sprinkling of holy water, an acolyte stood before the altar and read Ex. 15:27–16:10, and then, with no intervenient chant, the deacon at once read the account of the entry from the twelfth chapter of the Gospel of John. That Fourth Gospel establishes a chronological connection between the triumphal entry and the passion that Matthew and the other synoptic gospels do not (an oddity evidently overlooked in the modern rite in which the synoptic accounts of both the entry and the passion are read over three years). After this gospel, the flowers and branches were exorcized, blessed, aspersed and censed. After a further prayer, the palms were distributed to the people while two antiphons were sung.

Although not mentioned in the oldest (thirteenth century) of the manuscripts used by J. Wickham Legg in his edition of the *Sarum Missal*,[9] later manuscripts describe the preparation of a *feretrum*[10] with relics, from which, in a pyx, hung the Blessed Sacrament. While the distribution proceeded, this was carried in a separate procession to the place of the first station.

The distribution completed, the congregation and clergy processed, while antiphons were sung, to the place of the first station, where they met the previously transported Blessed Sacrament as the populace of Jerusalem met Jesus on the Mount of Olives. There the deacon read another gospel account of the entry, this time Mt. 21:1–9, the account read before the procession in the *Missale Romanum*. In the *Sarum Missal*, perhaps to conserve velum, that text is not presented with the rubric prescribing its proclamation at the first station, but rather a note included in the rubric directs the deacon to find the text in the proper for the first Sunday of Advent.[11] This suggests, of course, that that account of the entry into Jerusalem was already appointed for the first Sunday of Advent when the ceremonial of the Palm Sunday procession took shape. Moreover, in view of the clear redundancy with the earlier Johannine account, it may well be that the inclusion of this second gospel of the entry, Mt. 21:1–9, represents an accommodation to the rite followed at Rome in the thirteenth century.[12]

What is more interesting, perhaps, is the evidently older reading of that passage at Salisbury on the First Sunday of Advent, an appointment continued in the Book of Common Prayer until the 1979 revision of the American book. Although one cannot know how old this appointment of Matthew's account of the entry for the Advent liturgy really is, we do find it in the Comes of Murbach, a system of lections at the eucharist prepared, it is believed, to be used with the Frankish Gelasian Sacramentaries of the eighth century. That series of readings begins with the feast of the nativity, and presents at the end of the year a series of Sundays of the Advent of the Lord. There are five such Sundays. The gospel appointed for the first is Jn. 6:5–14 and that for the second of them is Mt. 21:1–9. When later development standardized an Advent of but four Sundays, the first, once known in Prayer Book tradition as "the Sunday next before Advent," its gospel still Jn. 6:5–14, gave way to make the old second Sunday the new "First Sunday of Advent," a change already evident in the *Sarum Missal* in the thirteenth century. The scheme laid out in the Comes of Murbach runs from the first *Parousia* to the second, beginning the year with the celebration of Christ's coming into history, and concluding the year with the celebration of the second coming at the *eschaton*. Professor J. Neil Alexander has shown this same pattern in other liturgical sources.[13]

Christine Mohrmann has observed that since the time of the Ptolemies, *Parousia*, like *epiphania*, was a technical term for the arrival or visit of a king.[14] That explains the appointment of our Lord's triumphal entry into Jerusalem as a sign of his coming *Parousia*. Other strains in the evolving liturgical year, however, would speak of the Sundays preceding the feast of the nativity as "Sundays of Annunciation," and would treat this as a time of preparation for the nativity festival, emphasizing the roles of St. John the Baptist and the Blessed Virgin in the mystery of salvation. In the end, the four Sundays of Advent found themselves at the beginning of liturgical books, and the First Sunday of Advent, its gospel in Anglican tradition the

Matthean account of Christ's triumphal entry into Jerusalem, came to be regarded as the beginning of the Christian Year.

By the thirteenth century, in any case, that passage of Matthew was read also at the first station of the Palm Sunday procession at Salisbury. At its conclusion, the procession, led by the shrine with relics and the Blessed Sacrament, carried on the shoulders of two priests, went to the place of the second station, where *Gloria, laus et honor* was sung. The third station was at the west door of the cathedral, and there the shrine with the Blessed Sacrament was held on high by those carrying it, and the procession entered the cathedral, all bowing to pass beneath it. A fourth and final station was at the rood in the cathedral, which was then unveiled before the beginning of the liturgy of the Passion.

This custom of carrying the Blessed Sacrament in the Palm Sunday procession has been attributed to Lanfranc, Abbot of Bec, although that is difficult to establish with certainty.[15] It was, in any case, but one occasion on which the Eucharist might be carried in procession. Nonetheless, it is difficult to read the twenty-sixth and twenty-ninth of the Forty Two Articles of 1553[16] (or their later parallels in the Thirty Nine Articles) without suspecting that their opposition to the carrying about and lifting up of the sacrament reflects a further theological agenda in the reformers' abolition of the Palm Sunday procession. Such a treatment of the sacrament would be totally incompatible with the receptionist eucharistic theology set forth so forcefully in the Prayer Book of 1552.

The abolition of Palm Sunday by the English reformers, as noted above, left this Sunday next before Easter focused entirely on the Passion of St. Matthew. This had been the case at Rome from at least the time of Leo I, judging from his sermons, and the blessing of palms and procession came to that city late, imported from Frankish and Germanic territories. The old Gelasian Sacramentary knows this Sunday as *Domenica in Palmas de Passione Domini,* and *Domenica in Palmas* (or a variant) appears as a title in Gregorian Sacramentaries of the ninth century, none of them a Roman document, but these give only the prayers for the mass, none of which refer to palms or the entry. In a few later manuscripts there is a preliminary *benedictio palmarum,* but this is clearly an addition.[17]

The Romano-Germanic Pontifical,[18] produced at Mainz around the middle of the tenth century, would provide the foundation for the Palm Sunday rite found later in the Roman Pontifical of the twelfth century and later Roman tradition, although for the opening rite the Mainz pontifical appoints the gospel of the entry according to Mark, rather than Matthew.[19] In spite of this and other differences, it is clear that the core of the Palm Sunday rite made familiar to later generations in the *Missale Romanum* of Pius

V came to Rome with the Ottonian emperors, as but one example of the liturgical change wrought by German influence.

Behind that Germanic tradition there is an earlier but incomplete blessing of palms in the Gallican Bobbio Missal from the late seventh century. The earliest complete ordo for the blessing and procession is found in Spain, in the sixth-century Mozarabic *Liber Ordinum*.[20] Here the palm blessing and procession are prefixed to an older liturgy focused on the delivery of the creed, *traditio symboli*, a climax to the lenten catechetical program customary in many churches on this Sunday at the head of Holy Week. The gospel appointed for that older mass (Jn. 11:55–12:13) seems to have been chosen in consideration of the Johannine reference to the proximate Passover, and ends just at the point of the beginning of the entry into the city.

There is virtually universal agreement that the introduction of a Palm Sunday procession in the West was an influence from pilgrims to the Holy City who had participated in such a procession there. Indeed, our earliest mention of such a procession is from the travel diary of such a pilgrim, Egeria,[21] a native of a western European locale, perhaps Gaul or Spain. Probably a religious, her description of the liturgical life of Jerusalem is now believed to pertain to the year 383.[22] She describes a gathering on the Mount of Olives in the early afternoon of the Sunday at the head of "Great Week," or Holy Week (31.1). Her account assigns no special designation to that Sunday, and nothing seems unusual about the morning liturgy. However, at one o'clock in the afternoon, all gather at the church called Eleona on the Mount of Olives. There, hymns and psalms are sung, lessons are read, and prayers are offered. At about three o'clock this activity moves to the nearby place of the Ascension, Imbomon, and at about five o'clock, after a reading from Mt. 21,[23] the procession descends to the city, all carrying branches and singing Psalm 118, arriving at Golgotha for the evening office, Lucernare.

Although Egeria insists endlessly that antiphons, hymns and readings are "appropriate to the day and the place," she is seldom more specific regarding scriptural texts. For more information on those, we are dependent upon the Jerusalem lectionaries of the first half of the following fifth century, preserved to us in Armenian translations. The editor of the best of those manuscripts, Dom Athanase Renoux, observes that by the early fifth century the gathering on the Mount of Olives has been shortened by two hours and that there are no scripture readings mentioned there. By contrast, the morning liturgy at the Martyrium (the basilica at Golgotha) has taken its theme from the increasingly popular afternoon exercise, and now refers to this Sunday as "the day of palms," and Christ's entry into Jerusalem, which in Egeria's late fourth-century account found its only commemoration at the afternoon function on the Mount of Olives, has now, in the early fifth century, become the theme of the morning liturgy at the Martyrium. The gospel appointed for the morning liturgy is Matthew's account of that entry, Mt. 20:29–21:17.[24]

Because Egeria's is our earliest account of that procession, it has become a commonplace to assert that the liturgical celebration of Christ's triumphal entrance into Jerusalem originated in the Holy City. In fact, although the procession probably did originate there, there is reason to suspect that what we find reported by Egeria represents an accommodation to the expectations of pilgrims, bringing to Jerusalem with them their sense of what events particular days commemorate. What we see in Jerusalem, in other words, is sometimes an acting out in the historical locales of scriptural themes established for those days in other liturgical traditions, traditions that shaped the expectations of pilgrims to Jerusalem. For reasons that I hope will become clear, this question of the hagiopolitan origin of the commemoration of the triumphal entry will require a summary, at least, of a perhaps complex argument that I have presented elsewhere.[25]

As we noted above, there is no suggestion in Matthew's gospel that the triumphal entry occurred in close temporal proximity to the passion. That use of Matthew, Jerusalem's favored gospel, would pose no serious problem if Jerusalem's celebration of the entry were following a custom established elsewhere, and based on the chronology of the Fourth Gospel. There is no reason, however, to predicate the commemoration of Christ's entry into Jerusalem on the Sunday before Easter as a totally new liturgical phenomenon on the basis of the Gospel of Matthew. If this observance originated in Jerusalem, affection for Matthew's gospel notwithstanding, one would expect the account of the entry from the Gospel of John, the only gospel to establish such a chronological connection to the passion.

It was, in fact, a passage from the Gospel of John that was read the previous day, the Saturday of Lazarus, in Bethany, atop the Mount of Olives. Here, however, Egeria's report is specific only with regard to an announcement of Pascha read at the dismissal from the liturgy at the Lazarium, the tomb of Lazarus. Egeria says: "Then at the dismissal a presbyter announces Easter. He mounts a platform, and reads the Gospel passage which begins, 'When Jesus came to Bethany six days before the Passover'" (29.5). She then adds, "They do it on this day because the Gospel describes what took place in Bethany 'six days before the Passover,' and it is six days from this Saturday to the Thursday night on which the Lord was arrested after the Supper" (29.6). This was not the only reading from John on that day, because before the procession arrived at the Lazarium there was a preliminary station at the point where Mary met Jesus and reported Lazarus's death. This was about a half mile before the Lazarium. Some part of Jn. 11 was read there, but how much is not clear.[26] Perhaps the account of the raising of

Lazarus was read when the procession arrived at the Lazarium, but we are not told.

What is clear is that in the fifth-century lectionaries there is no further mention of that preliminary station, and the passage announcing the coming Passover, Jn. 11:55–12:11, is no longer read at the dismissal, but is the gospel appointment for the liturgy at the Lazarium, although what it recounts is not the miraculous raising of Lazarus from the dead, but a subsequent visit of Jesus to Bethany, the occasion of his anointing by Mary. What had been a commemoration of the raising of Lazarus has in just a few decades become oriented entirely toward the coming Pascha and there is no mention on this Saturday before Great Week of the raising of Lazarus. We have two sermons for that Saturday from the great fifth century Jerusalem preacher, Hesychius, and of them the editor of Hesychius's sermons, Michel Aubineau, says: "it seems indeed that the liturgical feast of the Saturday was oriented rather toward the proximate 'Great Week,' toward Pascha and the Passion of the Lord."[27] Here again, the ephemeral celebration of the raising of Lazarus at Bethany, reported by Egeria, can best be understood as a response to the expectations of pilgrims whose native liturgical tradition knew this Saturday to be an important festival celebrating the miraculous event at Bethany. This observance was not native to Jerusalem, where the gospel account of the raising of Lazarus was read on the fifth day of the Epiphany octave in Egeria's time, and a day later in the Armenian lectionaries.

At Constantinople, on the other hand, the six weeks of Lent are given to a course reading of Mark on all Saturdays and Sundays, the only days on which eucharist was celebrated during Lent. On the fifth Sunday of Lent the gospel reading is Mk. 10:32–45, and on the following Saturday, the next celebration of eucharist, Mark is dropped abruptly in favor of John for the next two days, the account of the raising of Lazarus on Saturday and the triumphal entry into Jerusalem on Sunday. Then the Constantinopolitan cursus takes up the Jerusalem gospel lections from Matthew for Great Week itself. This use of the Gospel of John on these two days is compellingly suggestive, in my view, that it was the liturgy of Constantinople that prompted the afternoon commemoration of the raising of Lazarus at Bethany on the Saturday before Great Week and the celebration of Christ's triumphal entry into Jerusalem on the following day in the liturgy of Jerusalem in the late fourth century, as reported by Egeria.

Apostolic Constitutions V.13 orders a two-day hiatus between the fast of forty days and the six days of the paschal fast in Holy Week. That suspension of fasting on the Saturday and Sunday between the fast of forty days, ostensibly predicated upon the imitation of the fast of Jesus, and the older paschal fast, one or two days extended to six from the first half of the third century, would correspond to the peculiar two-day switch to John's gospel at Constantinople. That correspondence, however, is not itself an explanation. Why, on these two days, did Constantinople switch from the course reading of Mark to the accounts of the raising of Lazarus and the entry into Jerusalem from the Gospel of John?

The answer to that question, is, I believe, to be found in ante-Nicene Alexandria. A range of consistent sources from the third to the fourteenth centuries was given close study by René-Georges Coquin in an essay published in 1967.[28] This material suggests that the early Alexandrian fast of forty days began on the day following the Epiphany celebration of Christ's baptism, thus following exactly the Markan chronology, according to which the temptation of Jesus followed immediately upon his baptism in Jordan. In the sixth week of that fast, baptism was conferred, and that initiatory season was brought to a close on the following Sunday by the Feast of Palms. Such is the testimony of Abu-'l-Barakat, the highly respected fourteenth century author of the encyclopedia of Coptic Church practice entitled *The Lamp of Darkness*. Of the custom of conferring baptism on the Friday before that Feast of Palms, he repeats the curious legend, reported four centuries earlier by Macarius, the Bishop of Memphis, that this is said to be the day on which Jesus conferred baptism.

That legend, given the gospel records, made no sense at all until the 1973 publication by Professor Morton Smith of what is now known as the Mar Saba Clementine Fragment.[29] Although Professor Smith's analysis of the document raised many questions, by now the document itself is generally accepted to be of at least the third century, if it is not, indeed, the work of Clement himself. In what purports to be a letter of Clement of Alexandria, the author gives the text of a pericope from a version of the Gospel of Mark peculiar to the Church of Alexandria, and kept secret save for its use at the baptismal liturgy. It describes Jesus raising a young man from the dead at Bethany in response to his sister's pleading, and the performance of some sort of initiatory ritual (including baptism?) with him six days later. Although the young man is not named, this is clearly a variant of the story of the raising of Lazarus recounted in the Fourth Gospel. The author of the letter locates the pericope in this Alexandrian version by citing Mk. 10:32–34, after which comes the text of the "secret gospel." The gospel continues, the author tells us, with: "'And James and John come to him,' and all that section." (Mk. 10:35–45) If one conjectures that the remainder of chapter 10 was read on the following day, then Mk. 11 would describe the entry into Jerusalem on the Sunday Feast of Palms.

At some point in the fourth century, probably after the Council of Nicea and perhaps as a dimension of the paschal settlement there,[30] this Markan cursus was adopted for the fast of forty days at Constantinople, but with two differences: it no longer followed the Epiphany, but preceded the paschal fast; and the peculiar pericope imbedded in Mk. 10:32–45 (read on the fifth Sunday of Lent at Constantinople) has vanished, to be replaced by its only canonical parallel in Jn. 11 at the next eucharist on the following Saturday. It is John's account of the entry, as well, that is read on the following day. The canonical account of the Bethany miracle makes no reference to any initiatory ritual, but in the typikon for Hagia Sophia, copied in the tenth century but clearly replicating much earlier material, the Saturday of Lazarus is still a major baptismal day on which the patriarch confers baptism in the Little Baptistry and celebrates eucharist, although it is but a week before the great baptismal event at the Paschal Vigil.[31] The most probable explanation of this curiosity is that it continues the old Alexandrian baptismal day on the sixth day of the sixth week of the fast, though Constantinople's prohibition of eucharist on fast days moved the baptism and the eucharist that followed to Saturday.[32]

While it is likely that this Constantinopolitan recasting of the old Alexandrian cursus occurred after 325, it seems likely that it was fairly early in the fourth century. The conclusion of the Fast of Forty Days with a Sunday Feast of Palms seems forgotten by the end of the century. A sermon of John Chrysostom preached at Constantinople on the Saturday of Lazarus treats that day and the Sunday following as a unit, and sees these not as marking the end of the Forty Days, but already as oriented toward the coming Great Week, as was the case at Jerusalem. His words make it clear that there was no palm procession, and can easily suggest some resentment of the popularity of Jerusalem's liturgical employment of the sacred topography of the city and its environs.[33] Nonetheless, it is clear that John's account of the entry was the gospel of that Sunday. He makes no reference to the conferral of baptism on this day, but the literature does begin to yield such references to the *prophotismata* on the Saturday of Lazarus in the sixth century.

If we have understood it rightly, the early Alexandrian Feast of Palms reported by Abu-'l-Barakat made no claim to historical accuracy. It was simply the point reached in the course reading of Mark at the end of the Fast of Forty Days. However, the suppression of Alexandria's "secret gospel," and the substitution of Jn. 11:1–45 would introduce a chronological note, setting the proximity of events in Bethany to the coming Passover. With that came the setting of a like proximity of the entry into Jerusalem to the coming Passover and Passion of the Lord. It seems impossible, at present, to determine whether that was a fortuitous result of the introduction of the readings from John at the end of a Lent transferred to its pre-paschal position for independent reasons, or whether it was the introduction of the

Johannine readings that drew the season to its pre-paschal position. In any case, by the end of the fourth century, pilgrims to Jerusalem from Constantinople seem to have prompted the dramatic recreation of events in John's gospel on the two days before Great Week at Jerusalem: the raising of Lazarus on Saturday, and the procession with palms down the Mount of Olives on Sunday, both exercises in the early afternoon, outside the normal hagiopolitan liturgical schedule. By the early fifth century this had changed at Jerusalem. The Saturday of Lazarus is no longer the commemoration of the miraculous raising of Lazarus from the dead, but is rather a day oriented toward the coming Passover, the gospel for the day Jn. 11:55–12:11, still the gospel for this Saturday in the Armenian Church. As for the following day, the gospel account of the entry into Jerusalem was no longer read in the afternoon on the Mount of Olives, as had been the case in the late fourth century. Rather, the day is now called "the Day of Palms," and that account of the triumphal entry from the Gospel of Matthew is the gospel for the morning liturgy at the Martyrium, the basilica on Golgotha. Still, in the afternoon, now two hours later, all the populace gathered on the Mount of Olives and made a great procession with palms, singing Psalm 118, down to Golgotha for the evening office. This procession, as distinct from the commemoration of the triumphal entry, would remain Jerusalem's contribution to liturgical history.

Pilgrims would carry the memory of their participation in that procession back to their homes, including, eventually (but no longer), Constantinople. The procession appears in the West first in sixth-century Spain, preceding a liturgy of the delivery of the creed, whose gospel stopped just short of the triumphal entry. A similar liturgy, but with the gospel extended to include the entry, seems to have obtained a century later in Gaul's Bobbio Missal. By the tenth century, the commemoration of the entry with an elaborate procession is found in Germany, leading into the liturgy of the Sunday of the Passion. With minor changes, this passed to Rome with the Ottonian emperors, and later Roman liturgy will present the dual theme familiar to us today. That German pattern, first set forth in the Romano-Germanic Pontifical of the tenth century, is still evident in Roman *ordines* of the thirteenth century.

English cathedrals, however, had a different rite, as did many cathedrals on the continent. That at Salisbury commended itself to most of the country by the sixteenth century, and its blessing of palms and carrying about and lifting up of the Blessed Sacrament drew the ire of English reformers. Abolished, but hardly forgotten, Palm Sunday went into an eclipse in English church life. Nonetheless, in the nineteenth century, aided no doubt by the traditionalist bias of the Oxford Movement, and given expression by such poets as Keble and Milman, the joint commemoration of the entry into Jerusalem and the passion of our Lord found its way slowly back into English church life. The pre-reformation rite of Salisbury had taken its gospel for the entry from John, as had Constantinople before (although the passages differ by a few verses). The chronological link made in that gospel established this Sunday at the head of Holy Week as the day on which the Lord made his triumphal entry into Jerusalem. That would suffice to set and fix the day, whatever gospel was read, even if it were Matthew, as at Rome and Jerusalem, or another synoptic gospel as in tenth-century Germany. In fact, by medieval times variations in gospel chronologies were seldom noticed, and any possible incongruity was bridged by such liturgical poets as Theodulph of Orleans and, later, Henry Hart Milman. These enriched and, to a degree, even shaped the tradition that now finds such rich expression in the American Book of Common Prayer. It is a tradition of great length and complexity, but all the richer for that.

Notes

1. Marion J. Hatchett, *Commentary on the American Prayer Book* (New York: The Seabury Press, 1980).

2. Hatchett, *Commentary*, 217.

3. Vernon Staley, ed., *Hierurgia Anglicana, Part III*. The Library of Liturgiology & Ecclesiology for English Readers, Volume V (London: Alexander Moring, Ltd., 1904) 259–263.

4. John Keble, *The Christian Year* (London: Methuen, 1895) 92.

5. *The Hymnal 1940 Companion* (New York: The Church Pension Fund, 1949) 49.

6. For the above precisions on revisions of the lectionary for Morning Prayer, I am indebted to the Bishop of Bethlehem, the Rt. Rev. Dr. Paul Marshall, who was kind enough to provide the information in a personal communication.

7. Cited here from Hatchett, *Commentary*, 225.

8. Archdale King, *Liturgies of the Past* (London: Longmans, Green, 1959) 279.

9. J. Wickham Legg, *The Sarum Missal, edited from three early manuscripts* (Oxford: Clarendon Press, 1916) 94, n. 5.

10. A shrine or reliquary, sometimes (as here) borne as a litter. A much earlier *ordo* for Palm Sunday refers to such a litter, bearing the Gospels as sign of Christ, as *portatorium*.(Ps. Alcuin, *De divinis officiis*, XIV. *PL* 101.1201).

11. In Legg's primary ms.: *Require hoc evangelium in dominica I. adventus domini.* Legg, *The Sarum Missal*, 95.

12. See S. Van Dijk [and J. H. Walker], *The Ordinal of the Papal Court from Innocent III to Boniface VIII and Related Documents*. Spicilegium Friburgense 22 (Fribourg: The Univ. Press, 1975) 210–215.

13. J. Neil Alexander, *Waiting for the Coming: The Liturgical Meaning of Advent, Christmas Epiphany* (Washington, D.C.: The Pastoral Press, 1993) 17–20.

14. C. Mohrmann, *Études sur le Latin des chrétiens*, Tome I (Rome: Editioni di Storia e Letteratura, 1961) 249.

15. The matter is discussed by H. Philibert Feasley, O.S.B., in "Palm Sunday," *The*

Thomas J. Talley

Ecclesiasticl Review XXXVIII.4 (April 1908) 372.

16. Edgar C. S. Gibson, *The Thirty-Nine Articles of Religion of the Church of England,* Vol. I (London: Methuen, 1896) 81, 83.

17. Jean Deshusses, *Le Sacramentaire Grégorien: ses principales formes d'apres les plus anciens manuscrits, tome I.* Spicilegium Friburgense 16 (Fribourg; Éditions Universitaires, 1971) 693.

18. C, Vogel-R. Elze, *Le Pontifical Romano-Germanique du dixième siècle, II*. Studi e Testi 227 (Città del Vaticano: Biblioteca Apostolica Vaticana, 1963) 40–51.

19. Cf. M. Andrieu, *Le Pontifical Romain au moyen-âge: Tome I, Le Pontifical Romain du XII* siècle*. Studi e Testi 86 (Città del Vaticano: Biblioteca Apostolica Vaticana, 1938) 211.

20. D. Marius Ferotin, ed., *Le Liber Ordinum.* Monumenta Ecclesiae Liturgica, Vol. V (Paris: Librairie de Firmin-Didot, 1904) cols. 178–187.

21. The currently agreed upon name. She has also been known to earlier scholars as Etheria, Eucheria, and Sylvia. The most convenient English translation is that of John Wilkinson, *Egeria's Travels in the Holy Land* (Jerusalem: Ariel, 1981). References in parentheses are to standard chapter and verse divisions in the text.

22. Paul Devos, "*La date du voyage d'Égerie,*" *Analecta Bollandiana 85* (1967) 165–194.

23. Egeria's text (31.2) alludes to Mt. 21:15, but there is no further specification of the reading.

24. A. Renoux, *Le Codex Arménien Jérusalem 121, II.* Patrologia Orientalis XXXVI.2, No. 168 (Turnhout: Brepols, 1971) 257, 259 and notes.

25. T. Talley, "The Origin of Lent at Alexandria," *Studia Patristica* XVII.2 (Oxford and New York: Pergamon, 1982) 594–612. [Reprinted in T. Talley, *Worship: Reforming Tradition* (Washington, D.C.: Pastoral Press, 1990) 87–112.]

26. Egeria (29.4) says of this preliminary station, "All the monks meet the bishop when he arrives there, and the people go into the church. They have one hymn and an antiphon, and a reading from the Gospel about Lazarus's sister meeting the Lord." (Wilkinson, *Egeria's Travels,* 131).

27. M. Aubineau, *Les Homélies festales d'Hésychius de Jérusalem.* Subsidia Hagiographica 59 (Brussels, 1978) 388.

28. R.-G. Coquin, "*Les origines de l'Épiphanie en Égypte,*" in B. Botte, E. Mélia, etc., edd., *Noël, Épiphanie, retour du Christ. Lex Orandi 40* (Paris: Cerf, 1967) 139–170. The relevant source materials include a homily of Origen, the Canons of Hippolytus, a Coptic codex of the fifth–sixth century, the *Annals* of Eutychius, a letter of Macarius of Memphis, and *The Lamp of Darkness* by Abu-'l-Barakat.

29. M. Smith, *Clement of Alexandria and a Secret Gospel of Mark* (Cambridge, Mass.: Harvard University Press, 1973). The translation of the fragment is on 446 f.

30. See R.-G. Coquin, "*Une Réforme liturgique du concile de Nicée (325)?*" *Comptes rendus, Académie des Inscriptions et Belles-Lettres* (Paris, 1967) 178–192.

31. Juan Mateos, S.J., *Le Typikon de la Grande Église, Tome II.* Orientalia Christiana Analecta 166 (Rome: Pont. Institutum Orientalium Studiorum, 1963) 62–65. On the Saturday of Lazarus, as on other major baptismal days, the usual entrance chant, Trisagion, is replaced with the baptismal troparion, "You who have been baptized into Christ have put on Christ." That substitution is still made in the Byzantine rite today.

32. This is not the only vestige of the old Alexandrian baptismal day, though it was moved from Friday to the preceding Sunday by the 14th century. In current Coptic practice, the Sunday before Palm Sunday is "The Sunday of Baptisms," and baptism is forbidden between Palm Sunday and Pentecost.

33. See T. Talley, *The Origins of the Liturgical Year,* Second, Emended Edition (Collegeville, Minn.: The Liturgical Press, 1991) 186 ff. By the time of the tenth-century typikon of Hagia Sophia, a procession has appeared, and has been in place long enough to require explanation of variant stations. It has since disappeared from the Byzantine rite. See Juan Mateos, *Le Typikon de la Grande Église, II.* Orientalia Christiana Analecta 166 (Rome: Pont. Institutum Orientalium Studiorum, 1963) 64–67.

"The Fruits of Life O'erspread the Board": Isaac Watts's Hymns for the Lord's Supper

Daniel B. Stevick

CONGREGATIONS REQUIRE a generous supply of hymns–three or four every Sunday at a minimum. Some hymns are chosen because they relate to the season or the day's Scriptures, while some interpret the eucharist. Persons planning liturgical events expect an adequate provision in the Hymnal, and those who use Marion Hatchett's indispensable *Liturgical Index to the Hymnal 1982* will find it. But if congregations depend on the *Hymnal*, what do the hymnal-makers depend on? If there are to be at hand singable, believable hymns to support the eucharistic action and to express its meaning and tone, where do such hymns come from? The persons who compile the hymnals must draw on a well-stored tradition. A succession of poets have explored what hymns in English for the Holy Communion might appropriately say, what meaning system they should imply, what vocabulary they should use, in what voice they should speak, and what emotions they should express. These poets will have many failures, and some experiments will not work, but there are also discoveries and achievements. Gifted persons have been able to express their ideas and devotion in convincing hymns. Then once someone has done it, it all seems self-evident, and others can do it too.

In the matter of writing hymns in English for the eucharist, it was the early eighteenth-century Independent, Isaac Watts, who pioneered.

Isaac Watts and his Hymns

This essay will look at the group of hymns "Prepared for the Lord's Supper" that Watts issued in 1707. There had been at least two earlier collections of hymns for the Holy Communion—one by a Presbyterian, Joseph Boyse, 1693; and another by a Baptist, Joseph Stennett, 1697. These hymns were generally pedestrian and stylistically awkward, but their existence is a reminder that with respect to singing congregational hymns and specifically hymns for the sacrament, dissenters were ahead of the established Church. English Christians were generally reluctant to accept for congregational singing anything other than the psalms, usually in the jog-trot metrical version of Sternhold and Hopkins, 1562, which was in Watts's time being gradually supplanted by the less amateurish New Version by Tate and Brady, 1692. Watts, striking off on new lines, wrote hymns which were not versified psalms, but independent compositions by which congregations could name their beliefs and their experience. He can justly be called "the creator of the modern English hymn,"[1] but he should further be honored as the writer of the first set of English hymns for the Holy Communion that might lay claim to distinction of thought and expression.

Watts was born in 1674 in Southampton to a Nonconformist family and was educated at the academy at Stoke Newington—one of dissenting academies which were in the late seventeenth and eighteenth centuries preparing a substantial portion of the leaders of English society. (His mind was shaped more by the seventeenth century than by the eighteenth century.) In 1702 he became pastor of the Independent congregation at Mark Lane in London. His health was always frail, and in 1712 he resigned his pastorate and went to live in the home of Sir Thomas Abney in Stoke Newington, where he died in 1748. The revered Dr. Watts was given a monument in Westminster Abbey.[2]

He was by temperament an educator, and his writings include widely used textbooks on logic and grammar as well as philosophical, theological and practical works. However, his lasting achievement was his hymns. He began writing hymns as a young man, evidently out of his dissatisfaction with the metrical Psalter. He published some of his early poetry in *Horae Lyricae*, 1706. His principal collection, *Hymns and Spiritual Songs*, was issued first in 1707, enlarged in 1709, and subsequently printed many times in Britain and America through the nineteenth century. Watts the hymn writer should be remembered also for his small book *Divine Songs for Children*, 1715. Its lively, but moralistic, hymns were an early effort to write religious songs for children; it too was a best-seller. In 1719 Watts issued a versified and christianized version of the psalms on which he had worked for many years. His *Hymns and Spiritual Songs* and his *The Psalms of David Imitated* were often printed in a single volume. The book, which contained only the words of the hymns and was sometimes printed in virtually microscopic typeface, was owned and carried to church and cherished in thousands of families. All in all Isaac Watts wrote nearly seven hundred hymns, producing virtually all of them quite early in his career.

Watts's practical aim was to raise the level of congregational singing. He began the Preface of his *Hymns and Spiritual Songs* with the pungent sentence, "While we sing the praises of our God in his church, we are employed in that part of worship which of all others is the nearest a-kin to heaven; and it is a pity that this, of all others, should be performed the worst upon earth."[3] As an aid to popular use, he kept his work simple, using only three meters. (Thirteen hymns are in common meter, nine in long meter, and three in short meter; these new hymns could be sung to familiar psalm tunes.) Watts's hymns are nearly all in iambic rhyming quatrains. (Watts always rhymed his second and fourth lines, but he sometimes left his first and third lines unrhymed. Some of his rhymes are quite rough.) Most of his lines end in a stop; he is writing for congregations in which hymns would be "lined out" by a precentor and repeated by the congregation, and "run-on" lines might be confusing. Alliteration would make lines stick in the memory, and Watts used it, albeit sparingly: "The price of pardon was his blood,/ His pity ne'er withdrew," (4:4.3–4), or "Let sinful sweets be all forgot," (6:4.1), or "And the large load of all our guilt/ Lay heavy on him too," (16:4.3–4). He remarks that he held in check his use of literary, unusual or consciously poetic speech. "The metaphors," he says, "are generally sunk to the level of vulgar [common] capacities. I have aimed at ease of numbers [meter], and smoothness of sound, and endeavoured to make the sense plain and obvious. If the verse appears so gentle and flowing as to incur the censure of feebleness, I may honestly affirm, that sometimes it cost me labour to make it so."

Few of Watts's hymns are excessively long, but as a further aid to congregational use, he often put some stanzas in brackets ("crotchets" in the eighteenth century). Occasionally more stanzas of a hymn were set in brackets than were not. The parts so designated might, in the author's judgment, "be left out in singing without disturbing the sense." These stanzas, he explained further, may "contain words too poetical for meaner understandings." Groups which economized by adopting Watts's suggested deletions often would have omitted some fine stanzas.

Watts's style is thus plain. His vocabulary is concrete and heavily Anglo-Saxon, and many lines and whole stanzas are almost entirely of words of a single syllable. The passage of time and changes in the language have made a few of his expressions sound awkward or even comic.[4] Yet within his self-imposed limitations he achieves a wide variety of thought and emotional tone, and he has a gift for the arresting phrase, couplet or stanza. When his verse succeeds, it has the feeling of rightness and inevitability that is the mark of well-crafted poetry.

Hymns and Spiritual Songs is in three sections. The 150 hymns of Book I are largely verse paraphrases of or reflections arising from specific biblical texts. The 170 hymns of Book II are more thematic, and Watts usually supplies a topical heading for each. Book III, which is our present interest, consists of 25 hymns "Prepared for the Lord's Supper." Watts intended, according to his Preface, that these hymns be used so that "in imitation of our blessed Saviour, we may sing an hymn after we have partaken of the bread and wine." These hymns, like those of the previous books, are given headings to indicate their theme or the biblical text to which they refer. Watts says that "above an hundred" hymns in Books I and II might also be suitable for the Supper, but these twenty-five which speak specifically to the sacrament of the table are placed together. Watts ends the entire work with twenty doxologies.

Watts's "Hymns Prepared for the Lord's Supper"

The twenty-five hymns of Book III represent a significant achievement. Nothing remotely equaling them had appeared before, and they would only be at least partially surpassed a generation later by Charles Wesley's remarkable *Hymns on the Lord's Supper,* 1745. But Wesley could not have done what he did without the model that Watts had provided. Wesley's 166 hymns can, of course, speak of matters which find no place in Watts's much smaller collection. Yet there are emphases in Watts that are not found in Wesley, and no hymn in Wesley's volume comes up to the standard of Watts's Hymn 7, "When I survey the wondrous cross."

Watts's hymns are not all of equal merit, but the best are very good indeed, and the failure rate of hymns by even the best of hymnodists is quite high. The hymns, even though they all gather around a single subject, show a rich variety. Many of them are headed by a theme or a biblical reference which indicates their focus. Watts is not didactic; since he is writing hymns, his affirmations about God, Christ, the human condition, redemption, the sacrament, and Christian life are made indirectly, embedded in doxology.

When Isaac Watts, that doughty Independent, in his "Hymns Prepared for the Lord's Supper" provides words to stimulate and carry the sacramental spirituality of his fellow Christians, what did he say? It would be interesting to answer by looking at the hymns individually, for the texts are hard to come by, and most of the hymns have features worth remarking. But for this brief essay, we shall simply identify some of Watts's principal themes and cite some of his more memorable and expressive lines:

Joy, Satisfaction and Love

A running theme of the sacramental hymns is joy; the word "pleasure" recurs often, beginning with the second hymn which says "Pleasure and love fill every mind" (2:6.3). A reader who comes to these hymns expecting something dour and burdened with penitence will be surprised. In Watts, the Puritan-derived eucharistic piety of Independency has become humane and affirmative; it celebrates "our joy for pardon'd guilt" (4:8.3) and says that "new blessings flow, a sea of joy without a shore," (22:4.3–4).[5] If one were to see in isolation the splendid line "where the fresh springs of pleasure rise," one might forgiven if one guessed "Blake." But it is Isaac Watts describing the Supper of the Lord (5:2.3). Bernard Manning, in his appreciative essay on Watts, says that "the note of cheerfulness" is "perhaps the most distinctive note in Watts's poetry."[6]

The "generous wine" of the Supper, Watts says, surpasses all other delights:

> On earth is no such sweetness found,
> For the Lamb's flesh is heavenly food;
> In vain we search the globe around
> For bread so fine, or wine so good. (18:3)

Later in the same hymn Watts exclaims, "Joy to the master of the feast" (18:5.1).

Hymn 8 describes the Supper in terms of "The Tree of Life," its rich language suggesting Eden, primal beginnings, and the tree of life in heaven, ultimate endings. It opens "Come let us join a joyful tune," and it speaks of the "dear refreshments" that are found in "this immortal food." Sitting in the shade of Jesus, the Tree of Life, "His fruit is pleasing to the sight,/ And to the taste as sweet" (8:1.1; 2.3–4; 5.3–4). In one of his best lines, Watts says, "'Tis a young heaven of strange delight" (8:5.1).

In another hymn, in lines fairly bursting with sensuous vitality, Watts says:

> The tree of life adorns the board
> With rich immortal fruit,
> And ne'er an angry flaming sword
> To guard the passage to't.

The cup stands crown'd with living juice;
The fountain flows above,
And runs down streaming for our use
In rivulets of love. (20:2–3)

The communicant who finds delight in the eucharistic meal also comes to it for food and nourishment. The banquet gives both pleasure and sustenance. The Supper upholds "dying men" so that they will not faint again (5:4). At the Supper "we on the rich provision feed" (6:3.2). At Christ's table "The fruits of life o'erspread the board,/ The cup o'erflows with heavenly love" (12:1.3–4). The King descends from heaven and bids his friends eat and drink salvation (15:4). Jesus' table "is divinely stored" (18:1.2). Of course, the motifs of pleasure and of feeding mingle:

The food's prepared by heavenly art,
The pleasure's well refin'd,
They spread new life thro' every heart,
And cheer the drooping mind. (20:4)

Jesus' meal both feeds and gives pleasure, for it is an act suffused by love. (Nineteen of these twenty-five hymns mention love.) "Mingled with love the fountain flow'd/ From that dear bleeding heart of thine" (18:2.3–4). Moreover, in striking lines Watts says that it is not only love that set the feast, but it is on account of love that we are present at it: "'Twas the same love that spread the feast,/ That sweetly forc'd us to it" (13:5.1–2).

Christ and the Cross

This Supper is a feast of Christ. To know it truly is to know him. When Watts speaks of Christ, his approach is fundamentally incarnational.

What shall we pay th' eternal Son
That left the heaven of his abode,
And to this wretched earth came down
To bring us wanderers back to God. (12:5)

He speaks of the grace of Christ in his coming:

How condescending and how kind
Was God's eternal Son!
Our misery reach'd his heavenly mind,
And pity brought him down. (4:1)

At one point Watts exclaims: "How cheerfully he came!" (9:2.4).

232

The one who came is described in a variety of phrases. To list a few: He is the descending God (2:2.4); God's eternal Son (4:1.2; 12:5.1); the eternal Word (5:1.1); the pledge of eternal life (5:5–6); the Lord of life (6:3.1); the coming one (6:6); the young prince of glory[7] (7:1.2); Christ my God (7:2.2); the ambassador of peace (9:2.3); this dying Lamb (14:4.1); or this dying Lord (23:1.3); our light, our morning star (14:5.1); the bleeding Prince of Love (16:2.2); the master of the feast (18:5.1); our dearest Lord (19:1.1); Jesus the God (21:2.1; 3.1); the Victorious God (21:11.1); the prince of heaven (22:2.2); and Jesus, our incarnate God (22:5.4).

As these name-phrases will have indicated, Christology and soteriology cannot be separated. The one who came to save, and salvation of an alienated world required a cross. The first hymn sets Jesus' institution of the Supper in the context of the passion events:

> 'Twas on that dark, that doleful night
> When powers of earth and hell arose
> Against the Son of God's delight,
> And friends betray'd him to his foes. (1:1)

Watts says repeatedly that Jesus' death brought life to others: "For us his vital blood was spilt,/ To buy the pardon of our guilt" (1:5.1–2). He has Christ say of himself, "'For you, the children of my love,/ It was for you I dy'd" (21:5.1–2).

In a striking hymn, Watts begins with nature as a revealer of God. In prior generations the theological tradition had said that God is made known in "the Book of Nature" and in "the Book of Scripture." In seventeenth and eighteenth century thought, however, natural revelation had become the preoccupation of religious thinkers. Watts affirms nature; it is the context of human life; and every creative act of God is revelatory:

> Nature with open volume stands
> To spread her Maker's praise abroad;
> And every labour of his hands
> Shows something worthy of a God. (10:1)

But by itself the Book of Nature is inadequate. The character of God–grace and glory, the whole divine name, power wisdom and love–is shown, not in nature, but in the cross. The hymn continues:

> But in the grace that rescu'd man
> His brightest form of glory shines;
> Here on the cross 'tis fairest drawn
> In precious blood and crimson lines. (10:2)

Watts speaks often of Jesus' "wounds" and his "blood"–using both terms as shorthand for the redemptive acts. This language was a convention of earnest Christians of the period, but it must be said that Watts is more restrained than many of his contemporaries, Charles Wesley in particular. It was common to emphasize the importance of Christ's blood by exaggerating its quantity–something that Watts does not do. In these hymns no one plunges into Christ's blood.

It seems that Watts held some version of a penal substitutionary theory of the atonement; he speaks of an offended God punishing the innocent Savior so that the guilty can go free:

> For us his flesh with nails was torn,
> He bore the scourge, he felt the thorn;
> And justice pour'd upon his head
> Its heavy vengeance in our stead. (1:4)

and:

> Rebels, we broke our Maker's law;
> He from the threatening set us free,
> Bore the full vengeance on his cross,
> And nail'd the curses to the tree. (22:3)

This strange joining of "grace and vengeance" (10:4.2) was in Watts's day widely understood to be no more than Christian orthodoxy and the teaching of the New Testament. Yet in a group of hymns that say as much as these do about the cross, it is notable that this theory figures as little as it does. Watts in his hymns seems to prefer to sing another account of the atonement.

Watts celebrates the reality that today goes by the name "Christus Victor." Christ comes to liberate humanity held in bondage. "Dying he conquer'd hell and sin,/ And made his triumph there" (16:5.3–4). Watts has Jesus say of himself:

> "When I came down to free your souls
>   From misery and chains . . . .
>
> When hell and all its spiteful power
>   Stood dreadful in my way,
> To rescue those dear lives of yours
>   I gave my own away.
>
> But while I bled and groan'd and dy'd,
>   I ruin'd Satan's throne,
> High on my cross I hung and spy'd
>   The monster tumbling down." (21:6.3–4; 8–9)

Christ having overcome the race's ancient enemies, the Holy Communion is a victory banquet to which believers are invited:

> "Now you must triumph at my feast,
>   And taste my flesh, my blood;
> And live eternal ages blest,
>   For 'tis immortal food." (21:10)

To speak of divine redemption of sinful humanity carries Watts beyond our common sense, rational world, and he must speak in paradox–Jesus' cruel thorns yield our heavenly crowns; our life is from his dying; his loss and wounds are our gain and wholeness:

> From all his wounds new blessings flow,
> A sea of joy without a shore. (22:4.3–4)

> Thy cruel thorns, thy shameful cross
>   Procure us heavenly crowns;
> Our highest gain springs from thy loss,
>   Our healing from thy wounds. (23:3)

Or he may express it as an exchange:

> It cost him death to save our lives,
> To buy our souls it cost his own. (12:6.1–2)

The paradoxes of the cross are not explained; puzzles can be explained, but not paradoxes. Watts simply states them in their mystery and suggestion, leaving them to do their work deep in the imaginations of devout congregations.

Only a few of Watts's twenty-five hymns are in praise of the Holy Communion. Most are not about the sacrament, and several do not even mention it expressly. One does not so much look at the rite as look through the rite to Christ. It is the way of these hymns to stand at the Holy Communion and celebrate Christ's love and redemption.

No doubt the most notable instance of this approach is Hymn 7, "When I survey the wondrous cross"–clearly the prize of the collection. This hymn is universally recognized as one of the great hymns in the language. Erik Routley says that it "is the most penetrating of all hymns, the most demanding, the most imaginative. It is these things precisely because its style is so simple. It is drawn throughout in strong, clear, simple lines and colors."[8] However, it is seldom realized that "When I survey the wondrous cross" was a hymn written for the Lord's Supper.

The hymn is confessional–all of it in the first-person "I" voice. It is also visual; the speaker sees, "When I survey . . ." and calls on others to see as well, "See from his head, his hands, his feet . . ." (7:1.1; 3.1). The communicant, at the sacrament, is in the presence of the cross. In looking at the cross, one looks at the reality to which the sacrament looks. The hymn moves between external event and inward response, first looking:

> When I survey the wondrous cross
> On which the prince of glory dy'd. (1.1–2)

> See from his head, his hands, his feet,
> Sorrow and love flow mingled down. (3.1–2)

and then reflecting on what has been seen:

> My richest gain I count but loss,
> And pour contempt on all my pride (1.3–4)

> Did e'er such love and sorrow meet?
> Or thorns compose so rich a crown? (3.3–4).

Watts is circumstantial, even graphic, in this hymn, speaking of Jesus' "five wounds"–his head, his hands and feet. Lines that are sometimes omitted (by Watts's permission) say "His dying crimson like a robe/ Spreads o'er his body on the tree" (4.1–2). But Watts sees the cross, even in its horror, as a demonstration of love–love that is "so amazing, so divine," and love that is mingled with sorrow (5.3; 3.2–3).

At the head of the hymn Watts sets the title "Crucifixion to the World by the Cross of Christ" and refers to Gal. 6:14. He means for the hymn to express Paul's great wish, "But God forbid that I should glory, save in the Cross of our Lord Jesus Christ, by whom the world is crucified unto me, and I unto the world" (AV). The cross is not simply something that happened to Jesus; it is something profound and revolutionary that happens within a believer. In the light of Christ's cross, life's priorities are reassigned; one's values are revalued. "My richest gain I count but loss" (1.3); "All the vain things that charm me most,/ I sacrifice them to his blood" (2.3–4), and climactically:

> Were the whole realm of nature mine
> That were a present far too small;
> Love so amazing, so divine
> Demands my soul, my life, my all. (7:5)

In this hymn, Watts describes the cross as "the death of Christ my God" (2.2)–words which familiarity should not be allowed to dull. In this line as well as in several later lines Watts reiterates the surprising, even shocking, "crucified God" motif. He speaks of "that cross where God the Saviour lov'd and dy'd" (10:5.2). He says "Jesus, the God that fought and bled/ And conquered when he fell" (21:2.2). He exclaims "Blest fountain! springing from the veins/ Of Jesus our incarnate God" (22:5.3–4). Watts writes as a poet, not as a discursive theologian. He does not explain his thought or indicate what he makes of the long-held teaching of divine impassibility. But taking with utter seriousness the incarnation, he says that the one who died was divine. The cruel death that belonged to the experience of the human Jesus somehow belonged also (if one may put it so) to the experience of God. Human redemption was won with a cost, and the cost was borne by the redeeming God.

> It cost him death to save our lives,
> To buy our souls it cost his own;
> And all the unknown joy he gives
> Were bought with agonies unknown. (12:6)

Wesley would say this sort of thing repeatedly and forcefully in his *Hymns on the Lord's Supper* thirty-five years later, but was anyone else saying it in 1707?

When Watts speaks of the cross he often uses dramatic, graphic terms, seeking to convey the shocking reality of a terrible, yet saving death. In one memorable line he says, "On the cold ground his life was spilt" (9:5.3). However, the cross is transformed into a sign of God's loving kindness, and in what may be the best lines of the collection, Watts exclaims with great tenderness and serenity:

> O the sweet wonder of that cross
> Where God the Saviour lov'd and dy'd!
> Her noblest life my spirit draws
> From his dear wounds and bleeding side.
>
> I would for ever speak his name
> In sounds to mortal ears unknown,
> With angels join to praise the Lamb,
> And worship at his Father's throne. (10:5–6)

The Supper of the Lord

It may suggest the richness of Watts's understanding of the Holy Communion to list and loosely group some of his descriptive expressions:

Watts speaks of the Holy Communion as "this living branch of sovereign power" (8:8.3); "his [Christ's] board" (8:1.4; 16:3.2); "his royal board" (15:1.3); "our Father's board" (23:1.1); "thy table" (18:1.2); "the Lord's own table" (24:1.3); "this dear covenant of thy blood" (3:2.1); "repeated seals of Jesus' dying love" (4:7.1–2); "dear refreshments" (8:2.3); "this immortal food" (8:2.4; 21:10.4); "this heavenly food" (18:3.2); "the sacred feast of his redeeming grace" (11:1.3–4); "the solemn feast where sweet celestial dainties stand" (20:2–3); "this soul-reviving wine" (17:2.1); "this banquet . . . of heavenly things" (17:3.1–2); "our Saviour's blood" which is "generous wine" (18:2.1–2); "this triumphal feast" which "brings immortal blessings down" (21:3.2–3). This catalog of phrases could easily be doubled in length.

Other than mentioning frequently the bread and wine, Watts says little about the sacramental words, setting, actions or community; he is more interested in the interior than in the exterior of the eucharist. He affirms that communicants partake of Christ: "Thy sacred flesh our souls have eat[en],/ 'Tis living bread; we thank thee, Lord!/ And here we drink our Saviour's blood,/ We thank thee, Lord, 'tis generous wine" (18:1.3–2.2). His sacramental realism can be almost physical:

> Here we have seen thy face, O Lord,
> And view'd salvation with our eyes,
> Tasted and felt the living word,
> The bread descending from the skies. (14:3)

In another hymn Watts says:

> We touch, we taste the heavenly bread,
> We drink the sacred cup;
> With outward forms our sense is fed,
> Our souls rejoice in hope. (24:2)

In these lines he seems to be following the idea associated with Calvin, and repeated by many English writers on the sacrament, both Puritan and Anglican, that as our bodies are fed at the Lord's Supper by the elements of bread and wine, so, in a somewhat parallel way, our souls are fed by the body and blood of Christ.

Hymns do not define; they suggest and celebrate. But Watts obviously thinks of Christ as in some sense present in the sacrament:

> From the high-way that leads to hell,
> From paths of darkness and despair,
> Lord, we are come with thee to dwell,
> Glad to enjoy thy presence here. (12:4)

Watts says repeatedly that at the Supper, communicants are fed by the body and blood of Christ: "Thy blood like wine adorns thy board,/ And thine own flesh feeds every guest," (19:1.3–4). The sacramental elements are "this immortal food" (17:2.4). Watts remarks that "in lively figures" (that is in vital symbols) "here" (in the Supper) "we see" (by faith) "the bleeding Prince of love" (16:2.1–2). In the seventeenth and eighteenth centuries, it was common in both Anglican and Puritan traditions to attach significance to the actions of breaking the bread and pouring out the wine, and very likely these ritual gestures were what Watts had in mind as "lively figures" which conveyed the reality of Christ's sacrificial work. In a later hymn he speaks of these two actions as though he considered them constitutive of the sacrament:

> How are thy glories here display'd,
>   Great God, how bright they shine,
> While at thy word we break the bread,
>   And pour the flowing wine. (25:1)

While Watts says that Christ is present at our feast, it seems more important for him to say that the Supper is Christ's feast to which he invites, "Jesus the God invites us here/ To this triumphal feast" (21:3.1–2). Watts says gratefully:

> Here we have seen thy face, O Lord,
> And view'd salvation with our eyes,
> Tasted and felt the living word,
> The bread descending from the skies.

> Thou hast prepar'd this dying Lamb,
> Hast set his blood before our face,
> To teach the terrors of thy name,
> And show the wonders of thy grace. (14:3–4)

At one point Watts speaks of the Supper as a sacrifice: "Thy saints attend with every grace/ On this great sacrifice," (25:3.1–2). One would like to know more of what he understood by the expression, but the line stands alone.

In speaking of the union of Christ and the church, Watts uses the image (from Hebrews) of children of a family and Christ as the elder brother. Then he turns to the image (from Paul) of body and members. Having spoken of the sacramental body, he brings in the ecclesial body; and having spoken of the sacramental bread, he says that "We are but several parts/ Of the same broken bread" (2:4–5). The thought is not fully developed, but he seems to be saying that the body and the bread which are Christ are at the same time the church. The lines echo St. Paul's emphasis on the one bread (1 Cor. 10:16–17), and they have the sound of the Augustinian point that if it is Christ's body on the altar, and if you are Christ's body, "It is yourselves upon the altar."

The purpose of the sacrament, as Watts presents it, is the believer's union with Christ: "union with our living Lord,/ And interest in his death" (2:3.3–4). To describe this union, Watts uses interpersonal terms rather than anything that sounds metaphysical. He speaks of the sacrament as a covenant to which one sets one's name–"I seal th' engagement to my Lord" (3:2.3).

In one hymn, Watts describes the relation of Christ and the Christian in the eucharist using the language of the Song of Songs:

> There the rich bounties of our God
> And sweetest glories shine,
> There Jesus says, that "I am his,
> And my beloved's mine." (11:2)

In Book I, in his hymns on biblical texts, Watts freely christianizes the Song of Solomon, bringing in sacramental imagery, as in, "With living bread and generous wine/ He cheers this sinking heart of mine" (Bk. I, 68:5.1–2). Reciprocally, when he writes about the eucharistic meal as a sign of love, he can express his thought in imagery from the Song of Solomon.[9]

It may be observed that Watts's eucharistic theology, for all that it affirms, makes no use of the book of Hebrews and its presentation of Christ's heavenly high priesthood. Such an emphasis had been virtually taken for granted in the sacramental thought of a long tradition of Church of England theologians–Jeremy Taylor, John Cosin, Herbert Thorndike, and a score of others.[10] It would figure strongly a generation later in Charles Wesley's *Hymns on the Lord's Supper*. To writers in this high Anglican tradition, such an emphasis seemed essential to a full account of the eucharist, for it served to tie what the church does now at the sacramental table with what the living Christ is always doing in the holy place in heaven. Of course, Isaac Watts would affirm everything that the book of Hebrews says about Christ's high priestly work and his presentation of himself on the cross and in heaven as the final sacrifice. It is just that he (with the dissenting tradition generally) thinks that the christology of Hebrews has nothing to do with the Lord's Supper. Traditionally this has been one of the marked differences between eucharistic thought in catholic-minded Anglicanism and in evangelical Anglicanism and dissent. The high Anglicans would identify the absence of Christ's priestliness as an important omission in evangelical and dissenting thought on the sacrament; dissenters and evangelicals, for their part, would hear what the Anglicans say and think it exegetically and theologically unsupportable.

Daniel B. Stevick

Praise and Self-Dedication

The devout communicant responds to the grace of redemption and of the sacrament with praise and dedication to Christ.

> Thy light, and strength, and pardoning grace,
>   And glory shall be mine;
> My life and soul, my heart and flesh,
>   And all my powers are thine. (3:3)

Watts says in many ways, often at the end of a hymn, that the amazing, divine love demands "my soul, my life, my all" (7:5.4–5). He asks what we can give for "favors so divine," and answers that we would devote our hearts "to be for ever thine" (21:11.2–4). In the language of doxological excess, he says:

> In vain our mortal voices strive
> To speak compassion so divine;
> Had we a thousand lives to give,
> A thousand lives should all be thine. (22:6)

Several of the hymns conclude with a stanza of doxology, acknowledging that even the best expression of praise is not equal to the subject:

> We give thee, Lord, our highest praise,
>   The tribute of our tongues;
> But themes so infinite as these
>   Exceed our noblest songs. (21:12)

These hymns, despite their attractive features, are no longer sung in congregations. Only two of them—certainly two of the best, 434, "Nature with open volume stands," and 474, "When I survey the wondrous cross"—are in *The Hymnal 1982*. (Both of them have a stanza deleted.) When hymns have dropped from use, it is difficult to reinstate them. In the case of hymns from the early eighteenth century it is almost inevitable that features of their thought and expression will have become dated.

If these hymns, or most of them, cannot be entered in the church's current repertoire, it does seem important that they become known at least as a subject for historical understanding. They express the affirmative sacramental thought and spirituality of early eighteenth century Independency, and they occupy an honored place at the head of the tradition of eucharistic hymns written in English. Knowing how easily hymns on the Lord's Supper can slip into sentimentality or false posturing and how difficult it is to craft lines that are technically accomplished and yet vital, it

241

seems important to identify Watts as one who did the task well and did it first. His ideas and his style place him in the thought and piety of his time and tradition. Yet his work was non-polemic, nonpartisan, catholic. He sang of Christ, the gospel and the sacrament as we do today. His work—either as texts to be understood or as hymns to be sung as acts of devotion—can leap across the almost three centuries that separates it from us in calendar time and inform our minds and "raise our souls a little above this earth."

Notes

1. The words are the opening sentence of the entry on Watts in *The Hymnal 1940 Companion*, (New York: Church Pension Fund, 1951) 586. Similar tributes are common. Bernard Manning, in his splendid chapter on Watts in *The Hymns of Wesley and Watts* (London: Epworth Pr., 1942) 81, says, "To Watts more than to any other man is due the triumph of the hymn in English worship."

2. The literature on Watts is not large. The major studies are A.P. Davis, *Isaac Watts: His Life and Works* (New York: The Dryden Press, 1943) and Harry Escott, *Isaac Watts Hymnographer* (London: Independent Press, 1962). The well-written small book by Bernard Manning cited above contains only one chapter on Watts, but it is full of appreciative insight. None of these works gives any special attention to Watts's sacramental hymns.

3. Quotations from Watts are all from an edition of his *Works* prepared as a tribute to him by two Independents of the next generation, David Jennings and Philip Doddridge, who were Watts's literary executors. This edition of 1753 was given a splendid printing in six volumes by John Barfield (London, 1810). The poetry is all in Vol. IV. In this essay, quotations from the hymns "Prepared for the Lord's Supper" are identified by hymn number, followed by a colon; stanza number, followed by a period; and line number. Thus the lines "While all our hearts and all our songs/ Join to admire the feast," are from Hymn 13, stanza 3, lines 1–2; which is noted 13:3.1–2.

4. Two words which are fairly common and which make the hymns in which they occur unusable are "bowels" and "worms." Watts uses "bowels" often to speak of God's or Christ's compassion. It traces to the English Bible (for example the AV of Phil. 1:8, "I long after you all in the bowels of Jesus Christ") in which it translates the Greek *splanxna*, the "nobler viscera," which in the phsysio-psychology of the time was thought of as the seat of the higher and tenderer emotions. Watts uses "worms" to describe the lowliness of humanity. This word too would have its place in religious vocabulary through the Bible, perhaps especially the penitential Psalm 22, which says in vs. 6, "I am a worm and no man." Changes in speech and sensibility have made it impossible to use these words in congregational hymns, but Watts would no doubt have thought of them as legitimated by the Bible.

5. This celebratory tone was not unique to Watts. Philip Doddridge (1702–1751), a younger writer in Watts's own tradition, is remembered for a hymn which opens "My God, thy table now is spread,/ thy cup with love doth overflow," and goes on to speak of the "joyful guests" at God's table (Hymn 321 in *The Hymnal 1982*).

6. Manning, 79.

7. Watts original (1707) text for the second line of "When I survey the wondrous cross" was "Where the young Prince of glory died." However, in the 1710 edition he changed the line to read "On which the prince of glory died." This duller wording has persisted and still appears in most contemporary hymn books. Perhaps editors thought

that it represented Watts's own second thoughts. However, the Episcopal Church's *Hymnal* (1940 edition, followed in the matter by the 1982 edition), defying long custom, has returned to Watts's first thoughts.

8. Erik Routley, *Hymns and the Faith* (Greenwich, CT.,The Seabury Press, 1956) 112. Routley's comment on the simplicity of the hymn may be supported by the observation that of its 139 words only 18 are of more than one syllable.

9. The relation between Watts's sacramental hymns and his hymns on the Song of Songs is developed briefly in Escott, 54–56.

10. This tradition has been surveyed in two recent books: Kenneth Stevenson, *Covenant of Grace Renewed: A Vision of the Eucharist in the Seventeenth Century* (London: Darton, Longman and Todd, 1994); and H.R. McAdoo and Kenneth Stevenson, *The Mystery of the Eucharist in the Anglican Tradition* (Norwich: Canterbury Press 1997).

"With Eloquence in Speech and Song": Anglican Reflections on the Eucharistic Hymns (1745) of John and Charles Wesley

J. Neil Alexander*

*L*ESSER FEASTS AND FASTS, the calendar of commemorations used in the Episcopal Church, assigns to the lesser feast of John and Charles Wesley (March 3) the following collect:

> Lord God, who didst inspire thy servants John and Charles Wesley with burning zeal for the sanctification of souls, and didst endow them with eloquence in speech and song: Kindle in thy Church, we beseech thee, such fervor, that those whose faith has cooled may be warmed, and that those who have not known thy Christ may turn to him and be saved; who liveth and reigneth with thee and the Holy Spirit, one God, now and for ever. Amen.[1]

This collect is certainly not one of the more inspired prayers in the Anglican liturgical tradition. It is a prayer sadly lacking any element of thanksgiving, traditionally a principal element in the church's witness to the living faith of those who have died in Christ. The prayer's petition to "warm up" those who have "cooled down" in the faith is, I suspect, a near-charming and irresistible reference to Aldersgate. But the Wesleys' eloquence in speech and song–John

*An earlier version of this essay was presented as a paper read to the Charles Wesley Society at its Sixth Annual Meeting, October 1995, at the Divinity School of Duke University, Durham North Carolina. That version is published in the *Proceedings of the Charles Wesley Society II (1995) 35–50*. The author gratefully acknowledges the permission granted by the Society to reprint this essay here in honor of one whose study of the hymns of the church has enriched the lives of several generations of American Episcopalians.

in speech and Charles in song is perhaps the intent—captures not only their faithful efforts to secure the tradition that was their inheritance, but their struggle to enable that tradition to live and flourish in their own day, and to be advanced with integrity for the benefit of those who were to come after them. It is perhaps that aspect of the lives of the Wesleys—their respect for the tradition that shaped them, their desire that the tradition prosper for the sake of the gospel, and their heartfelt yearning to reform that tradition from within —that will guarantee in perpetuity a place for them in the hearts of Anglicans.

An investigation of the eucharistic hymns of John and Charles Wesley from an Anglican perspective seemed, at the outset, a great deal more straightforward than it has turned out to be. My immediate thought was to place the Wesleys, particularly John, in the context of the patristic revival in Anglicanism in the seventeenth and eighteenth centuries, and to demonstrate, at least suggestively, how dependent are the *Hymns on the Lord's Supper 1745*, on that literature with which both the Wesleys and Daniel Brevint would have been thoroughly familiar. Alas, Geoffrey Wainwright, in his characteristically detailed and insightful fashion, has recently completed just such a study.[2] But I am emboldened by the admonitions of Robert Taft who repeatedly reminds us that scholarship moves forward not because of the generation of new data ("there's nothing new under heaven") but by creating new structures of intelligibility for what we already know and by asking new questions.[3] So in that spirit, let us proceed.

The eighteenth century is surely the most neglected period in Anglican history and theology. Even the most cursory review of the literature reveals extensive interest and scholarship in the documents of sixteenth and seventeenth centuries and again in the nineteenth century, but very little work in the eighteenth-century sources. We have historians who specialize in early classical Anglicanism of the sixteenth and seventeenth centuries, and still more it seems who focus their attention on the Tractarians and the Oxford Movement, but few claim serious expertise the eighteenth-century materials. In fact, in informal conversations with my colleagues in the field of Anglican Studies, we could identify scholars who had written about eighteenth-century topics, but no one came immediately to mind that we readily associate with critical study of eighteenth-century sources. Everyone seems to be tidying things up after the seventeenth century, or setting the table for the turmoil of the nineteenth. I am sad about this state of affairs because the brief detour into the eighteenth century this study has provided has shown me what I should have known more clearly: that the eighteenth-century sources have been well-trodden by Wesley scholars and those of other disciplines, but those same sources have not received the attention they deserve from scholars who read with Anglican glasses.

The reason for this seems obvious: the nineteenth-century experience of Anglicanism—the Tractarians, the Oxford Movement, the Cambridge-Camden Society, the Gothic revival, and nineteenth-century romanticism in general—caused in much of Anglicanism a selective return to the formulations of earlier times, particularly those of the "high church" Caroline divines of the seventeenth century, fortified by a greater, though not always accurate, understanding of the early church. For many nineteenth-century Anglicans, especially those influenced by that century's catholic revival, the eighteenth century and the movements it produced were precisely the problem to be dealt with by, in their minds, getting back to basics.

The impact of all of this is still being felt today. At least among "Scottish Non-Juring American Episcopalians" it is very difficult to get a sufficient distance on our post-Tractarian experience in order to get a quality reading of pre-Tractarian sources. It is always a jolting experience for a newcomer to the primary sources when he or she discovers that the so-called "catholic" eucharistic theology of the Caroline divines still bears many of the marks characteristic of the Protestant theological debates of the sixteenth century. Such discoveries will often break their post-Tractarian hearts.

I shall not spend any time reviewing the impact upon the Wesleys of the revival of patristic studies in the Church of England in the seventeenth and eighteenth centuries. That material is well-known and it has recently received a fresh reading at the hands of Professor Geoffrey Wainwright of the Duke faculty, and Professor Ted Campbell of Wesley Theological Seminary in Washington.[4] In the last few years, however, several Anglican scholars have given their hand to a reappraisal of eucharistic theology prior to the nineteenth century. John Booty's long-awaited commentary on Book V of Richard Hooker's *Of the Laws of Ecclesiastical Polity* is an essential companion for anyone who wants to understand the eucharist in Anglicanism.[5] A 1993 work by Dr. Christopher Cocksworth entitled, *Evangelical Eucharistic thought in the Church of England,*[6] is a careful study of the role played by Evangelicals in the debates over eucharistic theology and practice from the sixteenth century to the present. In 1994, Dr. Kenneth Stevenson, now Bishop of the Diocese of Portsmouth, England, published a study of the eucharistic theology of the Caroline divines under the title *Covenant of Grace Renewed.*[7] It is the first work in decades by an Anglican that has given significant treatment to Daniel Brevint. Also in 1994, Archbishop Henry McAdoo published a brief, but important, study of Brevint and the Wesleys.[8] And earlier this year, McAdoo and Stevenson jointly published *The Mystery of the Eucharist in the Anglican Tradition,*[9] a work in which the Caroline divines and Daniel Brevint play an important role.

I trot out these names and titles for two reasons. First, I want to acknowledge my dependence upon these sources in the preparation of this essay. Trying to discover what, if anything, current scholarship might be offering to the discussion at hand, was clearly an important part of my preparation. But more to the point, I want to suggest that we are, one hopes, at the beginning of a resurgence of interest in the sources of Anglican eucharistic theology prior to the nineteenth century. Even Daniel Brevint, whose influence upon the Wesleys has been well-known for some time, by comparison to his contemporaries, is relatively unknown among Anglicans. (This latter point is not only supported by a review of the literature, but in an unscientific poll conducted during the preparation of this essay. I have repeatedly inquired of Anglican historians, theologians, graduate students, and others well-read in the sources, asking, "What can you tell me about Daniel Brevint?" Without exception I received the reply, "Daniel, who?") Even so standard a work as C.W. Dugmore's *Eucharistic Doctrine in England from Hooker to Waterland*,[10] published in 1942, never once mentions Daniel Brevint.

It is important, therefore, to look into this recent Anglican literature on Daniel Brevint and seventeenth-century eucharistic theology in England. Have the scholars mentioned above brought any precision to our understanding of Brevint as one of the principal links between the Caroline divines and the eucharistic theology of the Wesleys?

Since the main lines of Brevint's biography appear to be largely unknown, it is important to put a few notes into the record. Daniel Brevint was born in the Channel Islands, a territory greatly influenced in the sixteenth and seventeenth centuries by the French Reformed (Huguenot). Even after Elizabeth I placed the parishes in the Channel Islands under the direct control of the Diocese of Winchester, it was not until after the Restoration that "the religion of the realm and the Book of Common Prayer" was fully established there. In addition to having Huguenot parents, Brevint took his first degree in philosophy at the French Protestant University in Saumur (1624). Some years later (1636), he was admitted to Oxford and in spite of haggling from Archbishop Laud about the credibility of his French academic credentials, he received the master's degree (1638). After a short stay at Oxford as a university fellow, he retreated first to the Channel Islands, and eventually back to France in 1650/1651 to escape the Civil War. He found refuge in the Anglican community in Paris where he became acquainted with the exiled Charles II and became a good friend (some would say protégé) of John Cosin, the future Bishop of Durham who will come to play such an important role in the formation of the 1662 Prayer Book. It was during his Paris exile that Brevint received holy orders at the hands of Thomas Sydserf, the exiled Scottish bishop of Galloway, the diaconate and the priesthood being conferred in the same rite.[11]

These particular aspects of Brevint's life are important for the interpretation of his work. Although Brevint would return to England and enjoy the support of the crown, first as a parish priest and prebendary of Durham and later as Dean of Lincoln, his French Reformed background and Protestant university education remained a moderating influence on his thought throughout his life. Brevint's contempt for Roman Catholicism is well known by way of his polemical writings and his uneasiness with the theology of more radical Protestantism can also be documented. While taking his first degree Brevint would have come into contact with a group of French Calvinist scholars who were attempting to revise and expand the eucharistic thought of John Calvin on the basis of the rapidly expanding knowledge of the ancient sources. This group, led most notably by Philippe du Plessis-Mornay, held that the eucharist could be a sacrifice as long as it was understood to be "a commemoration of the cross, the sacrifice of thanksgiving and intercession, the offering of the gifts, and the sacrifice of the worshippers"–all themes that make their way into the work of Brevint, all themes that struggle to find a balance between the hard objectivity of post-Tridentine Roman Catholicism and the soft subjectivity of the more radical parties of Protestantism. (It is important to note here that the work of members of this same group also influenced others in England, a fact particularly visible in the work of Jeremy Taylor.)

At this point, it is important to backtrack slightly and examine Brevint's relationship with John Cosin, his fellow exile in Paris. Cosin was roughly 20 years Brevint's elder and most of Cosin's personal history is associated with the Diocese of Durham. He moved through the ranks from domestic and hospital chaplaincy, to parishes small and large, and finally to become Archdeacon of Durham East. Bishop (not yet Archbishop) William Laud recommended Cosin to be the master of ceremonies at the coronation of Charles I (1626). That was the first of several liturgical extravaganzas orchestrated by Cosin that made a positive impression on the crown. Cosin's pre-exilic reputation as the liturgical animateur of Durham included, in the minds of his antagonists, such detestable enormities as "comely and large surplices with wide and large sleeves," copious copes, fully sung Prayer Book services including the choral rendition of the ordinary, and the restoration of a second ambo from which to read the prayers of the liturgy, ostensibly to dilute the Puritan emphasis on preaching associated with a singular pulpit.[12] It was, however, Cosin's obsession with candles that might well be regarded as his pre-exilic claim to fame. Durham Cathedral's 1628 celebration of Candlemas–(February 2)–so outraged the Puritan Peter Smart that in July of the same year he was still so angry that he both preached about it and filed a formal complaint with Parliament. In the sermon, Smart wrote:

> On Candlemas Day last, Mr Cosins, in renewing that Popish ceremony of burning candles in the honour of Our Lady, busied himself from two on-the-clock in the afternoon till four in climbing long ladders to stick up wax candles in the said Cathedral Church. The number of all of the candles burnt that evening was 220, besides 16 torches, 60 of those burning tapers and torches standing upon or near the high altar.[13]

What Smart seems to have missed, according to Bishop Stevenson, is that in spite of appearances (and a truly passionate love of candles!) Cosin had a moderating influence upon the celebration of Candlemas if one holds in mind certain comparisons: the service for which Cosin was climbing the ladder in preparation was no doubt Evensong, not the eucharist which would have been the decided preference of the strongly catholic camp. Furthermore, it is Cosin who seems to be responsible for the shift in emphasis in the Anglican liturgical tradition from the Feast of the Purification of the Blessed Virgin Mary, to the Feast of the Presentation of Jesus in the Temple, a change that was formally executed by Cosin during the preparation of the 1662 Prayer Book.

Whatever Cosin's catholic leanings, particularly with respect to liturgy and ritual, a decade or so in exile seems surely to have had a moderating influence upon him. Perhaps it was just maturity, or simply political prowess, but the John Cosin we see in 1660 has calmed down considerably from earlier years. He is still a reformed Catholic, in the best sense, and he certainly carries that banner (or was it a candle?) into the negotiations with the Puritans and others that will produce the 1662 Prayer Book. He continues to be a man very anxious about the Puritan agenda, and given his loyalty to the crown, that anxiety probably has as much to do with politics as it does with liturgy and ritual.

This detour into the life of John Cosin is important if, in fact, his relationship with Daniel Brevint was as close as is often presumed. Cosin was both the presenter and preacher at Brevint's ordination in Paris, and upon their return to England, Brevint succeeded Cosin as the incumbent of Durham's Brancepeth parish and served Durham Cathedral during Cosin's episcopate. In the years of their close, perhaps daily association, for a decade in Paris and for another in Durham, Cosin and Brevint seem to have matured together into a balanced, reformed Catholic position. Both remained anti-Roman to the day they died and at the same time possessed a fear of more radical Protestantism. One can almost hear late night conversations between the two of them: Cosin expounding the virtues of a liturgically rich reformed Catholicism very much within the mainstream of the Church of England, and Brevint thinking out loud about how much his thinking had changed since his days as a minister in the French Reformed

Church. A most significant learning from recent Anglican scholarship on Daniel Brevint is that if we are going to know him, we must know John Cosin as well. Cosin is known among Anglicans mainly for his liturgical leadership at Durham and as a major player in the preparation of the 1662 Book. With a few exceptions, his devotional and theological writings, and other aspects of his life, have not received the scholarly attention they deserve; and while I am optimistic that such work is beginning, I remain convinced that until we more thoroughly unpack John Cosin, we shall know Daniel Brevint only in a preliminary way.

At this point it is tempting to launch into an analysis of Brevint's treatise, *The Christian Sacrament and Sacrifice,* and compare its structure and content with that of the Wesleys' *Hymns for the Lord's Supper 1745.* But such comparative work is very welltrodden territory and little would be served by rehearsing those findings again, as important as they are. The Wesleys' attachment of an abridgement of Brevint's treatise to their collection of eucharistic hymns, their organization of the collection following Brevint's structure, and most importantly, the way the Wesleys carried forth many of Brevint's themes in the devotional poetry of the hymns, represents data that is just about as secure as it gets.

So perhaps there is another question that should be raised: does the treatise of Brevint, in fact, represent an accurate synthesis of late seventeenth-century Anglican eucharistic theology? There appears to be a widespread assumption in the literature that it does, and while there are a number of studies that trace discreet lines of thought, I am unaware of any one work that attempts to provide a comprehensive analysis of Brevint against the background of seventeenth-century theology. Does his work represent simply a compilation of disparate seventeenth-century themes, or is there evidence of development of original thought? Does his work represent only the Catholic stream of the seventeenth century, or are there also Protestant, perhaps even Puritan, voices imbedded in his prose that we have failed to see because of our own post-Tractarian biases? And another question, of a different sort, has also been something of an irritant to me: Since the form of the treatise attached to the *Hymns for the Lord's Supper* is an abridgement of Brevint's original, has anyone compared the original with the abridgement to determine whether any of the deletions are significant? If the Wesleys excised mostly prosaic clutter, that's one thing; but, other deletions might in fact tell us something rather significant about the thinking of the Wesleys in the mid-1740s. (I suppose it goes without saying that these and many similar questions may be exhaustively covered in literature unavailable to me; I do wish, however, that they had occurred to me sooner.) With those questions and caveats in place, I want to raise, as briefly as possible, two points often raised in the literature on the relationship between Brevint and the Wesleys, and then ask two academically perilous questions that I believe require further exploration.

Most would agree that the central theme of Brevint's treatise is the eucharist as the meeting place between heaven and earth, the unity of sacrament and sacrifice, God's board and the Heavenly Altar. Archbishop McAdoo has called attention to this theme in other seventeenth and early eighteenth-century literature[14] That it had captured the imaginations of many can be noted most easily in the frontispiece of (Charles) Wheatley's *A Rational Illustration of the Book of Common Prayer* (2e. 1714). According to McAdoo's description, the drawing illustrates "the communicants kneeling on the chancel floor before the rails of the altar at which the celebrant is consecrating the elements. Above him in a cloud of glory stands the Savior, hands raised before the heavenly altar." The lettering in the halo refers us to the Epistle to the Hebrews. In the 1611 Authorized Version, these passages read:

> But Christ being come an high priest of good things to come, by a greater and more perfect tabernacle, not made with hands, that is to say, not of this building. (Heb. 9:11)

> It was therefore necessary that the patterns of things in the heavens should be purified with these; but the heavenly things themselves with better sacrifices than these. (Heb. 9:23)

> Wherefore he is able also to save them to the uttermost that come unto God by him, seeing that he ever liveth to make intercession for them. (Heb. 7:25)

Notice how Brevint's text reads almost like a description of the Wheatley illustration:

> So let us ever turn our eyes and our hearts toward Jesus our eternal High Priest, who is gone up into the true sanctuary, and doth there continually present both his own body and blood before God, and (as Aaron did) all the true Israel of God in a *memorial.* In the meantime we, *beneath in the church*, present to God his body and blood as a *memorial,* that under that shadow of his cross, and figure of the Sacrifice, we may present ourselves in very deed before him. [VI.3]

And, of course, this same picture can be detected in the *Hymns:*

> Yet may we celebrate below,
> And daily thus thine offering show
>   Expos'd before thy Father's eyes;
> In this tremendous mystery
> Present thee bleeding on the Tree
>   Our everlasting sacrifice. (Hymn 124)

With solemn faith we offer up,
　　And spread before thy glorious Eyes
That only ground of all our hope,
　　That precious, bleeding sacrifice,
Which brings thy Grace on Sinner down,
　　And perfects all our Souls in One. (Hymn 125)

Father to Him we turn our Face
　　Who did for all atone,
And worship tow'rd thy Holy Place,
　　And seek Thee in thy Son,

Him the true Ark and Mercy-seat
　　By faith we call to mind,
Faith in the blood atoning yet
　　For us and All Mankind.

The Lamb his Father now surveys,
　　As on this Altar slain,
Still bleeding and imploring Grace
　　For every Soul of Man. (Hymn 126)

The holy sacrament [writes Brevint] is the *table* purposely set to receive those mercies that are sent down from his *altar* . . . Here then I wait at the Lord's table which . . . *offers* me the richest gift . . . the Lord Jesus *crucified* . . . bless thine ordinances, and make it an *effectual* means of thy grace . . . Come in thou eternal priest; but cleanse thy house at thy coming.[IV.8]

This is beautifully captured by the Wesleys:

Saviour, and can it be
　　That Thou should dwell with me?
From thy high and lofty Throne,
　　Throne of Everlasting Bliss,
Will Thy Majesty stoop down
　　To so mean an house as this?

Yet come Thou heavenly Guest,
　　And purify my Breast,
Come Thou great and glorious King,
　　While before thy Cross I bow,
With Thyself Salvation bring,
　　Cleanse the House by entering Now. (Hymn 43)

This eucharistic intersection between heaven and earth is not only Brevint's "master theme," to use McAdoo's apt phrase, but it is a theme that runs consistently through the texts of the seventeenth century: it is there in the sermons of Lancelot Andrewes, in the *Mensa Mystica* of Simon Patrick, and, prior to Brevint, gets its most eloquent formulation from the pen of Jeremy Taylor. Note the following excerpt from Taylor's *The Worthy Communicant*:

> For when Christ was consecrated on the cross and became our high-priest, having reconciled us to God by the death of the cross, he became infinitely gracious in the eyes of God, and was admitted to the celestial and eternal priesthood in heaven; where in virtue of the cross He intercedes for us, and represents an eternal sacrifice in the heavens on our behalf. That He is a priest in heaven, appears in the large discourses and direct affirmatives of St Paul; that there is no other sacrifice to be offered but that on the cross, it is evident, because 'He hath but once appeared in the end of the world to put away sin by the sacrifice of himself;' and therefore since it is necessary that he hath something to offer so long as he is a priest, and there is no other sacrifice but that of Himself offered upon the cross; it follows that Christ in heaven perpetually offers and represents that sacrifice to His heavenly Father, and in virtue of that obtains all good things for His Church.
>
> Now what Christ does in heaven, He hath commended us to do on earth, that is, to represent His Death, to commemorate this sacrifice, by humble prayer and thankful record; and by faithful manifestations and joyful Eucharist to lay it before the eyes of our heavenly Father, so ministering His priesthood, and doing according to His commandment and His example; the church being the image of heaven, the priest the minister of Christ; the holy table being a copy of the celestial altar, and the eternal sacrifice of the lamb slain from the beginning of the world being always the same; it bleeds no more after the finishing of it on the cross; but it is wonderfully represented in heaven, and graciously represented here; by Christ's action there, by His commandment here.[15]

While not everyone's prose (or vision of the priesthood of Christ) soars to quite the same level as Jeremy Taylor's, even those of less-mediatorial sympathies would have known well the Prayer Book collect for the feast of the Lord's Ascension:

> Grant, we beseech thee, Almighty God, that like as we do believe thy only-begotten Son our Lord Jesus Christ to have ascended into the heavens; so we may also in heart and mind thither ascend, and with him continually dwell, who liveth and reigneth with thee and the Holy Ghost, on God, world without end. Amen.

This picture of the eucharist, as the intersection of heaven and earth, visible in the writings of a number of seventeenth-century writers, does in fact, in my judgment, receive its fullest expression from Daniel Brevint. It is, of course, not Brevint's only theme. Almost inseparable from it, and visible already in the texts cited, is Brevint's retrieval of eucharist as sacrifice and the relationship of eucharist as sacrifice to eucharist as sacrament. Also intertwined with the eucharist as sacrament and sacrifice is, of course, Brevint's concern for the nature of Christ's presence. One can, for example, detect the three of these themes coming together in Brevint's words:

> His body and blood have everywhere, but especially in this sacrament, *a true and real presence*, when he offered himself upon earth . . . and since he is gone up, he sends down to earth the graces that spring continually both from his everlasting sacrifice, and from the continual intercession that attends it.[16]

The maddening thing, at this point, is that Brevint is unwilling to get back into the theological debates of the sixteenth century about the manner of Christ's presence. But here again, as a man of his time, he stands in a secure tradition. It was clearly of deep concern to the Catholic tradition within seventeenth-century Anglicanism to speak of "the true and real presence" of Christ in the sacrament, but unlike their fifteenth- and sixteenth-century forebears, they were not going to sharpen their philosophical tools by debating "the shelf life" of the real presence. "*Mysterium est,*" writes Jeremy Taylor, "it is a sacrament and a mystery: sensible instruments consigning spiritual graces."[17] And Brevint follows in his train:

> I come then to God's altar, with a full persuasion, that these words, *this is my body*, promise me more than a *figure*; that this holy banquet is not a bare *memorial* only, but may actually convey . . . many blessings to me . . . Indeed, in what *manner* this is done, I know not; it is enough for me to admire. (IV.3)

As Archbishop McAdoo has observed, "Brevint is in the Anglican tradition from Andrewes onwards through such as Bramhall, Thorndike, and Taylor in refusing any mandatory definition of what Hooker calls 'the manner How.'"[18] And, of course, the eucharistic hymns of the Wesleys stand very much in this same tradition. So strong is this idea in Hymn 57 that it is worth quoting in full:

> O the depth of Love Divine,
>   Th' Unfathomable Grace!
> Who shall say *how* Bread and Wine
>   God into Man conveys?
> *How* the Bread His Flesh imparts,
>   *How* the Wine transmits His Blood,
> Fills his Faithful Peoples Hearts
>   With all the Life of God!
>
> Let the wisest Mortal show
>   *How* we the Grace receive:
> Feeble elements bestow
>   a Power not theirs to give:

Who explains the Wondrous Way?
    How thro' these the Virtue came?
These the Virtue did convey,
    Yet still remain the same.

How can heavenly Spirits rise
    by earthly matter fed,
Drink herewith Divine Supplys
    And eat immortal Bread?
Ask the Father's wisdom *how*,
    Him that did the Means ordain
Angels round our Altars bow
    To search it out, in vain.

Sure and real is the Grace,
    The Manner be unknown;
Only meet us in thy Ways
    And perfect us in One,
Let us taste the heavenly Powers,
    Lord, we ask for Nothing more;
Thine to bless, 'Tis only Ours
    To wonder, and adore. [Italics added.]

I believe it is fair, on the basis of this one very narrow trek through the sources, to concur with what seems to be the conventional wisdom that understands Daniel Brevint as a worthy representative of the Catholic vision of the eucharist in seventeenth-century Anglicanism. But let me hasten to add, once again, that there is much work still to be done on Brevint and his connection to the works of those who went before him and those who were his influential contemporaries. I am thus far unsatisfied that Brevint's work has received the sort of "text-grinding" in the Puritan and Huguenot sources comparable to the work that has been done on the texts of the Caroline divines of the Catholic sort.

At this point, I shall change gears a bit, and do what is perhaps more characteristic of a liturgiologist, that is, address the topic before us from the standpoint of the Book of Common Prayer. This approach is, of course, not new, and there is a good bit of literature that places the eucharistic hymns of the Wesleys in their Prayer Book context. In my survey of this literature, I have been fascinated to discover that in several cases the comparisons have been alongside a Prayer Book eucharistic structure, generally unidentified, but presumably that of 1662. In a couple of other cases, I have noted that the comparisons were against a liturgical structure similar to the aborted 1637 Scottish Book (or one of the "amplified editions" of that text that were the

"Wee Bookies" utilized by the Non-Jurors in route to the Scottish Liturgy of 1764, and eventually the first American Prayer Book of 1789), but nearly all of the references are simply to "the Prayer Book" as though that were some sort of generic text that has remained unchanged.

Everyone knows, of course, that liturgical historians can get real fixated on the smallest of details and can ruin an otherwise pleasant party. But it does make a difference if one is comparing the *Hymns on the Lord's Supper 1745* with the Prayer Book, which Prayer Book one is talking about. It is not helpful to refer to the Wesleys' fondness for "the epiclesis of the Prayer Book" when, in fact, the 1662 Prayer Book did not (and does not) have one. Nor, is it helpful to suggest that John Wesley was so fascinated with the epiclesis that he made sure to add one to the 1784 Prayer Book he prepared for the United States. I do not consider myself an expert on Wesleyan epicleses, but I have consulted Professor James White's new edition of Wesley's 1784 Prayer Book and for the life of me, I cannot find an epiclesis.[19]

And on the subject of the anamnesis and oblation: first, it makes a great deal of difference whether one sees them as inseparable parts of a unified liturgical syntax, that is, *that oblation is the natural consequence of anamnesis*; and second, it is a matter of no small magnitude whether the anamnesis and oblation are parts of the whole action of eucharistic praying, *whether or not (and in what sense) one understands the institution narrative to be consecratory*. Then, there is also the structural relationship between the anamnesis/oblation and the epiclesis. For example, in 1662, the "prayer of consecration" ends with the institution narrative, followed by the "Amen," after which the elements are delivered to the people. The so-called "anamnesis and oblation" follows the reception of the elements. There is no epiclesis before or after the reception of communion. This stands in contrast to other Prayer Book structures in which the anamnesis and oblation follow the institution narrative, and in which the position of the epiclesis is before the institution narrative (as is 1549) or after the oblation of the gifts of bread and wine (as in the Scottish Liturgy of 1764 and the first American Prayer Book of 1789).

The fact that any number of the Wesleys' *Hymns on the Lord's Supper 1745* can be traced, either thematically or textually, to the 1662 Prayer Book, is in fact, very useful. But far more important, I believe, would be an analysis of the Wesley hymns from the standpoint of the rich liturgical ferment going on among the Non-Jurors. We know, of course, that early on both of the Wesleys had plenty of alliances with the Non-Jurors and, at least up to the publication of the eucharistic hymns in 1745, seem to have been captivated by their general theological orientations. This liturgical research and ferment, the work of Thomas Deacon on *Apostolic Constitutions VIII*[20] and of Thomas Rattray on *The Liturgy of St. James*,[21] to mention only two representative works, seems clearly to have influenced the Wesleys in their preparation of *Hymns on the Lord's Supper.*

But again, let me emphasize the structural implications of these questions: the fact that one finds textual or thematic similarities between an epicletic text from the Prayer Book and a Wesley hymn that invokes the Holy Spirit is only the beginning of the story. Since there is no epiclesis in 1662, then the Wesleys are perhaps interested in the epiclesis before the institution narrative in the 1549 Book (a Book for which the Non-Jurors had no small degree of affection), or perhaps they were interested in the restoration of the post-anamnesis/oblation position for the epiclesis, an issue that was very much on the front burner during the days of their Non-Juror associations. Asked another way, is the epiclesis the Wesleys have in mind structurally before the institution narrative (as in 1549), or are they anticipating what will eventually be the solution in the Prayer Books of Scotland (1764) and America (1789), that is, placing the epiclesis not only after the institution narrative, but after the anamnesis and the oblation of the bread and wine as well? On the basis of Hymn 72, the "epiclesis hymn" quoted most often in the literature, such a question seems impossible to answer:

> Come, Holy Ghost, thine influence shed,
> And realize the Sign,
> Thy Life infuse into the Bread,
> And Power into the Wine.
>
> Effectual let the Tokens prove,
> And made by Heavenly Art
> Fit Channels to convey thy Love
> To every Faithful Heart.

But in the stanzas of several other hymns, one sees structural similarities that are closer to patterns emerging among the Non-Jurors than to the 1662 Prayer Book itself. For example:

Then let us go, and take and eat	*Institution Narrative*
The heavenly, everlasting meat,	
For fainting souls prepared;	
Fed with the living Bread Divine,	
Discern we in the sacred sign	
The Body of the Lord.	
Then let our faith adore the Lamb	*Anamnesis*
To-day as yesterday the same,	
In Thy great offering join,	*Oblation*
Partake the sacrificial food,	*(The result*
And eat Thy flesh and drink Thy blood,	*of) Epiclesis*
And live forever thine.	*Doxology*

It does not require too much imagination to see in the structure of these two stanzas the institution narrative, anamnesis, oblation, and (the result of) epiclesis, and even doxology, in that order. I am not inclined to believe this was a accident. I believe it suggests, fairly strongly, that the liturgical developments in England and Scotland (perhaps even biases) of the more "catholic" Non-Jurors of the early seventeenth century were well known to the Wesleys and to some degree embraced by them.

I am not well-enough acquainted with the entirety of the Wesley hymns to know whether this might prove to be a new and useful avenue for the analysis of the texts. But I hope it points to an important point: textual comparisons that pay attention only to "echoes in language" (words) and fail to pay sufficient attention to ritual structures into which that language is placed, may well be missing the more important point. An epiclesis—whether single, double, or split—is not *just* an epiclesis. Quite apart from the specific formulation of the words, the *position* of the epiclesis within the liturgical-sacramental syntax of the total eucharistic action tells one at least as much about what is believed to be happening sacramentally as the precise meaning of the words themselves.

The Anglican and Wesleyan traditions, because of our common heritage, must often tolerate with grace the insinuations from others—particularly those of the confessional traditions—for not having theological positions than can be pinned down with philosophical sophistication and precision. Although I would be inclined to debate what they *really* mean by that, it is true that we do not do as well as others when it comes to a tidy history of doctrine, nor do we excel quite as well as, say, Roman Catholics or Lutherans, when it comes to creating "agreed statements" on fine points of doctrine and practice. At this point in my life, I prefer to embrace this is a strength, not as a weakness. I find it helpful to look back at the theological inheritance of the seventeenth century, for example, and see the struggle between the Caroline divines of a sacra-mental-liturgical persuasion and their colleagues of more Puritan convictions, and honor both sides as part of our common history—both sides deeply committed to the pursuit of the truth as it was known to them, not as truth *per se*, but as the love of God in Jesus Christ. That there needed to be, indeed *had* to be an eighteenth-century evangelical revival is not to be regarded as an unfortunate historical blemish, but, in fact, as a period of great strength that, despite our sad divisions, left us all stronger and more deeply committed to the gospel "as we have received it," to paraphrase the Prayer Book. And in time, there *had* to be a Catholic revival—complete with little parish churches that deep in their hearts wanted to be great cathedrals with pointed windows, stained glass, chasubles, incense, and all that—to irritate us, and remind us, that life in God is not limited to the parameters of one's own faith experience.

Bishop Stevenson has suggested that the *Hymns on the Lord's Supper*, indeed the entire corpus of Wesley hymnody, might well be understood as a *supplement* to the Prayer Book tradition, not only to enhance it, but also to provide for what may be lacking.[22] I suspect that the point the bishop is making is that there are limits to the ability of speculative theology to capture the wonders and graces of the Holy Eucharist, so the church turns first to prayer and then to song—each with its own language and affections—in an effort to give voice to the unspeakable mystery of it all.

Dr. Cocksworth expressed it this way:

> On one level (generally corresponding with his writings), Wesley's doctrine may be stated quite precisely. However, on another level (generally corresponding with the hymns), the reality of the eucharistic mystery cannot be fully known by a spotlight on one or two systematic points; it is too diverse and complex—like a beam refracted through a prism into several colourful rays.[23]

There was a time in my own theological formation when uncertainty was an intolerable burden; but by God's mercy I have grown out of that, and now prefer to wallow around and delight in the rich ambiguity of it all. I have always suspected that was what Charles had in mind when he wrote:

> Changed from glory into Glory
> Till in Heaven we take our place
> Till we cast our crowns before Thee,
> *Lost* in wonder, love and praise.

Notes

1. *Lesser Feasts and Fasts, 1991* (New York: Church Hymnal Corporation) 159. Charles Wesley died on March 29, 1788 and John Wesley died on March 2, 1791. The Episcopal Church commemorates them on March 3, the date nearest the death of John that is open in the calendar. March 2 is kept as the commemoration of Chad, the seventh century Bishop of Lichfield.

2. Geoffrey Wainwright, "Our Elder Brethren Join: The Wesleys' *Hymns on the Lord's Supper* and the Patristic Revival in England," *Proceedings of the Charles Wesley Society I* (1994) 17-47.

3. Robert Taft, S.J., "The Structural Analysis of Liturgical Units: An Essay in Methodology," *Beyond East and West: Problems in Liturgical Understanding* (Washington: The Pastoral Press, 1984) 151–164.

4. Ted A. Campbell, *John Wesley and Christian Antiquity: Religious Vision and Cultural Change* (Nashville: Kingswood Books (Abingdon), 1991).

5. John E. Booty, "Introduction," (Vol. VI, Part 1) 183–231; and "Commentary," (Vol VI, Part 2) 653–832, in W. Speed Hill (et.al), (ed.) *The Folger Library Edition of the Works of Richard Hooker VI* (Binghamton: New York: Medieval and Renaissance Texts and Studies, 1993).

6. Christopher J. Cocksworth, *Evangelical Eucharistic Thought in the Church of England* (Cambridge: Cambridge University Press, 1993).

7. Kenneth Stevenson, *Covenant of Grace Renewed: A Vision of the Eucharist in the Seventeenth Century* (London: Dart, Longman, and Todd, 1994).

8. Henry Robert McAdoo, "A Theology of the Eucharist: Brevint and the Wesleys," *Theology XCVII* (July/August 1994) 245–256.

9. H.R. McAdoo and Kenneth Stevenson, *The Mystery of the Eucharist in the Anglican Tradition* (Norwich: The Canterbury Press, 1995).

10. C.W. Dugmore, *Eucharistic Doctrine in England from Hooker to Waterland.* (London: SPCK, 1942).

11. Stevenson, *Covenant of Grace Renewed,* 85. I acknowledge my dependence upon his reconstruction of the details of Brevint's background and relationship with John Cosin.

12. Stevenson, *Covenant of Grace Renewed,* 88.

13. Cited in Stevenson, *Covenant of Grace Renewed,* 90.

14. McAdoo, "A Theology of the Eucharist: Brevint and the Wesleys," *Theology XCVII,* 246ff. I acknowledge my dependence upon McAdoo's analysis of this material.

15. Cited in McAdoo and Stevenson, *The Mystery of the Eucharist,* 153–154.

16. Daniel Brevint, *The Christian Sacrament and Sacrifice.* Abridged by John Wesley and attached to John and Charles Wesley, *Hymns on the Lord's Supper, 1745.* Facsimile of the 1745 Farley Edition: The Charles Wesley Society (1995) 15.

17. Cited in McAdoo, "A Theology of the Eucharist," 251.

18. McAdoo, "A Theology of the Eucharist," 252.

19. *John Wesley's Prayer Book: The Sunday Service of the Methodists in North America.* With Introduction, Notes, and Commentary by James F. White (Cleveland: OSL Publications, 1991).

20. Thomas Deacon, *A Compleat Collection of Devotions* (London, 1734); see also *A Full, True, and Comprehensive View of Christianity* (London, 1747).

21. Thomas Rattray, *The Ancient Liturgy of the Church of Jerusalem, being the Liturgy of St. James* (London, 1744).

22. McAdoo and Stevenson, *The Mystery of the Eucharist,* 172.

23. Cocksworth, *Evangelical Eucharistic Thought,* 68.

Returning to Our Musical Roots: Early Shape-Note Tunes in Recent American Hymnals

Harry Eskew

Since the publication of Alex Haley's *Roots* (1976) and its popular television miniseries (1977), Americans have become increasingly interested in digging into their family trees. This same process has been occurring in American music, for Americans have been discovering many of their musical roots in folk music. In the decades after the Civil War, Americans discovered the rich store of African-American song that developed during the days of slavery in the South. From the 1870s the touring Fisk Jubilee Singers made the black spirituals widely known in this country and in Europe. In the second decade of this century the British folksong scholar Cecil Sharp came to the southern Appalachians and collected and published a sizable body of traditional English ballads that had been brought across the Atlantic and preserved among the isolated mountain folk.[1] In addition to the discovery of African-American song and the Anglo-American ballad, there is a third body of folksong that came to be known to the American public beginning in the 1930s—Anglo-American folk hymnody of the shape-note tradition reflecting oral traditions with such characteristic traits as modal melodies and gapped scales. It is this sacred folksong and the story of its discovery and subsequent spread and incorporation into congregational song which is the focus of this essay.

Discovery of Folk Hymnody

In the 1930s the shape-note tradition of singing was virtually unknown outside of the circles of those singers who grew up with it in the South. Such well known singing-school shape-note tunebooks as *The Southern Harmony* (1835) and *The Sacred Harp* (1844) were not even mentioned in the histories of American music of that time. A key year that marks the beginning of the discovery of our rich heritage of shape-note folk hymnody is 1933, the year in which the University of North Carolina Press published *White Spirituals in the Southern Uplands: The Story of the Fasola Folk, Their Songs, Singings, and "Buckwheat Notes."* The author, George Pullen Jackson, was not by training a musicologist or hymnologist; he was a professor of German, serving from 1918 to 1943 as chairman of the Department of German at Vanderbilt University in Nashville. It was, however, his second career, as a historian of American sacred folksong, for which Jackson became widely known.

Jackson relates how he discovered the shape-note singing tradition in the opening pages of his *White Spirituals:*

> The word "Fasola" is not of my making. Neither is it to be found in any dictionary. But ask almost any real country person of mature years anywhere in the wide stretches of the southern states—the hilly and mountainous regions principally, which make up the far greater part of that section—if he knows anything about fasola singers, and he will very likely be able to direct you to one of them, or perhaps to a group in a "singin'."

Jackson then described how he had lived in the South for years unaware of the fasola singing tradition until he learned about it from John W. Barton of the Ward-Belmont School:

> Dr. Barton described one of the fasola "singin'-all-day-and-dinner-on-the-grounds" conventions which he had observed in Texas and told of the singers' claims to an art of song which had come down in direct line from the earliest music of the world, as that earliest music had been revealed in the Bible and by subsequent history. He told also of their strange notation and of a music theory, singing schools, teachers, and song books which were exclusively the rurals' own, making these people, in effect, as contrasted to music and musicians as they are known in occidental urban culture, a sort of "lost tonal tribe."
>
> There was, I soon found out, a large ingredient of truth along with the manifest element of romance in the country songsters' claims. There was so much truth, indeed, and truth that has impressed me as being so important and interesting, culturally and historically, and so completely unknown to the archivists of culture-lore, that its story on the following pages can need no apology.

In his *White Spirituals,* Jackson sought to tell the American public what he had discovered in his quest for the roots of American sacred folksong.

Harry Eskew

It has been my good fortune, and good fun, incidentally to have uncovered a goodly batch of the aged handbooks of spiritual folk-song which seem to have completely escaped all other collectors and all other diggers into American institutions. How and where I found them, what strange sorts of songs they contained, whence the unique notation in which the songs are recorded, who made, collected, and sang them, how, when, and where they came into being, and how and where their singing persists at present—these are a few of the problems which have claimed my interest for a number of years and have provided matter for discussion in *White Spirituals*.

Folklorist Don Yoder described the reception of *White Spirituals* in his introduction to the 1964 reprint[2] of Jackson's book:

White Spirituals was an immediate success. It was widely reviewed both here and in Britain and received favorable notice everywhere. The sense of discovery, of something new, something important to America, is commented on many times.

Having written a history of the shape-note tradition in his *White Spirituals*, Jackson then provided hundreds of examples of sacred folksongs in several of his later books: *Spiritual Folksongs of Early America* (1837), *Down East Spirituals and Others* (1939), and in his last book, *Another Sheaf of White Spirituals* (1952).

In addition to telling the story of this southern sacred folksong to those outside of this culture, Jackson sought to encourage the survival of shape-note singing. Yoder describes how Jackson was equally at home in the world of the symphony orchestra and in the world of the rural singings.

If Jackson was concerned to evangelize urban America on its native folksong heritage, he likewise worked with his rural friends—the "fasola people," as he liked to call them—to prolong the life of this most widespread of America's native song traditions. "Uncle George," or "Pappy Jackson," as he came to be called in affectionate Southern fashion, sang along with and led in singing those summer-day assemblies of rural singers in the little county-seat towns of the South—those occasions of "singin'-all-day-and-dinner-on-the-grounds" that he has described so winsomely and so revealingly. If the coat-and-tails academic Jackson may be seen in his organization of the Nashville Symphony Society and the Vanderbilt Choir, an equally authentic shirt-sleeve variety "Uncle George" Jackson is seen organizing the Tennessee Sacred Harp Singin Association, and the Old Harp Singers, a group which toured the nation singing the white spirituals of the South. In all of this, as in his books, with their understanding of the rural psychology that kept these songs alive into the twentieth century, one senses the warmth of the man.

In addition to George Pullen Jackson, others were active in bringing the early shape-note folk hymns to public attention. In 1934 the Virginia composer John Powell edited *Twelve Folk Hymns*, harmonized by Powell along with Annabel Morris Buchanan and Hilton Rufty, and published by

J. Fisher and Brother of New York City. This same publisher in 1938 brought out Annabel Morris Buchanan's *Folk Hymns of America*, containing her harmonization of LAND OF REST, which has been used for "Jerusalem, My Happy Home" in several hymnals.[3] Mrs. Buchanan, co-organizer of the White Top Folk Festival in the mountains of southwestern Virginia in 1931, also wrote an important pioneering article on American folk hymns for the 1943 reference work, Oscar Thompson's *The International Cyclopedia of Music and Musicians* (New York: Dodd, Mead and Co.).

The 1930s were not only important in the publication of books about American folk hymns and the publication of choral arrangements; this decade was also an important time for the republication of *The Southern Harmony* and *The Sacred Harp*. In 1936 the Denson revision of *The Sacred Harp*, entitled *The Original Sacred Harp*, was published. This twentieth-century edition, revised again in 1960, 1967, 1971, and 1991, is the most widely used edition of *The Sacred Harp*. In 1939 a reprint of the 1854 edition of *Southern Harmony* was published by Hastings House of New York, especially to provide copies for the annual Big Singing Day each fourth Sunday in May at Benton, Kentucky. When this reprint appeared, a story on the Benton singing appeared in *Time* magazine (June 12, 1939, 67).[4] Thus the shape-note heritage was gradually becoming known to the American public at large, beginning in 1933 with Jackson's *White Spirituals*.

The early shape-note tradition also received attention from America's composers. As early as 1928, five years before Jackson's *White Spirituals*, Virgil Thomson completed his *Symphony on a Hymn Tune*, which consists of a set of variations on the tune FOUNDATION (How Firm a Foundation).[5] Thomson's symphony was followed in 1937 with his choral arrangement of *My Shepherd Will Supply My Need*, based on the folk hymn tune RESIGNATION taken from *Southern Harmony*, and in 1949 by *Hymns from the Old South*,[6] which included shape-note settings of "Morning Star," "Greenfields," and "Death, 'tis a Melancholy Day."

A number of other American composers took the early shape-note tunes and arranged them for choirs. These tunes have taken their place in the standard repertory along with the black spirituals. Particularly noteworthy are the choral arrangements of Alice Parker and Robert Shaw recorded in the 1960 Shaw Chorale album *What Wondrous Love*. These included, in addition to "Wondrous Love," such well known folk hymns as "The Morning Trumpet," "Samarantha" ("His Voice as the Sound"), and "Amazing Grace." A second album of Alice Parker's beautiful choral arrangements of early American folk hymns sung by the Shaw Chorale, *Sing to the Lord*, was released in 1967. Alice Parker continued her interest in the early shape-note tradition, composing an opera, *Singers Glen* (1978), based on the life of Joseph Funk, a

Mennonite from the Shenandoah Valley of Virginia, and utilizing music from Funk's shape-note tunebook *New Harmonia Sacra* (1832).[7]

Probably no one in recent times has done more to promote this early tradition of shape-note singing than Hugh McGraw of the Sacred Harp Publishing Company, Bremen, Georgia. He has led Sacred Harp singing at numerous conferences, such as those of The Hymn Society in the United States and Canada, the Sonneck Society for American Music, and the summer Church Music Conferences of the Southern Baptist Sunday School Board. He also led Sacred Harp singing at Expo 67 in Montreal, and at the Smithsonian Institution's Festival of American Folklife in 1970, 1976, and 1982, when he was awarded a National Heritage Fellowship by the National Endowment for the Arts. McGraw's leadership of this movement also resulted in the establishment of a Sacred Harp Museum near Carrollton, Georgia, and of a Sacred Harp Foundation.

A particularly remarkable development of the Sacred Harp singing movement in the 1980s and 1990s has been the spread of this tradition outside of its home in the rural areas of the South. Sacred Harp singing has spread to the Northeast, the Midwest, and to the West Coast. Perhaps the most enthusiastic Sacred Harp singers are those in Chicago who host an annual Midwest Convention.[8] Thus the shape-note folksong singing tradition of the South has become a national phenomenon with singers participating from practically every region of this country.

Shape-Note Folk Hymns in American Hymnals

Before the 1930s, few major American hymnals included a significant number of texts and/or tunes from the shape-note folk-hymn tradition. In the latter half of the twentieth century practically every major American hymnal has included a larger selection of American folk hymns than its predecessor. A comparison of such major denominational hymnals as *The Methodist Hymnal* (1935) and *The Methodist Hymnal* (1964) (later retitled *The Book of Hymns*), the Southern Baptist *Baptist Hymnal* (1956) and *Baptist Hymnal* (1975), and *Service Book and Hymnal* (Lutheran, 1958) and *Lutheran Book of Worship* (1978) show the latter hymnal in each case with a significantly larger number of American folk hymns. To illustrate the growing acceptance of American folk hymnody in hymnals of recent decades, the remainder of this essay will focus on a comparison of the inclusion of this tradition in the Episcopal hymnals of 1940 and 1982.

The Hymnal 1940

The Hymnal 1940, published by the Episcopal Church in 1943, included only four early folk hymn tunes, each one set to texts not associated with tunes of the American folk hymn tradition. KEDRON (to a translation from Clement of Alexandria, "Sunset to sunrise changes now") (H40–81), is a melody in the Aeolian mode published as early as 1799.[9] A second tune, LAND OF REST (to the late sixteenth- or early seventeenth-century English ballad text, "Jerusalem, my happy home," H40–585), is a pentatonic (five-note) melody published in 1836.[10] The other two folk hymn tunes in *The Hymnal 1940* consist of the same tune used twice: MORNING SONG, also in the Aeolian mode, was first published in 1820.[11] MORNING SONG serves as the musical setting in *The Hymnal 1940* for two twentieth century texts: "O holy city, seen of John" (H40–494) by Walter Russell Bowie, and "Awake, awake to love and work" (H40–156) by Geoffrey A. Studdert-Kennedy.

The Hymnal 1982

In contrast to *The Hymnal 1940, The Hymnal 1982* includes a much larger selection of early American folk hymns, primarily tunes from early nineteenth-century shape-note tunebooks, increasing from three to twenty. The tunes KEDRON, LAND OF REST, and MORNING SONG are still included, each serving as musical settings for two texts.[12]

Six of the twenty folk hymns in *The Hymnal 1982* have received ecumenical acceptance in recent American hymnody, appearing in practically every major denomination's hymnal. Of these six folk hymns, two of the tunes are used twice and four of these consist of both texts and tunes from the early shape-note tradition. The most popular, "Amazing grace, how sweet the sound" (NEW BRITAIN, H82–671), is a text by the Anglican clergyman John Newton, first published in *Olney Hymns* (London, 1779). Its pentatonic folk tune NEW BRITAIN was published in America with other texts as early as 1829,[13] but first published with "Amazing Grace" by William Walker in the first edition of his *Southern Harmony* (Spartanburg, SC; printed by Nathan Whiting, New Haven, CT, 1835). "Amazing Grace," beloved by people of many cultures and nationalities, is the subject of an extensive television documentary by Bill Moyers.[14]

A second among these six folk hymn settings is "How firm a foundation, ye saints of the Lord" (H82–636), an anonymous text first published in London Baptist pastor John Rippon's *A Selection of Hymns from the Best Authors* (London, 1787). In *The Hymnal 1940* this text was set to LYONS, with ST.

DENIO listed as an alternate tune. In *The Hymnal 1982* this English hymn is set to the early American pentatonic folk tune FOUNDATION,[15] the tune used with this text in early shape-note tunebooks and now found with this text in most recent American hymnals.[16]

A third of these ecumenically accepted folk hymn settings is "Come, thou Fount of every blessing" (H82–686), a text written in 1758 by the English Baptist pastor Robert Robinson and associated with the tune NETTLETON, first published with this text in John Wyeth's *Repository of Sacred Music, Part Second* (Harrisburg, 1813), and subsequently reprinted often during the following decades in shape-note tunebooks of the Midwest and South.

The fourth of these five folk hymns is "What wondrous love is this, O my soul, O my soul" (WONDROUS LOVE, H82–439), with both text and tune from the early South. The anonymous folk text, in the same meter as the ballad "Captain Kidd," first appeared in Virginia and Kentucky in two hymnals published in 1811.[17] The haunting hexatonic (six-note) melody in the Dorian mode of WONDROUS LOVE is widely considered one of the most beautiful of the early American folk hymns. WONDROUS LOVE first appeared in print in 1840 [second] edition of William Walker's *Southern Harmony*.[18]

The fifth of the folk hymns of ecumenical acceptance in *The Hymnal 1982* is HOLY MANNA, a pentatonic melody which was first published in Tennessee in 1825, ascribed to William Moore in his *Columbian Harmony*.[19] In Moore's tunebook and other early shape-note collections, HOLY MANNA is associated with a camp meeting text, "Brethren, we have met to worship."[20] In *The Hymnal 1982* HOLY MANNA is associated with two very different hymn texts: John Mason Neale's translation of a twelfth century Latin hymn, "Blessed feasts of blessed martyrs" (H82–238) and the American Catherine Cameron's hymn of 1967, "God, who stretched the spangled heavens" (H82–580).

The sixth of the folk hymns of ecumenical acceptance in *The Hymnal 1982* is LAND OF REST, the only one in this group to be carried over from *The Hymnal 1940*. Here it is set not only to "Jerusalem, my happy home" (H82–620), but also to Brian Wren's communion text of 1968, "I come with joy to meet my Lord" (H82–304).

Several hymn texts included in *The Hymnal 1940* have been carried over into *The Hymnal 1982*, but set in the latter hymnal to tunes of the American folk hymn tradition. One example already mentioned is "Blessed Feasts of blessed martyrs," set to HOLY MANNA (H82–258). Reginald Heber's Epiphany hymn, "Brightest and best of the stars of the morning" is given its usual nineteenth-century tune, MORNING STAR (H82–117), as its first tune. A second tune is provided from the American folk tradition, STAR IN THE EAST (H82–118), an Aeolian mode melody taken from the first edition of Walker's *Southern Harmony*.[21] In addition to its unison setting with a choice of guitar or keyboard accompaniment, *The Hymnal 1982* provides William Walker's three-part harmonization of STAR IN THE EAST, with the melody in the tenor, the usual voice part carrying the melody in this early American tradition.[22] Another text from *The Hymnal 1940* given an American folk hymn tune in *The Hymnal 1982* is John Keble's "New every morning is the love" (H40–155, H82–10). Keble's hymn in the latter hymnal is set to KEDRON, and its tune used in *The Hymnal 1940*, MELCOMBE, is cited as an alternate tune. KEDRON is given with guitar chords, and an alternative harmonization is cited (H82–162). One more text from the earlier Episcopal hymnal now given an American folk hymn setting is Frances R. Havergal's "Jesus calls us o'er the tumult" (H40–566, H82–550). This hymn's two tunes in *The Hymnal 1940* (CHESTER and GALILEE) are replaced with two other tunes in *The Hymnal 1982*. The first is David Hurd's recent tune ST. ANDREW, a unison melody with free accompaniment, and the second is RESTORATION, a pentatonic tune first published in 1835 in William Walker's *Southern Harmony*. Two harmonizations of RESTORATION are supplied, one similar to that of Walker and an alternate accompaniment written for *The Hymnal 1982* by Margaret Mealy.

One more category for text associations of folk hymn tunes in *The Hymnal 1982* consists of seven hymn texts not found in *The Hymnal 1940* which have been set to tunes of this early American tradition. The oldest of these texts, "Now let us all with one accord," (H82–147) is a translation from the Latin attributed to Gregory the Great, set to BOURBON, a pentatonic tune first published in Freeman Lewis's *Beauties of Harmony* (Pittsburgh, 1814). The tune BOURBON is used a second time as the setting for Connecticut Episcopalian minister Charles W. Everest's "Take up your cross, the Savior said" (H82–645). Also from *Beauties of Harmony* is the hexatonic tune DUNLAP'S CREEK (H82–276), set to Cecil Frances Alexander's hymn for the feast day of St. James, "For thy blest saints, a noble throng."

One of these seven texts set to melodies from the American folk tradition was published with its tune in an early shape-note tunebook. Charles Wesley's text, "Come away to the skies," was published with the tune MIDDLEBURY in the second edition (ca. 1821–1824) of the Shenandoah Valley tunebook, *Supplement to the Kentucky Harmony* by Ananias Davisson. Wesley's text, originally written as a birthday hymn for his wife, exudes a joy appropriate for Easter. MIDDLEBURY (H82–213), with its unusually wide range (an octave and a fourth) and its repeated upbeat rhythms, captures the joyful mood of Wesley's text in a wonderful way. *The Hymnal 1982* not only provides Jack W. Burnam's harmonization of MIDDLEBURY but also gives chord indications for guitar and an accompaniment in a higher key for hand bells by Marilyn Keiser.

Harry Eskew

Three of the texts not in *The Hymnal 1940* set to tunes from the shape-note tradition in *The Hymnal 1982* are texts written in the twentieth century. One of these, already mentioned in the group of ecumenically accepted tunes, is "God who stretched the spangled heavens" of Catherine Cameron, set to HOLY MANNA (H82–580). A second text from this century is Rosamond E. Herklots's "Forgive our sins as we forgive" set to DETROIT (H82–674), a hexatonic melody from Ananias Davisson's *Supplement to Kentucky Harmony* (Harrisonburg, VA, 1820). The third of these twentieth-century texts set to folk hymn melodies is "All who love and serve your city" by the hymnologist and hymn writer Erik Routley, set to the tune CHARLESTOWN (H82–571), a hexatonic tune published in Amos Pilsbury's *The United States Sacred Harmony* (Charleston, SC, 1799), the round-note tunebook that also included KEDRON.

Conclusions

The discovery of American folk hymnody is undoubtedly one of the signal events influencing the development of hymnody in the latter half of our century. Much of the credit for this discovery belongs to George Pullen Jackson, who through his publications beginning in 1933 sympathetically told the story of this tradition and made it widely accessible through his books. The tradition of American folk hymnody, which appeared in numerous shape-note singing-school tunebooks in the early nineteenth century and which have survived largely through Sacred Harp singings in rural sections of the South, has experienced expansion into urban areas from coast to coast in the latter decades of this century. In addition to its life in these singing sessions, this tradition has had a significant impact on major American hymnals which has been felt in the latter half of this century, for practically every mainstream denominational hymnal has included more American folk hymnody than the hymnal it replaced. This increase in American folk hymnody is well-illustrated by comparing the Episcopal hymnals of 1940 and 1982, in which the number of these folk hymns to be included grew from four to twenty, with several tunes associated with more than one text. Although several well-known hymns with both text and tunes from the early nineteenth-century tunebooks (such as "Amazing Grace," "Come, thou fount of every blessing," "How firm a foundation," and "Wondrous Love") have been added to *The Hymnal 1982*, in most cases the American folk hymn tunes have been appropriated for use with hymn texts from a wide range of periods and traditions. As a result of this return to our musical roots, congregations throughout our country are rediscovering some of the rich treasures of American folk hymnody when they join their voices in singing as they worship from week to week.

Notes

1. Cecil J. Sharp, *English Folk Songs from the Southern Appalachians* Maud Karpeles, ed. (London: Oxford University Press, 1932).

2. Hatboro, PA: Folklore Associates.

3. See *The Hymnal 1940* (hereafter H40), no. 585 and The *Hymnal 1982* (hereafter H82), no. 620. LAND OF REST is also used as the tune for Brian Wren's communion text, "I come with joy to meet my Lord." (H82–304).

4. A recent comprehensive study of this singing is Deborah Carlton Loftis, "Big Singing Day in Benton, Kentucky: A Study of Ethnic Identity and Musical Style of Southern Harmony Singers" (Ph.D. dissertation, University of Kentucky, 1987).

5. H82–636.

6. Published by H. W. Gray.

7. Funk's *New Harmonia Sacra* is still in use in Shenandoah Valley singings. This, the earliest of all shape-note tunebooks still in use, is in its twenty-fifth edition, published in 1993 by Good Books, Intercourse, PA 17534.

8. Information on Sacred Harp singings is found in an annual publication, *Sacred Harp Singings,* available from Jeff and Shelbie Shepperd, PO Box 5246, Glencoe, AL 35905.

9. In Amos Pilsbury's round-note *United States Sacred Harmony,* but later often reprinted in shape-note tunebooks.

10. LAND OF REST appears in both *The Hymnal 1940* and in *The Hymnal 1982* in Annabel Morris Buchannan's harmonization from her *Folk Hymns of America.*

11. In John Wyeth's *Repository of Sacred Music, Part Second* (Harrisburg, PA, 1813, 1820 ed.). This edition was reprinted in 1964 by Da Capo Press of New York.

12. American folk hymns and their texts in H40 and H82 are listed at the close of this essay.

13. In *Columbian Harmony, or Pilgrim's Musical Companion* by Benjamin Shaw and Charles H. Spilman (Cincinnati, 1829) in variant forms under the names ST. MARY'S and GALLAHER.

14. This 87-minute documentary, *Amazing Grace with Bill Moyers,* is available as PBS Home Video 123 (Beverly Hills, CA: Pacific Arts, 1990).

15. First published in the Shenandoah Valley in Joseph Funk's shape-note tunebook, *Genuine Church Music* (Winchester, VA, 1832).

16. *The Hymnal 1982* lists LYONS as an alternative tune.

17. The second edition of Stith Mead's *A General Selection of the Newest and Most Admired Hymns and Spiritual Songs Now in Use* (Lynchburg, VA) and Starke Dupuy's *A Selection of Hymns and Spiritual Songs* (Frankfort, KY).

18. Walker indicated WONDROUS LOVE to be "Arranged by James Christopher, of Spartanburg, S. C. A very popular old Southern tune." William Walker, *Christian Harmony* (Spartanburg, SC, but printed at Philadelphia, 1867) 359.

19. (Cincinnati: Printed for the compiler by Morgan, Lodge, and Fisher). Moore lived in Wilson County, Tennessee, but since this county was home to at least four William Moores, the exact identity of the compiler is unknown.

20. This camp meeting text is found in *The Baptist Hymnal* (Nashville: Convention Press, 1991) 379.

21. The earliest printing of STAR IN THE EAST, cited by Marion Hatchett is in the "Sixth Edition, Enlarged and Improved" of *The Temple Harmony* (Hallowell, ME, 1826) a round-note tunebook of Japheth Coombs Washburn. This tune was later published in numerous shape-note tunebooks. Marion Hatchett, "118 *Brightest and best of the stars*

of the morning," The Hymnal 1982 Companion, Vol. 3A, Raymond F. Glover, ed. (New York: The Church Hymnal Corporation, 1994) 245.

22. The editorial policy in most hymnals, including *The Hymnal 1940* and *The Hymnal 1982,* is to invert the tenor and soprano lines in early American tunes so the original tenor melody is assigned to the soprano an octave higher and the soprano part is lowered an octave to become the tenor part.

Appendix

American Folk Hymnody in *The Hymnal 1940* and *The Hymnal 1982*

I. *The Hymnal 1940:*
    KEDRON – "Sunset to sunrise changes now" (81)
    LAND OF REST – "Jerusalem, my happy home" (585)
    MORNING SONG – "O holy city, seen of John" (494), "Awake, awake to love and work" (156)

II. *The Hymnal 1982:*
    BOURBON – "Now let us all with one accord" (147), "Take up your cross, the Savior said" (645)
    CHARLESTOWN – "All who love and serve your city" (571)
    DETROIT – "Forgive our sins as we forgive" (674)
    DUNLAP'S CREEK – "For thy blest saints, a noble throng" (276)
    FOUNDATION – "How firm a foundation, ye saints of the Lord" (636)
    HOLY MANNA – "Blessed feasts of blessed martyrs" (238), "God, who stretched the spangled heavens" (580)
    KEDRON – "New every morning is the love" (10), "Sunset to sunrise changes now" (163)
    LAND OF REST – "I come with joy to meet my Lord" (304), "Jerusalem, my happy home" (620)
    MIDDLEBURY – "Come away to the skies" (213)
    NETTLETON – "Come, thou fount of every blessing" (686)
    NEW BRITAIN – "Amazing grace, how sweet the sound" (671)
    RESTORATION – "Jesus call us o'er the tumult" (550)
    STAR IN THE EAST – "Brightest and best of the stars of the morning" (118)
    WONDROUS LOVE – "What wondrous love is this, O my soul, O my soul" (439)

Americans in the
English Hymnal of 1906

David W. Music

THE *ENGLISH HYMNAL* OF 1906 has long been recognized as one of the landmark hymnals of the twentieth century. Compiled and edited primarily by Percy Dearmer and Ralph Vaughan Williams, this collection was remarkable on several counts. Unlike many of its immediate predecessors, the *English Hymnal* was designed mainly for the congregation rather than the choir and was one of the first hymnals to provide tunes in unison settings and lower keys. The book was perhaps the most eclectic hymnal that had been published to that time, drawing from a wide variety of traditions and sources. It introduced—or reintroduced—into common use many historic styles of hymnody and served as the source for new texts and tunes that became part of the standard congregational repertory of the twentieth century.[1] The hymnal was distinctly liturgical in tone, offering "hymns with specific liturgical functions" rather than "hymns that could be used within the liturgy."[2] In spite of its eclecticism, the book was also extraordinary for its character as a national hymnal (implicit in its very title), emphasizing the contributions of the English people to the song of the church. The result of these innovations was a hymnal that not only proved to be popular in the churches, but one that served as a model for succeeding generations of hymnals in both Great Britain and North America.

One aspect of the *English Hymnal* that is often overlooked is the contribution made to its pages by authors and composers of the United States. Americans, of course, had been using psalm and hymn texts and tunes of

British origin in their worship since the first English settlers arrived in the New World. Beginning with the *Bay Psalm Book* of 1640, Americans had also been making their own contributions to the repertory of congregational song. However, hymns by Americans were seldom included in British collections. Indeed, in the words of Percy Dearmer, during the nineteenth century "the modern American school [of hymnody] was hardly consulted–if at all–by Anglican compilers; and, as it happened, it was just in America that the best hymns, and those which are most in accord with the convictions of the present age, were then being written."[3] It was left to the *English Hymnal* to become one of the first influential British collections to make extensive use of American materials in its pages.

The purpose of this study is to call attention to the presence of these American contributions in one of the most significant English hymnals of the twentieth century. In this context, a text or tune is considered to be of "American origin" if it were written by a native of the United States or by an immigrant to America. In the latter case, the text or tune must have been written after the author or composer left his or her native country for the United States, and its first publication must have been in the New World. For example, George J. Webb is said to have written the tune WEBB "in 1830 as he sailed from England to Boston";[4] therefore, WEBB is here considered to be an American tune, particularly since its first publications–both as a secular and a hymn tune–occurred in America. On the other hand, the composer of MAIDSTONE, Walter B. Gilbert, was an Englishman who immigrated to America after he composed and published this particular tune; thus, MAIDSTONE is considered to be non-American in origin.

The use of American tunes in the *English Hymnal* was noted in Vaughan Williams's preface to the music, in which he specifically pointed out "Lowell Mason's tunes, certain tunes from 'Sacred Songs and Solos,' and a few 'Western melodies' in use in America as hymn tunes" (p. xvi). No equivalent mention of the use of American texts was made in the general preface to the book. Hymns of American origin were not specifically identified as such in the *English Hymnal* except when the writer was a bishop in the Episcopal Church, in which case the site of his bishopric was listed in the index of authors (e.g., "Brooks, Phillips, Bishop of Massachusetts," 944).

Thirty-two texts and 15 tunes in the *English Hymnal* have been traced to American origins. These texts and tunes, together with their authors and composers, are listed in table 1.

Table 1

Text	Author	Tune	Composer	# in English Hymnal
All things are thine no gift have we	Whittier, J. G.			173
City of God how broad and fair	Johnson, Samuel			375
Dear Lord and Father of mankind	Whittier, J.G.			383
Eternal ruler of the ceaseless round	Chadwick, J.W.			384
Father hear the prayer we offer	Willis, Mrs. Love M.			385
Father to thee we look in all our sorrow	Hosmer, F.L.			538
Fling out the banner let it float	Doane, G.W.			546
God be with you til we meet again	Rankin, J.E.			524
Ho my comrades see the signal	Bliss, P.P.	HOLD THE FORT	Bliss, P.P.	570
I hear thy welcome voice	Hartsough, Lewis	I HEAR THY WELCOME VOICE	Hartsough, Lewis	573
I look to thee in every need	Longfellow, Samuel			406
I love to hear the story	Miller, Emily			594
Immortal love for ever full	Whittier, J.G.			408
It came upon the midnight clear	Sears, E.H.			26
Jesus these eyes have never seen	Palmer, Ray			421

Text	Author	Tune	Composer	# in English Hymnal
Lord of all being throned afar	Holmes, O. Wendell			434
My faith looks up to thee	Palmer, Ray	OLIVET	Mason, Lowell	439
O little town of Bethlehem	Brooks, Phillips			15
O Lord and master of us all	Whittier, J.G.			456
O north with all thy vales of green	Bryant, W. Cullen			550
O thou in all thy might so far	Hosmer, F.L.			463
Once to every man and nation	Lowell, J. Russell			563
Safe in the arms of Jesus	Van Alsyne, Frances J.	ARMS OF JESUS	Doane, W.H.	580
Saviour sprinkle many nations	Coxe, A. Cleveland			551
Stand up stand up for Jesus	Duffield, George	MORNING LIGHT	Webb, G.J.	581
Still will we trust though earth seem dark and dreary	Burleigh, W.H.			482
Take up thy cross the Saviour said	Everest, C.W.			484
The summer days are gone again	Longfellow, Samuel			288
Thy kingdom come on bended knee	Hosmer, F.L.			504
'Tis winter now the fallen snow	Longfellow, Samuel			295

Text	Author	Tune	Composer	# in English Hymnal
Who is he in yonder stall	Hanby, B.R.			612
Who is this with garments gory	Coxe, A Cleveland			108
		ADVENT	Plymouth Collection	342
		ALL SOULS	Yoakley, J.	429
		BENEATH THE CROSS	Sankey, I.D.	App 22
		IVES	Ives, Elam, Jr.	582
		MISSIONARY HYMN	Mason, Lowell	577
		MONTGOMERY	Woodbury, I.B.	391
		PLEADING SAVIOUR	Plymouth Collection	593
		TELL ME THE OLD, OLD STORY	Doane, W.H.	583
		THE NINETY AND NINE	Sankey, I.D.	584
		ZUNDEL	Zundel, John	615

Table 1 reveals that the American hymns in the *English Hymnal* were written by 23 different poets and 10 named composers.[5] Twenty-seven of the American texts were linked with tunes that were not of American origin, while 10 American tunes were set to non-American texts; five hymns were completely American in both words and music. Five American authors were represented by two or more texts: John Greenleaf Whittier (4), Frederick L. Hosmer (3), Samuel W. Longfellow (3), A. Cleveland Coxe (2), and Ray Palmer (2). Three American composers were drawn upon for two tunes each: William H. Doane, Lowell Mason, and Ira D. Sankey.

While a number of the American authors and composers whose works were used by the compilers of the *English Hymnal* are quite well-known in hymnic or literary circles, several of them are considerably more obscure. Table 2 presents a brief biographical sketch of each of the text and tune writers, with reference to a source in which more information can be found.

Table 2

Brief Biographies of American Authors and Composers in the English Hymnal

Key to sigla: BaptHyBkComp=R. W. Thomson, ed. *The Baptist Hymn Book Companion,* rev. ed. London: Psalms and Hymns Trust, 1967.

H40Comp=[Leonard Ellinwood, ed.]. *The Hymnal 1940 Companion,* 2nd ed., rev. New York: Church Pension Fund, 1951.

H82Comp=Raymond F. Glover, gen. ed. *The Hymnal 1982 Companion,* vol. 2. New York: Church Hymnal Corporation, 1994.

HandBaptHy=Jere V. Adams, ed. *Handbook to The Baptist Hymnal.* Nashville: Convention Press, 1992.

Bliss, P. P. (1838–1876). Gospel song author/composer and evangelistic singer, co-compiler with Ira D. Sankey of *Gospel Hymns and Sacred Songs* (1875). [HandBaptHy]

Brooks, Phillips (1835–1893). Episcopalian. Minister at churches in Philadelphia and Boston, Bishop of Massachusetts, renowned preacher. [H82Comp]

Bryant, William C. (1794–1878). Distinguished poet, founder of *New York Review* and editor of *New York Evening Post.* Author of "Thanatopsis." [H40Comp]

Burleigh, William H. (1812–1871). Unitarian. Journalist, temperance and antislavery activist, publisher of *Christian Witness* and *Temperance Banner* (Pittsburgh), editor of *Christian Freeman (Charter Oak).* [H82Comp]

Chadwick, John W. (1840–1904). Unitarian. Minister at Second Unitarian Church, Brooklyn, for 40 years. [H82Comp]

Coxe, Arthur Cleveland (1818–1896). Episcopalian. Minister at churches in Hartford, Connecticut; Baltimore; and New York City. Bishop of Western New York. [H40Comp]

Doane, George W. (1799–1859). Episcopalian. Minister at churches in New York City and Boston, professor at Washington (Trinity) College, Hartford, Connecticut, Bishop of New Jersey. [H82Comp]

Doane, William H. (1832–1915). Baptist. Businessman in Connecticut, Illinois, and Ohio. [HandBaptHy]

Duffield, George, Jr. (1818–1888). Presbyterian. Minister at churches in New

York, New Jersey, Pennsylvania, Michigan, and Illinois. Editor of *Christian Observer*. [H82Comp]

Everest, Charles W. (1814–1877). Episcopalian. Minister at Hamden, Connecticut

Hanby, Benjamin R. (1833–1867). United Brethren. Minister at churches in Ohio, music editor for John Church and Root and Cady publishing houses, composer of the popular Christmas song "Santa Claus [Up on the Housetop]." [HandBaptHy]

Hartsough, Lewis (1828–1919). Methodist. Minister and denominational worker in New York, Utah, and Iowa. Music editor of Joseph Hillman's *The Revivalist* (1868). [HandBaptHy]

Holmes, Oliver Wendell (1809–1894). Unitarian. Professor at Dartmouth and Harvard, co-founder of *Atlantic Monthly*. Author of "The Chambered Nautilus." [H82Comp]

Hosmer, Frederick L. (1840–1929). Unitarian. Ministered at churches in Massachusetts, Illinois, Ohio, Missouri, and California. [H82Comp]

Johnson, Samuel (1822–1882). "Never definitely connected with any religious denomination," though "regarded as a Unitarian" [H40Comp]. Ministered at Free Church in Lynn, Massachusetts.

Longfellow, Samuel (1819–1892). Unitarian. Ministered at churches in Massachusetts, New York, and Pennsylvania. [H40 Comp]

Lowell, James Russell (1819–1891). Professor at Harvard, United States Minister to Spain, ambassador to England, editor of *Atlantic Monthly* and *North American Review*. [H40Comp]

Mason, Lowell (1792–1872). Presbyterian. Church organist and choir director in Georgia and Massachusetts, conductor of Boston Handel and Haydn Society, founder of Boston Academy of Music, and leader in music education in the United States. [HandBaptHy]

Miller, Emily (1833–1913). Dean of Women at Northwestern University, co-editor of *Little Corporal*. [BaptHyBkComp]

Palmer, Ray (1808–1887). Congregationalist. Minister at churches in Maine and New York, Corresponding Secretary of American Congregational Union, New York City. [H82Comp]

Plymouth Collection (1855). Hymnal by Henry W. Beecher, Charles Beecher, and John Zundel. One of the first standard hymnals to print words and music together on the same page.

Rankin, Jeremiah E. (1828–1904). Congregationalist. Minister at churches in New York, Vermont, Massachusetts, Washington, D. C., and New Jersey. President of Howard University. [H82Comp]

Sankey, Ira D. (1840–1908). Methodist. Evangelistic singer with Dwight L. Moody, compiler of *Sacred Songs and Solos* (1873), and co-compiler of the influential *Gospel Hymns* series (1875 and following). [HandBaptHy]

Sears, Edmund H. (1810–1876). Unitarian. Minister at churches in Massachusetts, co-editor of *Monthly Religious Magazine*. [H82Comp]

Van Alstyne, Frances Jane (1820–1915). Methodist. Better known as "Fanny Crosby." Teacher at New York City School for the Blind, prolific writer of gospel song texts. [HandBaptHy]

Webb, George J. (1803–1887). Swedenborgian. Emigrated to United States from England in 1830. Organist at Old South Church, Boston, for 40 years, co-founder of Boston Academy of Music, president of Boston Handel and Haydn Society. [H82Comp]

Whittier, John Greenleaf (1807–1892). Quaker. Editor of *Pennsylvania Freeman* and *National Era*. Author of "Snow-Bound." [H82Comp]

Willis, Love Maria (1824–1908). Wife of an M.D. and resident of New Hampshire and New York. [BaptHyBkComp]

Woodbury, Isaac B. (1819–1858). Music teacher and church music director in Massachusetts, Vermont, and New York, editor of *New York Musical Review*. [H40Comp]

Yoakley, John (1860–1932). Episcopalian. Organist at churches in Ohio. [BaptHyBkComp]

Zundel, John (1815–1882). Native of Germany, immigrated to United States in 1847. Organist at churches in New York and Detroit. [H82Comp]

American Texts

Among the American text writers represented in the *English Hymnal* several were major literary figures whose works are widely anthologized in collections of poetry, including Bryant, Holmes, Lowell, and Whittier. A number of others (mostly Unitarians), may be described as social gospel hymnists: Burleigh, Chadwick, Hosmer, Johnson, Longfellow, and Sears. Dearmer suggested that:

> The Church of England hymn-books of the 19th century ignored the beauty of Whittier's work, as also that of other New England poets and hymn-writers, perhaps because Whittier was a Quaker, Longfellow and others Unitarians—and Lowell because he was an American.[6]

On the other hand, the inclusion of such authors in the *English Hymnal* is not surprising, given Dearmer's social bent. A third group of what might be called "standard" hymn writers were bishops and ministers of the Episcopal church: Brooks, Coxe, G. W. Doane, and Everest. A stark contrast to these three groups was provided by several writers of gospel songs such as Bliss, Duffield, Hanby, Hartsough, Rankin, and Van Alstyne. A comparison of the American textual contributions to the *English Hymnal* with those in its illustrious predecessor, *Hymns Ancient and Modern*, is instructive. Only two American hymns appeared in the first (1861) edition of *Hymns Ancient and Modern*: George W. Doane's "Thou art the way: by thee alone" and C. W. Everest's "Take up thy cross, the Saviour said."[7] The number of American contributions gradually increased through subsequent revisions and enlargements, so that the 1904 edition featured 12 texts of American origin: "Rescue the perishing" (Van Alstyne), * "Saviour, sprinkle many nations" (Coxe), "Thou art the way" (G. W. Doane), * "Stand up, stand up for Jesus" (Duffield), * "Take up thy cross, the Saviour said" (Everest), "Return, O wanderer" (Hastings), "Holy Spirit, truth divine" and "Now on land and sea descending" (S. Longfellow), * "I love to hear the story" (E. Miller), "Jesu, thou joy of loving hearts" (trans.) and "Lord, my weak thought" (Palmer), and "Lift your glad voices" (H. Ware). The 1904 *Hymns Ancient and Modern* also included three American tunes: RESCUE (W. H. Doane), *MORNING LIGHT (Webb), and *MISSIONARY (L. Mason).[8]

The American texts in the 1904 *Hymns Ancient and Modern* certainly represented a sizeable recognition of New World hymnody for a British hymnal of that era. However, the *English Hymnal*, published only two years later, included nearly three times as many American texts. Furthermore, the *English Hymnal* used only four of the American texts that had appeared in the 1904 *Hymns Ancient and Modern*, demonstrating that–in this area, at least–Dearmer relied very little on the earlier book for guidance in the inclusion of American hymns.[9]

A more apt comparison might be made with W. Garrett Horder's *Worship Song*, published the year before Dearmer and Vaughan Williams's effort (1905). Twenty-three texts by American authors were common to *Worship Song* and the *English Hymnal*, a number of which appear to have been introduced to Britain through the pages of the 1905 book or one of Horder's earlier collections.[10] However, while it is probable that Dearmer took some of the American hymns common to the two books directly from Horder, it is evident that he did not do so in all cases, for the *English Hymnal* versions occasionally contain stanzas that are not found in *Worship Song*.[11]

Furthermore, nine hymns–nearly thirty percent of the American texts in the *English Hymnal*–were not found in *Worship Song*. Horder's significant role in the introduction of American hymns to British hymnals is obvious, but the inclusion of such works in the highly successful *English Hymnal* ensured their consideration for a place in subsequent British and American hymnals.

American Tunes

The American tunes in the *English Hymnal* fall principally into four categories: the standard nineteenth-century (Victorian) type tune, melodies by Lowell Mason and his associates, gospel songs, and folk hymn tunes. The standard nineteenth-century type tunes include Yoakley's ALL SOULS and Zundel's ZUNDEL. Mason's well-known MISSIONARY HYMN and OLIVET were printed, as were tunes by two of his associates, George J. Webb (WEBB) and Elam Ives, Jr. (IVES), and one by his contemporary Isaac B. Woodbury (MONTGOMERY).

The two categories of American tunes whose presence is most surprising are the gospel songs and folk hymns. Six gospel songs by four different composers (Bliss, W. H. Doane, Hartsough, and Sankey) are found in the *English Hymnal*. Gospel hymnody had made a tremendous impact in Britain during the Moody-Sankey revivals of the 1870s. However, this style had had singularly little effect on standard British hymnals,[12] and one would not expect to find a composer such as Vaughan Williams looking with much favor on these songs, particularly given his comments in the preface to the *English Hymnal* about the "languishing and sentimental hymn tunes which so often disfigure our services" (p. xi) and his attempt "to set a minimum standard in the music selected for this work" (p. xii). Indeed, his opinion of gospel songs is probably evident from their placement in the book: all but one of them appeared in the "Mission Services" section of the hymnal; the single exception, Sankey's BENEATH THE CROSS, was printed in the appendix of "additional tunes which do not enter into the general scheme of the book" (p. 903), or, as Vaughan Williams and his associates nicknamed it, the "Chamber of Horrors."[13] Vaughan Williams probably thought that the gospel songs could do little harm in such surroundings, but the fact that they found a place at all in the *English Hymnal* is remarkable. It is also instructive to note that most of the gospel songs in the *English Hymnal* were among the most widely known examples of the genre. Doane's TELL ME THE OLD, OLD STORY and Hartsough's I HEAR THY WELCOME VOICE still appear in some late-twentieth-century hymnals;[14] Sankey's THE NINETY AND NINE, Bliss's HOLD THE FORT, and Doane's ARMS OF JESUS are seldom sung today, but in the late nineteenth and early twentieth centuries these songs were spectacularly popular.[15] The *English Hymnal* specifically credited each of the gospel songs to Ira Sankey's *Sacred Songs and Solos*. Further analysis reveals that all appeared in the 271–piece collection that constituted *Sacred Songs and Solos No. 1* (1877). Vaughan Williams introduced a few minor alterations into the harmonizations of the tunes; in two instances (BENEATH THE CROSS and HOLD THE FORT) he doubled the time values of the notes.

The incorporation of two American folk hymn tunes into the *English Hymnal* is also unusual, but for a different reason than the inclusion of gospel songs. Vaughan Williams's love for and use of British folk tunes in the *English Hymnal* is well known, and it is not surprising that he would be attracted to American tunes of the same type. What is remarkable is that he was able to find American folk hymn tunes at all. Gospel songs might have been disdained by cultivated English musicians of the early twentieth century, but there was no question of their popularity; indeed, it was difficult to escape them. On the other hand, by 1906 the many American folk hymns that had been published during the first half of the nineteenth century were virtually unknown, even in the New World, their place as the popular religious expression of most Americans having been taken over by the gospel song, and their venue having been relegated largely to isolated shape-note "singings" in rural areas. It was not until 1933, when George Pullen Jackson issued his *White Spirituals in the Southern Uplands* that Americans began rediscovering this folk hymn heritage in a significant way, and even after the publication of Jackson's book it was some time before folk hymns began making a real impact on American hymnals. Yet 27 years before Jackson's book was issued, two of these tunes appeared in a British hymnal.

The two American folk hymn tunes utilized by Vaughan Williams, ADVENT and PLEADING SAVIOUR, were drawn from the *Plymouth Collection of Hymns and Tunes,* edited by Henry Ward Beecher, Charles Beecher, and John Zundel (New York: A. S. Barnes, 1855). The *English Hymnal* followed the *Plymouth Collection* in labeling ADVENT a "Western Melody," a nineteenth-century euphemism for "folk hymn." PLEADING SAVIOUR received no such source notation in the *Plymouth Collection*–in the *English Hymnal* it was credited merely to *"Plymouth Collection (U.S.A.), 1855"*–but its folk basis is obvious from its pentatonic melody and simple form. Vaughan Williams made no changes in the melodic forms of ADVENT and PLEADING SAVIOUR as found in the *Plymouth Collection,* but in both cases he completely reharmonized the tunes.[16] Vaughan Williams's harmonization was reprinted verbatim (but with a different text) in *The Hymnal 1940.*[17]

The *Plymouth Collection* also served as Vaughan Williams's source for the tune IVES, and probably for ZUNDEL (=EMILIE, no. 285 in *Plymouth Collection*) and MISSIONARY HYMN as well. IVES has been categorized as one of the *English Hymnal*'s American folk hymns.[18] However, in the *Plymouth Collection* IVES is attributed to "E. Ives, Jr. Beethoven Collection" (402). Elam Ives is not known to have been a collector of folk hymns, nor does his eponymous tune include characteristics that link it with American folk hymnody. It is perhaps better to consider this a "composed" tune.

Text-Tune Pairings

Many of the text-tune pairings involving American hymns in the *English Hymnal* were already customary in 1906, e.g., Lowell Mason's OLIVET with Ray Palmer's "My faith looks up to thee" or W. H. Doane's TELL ME THE OLD, OLD STORY with the Englishwoman Katherine Hankey's hymn of the same first line. In some cases, however, Vaughan Williams chose new couplings for words and music.

Three of these new combinations are of special interest because of their subsequent history. In America, Phillips Brooks's Christmas hymn "O little town of Bethlehem" had been sung almost exclusively to Lewis Redner's ST. LOUIS since the first publication of the text and tune together in William R. Huntington's *Church Porch* (1874). However, Vaughan Williams evidently found ST. LOUIS to be wanting, and, since the hymn was "hardly known in England" at this time,[19] he set "O little town of Bethlehem" to the English folk melody FOREST GREEN instead. This linkage was followed in other British hymnals and in popular programs such as the annual Festival of Lessons and Carols from King's College, Cambridge. Thus, Vaughan Williams's pairing of Brooks's text and FOREST GREEN has become standard in Britain. ST. LOUIS still holds sway in the United States, though the use of FOREST GREEN in American hymnals appears to be growing, with some books giving both ST. LOUIS and FOREST GREEN as settings for "O little town of Bethlehem" or at least cross-referencing the tunes.[20] ST. LOUIS has been criticized as having "nothing of the craftsmanship one associates with great music" and "the added misfortune of being undeservedly popular,"[21] while the coupling of FOREST GREEN with "O little town of Bethlehem" has been called "one of the many happy inspirations of the music editor, Vaughan Williams."[22] In strictly musical terms, FOREST GREEN is undoubtedly the superior melody; on the other hand, ST. LOUIS seems more in keeping with the sentimental nature of Brooks's text.

Vaughan Williams was also the first to link Orlando Gibbons's SONG 1 with Chadwick's "Eternal ruler of the ceaseless round."[23] This combination has been repeated in *The Hymnal 1982* (no. 617) among other books.

Another new text-tune pairing in the *English Hymnal* that is of interest involves one of Vaughan Williams's own compositional efforts. Four tunes by the music editor appeared in the book, all of them being modestly designated "anon.": DOWN AMPNEY (152), RANDOLPH (524), SALVE FEST DIES (175, 216, 225), and SINE NOMINE (641). RANDOLPH set the American Jeremiah Rankin's gospel song text "God be with you till we meet again," which had first been published in J. W. Bischoff's *Gospel Bells* (1880) to a tune by William

G. Tomer. Tomer's setting was characterized by gentle, but rather dull, note repetitions in the stanza, while the refrain was full of athletic leaps that seem out of character with the text and the earlier part of the tune; in fact, some American hymnals that contain this tune omit the refrain altogether.[24] Vaughan Williams omitted Rankin's refrain and wrote a simple, tender setting that has gained acceptance in a number of American hymnals.[25]

Conclusion

The *English Hymnal* was one of the most forward-looking hymnals to be published in either Great Britain or the United States during the early twentieth century. Among the many reasons for this hymnal's progressive nature is the appearance in its pages of a substantial body of American texts and tunes. Since the American hymns included in the *English Hymnal* were not original to that collection, the direct impact of Dearmer and Vaughan Williams's work in this regard is difficult to measure; later collections that included these same hymns might have taken them from other sources. However, there seems to be no reason to question Dearmer's own testimony that it was through the pages of the *English Hymnal* that several "exceptionally fine hymns from America" came "into general use in England."[26] The important role of the American contributions to the *English Hymnal* is also evident in the lasting influence of some of the book's combinations of American texts with specific tunes. In this, as in so many areas, the *English Hymnal* continues to have a significant impact on Christian congregational song.

Notes

1. Among the historic styles that were incorporated were melodies by English Renaissance composers such as Thomas Tallis and Orlando Gibbons. For new material that has seen extensive use in the twentieth century one needs look no further than Vaughan Williams's tune SINE NOMINE.

2. Robin A. Leaver, "British Hymnody, 1900–1950," in Raymond F. Glover, gen. ed., *The Hymnal 1982 Companion* vol. 1 (New York: Church Hymnal Corporation, 1990) 492.

3. Percy Dearmer, *Songs of Praise Discussed: A Handbook to the Best-known Hymns and to Others Recently Introduced* (London: Oxford University Press, 1933) 5.

4. Carlton R. Young, *Companion to The United Methodist Hymnal* (Nashville: Abingdon Press, 1993) 608.

5. The composers of the folk hymn tunes ADVENT and PLEADING SAVIOUR are not known. A handful of authors and composers in the *English Hymnal* have not been identified, including Harriet Packer, R. S. Genge, W. Griffith, H. A. Jeboult, G. E. W. Malet, and W. R. Waghorne.

6. Dearmer, *Songs of Praise Discussed*, 257.

7. According to Maurice Frost, ed., *Historical Companion to Hymns Ancient & Modern* (London: William Clowes & Sons, 1962) 255, Doane's "was the only American hymn

in the original edition of *Hymns A. & M,*" while Dearmer, in *Songs of Praise Discussed,* observed that Everest's text was "brought into popularity [in England] by the original edition of *Hymns Ancient and Modern* (1861)" (76). An examination of the 1861 (273–hymn) edition of *Hymns Ancient and Modern* reveals the presence of both pieces (nos. 162 and 165).

8. Asterisks indicate texts and tunes that also appeared in the 1906 *English Hymnal.*

9. The *English Hymnal* also used five times as many American tunes as *Hymns Ancient and Modern;* only two of the tunes found in the 1906 book were common with the earlier collection.

10. See Dearmer, *Songs of Praise Discussed,* 174 ("Once to every man and nation") 259 ("Eternal ruler of the ceaseless round"), and 281 ("I look to thee in every need").

11. To choose two examples from hymns by Whittier, see "Dear Lord and Father of mankind" (St. 2 in *English Hymnal*) and "Immortal love, for ever full" (St. 7 in *English Hymnal*).

12. For example, only one gospel hymn and tune, "Rescue the Perishing"/RESCUE, was published in the 1904 edition of *Hymns Ancient and Modern.* F. M. Bird observed in John Julian's *A Dictionary of Hymnology* (London: John Murray, 1892) 59, that "the *Gospel Songs* of our [American] revivalistic schools are the mainstay of similar efforts in the mother country," but these were printed in collections that were almost wholly devoted to such songs rather than in standard hymnals.

13. Michael Kennedy, *The Works of Ralph Vaughan Williams,* new ed. (London: Oxford University Press, 1980) 571.

14. See *Trinity Hymnal. Revised Edition* (Atlanta: Great Commission Publications, 1990) no. 625, and *The Baptist Hymnal* (Nashville: Convention Press, 1991) no. 302.

15. See Mel R. Wilhoit, "'Sing Me a Sankey': Ira D. Sankey and Congregational Song," *The Hymn 42* (January 1991) 17.

16. For additional information on PLEADING SAVIOUR and a facsimile of the *Plymouth Collection* printing see M[arion] H[atchett]'s article on "Jesus, thou divine Companion: Music" in *The Hymnal 1982 Companion,* vol. 3B, no. 586.

17. Hatchett, *Hymnal 1982 Companion,* vol. 3B, no. 586.

18. See *The Hymnal 1982 Companion,* vol. I, pp. 488, 515.

19. Dearmer, *Songs of Praise Discussed,* 55.

20. For example, *The Baptist Hymnal* (1991) prints only ST. LOUIS (no. 86) while *The Hymnal 1982* (New York: Church Hymnal Corporation, 1985) includes both tunes (nos. 78 and 79), and *The United Methodist Hymnal* (Nashville: United Methodist Publishing House, 1989) gives only ST. LOUIS but with the note "Alt. tune: FOREST GREEN" (no. 230).

21. Stanley L. Osborne, *If Such Holy Song: The Story of the Hymns in the Hymn Book 1971* (Whitby, Ont.: Institute of Church Music, 1976) no. 421.

22. Wesley Milgate, *Songs of the People of God: A Companion to the Australian Hymn Book/With One Voice,* rev. ed. (Sydney: Collins Liturgical Publications, 1985) 111, quoted in Young, *Companion to The United Methodist Hymnal,* 519.

23. *The Hymnal 1982 Companion,* vol. 3b, 1134.

24. See *The Hymnal for Worship and Celebration* (Waco: Word Music, 1986) no. 602.

25. See *Psalter Hymnal* (Grand Rapids: CRC Publications, 1988) no. 316; *The Presbyterian Hymnal: Hymns, Psalms, and Spiritual Songs* (Louisville: Westminster/John Knox Press, 1990) no. 540; and Jeffery Rowthorn and Russell Schulz-Widmar, *A New Hymnal for Colleges and Schools* (New Haven and London:Yale University Press, 1992) no. 344.

26. Dearmer, *Songs of Praise Discussed,* 251; see also 55, 293, 308.

"Always and Everywhere": The 1979 Book of Common Prayer and the Promise of a Liturgical Evangelism

Joe G. Burnett

MY FIRST ENCOUNTER with the word "eucharist" was at a seminary chapel service at Southern Methodist University in Dallas. The service was right out of the back of the hymnal, the same one I knew so well from years of quarterly communion services attended while growing up in a Mississippi Methodist parsonage. Except that here, at Perkins Chapel, the service was sung. The presiding elder, the "celebrant," wore simple vestments; but still they were "vestments," garb I had never seen in any Mississippi Methodist church. I had heard sermons before preached on the topic "the blood of Christ," but not with a connection extolled between that and the element used in communion.

We broke bread that day from a common loaf and communed with a common cup. And I shall never forget the hymn we sang as we approached the altar rail to receive:

> O the depth of love divine, Th' unfathomable grace!
> Who shall say how bread and wine God into man conveys!
> How the bread his flesh imparts,
> How the wine transmits his blood,
> Fills his faithful people's hearts with all the life of God![1]

This text, written by Charles Wesley, speaks of the mystery of Christ's "real presence" in the eucharist. And that morning, for the first time in my life, I recognized it: the risen Christ present in fullness and in power "in the breaking of bread and in the prayers."

This profound moment initiated my pilgrimage into the sacramental faith and life of the Episcopal Church. What I experienced there, but did not then have words to express, was that "theology is worship remembered." *Lex orandi lex credendi*: The rule of prayer [is] the rule of belief. However articulated, it is widely recognized that one way of understanding the development of Christian doctrine is to look at the liturgy and worship of the Christian community. Liturgy predates even Scripture, and the full extent to which the church's corporate prayer has molded Christian thought throughout the centuries has probably yet to be fully documented and appreciated.[2]

In recent years, however, a great deal of progress has been made in understanding the relationship between liturgy and Christian education,[3] between liturgy and pastoral care[4] and between liturgy and the Christian's moral, social and political life.[5] In the course of this work it has become clear that the ancient dictum concerning worship and Christian believing may also be appropriately applied to the disciplines of pastoral theology; i.e., worship is formative not only for Christian self-understanding[6] but also for Christian ministry. Thus not only the *theology* but also the *ministry* of the Christian community can be understood as "worship remembered." In other words, pastoral theology is systematic reflection on the praise of God in action.[7]

The purpose of this essay is to consider in some preliminary ways the link between worship and *evangelism*, particularly as experienced in the Episcopal Church in the light of the baptismal and eucharistic liturgies of the 1979 Book of Common Prayer. In so doing it will first be necessary to touch on some crucial questions that have emerged as this church has sought, especially during the last quarter century, to embrace with greater fervor the ministry of evangelism, culminating in the now-waning days of what has been called "the decade of evangelism." Finally, I will suggest in broad terms how our theology and practice of evangelism might thus be re-visioned as we approach the dawn of a new millennium.

I hasten to add that such a consideration of the relationship between liturgy and evangelism is no new undertaking. Some thirty-five years ago James F. White suggested "that the roots for the evangelism of our time lie in a new understanding of liturgy."[8] His insight, in my opinion, still invites further serious reflection and exploration. In this brief context I shall endeavor to outline the theological rationale for such a proposal, and on that basis to suggest several salient points of contact between liturgy and evangelism, and their possible implications, particularly as they impinge on the life and witness of the Episcopal Church.

James Fenhagen has recently voiced what many others have no doubt observed, that the Episcopal Church moving into the next century is a vastly different church from what it was when the revision of the 1928 Prayer Book began. "We are now a church deeply influenced by those Baptismal and Eucharistic liturgies that have become our common experience."[9] These new liturgies, Fenhagen continues, "have caused us not only to worship differently but to think and act differently."[10] I think he is correct, and his remarks touch on the very heart of my contention. Now more than ever I am persuaded that, while we have gained immeasurably from the efforts of many dedicated lay and clergy advocates who rightly saw the need for this branch of the Anglican communion to reclaim the fullness of the gospel's outreaching power, we have yet to be confidently clear about underlying dimensions of a properly conceived ministry and theology of evangelism in our tradition. I will argue that it is our liturgical life which is the essential foundation upon which all such efforts can be, should be–and, in fact, are inevitably–constructed. Understanding this foundation in depth, and affirming it in practice, can help reshape, transform and empower all our evangelism ministries.

Evangelism and Church Growth in Biblical and Theological Perspective

Of definitions of evangelism there seems to be no end.[11] However, I have long found one of the most helpful starting points in an often overlooked scriptural foundation–Paul's great summary of the gospel in his Second Letter to the Church at Corinth:

> All this is from God, who reconciled us to himself through Christ, and has given us the ministry of reconciliation; that is, in Christ God was reconciling the world to himself, not counting their trespasses against them, and entrusting the message of reconciliation to us (2 Cor. 5:18–19, NRSV).[12]

This is not only a succinct definition of ministry, but of evangelism as well: Evangelism *is* the message *and* ministry of reconciliation. It seeks what God seeks–if one may put it so boldly–in that it aims toward the restoration of human wholeness (the individual dimension) and genuine human community (the corporate dimension), "in" Christ, and "under" God, and "through" the Spirit. It has to do with the proclamation in word and deed of the gospel of God's unbounded, liberating, and reconciling love–decisively represented in the event of Jesus Christ. Paul VI was correct in declaring that "evangelizing is in fact the grace and vocation proper to the church, her deepest identity. She exists in order to evangelize . . . "[13] Evangelism is the church's existential orientation.[14]

Since 1973 the Episcopal Church has officially defined evangelism as "the presentation of Jesus Christ, in the power of the Holy Spirit, in such ways that persons may be led to believe in him as Saviour and follow him as Lord within the fellowship of his Church."[15] This classic statement attributed to William Temple and used as the touchstone of Episcopal Church efforts is one which seems consistent with the church's understanding of the charge given by the risen Jesus in Mt. 28:16–20,[16] about which I will say more later. But what are the critical factors involved when a congregation, called and empowered by the gospel to evangelize, is awakened to the need so to equip itself for this preeminent task? And, if such a congregation enjoys growth in numbers as a perceived result, can it be assumed correctly that evangelism was done "successfully?" If growth does not occur, will a ministry of evangelism correctly be presumed lacking or in some way deficient?

These and other considerations beg for our attention, since during these past years the Episcopal Church, along with most other mainline churches, has become much involved in the "Church Growth" movement.[17] In the late 1970s (ironically around the same time as the final stages of the adoption of the new Prayer Book) numerous lay and clergy leaders from around the country began receiving extensive training in the diverse ministries and methods emanating from the Church Growth school.[18] I myself attended or shared leadership in a variety of regional events geared toward inculcating and applying the principles and practices of Church Growth strategy–albeit shaped insofar as possible to accommodate the unique dimensions of Episcopal Church polity and ethos. I did then and still do rejoice in the progress made as a result of this and similar subsequent emphases. However, like William J. Abraham, commenting on this particular "birthing" of interest in evangelism, I also continue to harbor mixed feelings of gratitude and concern.[19]

There is no question that the Church Growth movement has had a profound impact. Through its unequivocal insistence on the numerical growth of the church as the litmus test for authentic evangelism, it has sharply raised the question of the ecclesiological community's *raison d'etre*. The debate in missiology will never be the same. Second, its relentless development and employment of analytical tools (and the data they yield) have resulted in more sophisticated quantification of ministerial (pastoral) action. It has also pioneered deeper structural-functional understanding of congregational systems, thus providing a new context for planning, implementing, and evaluating the church's ministry and mission. And it has emphasized thereby the fact that numbers and parish statistics do make a critical difference, as revelatory symbols of the inner life and history of a community of faith. Finally, Church Growth methodology has helped us all better define and describe the behavior and interrelationship of groups in church life.[20]

However, as William Abraham suggests, there are serious biblical, theological, and methodological questions to be asked.[21] Though this is not the place for a thorough critical review of such issues, it is necessary to summarize the relevant primary areas of debate, since the bulk of efforts in "evangelism" ministry in the Episcopal Church have revolved around a modified version of church growth philosophy and practice.[22]

First and foremost is the question of scriptural foundations. As far as the proponents of Church Growth are concerned, there is no question as to its biblical basis. Waving the so-called "Great Commission" of Jesus like a banner, Donald McGavran and Win Arn state that "the New Testament is a series of Church Growth documents . . . written by Church Growth people to Church Growth people to help the church grow."[23] And on this point, C. Peter Wagner is uncompromising: the end justifies the means.[24] The aim is growth, motivated by God's will and command to seek and save the "lost." Whatever furthers that aim shapes missionary endeavor. In his controversial book, *Church Growth and the Whole Gospel,* Wagner argues that the urgency of the "evangelistic mandate" roots in one of what he considers to be the "five theological non-negotiables underlying the Church Growth movement," namely, "the ultimate eschatological reality of sin, salvation, and eternal death." Those who, for *whatever* reason, "have not put their faith and trust in Jesus as Savior and Lord are now alienated and will be alienated throughout all eternity."[25] If one begins with Wagner's eschatological premise, one cannot help but adopt as one's aim the adding of more and more numbers of persons to the rolls of those being "saved." Church Growth, and that alone, is deemed faithfulness to God.[26] So *growth,* not the gospel, is in danger of becoming the norm. In fact, growth *becomes* the gospel, and the gospel becomes growth.

Certainly there is broad agreement as to the intense missionary character of the Scriptures, but is this an exegetically adequate characterization of the "thrust" of Scripture? David J. Bosch, in his book *Witness to the World,* notes that it is traditional in Protestant circles to lay as a first step a "biblical foundation" of mission, but he cautions that we may not find in the Bible "any carefully defined and unalterable notion of mission, but rather a variety of emphases and approaches within the wider framework of an understanding of mission as God's concern with the world."[27] A different method is necessary—"that of trying to establish the central thrust of Scripture."[28] In this regard, Mortimer Arias, sometime Methodist Bishop of Bolivia, has offered an insightful critique of much casual use of Mt. 28:16–20:

Yes, we have what has been called the Great Commission. I would prefer to call it the *Last Commission* given by our resurrected Lord. In no part of the New Testament is it called the *Great* Commission . . . There is a *Great Commandment,* however, "To love the Lord your God . . . " And a second, which is like the first, says Jesus: "to love your neighbor . . . "

> . . . This is the distinctive mark, the sign, of the evangelistic community: "In this they will know you are my disciples: "If you love . . . "(Jn. 13:35). "To make disciples" is all right, this is part of the commission, but first we have to *be* disciples in the way Jesus defines a disciple.[29]

This then raises a further question regarding the implications of Church Growth for the development of personal Christian faith and life. McGavran claims that there is a two-stage process of becoming a mature Christian, which he calls "discipling" and "perfecting." Discipling is used to signify the point at which a people make an initial decision for Jesus Christ. Perfecting, theoretically, has to do with the ongoing work of nurture which leads to Christian maturity and moral awareness. The problem here goes back to the unqualified emphasis on growth. In the press to "win" more and more persons, "discipling" increasingly becomes all the church has time for. The system itself requires for its sustenance that almost all of the nurture be channeled toward enabling the recently discipled to disciple still others–and so on, and so on.[30] The resulting repetitive cycle tends to yield a shallow "conversionist" agenda which has the effect of stifling any meaningful development of "Christian maturity and moral awareness." The late Urban T. Holmes, who rightly called Church Growth a mission of "recruitment," once observed: "Church Growth runs a real risk of creating a situation that thwarts a perfecting consistent with biblical norms of renewal."[31] Furthermore worship in such an intense evangelical context inevitably becomes primarily an opportunity for *persuasion*–of the unchurched to come and stay, and of the churched to persevere in their efforts at discipling.

Perhaps the most significant area of concern relates to what has been called the *homogeneous unit* concept. McGavran's classic claim, more central to the movement than many adherents have been willing to acknowledge, is that people "like to become Christians without crossing racial, linguistic, or class barriers."[32] Peter Wagner unfolds the evangelistic application of this observation by insisting that there is nothing inherently wrong in affirming and seeking to preserve group and/or racial identity. Furthermore, he says it is clear that such group consciousness can enhance Church Growth among the ethnic and socioeconomic layers of a culture.

While it is one thing to recognize this factor as an *element* of growth, it is something else again to exploit and promote it. Wagner seems to view cultural, social, and even economic distinctions between ethnic groups as somehow inherent in the fabric of humanity, when in fact they may be in part the outworking of previous injustice or purely circumstantial factors.[33] While taking seriously the glorious and infinite diversity of the natural ties that bind persons to persons, we should recognize that there is a very fine line between this phenomenon and the reality of human sin. The gospel certainly does not undermine the basic integrity of human culture and communities. But it is equally certain that the gospel strikes at the roots of human pride, hatred, and injustice, whether these emerge within, between, or because of these cultures and communities.[34] Again, in the final analysis, the reigning goal of growth means that the *homogeneous unit* principle is not justifiable fully on its own terms, but only because it can be shown to be a means to more rapid numerical increase. Thus it is, at one and the same time, both the fundamental methodological principle, and the cardinal theological capitulation, of the Church Growth movement.

Such an understanding of the centrality of growth also has serious ecclesiological implications. Church Growth has equated salvation, for all practical purposes, with membership in the visible church.[35] Such an approach, argued the late Latin American theologian, Juan Luis Segundo, mistakenly identifies the church as the "locus" of salvation. The "community called church," Segundo maintained, is not called to be the community of all humankind; rather, it is to be a "sign," a sacramental expression of the reality of God's salvation and the *destiny* of the human community. It is as "salt" to food; or "leaven" to dough. "It produces a change, turning the whole mixture into something else: not into leaven, but into a loaf of bread."[36]

Finally, I would also suggest that the practice of Church Growth *in a well-churched environment* has a potentially negative impact on an authentic Christian evangelism. To say that "the United States of America is a well-churched nation" is *not* to say, according to David Lowes Watson, that almost everyone goes to church.[37] Citing studies of this phenomenon,[38] he points out that the key elements of such an assertion are (a) the affiliation of an overwhelming majority of Americans with some form of organized religion, and (b) the indications that those who are not so affiliated neverthe-less have a basic familiarity with Christianity. Even in what has come casually to be called the "post-Christian" era, there is evidence that even the so-called "unchurched" are yet part and parcel of the church's orbit.[39]

The implications for the meaning and practice of evangelism in such a setting are clear. In a non-Christian culture the very planting of a Christian church, with its attendant ministries and numerical expansion, can be understood as evangelism—simply because for a member of such a culture to become a *church* member represents a fairly explicit embracing of the Christian gospel and world view. However, the same cannot confidently be said about the planting and/or growth of the church in a society like ours. The difference is due to the fact that in a culture where the historical and social interrelationships of church and culture are as complex and as deep as the aforementioned findings suggest—where even the *un*churched are often *formerly* churched—it is too much to assume that the "conversion" of the unchurched to the church is at the same time conversion from unfaith to the circle of faith. In short, in such a "Christianized" context the rigorous application of Church Growth principles can leave vital dimensions of the gospel message, and the response for which it calls, untouched and unfulfilled.[40]

In the final analysis I believe Church Growth may be shown to be essentially *church development*—an ongoing systematic process of recruiting, receiving, retaining, and deploying new church members. As such it functions *in connection with*, but also needs to be understood *as distinct from*, evangelism. Both ministries have their respective fields of focus—fields that are at once inseparable and yet distinct. Both ministries as well have the same fundamental criterion—the gospel itself—for their sound undertaking in and on behalf of the church. However, unless their vital connections *and* distinctions are made clear, they both may suffer by being neither defined nor practiced in sufficient depth.

In his passionate essay on contemporary missiology, *Christ Outside the Gate*, the late Orlando Costas wrote that

> God's mission has as its ultimate and definitive goal the full manifestation of the messianic kingdom, understood as a new order of life characterized by love, freedom, justice and peace. The church is the firstfruits of that new order: it anticipates the messianic kingdom in its life and proclaims it in its mission.[41]

Church growth is not therefore the object of mission but a *sign*, a "provisional goal," of mission. The *community's organic* development is as important as its *numerical* growth:

> If there is one thing that the book of Acts and the New Testament epistles make clear it is that the kingdom takes shape in the system of relationships that is produced by the call to faith and repentance. The liturgical celebration, internal discipline, stewardship, leadership training—all of which are aspects of the internal life of the church—are an essential, indispensable part of the mission, not some extraneous imposition. The evidence and goal of growth in the faith is that the whole body should participate in mission. Also, the proclamation of the kingdom carries within it the invitation to participate in the life of the kingdom *now* in the community's experience of faith. Without a vibrant community, which stands behind the proclamation and receives those who are called, the numerical element becomes a mere consumer production.[42]

Thus, we are ready to proceed to a consideration of the church's worship as the primary key to a faithful understanding of the message and ministry of evangelism.

Liturgy and Christian Formation

The church at worship is the church gathered at the center of its life and power. It is the church "realizing" itself, the church taking form; or, rather, it is the experience of Jesus as the Christ taking form in the church in word and sacrament.[43] Corporate worship is the community's re-presentation, in kerygmatic proclamation and sacramental celebration, of the death and resurrection of Jesus Christ. Through participation in worship—in the word read and proclaimed, in intercession, in praise, thanksgiving, and communion—the church's members offer themselves anew and are empowered anew for what Henri Nouwen has called "service and prayer in memory of Jesus Christ."[44] Hans Küng reminds us that "the word *ecclesia* means both the process of assembling together and the concrete assembly itself. The church exists as assembly because of the constantly renewed process of assembling."[45]

Liturgy is preeminently the "place" where the unique resources of the church's heritage of faith and life are brought to bear on the human situation in which and out of which the community gathers for prayer and praise. In that sense worship is a kind of *anamnesis* of the Christian tradition, a recalling of foundational events and interpretations into present experience and awareness. It is the "lens" through which the historic witness of faith can be brought into focus, and reappropriated by the community, so that the *doxa* of the past has a bearing on the *praxis* of the present, and—vice versa—the *praxis* of the past informs the *doxa* of the present.

And what of the present—the present life in the world and in the human community? James Fenhagen has said that "religious truth is normal experience understood at full depth."[46] All human experience lends itself to theological reflection of one kind or another. And the community gathered for worship is the community of those drawn *from*, or called out of, the world (*ecclesia*), worshiping *in* the world, and being sent constantly back *to* the world.[47] In worship we are dealing with whole persons, with minds and bodies, in their individual and corporate identities, at once spiritual and secular. These are persons who see themselves to some degree attempting to live out the gospel in human society, persons engaged by the witness in the midst of human existence. Such a community of persons assembled for worship need not, should not, indeed cannot really exclude the cultural *milieu* out of which and in which they live and work. The liturgy, then, is "for the life of the world."[48] Yet it is also *from* the life of the world. In part worship depends for its integrity on its very own "worldliness."[49] As James White has pointed out:

It is when God is worshipped in accordance with his nature that worship becomes truly worldly. This comes when we take seriously the worldliness of God, that all that is depends on his constant creating and redeeming activity. Here then the world is granted the full seriousness and the only seriousness that it deserves as the arena of God's action. At its very heart is history, both past and present."[50]

And, we might add, the future. Worship strains as much toward the future as it recalls the past and gathers up the present. In the eucharist, for instance, the sacramental signs of bread and wine are striking in their ambiguity: They are *already* the first fruits of the coming new age, the body and blood of the risen and coming Lord; but they are also *not yet*—for they remain bread and wine. And the presence of the kingdom, however real, is not a full and final presence. As such the eucharist—indeed, worship in any sense—is an act of and in hope, a bold affirmation of "the divine *pronoia*."[51]

And what, or who, is being shown forth in that future? Is it not the evangel, Jesus Christ and his gospel, whose history and whose presence and whose future are being proclaimed and re-presented "until he comes?" Harmon Smith claims that

> this is why eucharist is the most significant moral act of the church. In the eucharist we have our unity with—and with one another in—God. We have eaten an eschatological meal; a new age, a new history, has really dawned with Jesus' presence among us; and we long for unity and peace and fellowship between and among all of God's creation.[52]

This is the final ground and ultimate meaning and impelling force of a "liturgical" evangelism.

In this light it is now possible to lay out in a preliminary way some fundamental dimensions of an evangelism rooted in the church's worship. At the outset it must be made clear that such an understanding is not intended to reflect the prevalent notion that worship is evangelistic simply because in such a setting persons may respond to the preaching of the word. As suggested earlier, this view of worship sees it primarily as an occasion for persuasion, and the form of "evangelism" presupposed in such a setting is no longer very helpful in a well-churched context. This whole approach easily degenerates into a closed circle, with the faithful addressing the faithful, and thus limits the witness of faith to those who happen already to be predisposed toward attending church services.

I would concur with James White that the first great role of Christian worship with regard to evangelism is that of "formation."[53]

> Becoming a Christian is not simply a matter of acquiring the necessary information, as might be the case in becoming a licensed electrician. It is a matter of formation in which one's stance on life, his style of living, becomes

changed. Formation or nurture is the gradual and often imperceptible change of one's being . . . In the terms of Jonathan Edwards, one's "strongest motive" is changed. This means that worship . . . changes one's future.[54]

Wayne Meeks has shown how crucial ritual was for the Pauline churches. The coming together of those early believers was certainly for the "building up" of the Body of Christ, but Meeks asserts that this "*oikodomé* was more than just social cohesion."[55] In it the community's ethos is formed, "attitudes and dispositions take form: the kinds of behavior 'worthy of the way you received Christ' are learned."[56]

David J. Bosch reminds us of the "scope" of mission as articulated by the Willingen conference: witness, proclamation, fellowship, and service. But Bosch would add a fifth aspect—*leitourgia*—"the encounter of the Church with her Lord. This is, in the last analysis, the fountain of the entire mission of the Church and the guarantee of her distinctiveness."[57] Worship is the fountain of mission because worship *forms the people of mission.* White points out that this is not so much a deliberate and conscious purpose of worship as it is a subliminal and long-term effect. Worship enables us to appropriate and hold as our own the essentials of the Christian story, thus enabling it to become *our* story. White insists that one does not do evangelism; rather one becomes an evangelist:

> Evangelism is a matter of being, and it is worship that, to a large measure, forms this being. Worship assists in the formation of the new being in Christ, who alone can witness to the world . . . In constantly rehearsing and rediscovering what he already is, a recipient of God's loving action, one becomes equipped to live the life of an evangelist in the world.[58]

This formative character of Christian worship is first manifested in the liturgy of initiation. Hugh Riley, in his monumental work on *Christian Initiation,* examines the work of Cyril, Chrysostom, Theodore, and Ambrose, and shows how their use of the liturgy of Baptism made the liturgical symbols, actions, and words both life-transforming and world-engaging: ". . . the life, cross and death of Jesus, which once took place in the past, reveal themselves again in the encounter of the Christian with the radical challenges which the secular city provides. And [they show] this precisely by recourse to the meaning of the words and symbolic actions of the liturgy . . . "[59] Theodore Eastman speaks of Baptism as inaugurating and commissioning a "missionary exodus" into the world.[60] Certainly in this, the fundamental Christian sacrament, the liturgy leaves an indelible imprint of the missionary character of the gospel, as well as of the missionary tasks of those who are brought under its hegemony in and through baptism.

In the celebration of Holy Baptism in the Book of Common Prayer the candidates and people together affirm promises regarding the continuing shape of their lives as they seek to appropriate the meaning of this "new birth" in accountable discipleship:

Celebrant	Will you continue in the apostles' teaching and fellowship, in the breaking of the bread, and in the prayers?
People	I will, with God's help.
Celebrant	Will you persevere in resisting evil, and, whenever you fall into sin, repent and return to the Lord?
People	I will, with God's help.
Celebrant	Will you seek and serve Christ in all persons, loving your neighbor as yourself?
People	I will, with God's help.
Celebrant	Will you strive for justice and peace among all people, and respect the dignity of every human being?
People	I will, with God's help. [61]

Later in a series of prayers one petition reads: "Send them into the world in witness to your love."[62] Following the baptism, as the new initiates are welcomed into the fellowship of the body of Christ, they are at the same time charged once more with the profound agenda of Christian evangelism: "We receive you into the household of God. Confess the faith of Christ crucified, proclaim his resurrection, and share with us in his eternal priesthood."[63]

Yet what baptism does "once and for all"—albeit renewed in each profession of vows as the community witnesses the baptism of others—the eucharist rehearses throughout the Christian life. It, too, is a sacrament of formation par excellence. Browne Barr has said that

> the formation of Christian worship with the Lord's Supper as its holy center sets forth who we are. It establishes *identity*. It reflects explicitly or implicitly Christ's work, the drama of the world's redemption and our salvation . . . So Wesley declared that the Eucharist is 'the chief form of evangelism and conversion.'[64]

"We understand Christian Liturgy," claims Harmon Smith, "as the means by which we are habituated to the heart, and brought into the life, of God." So the "eucharist . . . means to locate our lives within the life of God as we have been given to know this in the life of Jesus."[65]

Thus the primary context for a liturgy-based evangelism is an understanding of the *formative* role of Christian worship, particularly with regard to the primary sacraments and services of baptism and the eucharist. Liturgy forms and shapes the "evangelistic" consciousness of the people *of* and *in* worship, rehearsing and renewing for them the essential aspects of the gospel which is at its heart a missionary one. What is necessary now is to spell out in more specific terms the unique points of convergence between the liturgy and the ministry of evangelism it engenders.

Liturgy and Evangelism

First, God is a "sending God," an "urgent God,"[66] and the liturgy echoes this movement in numerous ways. In addition to the sections from the baptismal service earlier noted, there are also explicit references in the eucharist to the outward thrust from liturgy to life, from worship to mission, from *anamnesis* to evangelization. In Eucharistic Prayer *A* in the Book of Common Prayer we ask God through the power of the Holy Spirit to sanctify our gifts of bread and wine, but also to "sanctify us . . . that we may faithfully receive this holy sacrament and serve you in unity, constancy, and peace . . . "[67] The post-communion prayer asks God to "send us out to do the work you have given us to do, to love and serve you as faithful witnesses . . . "[68]

A second point of convergence has to do with the theological content of the liturgy as a vehicle for the gospel. In the eucharistic prayers, for example, we see encapsulated the fundamental Christian story. Through these gospels "in miniature" the essential elements of the tradition are vividly and succinctly communicated over and over again in the daily or weekly round of prayer:

> Holy and gracious Father: In your infinite love you made us for yourself; and, when we had fallen into sin and become subject to evil and death, you, in your mercy, sent Jesus Christ, your only and eternal Son, to share our human nature, to live and die as one of us, to reconcile us to you, the God and Father of all.

> He stretched out his arms upon the cross, and offered himself, in obedience to your will, a perfect sacrifice for the whole world.[69]

> We give thanks to you, O God, for the goodness and love which you have made known to us in creation; in the calling of Israel to be your people; in your Word spoken through the prophets; and above all in the Word made flesh, Jesus, your Son. For in these last days you sent him to be incarnate from the Virgin Mary, to be the Savior and Redeemer of the world. In him, you have delivered us from evil, and made us worthy to stand before you. In him, you have brought us out of error into truth, out of sin into righteousness, out of death into life.[70]

A third link between liturgy and evangelism is seen in the common emphasis on the eschatological tension of human existence.[71] As has already been stated, worship is a prime sign of the "betweenness" of our age. In living remembrance the church shows forth the death of Christ "until he comes." In the eucharist we experience a pledge of the coming kingdom, a foretaste of the messianic banquet. Herein is the very dynamic of grace–that while the kingdom's coming is not finally contingent upon our effort or merit, but is first and last the gracious gift of God in Christ, nevertheless it is one which must ever be received and reappropriated anew. For the time being we live in the painful and joyful tension between the *now* and the *novum,* and out of that middle ground we are called in thanksgiving and remembrance, in confidence and hope, in faith and in freedom, to announce the impending arrival of a new age and to invite others to be a part of the new order:

> Insofar as we receive it, the liturgy shapes us to be the reconstituted family of God, the people of God's new age, the *ecclesia theou.* It forms our lives morally by providing the essential means whereby Jesus' life becomes our life, his story becomes our story, his work becomes our work. It recapitulates the story of God's continuing effort to show the world its true destiny and claim it by God's faithful love. It tells us who we are and who we are meant to be if we purpose to understand and intend ourselves as disciples of Jesus, God's Christ.[72]

The memorial acclamation in Eucharistic Prayer A articulates this eschatological nerve of the liturgy: "Christ has died. Christ is risen. Christ will come again."[73]

A fourth significant element in this relationship between liturgy and evangelism can be seen in the way in which the celebration of baptism and the eucharist become forms of proclaiming the kingdom which involve us in the struggle for justice. Jürgen Moltmann has maintained that "the Kingdom of God is not only announced and believed, but also eaten and drunk."[74] Two passages from eucharistic prayers in the Book of Common Prayer reflect this theme in explicit ways:

> Lord, God of our Fathers; God of Abraham, Isaac, and Jacob; God and Father of our Lord Jesus Christ: Open our eyes to see your hand at work in the world about us. Deliver us from the presumption of coming to this Table for solace only, and not for strength; for pardon only, and not for renewal. Let the grace of this Holy Communion make us one body, one spirit in Christ, that we may worthily serve the world in his name.[75]

> Father, you loved the world so much that in the fullness of time you sent your only Son to be our Savior. Incarnate by the Holy Spirit, born of the Virgin Mary, he lived as one of us, yet without sin. To the poor he proclaimed the good news of salvation; to prisoners, freedom; to the sorrowful, joy. To fulfill your purpose he gave himself up to death; and, rising from the grave, destroyed death and made the whole creation new.[76]

James White argues that the eucharist is celebrated both as judgement and as promise, and that in it we have represented "a much more radical vision for humanity than any social reformer has hoped to bring about . . . "[77] Thus we have a celebration that is in and of itself a proclamation of justice. And evangelism, if it is understood to be an announcement of this "new being," or "new world," or "new age,"[78] is thereby carried out in the very act of making eucharist.

Finally, the relationship between liturgy and evangelism is made visible in the act of gathering and celebrating. Much is made of the "four-fold shape" of liturgical action in the eucharist wherein we do as Jesus did: We take bread, we bless the bread (give thanks), we break the bread, and we give or share the bread. Traditionally this sacramental pattern has been interpreted as describing the spiritual experience of the assembly itself: we are taken, blessed, broken, and given, and in so doing we are sent into the world to be and bear the gospel. Thus, even more important than the benefit derived by each individual in the reception of communion is the event of gathering and the celebration itself—gathering in the name of Jesus as the community of Jesus to eat and drink with Jesus. "Gathering," says Harmon Smith, "is a moral act."[79] And what Aidan Kavanagh says about the baptismal and initiation process may also be applied to the worship of the eucharistic assembly: It "constitutes the Church's radical business for the good of the world itself."[80]

The Promise of a Liturgical Evangelism

The idea of a "liturgical" evangelism is not new.[81] Robert Webber has explored the implications of worship for evangelism, emphasizing the liturgical character of the process of initiating persons into the life of the community of faith.[82] More recently, Patrick R. Keifert has echoed this perspective, which attempts to utilize catechetical patterns discerned in the *Apostolic Tradition* of Hippolytus.[83] Both authors, however, seem to base their theses on an understanding of worship as, itself, the "moment of evangelism,"[84] or as an element in a catechetical process. Doubtless there are those persons for whom *an* experience or *a series* of experiences in worship directly awakens faith and conveys a call to discipleship. And, to be sure, worship *is* formational, supporting and anchoring any catechumenal model designed to instruct and incorporate new members. But the "liturgical" evangelism of which I speak is something more altogether—an underlying ritual and ceremonial structure which shapes and transforms the body of Christ for these defining missional tasks. Such a view holds, as White so pointedly declared, that the worship life of a consciously liturgical community functions in this regard *ex opere operato*. The community's liturgy affects what Terry Holmes called the communicant's—and the community's—"deep memory":

> The sacramental life of the Church is the heart of the Church's performance where the symbols of Christ's passion reach and touch the deep memory of humankind and transform our vision to our roots. We live by the memory of the death and resurrection of Jesus. It is our root metaphor. It evokes the social drama from which we live as Christians. We become, by our participation, sacraments of Christ.[85]

Joe G. Burnett

While I am in sympathy with the general intent of Keifert's work–wrestling with the issue of "hospitality to the stranger" in the context of modern worship–it strikes me that his view of worship is, ultimately, a utilitarian one bordering on the gratuitous. In considering his assessment of the origins and directions of the various "currents" of modern liturgical revision, one can almost imagine a ruling liturgical *intelligentsia*, arbitrarily picking and choosing their textual ingredients from a cafeteria of two millennia of liturgical options. He suggests that much of what has passed for genuine renewal in liturgy may simply be "copied from the rites of some idyllic golden age of the church,"[86] and, further, that "the logic of worship is grounded neither in tradition nor in practical novelty but rather in God and the presence and actions of God in worship."[87] Yet I would argue that what we have harvested in our century of reform, far from being a designation based on esoteric liturgical taste, is precisely the latter–the theocentric fruit of a dynamic, evolving tradition of corporate prayer, liturgical memory, theological reflection, and pastoral action.

This has perhaps been best expressed by Michael Moriarty in his recent analysis of what he calls "a generation of change in the Episcopal Church." Moriarty reminds us that "in a way that is true for no other church, Episcopalians define themselves by their liturgy." The Book of Common Prayer "is not only a grammar for the church's conversation with God, but an arbiter of doctrine and polity, a definer of corporate identity, and a *vade mecum* for the individual soul's journey."[88] In reviewing the steps toward the most recent revision, he goes on to maintain that "the liturgical movement was just that–a movement, not an organization. It had no single point of origin, no unanimous program, no leaders empowered to set policy and exact obedience."[89]

> By returning the liturgy to its sources in the Bible and early tradition, the liturgical movement rediscovered not only a broader tradition, but also a grammar for engaging contemporary issues. Active participation in and comprehension of the liturgy, it was thought, would renew the structures of the church as well as create a new consciousness in individuals, who in turn would affect the structures of society by living out the implications of liturgy.[90]

"Episcopalians love the Prayer Book,"[91] says Moriarty. And, I would conclude, hidden in that love is a crucial clue for our church as we seek to chart the contours of an evangelism for the new millennium. Despite increasing emphasis on racial, social, and cultural diversity in its ministry and mission–especially in the years since the adoption of the 1979 Book of Common Prayer–the Episcopal Church largely remains a relatively literate and liberal ecclesial body. The complexity of our theological heritage, our liturgical life, and our socioeconomic profile makes us somewhat less immediately accessible than many of the other communions which comprise American Christendom. Therefore, developmental models (such as those provided by Church Growth) which have led some churches and denominations to experience record levels of numerical growth, particularly in areas with favorable demographics, simply will not yield the same results for us. Like it or not, the Episcopal Church does not seemed destined to be a fast growing church. Rather, our role in the panoply of religious groups in this country seems to continue to be that of a "second step" church, one that persons come to after a period of inactivity in some other church, or as a means of pursuing a richer, deeper spirituality than they have found in other faith communities.

Here, I would argue, is precisely where we need to focus our developmental efforts. Here is our first and greatest opportunity in terms of "church growth." We must equip ourselves to recruit, receive, and retain those persons who come to us seeking space and depth; those persons who come in search of a community of moderation and maturity; those persons who long for a community of fellow pilgrims who can serve as companions on a common spiritual journey. Such a process, I have maintained, finds its mainspring in the ongoing worship of the baptized, eucharistic community. It is grounded in a conception of the church which has always been central to Anglican Christians. It does not mean that we abandon or neglect specific programmatic efforts in the arena of evangelism and church development, nor does it require us in any sense to draw back from our commitments to justice and full inclusion. What it does call us to do is to embrace with even more intensity and intentionality the liturgical foundations of those missional tasks, and train all our catechetical energy on making the connections visible and compelling.[92]

I began with a personal story of what became for me a pivotal experience in worship. Not only was the seminary chapel service itself important, however, but also the years of Sunday services, the week-in and week-out routine of being in worship. That, above all else, enabled me to appreciate and appropriate the significance of what I described earlier as having happened "for the first time in my life." I was *formed* in worship; and, in worship, I was *re-formed.* Paulo Freire has spoken of *praxis* as the unity of action and reflection, and of the point at which *praxis* unites with the mission of the church as the point of *conscientization,* or reformulation.[93] The thrust of my argument has been that worship—or worship remembered—is a concrete "place" where such reformulation can occur. Here is a prime coincidence of person, witness, and existence. Here the self-understandings of the individual and the community, celebrating "always and everywhere" in response to God's self-giving love in Jesus Christ—and in the power of the

Spirit—are uniquely open to conversion and transformation, uniquely equipped for action and re-action. Here, in this event or series of events, is a powerful process of formation which gathers, shapes, sends, and sustains us. In worship, we are evangelized, and in turn equipped for the ministry of evangelism.

On the cusp of the modern liturgical movement, James White asserted in 1964 that "liturgy *is* evangelism."[94] In 1976, writing to educate new generations about the changes taking place in the church all around them, Marion J. Hatchett assured the faithful that

> the revisions of the various churches now in process are being carried out with the expressed aim of returning to the sources, the Biblical and Patristic heritage, incorporating the results of liturgical scholarship, and adapting to present conditions and missionary and pastoral needs. There have been attempts to make the language intelligible, to incorporate the social concerns of the day, and to allow for more flexibility to meet the needs of particular worshiping communities. There have been attempts to restore to the liturgies something of the missionary, proclamatory, educational, and pastoral aspects, which have been missing or overclouded for some centuries.[95]

We still have much to learn from the genius of their common insight, but I am convinced that one implication is inescapable: If we will deeply attend to our liturgical life,[96] if we will give to our liturgy and worship the same energy and care that we have expended in this church on congregational development, then our liturgy will make of us the evangelists—and disciples—we need to become.

Notes

1. Charles Wesley, "O the Depth of Love Divine," Hymn no. 332 in *The Methodist Hymnal* (Nashville: The Parthenon Press, 1964, 1966).

2. One very important analysis of this is the systematic theology of Geoffrey Wainwright, in *Doxology: The Praise of God in Worship, Doctrine, and Life* (New York: Oxford University Press, 1980). See also Leonel Mitchell, *Praying Shapes Believing: A Theological Commentary on The Book of Common Prayer* (Harrisburg, Pennsylvania: Morehouse Publishing, 1985).

3. See, for example, John Westerhoff, *Will Our Children Have Faith?* (New York: The Seabury Press, 1976). Westerhoff has argued that worship is a prime ingredient in the socialization process which is at the heart of human cultural, intellectual, and spiritual development.

4. William Willimon has creatively uncovered the striking implications of liturgical life and practice for mutual ministries of Christian caring, in *Worship as Pastoral Care* (Nashville: Abingdon, 1979).

5. See Harmon L. Smith, *Where Two or Three are Gathered: Liturgy and the Moral Life* (Cleveland: The Pilgrim Press, 1995); see also Willimon, *The Service of God* (Nashville: Abingdon, 1984).

6. See Schubert M. Ogden, "What is Theology?" *Perkins Journal*, XXVI.2 (Winter, 1973) 2.

WITH EVER JOYFUL HEARTS

7. I base this affirmation in part on the Introduction to Wainwright's *Doxology*, 1–12.

8. James F. White, "Liturgy is Evangelism," *The Christian Advocate* (Dec. 1964) 9.

9. James C. Fenhagen, "The Book of Common Prayer and the Pastoral Ministry of the Church," *Sewanee Theological Review*, Pentecost 1993 (Volume 36, No. 3) 296.

10. Fenhagen, 289.

11. See, for example, John H. Westerhoff, "Evangelism, Evangelization, and Catechesis: Defining Terms and Making the Case for Evangelization, in *Interpretation: A Journal of Bible and Theology*, Vol. XLVIII, No. 2 (April 1994) 156–165. Indeed, the articles in the entire issue reveal the broad diversity of views. See also the review of various ecclesiastical definitions of evangelism in Ben Johnson, *An Evangelism Primer: Practical Principles for Congregations* (Atlanta: John Knox Press, 1983) 6–9.

12. For a distinctive and creative analysis of the biblical roots of evangelism, see Walter Brueggemann, *Biblical Perspectives on Evangelism: Living in a Three-Storied Universe* (Nashville, TN: Abingdon Press, 1993).

13. Pope Paul VI, *On Evangelism in the Modern World* (Washington: United States Catholic Conference, 1976) 12.

14. The choice of the word "orientation" in this context is meant to suggest a determining position, not unlike Seward Hiltner's use of the term "perspective" in *Preface to Pastoral Theology: The Ministry and Theory of Shepherding* (New York: Abingdon Press, 1958).

15. See A. Wayne Schwab, *Handbook for Evangelism*, rev. ed. (New York: The Episcopal Church Center, 1989) 1. This definition is a slightly revised form of the 1918 report of the Committee of Inquiry into Evangelism in the Church of England which was chaired by William Temple, later to become Archbishop of Canterbury.

16. In this context it should be pointed out that the Reverend A. Wayne Schwab, the indefatigable progenitor of renewed efforts in evangelism ministries in the Episcopal Church, has argued that this statement needs to be understood in the context of Jesus' prophetic pronouncement in Lk. 4:17–21, *and* against the backdrop of Matthew's "great commission," thus affirming *deeds* and *words* as "inseparable aspects of the mission of God's people" (Ibid.). The intent of Schwab's assertion was to safeguard against evangelism being reduced only to a simplistic, personalistic, and conversionist agenda, devoid of social concern. Our success in this regard is yet a matter for analysis and debate.

17. The term "Church Growth" can be understood in several different ways. See, for example, John H. Yoder, "Church Growth Issues in Theological Perspective," in *The Challenge of Church Growth: A Symposium*, ed. By Wilbert R. Shenk (Scottsdale, Pennsylvania: Herald Press, 1973) 25–27. In this volume, one of the earliest critiques of the movement–and still, in my opinion, the definitive one–Yoder's article begins by distinguishing four levels of usage for the term. When I employ it exclusively in Yoder's fourth sense as having to do "with a specific set of institutions and persons," I will capitalize it, even though not all advocates do so consistently.

18. Seminal works in the field include Donald A. McGavran, ed., *Church Growth and Group Conversion* (Lucknow, India: Lucknow Publishing House, 1962); Donald A. McGavran, *The Bridges of God* (n.p.: World Dominion Press, 1955); *Understanding Church Growth*, 1st rev. ed. (Grand Rapids, Michigan: William B. Eerdmans Publishing Company, 1980); C. Peter Wagner, *Our Kind of People: The Ethical Dimensions of Church Growth in America* (Atlanta: John Knox Press, 1979).

19. William J. Abraham, "A Theology of Evangelism: The Heart of the Matter," in *Interpretation: A Journal of Bible and Theology*, April 1994 (Vol. XLVIII, No. 2)118.

304

20. I continue to find Peter Wagner's simple equation very instructive for the proper balance of a congregation's expanding, nurturing, and sustaining activities: *celebration* (worship) plus *congregation* (educational units) plus *cell* (small groups) equals *church.* See C. Peter Wagner, *Your Church Can Grow: Seven Vital Signs of a Healthy Church* (Glendale, California: G/L Publications, 1976) 97–109.

21. Abraham, "A Theology of Evangelism," 118.

22. See Schwab, *Handbook for Evangelism.* As an example, note that except for a brief discussion of dimensions of "proclamation," the other "basic steps in evangelism" presented are "new member ministry," "ministry with the lapsed," "founding new congregations," and "parish revitalization and spiritual direction."

23. Donald A. McGavran and Winfield C. Arn, *Ten Steps to Church Growth* (San Francisco: Harper & Row) 24. See also McGavran, *Understanding Church Growth,* 7: "Church Growth is basically a theological stance. God requires it. It looks to the Bible for direction as to what God wants done."

24. Wagner, *Your Church Can Grow,* 136–137.

25. Wagner, *Church Growth and the Whole Gospel: A Biblical Mandate* (San Francisco: Harper & Row, 1981) 52.

26. McGavran, *Understanding Church Growth,* 5–8.

27. David J. Bosch, *Witness to the World: The Christian Mission in Theological Perspective* (Atlanta: John Knox Press, 1980) 43.

28. Bosch, *Witness,* 48. See also Ferdinand Hahn, *Mission in the New Testament,* Studies in Biblical Theology, No. 47, trans. Frank Clarke (London: SCM Press, Ltd., 1965).

29. Mortimer Arias, "In Search of a New Evangelism," *The Perkins School of Theology Journal* XXXII.2 (Winter 1979) 17–18.

30. McGavran, in *Understanding Church Growth,* as much as says that the danger of perfecting is that it undermines the will and desire to disciple. See Chapter 15: "Halting Due to Redemption and Lift."

31. Urban T. Holmes, *Turning to Christ: A Theology of Renewal and Evangelization* (New York: The Seabury Press, 1981) 134. Holmes's book is one of the more creative attempts to address evangelism in a liturgical context.

32. McGavran, *Understanding Church Growth,* 223. A more recent and controversial apology for this concept can be found in Wagner, *Our Kind of People.*

33. See Wagner, *Church Growth and the Whole Gospel,* 41. In my opinion, it is one thing to say that groups need not compromise authentic cultural traits, or be swallowed up willy-nilly by a larger group. It is something else again when cultural traits contradict the gospel, or when genuine attempts at social integration are discouraged. Wagner's argument–his citing of theologians and social scientists notwithstanding–fails to take seriously the complexity and continuing implications of *past* social injustice in the *present* relations of homogeneous units. He also underestimates the propensity of certain groups, on the basis of these complex relations, to seek to gain or maintain social superiority and/or economic control.

34. It should be noted that the *homogeneous unit* concept is often descriptively accurate, and may rest on dimensions of group identity other than racial or cultural. In the Episcopal Church, for example, I will argue that our seeming diversity is often misleading. A given congregation may be populated by *seemingly* diverse elements–young and old, black and white, even upper and lower income groups–but may upon closer inspection reveal underlying dimensions of commonality in such areas as education and the arts, political awareness and activism, or even liturgical

sensibility and taste. The issue is how we go about expanding our membership base without compromising the universality of the gospel invitation.

35. Wagner, *Church Growth and the Whole Gospel,* 161.

36. Juan Luis Segundo, *A Theology for Artisans of a New Humanity,* Vol. I: *The Community Called Church,* trans. John Drury (Maryknoll, New York: Orbis Books, 1973) 83.

37. David Lowes Watson, "The Church as Journalist: Evangelism in the Context of the Local Church in the United States," *International Review of Mission,* LXXII (January, 1983) 57.

38. J. Russell Hale, *The Unchurched: Who They Are and Why They Stay Away* (San Francisco: Harper & Row, 1980); The Princeton Research Center and The Gallup Organization, Inc., *The Unchurched American* (Princeton, N.J.: PRRC, 1978).

39. J. Russell Hale, *The Unchurched,* pp. 99–110.

40. See, for example, Robert K. Hudnut, *Church Growth is Not the Point* (New York: Harper & Row, 1975).

41. Orlando E. Costas, *Christ Outside the Gate: Mission Beyond Christendom* (Maryknoll, New York: Orbis Books, 1982) 43.

42. Costas, *Christ Outside,* 47.

43. See Dietrich Bonhoeffer, *Ethics,* tr. Neville Horton Smith, ed. by Eberhard Bethge (New York: Macmillian Publishing, 1955) 83: "'Formation' . . . means in the first place Jesus' taking form in His Church. What takes form here is the form of Jesus Christ Himself . . . The Church, then, bears the form which is in truth the proper form of all humanity."

44. Henri Nouwen, *The Living Reminder: Service and Prayer in Memory of Jesus Christ* (New York: The Seabury Press, 1981). See also Harmon L. Smith, *Where Two or Three Are Gathered,* 70: "The liturgy trains us to see, to discern ourselves, the church, and the world—indeed all of life and reality—as formed by the Gospel. Because the liturgy is formed by the story of Israel, and the story of the life, ministry, death, resurrection, and ascension of Jesus, its power forms us in its image, after its assumptions, according to its norms."

45. Cited in James D. Anderson and Ezra Earl Jones, *The Management of Ministry* (New York: Harper and Row, 1978) 48–49. See also John Deschner, "What Does Practical Theology Study?" *Perkins Journal,* XXXV.3 (Summer, 1982) 11: "The church is not adequately understood simply in terms of mission, task, action . . . The church is even more basically the community of worship . . ."

46. James C. Fenhagen, *Mutual Ministry: A New Vitality For the Local Church* (New York: The Seabury Press, 1977) 78.

47. See Geoffrey Wainwright, *Doxology,* 8: "Into the liturgy the people bring their entire existence so that it may be gathered up in praise. From the liturgy the people depart with a renewed vision of the value-patterns of God's kingdom, by the more effective practice of which they intend to glorify God in their whole life."

48. See Alexander Schmemann, *For the Life of the World: Sacraments and Orthodoxy,* 2nd rev. ed., (Crestwood, New York: St. Vladimir's Seminary Press, 1973).

49. But see also Smith, *Where Two or Three Are Gathered,* 79: "The fact of the matter, of course, is that the church is *in the world,* and has its life among those who exercise their freedom not to have their lives ordered by God. The real and urgent question for the church from the beginning is how it can be *in* but not *of* that environment."

50. James F. White, *The Worldliness of Worship* (New York: Oxford University Press, 1967) 78.

Joe G. Burnett

51. White, *Worldliness.* 73.

52. Smith, *Where Two or Three Are Gathered,* 65.

53. White, *"Liturgy is Evangelism,"* 10.

54. White, *Worldliness,* 26.

55. Wayne A. Meeks, *The First Urban Christians: The Social World of the Apostle Paul* (New Haven: Yale University Press, 1983) 145.

56. Meeks, *First Urban,* 145–146.

57. Bosch, *Witness,* 227.

58. White, *Worldliness,* 103–104.

59. Hugh Riley, *Christian Initiation* (Washington, D.C.: The Catholic University Press/Consortium Press, 1974) 453.

60. Theodore Eastman, *The Baptizing Community* (Minneapolis: The Seabury Press, 1982) 51–52.

61. The Book of Common Prayer (New York: The Church Hymnal Corporation, 1979) 304–305.

62. Prayer Book, 306.

63. Prayer Book, 308.

64. Browne Barr, *High Flying Geese: Unexpected Reflections on the Church and its Ministry* (Minneapolis: The Seabury Press, 1983) 20.

65. Smith, *Where Two or Three Are Gathered,* 60, 64.

66. Barr, *High Flying Geese,* 36. Barr's citation is of P.T. Forsyth's Lyman Beecher Lectures on "Positive Preaching and the Modern Mind" (New York: Hodder & Stoughton, 1907) 44.

67. Prayer Book, 363.

68. Prayer Book, 366.

69. Prayer Book, 362.

70. Prayer Book 368.

71. See Geoffrey Wainwright, *Eucharist and Eschatology* (New York: Oxford University Press, 1981) 6. Wainwright says that the "recovery of a healthy eschatological understanding of the eucharist" will have important "consequences for the church's *mission* as the messenger of the kingdom, and for the church's *unity* as the body of Christ." See also 153: "Suffice it to recall that the eucharist *announces and initiates,* or (as we should rather say in the case of the eucharist) *furthers,* the coming of the kingdom of God."

72. Smith, *Where Two or Three Are Gathered,* 54.

73. Prayer Book, 363. Smith, *Where Two or Three Are Gathered,* says that we celebrate the eucharist "to be formed into a people to whom Jesus can come again . . . " and "to signify that we are such a people to whom he can come again . . . " and "to acknowledge ourselves as a people who welcome Jesus' coming again" (65).

74. Jürgen Moltmann, "The Life Signs of the Spirit in the Fellowship Community of Christ," in *Hope for the Church: Moltmann in Dialogue With Practical Theology,* ed. Theodore Runyon (Nashville: Abingdon Press, 1979) 54.

75. Prayer Book, 372.

76. Prayer Book, 374.

77. White, *Sacraments as God's Self Giving* (Nashville: Abingdon Press, 1983) 110–111. However, White, along with theologian Jürgen Moltmann, cautions that the sacraments must be constantly reinterpreted and reconsidered in the light of Scripture–"Christianized" is Moltmann's term–in order that their power of signification is not compromised or made to appear magical. See Moltmann, *Hope for the Church,* 54.

78. See Alfred C. Krass, *Five Lanterns at Sundown: Evangelism in a Chastened Mood* (Grand Rapids: William B. Eerdmans Publishing Company, 1978).

79. See Smith, *Where Two or Three Are Gathered,* 72.

80. Aidan Kavanagh, *The Shape of Baptism: The Rite of Christian Initiation* (New York: Pueblo Publishing Company, 1978) 115. See also Rafael Avila, *Worship and Politics* (Maryknoll, New York: Orbis Books, 1981) 89–90.

81. See my article, "Christ Has Died, Christ Is Risen, Christ Will Come Again: Toward a Liturgical Evangelism," *Journal of the Academy for Evangelism in Theological Education* (Vol. One, 1985–86) 46–58. Revised portions of this article appear in the current essay.

82. Robert Webber, *Celebrating our Faith: Evangelism Through Worship* (San Francisco: Harper & Row, 1986).

83. Patrick R. Keifert, *Welcoming the Stranger: A Public Theology of Worship and Evangelism* (Minneapolis: Fortress Press, 1992).

84. Keifert, *Welcoming,* 3.

85. Holmes, *Turning to Christ,* 87–96.

86. Keifert, *Welcoming,* 54.

87. Keifert, *Welcoming,* 6.

88. Michael Moriarity, *The Liturgical Revolution: Prayer Book Revision and Associated Parishes: A Generation of Change in the Episcopal Church* (New York: The Church Hymnal Corporation, 1996) 1.

89. Moriarity, *Liturgical Revolution,* 7.

90. Moriarity, *Liturgical Revolution,* 7

91. Moriarity, *Liturgical Revolution,* 1.

92. See Orlando E. Costas, *The Integrity of Mission: The Inner Life and Outer Reach of the Church* (New York: Harper & Row, 1979) 91: "There is no dichotomy between worship and mission. Worship is the gathering of the people sent into the world to celebrate what God has done in Christ and is doing through their participation in the Spirit's witnessing action. Mission is the culmination and anticipation of worship."

93. See Paulo Freire, *Pedagogy of the Oppressed,* tr. Mary Bergman Ramos (New York: Herder and Herder, 1970) esp. 75, 100ff., 120, 158.

94. White, "Liturgy *is* Evangelism," 9.

95. Marion J. Hatchett, *Sanctifying Life, Time, and Space: An Introduction to Liturgical Study* (New York: The Seabury Press, 1976) 162–163.

96. For one example of the kind of attention needed, see Paul Marshall, "Trite Rite: Field Notes on the Trivialization of Christian Initiation," in *Leaps and Boundaries: The Prayer Book in the 21st Century,* ed. Paul V. Marshall and Lesley Northup (Harrisburg, PA: Morehouse Publishing, 1997) 71-80.

The 1892 Prayer Book, Prayer Books for the Twenty-First Century and Willow Creek Church: A Cautionary Tale

George Wayne Smith

THE 1892 BOOK OF COMMON PRAYER was the first complete revision in the American Prayer Book tradition. It resulted from a decades-long theological battle and, perhaps to an even greater extent, from new societal pressures. The champions of a renewed sacramental theology, led by William Augustus Muhlenberg, had urged liturgical reforms allowing flexibility in planning, for they wanted the freedom to put the eucharist at the center of a worshiping life. Since the 1840s these forces had been urging the General Convention of the Episcopal Church to reshape the Prayer Book accordingly. The great rallying cry, however, was flexibility, not the eucharist, and that cry emerged from a church in the midst of a changing society. The bustle and expansiveness of nineteenth-century American life made for a nation self-assured and optimistic. These qualities also left people distracted and enervated from all the busy-ness and bustle. A frontier people who in 1858 could attend to every word of the Lincoln-Douglas de-bates—carefully crafted and nuanced rhetorical pieces lasting two-and-a-half hours—began to lose their edge and their attention span. The 1789 Book, heretofore the only Book in the American tradition, followed the pattern set by the earlier Books in the English tradition. Its rubrics required lengthy Sunday worship, about as long as one of those 1858 debates, with a rhetoric and pace all its own. Sunday worship, to state it bluntly, was boring. People had become too busy and too distracted for a loquacious style. Prayer Book revision, then, became a pastoral necessity as well as a theologically based hope. The 1892 Prayer Book emerged to legitimize forty years of incremental liturgical change.

At the end of the twentieth century, the Episcopal Church finds itself in a situation not all that different. If the forebears of this generation were distractible, its children are even more so. Attention spans may be as long as the customary time between television commercials—some nine to eleven minutes—or as long as it takes to read the snippet-sized news articles in *USA Today*. Alternatively, the usual attention span may be about as long as the text and images between hypertext links on a web document. The pastoral necessity before the church at the turn of this century—and millennium—lies, as always, in teaching and learning the lore of the people of God. Such lore is now taught and learned among people who know how to use the remote control and to surf the web—and therein lies the challenge.

Then there are those who argue, convincingly, that the end of this century marks the turning of an epoch. The sureties of enlightenment ideals and modernist progress have eroded, to the point that many name this new era "postmodern," for it comes on the heels of modernity's demise. If the new era is postmodern, it is also likely post-Christian, for the certitudes of church's place in culture—as partner with state and its culture, as sponsor and guardian of morality, as established institution—are disappearing or are already gone. This post-Christian, postestablisment situation requires the church to find new bases for credibility besides the institutional ones, in a time when institutions are themselves held in question.[1]

An incarnational church knows the culture in which it lives, and various movements of the church show thoughtful responses to the world around us. The 1979 Prayer Book, for example, may be the first postmodern and postestablishment Book in the entire Anglican tradition, for it provides a heretofore unknown flexibility in worship, and it sheds the establishment (or quasi-establishment) assumptions of earlier Books. Anglican expressions of postmodernity do not begin and end with the 1979 Prayer Book, however. Liturgical experimentation has by no means come to an end with the 1979 Book; if anything, the parishes of the Episcopal Church have become emboldened to extend the experimentation *as one of the norms of postmodern church practice.* The publication of supplemental liturgical texts, such as *Enriching Our Worship,*[2] the most recent in a series beginning in 1988, illustrates the norms of creativity and ongoing experimentation in worship. Fewer and fewer parishes have a single book of song, the official *Hymnal 1982,* in their pews. Postmodern culture demands a greater variety than one hymnbook could possibly provide. If one technological revolution—the

invention and widespread use of the movable type printing press–presaged
the liturgical revolution that was the English reformation, then perhaps
another technological revolution–the computerized media, emerging too fast
to keep track of–presages another revolution, equally epochal.

Evangelism in this cultural setting requires an invitation secular people
can understand. It also requires a savvy unfamiliar within the Anglican
heritage. With the demise of church as cultural sponsor, church can no
longer take for granted that secular people will know the lore of Scripture,
for example. Thus couching an invitation in scriptural language may have
little or no meaning for people outside the church. Episcopalians, with a
legacy of incarnational theology, are well-positioned to issue the invitation
in language faithful to our lore but still comprehensible to secular people.
Doing so is probably one of the great challenges ahead.

Then there is Willow Creek Church in Palatine, Illinois–not an Episcopal
Church, not a church of any mainline denomination, not a church of *any*
denomination, but a church representing phenomenal growth in numbers
since its founding in 1975. Willow Creek has become emblematic of a style
of worship designed specifically for *seekers* in the postmodern setting. Willow
Creek's "seeker services" are

> four identical weekend services in the main auditorium. Using drama, multi-
> media, contemporary music, and a message that connects with people's lives, the
> ageless wisdom of Scripture is presented in a creative, yet straightforward way.[3]

Saturday and Sunday worship is for seekers and includes a service called
"Axis," designed especially for Generation X.

> Not just another service, Axis is a truly alternative experience for people
> basically in their twenties, single or married, with kids or without. This place
> speaks the language of Generation X.
>
> The music is edgier, as is the style of service and dress, for that matter. Topics
> include marriage, careers, sexuality, social issues, and others of special interest
> to this age group. In short, Axis is church tailored to the needs of a new
> generation.[4]

Worship for the faithful, on the other hand, is on Wednesday and Thursday
evenings. Around seventeen thousand people worship at one of the weekend
services; around seven thousand worship during the week.[5] This community
expresses its focus and purpose at the weekend seeker services. This is why
there is a Willow Creek Church–to invite and welcome secular people.

The nineteenth-century revival movement did not draw in many
Episcopalians as active participants, but its existence *as a cultural phenomenon*
helped shape Episcopalians' desires for more flexible worship. In the same
way, few Episcopalians may actually join the Willow Creek Network, but

that organization's existence as a cultural phenomenon (and its success in drawing large numbers) may help shape yearnings for cultural relevancy in worship and subsequent church growth.

In this time of ongoing liturgical renewal and cultural challenges in a postmodern era, the Episcopal Church's experience with the 1892 Prayer Book may prove helpful as a point of reflection.

The 1892 Book of Common Prayer

The reader scanning the text of the 1892 Prayer Book for dramatic changes, or for the most part, even noticeable ones, will be disappointed. The familiar legacy of Tudor English and Cranmerian arrangement remain intact. The Book looks and feels like its predecessors—perhaps one of the reasons it was received by the Episcopal Church in such an irenic spirit. If anything, the *modesty* of alteration stands out, especially as the Book completes the work of four decades' consideration. Leaders like William Augustus Muhlenberg brought their intellect and passion to bear on the bishops and on General Convention all these years—and still the reader must attend to subtitles to recognize any change at all.

Yet changes there are—the recovery of canticles for Evening Prayer and the restoration of the *Benedictus* to Morning Prayer (the 1789 Book having excised them), small additions permitted in the Burial Office, inclusion of new prayers and thanksgivings, and an expanded service for Ash Wednesday, among the most noticeable. The Book also provides for the optional omission of the Decalogue and the Exhortation at Communion, under certain circumstances. It is the rubric in the front matter of the Book, however, that legitimizes a change first permitted (with the ordinary's approval) in 1856:

> The Order of Morning Prayer, the Litany, and the Order for the Administration of the Lord's Supper or Holy Communion, are distinct Services, and may be used either separately or together; *Provided*, that no one of these Services be habitually disused.[6]

This brief direction shapes the rationale for worship in the late nineteenth century.

Small changes and brief directions may leverage larger ones. Nuanced distinctions may provide grounds for future polarizations. A student of Marion Hatchett would know the shortcomings of the 1892 Prayer Book. Dr. Hatchett takes care to detail the consequences of seemingly insignificant changes wrought by this Book. Insofar as this Book receives more attention than most others in Dr. Hatchett's lectures, it does so because it aptly provides a negative, though well-intentioned, example.

The 1892 Prayer Book, in that one brief rubrical statement, loosened the strictures for Sunday worship. Good pastoral intentions and the substantial eucharistic theology of Muhlenberg undergirded this shift, for Sunday morning worship following the earlier Prayer Book template was too long and too wordy for the new cultural setting of late nineteenth-century America. The industrial revolution, after a century of settling in, had left most people too busy, too restless, and robbed of the necessary virtue of leisure for a word-intensive two and a half hours on a Sunday morning. The agrarian setting that might provide Sunday leisure for such a pattern of worship was in serious decline in late nineteenth-century America. A leisured aristocracy, small though widespread in the English countryside, never found much credibility in the United States outside isolated pockets with a distinct colonial heritage. Besides, the Anglican scheme of worship–full Morning Prayer, litany, sermon, and ante-Communion–never caught on in the American frontier experience. The more flexible and lively traditions of worship, especially Methodist and Baptist, became normative, as did the more ecumenical model of worship in the revival style. Stodgy Anglican worship did not stand a chance in city, town, or country. It was too much and too dull for most people. For Episcopalians, change became a pastoral necessity. They were in danger of boring themselves out of existence.

The latter half of the nineteenth century thus saw an increasingly evident pastoral need for greater flexibility in the liturgy. The Bishops and Deputies of General Convention began to consider this need, first in 1853, in general terms, and with an eye toward Prayer Book revision, beginning in 1868.[7] Pastoral needs did not exist apart from other concerns. A renewed and sacramentally based piety, urged by disciples of the Oxford Movement and their heirs, provided a theological framework for questioning the traditional Anglican practice. Not only was the old and loquacious style of worship pastorally inadequate; it also detracted from sound sacramental and theological principles, or so argued the various high church parties. They wanted the eucharist and its celebration, unencumbered. So William Augustus Muhlenberg, in a memorial to General Convention in 1853, made his famous request for greater flexibility in Sunday worship, with special attention to eucharistic celebration. In 1856 the bishops meeting at General Convention resolved to permit the breakup of the threefold Anglican norm for Sunday worship–Morning Prayer, litany, ante-communion–into its component parts, as long as the diocesan bishop would approve.[8] Some communities, such as Muhlenberg's Church of the Holy Communion in New York City, began Sunday celebrations of the eucharist every week, apart from the larger framework of Morning Prayer, litany and sermon. As has been typical in the history of Prayer Book revision, full legitimization followed emerging practices, and new practice has seldom awaited full Prayer Book authorization. Anglicanism has within its corporate memory this creative principle.

General Convention in 1892 brought closure to forty years' efforts at Prayer Book revision. A new Prayer Book, only the second Book in the American tradition and the first since 1789, came out of that Convention. Final approval came with remarkably little dissension, and the few procedural objections were easily set aside early in debate. The lengthy report from the commission charged with drafting a new Prayer Book presented a rationale replete with details of orthography–spelling and punctuation! The departure from an earlier usage inherited from the English style for a more identifiably American one required an explanation and a style sheet, as if such a move might be controversial. The most substantive disputes concerned a few points in an expanded Ash Wednesday service and the canonical details for keeping a standard copy of the Prayer Book, the one to which all other copies must conform. Such was the extent of debate. The essential changes, concerning the shape of Sunday worship, were noncontroversial.[9]

Thus a small set of pastorally necessary and theologically desirable practices received full authorization through the 1892 Book. The General Convention ratified the Book, and the Episcopal Church received it gladly, for it resulted from an unusual consensus among the various parties in the church. Most Episcopalians wanted some flexibility in worship, but the various parties looked to the Cranmerian status quo as a zone of safety for their own beliefs. Episcopalians–High Church and Low, Catholic and Evangelical–had grown accustomed to reading into the Prayer Book their own sets of beliefs and practices. Distinctively, the Prayer Book legacy proved flexible enough for just that. So most Episcopalians wanted change–but not too much. The 1892 Prayer Book met this need, no more and no less, and thus was well received. The Episcopal Church had the Book for new pastoral needs and theological concerns, and the various parties could agree on it.

Over the ensuing decades, however, the shortcomings of this revision became evident, for the small changes in this Prayer Book did leverage larger ones. They are chiefly two.

First, the choice among liturgical practices allowed further polarization of already existing factions, the evangelical and broad church, on the one hand, and the catholic, on the other. The first groups, with a great love for the Scripture and preaching, almost invariably chose Morning Prayer for the Sunday service. The second group–tractarians, ritualists, and later on, those influenced by the liturgical renewal movement of the twentieth century –chose the Holy Communion service. "Churchmanship" marked the fault line in Episcopal Church politics, and the choices for Sunday worship became party emblems. People knew what it meant to be part of a Morning Prayer or "low church" parish, and they knew its counterpart in the "high church" parish that celebrated eucharist at the main service every Sunday. The choices forced by the 1892 Prayer Book, a book ironically affirmed by a consensus of the Episcopal Church, actually enabled ongoing conflict.

Second, as tedious as it had become, the traditional Anglican structure for Sunday worship preserved, at least symbolically, two points of reference for the Christian life—word and sacrament. The points of reference were completely in view whenever there was Morning Prayer, Litany, and Communion, and present by symbol whenever there was Morning Prayer, Litany, and ante-communion. Admittedly, the incomplete symbol of a symbolic meal, interrupted before brought to completion, was less than satisfactory, both in theology and in practice, with the use of ante-communion; at least the traditional schema, including the liturgy of the word from Holy Communion, held out the holy meal's first acts and anticipation. The new routines of Sunday worship epitomized in the 1892 Book, breaking apart a centuries-long practice, symbolically set word against sacrament, instead of holding them in creative tension. For practical purposes, communities now had to choose between the two. Those who celebrated the eucharist every Sunday regularly heard two relatively short readings from Scripture—and almost never heard anything from the Old Testament. At least they had the sacrament. Those who worshiped at Morning Prayer, on the other hand, had a word-rich service, with lengthy readings (including the Old Testament), canticles, and psalms—but typically received communion infrequently at best.

The decades of liturgical renewal in the twentieth century had to take into account the unintended consequences from the 1892 revision. The 1928 Prayer Book, the last American Prayer Book with Tudor language and Cranmerian structures as the norm (and some would say, the last Prayer Book before the demise of establishment and modernity), did not address the consequences. The 1979 Prayer Book did—but not by way of imposing again the threefold act of Sunday worship (office, litany, eucharist) on Episcopalians. This Prayer Book looks behind reformation practices to the longer tradition, to reshape a word-rich eucharistic liturgy. The eucharistic lectionary requires two and appoints three longish readings (always including an Old Testament reading among the options) and a psalm for every Sunday and major holy day. It provides a framework with many options and underutilized flexibility. This word-rich eucharistic celebration is named as the norm for Sunday and holy day worship.[10]

The Book of Common Prayer 1979 probably fulfills William Augustus Muhlenberg's quest for consistent eucharistic practice and flexible pastoral adaptation better than did the 1892 Book, a direct outcome of his work. Muhlenberg shepherded the changes in the 1883 book for trial use, known as *The Prayer Book Annexed*, providing clear guidelines for innovation and flexibility in liturgical practice. Though well-received by the church, The *Book Annexed* proved too bold to win the support of General Convention in subsequent years. The Prayer Book finally approved had little more flexibility than rubrical permission for the shortened Sunday service. The 1979 Book meets and exceeds Muhlenberg's criteria for flexibility and normative eucharistic practice. But even Muhlenberg's boldest work did not anticipate the unintended consequences of a shortened service—the hardening of party lines and the loss of that dual focus, word *and* sacrament, rather than the forced choice of one or the other.

The Current Situation

Loss of historical perspective may cause Episcopalians to forget that other eras besides our own were times of rapid liturgical change and creativity. Certainly the reformation years were such, and so were the years of the Nonjurors' influence in England, Scotland, and (to a lesser extent) in the United States. The four decades culminating in the 1892 Prayer Book were rich ones for the church's liturgical life. That the resulting Prayer Book was a modest revision, resulting perhaps from a loss of nerve by the church's leaders in General Convention, should not detract from this period's creativity. The creative foment of the times, the desire to take into account the various new learnings, the societal seachange experienced, a sense of inadequacy in temperament and in worship styles for competing in the public square, the fractious nature of the church, an overwhelming desire for consensus in the face of that nature, the realities of liturgical change to adapt to and the likelihood of more change, the need for the church to define flexibility in its worshiping life—all these mirror a current situation.

The Episcopal Church will soon end a "Decade of Evangelism" with little perceived success and a greater degree of internalized guilt than before, for Episcopalians are not good at the disciplines of evangelizing. These waves of little success and much guilt may lead Episcopalians to look with longing, or alternatively, with revulsion, at the life of a ministering community like Willow Creek Church. Episcopalians may yearn for something *big* like that, something vibrant, something capable of catching the ever-diminishing attention span of folks in American cultures. Or Episcopalians may resist anything at all like Willow Creek Church and retreat to the comfort of nonthreatening Anglican practice. Waves of dependency and counter-dependency strike Episcopalians when looking on phenomena like Willow

Creek Church. I suggest that Episcopalians look neither with longing nor with revulsion—but that we look nonetheless and look carefully. Many parish communities are already considering and implementing models for alternative, highly innovative worship, and doing so out of good intentions and evangelical desire. The experience of the 1892 Prayer Book and its aftermath may help Episcopalians seeking new flexibility in worship recognize some pitfalls and possibilities in such an enterprise.

Furthermore, the long season of liturgical renewal begun in the twentieth century will surely continue into the twenty-first. Insights from that long season of renewal in the nineteenth century might give a helpful perspective to Episcopalians anticipating a new Prayer Book—or at least several more waves of new liturgical materials. General Convention in 1997 mandated the Standing Liturgical Commission to submit to the next Convention (in the year 2000) a first reading for a constitutional amendment clarifying authorization and use of additional (i.e., non-Prayer Book) resources for worship—and to submit a plan for future revision of the liturgy.[11] Further liturgical reform is in our future, and it likely will involve electronic media supplementing *or replacing* the customary Prayer Book between hard covers familiar in Anglican practice since the sixteenth century.[12] A next wave of reform may prove even more revolutionary, for it will present the church not only with new content but with a new process and medium for making sense out of it.

How, then, does the church's experience with the Book of Common Prayer 1892, both before and after, help make sense of the current situation? I offer some provisional suggestions.

First, Episcopalians were right to make a pastoral response toward liturgical flexibility within a rapidly changing cultural setting. Such a movement is not at all inimical to the Anglican spirit, as the 1892 Book exemplifies. Moreover, the pastoral response of the time was not a movement apart from theological reflection. Integrative thinking marked the movement, and liturgical revision was not rooted in the academy. It emerged in the parish. The best theologian-pastors of the time, led by William Augustus Muhlenberg, brought their unrelenting intellect and passion to insist on liturgical change. *And they still did not get everything right.*

This leads to a second point—the anticipation of unexpected consequences. The revisers behind the 1892 Prayer Book did their work in all good intent for pastoral and theological reasons, and they worked at it for forty years. They still could not have anticipated the consequence of a church further polarized around choices that the 1892 Book forced, or the spiritual impoverishment over the long term that came with the desired shortened liturgy—one grounded in word *or* sacrament but not necessarily both. Perhaps those charged with revising the rites can learn to imagine possible consequences and play "What if?" toward a good end, with every revision proposed. Trial usage has become customary in the Episcopal Church, and certainly trial usage of new materials helps ferret out some of the more evident miscues in newly revised rites. Remember that *The Prayer Book Annexed* was in effect a book for trial usage, and even in nine years of its use before the 1892 Book was ratified, the church did not *and could not* recognize some of the consequences inherent in the most basic change in the Book, namely, a more flexible Sunday liturgy. Perhaps exceptional care in discernment among a wide range of people in the academy and parishes, among the baptized and the ordained, among people of various cultures can help name consequences more adequately. Perhaps modesty in approach can also help Episcopalians admit the inevitable, for even with the best of plans and the widest participation, we cannot anticipate every consequence of liturgical reforms we make. Small changes may leverage larger problems we cannot at the time recognize. Hubris serves no one well, and a legacy of Prayer Book revision in the past should help prepare the way for the *next* revision to come, for in this tradition, every Prayer Book has proved provisional.

A grounding in the basics of Anglican tradition and practice—not a perfect tradition, but it happens to be the one Episcopalians get to live in—may also help avert missteps. The loquacious, threefold practice of office, litany, ante-communion *had* grown stodgy by nineteenth-century standards; even so, there must have been something valuable in a practice that had lasted three hundred years and more. Identifying that which has value from the longer tradition—in this case, a word-rich liturgy within the context of sacramental worship—can help mark the way forward in reshaping the worshiping life of a church. Mimicking or sustaining patterns grown stodgy serves no one, but knowing what is valuable from the legacy of our forebears has a way of helping Christian folk find a way toward a future. That pattern of office, litany, and ante-communion did not work a century ago, and it certainly would not work now. But a rich liturgy of the word and its counterpart in a sumptuous liturgy of the table, ideals from that old pattern, might serve as good markers for any liturgical revision in current Anglican practice. There are various ways, and creative ones, to reshape the Sunday liturgy; perhaps any reshaping should meet these basic criteria from the tradition—word and sacrament.

Oddly enough, the 1892 Prayer Book represented a clear consensus at the time of its ratification. That consensus transformed into division *and did so around the very points of agreement.* The "lowest common denominator," however, does not always make the best consensual choice. One wonders what would have happened in the more radical—and widely acclaimed—*The Prayer Book Annexed* had been more fully incorporated into Prayer Book revision. A small but vocal minority forced the more conservative revision resulting from the forty years' effort at Prayer Book reform. The General Convention gave that small minority inordinate power by meeting their demands for a conservative reform. Even that did not prevent the further polarization of church life for two generations. I say this not to suggest that emerging majorities should ignore the voices of pesky minorities. Quite the contrary. My point is instead that reaching genuine consensus is tricky— much trickier than up-or-down votes allow. The 1892 Prayer Book was by all accounts a consensual document. Today's consensus, however, can provide the platform for tomorrow's division. Consensus is achieved over time, not by the votes of one General Convention or even two.

Liturgy shapes believers, who in turn shape liturgy anew in their desire for ever more adequate and eloquent praise of God—and praise that fits the lives of the people offering it. Such has been the steady rhythm in the Prayer Book heritage. With a few exceptions, this rhythm has been rather a slow one. Occasionally in Anglican history, movement of believers to reshape their worshiping life has been quick and dramatic. The first Book of Common Prayer 1549 gave way quickly to that of 1552. But more typically, it takes more years than three and even decades for the liturgy to have its way with believers, who may in turn discern the need to have their way in shaping a new liturgy as a consequence. For example, after twenty years of living with the 1979 Prayer Book, Episcopalians are just now getting an adequate sense of what needs reshaping in this Book. The rites of initiation, necessarily ambiguous in relation to confirmation, at least at the time, now beg reworking. A next revision will have to take that insight into account. The eucharistic prayer cast in the most expansive and cosmic language, Prayer C of Rite II, the most contemporary sort of expression with the time of its writing, now seems a little dated and a very much a product of its time—and is recognized as the most gender-specific of the Rite II prayers. Celebration of New Ministry, participatory to the extent that none of its predecessors was, has not worn well. It now seems more clerical and triumphalist than is fitting.

Liturgy has consequences because language has consequences, not all of which reveal themselves at once. Often the liturgy and its language have to settle into the lives of people praising God for years before the people can judge the adequacy of it, what works, what does not. The 1892 Prayer Book worked—and it did not work. What worked was obvious. A shortened, more flexible service worked. I suspect such a service will still work. No one (well, almost no one) clamors for a longer Sunday liturgy done in a more rigid style. That is not the future of liturgy in the Episcopal Church. Greater flexibility and more choices are our future—and a necessary one. Even Willow Creek Church will provide challenges and a source of learning for the Episcopal Church. Prudent, discerning incorporation of those learnings, not an unthinking emulation of the model, will show a way forward. With an eye toward the 1892 Prayer Book and its revision necessary in its time, perhaps Episcopalians can be alert to various consequences in the years of liturgical reform ahead of us. Does increasing flexibility in worship truly support diverse and en-Spirited expressions of praise as each worshiping community sees fit—or does it merely provide a framework for polarization within the church and the further demise of consensus? A hard question for a church already feeling its divisions too well.

Notes

1. For an overview of postmodernity, see Albert Borgmann, *Crossing the Postmodern Divide* (Chicago: University of Chicago Press, 1992).

2. *Enriching Our Worship: Supplemental Liturgical Materials* prepared by The Standing Liturgical Commission (New York: Church Publishing Incorporated, 1998).

3. HTML document, "Church Services at Willow Creek," http://www.willowcreek.org.

4. HTML document, "Church Services at Willow Creek: GenX, " http://www.willowcreek.org.

5. HTML document, "Frequently Asked Questions," http://www.willowcreek.org.

6. Paul V. Marshall, *Prayer Book Parallels: Anglican Liturgy in America*. 2 vols. (New York: Church Hymnal Corporation, 1989) 1:72.

7. William Sydnor, *The Real Prayer Book: 1549 to the Present* (Wilton, Connecticut: Morehouse-Barlow, 1978) 61–69.

8. Byron D. Stuhlman, *Eucharistic Celebration 1789–1979* (New York: Church Hymnal Corporation, 1988) 96–97.

9. *Journal of the General Convention 1892,* pages 145, 195, 557–623. My thanks to the staff at the Archives of the Episcopal Church, Austin, Texas, for providing these materials for this essay.

10. The Book of Common Prayer 1979, 13. In this Book, the first two sections are historic in nature, the Preface to the first American Prayer Book and its Ratification. The next section, "Concerning the Service of the Church," describes current principles for Prayer Book practice. This norm about eucharist—word-rich in this Book—on Sunday and Holy Day is named *in the very first sentence.*

11. HTML Text, "Resolutions Proposed to the 72nd General Convention of the Episcopal Church, C021s, Amended and Adopted." http://www.dfms.org.

12. Ibid. The 1997 resolution of General Convention *requires* that new liturgical revisions be distributed "in a variety of forms, including multimedia and electronic options."

A Perspective on the Relation of the Prayer Book to Anglican Unity

Louis Weil

A RECENT ARTICLE by Professor Marion Hatchett is a strong reminder of the particular gift which he has brought to liturgical studies in the Episcopal Church during his long career as teacher and scholar. In an article entitled "Unfinished Business in Prayer Book Revision," Professor Hatchett offers a masterly reminder that the shaping of its public worship is an ongoing aspect of the church's life, a work that is never *finished.* I would apply the often quoted words of the architect Ludwig Mies van der Rohe that "God is in the details" to the work of Professor Hatchett. Over the past decades he has shown a marvelous ability to hold together a dazzling range of details which some might see as minutia, but which we who have profited many times from his scholarship see as the constitutive elements which shape the larger liturgical picture. His work has indeed shown that God is in the details.

In this recent article, Professor Hatchett reveals to readers the extent to which we may now see the Book of Common Prayer of 1979 as a work in progress.[1] In doing so, he also shows how profoundly the process of liturgical revision has changed since the Episcopal Church went through the stages of trial use in the sixties and seventies. At that time, our point of departure for such revision tended to remain, at least in principle, the work of Archbishop Thomas Cranmer in the Prayer Books of 1549 and 1552. As the work of revision went on at that time, however, many of us came to realize that we had arrived at a point in the evolution of our liturgical tradition that, in the words of one of my colleagues, "the last band-aid had been placed on Cranmer's work." The rearrangement and supplementing of this legacy would no longer be adequate to the needs of the church. This was, of course, not an easy conclusion since Cranmer had loomed so large in the entire history of the Prayer Book, even when a particular province produced a book with alterations of which the archbishop would not have approved. It was generally acknowledged that the Prayer Book served as a symbol of Anglican unity, and thus if particular provinces strayed too far from this model, wherein would we find our unity?

Toward the end of a study of the eucharistic rites of the Anglican churches in Africa, the English liturgist Phillip Tovey poses this question and then continues with a comment which some Anglicans would find disturbing. He writes:

> If the Book of Common Prayer ceases to be the norm throughout the Anglican Communion, what is it that holds it together? Anglicans are only just beginning to realize that a Communion of one form of worship is in fact a myth that has never existed.[2]

Tovey's comment is I believe, correct, but I would not use the word "myth" with the negative tone which it carries in the quotation. Yes, the Prayer Book has been for Anglicans a powerful and effective myth, a fundamental symbol of Anglican identity. Although that myth has often been invoked in a literalistic way which implied that Prayer Books of the various provinces were more similar than they actually were, Anglicans all over the world would carry this bound volume to church or reach forward from their pew to pick up a copy from the rack with confidence that this was the book familiar to them during years or even decades of public prayer. This fact played a significant role in the cohesion of the Communion all over the world. Whatever the local variations might be, it was my experience that any Anglican would respond that the Prayer Book was the basis for their parish's worship. During recent decades, however, that situation has gradually but dramatically changed.

An essay by Paul Gibson, the former Liturgical Officer of the Anglican Church of Canada, recognizing this new situation, echoes Tovey's question by asking, "Now that provincial and contemporary liturgies are replacing the Book of Common Prayer, . . . what will hold Anglicanism together?" Gibson responds that the real issue beneath this question is that of authority: the Book of Common Prayer has provided a unifying authority for both doctrine and worship. In both of these areas, however, that authority has been partially eclipsed by the emergence of issues about which the church's leaders are sharply divided.[3] In his discussion of the understanding of authority in Anglicanism, Gibson makes the interesting observation that "as the official status of the Articles (of Religion) went down (as a defining document of Anglican theology), the unofficial status of the Book of Common Prayer became, by a process of consensus, the organ of normative authority in the Anglican Communion."[4] What is most interesting about this observation is that it reminds us that the Book of Common Prayer has not always been understood as the fundamental symbol of Anglican unity; that is an attitude which emerged gradually to fill, as it were, a vacuum created when the Articles of Religion lost their binding authority with regard to doctrine, and in many provinces ceased to require assent by ordinands at the time of ordination.

When we consider the very rich body of apologetical literature produced in defense of the Book of Common Prayer, the major themes concern the beauty of the Prayer Book and its usefulness as a basis for both corporate and private devotion.[5] These writers were concerned with the Prayer Book not as an instrument for political conformity nor even for ecclesiastical unity, but as the foundation for an authentic piety. Its preservation was viewed as a providential gift from God to the English Church.[6] The idea of the Prayer Book as a symbol of Anglican unity could be born only when the idea of Anglicanism as a communion of national, autonomous churches might seek to name those aspects of its occlusal life which could serve in that way. In this perspective, the Prayer Book as a symbol of unity seems really to be a development of the later nineteenth century, and as this symbol always involved an awareness of a family of Prayer Books authorized in the various provinces. The symbol involved diversity from the start. It is evident, of course, that the earliest of the books produced outside of England were nevertheless quite dependent upon the work of Thomas Cranmer and the later evolution of the books authorized after those of 1549 and 1552. This basic conservatism about Cranmer's work is easy to explain on the simple basis of the beauty of his vernacular forms. It was not without reason that Anglican apologists had emphasized this quality in our liturgical tradition.

In his essay, Paul Gibson notes that the current situation in which provincial rites are beginning to replace the inherited tradition is a serious matter for Anglicanism. He writes, "The Prayer Book tradition has been the outward form of an occlusal culture, the basis of an aesthetic, the theological definition of a social order. It has been all this and much more, and it is under serious pressure on three fronts today."[7] Gibson then goes on to discuss the three major forces which are acting upon the inherited Prayer Book tradition of Anglicanism: first, he notes the social realities with which we live today and which the Prayer Book often ignores from its lofty perspective of an elitist and ordered society. If we were to note those members of our society whose lives seem quite foreign to the those of the

Prayer Book—the marginalized, the dispossessed, the abused, the destitute—the list would in fact be incredibly long. Gibson is pointing to what we might call the sociological realities of the church in the world, and the imperative for us that our public prayer reflect this world honestly. Second, Gibson names the impact of ecumenical convergence as a major factor impelling us toward new models of corporate prayer. One of the great discoveries of the ecumenical work of the twentieth century has been the enormous ground which most Christians share, even when denominational separation implies otherwise. The renewal of the liturgy in our various traditions has built upon this awareness to propose the use of common forms of prayer which, while not resolving some major areas of theological dispute, open for us a place where our shared faith in Jesus Christ may find a united voice. Third, Gibson speaks of the impact of cultural pluralism not only upon our world but specifically upon Anglican models of liturgical prayer. For more than four centuries, Anglican worship has been essentially shaped by its origins in English culture. The missionary outreach of Anglicanism in the eighteenth and nineteenth centuries was, understandably, deeply affected by the dominant political role which England held around the world. The missionaries— perhaps often unconsciously—carried that culture with them, but more than that, their culture was held as superior to other cultures and thus was thought to have an inherent right to inhibit or subjugate those other cultures. In the last decade alone, between the Lambeth Conference of 1988 and that of 1998, the dramatic cultural shift within the Communion has become abundantly evident.[8]

All three of these factors are, of course, quite important. All three create imperatives for the church today to look at its inherited liturgical traditions with new insight and to foster new priorities in future liturgical evolution. But it is the third, the cultural issue, upon which I wish to focus in this essay. Without cultural pluralism, or without the recognition of the value of cultural pluralism as the context for a deeper engagement of the gospel in our time, I believe that it would be possible for the first two factors mentioned by Gibson to be domesticated. It would, for example, be easy to see the sociological imperatives of our own society as the universal agenda for these issues without acknowledging that these factors play themselves out quite differently in different cultural contexts. It is arrogant to presume that appropriate responses to these realities in our culture can offer a universal blueprint to be utilized in very different cultures from our own. Our world is much more complex than that. So, too, with the second issue, that of ecumenical convergence. If we do not look at that development in the light of a multicultural world, we might easily see the goal of ecumenism as little more than the consolidation of first-world churches. I have come to realize in recent years that the ecumenical horizon must be wider and the goals of dialogue much more profound than those of us who have been involved in the ecumenical movement could possibly have imagined a few decades ago.

It is, I believe, that multicultural dimension of our world which poses the greatest challenges and the highest goals for the continuing renewal of the church and its worship. Using an image which I have often offered to students, the early stages of liturgical renewal were like the journey of a person setting out to climb a glorious mountain which dominates the horizon. This was the common renewal which all of the liturgical traditions have been involved in for many years. Its goal was to restore the integrity of the rites received from the tradition. On the whole, we have conquered that mountain, and the authorized Books reflect the fruits springing from an enormous common ground of historical and theological scholarship. But when we arrived at the summit of that mountain, suddenly several other yet more glorious mountains came into view—mountains which we could never have seen had we not climbed to the top of the first. That, I believe, is the situation of the church as it stands before the social and cultural complexity of our world. The horizon has now become much wider than we could perceive earlier: how do we live the gospel in a multicultural and rapidly changing world? And how do we proclaim the gospel in a multi-religious world in which we have come to recognize the authenticity and truth professed and lived in other forms of religious faith? And how do we respond to God in forms of worship which are honest about that world?

My own commitment to the impact of cultural pluralism upon Anglican liturgical practice began early in my own ordained ministry. During my final year in seminary, I had agreed to begin my pastoral ministry in Puerto Rico in response to an effort by the bishop there to intensify the presence of the Episcopal Church in that area. I arrived in Puerto Rico only a few days after my ordination to the diaconate. Quite unconsciously, I was the bearer of my culture. In fact, I believe that even as late as the 1960s this was still the expected model for missionaries going to serve in overseas dioceses. Prophetic voices had been attempting to bring a judgment upon this mode, but these voices were scarcely noticed by the administrators who oversaw the sending out of missionaries. In retrospect, I realized later that the sign of a culpable indifference to the local culture was to get what I needed in a five week intensive program. Fortunately, as a musician, I was sensitive to the unique sounds of Spanish inflection, and by the end of a torturous first year had become reasonably adept with the language. This cavalier attitude toward language on the part of the "mother church" remains for me a powerful expression of the failure to take the local culture seriously.

As my knowledge of Spanish grew, I came to realize that the translation of the American Book of Common Prayer of 1928 was often defective. It could have been called "Spanglish" since the text was often a transliteration rather than a translation. The printing of the Prayer Book was also intended to replicate to the greatest degree possible the appearance of the American book, in size, binding and layout. I have no way of knowing to what degree this was conscious and intentional or simply based upon the presupposition that the American book served the same role which the *missa normativa* was seen to hold for the Roman rite.

Only a few months after my arrival in Puerto Rico, a new and long-awaited hymnal was published. As a trained musician and previously a parish organist, I was anxious to see this new resource. I commented later to the Bishop of Puerto Rico that within one hour of studying the new hymnal, I had a long enough list of errors to have stopped publication. Although at the time I was simply irritated by the poor editorial work, the inconsistent use of phraseology and elision, and the faulty musical layout, I realized later that the poor quality of the hymnal in Spanish (1961) was again an indication of a failure to take the local culture seriously. Both for the Prayer Book and the hymnal, the level of editorial carelessness alone would have been unimaginable for official liturgical books published in the United States.

All of this is said not to condemn the Episcopal Church of that time for failures as though these failures were not to be found in other denominations. As far as I could observe from my own experience at that time, this attitude was universal in all denominations with foreign missionaries in Latin America. The Roman Church had the advantage of a long tradition of pastoral presence in Latin America, so when Vatican Council II authorized the use of vernacular there were some resources already in place. But even in this case, the Roman rite was considered to be the defining source for all liturgical rites. The idea of locally developed rites would have appeared to all of us as dangerously radical. During my years in Puerto Rico, up until 1971, we continued to use these two volumes—the Prayer Book and the Hymnal—as the basic resources for all liturgical celebrations. By the early seventies, however, more radical questions were being posed which would take the local culture and its own unique character as a constitutive aspect of the liturgy.

Once I was back in the United States, I had two other experiences which helped to shape my attitude toward the imperatives of culture. The first was my acceptance of an invitation from the Bishop of Ecuador in 1975, to go into the interior of his diocese to work with a small group of Quetchua Indians who were in an early stage of formation with a possible goal of ordination later on. My first task was to give them a basic sense of the role of liturgy in the life of the church and a grounding in the theology of the sacraments. But another task which the bishop asked me to undertake with the group was the preparation of a eucharistic rite in Quetchua. Spanish was the second language for me and for men in the group. I knew no Quetchua and they knew no English. Our point of departure was then the trial-use rite which later became Rite II in the Book of Common Prayer of 1979. We had to work very carefully with the language, exploring the sense and nuance of a Spanish translation of the eucharistic prayer in order to have some confidence in the Quetchua translation which we were aiming to produce. By that time, my knowledge of Spanish was fairly reliable. One of the delights of this experience was to hear, as the text in Quetchua developed, the beauty of the sound of the language, what I came to hear as its "music." Although we were able to complete our task with some level of confidence, and I did hear later that the text became the version used for the celebration of the eucharist in Quetchua communities, it became obvious to me that the real task was not translation and adaptation but rather the development of new rites from within the framework of Quetchua language and culture. In other words, the true goal had to be an authentic indigenization, and that could not come about through the adaptation of a North American rite.

The other experience which I had during this period was my appointment as liturgical consultant for two projects of the Standing Liturgical Commission in the early eighties. The Commission was committed to the preparation of a Spanish translation of the by-then-authorized American Book of 1979. When the committee gathered to begin this work, we were told by Canon Charles Guilbert, the Custodian of the Book of Common Prayer, that our task was defined as an exact translation of the authorized Book of the United States. We questioned how much latitude there would be, and we were told that although the best translation possible was the goal, we were not to stray beyond the actual text of the 1979 Book.

A short time later, while the Spanish project was still going on, I was asked to serve on a second committee whose task was to prepare a new Book in French for use in Haiti and some of the French-speaking dioceses of Africa. Within perhaps no more than a two year interim, however, the mentality toward adaptation had changed. The chair of the committee was a French Roman Catholic priest, Jacques Gres-Gayer, who had an extensive knowledge of the Anglican tradition. He pressed for greater flexibility in the preparation of the French version so that we might produce a book which would correspond closely to the American book but which would not sacrifice idiomatic French in the name of fidelity to the 1979 Book. This meant that texts which were already available in the authorized French translation of the Roman Rite would be available to us.

It is interesting to note that dissatisfaction with the Spanish version was already in evidence in the late eighties when I did clergy conference in Guatemala. At a eucharist celebrated by the Bishop of Guatemala, the text used was one which had been locally developed. The French version, being more idiomatic, was received as a more successful model of adaptation. What was happening in the eighties in this regard was the growing awareness that the Anglican Communion could no longer find its identity within an Anglo-American cultural framework. If the church was to develop authentically in other cultural contexts, it would have to take those cultures seriously. During this same period, while attending a conference in Toronto, I had a conversation with a much respected parish priest there. Toronto is a highly multicultural, international city, and I raised the question with the priest about the adaptation of Anglican liturgy to this diverse cultural context. He responded that he did not feel that Anglicanism was capable of such a level of adaptation, and that its English historical origin was an essential part of its identity. I realized that this is truly the issue before us: is our tradition capable of taking root authentically in a wide range of cultures and fulfill the catholic identity which it claims, or is it doomed in the twenty-first century to become an enclave of nostalgic Anglophiles? My own belief is that the essential characteristics of the religious tradition which we know as "Anglicanism" is accidentally English. Although one would be mad not to acknowledge the dramatic impact of the British origins of our tradition, the essential dynamics of that tradition are, I believe, quite capable of incarnation within cultures which are quite distinct from the Anglo-American context. For this to happen on a larger scale than has occurred up until now, the constitutive national churches which make up the Anglican Communion must be willing to scrutinize the tradition for those aspects of the tradition which are foundational for its occlusal life and to find coopera-tive means to build up those dimensions as the common ground of Anglican identity. Along with this, however, there must be a much greater affirmation of the potential for all cultures to proclaim and celebrate the sign of Christian faith, and to support a wide latitude in that regard. We are not called to be the curators of a liturgical museum, no matter how beautiful the treasures of the church's past may be.

This change of perspective has been developing in the Anglican Communion during the latter half of this century. As recently as 1948, the stability of Anglican worship seemed as secure as ever in its history. At the Lambeth Conference of that year, the bishops resolved "that the Book of Common Prayer has been, and is, so strong a bond of unity throughout the whole Anglican Communion that great care must be taken to ensure that revisions of the Book shall be in accordance with the doctrine and accepted liturgical worship of the Anglican Communion" (Resolution 78a). It was easy for the bishops to make such a resolution in 1948, since the ethos of the Anglican rites all over the world was very much the same. Just ten years later, however, at the Lambeth Conference of 1958, Article XXXIV of the Articles of Religion, which had been the original justification for the formation of the English Church's own rites at the time of the separation from Rome, was now seen in terms of its relevance to the situation in the twentieth century. The article reads as follows:

> It is not necessary that traditions and ceremonies be in all places one, or like; for at all times they have been divers, and may be changed according to the diversity of countries, times, and men's manners, so that nothing be ordained against God's word . . . Every particular or national church hath authority to ordain, change, and abolish, ceremonies or rites of the church ordained only by man's authority, so that all things be done to edifying.

At Lambeth 1958, the bishops accepted the fact that this article suggested considerable adaptation among the various national cultures of the numerous provinces of the Anglican Communion. One may see now that the handwriting was clearly on the wall and that a time of profound liturgical change lay before them.

An interesting document was issued in 1965, entitled "The Structure and Contents of the Eucharistic Liturgy." The document marked the completion of the liturgical work of the 1958 Lambeth Conference. In the face of substantial liturgical changes which had taken place during the preceding decade, the document sets forth the traditional structural elements of the eucharistic liturgy in the expectation that a certain ritual unity may be maintained with regard to the structure of the rite. Concerning this issue we may note that the report of the Lambeth Conference of 1958, made the following observation:

> There are reasons for hoping that it is now possible to work toward a liturgy which will win its way throughout the Anglican Communion. The Committee would not suggest a return to those rigid and legalistic ideas of uniformity which prevailed for some centuries. It recognizes that even in the sacrament of unity there is a place for variations of rite to meet local situations and needs. What is urged is a basic pattern for the service of holy communion itself to all provinces.[9]

The suggested pattern appeared later in the previously mentioned document which was published in 1965. Interestingly, this document takes as its norm the eucharist of the "primitive church" rather than any of those rites which had been developed in the national churches of the Anglican Communion nor from the heretofore foundational work of Thomas Cranmer in the books of 1549 and 1552. The proposed pattern lists the following elements: (1) Preparation; (2) Service of the Word of God; (3) Great Intercession; (4)

Service of the Lord's Supper; (5) Dismissal. This pattern, of course, opens up a narrow range of inherited Anglican liturgical forms. The pattern also had important ecumenical implications in that it offered a common ground upon which Christians in a variety of traditions would find a fundamental agreement. The purpose was not to abolish the idea that the liturgy is a source of unity for Anglicans, but that this unity was not to be found in the insistence upon common texts but in the use of a common liturgical structure. The idea of unity through conformity, which had always been a fundamental principle of Anglicanism through allegiance to the Book of Common Prayer, is thus dismissed, and in its place a new basis is proposed which would serve not only within the Anglican Communion but in its relations to other Christian traditions as well.

At a meeting of the International Anglican Liturgical Consultation in Dublin, Ireland, in 1995, among the principles and recommendations commended by the group to the entire Communion, item 2 repeats this same perspective: "In the future, Anglican unity will find its liturgical expression not so much in uniform texts as in a common approach to eucharistic celebration and a structure which will ensure a balance of word, prayer, and sacrament, and which bears witness to the catholic calling of the Anglican communion."[10]

This approach, of course, opens the horizon for an unprecedented liturgical diversity, but it is also an approach which takes seriously the importance of multiculturalism for liturgical developments in the future. It is also an approach which has been gaining ground ecumenically. It suggests that the unity of the church is not grounded in conformity to a particular liturgical model but rather in the identity which we share through baptism. This approach is found not only in the Anglican documents cited, but also in the documents of Vatican Council II. In the *Constitution on the Sacred Liturgy* we find:

> Even in the liturgy, the church has no wish to impose a rigid uniformity in matters which do not implicate the faith or the good of the whole community; rather does she respect and foster the genius and talents of the various races and peoples. (Article 37)

Although this principle has met with resistance to some of the efforts for its implementation in the Roman Church, it does indicate, as do the Anglican documents, that an important page has been turned in the evolution of the liturgy, and that henceforth culture must be taken seriously, and that diversity is not the enemy of unity.

Anglican theology has usually been understood as grounded in the Incarnation, a theology which sees the created world as the place in which we encounter God's presence and activity. The implications of such a theological approach are far-reaching, but one incident in my memory serves as a powerful example of this theology in relation to the issues of cultural diversity. The incident took place in Haiti back in the 1950s. A group of Haitian artists asked for permission to paint some murals on the wall of a newly built gymnasium of the school attached to the Roman Catholic cathedral. The director of the school told the artists that Haitian art is pagan and could not be placed in a building used by Christians. The Anglican bishop of Haiti heard of this incident, and invited the leader of the artists to his office. The bishop was a man of deep aesthetic sense, and in order to demonstrate his conviction that all art may become the means by which the gospel of Christ is proclaimed, he offered to the artist the whitewashed walls of the interior of Holy Trinity Cathedral. He made only one stipulation: "Remember that this is a place of worship for Christians." The murals which the artist painted are now known all over the world as important examples of Christian art. They depict events in the life of Christ, but in them the Lord is seen to be incarnate among the people of Haiti: it is in Haiti that he is born, in Haiti that he is crucified, in Haiti that he rises from the dead and ascends to the Father. When Haitian people gather in the cathedral for worship, they find a God who is not a foreigner to them and to their culture. It is on this same basis that the inculturation of the liturgy is an imperative.

The incorporation of such diversity will mean an end to the Book of Common Prayer as we have known it, but not necessarily an end to the understanding that liturgy is at the heart of Anglican identity. The implementation of this new vision is an enormous task which will require the gifts of people in every province of our communion. As we said at the beginning of this essay, the evolution of the church's worship is never finished: it is an on-going dimension of both Christian faith and practice, and thus a reminder that our unity in faith is not something which we create but rather a gift which God gives to the Church.

Notes

1. Paul V. Marshall and Lesley A. Northup (eds.), *Leaps and Boundaries. The Prayer Book in the 21st Century* (Harrisburg, PA: Morehouse Publishing, 1997) 3–41.

2. *Inculturation: The Eucharist in Africa* Alcuin/GROW Liturgical Study 7 (Bramcote, Nottingham: Grove Books, 1988) 39–40.

3. 'What is the future role of liturgy in Anglican unity?" in *Liturgical Inculturation in the Anglican Communion,* David R. Holeton (ed). Alcuin/GROW Liturgical Study 15. (Bramcote, Nottingham: Grove Books, 1990) 17–22.

4. Gibson, 20. Words in parentheses added for clarity.

5. A convenient survey of this literature is available in *Prayer Book Spirituality,* J. Robert Wright ed.(New York: Church Hymnal Corporation, 1989). In addition to offering substantial quotations from this literature, Wright gives a list of authors with the titles of their work.

6. Note, for example the title of Tract 86 of the Oxford Movement's Tracts for the Times : "Indications of a Superintending Providence in the Preservation of the Prayer Book and in the Changes which it has undergone" (London: Gilbert & Rivington, 1842).

7. Gibson, 20.

8. The impact of this shift has been explored in depth by my colleague John L. Kater, Jr., in an essay entitled "Faithful Church, Plural World: Diversity at Lambeth 1998," which I have read in draft and which will be published in the *Anglican Theological Review*, January 1999.

9. *Lambeth Conference 1958* (SPCK, 1958) 2.81.82.

10. *Renewing the Anglican Eucharist. Findings of the Fifth International Liturgical Consultation*, Dublin, Eire, 1995. David Holeton, ed. (Cambridge, UK: Grove Books, 1996) 7.

Good Theology, Bad Ritual: What Liturgy Can Learn from Ritual Studies

Lesley A. Northup

ABOUT A YEAR AGO, a colleague had occasion to review my *curriculum vitae* and found herself at something of a loss. "Let's see. You got your degree in theology from a Catholic university; you specialized in liturgical studies; and now you're doing ritual studies. What is it you do, exactly, anyway?" It seemed to me that if this seminary-educated, active-Catholic faculty member could be uncertain about the relationship of theology, liturgiology, and ritology,[1] many other scholars are also confused. These categories entwine each other so mystifyingly that virtually no one can unravel the knot and identify where one field begins and another ends. While it is easy to dismiss such confusion as a typical case of academic muddle, this particular muddle has, I believe, contributed to the inability of many "liturgical" churches to articulate a coherent and comprehensible message, to attract and keep members, and to capitalize on the advantages of traditional praxis.

Let's face it: liturgics, as a discipline, has had a hard time finding and claiming its niche. Decades after the liturgically booming 1960s and 1970s, filled with discovery and opportunity and creative ferment for those with a hand in defining worship, William Reed Huntington's dismal, century-old prediction seems all the more prophetic:

> Remembering that in favorite studies, as in crops, there rules a principle of rotation, fashion affecting even staid divines with its subtle influence, we may look to see presently a decline of interest in this particular department of inquiry.[2]

Indeed, by comparison with say, anthropological ritual study, liturgics would appear to have made little headway since Huntington's time, when "the Patagonian naturalist secures recognition and is decorated, [while] every jaunty man of letters feels at liberty to scoff at the liturgiologist as a laborious trifler."[3]

Today, in illustration, one large Episcopal seminary has never replaced its retired liturgical scholar, another has never had one at all, and the faculty member hired to teach liturgics at another has announced that he prefers henceforward to be known as a theologian. There is no longer a prestigious publishing outlet for serious scholarly work in liturgics, and what was once considered a premier journal in the field, *Worship,* was scoffed at by my colleague as a "popular" periodical for "practitioners." As a respected discipline, liturgical studies seems to have been more or less abandoned by Anglicanism (in which its function is generally understood to be *ad hoc* and revisionary), and discouraged by Roman Catholicism (in which it is variously depicted as threatening, vaguely inappropriate, and largely to blame for Vatican II). Practical liturgists in both camps emerge principally from the ranks of clergy and active laity, rather than those of scholars, and the work of current liturgical researchers and theorists commands little interdisciplinary or even ecclesiastical attention.

I offer no apologia for liturgiologists here, who in large part have dug the hole into which they have fallen. Unlike their creative predecessors in the age of revision, today's scholars seem mired in arcane textual analysis and a kind of academic ennui, all too often intimidated and diverted by the reactionary mandates of their church hierarchies. What exciting new liturgical insights or projects have emerged in the last twenty years? Still, current liturgical scholars, among whom I count myself, cannot be held fully accountable for the decline of the field. The problem is not personal, but academic. Liturgiology has long suffered from an identity crisis engendered by its inability to define itself among other disciplines and to carve out an appropriate role in ongoing research into rituals of worship.

Back in 1979, Ron Grimes attempted to introduce order into the discussion by describing liturgy as one "mode of ritual sensibility" among several.[4] In Grimes's schema, liturgy (in contrast to, for example, celebration or decorum) is that category of ritual behavior that deals with cosmic necessity and invokes reverence, meditation, and "structured waiting." In short, for Grimes, liturgy is "religious" ritual, concerned with ultimate things (though not necessarily only Christian ones.) This distinction is probably one with which most of us would feel fairly comfortable, though there does seem to be some overlap with other possible categories (such as ceremony or magic).

In the same year, ecological anthropologist Roy Rappaport offered in "The Obvious Aspects of Ritual" a controversial, formal definition of liturgy that set out its ritual distinctiveness in terms of discourse and performance theory. He makes a distinction between "indexical" rituals, which express information about the participants themselves and their place in the social order, and "canonical" (roughly, liturgical) rituals, which refer to relatively invariant and durable messages beyond the immediate context. Canonical rituals effect the acts they describe; that is, they are performatives. They have intrinsic moral authority in that they bind the participant to some obligation. Ultimately, they produce "sanctity" because of their "unquestionableness."[5] This important essay outlined a structural analysis of liturgy, without regard to its content (sacred things), as a kind of morally imperative ritual. Still, Rappaport tended to use the terms ritual and liturgy interchangeably, leaving the boundaries of the two in very soft focus.

In 1992, an interdisciplinary conference sponsored by the Notre Dame Center for Pastoral Liturgy elicited a series of papers nominally on the topic "reclaiming our rites." It was clear, however, that before launching into analyses of the state of liturgical revision, many of these scholars felt the need to clarify their own and their disciplines' definitions of liturgy. The result, though it may not have been the intended one, was the most serious collective consideration to date of the relationship between liturgics and ritual studies.[6]

A key voice in that discussion belonged to Rappaport, who further developed his earlier definition of liturgy over against ritual, suggesting that liturgical rituals belong to orders, or larger groups of rituals he called "logoi"–roughly, rational world views.[7] To enact these rituals is to create the reality they describe. The divinities of dead cultures are themselves just as certainly dead, because "they are no longer given voice by anyone's breath and no longer enlivened by anyone's body."[8] The kind of ritual called liturgy, then, establishes a fundamental truth condition. With such a profound ontological responsibility on the line, liturgiologists, he suggests, have a particular duty to create and authorize rituals that avoid deception and falsehood.[9]

If Rappaport held liturgical scholars morally accountable, Roman Catholic liturgiologist Aidan Kavanagh was clear that they had abrogated this trust. For him, the tendency of "educational elites whose certification is academic and political rather than ecclesial"[10] to focus on texts, rather than performance, did not so much disenfranchise performance as lead to an unhealthy proliferation of new texts and orders. Kavanagh averts to Rappaport's definition of canonical ritual to bolster his complaint, but ultimately rejects Rappaport's claim that creating liturgy is precisely the province of those who can both limit the unholy power of unskilled and unscrupulous authorities and produce rituals that generate the moral assent, through participation, of the people.

Catherine Bell, who also spoke at the Notre Dame conference, investigated the role of "ritual experts" in defining and shaping liturgical ritual.[11] Acknowledging that ritual experts[12] come in various guises, including charismatic though not necessarily learned figures, she nonetheless held liturgiologists singularly responsible for scholarship and commentary on worship:

> The general invisibility of professional ritualists helps to promote the old but still powerful model in which the only effective or authentic ritual is that which rises up spontaneously from the community by means of faceless social forces ... If they are right, then liturgists will have a hard time understanding where they have come from and making sense of what they can actually do. But I don't think they are right. The role of ritual experts in devising and decreeing rites is in fact much more widespread, dynamic, and complicated than most current models would lead us to suppose.[13]

For Bell, it is specifically the job of liturgiologists to become ritual experts and to lead the process of ritual creation. Noting that liturgical scholars now have access to the social sciences (major contributing disciplines to the development of ritual studies), she claims that this knowledge has differentiated liturgiologists from "more traditional church scholars and legitimated [their] relative authority."[14] Like Rappaport, Bell wants liturgical experts to exercise their authority in the creation of new rites, rather than cede it to some unspecified popular groundswell. She decries the lack of "liturgical authority, conformity, and dignity."

Generally, the consensus at the 1992 conference was that liturgics (1) is not the same thing as ritual studies; (2) is distinct from other kinds of ritual expertise in that it deals with matters of ultimate importance to the ritual participants; (3) should be devised, and even imposed, only by competent authority. Quite pronounced was the effort to define liturgics, and even its scholarly resources, as distinct from ritual studies.[15] Absent was any substantive discussion of where liturgical experts were expected to turn for their ritual acumen—that is, what field(s) of knowledge legitimately underlie their supposed authority. Bell suggests that liturgical studies "may well want to backtrack and explore how those problems may result in part from its own perspective on ritual."[16]

Liturgy and Theology

Bell, in her clarion call to liturgiologists, is clear that they ought not to depend too heavily on the social sciences: "Why is [liturgical studies] so willing to take social scientific expertise at its word and believe that social science really has a clue as to which cultural forms express what?"[17] She disparages the idea that following the lead of "disinterested theoreticians of ritual dynamics"[18] would be a useful direction for liturgical studies. Instead, she suggests that liturgical studies has generally been understood as a branch of theology[19]–theologians being the "traditional church scholars" to whom she refers.

The distinction between theology and religious studies, like the differentiation of liturgics and ritual studies, has been hotly debated of late.[20] The question centers on whether theology can transcend its customary role as a self-focused ecclesial discipline–that is, whether it has a legitimate claim to be considered a subfield of the academic study of religion. The key issue is that the truth claims of theology are set forth as normative and its critiques as evaluative, whereas religious studies attempts to be objective. Leaving aside the postmodern (and feminist[21]) argument against the possibility of such a thing as objectivity, the controversy hinges on whether theology, an undertaking reserved to believers of one kind or another, can achieve a comparative view of why and how human beings are religious, and convey it without prejudice or proselytizing. This concern has been exacerbated by the actions of the Vatican and other authoritative religious bodies in shutting down academic freedom and dissent in educational institutions under their control.

It is probably fair to say that the assumptions undergirding religious studies and theology differ substantively, as do their goals. Religious studies assumes that the human person is in some way naturally religious, and seeks (among other things) to understand and explicate that phenomenon, apart from any question of the veracity of the claims of various religions. Theology, on the other hand, starts with the foundational condition that some form of active divinity does, in fact, exist, and attempts to explicate a series of truth claims. Practically speaking, the latter also has been principally a Christian endeavor, with a methodology and language that make discussing other religions difficult at best.

Liturgiologists, on the whole, have stowed their gear in theology's boat, as Bell implies. While at one time most liturgical study relied on a historical, textual approach, since the frenzy of liturgical revision the majority of publications in the field have reflected an emphasis on "liturgical theology."[22] This content-specific approach to religious ritual is unsurprising, considering that most liturgiologists are ordained clergy or members of religious orders, with ecclesiastical affiliations, primary training in theology, and STD or ThD degrees. The principal centers of graduate education in liturgics are also church-affiliated institutions: Notre Dame, Catholic University, Drew University, the seminaries, and so on.

Obviously, in liturgics as in other fields, approaches and interests vary. The discipline includes historians as well as theologians, theorists as well as practitioners. In this, the age of the liturgical theologian, there are still textual researchers about. Still, despite this diversity, theology drives liturgics–or perhaps more accurately, a theological attitude drives liturgical studies. The doctrinal content of rituals of worship continues to rationalize what is done, how it is done, and what it is supposed to mean.

This is problematic on several counts. From a purely academic stand-point, if liturgy is essentially a subfield of theology, then it runs the risk of being academically marginalized, as (rightly or wrongly) theology has been. This is all the more likely if Bell is right in claiming that liturgics is distinct from ritual studies "by virtue of its comprehensive framework and its ultimately pastoral objectives. . . to encourage appreciation, understanding, and participation in Christian worship," and that its primary concerns are such issues as "the crisis in the churches" and the failure of some liturgical reforms.[23] If it is true, as Bell concludes, that liturgics "can be distinguished from the scholarship of those working in an exclusively academic context,"[24] then liturgiology has already come to the pass Huntington foresaw.

Another problem is that an overreliance on the relationship of liturgy and theology promotes an insularity that leads to ritual Balkanization, a narrow view of truth claims, and the worst kind of liturgical arrogance. Theology is hardly the discipline most likely to give the scholar an unobstructed view of the liturgical horizon, since it demands as its *sine qua non* a non-rational, singular commitment of faith. From that presumptive stance, it is difficult to be open to the insights of either other religions or other disciplines. This may account, in part, for the difficulty Christian liturgiologists have encountered in recruiting colleagues from other traditions into organizations like the North American Academy of Liturgy.

A closely related difficulty is that the theological environment hinders deep liturgical investigation, placing truth boundaries around the work of liturgical scholars and forcing them to work in something of an intellectual vacuum. Consequently, liturgics becomes a reactionary field that, even when other ritual considerations urge significant change, tends to be content to fiddle with symptomatic details rather than opt for a full cure. Theology, by its nature the study of immutable things, tends to produce a surfeit of immutable thinking. In a theological atmosphere, ritual change, admittedly an undertaking requiring care and caution, takes on the mien of a dangerous enemy. Liturgiologists are easily caught in this bind; for example, a recent volume on the prospects for liturgical revision in ECUSA was circumscribed with so many official caveats to avoid controversy that only the most conservative and least challenging articles were included.

Even more worrisome is a concomitant concern: ritual participation is limited when worshipers are given official theological explanations of the rite, rather than being encouraged to uncover meaning through their active participation. When a theological agenda drives the understanding of ritual behavior, little room is allowed for interpretation. Liturgy becomes text, not action; worshipers become observers, not participants. With congregations trained to be audiences rather than participants, it should not be surprising that new Christian religious services of the Willow Creek sort, geared to providing entertainment, are enjoying great popularity.

Many theologically oriented liturgiologists would question whether the goings-on at places like Willow Creek really are liturgy at all; bound by a confessional perspective on what constitutes legitimate forms of worship, liturgical scholars are often slow to acknowledge new or unofficial ritual practices. Consequently, while authorized rites have been dissected and analyzed *ad nauseam*, relatively little attention has been devoted to behaviors usually designated as "extra-liturgical"–the little tradition rituals that, a broader view of ritual studies tells us, frequently constitute the most meaningful activities of the faithful. How much research have liturgiologists done on indigenous festivals, rosaries, and personal devotions; on snake-handling, spirit-protection, and glossalalia?

This hesitation to deal with unofficial rites reflects the popular confusion about ritual authority that is highlighted by an overly theological approach to liturgy. When the creation and authentication of liturgy is understood to be the province of an ecclesiastical hierarchy, then the people in the pew are not really free to exercise their own construction of ritual tradition.[25] They are led to believe that acceptable liturgical innovation and change are generated only from on high, and that homegrown rituals are inferior and nonessential. Although people nevertheless ritualize, they seldom own their prerogative to create an appropriate ritual.

Another problem arises when the conjunction of theology and liturgy leads to a muddling of the categories of orthodoxy and orthopraxy. Christianity, particularly, has become concerned with the former, emphasizing correct belief rather correct action, and ascribing a doctrinal underpinning to ritual action. In Anglicanism, the Book of Common Prayer has been elevated, via the old cliché *lex orandi, lex credendi*, as a model of orthopraxy, in which ritual behavior leads to belief. Nevertheless, ritual in this tradition is not allowed to express its own meaning; instead, credal statements and theological coherence determine the form, order, and interpretation of Anglican liturgical activities.

Aside from these overarching concerns, there are also pragmatic and pastoral problems that result from the bedding down of liturgy with theology. One is the difficulty that various liturgical professionals encounter finding useful employment. Only in Roman Catholicism has an appropriate place been found for liturgists—lay and clerical designers, consultants, and leaders of worship with the credentials to back up their skills. There, they have found some acceptance in diocesan offices and large parishes. In the Episcopal Church, it is rare to find a working liturgist. It is all too often assumed that even minimal theological schooling is sufficient qualification for liturgical leadership. Liturgical training at the seminary level is frequently conflated into sacramental theology, and all too often faculty are theologically trained, with liturgics as only an ancillary interest. This denigrates the field and provides the necessary backdrop for its demise.

Liturgy as Ritual

If it is to emerge from its self-imposed position as the stepchild of theology, a primer of local ritual useful only as an intramural adjunct of pastoralia, liturgical studies must step beyond the restrictions of denominational theology and identify more fully as a part of ritual studies. It need not wholly embrace the social sciences approach so fiercely championed by the North American Association for the Study of Religion,[26] though a good dose of empirical sensibility and field methodology would not hurt. It need only recognize its place, as Grimes would have it, as one—quite possibly the most prominent—type of ritual.

This is all the more important at this time. The towering generation of liturgiologists responsible for the revision movement is stepping aside, leaving an insufficient legacy of trained replacements. As seminaries and bishops downgrade the importance of liturgical study and as worshipers continue to bleed from the mainline liturgical churches, fewer young scholars are drawn to liturgiology. Renovating our understanding of the field to embrace wider influences than theology can only generate more interest and attract the bright, interdisciplinary scholars needed to bring fresh approaches to the study of worship. If liturgical research *per se* is somewhat stagnant right now, great excitement is being generated with each new wave of ritual studies insights. This is the field in which discoveries important to the future of worship are being generated. The liturgiologist who is not fluently conversant with ritual studies will soon become an anachronism.

In the Episcopal Church, if we take seriously our constant refrain that we are a church in which practice precedes doctrine—that is, if we are indeed an orthopraxic body—then we have a responsibility to consider very seriously what it is that we do, what we convey when we do it, and whether it is effectively done. Ironically, this is one of those situations in which we may appear to be more Catholic than the Pope—the Pope, as well as other Roman Catholics, has doctrine to guide his liturgical life; Anglicans, lacking dogma (if not dogmatism), must place primary importance on liturgy as the guide to right action and right belief.

It is on just this point that so much of the media-hyped ECUSA controversy turns. Again, the core question concerns authority. The subtly nuanced balancing act that gives primacy to the Book of Common Prayer has been tattered in the eyes of traditionalists by the very notion of liturgical revision, no less its actualization. Without confidence in the continuity of worship, many of the faithful, in search of solidity, are turning instead to a reconstructed fundamentalism. This is in large part a failure of liturgy, and of its scholars, who have been unable to convey adequately the values and principles that underly "good" liturgy. And no wonder—those foundational principles have been dictated more by the prevailing theological idiom than by what is known to be effective ritual. If liturgiologists are to have a serious impact on the future of religious ritual, they must stop allowing the theological tail to wag the ritual dog, and must turn to ritual studies for the foundational understandings behind the rituals they create and revise.

The Failure of Liturgics

A theological rationale can mask a number of ritual absurdities in the liturgy. Over the centuries, a finely honed Hellenistic sophistry has managed to reinterpret fairly obvious ritual acts in such a way as to put a safe distance between Christians and "pagans." Where every other culture in the world has rites of passage, for example, Christianity just happens to have rituals at the same personal milestones—birth, marriage, death, and so on—but, according to liturgical theologians, they are definitely not rites of passage, but sacraments. Though countless other religions have understood symbolic ritual meals of human flesh as precisely that, the eucharist is a meal presumed to be so spiritually unique and pure that any imputation of cannibalism is dismissed as blasphemous, simplistic ignorance. While worship around the world celebrates the body in dance, gesture, touch, and a hearty recognition of sexuality and fertility, Christian ritual still clings to a lifeless and spiritualized liturgical tradition in which the body is concealed, restricted, ignored, and suspected.

Examples of ineffective, overly theologized liturgical problems abound. Many stem from a seeming inability, or unwillingness, to develop a symbol set that has power and resonance in our time. Handcuffed by classical Greek philosophical terminology and our unwillingness to offend, we continue to try to worship a mystifyingly obscure God who is three persons in one substance, simultaneously divine and immutable, *ganz andere, mysterium, tremendum et fascinans.* We decry the loss of believers from the mainline traditions and mock the booming megachurches and reconstructionist sects, but need only look at the way in which they address God—familiarly, vernacularly—to understand why people flock to them in droves.

Is this a dumbing-down of religion? Possibly. But more likely it represents the development of ways of talking about and to God that ring true for today's believers. There is nothing sacrosanct about the classical period; there is no evidence that the Greeks knew more about God than any number of other cultures. Indeed, given the survival record of Greek religion, quite the opposite would seem to be the case. Still, under the delusion that God somehow requires this kind of description, we continue to burden the faithful in worship with a language and conceptual system utterly foreign to their understanding, their experience, and their intuition. Removing "thee" and "thou" scarcely scratches the surface of the problem.

Our enslavement to ancient ontological metaphors is even more distancing and dangerous when we take them literally. The modern, empirical sensibility has little tolerance and less understanding of poetic expression and the literary character of sacred texts. Read literally, Scripture allows only two options: apostasy or fundamentalism. But ritual is precisely the venue in which the figurativeness of our texts should be conveyed, explored, and celebrated; it is ritual that uncovers the deeper meaning of the tropes that describe the object and practice of faith. If today's worshipers have difficulty perceiving the truth in myth, it is largely a failure of literal-minded and unimaginative liturgies, and a theological bias that assumes that ritual action must be interpreted doctrinally, rather than experientially.

A similar difficulty arises when liturgy is driven by rubrics to enforce exactitude—that is, when liturgical efficacy is understood to reside in form. In the Roman tradition, this reinforces doctrine and systems of control; the result has historically been a sacramental practice that is clearly (despite all arguments to the contrary) magical in emphasis—sacraments *do* and *change* things through the intervention of a specially trained, appointed, and empowered priest. In Anglicanism, at least when it isn't aping such Roman anachronisms, the need to follow the liturgical rules seems more driven by a sentimental attachment to English customs and a false notion of uniformity. (Thus, for example, we continue to imagine that there is such a thing as a "common" Prayer Book.)

Regardless of their rationales, rule-driven Christian liturgies may reflect good theology, but they constitute poor ritual. Unlike Jews or Muslims, for whose rituals the rules are numerous and specific, Christians—lacking 613 instructions—have at best been able to painstakingly reconstruct only the general outlines of their early liturgies, which were surprisingly free of set forms, gestures, and texts. Today's liturgies, no doubt in part to preserve a certain felicity of expression and a quaint idea of liturgical decorum, have instructions for posture, hymnody, vocal participation, and movement (or lack thereof), as well as for sacramental acts. These are supplemented by unwritten rules that stipulate dress codes, behavior at communion, acceptable ways to pass the Peace, what to do when arriving late, and other conventions. It's no wonder that Anglicans are counted among God's frozen people—and as little wonder that charismatic forms of worship, which allow for spatial and spiritual freedom, are burgeoning in the "liturgical" churches.

A somewhat related problem stems from an emphasis on text over action. While performance theory increasingly informs research into ritualizing and shifts the focus of effective ritual from word to act,[27] the various forms of catholic liturgy remain mired in books, readings, manuals, speeches, and a central symbolization of the founder as the "Word."[28] Not only does this produce static, inaccessible, and pedantic liturgy (and symbols), but it deprives worshipers of the opportunity to participate physically, spontaneously, or even idiosyncratically in what should be a powerfully moving experience.[29] Moreover, despite the efforts of liturgical revisers to structure the eucharistic liturgies of the 1960s and 1970s as a logical progression from word to sacrament, the "service of the word" tends to expand, as presiders add announcements, children's homilies, special mini-liturgies, and other verbose accretions before the "service of the table." It used to be said that Anglicans didn't know how to get in or out of their liturgies, sprouting appendages (preservice hymn practice, litanies, the Last Gospel, a departing prayer) at either end; now the most vulnerable location for fat to accumulate appears to be the middle. In any case, the extra bits always seem to be words, words, words—rarely do they allow people to do anything but be passive observers.

Good ritual requires that people *do* things. Although listening and speaking and reading are, of course, doing something, in the general realm of activity they are pretty tame. To work well, ritual must work through and with the body; it must involve more than the intellect. This focus on word over act again highlights the failure of theology to serve as an adequate foundation for liturgical development. As Mary Collins warns, ritual is essentially bodily and nondiscursive, "inaccessible to ordinary theological methods, which work with texts."[30]

It is not simply textuality, but also the highly negative view of the body bequeathed by theology that has leeched from liturgy the action orientation implicit in the command to "Do this" that stands at the heart of the eucharist. Anglicans succumbed to the body-bashing of classical theologians and to a pulpit-led Victorianism that circumscribed behavior in houses of worship, then took along with them everyone who wanted to conform to the image of a proper American Christian. Only those Christians perceived to be without a stake in upward mobility risked fully embodying their worship: African-Americans, rural Appalachians handling snakes and strychnine, Pentecostals drawn (at least initially) from the ranks of the poor. Ironically, it is to those forms of worship that the educated and elite are now turning in droves, seeking an authentic expression of religious experience in dance, glossalalia, interpersonal touch, laughing, thespian roles, drumming, and so on.

If liturgical theologians will not give it to them, congregations will try to achieve some measure of bodily engagement on their own. Recent complaints about "the chaos that erupts at the exchange of the Peace"[31] fail to recognize the non-official adaptation occurring as people seek a more embodied manifestation of community, belonging, joy, and forgiveness. At the relatively new parish of St. Gregory of Nyssa in San Francisco, the Bible is passed, like the Torah, for worshipers to touch and kiss; ancient processional movements draw congregants from one area of the church to another, accompanied by hand drums; and participants grasp each other's shoulders as they dance around the altar. People stand, up against one another and in changing configurations; the celebrants are in constant but more or less dignified motion; there is a comforting but compelling mix of informality and mystery. The liturgy succeeds largely because of its forthright appeal to the senses, with dazzling color, fragrant incense, catchy yet venerable music, and lots of simple but compelling movement. While this may not be everyone's idea of good liturgy, it is certainly effective ritual.

Good liturgy demands this sort of involvement, both physically and intellectually, both personally and corporately. While liturgical theology has stressed, correctly, the corporate nature of Christian worship, it has in its zeal entirely overlooked the need of individuals to be deeply and personally affected by religious ritual. As a result, churchgoers as often as not find greater emotional satisfaction in the assembly—in gathering with the community of friends, business associates, and neighbors that attend the church—than they do in the ritual itself. It should come as no surprise, then, that the Peace is one of the most popular of the liturgy's actions; not only do people get an opportunity to *do* something, they get to do it with their friends.

This communal context quite deliberately affords little opportunity for congregants to place themselves within the ritual performance as distinct persons. Indeed, focusing on the assembly has been considered one of the triumphs of liturgical renewal. Reestablishing the corporate nature of worship is sound liturgical theology. But it neglects any number of equally sound ritual principles that are the hallmarks of effective worship in many cultures.

To reopen a can of worms, let's start with the well-worn mantra, "rites of

344

passage." Unquestionably, this concept has been flogged to death in popular media, self-help tomes, and the workshop circuit. Of late, people are cheerfully creating all manner of self-generated, ego-pleasing rituals to see themselves through every life crisis and setback. But sheer cheesiness doesn't mitigate the impact and value of rituals that involve the self and mark significant changes in social and religious status.

The return of baptismal rites to their proper place within the eucharist is a case in point. Getting away from private Saturday "christenings" attended only by family has been an important reform. But is it necessary to throw the baby out with the bath water (so to speak)? Baptism as it is now constituted in the Prayer Book and performed in most of our churches is only referential in passing to the persons being baptized, for whom it should be a ceremony of enormous personal impact. This should be a moment engraved in the memory of the baptized and their sponsors—a ritual affirmation of a whole new life and status, a true experience of death and rebirth. Now it is just another brief action, undergone simultaneously by a number of (usually) cute infants, inundated with lots and lots of words.

To ritually minimize the singularly personal event of deep conversion is to rob initiation of most of its power. The ritual desirability of adult baptism insistently nags; no amount of vicarious pledging can rival a personal, ritualized act of commitment in imparting significance.[32] An adult expression of conversion can be a powerful, sustaining act, whereas most infants, once grown, are indifferent to their baptisms at best. Even in the case of infant baptism, which we assume to be a celebration of a new birth, it is safe to say that the arrival of the baby is a life-changing event for the immediate family—but that is not how we ritualize it.

Likewise, despite our theological, symbolic understanding of a few drops of liquid as representive of a body of running water, the impact of an actual body of water far exceeds that of a dribbling shell. Our symbols, again, must be not only intellectually accessible, but immediate and realistic enough to ritually stun us. For all our tinkering with the rites of initiation, we still have fallen far short of, say, the Marine Corps in fashioning a ritual that provokes a lasting sense of identity, loyalty, and belonging in new Christians.

A similar analysis reveals the same weakness in most of our rites. Confirmation, which most agree has little valid historical precedent, at least allows an opportunity for adult commitment and/or a recognition of adolescent transition. To say, as several ritologists have, that getting a driver's license is a ritual more fraught with significance for teenagers than any the church can offer is an indictment we ought to be hearing. Ditching confirmation altogether (politics be damned!) and experimenting with adult baptism in adolescence may be the answer, at least in part, to the persistent question of how to retain the young people who leave the church behind along with junior high.

It is certainly true, as Larry Hoffman points out, that the idea of a life cycle is "an anachronism unavailable to rabbinic [or Christian] thinking 2,000 years ago."[33] Hoffman points out that liturgies such as circumcision were not meant originally to celebrate life's highpoints. But there is wisdom, both ritual and psychological, in recognizing the necessity of people to understand themselves on a journey through life, at least at this point in human evolution. Joseph Campbell and numerous scholars of myth,[34] as well as reputable psychologists of both Jungian and other stripes,[35] have documented this basic human reality and demonstrated the importance of ritualizing it.

The questions cannot be avoided. How does the liturgy help with life's maturation process? Do Christians take a hero's journey? Certainly Jesus did. But to say that Jesus made the journey for us vicariously and that we no longer need to do it ourselves simply keeps people powerless and infantile in a world that already does more than enough of that. Individuals need to take that journey, and they will, with or without the church. So what can be done? Theological tidiness should not prevent the church from playing a major role in the inevitable ritualizing of major life events. Celebrate birth individually and festively. Initiate those who want a mystical experience of rebirth. Sanction marriage without stipulating conditions, and ritually acknowledge its dissolution, too. Why do we treat funerals differently than baptisms when they are ritually equivalent and complementary rites? And why do we ignore retirement, one of life's most unsettling changes of course?

The various rituals surrounding priesthood and its functions are another fertile locus of theological meddling with the principles of good ritual. It should be clear from almost universal experience, including our own, that effective rituals require competent leadership. Yet this principle is a favorite target of liturgical theologians. The current imbroglio turns on the phrase "priesthood of all believers," taking literally a metaphorical allusion and applying it to priestly practice. Bizarrely, this has led to the assumption that anyone can equally well perform any clerical act. Just as we learned during the sixties and seventies that not everyone can write good liturgical texts, so too we must accept that not everyone can lead worship.

To take another example, experimentation with women's liturgies has hinged, in part, on a feminist theological understanding of shared leadership. Despite efforts to create egalitarian leadership schedules, however, Kay Turner notes that what frequently emerges is the "prominence of one individual as instigator or leader of ritual,"[36] as natural talents and proclivities surface. Good theology, bad ritual. Feminist groups, having learned that good ritual demands skilled leadership, have consequently found other ways to share responsibility and authority.

A concomitant issue revolves around our difficulty in adequately grasping the fundamental distinctions between priestly and shamanistic leadership, a matter familiar to ritual studies experts. A priest is a professional ritual practitioner whose authority derives from certification by a religious institution. She or he is chosen, trained, and licensed in accordance with established procedures, and exercises the privileges of the office in specific, prescribed ways. Power comes from knowing the proper forms and rituals. A priest is not necessarily designated for priesthood from on high, or ontologically transformed. If priesthood is the model of ritual leadership the church wants, then that paradigm should be developed with some consistency—that is, let's train priests to do what priests do (lead worship), then let them do it.

Our problem is that we would also like to incorporate aspects of the shaman into our priests. We would like them to evidence special, individual commissions from God, and to have advanced access to the world of the transcendent. They should be healers, and should be set apart by their very nature, not by their roles or functions. Their credentials depend on their individual holiness, the theologians tell us, and their power comes from within. If this is the model of leadership the church prefers, then we must allow the emergence and accession of charismatic individuals who make their own rules and claim direct communication with the realms of the Almighty. Arguments about lay leadership, clericalism, and seminary training generally turn on the confusion of these two paradigms.

Conclusion

The fundamental principles of effective ritualizing dictate that ritual symbol and action should be clear, understandable, accessible, and transformative. These qualities suffuse the rituals of various peoples around the world, in both tribal and multicultural societies. They are much less evident in Christian liturgy, all the more so because they command so little respect from liturgical theologians, who often succumb to the temptation to see them as primitive or naïve. The peculiarly Christian arrogance that eschews straightforwardness in ritual as a kind of awkward early phase of liturgical development, now supplanted by Western intellect and polish, frequently blocks our appreciation of good ritual done well.

One corrective is for liturgical scholars to delve more deeply into the insights of the anthropologists, dramatists, psychologists, sociologists, semiologists, phenomenologists, and other experts who comprise the field of ritual studies. This may well require less reliance on the intricacies and denominational allegiance of theology, which distances liturgy from other religious ritual and distances the worshiper from an authentic experience of what is being invoked.

The contemporary search for "spirituality," often disparaged as trendy mush by traditionalists, speaks to people's need for ritual that is as involving as a dream, as personal as a loving relationship, as exciting as an encounter with the living God. This is hardly a trend; it is the universal search for meaning that runs throughout time and finds its expression in ritual. If "liturgical" Christianity is to remain, quite simply, viable, it will have to acknowledge this deeply rooted yearning and speak to it in the idiom of the era. To do so, it need not sacrifice tradition, integrity, or good taste. But it may require the emergence of its ritual scholars from behind the skirts of theology, and the development of liturgiology into a distinct, integrated, and broadly informed discipline.

Notes

1. A note on terminology: I use "liturgics," "liturgiology," and "liturgical studies" more or less interchangeably to refer to that branch of ritual knowledge related, loosely, to religious ritual (though this is further defined below). Liturgiologists, liturgical scholars, and liturgical experts are also generally synonymous as those who study, research, and write on the field. Following ecclesiastical usage, "liturgists" are designers and leaders of worship. "Ritology," a term coined by Ron Grimes, properly refers to ritual criticism or analysis; I have taken the liberty to use it here to include ritual studies scholars (for whom we have no other name, and who are all, in some way, ritual critics). Religious studies scholars are at times referred to as religionists in other writings.

2. William Reed Huntington, "Revision of the American Common Prayer," *American Church Review,* April 1881. Reprinted in Huntington, *A Short History of the Book of Common Prayer* (New York: Thomas Whittaker, 1893) 85.

3. Huntington, "Revision," 84–5.

4. Ronald Grimes, "Modes of Ritual Necessity," *Worship* 53/2 (1979) 126–141.

5. Roy A. Rappaport, "The Obvious Aspects of Ritual," in *Ecology, Meaning, and Religion* (Berkeley: North Atlantic, 1979) 175–221.

6. Some mention should be made of the Ritual, Language, and Action group of the North American Academy of Liturgy, which meets annually and at times has engaged this question head-on. The group itself is not so much interdisciplinary as interested in testing the liturgy-ritual studies matrix. While what is does is almost always fascinating, it has a tendency to shoot off in all directions at once, contributing to the muddle somewhat more than clarifying it.

7. Roy A. Rappaport, "Veracity, Verity, and *Verum* in Liturgy," *Studia Liturgica* 23:1 (1993) 35–50.

8. Rappaport, "Veracity," 40.

9. It is not entirely clear why politicians and others in positions of control do not share this mandate.

Lesley A. Northup

10. Aidan Kavanagh, "Textuality and Deritualization: The Case of Western Liturgical Usage," *Studia Liturgica* 23:1 (1993) 75.

11. Catherine Bell, "The Authority of Ritual Experts," *Studia Liturgica* 23:1 (1993) 98–120. See Bell's *Ritual Theory, Ritual Practice* (New York: Oxford, 1992) and *Ritual: Perspectives and Dimensions* (New York: Oxford, 1997) for further elaboration of her theories.

12. Bell clearly views ritual experts as scholars and leaders in the field, rather than the everyday practitioners described by Susan Starr Sered in *Women as Ritual Experts* (New York: Oxford, 1992).

13. Bell, "Authority," 100.

14. Bell, "Authority," 113.

15. While this is, as I have implied, a necessary task, suspicion nonetheless arises as to why these noted scholars, none of them themselves liturgiologists, were so anxious to put distance between their own fields and liturgics.

16. Bell, "Authority," 119.

17. Bell, "Authority," 114.

18. Quoting Mary Collins, Bell, "Authority," 114.

19. Bell, *Ritual: Perspectives*, 219.

20. See, for example, Charlotte Allen, "Is Nothing Sacred? Casting Out the Gods from Religious Studies," *Lingua Franca* (November 1996) 30–40; Schubert M. Ogden, "Religious Studies and Theological Studies: What Is Involved in the Distinction between Them?" *Council of Societies for the Study of Religion (CSSR) Bulletin* 24:1 (February 1995) 3–4; the ongoing dialogue between Francis Schüssler Fiorenza and Donald Wiebe in the *CSSR Bulletins* 22:2 (April 1993) and 23:1 (February 1994); and Robert A. Segal, "Fending Off d., 113. the Social Sciences," *CSSR* 19:4 (November 1990). The debate continues in various professional publications.

21. See, for example, Mary McClintock Fulkerson, *Changing the Subject: Women's Discourses and Feminist Theology* (Minneapolis: Fortress Press, 1994), or J.D.H. Amador, "Feminist Biblical Hermeneutics: A Failure of Theoretical Nerve," *Journal of the American Academy of Religion* 66:1 (Spring 1998) 39–57, among many other sources.

22. The 1980s and 1990s have seen such titles in this area as Geoffrey Wainwright's *Doxology*, Aidan Kavanagh's *On Liturgical Theology*, David Power's *Unsearchable Riches* and *Worship: Culture and Theology*, and Scott McCarthy's *Creation Liturgy*.

23. Bell, *Ritual: Perspectives,* 219–220.

24. Bell, *Ritual: Perspectives,* 219.

25. This is still a critical task, despite Bell's concern that homegrown liturgy is emphasized to the diminution of the liturgiologist. Liturgy must belong as much to the people as to the institution if it is to survive.

26. See Allen, "Nothing Sacred," for more on this organization and those who champion a severe social-science orientation for Religious Studies.

27. See, *inter alia*, Stanley Tambiah, "A Performative Approach to Ritual," reprinted in Ronald L. Grimes, ed., *Readings in Ritual Studies*, Upper Saddle River, NJ: Prentice-Hall (1996) 495–511; J.L Austin, *How to Do Things with Words*, New York: Oxford University Press (1962) and Ronald L. Grimes, *Ritual Criticism: Case Studies in Its Practice, Essays on Its Theory*, Columbia: University of South Carolina Press (1990).

28. Kavanagh (though he sees the problem very differently) lays the blames for textualization directly on liturgiologists, whose research is skewed in this direction. "Textualization," 70.

29. One Episcopal priest, establishing a new congregation in Jersey City, found the

Nicene Creed and the Prayer Book such impediments to new members that he jettisoned them. Steven Giovangelo, "Without Creed," *The Witness* (April 1998) 18.

30. Mary Collins, *Worship: Renewal to Practice*, Washington: Pastoral Press (1987) 97.

31. Gary Kriss, "So Many Distractions," *The Living Church* (8 February 1998) 13–14. Or similarly, Glendon C. Coppick, "Pike's Peace," *The Living Church* (17 May 1998) 12–13.

32. This inevitably points to the currently debated question of open table fellowship.

33. Lawrence A. Hoffman, "How Ritual Means: Ritual Circumcision in Rabbinic Culture and Today," *Studia Liturgica* 23:1 (1993) 87–another in the papers from the Notre Dame conference.

34. Joseph Campbell, *The Hero with a Thousand Faces* (Princeton, NJ: Princeton University Press, 3rd printing, 1973) is the best known example.

35. See, for example, Rollo May, *The Cry for Myth* (New York: Delta/Dell, 1991).

36. Kay Turner, "Contemporary Feminist Rituals," in Charlene Spretnak, ed., *The Politics of Women's Spirituality* (New York: Anchor/Doubleday, 1982) 228.

A Just-Making Presence: Worship and the Moral Life

Joseph Monti

I hate, I despise your festivals, and I take no delight in your solemn assemblies. Even though you offer me your burnt offerings and grain offerings, I will not accept them; and the offerings of well-being of your fatted animals I will not look upon. Take away from me the noise of your songs; I will not listen to the melody of your harps. But let justice roll down like waters, and righteousness like an everflowing stream. Amos 5: 21–24.

The Christian Religion is not simply a doctrine, it is a deed, an action: and not an action of the past, but an action of the present in which the past is restored and the future appears. Louis Bouyer, *Le mystère paschal,* 9–10.[1]

Liturgy is the work of the people. It is the opposite of lethargy.
Marion J. Hatchett, *Sanctifying Life, Time and Space,* 4.

Preface: Calling God Back to the Mountain

In *Teaching a Stone to Talk,* Annie Dillard likens mainline Christian worshipers in privileged mountaintop societies to "tourists on a packaged tour of the Absolute." She wants to know if we "have the foggiest idea of what sort of power we so blithely invoke," or do we in fact really not "believe a word of it." For if we did know, she says, ushers would "issue life preservers and signal flares" and we would be lashed to our pews. The real questions Annie Dillard is posing is whether we any longer have a sense of the sacred presence we are encountering, or have we "heard God's speech and found it too loud"; are "the very holy mountains" we have ascended now keeping

silent and the burning bush doused forever? Neither Dillard nor we are sure
of the answers to these questions, but we know what she is talking about and
wonder whether, in our ecclesiastical and suburban insularity, we are now
only talking to ourselves about ourselves—what Karl Barth worried about
when he spoke of our feigning conversation with God by speaking of
ourselves in a loud voice.[2] And with all the "noise" of our "solemn
assemblies" are we really only encountering silence? For centuries, Dillard
argues, Christian worship has been "trying to call God back to the mountain,
or, failing that, raise a peep out of anything that isn't us." Still, she advises,
we must "pray to this silence" and "quit [our] tents" for it is "God's
brooding." "Pray without ceasing," she says, for even "stones" can be taught
to talk again.[3]

Talking to God again, calling God's presence back to a mountain that has
ceased to be holy, experiencing the power of the words and acts of our
worship for truth and justice is the work of a church that desires to reassert
its authenticity and effectiveness in the twenty-first century and third
millennium of its founding. We must speak and act with passion and power
again, and pray in the face of God's silence and our own inauthenticity and
complicity with the power and principalities of our age. We have been given
both obligation and authority as keepers of powerful metaphors, symbols
and models of the divine presence—a presence that both comforts our
afflictions and thunders against the injustices of our age. Such a presence is
neither abstract nor undefined, but concrete and particular in the universe
of every face we encounter or could encounter.[4] Clearly in privileged
societies like our own, we have attempted to tame the words and acts of our
liturgies, rendering them predictable and above all insulated from the God
of fire, whirlwind, and mountain. But the paradox of power asserts itself
again: a God whose presence has no power to assert justice for the oppressed
also has no power to offer us safety and comfort in our own needs and
afflictions; no power to call us forth to new creations and new lives; no
power to transform and make us whole again and to conquer death with the
victory of new life. The presence of God made real and powerful in our
liturgical symbols is always a *just-making presence*—an empowerment of both
tenderness and strength, comfort and righteousness. Any separation of
liturgy from the worldly household of God's creation, or of our lives of
prayer from the obligations of our moral character is the fatal fracture that
lies just below the surface of our worship. The rage of the prophets was
perennial on this point and for our own good. If we continue to misunder-
stand, misinterpret and misapply our faith in this way—continue to substitute
formality for passion, stability for action—we will fail to call the divine
presence back to the mountain and the only sounds we will hear in our

solemn assemblies will be noise, symbolizing, and thus making present, nothing at all. Raimundo Panikkar comments: "It is a risky business to celebrate the Eucharist. We may have to leave it unfinished, having gone first to give back to the poor what belongs to them."[5]

Part I: Four Axioms of Sacramental Theology

None of these dire predictions of ancient and modern prophets are inevitable. All prophetic predictions are both warnings and comforts—warnings that the time is short, but comfort that there is still time. The church still has the time, the power, the authority and the obligation to renew its liturgical life. The most recent liturgical renewals of this century have been based on four axioms of sacramental theology. But another more radical renewal is needed, one that completes the divine presence through a justice that rolls "down like waters, and righteousness like an everflowing stream" (Am. 5: 24).

1) *Sacraments effect what they symbolize.* Sacramental action invites us into a transforming process of life and power—a vital and active presence that can carry us to new creations and new ways of being in the world. Any separation between the work of the sacrament and the dispositions of the participants must now be discounted. Our liturgies maintain their powers for transformation and new life through remembrances and anticipations of vital and moving traditions—traditions that are not simply of our own making, but ones in which we must participate. At the same time such traditions can and will become effete and moribund unless our participation empowers them in the concrete and particular instances of contemporary life. As acts of the church, sacraments may work *extra nos* but never *sine nos*. In effective liturgical action, both God and world are continually *re-presented* to each other. And as the nexus of this renewed presence—at the epicenter of this deep symbolism—we find effected the encompassing mystery of the church, a new people of God in Christ. Aidan Kavanagh summarizes: "The liturgy cracks open radical values, invites without coercing people into them, and celebrates their living presence deep within these values. Thus the liturgy does not merely talk about God but manifests the assembly's graced union . . . ." Effecting what they symbolize, sacraments are "more of God than about God."[6]

2) *Sacraments are acts of the church.* As "acts of the church," sacraments are both rites of "location" and "dislocation." They not only gather the church into a particular time and space, but also dislocate the people of God from all static identifications and canonizations of any particular time and space. Rowan Williams writes: "the sacrament of the Lord's supper" must be

"socially disturbing" and is "itself an act of renunciation" of the old and present order for a new creation and a new way of life.[7]

3) *The Church is "The Body of Christ" and "The People of God."* To be a people of God, the church must be on the move.[8] It is a people formed by the Spirit-of-God-in-Christ moving in and for the world. The church is the *Spiritual Presence*–the new "Body of Christ." Revitalized in the Spirit, the *body* of the church can be *effected* by neither flesh nor spirit alone, but rather through an incarnational mix of both. Therefore the church will be enacted as a social and political reality in all times and places, but in no particular time and place above all others. No particular age or epoch in itself–past, present or future–can claim to be paradigmatic. There can be no such priorities in the infinite mystery of God's presence. Responding to the call of *the just-making presence* is a constant task of the people of God in any and all times. All institutional structures and systems, all ritual, doctrinal and moral precedents will be interpreted by their service to this greater sacramental task. No less than the *Body of Christ* is at stake, rendered alive again in the Pentecost of a church which is always being cast beyond itself, always *coming-into-being* in and for a larger world. Daniel Berrigan asks: "Could it not profitably be thought that in the breaking of the bread and the pouring of the cup, Christ was swept into the deep, far beyond the simple table rite?"[9]

4) *Sacraments are for the people.*[10] Being swept into the deep by our baptism with Christ, we are all equal in our situation and need. We are in the throes of both sin and grace and we need liberation from the one and salvation in the other. The Christian liturgy, like Christian faith and church, is radically egalitarian. Being egalitarian, our differences, particularities, and peculiarities are not wiped out, but accepted for celebrating the infinite diversity of the new Body of Christ and the equal inter-dependency of all of its members (1 Cor. 12:12–27). This is especially the case for those some might consider "our less respectable members," but who, all the more, must be "treated with greater respect" (1 Cor. 12:23). On the other hand, our particularities and differences of race, gender, sexual orientation, social and ecclesiastical status and the like are wiped out once and for all for any purpose of structured hierarchy or negative discrimination. There is no doubt about this, although our failures, rooted in an array of hierarchical separations and discriminations, remain pervasive.

Part of the task of a just-making sacramental presence is to interpret texts and reconstruct rites that model new experiences of the Spirit's vitality. In most of the ages of the church, this new and radically egalitarian creation has been driven to the edges of the people of God. Strong traditions of counter-gospel hierarchies, patriarchies and "a complex social pyramid of graduated dominations and subordinations" have claimed the center—what Elizabeth Schüssler Fiorenza has called "kyriarchy."[11] Such "lordships" are countered repeatedly in texts such as the famous hymn of exaltation-in-humiliation of Phil. 2; or in Gal. 3:27–28, which must be read and preached, not only in the negative where in Christ there can no longer be discrimination based on race, gender, ethnicity, nationality, social status and the like, but also in the positive. For those who have gone to the depths and been clothed with Christ, there is a positive universe of *both* women and men, adults and children, races of all colors, cultures and nations of all ethnicities and classes, indeed of all beliefs, customs and orientations. Among and for such a people, worship must necessarily be *"proletarian," "communitarian," and "quotidian."*[12]

Our challenge is to engage and celebrate the breadth and inclusiveness that mark sacramental action—what Aidan Kavanagh calls "an analogical spread." Sacramental acts are intensifications and representations in epitome of new creations not yet fully accomplished in everyday life, but capable, in analogy and model, of offering new and more comprehensive ways of being in the world. As *the Body of Christ* and *People of God,* our analogies "spread" from eternity to time, divinity to humanity, sameness to difference. "Calling God back to the mountain" rendered just and sacred again, requires the work of a sacramental action of a people made whole and holy again by the reflections in an infinite diversity of human faces. *Sacraments are for the people,* and it is their needs that count. Justin Martyr's famous depiction of the president of the liturgical assembly applies here: "the curate of all who are in need."[13]

Part II: The Works of a Sacrament[14]

Sacraments "Reconfigure" the Literal in Terms of the Ideal

Sacraments are effective configurations and enactments of the religious beliefs and moral ideals of a people. Sacraments are thus vehicles more for the celebration of the ideals of faith and life than simple descriptions of literal realities. Sacraments *consecrate* life in new ways—both *making* life sacred and *drawing* its core sacredness to the surface of everyday awareness.[15] Furthermore, sacramental acts give us an opportunity for new ways of being precisely because of our dissatisfaction with the literal. The facts of our lives have become too distant from our ideals. We have become imprisoned by the negative powers and principalities of our age and we look for the promised liberation. Sacramental acts are always about liberation from the literal, the ordinary, and the expected—indeed, from the sinful assumptions and presumptions of life in any age. Sacraments *reconfigure* our character and frame new expectations of how we ought to believe and act.[16]

In terms of the ideals of our faith and life, there are three basic works of a sacrament—*metaphorical disclosure, symbolic designation,* and the effective *demonstration* of lives-in-acts.

The Metaphorical Dimension:
The Invitation to Faith and the Disclosure of Values

In the wresting of the figurative ideal from the literal facts of everyday life, sacraments function first metaphorically. It is the precise work of metaphor to disclose new dimensions of experience and meaning amid the "failure" of the literal. Metaphors linguistically probe heights and depths of meaning beyond the flat surfaces of life. In metaphor, we are claiming implicitly that "there is more going on than meets the eye"—or more precisely, more than the literal descriptions of our language can disclose. Metaphors dwell naturally in poetry and religion; and in the case of liturgical action, they disclose invitations to enter new worlds of faith and life that are beyond our sight and ordinary, everyday grasp.[17]

When we say, for example, that "life is sacred" or *we are* or *this is* "the Body of Christ," we are engaging in metaphorical counterpoint. Thus, in the face of the literal death-dealing of our age, or our own assaults on Christ's body, we assert again what we ought to value and how we constantly need to rename ourselves eucharistically as a people of God. With all of our infidelities and sins, we are never out of touch with the just-making presence unless we lose our sacramental ability to reconfigure both life and ourselves in the face of stark and literal realities. Thus to celebrate the eucharist or any other sacrament in the face of the weapons of death and destruction of our age is an appropriate, necessary, and effective liturgical act. Wherever else the Eucharist is to be celebrated, it must celebrate life amid such cultures of death.

The Symbolic Dimension:
The Designation of New Habits of Being and Virtue[18]

Still metaphors are essentially linguistic and depend on the twist and shock of new disclosure and recognition to accomplish their purpose. The inviting work of metaphor tends to be blunted by routine. To have staying power and to be effective the faith and moral ideals disclosed in sacraments must also become sedimented in the routine rituals of daily life. It is amid these necessary and ritualized routines that symbol emerges to augment and further the work of metaphor. Metaphor invites us into this process of symbolization linguistically in liturgical narrations and prayers. In turn our words are given more material substance, stability and regularity by the *designations* of our symbols and rituals. It is this recombination of word and rite that provide the space and time necessary for sacramental symbols to grow and become regular and effective—to become habits of being and virtue.

In this symbolic dimension, the ideals of faith and life disclosed by sacraments become foundational for individual and social character. Moral character requires not only the dramatic disclosure of new meaning, but also the assimilation of meaning in regular judgments and patterned ways of life. Virtue requires that what has been *disclosed* as meaningful also becomes *designated* as "tried and true."[19]

For example, the symbols and rituals of Christian marriage mean that getting married in the church is far more than simply a moral justification for physical intimacy, or necessarily a canonization of any singular way of physicality. Rather, getting married *in facie Ecclesiae* is to be designated sacramentally into a new state of being and character—to take on a new vocation and office for the sake of the whole church. It is the special role and task of married Christians to display and model what a virtuous life of love and physical intimacy looks like. It is in this sense that the secular reality of marriage is reconfigured sacramentally and presented symbolically as "a new truth" for all to see.[20]

However the power of symbolic designation can also be its weakness: the "tried and the true" can become stale and trite. New experiences of the just-making presence may call for conversion and change—new ways of life and habits of being and virtue replacing the old. When this happens new symbols and rituals are necessary to regularize these states and make them stable. It was on this basis that women have been included in orders, and the blessing of covenanted same-sex unions is being engaged. This is also why on a regular basis the linguistic power of new metaphors needs to be reasserted in the regular revisions of liturgies and prayer books.

Sacraments as Models:
The Demonstration of the Goods of Christian Faith and Life
When faith and value ideals, now disclosed metaphorically and designated symbolically, become systematized in analogical paradigms and patterned ways of life, sacraments become models. The values disclosed and the virtues designated by sacramental acts must also be regularly *demonstrated* and displayed as goods in our lives. Just as in marriage, all sacraments model and *demonstrate* faith and value-ideals in action—in the lives of people who, though centered as a liturgical community, live also beyond its boundaries.[21] Liturgical rites cannot exist for long as sacramentally effective acts if they are abstracted and disconnected from the ways that we conduct our everyday lives. Sacraments do not model a simple and perfect identification between liturgy and life, but rather an analogical one, and the same phenomenon of counterpoint that exists in metaphor and symbol remains. Thus in faithful liturgy we are instructed and drawn forward by models that are always more

ideal than the life we might experience day to day, including the life of a given congregation. It is in this sense that our sacramental-liturgical models are cast upon an eschatological horizon.

Accordingly, in our liturgies we not only declare that life is valuable or that our love is true, we must also demonstrate their value and truth—from birthdays to baptisms, from weddings to funerals. We demonstrate further the goods of life and love in modeling an entire array of life-affirming and compassionate activities—the care and nurture of children, and especially in the forgiveness of those who have offended us the most, life and love affirmed and demonstrated again as valuable even for one who has unjustly taken life away.

For sacramental liturgies to be effective, our claims must be vindicated and legitimated by our lives. Sacraments exist in liturgical communities and it is finally these communities that must, in their everyday lives, *effect what they symbolize* and model in act and deed what they pray. In this way the entire Christian narrative and journey from birth to death becomes visible, concrete, and tangible.[22]

Part III: A Just-Making Presence

Holy Saturday 1983: A Narrative[23]

Bill Wylie Kellermann narrates events of a Holy Saturday night in 1983 that clarify the relationship and the challenge of worship and the moral life. Kellermann, a United Methodist pastor, and a group of Catholic priests and lay workers gathered for the Easter Vigil in a cabin in the woods of northern Michigan. The location of their vigil on that cold night was no accident. "Less than a mile up the blacktop road," Kellermann writes, "was Wurtsmith Air Force Base, home of the 379th Bombardment Wing of the Strategic Air Command. Sixteen B–52s with nuclear mission targets in the Soviet Union sat on the runway." This group had been meeting for "study, prayer and discernment," and now on "the eve of the Resurrection" they "were gathered to act."

It would be hard to imagine a better time to enact the just-making eucharistic presence in such a place than on the eve of Jesus' paradigmatic passage from death to new life as the Christ. This small band of friends was holding a mirror of judgment to the ways of the old creation and bringing into bold relief how our liturgies are to model new ways of being at peace in a world awash with weapons of death and destruction.

> At 2:00 A.M. we began the liturgy of the Word . . . the Easter Vigil . . . A feast of faithfulness, passage, and hope . . . A communion of the living. A solidarity of the spirit, this prayer of passage, this claim upon the future.

> After singing a hymn, we exited into the night . . . single file from the road through the woods to the extreme end of the runway . . . .

358

At the barbed-wire fence we paused and circled in preparation for two symbolic deeds. The first was to light the Paschal candle . . . . The second, indeed one with the other, was to cut the fence . . . . Twang! The security of death guarding death was broken in liturgy. The wall was breached.

Thereupon seven of us began our three-and-a-half-mile trek toward the high-security areas, the loaded B-52's . . . .

We walked on mostly in silence, lying down periodically in a fumbling comedy, to avoid the view of patrolling security cars. As the nuclear storage bunkers came into sight, we arrived at a small building . . . . And here we carried the vigil liturgy another step forward: we renewed our baptismal vows.

I had not foreseen the personal power of that moment: to look down the runway toward the machines and their cargo, and there to *"renounce Satan and all his works."* There I promised in a way not fully understood before to *"persevere in resisting evil, and, whenever, I fall into sin, repent and return to the Lord."* A life may be called back to such moments, indeed may turn on them.

The sky had begun to lighten. Birds were rousing. Shivering, we conferred and decided we had enough of the dodging and weaving. We would proceed upright with dignity, in the manner of right worship. Here an astonishing phenomenon occurred, one reportedly not uncommon in such undertakings. We passed unseen! . . . It was as though the waters had parted. We walked unhindered to the open entrance of the high-security area where planes on alert stood ready to fly.

There, measured by a sudden flurry of activity within, we were finally noticed. Armored vehicles and pickup trucks rushed to surround us. We spread our altar cloth of intercession on the runway. About it we scattered blood, brought in small bottles to signify the blood of the innocents, the blood of the Lamb. Producing elements of the eucharist, we completed the service at gunpoint, surrounded by young airmen with automatic weapons.

We were a disheveled band. Bedraggled, dressed in plastic garbage bags as makeshift protection against the unexpected weather . . . . In weakness and exhaustion, we suffered a sense of our own foolishness . . . .

"Are you . . . base personnel?" "No." "Do you work on the base?" "No . . . ." "Well, would you pick up your trash and leave?"

It was clear almost immediately that our breach of security was so severe an embarrassment that should we simply depart quietly, no record or mention need come to the attention of community, public or even military higher-ups. We consulted among ourselves and declined. The liturgy was complete in its own right, but it had momentum and direction we did not intend to abandon. Herded into a bus, strip-searched, interrogated by various agencies military and civil, we were in the end dumped unceremoniously at the front gate without charges.

Kellermann concludes his narration with the fundamental question: "Was anything actually accomplished?"[24] This is the question of all who contemplate the relationship of God and world, liturgy and action, and the effectiveness of the just-making and divine presence among us. In the midst of the enormity of human sin and the powers and principalities we confront, it has become commonplace to hear, often sermonically, a more moderate and less ambitious gospel–one that inevitably lapses into a functional fideism that separates faith and life, believing and acting. We hear that our lives of faith are not about "doing" but rather about "being" and that our primary calling is to abide faithfully in the haven of God's word and the shelter of God's household, now insulated from the storms of outside and foreign worlds.[25]

There are both formal and substantive mistakes in this posture, and central concepts and experiences of our faith are severely misinterpreted. First, (B)being, grace, and presence are all closely intertwined, and are all acts. More specifically, grace, as Paul Tillich reminds us, is the "Spiritual Presence" of God *active* among us–"grasping . . . inspiring . . . transforming."[26] All (B)being exists in modalities–in frames, shapes, forms and postures. This is to say that (B)being is intentionally posited as an *active moving toward*–more a verb (*esse*) than a noun (*ens*), more a personally existing subject than merely a category of thought or specific material object. In this light, any separation between *essence* and *existence*, and *being* and *doing* needs reevaluation.

We can distinguish between *particular* actions as behavior and the foundations of *action* in the *Act* of (B)being and (P)presence. Faithful liturgy enacts sacramentally God-with-us-in-act. This does not mean that the spiritual and just-making presence of Divine (B)being and grace is one dimensional. Before (B)being can intentionally *move toward* another, it must be capable of *receiving from another.* It is to this extent that we find the foundation of passion that is necessary for all action, and which is itself a dimension of action–the divine-human ability to receive from and to be moved by an (O)other. Personhood is the most profound *mode* of (B)being and (P)presence, both of God and humankind, and is made whole in these dual and dialectical movements of passion and action. The radical egalitarian and liberating presence of faithful liturgy is justice in epitome and in *act*–this *praxis of justice*, concretely and sacramentally modeled, informs all of our subsequent works *for justice* in particular situations and circumstances.[27]

At this point, then, we can offer a preliminary answer to the question of whether the Holy Saturday Vigil of these friends–their sacramental enactment of life, peace and justice– "accomplished anything," even with its unceremonious ending. Rowan Williams speaks specifically to such questions: "It is this capacity to imagine a 'faithful people' that seems to me the most significant irritant offered by sacramental practice to the contemporary social scene."[28] Amid all of our infidelities and sinful complicities, and in the face of seemingly overwhelming powers of death and destruction, it is this sacramental capacity to imagine and enact a "faithful people"–albeit in miniature by this small band of witnesses–that continues to empower our liturgies, no matter how modest, to bring new life and to be "irritating" again to the powers that be.

This Holy Saturday assembly epitomizes the fundamental nature and dynamics of the eucharist. Emerging at the ruins of the literal, the status quo, and the assumptive patterns of accommodation that mark our lives among the powers and principalities, the eucharist, upon the horizon of Passover, is a meal on the run of a community on the move–one constantly assembling and reassembling itself. Eucharist can only be a temporary place and time of respite and renewal for the sake of a deeper narrative and longer journey. This is a *pilgrim feast* and we participate best by traveling light, with just enough baggage of precedent and panoply necessary for refocusing our story and renewing our journey.

"The World is the Host; It Must be Chewed:"[29]
The Political Nature of the Eucharist

There is an intrinsic affinity between sacramental action and our political and moral lives. Sacraments are about interconnection and enactments: spirit and flesh, grace and nature, God and world, divinity and humanity, church and society. Consequently liturgy expands relationships and connections to universal worlds beyond the locality and particularity of its own enactments. What begins as acts of the church in specific times and places–among a particular people in their own situations, needs, and circumstances–is transferred to the horizon of universal salvation, liberation, and justice for all. This transformation of the particular to the universal is the proper dynamic of sacramental action–what Rowan Williams has called "the symbolic range of our sacramental practice." To insure the effectiveness of that range, and to counter our own penchant to resist the implications and obligations of our own transformation, Williams calls for on-going "symbolic therapy . . .the need to resist anything that trivializes or shrinks the symbolic range of our sacramental practice"–for example, "baptism as essentially a mark of individual confession, the eucharist as a celebration of achieved *local* fellowship."[30]

Alan Neely has the same concern: "If the Eucharist is the center of the church's life why have all of us so spiritualized, depoliticized, and a-historicized the broken bread and poured out wine . . . ?" Summarizing the teaching of the Medellín Conference of Latin-American Roman Catholic bishops in 1968, Rafael Avila argues that liturgical celebration, and the eucharist in particular, cannot be "a parenthesis in our history in order to celebrate another history," but must be a "recapturing" of the necessary tension between what in fact is the case in many aspects of our daily lives and what *must be* the case when the eucharist is modeled faithfully as a just-making presence and "a school of liberation."[31]

The fact that there has been so much resistance in Christian history to the legitimate and faithful connection between the eucharist and the life of the *polis* begs for some explanation. First is our long-standing fear of the obligations that ensue when we accept the sacramental-incarnational nature of the new creation—a dynamic that requires that we model in our lives the *descent* of the Word made flesh into the heart of the human condition before we can *ascend* at the end of life's journey. Rafael Avila also suggests both subterfuge and confusion based on "the pretext that a mystical unity" has already been established: "Great doses of hidden manichaeism anesthetize the conscience of many Christians who prefer 'mystical' or merely religious community to human community."[32]

Another reason for our resistance to the political and moral dynamics of the *breaking of the bread* and the *pouring out of the wine* is the fear that our liturgies will continue to be seduced and co-opted into legitimating particular ideologies and political systems, becoming functional "agents of the state." Thus a movement of withdrawal from these dangers into new forms of insulated sectarianism has taken on new life. Despite serious risks for Christian faith and life in such accommodations to the state, any security gained in such a neo-sectarian posture is short-lived. Our words and rituals can be co-opted politically by both sectarian and universalist perspectives. The former is a lapse into bourgeois and suburban enclaves in retreat from the universal needs and obligations of proletarian life, while the latter turns to a falsifying abstraction and idealization of these same needs, embodied sacramentally in the faces of particular people in local situations and circumstances. Framing a critical tension between the particular and universal, the personal and the social is the formal sacramental task of faithful liturgy—effecting globally what we celebrate locally. Accordingly, we should fear less the politicization of the eucharist and more our failure to *eucharistize* the polis.[33]

From "The Civitas of World" to a "Suburban Captivity"
Aidan Kavanagh aptly describes how our liturgical practice has lapsed into our own North American brand of *bourgeois elitism*—what Gibson Winter has termed our "suburban captivity":

> We have moved out of the *civitas* of World into a suburbia of sovereign subjectivity where the air is better for genteel savages whose individuality is absolute, sovereign, and weirdly noble. From here the view is frosty clear and the old *civitas* can be seen for the trap and delusion it always was, a vast stew of

tarts, muggers, ethnics smelling of garlic or collard greens, religious primitives, and ward heelers—cosmic unfortunates for whom, tiresomely, we the enlightened are obliged to care until their ability to breed can be curtailed. Unless they can become aseptic and anonymous citizens of the new electronic city they have no business existing. They are evolutionary dead ends.[34]

If Kavanagh is close to being accurate, even if acerbic, we are in an ironic predicament that is accelerating toward the tragic. The richly diverse and multidimensional experience of life that is necessary for sacramental action to occur in the first place is being reduced to a homogeneous and one-dimensional caricature of both the sacred and the secular. From the vital inter-connections of spirit and flesh demanded by an incarnational church, we have unhinged the sacred from the secular and our faith from our lives in the world. In so doing Christian congregations often, in Kavanagh's terms, "float free of World and City, becoming thereby unworldly, spiritualized, abstracted, idealized, sectarian and gnostic." With such an unhinged and ethereal floating above the "malaise" of worldliness, we also remain ungrounded and disconnected with little ability to commit to much of anything because we can no longer verify or legitimate incarnationally—in time and place—the claims we make or the prayers we say. In such a non-sacramental milieu, trying to call God back to the mountain by multiplications of liturgies can only routinize this "self-aggrandizing solipsism." The more we pray, the more God retreats into silence. Our liturgies become aestheticized entertainment and anesthetized distraction.

If this sort of "suburban withdrawal" is our greatest danger, then Aidan Kavanagh's argument that the most promising milieu for symbolizing God's presence among us today remains rooted in the city gains force. I do not interpret Kavanagh as necessarily presenting a facile opposition between the urban and rural. Rather he is presenting the *civitas* as symbolic of a richly diverse and heterogeneous ethos—cities as places of great political and moral density and sacramental thickness, and where both the need and promise of liberation and justice are most profoundly symbolized for all: "We are God's finite extrapolation, as *civitas hominum* is the finite extrapolation of *civitas Dei*." In faithful liturgy a new city and a new world are modeled and our ordinary everyday perspective is inverted, "projecting World out of Gospel rather than Gospel out of World."[35] This is the proper priority of sacramental action and eucharistic dynamic.

Political and Moral Density and Sacramental Thickness
In order to project sacramentally a world out of gospel, our liturgies must have enough gravity to be vital to how we are to live our lives and encounter our deaths. As in all things liturgical, we are not first speaking literally. It is

often the case that the literal weight of massive church structures, or the sound and fury of only triumphalistic ritual mask the true gravity and vitality of human situations—whether of sorrow or joy—in a reduction to only taste and performance. The political and moral density and "sacramental thickness" necessary to call forth the just-making presence does not often occur in the permanence of structure, but rather in the multiple dimensions and infinite permutations of spirit and life. Certainly the biblical symbols of wind and breath are dense and thick enough to both blow down old barriers and to support new life. This is the density and thickness of the "Spiritual Presence."[36]

Aidan Kavanagh criticizes much modern "worship" as a "pastel endeavor." But Mary Gordon reminds us of the need for a more careful hermeneutic here. In an essay subtitled "In Praise of Watercolors," Gordon writes that she finally found her voice as a woman writer by a "stubborn predilection for the *minor*." She says that she finally learned to write about the affairs and issues of daily life and not about epic stories and heroic quests—not about great truths in the distant heavens, but about the close intimacies and needs of ordinary existence. "I discovered that what I loved in writing was not distance but radical closeness; not the violence of the bizarre but the complexity of the quotidian." Her father had a taste for the metaphysical; her mother taught her "to remember jokes . . . . I don't know what the nature of the universe is, but I have a good ear. What it hears best are daily rhythms . . . ." Indeed, the best liturgy is in watercolor and more in tune with the daily and deep rhythms of justice that pulsate in every day life than the thinner, more ethereal music of the metaphysical spheres.[37]

Similarly, for Regis Duffy, it is more the ethical than the metaphysical that will offer the best contest to our own lack of presence in worship. Being "at table with Jesus" requires a eucharist framed by deep "symbols of need"—"hunger and thirst, . . . sharing, remembering, thanksgiving, dying, obeying, living, sending."[38] The particular and personal faces that symbolize the universal needs of our world are all around us, and more dangerous to the status quo because of that fact.[39]

Liturgical Praxis: The Challenge of Transformation
Rosemary Haughton asserts that ritual "is directly and solely concerned with the occurrence of transformation."[40] From deep anthropological roots we experience the symbols and rites of our liturgical life as moving, dislocating, and transforming. In rites of initiation, in reconciliation and at the Lord's table, or in the other times and places of radical transition—marriage, ordination, sickness and final passage—we are in motion. With necessary respites along the way, "putting on Christ" sacramentally means being transformed by the just-making presence. Nor is openness to the dislocating

and ecstatic movements of the Spirit an option in our liturgical lives. Concerning our foundational obligations of forgiveness and reconciliation, Mt. 5:23–24 directs that we "leave (our) gift . . . before the altar"–not necessarily until we have grown "perfect" but until we are open to and desirous of these graces, or simply curious enough to investigate a community that models them.[41]

Wayne Meeks has pointed out that "almost without exception, the documents that eventually became the New Testament and most of the other surviving documents for the same period of Christianity's beginnings are concerned with the way converts to the movement ought to behave." And, he adds, "these documents were addressed not to individuals but to communities." This is not surprising in "a movement of converts." It also is not surprising that a movement that so often gravitates to the center of middle-class assumptions experiences a disconnection between its worship and its moral life. In order to read our texts and celebrate our rites with vibrancy and vitality, we need to re-identify Christianity *as a movement of converts*–a people in transition and transformation who still live as our founders lived on the "boundaries between the old world and the new." Liturgy is not faithfully celebrated only at the center, but also on the boundary and in the praxis of transformation.[42]

Megan McKenna argues that the Church, "especially in the United States, has based its criteria for celebration of the sacraments" on an intellectualist "rather than a conversional base that can be witnessed to and attested to in behavior." Accordingly, our liturgy seldom calls us to accountability and we have little reason, in Wayne Meeks's terms, to pay much attention at all to the "moral consequences of conversion" or to speak "the language of obligation." However it is only such accountability and obligation to what we claim and celebrate that fully enact the metaphors, symbols, and models of sacramental action. In this way the just-making presence of liturgy can create a new moral environment where all prior assumptions are called into question. For McKenna, "the ritual gives the model, as Jesus gives the norm, the ethic in flesh and blood." For Meeks, ritual is "the symbolic moral universe" and becomes "the grammar of Christian practice."[43]

"Be What You See. Receive Who You Are. ": Symbols and Commitment
"Be what you See. Receive who you are," St. Augustine enjoins *the Body of Christ.* It can only be a "distorted sacramental praxis," maintains Regis Duffy, that prevents the power of liturgy from effecting the commitments in our lives that our words and rites symbolize and model–a perversion and seduction of the heart of liturgy itself, using "rituals to escape the cost of commitment" and "using the signs of God's presence (liturgy) to avoid

(God's) presence." These are dangerous self-deceptions and we become content with only nostalgic memories of a once "living" God: "Christians of any epoch who use transforming symbols perversely to remain untransformed in their praxis are in trouble." The constant challenge for faithful liturgy is to keep "the symbols of our worship, with their prophetic meaning" connected to "the public sphere of praxis and values." The test of true and false presence is whether our liturgies flow from and direct us toward commitments to "the concretized stories of individuals and communities" (including our own), or whether they are framed as spectacles for our passive observation, pious edification, or private catharsis. "Real presence is a question of commitment," Duffy concludes, and it is only ritual posturing "and dishonest religious autobiography" that give us the hubris to think we can call up the just-making presence of God from the heights and depths of creation with so little asked of us in return.[44]

No commitment happens without passion or in the abstract. Without *passion,* either of pain or pleasure, we can no longer be acted upon, cannot receive, cannot be moved or *suffer* with each other and bear one another's burdens. Commitments come when we can see, feel, and touch each other and experience our lives symbolically in all of their complexity. Literalists cannot be liturgists, nor can the pure but abstract atmosphere of traditionalist "orthodoxy," or the blinding fear and rage of "white patriarchy" see or touch any longer the real *Body of Christ* symbolized in all races, genders, orientations, and situations. Joseph Gelineau epitomizes the range of life, passion and commitment that ought to be modeled in our liturgies when he depicts the psalms as "a series of shouts: shouts of love and hatred; shouts of suffering or rejoicing; shouts of faith or hope."[45]

"Practicing Ambivalence"

Amid these obligations of transformation and commitment, Wayne Meeks marks an important caveat. The liturgy and lives of the earliest converts were also practices in ambivalence being perched, as they were, on the boundaries between the old and new creations. The ethos of the new creation was not yet fully in place and there was competition for their attention and their character.

> If according to one interpretation of 1 Cor. 11:21, 33, the poorer members of the congregation were arriving at the Lord's Supper too late to share the food, it was probably because they were slaves in other households, or hired workers or artisans who could not leave their shops. A traveling apostle must deal with shipping practices on the Mediterranean or Aegean, or with safe procedures on overland roads and in seedy hostels. Onesimus might become Philemon's "beloved brother" as well as his slave, but did that mean he would now be freed? All the peculiar practices of Christians are embedded within a web of

practices that connected them with the world whose form (Paul had said) was passing away . . . . For most Christians . . . withdrawal from the world and ascetic warfare against it were not realistic options. For the vast majority, the Christian life was an amphibian life, life at the same time in the old world that was passing away and in the new world that was coming . . . .[46]

Modeling in the eucharist and other liturgies the new creation on the edge of the old made it necessary for these earliest converts to become adept in "practicing ambivalence," a situation and practice much like our own– dangerous, but vital, and demanding the most profound efforts of interpretation and discernment.[47]

The Moral Point of View and the Narrative Unfolding of Liturgy
The Eucharist as Memory and Anticipation: The Praxis of Narrative
The sacramental event of the eucharist is centered in the present, but framed by past and future time. It may seem more natural and faithful to stress the dimension of the past in liturgy, but in only one sense is this true. We may be "wired" to remember first, but it is a mistake to assume a one-dimensional criterion of the past as normative in our liturgical life; or worse yet, to assume a geneticist fallacy that considers truth and fidelity always closest to origins. A vital eucharistic and liturgical life will be based on a "time-full" pattern of narrative unfolding: always in the contemporaneous present, we remember the past in terms of its *unfolding* toward the future. Nor is it necessarily easier to remember what has "already happened" than to anticipate a future not yet fully upon us. Through repression and fantasy, both remembrance and anticipation are equally dangerous as are the constant seductions of the present. And no remembrance or anticipation is more dangerous to the status quo of the powers and principalities of the world than the eucharistic narrative of liberation and justice. To *remember faithfully* "the night before he died" is to radically transform the present and create new hope for the future.[48]

"The Dangerous Memory of the Freedom of Jesus Christ"[49]
The earliest proclamations of the gospel were in the form of proclamations of liberation–"For freedom Christ has set us free. Stand firm, therefore, and do not submit again to a yoke of slavery," proclaims Gal. 5:1. Freedom has many forms, but in epitome it is liberation–first from the enslavements of sin in all of its manifestations from personal vice to political oppression. As the liberator of the new creation–the new Adam and the new Moses–Jesus Christ ushers in a new way of being in the world beyond all oppression and death-dealing. What has been achieved in Christ is now being modeled in faithful Christian liturgy. It is "for freedom itself," Paul proclaims, not only

for particular acts of freedom that Christ has "set us free."

These radical proclamations of the demise of the old and the rise of the new order of freedom will necessarily be dangerous to forces that want to resist liberation and hold on to the old ways of enslavement, law, and power. Marked once and for all by the freedom and liberation of Jesus Christ, Christian liturgy is a radical and dangerous act. As Johann Metz indicates, the repression of such sacramental power is to be expected. This includes overt external prohibitions of eucharist and liturgy by government as well as by far more insidious and pervasive internal repressions where Christian communities themselves attempt to mute the power of the divine presence to enact justice. As a constantly repressed narrative of freedom and justice, liturgy is always about retrieval.

"The Future in the Memory of Suffering"[60]

> I, Paul, became a servant of this gospel. I am now rejoicing in my suffering for your sake, and in my flesh I am completing what is lacking in Christ's afflictions for the sake of his body, that is, the church. (Col. 1:23–24)

Johann Metz also sets the proper dynamic for the Christian anticipation of the future—the way we are to be cast forward and upon what horizon of interpretation and judgment we are to interconnect our past with our present and future. In the active remembrance of the paschal "passing" of Jesus to the Christ, we hold our future in view only "in the memory of suffering." Our way of liberation and freedom is necessarily a *via crucis*, not in a morbid "celebration" of suffering but rather in joyful anticipation of the passing of our suffering to liberation and new life. This alone can be "what is lacking in Christ's afflictions"—the passing to liberation and new life of those who are still suffering injustice, oppression, violence and death. What can only be *lacking* in the afflictions of the Christ is not the universality of redemption but only its particularity—the social, political and moral concreteness of freedom and justice. It is the work of liturgy, and the eucharist most especially, to keep the mystery of our general redemption—accomplished once and for all in Christ—connected to our obligations to the particularities of liberation and justice yet to be enacted, and in this way to model in full the completion of the new creation.

The Ethics of Lamentation and the Theology of Complaint

Still, liturgy must take care not to "level off" the fissures and fractures of life by a facile hermeneutic of word or rite. In an address delivered on Yom Ha-Shoah, 1989, Paul Ricoeur argues that remembering the victims of Holocaust is a moral duty especially as "there still exists throughout the world some declared and undeclared friends of the executioners who expect our forgetfulness." At the same time that we begin to repay our "*debt* to the victims" in our retelling and ritualization, we also, Ricoeur continues, "prevent their life stories from becoming banal"–a danger that "may be greater today than the danger of sheer forgetfulness." The most extreme case of such banality is the danger of "full explanation" wherein we render "intelligible," even "understandable" the Holocaust given this or that series of events–that is to say, monstrous evil "leveled off" by a theodicy of "explanation." There may be a logic to this evil, but it is a demonic one.[51]

The final form of forgetfulness and thus loss of the reality of the event of suffering in our narratives and rituals is the suggestion that somehow victims deserve their punishment because of some faithlessness or sin. Such is the rhetoric of retribution that also resonates throughout the sacred texts of most religions, including our own. In the midst of these theological debates, Ricoeur suggests a return to the biblical traditions of lamentation and complaint. Then, as in the rhythms and "shouts" of the Psalms, we can move

> back and forth from lament to praise and from praise to lament . . . . Whereas the theory of retribution makes victims and murderers equally guilty, the lamentation reveals the murderers as murderers and the victims as victims. Then we may remember the victims for what they are: namely, the bearers of a lamentation that no explanation is able to mitigate.[52]

This will mean that in the throes of the deepest lamentation and soulful complaint that an interrogation of God will ensue: *"Why my people? Why my parents? Why my child?"* Indeed, *"O Lord, how long?"* Thus our liturgy must allow and even frame the lamenting and complaining soul's struggles with God–with good and evil, victim and murder, and our own rage after retribution amid our obligation of forgiveness. We do not remain without guidance however from the biblical theology and ethic of lamentation and complaint:

> Whoever accuses God is far less godless than the one who does not care at all about God . . . . Lamentation needs memory as much as praise does. We remember "the six million" with all the more dedication if we acknowledge that God, whose blessing we remembered at Passover, is not the cause of suffering but rather the author of the Torah, which says: "Thou shall not kill."[53]

In the face of the human realities of lamentation and complaint, engaging eucharist and liturgy only in the dimensions of triumph and praise becomes a way of falsification.

However even within these norms, liturgy that engages evil, confronts murderers, judges injustice is necessarily at risk. John Navone reminds us that "the symbols of evil must be used wisely; otherwise they may bring upon their users the very evils they symbolize," and we begin to identify ourselves only ideologically and moralistically in terms of our external enemies—"purgation by scapegoat, congregation by segregation."[54]

The Moral Point of View and Narrative Unfolding

In comments suggestive of the narrative unfolding of good liturgy, Anne Lamott says that telling a good and true story requires *caring at the center*. And it requires an unfolding as well since we are always dealing with layers and with the ineffable—with heights and depths. "The truth doesn't come out in bumper stickers," she says, this is why a "whole book" may be required—a plot with characters that are alive and developing, and in whom we have a passionate interest beyond merely observing. In a good and true story we want our "characters to act out the drama of humankind," and we want to be with them as fellow actors. This is far more basic than sending a moral message, or even engaging in an ethical argument or judgment; but rather it is revealing "in an ethical light who we are . . . . So a *moral* position is not a message. A moral position is a passionate caring inside of you." Lamott's "instructions on writing and life" are about such "positions"—places upon which we stand and tell stories within which all else is interpreted. She concludes: "Tell the truth and write about freedom and fight for it . . . ."[55]

This is no more than to say that authentic moral practice requires, as Wayne Meeks has pointed out, a grammar and narrative provided by and large by Christian liturgy. In liturgy we use ritual to "reify the symbolic moral universe," and with such symbols as our language we plot the moral story of our lives, "not merely each individual, but humankind and the cosmos." And none of us are mere bystanders in this narrative unfolding, waiting for instructions from an intellectualist or spiritualist elite. "Each of us is called on to be a character" and we learn in this sacramental modeling what character and virtue are like overall.[56]

The Narrative Ethics of Testimony

A fundamental way in which we participate in the narrative unfolding and character "emplotment" of liturgy is by testimony. It is in testimony, Paul Ricoeur points out, that the "ideas, ideals and modes of being that the symbol depicts and discovers for us only as our most personal possibilities" are given the "sanction" of concrete and particular reality. Testimony is more than simple perception, but is "the story, the narration of the event" in which we have now become implicated. Thus testimony in liturgy creates a moral covenant between the worshipping community and its words and rituals, implicating us personally and practically in the narrative unfolding of the story of salvation—the story of liberation and justice. It is this narrative context of implicating testimony, Ricoeur concludes, that keeps our confessions from becoming gnostic. In the narrative unfolding of liturgy, we not only confess to what we have witnessed as chosen observers, but we testify in full that what we have seen and heard, what we are now narrating and modeling biographically, is a new way of being and acting in the world. All of the great testimonies of Scripture are such combinations of confession and narration: "'It is I, the Lord your God, who has led you out of the land of Egypt and out of the house of bondage'" (Ex. 20:2).[57]

The Poetics and Politics of Eucharist and Justice

I have argued that a new liturgical revolution is needed, one that makes thematic again the moral and political nature of the "just-making presence." Yet good liturgy often seems more poetic than political, more aesthetic than ethical. Therefore to conclude this argument, we need to reflect further on the intrinsic and classical ethical nexus between poetics and politics, especially in the contexts of the eucharist and justice.

Liturgy broadly understood is a type of poetic discourse and action, just as poetry is at its heart sacramental. Both poetry and liturgy are about configuring from ordinary and everyday events a new height and depth of experience. Classically, *poeisis* was a special act of creation—a new rendering of meaning and reality when the descriptions of ordinary language had failed. Paul Ricoeur argues that poetry is not just "one of the literary genres," rather "the category of poetics" exercises "a referential function that differs from the descriptive referential function of ordinary language and above all of scientific discourse." Poetics—in this instance what we might call *the poetics of sacramental acts*—offers different modes of reality and truth than those of only literal and scientific verification. Indeed, Ricoeur continues, "poetic discourse suspends this descriptive function" and offers in its stead another mode of reference and presence.

> Here truth no longer means verification, but manifestation, i.e., letting what shows itself be. What shows itself is in each instance a proposed world, a world I may inhabit and wherein I can project my ownmost possibilities. It is in this (sacramental) sense of manifestation that language in its poetic function is a vehicle of revelation.[58]

Both poetry and liturgy use, in Edward Farley's terms, "words of power" that both embody and inform action by motivation and implication. Good poetry and faithful liturgy both move us to act and implicate us in the new worlds *re-presented* in their words and rites. We can say that with respect to the making of justice and the moral life, the poetics of liturgy *gives rise to and invites obligation*[59]— that is, faithful and effective liturgy "re-configures" our character, twisting us from one referential locale into another, and draws us into the reality in question and its narrative unfolding. Within the fully sacramental context of liturgical poetics we are "tied" and "bound back" again in a religious and moral sense [*ob-ligare/re-ligare*] to the practical intentions and effects of our words and rites. What Ricoeur concludes about this *political* function of poetic discourse can be applied formally to the just-making presence of liturgy and sacramental action in general.

> My deepest conviction is that poetic language alone restores to us that participation-in or belonging-to an order of things which precedes our capacity to oppose ourselves to things taken as objects opposed to a subject. Hence the function of poetic discourse is to bring about this emergence of a depth-structure of belonging-to amid the ruins of descriptive discourse.[60]

However it needs to be emphasized that the power of such sacramental poetics can be used for re-presenting both good and evil. Being sacramental and liturgical is no guarantee of justice, peace, and life. What is being manifested must also be tested. The poetics in question must be filled with moral content and life. What has moved from and beyond the literal and descriptive must constantly return for verification and legitimation in practice. The lived poetics of a faithful eucharist promotes these tasks for Christians.[61]

"A Space on the Side of the Road": The Lived Poetics of the Eucharist
Kathleen Stewart titles her study of the Appalachian coal-mining region of West Virginia, *A Space on The Side of the Road: Cultural Poetics in an "Other" America.* Again, without much more adjustment than the well-placed parenthesis and emphasis, we can apply the "lived poetics" of Stewart's hermeneutic to the eucharist. "This [*the eucharist*] is a story about the fabulation of a narrative 'space on the side of the road' that enacts the density, texture, and force of a lived cultural poetics in the real and imagined hinterlands of 'America.'" This [*the eucharist*] is a story-in-act standing in opposition to the "chant of certainty" that makes up the standard account of American life. This [*the eucharist*] is a counter story, of an "other America" that, in its opposition to mainline assumptions can become "the site of an opening or reopening" of the standard account.

> In West Virginia, and in other like "occupied," exploited, and minoritized spaces, it [*the eucharist*] stands as a kind of back-talk to "America's" mythic claims to realism, progress, and order. But more fundamentally, and more critically, it [*the eucharist*] opens a gap in the order of myth itself–the order of grand summarizing traits that claim to capture the "gist" of "things." The "space on the side of the road" [*the eucharist*] is both a moment in everyday stories . . . and an allegory for the possibilities of narrative itself to fashion a gap in the order of things–a gap in which there is –"room to maneuver."[62]

Stewart's "West Virginia" stands for all locales of poverty, injustice and marginality. These are "decentered" and thus *eucharistic places* that stand in the face of all grand narratives and assumptive schemes, interrupting standard accounts and creating spaces for new stories embodied in local time and place. In these *eucharistic stories* of lived poetics, all claims of liberation and justice are cast upon a universal horizon of particular and local faces filled with "palpable desire" that defers and displaces the theoretic, the abstract, the overly consistent. The work of theory is both contained and rendered powerful again by its proper location in the midst of this lived poetics—between our desires for liberation at the beginning and our acts for justice at the end. In *eucharistic places*, "local voices are launched from within a space of contingency, and the 'truth' of things is lodged in the concrete yet shifting life of signs—a network of tellings and retellings, displacements and re-memberings." Here, in Appalachia and other de-centered liturgical sites—we are "flesh(ing) out the story of an 'Other America' in-filled with texture and the force of imagination and desire." *Eucharistic spaces* are spaces "of story, then, that both back talks 'America' and becomes the site of its intensification in performance." Such "space(s) on the side of the road" begin and end "in the eruption of the local and the particular;" but they emerge with universal implication for *being* and *things*. They emerge

> in imagination when "things happen" to interrupt the expected and naturalized, and people find themselves surrounded by a place and caught in a haunting double epistemology of *being* in the midst of things and impacted by them and yet making *something* of things. This is the space of the gap in which signs grow luminous in the search for their elusive yet palpable meanings . . . .[63]

The power to *sacramentally* translate the signs of everyday life into "luminous" symbols of universal meaning is at the heart of Stewart's cultural poetics just as it is in the eucharist and effective liturgy. Like the work of James Agee and Walker Evans before her, from Stewart's ethnographic study we can gain a desire for liberation and a passion for justice. In the poetics of justice, it is the stories of "ec-centric" and "off-center" ones—those on the sides of roads—that count.[64]

"Christ Stopped at Eboli"

Unless such people are brought to the center of our awareness and action by the poetics and politics of eucharist and justice, their affliction will remain "lacking" in the Body of Christ [Col. 1:23–24]. Carlo Levi writes of a poor village in southern Italy in the 1930s—one largely unchanged for centuries—where there was a saying among the people: "'Christ stopped short of here, at Eboli,' which means, in effect, that they have been bypassed by

Christianity, by morality, by history itself–that they have somehow been excluded from the human experience."

> "We're not 'Christians,'" they say . . . . "Christians," in their way of speaking means "human being . . . ." "We're not Christians, we're not human beings: we're not thought of as [humans] but simply as beasts, beasts of burden, or even less than beasts, mere creatures of the wild." Christ never came this far . . . into the desolate regions of Lucania . . . nor did time, nor the individual soul, nor hope, nor the relation of cause to effect, nor reason, nor history. Christ never came . . . . To this shadowy land, that knows neither sin nor redemption from sin, where evil is not moral, but is only the pain residing forever in earthly things, Christ did not come. *Christ stopped at Eboli.*[65]

But in the faithful eucharistic assembly Christ always stops, poetically but effectively, at these *other places*–stops to show us such places and send us to them.

The Eucharist as a Household of Inclusion: A Homeplace of Resistance
However, like Kathleen Stewart, bell hooks reminds us that places *on the side of the road* can also have value for refreshment and new life. In the quest for liberation and justice, it is sometimes easy to forget that these so-called *marginal* and *ec-centric* places have also for many been havens of safety, rest, and domesticity. There was a terrifying reality of "whiteness," hooks writes, and she learned as a black child to avoid encounter: it was a "survival strategy." But "the terror was made real," when she had to "pass through" a white area of town to reach her grandmother's house.

> It was a movement away from the segregated blackness of our community into a poor white neighborhood. I remember the fear, being scared to walk to Baba's, our grandmother's house, because we would have to pass that terrifying whiteness–those white faces on the porches staring us down with hate. Even when empty or vacant those porches seemed to say *danger*, you do not belong here, you are not safe.

> Oh! that feeling of safety, of arrival, of homecoming when we finally reached the edges of her yard, when we could see the soot black face of our grandfather, Daddy Gus, sitting in his chair on the porch, smell his cigar, and rest on his lap. Such a contrast, that feeling of arrival, of homecoming, this sweetness and the bitterness of the journey, that constant reminder of white power and control.[66]

Eucharistic Domesticity: "A Site for Subversion and Resistance"
As a third parallel in the poetics of eucharist and justice, we can refer to Edward S. Casey's comment on hooks's recollections:

> hooks's mother, Rosa Bell, stayed in the segregated part of town and created there a home-place that nurtured bell hooks and her siblings. Not only this, but the protective posture of staying put allowed the home-place to be what hooks

calls a "site of resistance" vis-à-vis the surrounding society in general and white racism in particular. In such a circumstance, "the task of making homeplace was not simply a matter of black women providing service . . . it was about the construction of a safe place where black people could affirm one another and by so doing heal many of the wounds inflicted by racist domination . . . . "The primacy of domesticity," writes hooks, is "a site for subversion and resistance." Turning and staying within–an in-version central to human in-habitation–ends by being a source of strength, capable of engendering a potent presence without.[67]

Like this homeplace of Baba and Daddy Gus, the eucharist is always the *Table of the Lord* to which all are invited–a domicile of inclusion and safety, an assembly for action.

Returning to the Center: A Renewed Normality
Nicholas Lash chides us for treating "the Christian story," and certainly the Christian liturgy, "as if it were only of significance for those whose private preference runs to an interest in something called 'religion.' We leave the story on one side when we discuss, evaluate and make plans for action in the ordinary, public world." What we should be doing, is enacting "the performance of a better myth, a more persuasive tale" than any of the standard accounts–that is, to "dramatize, enact, (and) display," in our liturgies and in our lives, new possibilities for humanity.[68]

In creating such a "contrast society," we are in Aidan Kavanagh's estimation returning to a new center, a new *orthodoxy* (or better, *orthopraxis*)–indeed, a renewed normality. It is as if effective and faithful liturgy has moved from the side of the road to the center. Those who have been on the edge are now in our midst. We who have been decentered are now recentered in a different place–moving from violence to peace, from hate to love, from slavery to freedom, from death to life. The *normal* injustices of the world–the way we have *done business* or *been realistic* in the past–have now been rendered abnormal; the care, compassion, and justice we once experienced as unexpected are now to be assumed. Kavanagh continues:

> From its normality arise not only the liturgy's primacy at the deepest level, but its immense power as well . . . . It is, in New Testament terms, *exousia*–literally something which surges up from the very depths of reality . . . . It is a Presence who, when asked its name, responds out of a burning bush with the most normal answer conceivable, "I am who I am . . . ."[69]

Faithful and effective liturgical rites begin as "resonances" of domestic normality, but end as new transactions with the just-making presence–oil and water as in a bath, bread and wine as at a dinner among friends, the touch of human hands, a kiss between lovers, benign gestures, words husbanded rather than squandered, smells and sights that speak, sounds of festivity .... *This* world is not at the periphery of reality but at its center. It is a City of God in the making . . .acts of supreme normality–and disconcertingly so for the powers and principalities of a world now rendered, in these sacraments of life, morbidly abnormal.[70]

Part IV: "Was Anything Actually Accomplished?"

A "Messianic Intermezzo"

Jürgen Moltmann refers to a faithful and effective eucharist as "the liberating feast"–a "messianic intermezzo" that "reveal[s] alternatives to the everyday world of work and makes them accessible." In its work for justice, however, such liberating freedom of Christ cannot become ponderous and grave. "The moral seriousness of liberation and improving the world has a tendency to totalitarianism," Moltmann continues, feeling such a weight of new obligation that "it leaves no time for festive joy." The "liberating protest" of the Christian eucharist, on the other hand, must also be the banquet feast that enacts and models the very experience of freedom itself. In this way, the eucharist becomes liberating and the protest against injustice and the obligations of justice are experienced as new ways of joyful presence. Sacraments effect what they "symbolize." Real life is not suspended in the liberating feast of the eucharist, it is reconfigured into a new reality, a new presence, a new normality.[71]

Thus the unceremonious, even comical ending of the small band of Holy Saturday protesters does not suggest that their eucharist on the tarmac was ineffective. Quite the contrary: they provided the alternative of life in the face of death with the entire range of emotion from the sublime to the ludicrous, marking both the grave reality and abysmal absurdity of such weapons of mass destruction. Moltmann argues that "oppressed people need (*both*) bread and circuses"–bread for new life and circuses (even with plastic costume), not as outlets only, but rather to demonstrate joyous and liberating alternatives to the deadly absurdities of violence and injustice.[72]

The Eucharist as Prismatic:
A Fragment of the World that Intensifies and Refracts

This eucharist of Holy Saturday 1983 was also effective because it was "a fragment of the world," an assembly of faith in a certain time and place that engaged the violence and death of the human city and transformed it through a feast of liberation–at least for those participating, and now for many who hear their story remembered and retold. But all celebrations need not display such an overtly thematic political and moral allusion to effect a just-making presence. While such eucharists in sacramental epitome–in the actual loci of death—must remain "normal," many if not most of our celebrations will be in more remote, suburban and "abnormal" places. The question then is how our more domestic feasts become the radical, liberating and just-making norm—become, in function and effect, prismatic fragments of the stark realities that confront the entire people of God in all types of places in the world.[73]

Joseph Gelineau argues that "the Paschal dynamics" of slavery to freedom and death to life must take over *in the place and people* of the celebration itself. The eucharistic mystery encompasses the entire range of human needs for redemption and liberation—no one can be left out just because they are not in *literal* attendance. We are in the midst of a *symbolic* event and *poetics* of action of great import: the justice absent in so much of God's household now through eucharistic poetics can be made present in the celebration itself and in the community assembled. Without this just-making presence, the eucharist fails to effect what it symbolizes—a "messianic intermezzo," a "liberating feast." Without local effect, sacramental action and eucharist remain dynamically incomplete—without the necessary "paschal dynamics" to send the community out again into the world of literal reality where issues of life and death are moving more quickly and starkly than ever before from *poetics* to *technics.*[74]

In one sense, all sacramental and eucharistic poetics are incomplete until we are *dismissed* back into the world of everyday life—*Ite missa est.* And so we ask, has the fragment of the world being split off in this particular celebration, now intensified sacramentally, been refracted with enough moral and political power to bring forth among us, the eucharistic assembly, "models which *induce* liberation"—models which allow the emergence of alternative ways of life in the world, new ways of liberation and justice?[75]

Both Strangers and Friends: The Capacity to Imagine

With the statement of these final criteria for a faithful and "effective" celebration, we are left with a note of "humble access," and a confession of the infinite ways to approach the divine and just-making presence and the incompleteness of our own faith and life. As I have argued, sacraments by definition can be neither perfectionist nor elitist, but must be radically egalitarian—more for sinners than saints. Joseph Gelineau concludes that we are to be welcoming of those, who for any reason, cannot fully join us:

> Because at the Lord's table there is also room for the passing stranger who is not directly concerned with the group choice, or the one who in conscience cannot accept it fully. The same communion welcomes those who cannot join fully. In the same communion there are those who have to struggle on other fronts according to different opinions.[76]

There can be no litmus tests of ideology, rule, or law for feasting at the Lord's Table, or for full participation in any of the sacraments. Rather in the name of the crucified and the sign of the cross, we must only be willing to tell stories that are authentic and truthful, to engage new journeys of transformation and change, and to accept invitations to be actors with others—a supporting cast, if you will—in the dramatic interplay of their lives. Such a desire for God and o(O)ther—both stranger and friend—and thirst for the rolling waters of justice is enough to begin. With this desire and thirst we may discover at last what we are doing in our worship, what keeps us coming back and in touch, and sometimes with that "ec-centric" stranger from "the side of the road" who may be—is most certainly—the Christ. Then we will be exercising our God-given sacramental capacity to imagine ourselves again as a faithful people.[77]

Postscript: Liturgy at Rest: "On the Porch: 3"

"The house had now descended:
All over Alabama the lamps are out."[78]

James Agee, along with Walker Evans, titled their monumental study of the depression South of 1936, *Let us Now Praise Famous Men* ("our ancestors in their generations" [Sir. 44:1–15]). However to complete the meaning of this project and manuscript, we need to read further in the chosen biblical text:

> But of others there is no memory; they have perished as though they had never existed; they have become as though they had never been born, they and their children after them. (Sir. 44: 9)

Agee and Evans present new and vivid images of life as lived in those times—in these times—a prismatic and intensified refraction of those for whom "there is no memory." I have preached on this text and their book as a sacramental imagination that enacts and re-presents:

> noble patriarchs of dirt, pain and sorrow, but also strong matriarchs, women with pained and weather-beaten faces, children with drooping and sad eyes, and, for the sake of relief, of a young boy, smiling, holding his dog. There are pictures of broken-down buildings and unpainted homes . . . pictures of iron beds and kerosene buckets, of general stores with Coca Cola signs, of a cemetery in a field with a fence that needs mending, of a wood-burning stove, and a decrepit St. Matthew School . . . . (And of) a baby lying on a plank floor on a piece of white cotton with another piece of cotton covering head to toe; and of two boots on dusty ground . . . (And a) final picture . . . of five gourds on a pole for homeless Martins to nest and roost—"even the birds of the air . . . ."

> . . . There is one picture of three black men sitting in front of a store and of a white man sitting apart in a car. And . . . of a black man driving a team of mules with a white girl in the rear. There are no pictures of white and blacks posed

together . . . . Even in the direst of common poverty, the powers that be enforce unnatural separations.

Still in all, these are noble, sad and famous pictures—famous men, women and children for whom, except for James Agee and Walker Evans (and others like them), there would have been no memory, as though they never existed, had never been born, they and their children after them.[79]

I bring up Agee and Evans at the end of this study not only to emphasize again the sacramental imagination's power for justice, but also, as a postscript, to emphasize how morally exhausting such vivid portrayals can be. After our more obvious collusions and accommodations with powers and principalities are confessed—among relatively decent people *like ourselves*—there remains the fear of being overwhelmed by the enormity of the obligations that will come upon us if we enter fully the just-making presence of faithful worship.

Agee's combination of artistic temperament with strong political and moral conviction is instructive. Courageously imagining ourselves again as a faithful people is a just-making act; it is the first and paradigmatic act of moral imagination that enables all further and necessary *actions*. Before justice can "roll down like an everflowing stream" it must also be still and deep, recollective and contemplative. Agee's final words capture the atmosphere of sacramental clarity, authenticity, and safety—the mergence of contemplation and action that also attends the just-making presence:

Our talk drained rather quickly off into silence and we lay thinking, analyzing, remembering, in the human and artist's sense praying, chiefly over matters of the present and of that immediate past which was part of the present; and each of these matters had in that time the extreme clearness, and edge, and honor, which I shall now try to give you; until at length we too fell asleep.[80]

Notes

1. Quoted in Robert Sokolowski, *Eucharistic Presence: A Study in the Theology of Disclosure* (Washington, D. C.: The Catholic University of America Press, 1994) 213.

2. Karl Barth, "The Word of God and the Task of Ministry" (1922), in *The Word of God and the Word of Man,* trans. Douglas Horton (New York: Harper Torchbooks, 1957) 196, 181–217.

3. Annie Dillard, *Teaching a Stone to Talk: Expeditions and Encounters* (New York: Harper & Row, 1982) 40, 69, 70, 71, 76.

4. Edward Kilmartin, S.J. speaks of how the Christian sacramental life takes human situations and makes them "situations of salvation," "times" and "signs of God's grace." In sacramental celebrations, particular situations are "no longer related to an undefined transcendence but concretely to God's loving presence and fidelity which comfort and call for decision." ["A Modern Approach to the Word of God and Sacraments of Christ: Perspectives and Principles," in Francis Eigo, O. S. A., ed., *The Sacraments of God's Love and Mercy Actualized.* (Villanova, PA. Villanova University Press, 1979) 77, 59–109.]

5. Raimundo Panikkar, "Man as Ritual Being" [*Chicago Studies 16*, (1977) 27], in William Crockett, *Eucharist: Symbol of Transformation* (New York: Pueblo Publishing Company, 1989) 263.

6. Aidan Kavanagh, *On Liturgical Theology* (New York: Pueblo Publishing Company, 1984) 116.

7. Rowan Williams, "Sacraments of the New Society," in David Brown and Ann Loades, eds., *Christ: The Sacramental Word* (London: SPCK, 1996) 89 (editor's note) 89–90, 94, 89–102.

8. The concept of the church as "the people of God" has now become foundational for liturgical and ecclesiastical renewal. An important source of this ecclesiology is the "Dogmatic Constitution on the Church" (*Lumen Gentium*, November 21, 1964) of Vatican II–a document whose profound implication has not yet been fully realized in the deconstruction of hierarchical and clericalist structures in the Roman and other Catholic churches, and among many other Christian denominations as well. For "a completely revised translation in inclusive language" of the basic documents of Vatican II, see Austin Flannery, O.P., ed., *The Basic Sixteen Documents of Vatican Council II*. (Newport, New York: Costello Publishing Company, 1996). The Council's "Constitution on the Sacred Liturgy (*Sacrosanctum Concilium*, December 4, 1963) remains a signature event in liturgical renewal in this century. In this regard, see also Mary Collins, O.S.B., "On Becoming a Sacramental Church Again," in David Efroymson and John Raines, eds., *Open Catholicism: The Tradition at its Best: Essays in Honor of Gerard S. Sloyan* (Collegeville, MN: The Liturgical Press, 1997) 111–128.

9. Daniel Berrigan, "Foreword," in John Dear, *The Sacrament of Civil Disobedience* (Baltimore: Fortkamp Publishing Company, 1994) xiii, xi–xvi.

10. Rendered traditionally in Latin, *sacramenti propter homines*, or "sacraments are for" and (literally) "on account of the people."

11. Elizabeth Schüssler Fiorenza, *Jesus, Miriam's Child, Sophia's Prophet: Critical Issues in Feminist Christology* (New York: Continuum, 1995) 14. With respect to liturgy in particular, Mary Collins notes such kyriarchy as a "privileging of the symbolic by office holders . . . ." Yet she also argues that "the power of the aesthetic is not 'power over'" and that a full "Catholic sacramental sensibility has opened worshipers to 'other meanings' than 'the Law of the Father,' and continues to do so." (In "On Becoming a Sacramental Church Again," 125.)

12. Aidan Kavanagh, *On Liturgical Theology*, 79.

13. "The First Apology of Justin Martyr," in Bard Thompson, ed., *Liturgies of the Western Church* (Cleveland and New York: Collins World, 1975) 9.

14. In parts of this section I reapply material presented in The Bradner Lectures for 1995 at the General Theological Seminary in New York City. The Bradner Lectures were adaptations from my *Arguing About Sex: The Rhetoric of Christian Sexual Morality* (Albany: State University of New York Press, 1995). Since I argued there that a mature ethical norm functions "sacramentally," I have been able to apply some of what I wrote about the formal structure and function of an ethical norm to liturgy and sacramental acts in general. In both treatments I also have been guided by a sacramental sensibility that was so thoroughly embedded in me by my own Roman Catholic tradition that no amount of dereliction on my part has been able to dispel it. For this undeserved grace I am most grateful.

15. In a general heuristic, sacramental theologies oscillate between more "catholic" traditions of "drawing to the surface" the sacred images and marks of grace that remain in creation after sin and more "protestant" traditions that emphasize the

coming of a "new creation." However all sacramental theologies share the note that consecration and sanctification are taking place in effective sacramental acts, and that this is the function and purpose of liturgy. It is to his credit that in his writing and teaching Marion J. Hatchett has moved easily between both of these poles while avoiding the ideological pitfalls of each. In his signature work, *Sanctifying Life, Time and Space: An Introduction to Liturgical Study* (San Francisco: Harper & Row, Copyright, Seabury Press, Inc, 1976), Hatchett sets out this comprehensiveness from the outset. Liturgy, he notes, is "a mirror of reality" and is "revelatory, as a source of light and life . . . " (7). At the same time "the whole of life, of time, of space is sanctified, *made* holy, by setting apart particular events, moments, and places" (12, emphasis added). Neither universalistic nor sectarian—"A religious sign, symbol, or sacrament has three frames of reference: the *world*, the *community*, the *eschaton*" (12). His approach to liturgy has also been marked by a robust gospel pragmatism where the proof of a liturgical rite is its meaning and effectiveness for the "upbuilding, and encouragement and consolation" of the church (1 Cor. 14:3). "Form follows function" (14) for Hatchett, and his impatience with all forms of narcissistic display and aestheticist pretension in liturgical celebration has been both edifying and legendary. In his scholarship and life, Marion Hatchett has exhibited the best of the Anglican/Episcopal "via media" and it is a pleasure to be his colleague and friend.

16. To have an adequate sacramental sensibility in the modern and postmodern worlds, several things are necessary: first, the literal must regularly fail to give an adequate account of our own life experience; and secondly, the world itself must *appear*, in Philip Wheelwright's words, as "a living reality." And in the face of postmodern challenges, a third quality is that we must care enough about our own experience of the world and that of others to continue to search for what Edward Farley has called "deep symbols." The principal characteristics of such a world of *height* and *depth*, Wheelwright goes on to say, are three: "it is presential and tensive; it is coalescent and interpenetrative; and it is perspectival and hence latent, revealing itself only partially, ambiguously, and through symbolic indirection." [*Metaphor and Reality* (Bloomington: Indiana University Press, 1968), 154, emphasis added]. It is only in such a world, phenomenally displayed in richly textured layers and multifaceted hues and dimensions—indeed, in *heights* and *depths*—that the work of sacraments and liturgy can take place. The fact that such a world is no longer the abiding assumption of our age leads Farley to an exploration of "the fate" of "words of power," or "deep and enduring symbols that shape the values of a society and guide the life of faith, morality, and action . . . ." [*Deep Symbols: Their Postmodern Effacement and Reclamation* (Valley Forge, Pennsylvania: Trinity Press International, 1996) 1].

17. Even though I do not believe that speculative metaphysics is necessary as a ground for either religion or sacraments, I do believe that at least we must make, as Philip Wheelwright suggests, "shy ontological claim(s)" (*Metaphor and Reality*, 162) first brought home to us in the figurative imagination of metaphor. The figurative language of metaphor and the metaphorical dimension of sacraments introduce us to worlds of imagination and obligation beyond our everyday sight: they give us a reach beyond our initial grasp and make conversion always an invitation and possibility. Wheelwright continues that such a richly textured world is "ultimately problematical" for all probing, and that there finally are only fragments for our grasp. But this too is a grace because there is always, in such a world, "something more than meets the eye, even the inner eye; the permanent possibility of extending one's imaginative awareness has no limits" (172). So too in our liturgical life it is always possible to say

and do something new—to find, amid our dissatisfaction with statistical realities and uncritical assumptions of everyday life, a metaphorical dimension that invites us into new worlds of faith and life, new and more vital relationships, new and more satisfying ties of obligation. This also recalls Paul Tillich's insistence on an eschatological horizon for Christian faith and life and his claim that our participation in the "Spiritual Presence" is always "in ambiguity and fragment." [*Systematic Theology* III (Chicago: University of Chicago Press, 1963) 138–141.]

18. For a more phenomenologically and existentially informed metaphysical/ ontological foundation for the "living reality" of sacramental acts, see Karl Rahner's "The Theology of the Symbol." [*Theological Investigations* Vol. IV, trans. Kevin Smyth, (Baltimore: Helicon Press, 1966) 221–252]. Here Rahner argues that "all beings are by their nature symbolic, because they necessarily 'express' themselves in order to attain their own nature" (224). Besides *being* in motion, all beings are multiple and, while called to communion, each bears the stamp of the finite, concrete, and particular and are "not simply and homogeneously the same in a deathlike collapse into identity" (225–226). The whole sacramental/symbolic process culminates in a communion of "knowledge and love" wherein *being* "expresses itself and possesses itself" by giving "itself away . . . into the 'other' . . . " (230).

19. Note the Latin *designare*—"to mark out," also "to point out the location," "to declare to be," "to name to a post or function," "to choose and set apart." *Designation* emphasizes the spatial and active dimensions of symbols—their visible and tactile presence beyond the verbal and auditory, their existence in visible and tangible rites and habits, and their naming/signing/symbolizing the physical stuff of everyday life for deeper experience, understanding and knowledge.

In a further comparison of symbol with metaphor, Paul Ricoeur argues: "there is something in a symbol (that) does not correspond to a metaphor . . . . Metaphor occurs in the already purified universe of the *logos,* while the symbol hesitates on the dividing line between *bios* and *logos.* It testifies to the primordial rootedness of Discourse in Life . . . . Symbols are bound within the sacred universe . . . . Symbols only come to language to the extent that the elements of the world themselves become transparent . . . This bound character of symbols makes all the difference between a symbol and a metaphor. The latter is the free invention of discourse; the former is bound to the cosmos" [*Interpretation Theory: Discourse and the Surplus of Meaning* (Fort Worth: Texas Christian University Press, 1976) 57, 59, 61–62, parens added].

20. See also Edward Schillebeeckx, *Marriage: Human Reality and Saving Mystery,* trans. N. D. Smith (New York: Sheed and Ward, 1965). And for more on the theology and ethics of Christian marriage as a sacramental office, vocation, and praxis in the Church, see my *Arguing About Sex.*

21. Note the Latin *demonstrare*—"to show," "to point out" and "manifest clearly, certainly, or unmistakably," "to illustrate." In this sense, disclosed and designated liturgically, sacramental models are "hands-on demonstrations" that show clearly how we are to believe and act as a new and renewed people of God. For a more complete discussion of model-theory in religion, ethics and theology, as well as more about the structure and function of metaphor and symbol, see Joseph Monti, *Arguing About Sex* (1995) 180–193, 147–211.

22. Still, there can never be any question of scale model perfection between our liturgies and our lives. However through analogy, what we model sacramentally remains empowering for conversion and transformation. Framed by the ever-present

distance between the ideal and the real, liturgy remains primarily the work of sinners rather than saints.

23. Bill Wylie Kellermann, *Seasons of Faith and Conscience: Kairos, Confession, and Liturgy* (Maryknoll, NY: Orbis Books, 1991) xix, xx–xxiii, italics added.

24. Bill Wylie Kellermann, *Seasons of Faith and Conscience*, xxiii.

25. For a good collection of reflections on "powers and principalities," see Bill Wylie Kellermann, ed., *A Keeper of the Word: The Selected Writings of William Stringfellow* (Grand Rapids, MI: Eerdmans, 1994. ("III Principalities and Powers") 185–292.

26. Paul Tillich, "Spiritual Presence," in *The Eternal Now* (New York: Charles Scribner's Sons, 1963) 84, 81–91. As *spirit*, the divine presence is ubiquitous and in no sense limited to traditionally sacred times and places. In "The Riddle of Inequality," Tillich writes: "There is no human condition into which the divine presence does not penetrate. This is what the Cross, the most extreme of all human conditions, tells us." [In *The Eternal Now*, 46, 36–46]. For a more systematic treatment of "The Spiritual Presence," see Tillich, *Systematic Theology* III, 111–161, and especially "The Media of the Spiritual Presence: Sacramental Encounters and the Sacraments," 120–128.

27. In "Sacraments of the New Society" (93), Rowan Williams points out that in the age of exploration and conquest "there was an immediate political linkage between being capable of receiving baptism and the capacity to be a 'citizen.' To be even potentially the object of affirming regard and adoption makes certain policies such as systematic enslavement of one group by another a good deal more problematic." Tragically however, "subsequent history shows how easily even grave theological tensions can be lived with, if the price is right . . . ."

28. Rowan Williams, "Sacraments of the New Society," 100.

29. John Updike, "The Music School," in Updike, *The Music School* (New York: Alfred A. Knopf, 1966) 190, 183–190.

30. Rowan Williams, "Sacraments of the New Society," 101, emphasis added.

31. Rafael Avila, *Worship and Politics*, trans. Alan Neely (Maryknoll, NY: Orbis Books, 1981) xii, (Alan Neely, "Translator's Foreword") 75–76, 81.

32. Rafael Avila, *Worship and Politics*, 100; 104.

33. *Eucharistize* is an archaic rendering (but with contemporary import) defined as "to consecrate as elements of the Lord's supper." In this sense, the city and world provide the elements for the church as the new body of Christ. For a further discussion of the challenge of neo-sectarianism, see Joseph Monti, "Dangerous Times and Obliging Places: A Response to the New Sectarianism," *Quarterly Review* (Winter 1993) 71–87, and Joseph Monti, *Arguing About Sex*, 4–50, 72–74, 82–86, 86–90, 331, 8.

34. Gibson Winter, *The Suburban Captivity of the Churches* (Garden City, NJ: Doubleday, 1961). Aidan Kavanagh, *On Liturgical Theology*, 33.

35. Aidan Kavanagh, *On Liturgical Theology*, 45, 44, 38, 42, 23–38, 39–51. But note also Wayne A. Meeks's point that like all who are perched on the boundaries between the old and new creations, there was also "a certain ambivalence about the towns, cities, and neighborhoods" in which most of the earliest converts to Christianity actually lived. However, despite their ambivalence, "it was in the neighborhoods and streets and households of those cities where the colonists of heaven had to rub elbows and do business . . . ." Such ambivalence about both city and world remains deep within the Christian story–a "love-hate relationship," like in many families, including the households of God. [*The Origins of Christian Morality: The First Two Centuries* (New Haven: Yale University Press, 1993) 12–13.]

36. In speaking of "sacramental thickness," I am recalling Clifford Geertz's

depiction of a hermeneutic of "thick description" in *The Interpretation of Cultures* (New York: Basic Books, 1973) 3–30. See also Edward Farley, *Deep Symbols*. For the relationship and difference between "structure" and "dimension" in terms of the phenomenology and theology of "The Spiritual Presence," see Paul Tillich, *Systematic Theology* III, 11–30.

37. Aidan Kavanagh, *On Liturgical Theology*, 60; and Mary Gordon, *Good Boys and Dead Girls* (New York: Viking, 1991)152, 150, 152, 148–152.

38. Regis A. Duffy, O.F.M., "At Table With Jesus: Sharing? Remembering? Thanksgiving? Dying? Obeying? Living? Sending?" (In Francis A. Eigo, O.S.A., *The Sacraments: God's Love and Mercy Actualized*, 111–142). A similar "priority . . . of the ethical over the ontological" is central to the work of Emmanuel Levinas. See for example, "Transcendence and Evil," in *Collected Philosophical Papers*, tr. by Alphonso Lingis (Dordrecht: Martinus Nijhoff, 1987) 183, 175–186.

39. Consequently, our liturgies are plagued by a familiar array of seductions: Duffy noting the "naive" and "dishonest use of religious symbols," our misreading of symbols, and "the ritual posturing that can pass for worship of God"; Kavanagh, how our symbols undergo "lingering deaths by trivialization"; and Juan Segundo, the logical result of trivialization, an aimless repetition resulting in "sacramental intoxication." Regis A. Duffy, O. F. M., *Real Presence*, 10, 17–18; 27; Aidan Kavanagh, *On Liturgical Theology*, 102; Juan Luis Segundo, S.J., *The Sacraments Today*, (in collaboration with the Peter Faver Center in Montevideo), trans. John Drury (Maryknoll, NY: Orbis Books, 1974) 34, and noted in David R. Newman, *Worship as Praise and Empowerment* (New York: The Pilgrim Press, 1988) 102, 157, 13. And for a challenging phenomenological ethic framed by the faces of those most in need, see Alphonso Lingis, *The "Community" of Those Who Have Nothing in Common* (Bloomington, IN: Indiana University Press, 1994).

40. Rosemary Haughton, *The Transformation of Man* (Paramus NJ: Deus Books, 1967) 248, and quoted in Kathleen Hughes, R.S.C.J., "Liturgy and Justice: An Intrinsic Relationship." [In Hughes and Mark R. Francis, C.S.V., eds., *Living No Longer for Ourselves: Liturgy and Justice in the Nineties* (Collegeville, MN: The Liturgical Press, 1991) 47.]

41. See Paul Tillich on the "ecstatic" (Gk *ek-stasis*] nature of the "Spiritual Presence," *Systematic Theology* III , 111–120, 129–138.

42. Wayne A. Meeks, *The Origins of Christian Morality*, 5, 12. On ritual, boundary situations, and thresholds or *liminality*, see Victor W. Turner, "Passages, Margins, and Poverty: Religious Symbols of Communitas," *Worship 46* (1972) 390–412, and noted in Hughes, "Liturgy and Justice," 47; see also Victor W. Turner, *The Ritual Process: Structure and Anti-Structure* (Chicago: Aldine Publishing Company, 1969), and noted in Hatchett, *Sanctifying Life, Time and Space*, 5.

43. Megan McKenna, *Rites of Justice: The Sacraments and Liturgy as Ethical Imperative* (Maryknoll, NY: Orbis Books, 1997) 5–6, 20; Wayne A. Meeks, *The Origins of Christian Morality*, 12, 14, 15, 91–110; see also J. A. Gimbernat, *"Predicación y crítica social,"* *Phase 10* (1970) 392; "The gospel is not a collection of recipes for the solution of problems, but an ethos that must be confronted with the experience of life." [In Joan Llopis, "The Message of Liberation in the Liturgy," trans. J. P. Donnelly, 73, in Herman Schmidt and David Powers, eds., *Politics and Liturgy*. Concilium Vol. 92 (New York: Herder and Herder, 1974) 65–73.]

44. Regis A. Duffy, O. F. M., *Real Presence: Worship, Sacraments and Commitment*, 16 (St. Augustine, Sermon 272); 18, 4, 6, 9, 13, 17, 22–23, 27, and 1–31.

45. Joseph Gelineau, *The Psalms: A New Translation* (Great Britain: Collins/Fontana Books, 1963) 5. See also the Latin, *pati, passio*–"capable of suffering," "endurance," "suffering" and *suffere*–"to bear (*ferre*), under (*sub*), hence to support." [In Eric Partridge, *Origins: A Short Etymological Dictionary of Modern English* (New York: Greenwich House, 1983) 475, 679.]

46. Wayne A. Meeks, *The Origins of Christian Morality*, 109.

47. Wayne A. Meeks, *The Origins of Christian Morality*, 109. For a note on the necessary relationship between "danger" and authenticity in Christian faith and life, see Paul Tillich, *Theology of Culture* (New York: Oxford University Press, 1959) 7. And for a good study of the need and practice of interpretation and discernment in the earliest Christian communities and now, see Luke Timothy Johnson, *Scripture and Discernment: Decision Making in the Church* (Nashville: Abingdon Press, 1996).

48. "Time-full" is a term of H. Richard Niebuhr in *The Responsible Self: An Essay in Christian Moral Philosophy* (New York: Harper & Row, 1963). For further discussion under the theme "The Church and the Conversation of History," see Joseph Monti, *Arguing About Sex*, 15–111.

49. Johann B. Metz, *Faith in History and Society: Toward a Practical Fundamental Theology*, trans. David Smith (New York, Seabury, 1980) 88–99. The entire chapter heading reads: "The dangerous memory of the freedom of Jesus Christ: The presence of the Church in society."

50. Johann B. Metz, *Faith in History and Society*, 100–118. The entire chapter heading reads: "The future in the memory of suffering: The dialectics of progress."

51. Paul Ricoeur, "The Memory of Suffering," in Ricoeur, *Figuring the Sacred: Religion, Narrative and Imagination*, ed., Mark I. Wallace, trans. David Pellauer (Minneapolis: Fortress, 1995) 289–290; 289–292.

52. Paul Ricoeur, "The Memory of Suffering," 290, 291.

53. Paul Ricoeur, "The Memory of Suffering," 291, 292. In the same vein Elie Wiesel comments: "I was much too religious not to question God" ("The Charlie Rose Show," Nov. 1995). See also Paul Tillich's interpretation of Rom. 8:26–27 in "The Paradox of Prayer": ". . . The Spirit helps us in our weakness." But that very Spirit also "intercedes for us with sighs too deep for words." "Sighing," Tillich continues, "is an expression of the weakness of our creaturely existence. Only in terms of wordless sighs can we approach God, and even these sighs are (God's) work in us." [Tillich, *The New Being* (New York: Charles Scribner's Sons, 1955) 135–138, emphasis/parens added]. And note Robert Gordis, in *A Faith for Moderns* (New York: Bloch, 1971): "The mystical classic, the Zohar, points out that when the heavenly gates are closed to prayers couched in words, they remain open to prayers couched in tears (Terumah). Quoted in David Birnbaum, *Good and Evil: A Jewish Perspective* (Hoboken, NJ: Ktav Publishing House, 1989). For an approach to theodicy interpreted in this light, see Joseph Monti "God in the Dock? Pastoral Ministry and the Justification of God in Late Modernity." *Anglican Theological Review LXXV*, No. 3, 315–344 (and from which much of this note is taken).

54. John Navone, "Evil and Its Symbols," in Herman Schmidt and David Powers, eds., *Politics and Liturgy*, 63, 62, 51–64.

55. Anne Lamott, *Bird by Bird: Some Instructions on Writing and Life* (New York: Anchor/Doubleday, 1994) 103, 104, 108, 109, emphasis added.

56. Wayne Meeks, *The Origins of Christian Morality*, 15, 17, 91–110, 189–210.

57. Paul Ricoeur, "The Hermeneutics of Testimony," in Paul Ricoeur: *Essays on Biblical Interpretation*, 122, 123, 130–131, 139, 133, 119–154.

58. Paul Ricoeur, "Toward a Hermeneutic of the Idea of Revelation," in Lewis S. Mudge, ed., Paul Ricoeur: *Essays on Biblical Interpretation* (Philadelphia: Fortress, 1980) 100, 100–101, 102, parens added, 73–118.

59. This parallels Paul Ricoeur's famous axiom *"Le symbole donne à penser"*–"The symbol 'gives rise to' and 'invites' the thought." ["The Hermeneutics of Symbols and Philosophical Reflection," in *The Philosophy of Paul Ricoeur,* edited by Charles E. Reagan and David Stewart (Boston: Beacon Press, 1978) 37]; See also, Paul Ricoeur, *The Symbolism of Evil,* trans. Emerson Buchanan (New York: Harper & Row Publishers, 1967) 347–357. And see also Edward Farley, *Deep Symbols,* 1, 3–8.

60. See Paul Ricoeur's discussion of revelation and "the poetic function" in "Toward a Hermeneutic of the Idea of Revelation." [In Paul Ricoeur: *Essays on Biblical Interpretation,* 101]. Contained here also is an outline of the reasons why scientific paradigms, no matter how artfully reconstructed or theologically attenuated, will never become congruent with the "poetic" center of religious experience and the church's liturgical life. Modes of being and discourse may coexist peaceably, but they are not interchangeable. For a display of the new, but uncritical, "coziness" between science and religion, see "Science Finds God," *Newsweek* (July 20, 1998).

61. The epitome of a poetics and liturgics of evil in our century, if not in human history, were the rituals of National Socialism.

62. Kathleen Stewart, *A Space on the Side of the Road: Cultural Poetics in an 'Other' America* (Princeton, NJ: Princeton University Press, 1996) 3, parens and emphasis added.

63. Kathleen Stewart, *A Space on the Side of the Road,* 3–4, emphasis added.

64. James Agee and Walker Evans, *Let us Now Praise Famous Men: Three Tenant Families* (New York: Ballantine Books, 1960, first published 1939). See also Karen Lebacqz, "Implications for a Theory of Justice," in Lebacqz, *Justice in an Unjust World.* [In Wayne G. Boulton, et. al., eds., *From Christ to the World: Introductory Readings in Christian Ethics* (Grand Rapids, MI: W. B. Eerdmans, 1994)255, 254–260]; and Gordon W. Lathrop, *Holy Things: A Liturgical Theology* (Minneapolis, MN: Fortress Press, 1993) 208.

65. Carlo Levi, *Christ Stopped at Eboli,* trans. Frances Frenaye (New York: Time Incorporated, 1964) xiii ("Editor's Preface") 1–2, emphasis added.

66. bell hooks, "Representations of Whiteness in the Black Imagination," in *Killing Rage: Ending Racism* (New York: Henry Holt, 1995) 45–46, 31–50.

67. Edward S. Casey, *Getting Back into Place: Toward a Renewed Understanding of the Place-World* (Bloomington & Indianapolis: Indiana University Press, 1993) 301–302. For a recent work on the theology and ethics of domesticity, see Thomas E. Breidenthal, *Christian Households: The Sanctification of Nearness* (Cambridge, MA: Cowley, 1997).

68. Nicholas Lash, "Eagles and Sheep: Christianity and the Public Order Beyond Modernity," in Lash, *The Beginning and the End of "Religion"* (Cambridge: Cambridge University Press, 1996) 236, 227, 236, 219–236.

69. Norbert Lofink, quoted in Walter J. Burghardt, S.J., *Preaching the Just Word* (New Haven: Yale University Press, 1996) 5; Aidan Kavanagh, *On Liturgical Theology,* 163, 164, and Chapter Eight: "Liturgy and Normality," 151–176.

70. Aidan Kavanagh, *On Liturgical Theology,* 157, 166, 168, 173, 165, 175. Orthopraxis –a critically informed "right" ethos and action of liberation and justice–is now in wide use in "Liberation Theology" and beyond. [See Gustavo Gutierrez, *A Theology of Liberation,* trans. Sr. Carida Inda and John Eagleson (Maryknoll, NY: Orbis Books, 1973) 10.]

71. Jürgen Moltmann, "The Liberating Feast," trans. Francis McDonagh, in Schmidt and Powers, *Politics and Liturgy*, 84 [quoting A. A. van Ruler, *Droom en Gestalte* (1947), and *Gestaltwerdung Christi in der Welt*] 77, 83, 84.

72. Jürgen Moltmann, "The Liberating Feast," 76, 76–77, parens added.

73. Joseph Gelineau, "Celebrating the Paschal Liberation," trans. V. Green, in Schmidt and Powers, *Politics and Liturgy*, 109, 111, 107–119.

74. Joseph Gelineau, "Celebrating the Paschal Liberation," 111, 112. See also Timothy F. Sedgwick, *Sacramental Ethics: Paschal Identity and the Christian Life* (Philadelphia: Fortress Press, 1987). And see Ernest Becker's analysis of radical evil where he notes, often with tragic results, the modern confusion of the symbolic and literal functions–such as when we literally plan for and technically carry out the destruction of others to symbolically gain life for ourselves. This is the new "ritual technics" of evil epitomized in categorical murders of racial, ethnic and religious identity, and in weapons of mass destruction. [*Escape from Evil* (New York: Free Press, 1975.)]

75. Joseph Gelineau, "Celebrating the Paschal Liberation," 115, 119.

76. Joseph Gelineau, "Celebrating the Paschal Liberation," 118. "The prayer of humble access" is traditional before communion in "Rite One" of the Book of Common Prayer (New York: The Church Hymnal Corporation, 1986).

77. Rowan Williams, "Sacraments of the New Society," 100. In "On Becoming a Sacramental Church Again," Mary Collins describes this "hope" as a "recovery of a genuinely sacramental liturgy that sanctions once again the play of the Christian religious imagination engaged in the demands of faith . . . " (p.114).

78. James Agee and Walker Evans, *Let us Now Praise Famous Men*, 17, 419.

79. Joseph Monti, "Let us Now Sing the Praises of Famous Men and of Others for Whom There is No Memory." Homily preached at The School of Theology, Sewanee Tennessee, November 1, 1991. Also contained in Joseph Monti, "Sermon: The Tent of Our Meeting," *Sewanee Theological Review 41:1* (1997) 10–15, parens and emphasis added.

80. James Agee, "On the Porch: 3," in Agee and Walker, *Let us Now Praise Famous Men*, 428, 419–428.

A Singing Clarity,
a Steady Vision:
Marion Hatchett's Work as a
Teacher of Liturgical Music

Carol Doran*

THE ASSOCIATION OF DIOCESAN Liturgy and Music Commissions included almost as many words in its Annual Award to Marion Hatchett in November 1997 as he spoke in his response to their presentation.[1] In naming the ways Dr. Hatchett has served the larger church and in listing his publications, the whereases became a dizzying recitation of more accomplishments, leadership, contributions and scholarship than any would imagine an individual able to achieve in a single lifetime. The award spoke good humor akin to Marion's own, and poignant acknowledgment that even those for whom the larger church holds towering respect may not be immune to the changes and chances of life.

Dr. Hatchett's contribution to the music of the Episcopal Church is not specifically mentioned in this award, even though the account of his service to the larger church indicates that he has served on the Standing Commission on Church Music, was Chairman of the Text Committee for *The Hymnal 1982* and Chairman of the subcommittee on Anglican Chant. He also continues to serve as a substitute organist in his local congregation. The list of his publications also indicates his interest in and knowledge of church music: *Music for the Church Year, Hymnal Studies Five: A Liturgical Index to The*

*The author wishes to express appreciation to Marian Barnett, Neil Alexander and Marion Hatchett for making available printed and recorded material used in this essay.

Hymnal 1982, Hymnal Studies Eight: A Scriptural Index to the Hymnal 1982, A Manual for Clergy and Musicians, A Guide to the Practice of Church Music, and "significant contributions toward *The Hymnal 1982.*"

Detailed though it is, even this careful accounting omits reference to Marion Hatchett's work as a teacher of music to seminarians during his thirty years at the School of Theology of the University of the South at Sewanee, Tennessee. There is no commendation in the award of his patient and systematic attention to the art, science and tradition of music within the wider discipline of liturgics. The extent to which his steadfast advocacy of music in theological education has influenced the church, while not widely realized, is immeasurable.

As Marion Hatchett's institutional teaching ministry of music draws to a close, however, we find particular reason to consider its significance. What is the value of a teaching ministry which intentionally forms future clergy for their responsibilities as "final authority in the administration of matters pertaining to music"?[2] What leads a recognized liturgical scholar consistently to allot significant time and effort to teaching future clergy about the church's music? And, given the rarity of fine music education for seminarians, which Marion Hatchett has built and consistently maintained for many years at Sewanee, what implications for the future of rich and creative liturgical practice in the Episcopal Church are raised when the one who originated and faithfully guided a seminary's music teaching ministry no longer participates in charting curricular direction.

Gifts and Training in Music

It is possible that many who know Marion Hatchett's work in liturgics may be unaware of his gifts and skills in music. In fact, his music training began in childhood when he studied piano, and continued with organ lessons while a student at Wofford College. During his own seminary training at Sewanee, Marion served as a student organist and has continued to play the organ during his many years of seminary teaching.[3]

Dr. Hatchett's convictions about the importance of music in the church are expressed most often in reasoned and direct statements:

> From the early days of the Church, music has been integral to the worship of God. Music gives solemnity, beauty, joy, and enthusiasm to the worship of the community. It imparts a sense of unity and sets an appropriate tone for a particular celebration. It is an effective evangelistic tool. It nourishes and strengthens faith and assists worshipers in expressing and sharing their faith. It heightens texts so that they speak more fully and more cogently. It highlights the basic structure of the rites. It expresses and communicates feelings and

meanings which cannot be put into words. As Messiaen expressed it, "The joy of music is that it can go beyond words–which are too precise. Music can express what there is in the soul." (*Newsweek,* November 23, 1970, 139) Music however must not dominate the liturgy; all elements of liturgy must work in harmony. Music, and the other arts, including speech, serve together in the liturgical action.[4]

Seeds of Hatchett's Concern for Music Education for Seminarians

But his steady work to develop the music component of the liturgics curriculum at Sewanee seems to have at its heart a conviction which exceeds logic. He acknowledges without hesitation that this concern for teaching seminarians music originated in a reaction to his post-seminary parish experience. When Marion Hatchett was deacon, or priest-in-charge, and later Rector of the Church of the Incarnation, Gaffney, South Carolina, (1951–57), after his seminary graduation, the quality of parish music was entirely dependent upon music leadership available from a nearby college. Liturgy often flourished or floundered on the basis of transitory student musical talent.[5] The parish grew to become self-supporting during the four-and-a-half years of Hatchett's leadership, but he did not escape the frustrating task of working with a new organist every year.[6]

In 1957 Marion Hatchett and Carolyn Carter Hatchett, who had been married in June, 1956, moved to Charleston, South Carolina, a major commercial and cultural center since colonial times. Here the musical challenge to liturgical renewal was the 1916 Episcopal *Hymnal* in the pew racks. Like many young clerics before him, Hatchett had to develop "in service" the skills necessary to maintain the shape of his own liturgical ministry and to provide patient and consistent catechesis for the people while in the midst of a reigning congregational consensus which strongly favored Victorian music.

In his subsequent seminary teaching and in his writing, Marion Hatchett has recognized the compelling need to draw seminarians into education in music so that they might be prepared for similar pastoral challenges. He has written:

> The rector has special responsibilities for the music program, for ultimately the rector is responsible for hiring and firing, for entering into contracts or letters of agreement with church musicians. The rector, as chair of the vestry, has some oversight of the music budget. As chair of the liturgy committee and as chief liturgical officer of the parish, the rector is in a position to exercise a tremendous influence on the music program.[7]

Priestly Formation at Sewanee

Marion Hatchett's own formation for professional ministry took place in the seminary to which he eventually would return as a member of the faculty. The School of Theology of the University of the South, Sewanee, Tennessee, was founded as a Theological Department of the University in 1878.[8] The department of Liturgics and Ecclesiastical Music was added very shortly after (in 1882–1883). The second bishop of Florida, John Freeman Young, taught a summer course in liturgics in 1882[9] and continued as a faculty lecturer and seminary choir director[10] until his death in 1885.[11] The inclusion of music in the liturgics course is indicated by Bishop Young's wide-ranging course bibliography, which lists two books on English church music: Jebb's *Choral Service*, and Dyce's *Common Prayer with Plain Tune*.[12]

But unfortunately, the ecclesiastical music aspect of the curriculum appears to have had an uncertain mandate. In the 1886–1887 catalog, the department of Liturgics and Ecclesiastical Music was listed, but faculty with responsibility for teaching courses in that area were missing. By the following year, 1887–1888, the department had disappeared.[13]

The teaching of liturgics appeared to be no more stable in the years that followed. Armentrout writes that the subject "in the early days" was taught within the lectures on "Ecclesiastical Polity,"[14] and later in classes designated "Theology," "Church Polity" or "Ecclesiastical History."[15] During the tenure of Dean William Porcher DuBose (1894–1908), there was no professor of liturgics at all and music education for seminarians was not available because of funding shortages.

Until 1961, the curriculum at Sewanee's School of Theology included music education for seminarians only on an intermittent basis. In 1931–1932 a course titled "Voice Culture," taught by Mr. Hirons, the University Organist, entered the curriculum. But in 1933–1934, these "Lectures and exercises in the fundamentals of voice production" became an elective and subsequently were not offered at all.[16] In 1936–1937, Professor Yerkes expanded the teaching of liturgics into a course called "History of Christian Liturgics" and added church music, "a study of Christian hymnody, psalmody and chanting of services."[17]

Although a number of other musicians have taught ecclesiastical music at Sewanee, their appointments have been part-time and, for the most part, short-lived. William Whitlock Lemonds, who taught from 1960–1963, achieved the rank of Associate Professor of Music, and Thomas Edward Camp, the librarian of the School of Theology, was also an instructor in Church Music, for a total of nine years, from 1958–1960 and 1966–1973.[18]

When Marion Hatchett entered the seminary as a student in 1948, the curriculum included two required courses in liturgy and a less stringent expectation that students "were supposed to gather together and practice the services and get some instruction in music." By Hatchett's own description, however, these sessions "had a low priority on the agenda of many students and attendance was very low normally." Although liturgies regularly were prayed in St. Luke's Chapel, few included music.

> When I was in seminary, either morning prayer or evening prayer was said in St. Luke's chapel every day. Frequently, but not with any regularity, Evening Prayer would be sung. There were two celebrations of Eucharist during the week. Typically there was no music with either of those.[19]

Scholarly Development

In 1938, a teacher and liturgist whose presence strongly influenced Marion Hatchett to pursue seminary education at Sewanee, joined the School of Theology's faculty.[20] Bayard Hale Jones (1887–1957) during his tenure on the national Liturgical Commission (1934–1957) had guided the work on the revision of the Daily Office lectionary, which was authorized in 1943. He also had made outstanding contributions to the Prayer Book Studies series which eventually led to the development of the present Book of Common Prayer.[21]

The weight of the Dr. Jones's influence on the young seminarian makes appropriate the inclusion here of excerpts from the minutes of the Standing Liturgical Commission, June 25–27, 1957, following his death:

> ... A life-long interest in liturgical studies, supported by an unusual equipment in languages both ancient and modern, gave to Dr. Jones a competence in his special field of learning, which in the annals of our Church, has been unexcelled. ... Dr. Jones' learning was matched by an unusual power of expression both in his speech and his writing—lucid, well-organized, trenchant and vivacious. He knew how to give clarity and life to complicated and technical subject matter. In his approach to liturgical questions he was never doctrinaire, nor partisan, and though he had strong convictions, based upon his extensive knowledge of facts, he was always reasonable, open-minded and fair in discussion, afraid neither of altering his views, nor of admitting his persuasion when convinced by the arguments of others. Questions submitted to him received thorough and prompt attention; his letters are testimony to the labor he exacted from himself to provide accurate and detailed information for those seeking his help and advice. He had little patience with obstructionist tactics or captious judgments; but his generous nature and keen sense of humor often cleared the atmosphere of tense situations. In all that he did for the Commission, Dr. Jones kept ever in mind the needs of the whole Church. His sympathy for divergent points of view, when honestly held, was one of his most unusual

qualities, and few men have had so intelligent a grasp of both the extent and the limits of comprehensiveness in the Church. Above everything else, he never sought advantage for himself, much less advantage for any party or partisan group, but worked only for the good of the Church in all its wholeness and fullness of truth. . . .[22]

Marion Hatchett studied liturgics and English church history under Bayard Jones. Both Jones's leading role in the movement toward Prayer Book revision and his "colorful character" impressed the young seminarian.

He was certainly one of the first American Episcopalians who was aware of Hippolytus or other things which have shaped revision in liturgy in the last several years. He took shots at preciousness and modeled a very straightforward, simple celebration of the Eucharist that had been thought out in terms of sacramental theology.[23]

At a time when no one who was teaching liturgy in the Episcopal Church had an earned doctorate in that subject, Bayard Jones had earned strong credentials as a liturgical scholar. His continuing scholarship, publications and teaching provided a substantial foundation for Massey Shepherd and the group of young liturgical scholars who began their own work in the late fifties and early sixties: H. Boone Porter, Leonel Mitchell, Thomas Talley, Louis Weil and Marion Hatchett.[24]

Hatchett entered the company of scholars in 1965 when, after fourteen years in parish ministry, he resumed full-time liturgical studies. He chose the General Theological Seminary for this work, drawn by the publications and the person of H. Boone Porter, who was professor of liturgy there.

Already I had known of him through some things he had published—for example, *The Day of Light.* I was very favorably impressed by him. He was a warm person and a meticulous scholar. He already was involved in liturgical revision at that point. He was on the Standing Liturgical Commission and was part of the first Trial Use. He continued very prominently in the process up to the approval of the proposed book. He was questioning the various new forms of ministry and eventually left teaching at General to head up Roanridge and then went on to be editor of *The Living Church.* He constantly challenged and stretched my thinking. I continue to find him a real source of inspiration.[25]

Early Years as a Sewanee Faculty Member

Marion Hatchett's appointment to the faculty of the School of Theology of the University of the South in January 1969, was as Assistant Professor of Liturgics and Music. He was the first full-time professor of this subject appointed since the death in 1957 of Dr. Bayard Jones.[26] The class schedule and requirements for liturgy and music that year were much as they had been when Hatchett had graduated from Sewanee in 1951. The catalog for that year states music requirements in general terms:

The students of the School of Theology are required to become familiar with the fundamentals of music and voice production with emphasis on the music of the Church as found in the *Hymnal 1940*, the Psalter, and the Choral Service.[27]

The seminary's intention to increase emphasis on liturgy[28] with the appointment of Marion Hatchett also included an increased emphasis on church music as a natural outcome of the young professor's understanding of the inherent partnership between the two disciplines. The catalog's outline of courses indicates the addition that year of a new course, "Choir and Church Music," where "Choir" previously had been. The "Church Music" course was

a survey of the development of Church Music, with particular emphasis upon the Anglican tradition. Discussion of the pastor's responsibility for congregational and choir music. One year. Required of Juniors and Special Students.[29]

He also offered a new one-term elective titled "The Choral Service," which was "Advanced training in the liturgical music for Morning and Evening Prayer, the Litany, and the Holy Communion."[30]

Hatchett's description of the continuing "choir practice" course, which seminarians did not take seriously even in his own seminary days, is indicative of the situation from which he has built the present curriculum in liturgics and church music.

Still the hour a week which was generally referred to as "choir practice" got very low attendance. In fact, we eventually "took roll" and two people actually flunked one year. But after two or three years of that curriculum with my giving an occasional lecture on music in the liturgy class, we did a major renovation of the curriculum.[31]

When Hatchett returned as a faculty member to Sewanee in 1969, the use of music in seminary liturgies also took essentially the same pattern as they had during his own student days: Morning Prayer five days a week, Evening Prayer once. Morning hymns and canticles were sung at least two or three days weekly. Evening Prayer had some music and frequently was sung; this liturgy also was the occasion for senior sermons.

Singing at the eucharist, however, was infrequent. The seminary chapel did not have eucharist on red-letter days. Nor were there any Holy Week liturgies. Students were expected to attend services at the university on red-letter days and would attend Holy Week liturgies at their field work parish.

Early Growth in the Music Program

From the earliest days of Hatchett's tenure, his teaching expanded beyond traditional lectures to draw students to share his passion for liturgy and to expand their understanding of liturgical and musical possibilities. During his first year as a faculty member, he led students in reconstructing and celebrating some historic rites.

> I remember when we had the first celebration of the Hippolytus's rite at the Sewanee Inn—how shocking and how thrilling that was for many. Then we went on to do various other rites, from the first century up through the Reformation and from various Prayer Books. This has tended to free students up. Even though by necessity some of the liturgies were hastily prepared, they seemed to get more out of them than simply reading the text.

> A number of students and other people as well have done historic liturgies in their parishes and have felt that they freed people up to face liturgical changes.[32]

His approach to teaching music to seminarians was equally innovative. With the assistance of his wife, Carolyn, who is a professional music teacher, Hatchett initiated an introductory (or makeup) course in reading music for incoming students who had little or no music reading ability. Their systematic and detailed approach to developing music reading uses musical examples from *The Hymnal 1982* in learning to sing and to play tunes at the keyboard.[33] Students are divided according to ability into groups of five or six which meet on three Saturdays for five hours early in the semester. This skill enables seminarians eventually to be confident and enthusiastic liturgical cantors and officiants.

Student appreciation of the importance of learning to read music was not always immediate.

> Some of them have confessed that while they had not much enthusiasm for music and certainly not for singing, they found that after they had gotten into the parish they were very grateful for the preparation they had had. And a couple who swore they would never sing ran into a situation shortly after graduation where being able to sing the prefaces and things like that was one of the prerequisites for anyone applying for the position they were being considered for.

> Even while they are students, the ability to read music has been helpful when, in the middler and senior year, they participate in liturgical planning meetings in the seminary, and when they are called upon to function as cantor or officiant in services that are sung.

> In any of our planning sessions, the student has to defend his or her choices in terms of text. Sometimes the student will add, "Here is a text that has two tunes, but this tune would be better in Advent or Lent and this one better during the

Great Fifty Days." This is illustrated by the difference between the tunes at numbers twenty-five and twenty-six in *The Hymnal 1982*. Twenty-five (Tallis' *Eighth Tune*), would be good for general use. Twenty-six (*Conditor alme siderun*), which is plainchant, is associated with an Advent hymn, "Creator of the Stars of Night" (*H82*, 60). This would be better for use in Advent for the *Phos Hilaron* text and maybe also for Lent. The *Tallis canon* tune would better suit more festal times or Ordinary time.[34]

Continuing Development

Comparisons of seminary curricula and course offerings in the succeeding years indicates the magnitude of change which accompanied the evolution of Sewanee's program of liturgical and musical education. The *Annual Catalogue, 1969–70* shows the addition of elective courses in "Christian Initiation," "The Eucharist in the Early Church" and "Liturgy and the Parish" taught by Professor Hatchett in addition to his continuing music teaching in the "Choral Service" and the required "Church Music" and "Choir Rehearsal" courses.

The *Bulletin* for 1972–1973 of the School of Theology at Sewanee carries a four-line "Worship" paragraph (7) which lists the sites of seminary worship services and is identical to information on this subject published in preceding *Bulletin* issues. But a second, new paragraph under "Curriculum" in that book (16, titled "Worship") indicates a changing institutional understanding of the role of the seminary's liturgical prayer in forming future church leaders.

St. Luke's Chapel is a teaching chapel where the community gathers in the presence of the risen Lord to acknowledge His Lordship and to receive His grace through His Word and Sacraments, in order to grow in a living relationship with Him and with each other, while at the same time becoming aware of both the why and how of worship. The skills of leading public worship are learned by experiences of exposure to various rites and to various styles of leadership. This happens through participation in the leadership roles, through critiquing the performances of others and receiving feedback upon one's own performances, and through developing guidelines for the planning of services and the evaluation of rites and ceremonies.

This volume also is the first to indicate the presence of a liturgics practicum in all three years. This practicum, which gives considerable attention to church music, is described in detail in the 1975–1976 issue of the *Bulletin*:

Students meet once a week for Liturgics Practicum. It is divided into three parts: the first is the practice of music to be used in the services of worship in the Chapel; the second is a presentation of the historical background of contemporary rites and ceremonies, as well as information about the seasonal emphases of the Church's worship and of the observance of specific Red Letter

Days; and the third is a cluster of special interest groups in the areas of basic rudiments of music, planning for services, chanting the choral service, altar guild instruction, and the liturgical year. The overall objective of Liturgics Practicum is to prepare the student for a leadership role in the direction and use of music within the liturgical worship of the Church. (15)

Hatchett speaks of the years when Dean George Alexander (1955–1972) and, subsequently, Dean Urban ("Terry") Holmes led the school as times of particularly significant progress in the teaching of liturgy and music. Attendance improved at the daily office, and eucharists with music were scheduled on red letter days. When it became clear that students involved in field work were not being exposed to the resources of the "Green Book," the seminary began scheduling the proper liturgies for Holy Week.[35]

The 1981–1982 *Catalog* includes a photograph of a liturgical celebration with the caption, "The Liturgy is Central in Seminary Life" (19). By the time of the publication of the 1982–1983 issue of this book, the entry titled "Worship" (17) had been expanded to reflect expectations of regular chapel attendance by students as well as liturgical planning and "supervised practical experience, particularly in relation to church music."

Another significant milestone in the liturgical life of the seminary came in the fall of 1984 when the community moved into its present building. In preparation for the move, the liturgical schedule was re-evaluated. The decision was made to include music in the liturgy of morning prayer four days a week, one of which would be a "sung" service with the psalms sung from either the plainchant or Anglican chant psalter; evening prayer would include music two days a week, one of which would be a "sung" service.

Music would also be integral to the principal eucharist of the week (eleven o'clock on Wednesday morning). The old "choir practice" was replaced by brief rehearsals prior to community liturgies. Simplified Anglican Chant was used for the psalter at Wednesday evening prayer. Learning was more by exposure and use than by scheduled practice periods. (More recently, a choir has been organized, directed by Susan Rupert, to lead the congregation in singing the Wednesday morning eucharist.)

At this time or earlier, the decision was made that each student would have to function musically in the chapel. Every student would have to sing at least one gradual psalm. Each student would have to sing at least one Morning Prayer and one Evening Prayer service. Thus, in effect, graduation requirements from that time forward included singing.[36]

The Present Situation

In the early 1980s, Sewanee's catalogs began to describe the seminary curriculum as "integrated." In 1988–1989, yet another curricular revision turned again toward a "basic core curriculum."[37] As the descriptive and organizing terms shift, however, the steady foundation of liturgical and musical education for seminarians not only remains firm, but gradually shows itself to be growing in strength and diversity.

> The [present] curriculum is grounded in worship. Students and faculty gather each day for morning prayer and for a weekly community Eucharist. Through participation in the church's liturgical life, students deepen their awareness of the meaning of worship and are provided opportunities to develop their skills in the ordering and conducting of a variety of prayer book rites. Students and faculty participate in planning, leading, and preaching in services. . . .[38]

Marion Hatchett teaches three major liturgics courses at the present time which include church music and are integral to the school's present curriculum.

Liturgics I includes among the learning objectives, "Preparation for singing in the services." Topics for class presentations include "Pointing and singing collects," "Practice as Cantor," "Singing the daily office (includes class assignment to prepare and sing certain selections from *The Hymnal 1982*)," "Singing the Prayers of the People," and "Music for the Proper Liturgies for Special Days." Susan Rupert assists Dr. Hatchett in working with students in class.[39]

For the Middler Liturgics course, on the development of the liturgy and liturgical theology, students are expected to buy both accompaniment volumes for *The Hymnal 1982* and to bring them to class (on specific days). *The Companion to The Hymnal 1982* is on the class reading list. Recommended reading includes, in addition to Dr. Hatchett's own books on music, five books on the music which is integral to the church's history. In dealing with each historical period at least one session is devoted to the church music of the period. Some examples: One day's lecture is titled, "The 1604, 1637 and 1662 BCP's and Church Music of the Sixteenth Century (Continental and Anglican)." Another day's lecture concentrates on "Anglican Eucharistic Prayers (1549–1928), Early American Folk Hymnody, and Church Music of the Nineteenth Century." Another day's lecture includes "Church Music of the Twentieth Century."[40]

The Senior Liturgics course includes reading assignments from *Hymnal Studies Three, Four, Five, Seven* and *Eight*, in addition to *Environment and Art in Catholic Worship*, *The Holy Eucharist (Altar edition)* and Dr. Hatchett's own books on music. Assignments direct students to practice altar edition music. On Day Seven presentations include "The Role of Music, Musical Ministries; Directors and Instrumentalists, including interviewing prospective organists, contracts and hiring and firing; Purchase and upkeep of organs. Day Eight considers "Evaluating hymns and other music; educating and inspiring a congregation, teaching new music and dealing with liturgical change" and the class on Day Nine covers "Singing Proper Prefaces (both simple and solemn tones)," with students expected to sing aloud in class.

The present curriculum continues the Practicum in Music Reading, which is as it has been from the beginning of the Hatchetts' work at Sewanee, a series of Saturday sessions which provide seminarians practical instruction in music and sight-reading. And there is a Practicum in Voice available as well. This latter course, taught by Susan Rupert, offers instruction in learning to sing the officiant's part in liturgical services.

About the liturgics and church music curriculum, one recent catalog notes the following:

> Over the course of three years the student is prepared to function liturgically in a parish through study of the development of liturgies, of liturgical theology, and of liturgical music from primitive cultures up to *The Book of Common Prayer* (1979) and *The Hymnal 1982* and beyond, and through study of the relationship of liturgy to preaching and pastoral care. In classes and through participation in worship planning meetings, the student is prepared for the planning of services. The student is prepared to administer a church music program and to sing the musical portions of the various rites. Practical experience in various liturgical ministries is gained through participation on the chapel ROTA.

A further note continues on the subject of the chapel ROTA:

> Though it carries no academic credit, participation on the chapel ROTA is required of all Master of Divinity (M.Div.) Students. Those on the ROTA for particular periods of time take part in the planning of services, prepare the service sheets, and function as officiants, as lectors, as cantors, as thurifers, as crucifers, as servers, and as ministers of Holy Communion in chapel services.

One has only to hold that 85-page ROTA (containing liturgical leadership assignments for August 27 through December 17, 1997) in one's hand to sense the seriousness with which responsibilities for leadership of daily seminary worship is undertaken. It should be said, however, that the choice of the engraving adorning its cover and the irony of the mischievously fabricated statement (a comment on the choir's authority?) describing the scene, add a healthy balance here. An ecclesiastical gathering involving hundreds of people within and without the rood screen is labeled:

> "The Sistine Chapel in a sixteenth century engraving. This engraving depicts a ROTA meeting in session. The choir sang (and adjudicated proceedings) from the small inset on the right wall."

Although Marion reports that the choice of the print and the "explanatory" note were the work of a student, faculty approval to print obviously came from one who is willing to aid and abet a trickster. His own restrained expressions of humor have been an effective tool in his teaching, both at Sewanee and in workshops and lectures presented to clergy and musicians across the country, particularly as he advises against liturgical extremes. "Thurifers should avoid 'around the worlds' in a small liturgical space," he says quietly.

The School of Theology also has two choral groups at the present time which are open to all students, their spouses, faculty and other community members. One group provides music for the community's Wednesday eucharist and the other sings a weekly choral evensong service.

The summer program at Sewanee's School of Theology was established in 1937 originally "to afford clergymen an opportunity for post-ordination study, in close personal contact with recognized leaders of theological knowledge and interpretation." During Marion Hatchett's tenure liturgical education offered in that program has been developed to include continuing education for musicians as well as clergy. "The Eucharist" course, for example, includes "the roles of the cantor and the choir" as a possible topic for discussion or for a class paper. The course description for the "Christian Initiation and the Pastoral Offices" course begins, "Theological, liturgical, musical and pastoral aspects of the rites of Christian initiation and of the principal Pastoral Offices . . . ." Those enrolled in that course are able to choose as a class project, "Music for weddings" or "Music for funerals."

Another graduate summer school course taught by Dr. Hatchett, "Liturgical Architecture, Furnishings, Vessels and Vestments," includes discussion of the placement of choirs and organs and of acoustics.

The summer school course which appears to contain the strongest music component by far is "The Church Year and the Daily Office." The classes treat psalms, canticles, office hymns, seasonal hymns, current hymnal revisions, as well as the significance of thematic and symbolic connections inherent in the themes of a number of new seasonable hymns (baptismal themes in Lent, for example, or Passover imagery). Discussions, papers or presentations for this course could include methods of singing the psalms, the role of a choir, metrical canticles, metrical psalms, and cathedral versus parish church music traditions.

An Inestimable Gift

How shall we appropriately describe the value of the program of liturgical and musical education for seminarians, in-service clergy and musicians that Marion Hatchett has built at the School of Theology at the University of the South? Something which cannot be replaced at any cost must be valued as priceless. Appropriating the concept of music education as integral to theological education, systematically building courses and programs by positioning one curricular element upon another, weathering the inevitable storms of criticism and resistance from both faculty and students—each of these is a remarkable achievement in itself. But when Marion Hatchett's scholarship and publications are added to that sum and his contributions to the Episcopal Church's liturgical renewal through the work of the Standing Liturgical Commission are tallied together, we must acknowledge all these with both awe and gratitude.

Marion Hatchett's ability and steadfast determination to pursue the solution to a presenting question or challenge has been applied with equal vigor whether encountering the mystery in an ancient liturgical manuscript or the need of the student body to learn to sing a new musical form. His scholarly publications attest to his steadfastness in the former matter; the multitude of slim three-ring folders containing gradual psalm texts together with photocopied simplified Anglican chants for use in community liturgies indicate his attentiveness to the latter.

He has done more than recommend that congregations be helped to learn new hymn tunes by hearing them played on the organ several weeks before they are asked to learn and sing them. He has produced a monumental notebook collection of chorale preludes for the organ, based on many of the tunes in the present hymnal, for the Sewanee chapel organist's use. Each time they are played, the point and value of the recommendation wordlessly is made.

But his strong ideas are not impervious to suggestions for change. An early decision to include the Palm Sunday Liturgy in the Holy Week schedule later was reconsidered and abandoned when it became clear that students were experiencing those (but not necessarily the Triduum) liturgies in their field work parishes. The original plan of scheduling liturgical responsibilities for students according to alphabetical order gave way to scheduling ROTA groups for seven-week periods so that their engagement with liturgical duties was more concentrated and their learnings made more secure by frequent repetition within a shorter period.

Certainly the experience of trial use and introducing the present Book of

Common Prayer has shown Marion's willingness to be flexible when substantial cause requires it. Working with *The Liturgy of the Lord's Supper* at the start of his seminary teaching, then introducing what he calls "the jolly green giant," and eventually the draft proposed Book of Common Prayer obviously put Marion into the role of advocate for change rather than for status quo.

And that ability to negotiate and manage change might be seen as one of the qualities which has enabled Dr. Hatchett to realize the program in liturgics and music which has been built at Sewanee. One wonders, for example, what might be a greater test of leadership than the challenge of introducing the use of incense in a seminary chapel where this practice previously had not been the local custom. Dr. Hatchett relates that when incense first was used in the seminary chapel in the early 1970s,

> A couple of faculty people and couple of students took great exception to its use. And there were people who coughed and carried on. [But after that class had graduated,] it was taken for granted by everyone that we would use incense on certain high days.[41]

Hatchett says that in general the faculty was "pretty responsive" to the changes he suggested.

> There was some negativity about changes in the chapel schedule, but most people went along with it. Some even were enthusiastic about it.

Marion Hatchett's ministry of music has been strongly hospitable and he has taught others that quality. His courses often require students to prepare the service sheet for a particular liturgy so that they might learn to produce clear layouts that enable people to participate more fully and easily in the liturgy. Even as he introduces students to the practical benefits of using new hymns as choir anthems and seeking opportunities to teach new music in informal situations, he has emphasized the ability of hymns to inform and inspire the people. The choice of hymns for liturgy is important because they are "people's 'take-home' package," he has said.

> The choice of hymns is almost more important than the choice of prayers or the production of the sermon. Just as the lectionary is designed to cover a broad range of scripture, so conscientious clergy and church musicians should make use of as broad a range as possible of the hymns in the hymnal and not just fall back on a few old tried-and-true favorites. It is not fair *not* to introduce as many as possible of the great hymns of the church to the people.[42]

The School of Theology of the University of the South undoubtedly has one of the finest and most comprehensive programs of liturgy and church music for the M.Div. curriculum of all the accredited seminaries in the Episcopal Church. The genesis of its growth and development may be traced to 1969, when the school appointed the Reverend Doctor Marion Josiah Hatchett to teach liturgics and church music. In building this program to its present strength, Dr. Hatchett, secure in his position as a respected scholar and liturgist, has graciously, steadfastly, and systematically included music education for seminarians in the vision of excellence toward which he has worked over the last thirty years. The church, through the work of the many clergy and musicians who have learned from him, has benefitted profoundly from his teaching ministry and the faith which has informed it.

Next spring both he and Carolyn will retire. We shall greatly miss them both.

Notes

1. *ADLMC Newsletter* (the newsletter of the Association of Diocesan Liturgy and Music Commissions), fourth quarter issue (1997) 8–11.

2. *The Constitutions and Canons of the Episcopal Church*, Canon 24, Section 1.

3. Telephone conversation with Dr. Hatchett, September 9, 1998.

4. Hatchett, Marion J. *A Guide to the Practice of Church Music* (New York, The Church Hymnal Corporation, 1989) 15.

5. Telephone conversation with Dr. Hatchett, September 9, 1998.

6. Ibid.

7. Hatchett, *A Guide to the Practice of Church Music*, 35.

8. Armentrout, Donald Smith, *The Quest for the Informed Priest: A History of the School of Theology* (Sewanee TN, 1979) iii.

9. Armentrout, *Quest*, 77.

10. Armentrout, *Quest, 89.*

11. Armentrout, *Quest*, p. 75.

12. Armentrout, *Quest*, 90.

13. Armentrout, *Quest*, 75.

14. Armentrout, *Quest*, 83.

15. Armentrout, *Quest*, 127.

16. Armentrout, *Quest*, 213.

17. Armentrout, *Quest*, 213.

18. Armentrout, *Quest*, 438.

19. Taped interview (tape one) with Marion Hatchett conducted by Marian Barnett in August 1998.

20. Hatchett, Marion J., "Bayard Hale Jones: A Reminiscence," *Sewanee Theological Review*, 39:2 (1996) 105.

21. Hatchett, "Bayard Hale Jones . . . ," 108–9.

22. Armentrout, *Quest*, 239.

23. Taped interview (tape one) with Dr. Hatchett conducted by Marian Barnett in August 1998.

24. Ibid.

25. Ibid.

26. Armentrout, *Quest*, 349.

27. *Announcements for 1969, 1970*, the School of Theology and Graduate School of Theology of the University of the South, Sewanee, Tennessee, 20.

WITH EVER JOYFUL HEARTS

28. Taped interview (tape one) with Dr. Hatchett conducted by Marian Barnett in August 1998.

29. *Announcements for 1969–1970,* The School of Theology and Graduate School of Theology of the University of the South, Sewanee, Tennessee, 30.

30. Ibid.

31. Taped Interview (tape one) with Dr. Hatchett conducted by Marian Barnett in August 1998.

32. Taped interview (tape one) with Dr. Hatchett conducted by Marian Barnett in August 1998.

33. Reading Music," an unpublished course of study developed by Carolyn Hatchett.

34. Taped interview (tape three).

35. Taped Interview (tape one).

36. Taped Interview (tape one).

37. Seminary *Catalog 1992–1993,* 9.

38. Seminary *Catalog 1993–1994,* 9

39. Dr. Hatchett's class syllabus, "Liturgics I" (Spring 1997).

40. "Middler Liturgics" class syllabus (Fall 1997–1998).

41. Taped interview (tape three).

42. Taped interview (tape two).

Marion Josiah Hatchett:
An Academic History
and Bibliography

Don S. Armentrout

MARION JOSIAH HATCHETT was born in Monroe, North Carolina on July 19, 1927, the son of Oliver Howard Hatchett and Myrtle (Harvey) Hatchett. Oliver Howard Hatchett was an ordained Methodist pastor. Marion Hatchett was confirmed in December 1946 while a senior at Wofford College, Spartanburg, South Carolina, from which he received his Bachelor of Arts degree in 1947. He received his Bachelor of Divinity degree (now the Master of Divinity) from the School of Theology, University of the South, in 1951. Hatchett was ordained deacon on June 13, 1951, and began his ministry as curate at the Church of the Advent, Spartanburg, and as deacon-in-charge of the Church of the Incarnation, Gaffney, and the Church of the Atonement, Blacksburg, all in the Diocese of Upper South Carolina, where he remained until November 1952.

Hatchett was ordained priest on June 25, 1952. In November 1952, he resigned as curate of the Church of the Advent, Spartanburg, to devote himself full-time to the Church of the Incarnation, Gaffney. He was priest-in-charge in Gaffney from 1952 until 1955 when the mission became a parish and he became the Rector. He served as Rector until March 1957. While in Gaffney, he met and on June 16, 1956, married Carolyn Carter of Lake City, South Carolina. They have three children: Martha Louise, born December 25, 1959; Ann Carter, born April 22, 1966; and John Kershaw Harvey, born September 27, 1972. When he came to the Gaffney mission in 1951, the Church of the Incarnation had 35 members and 25 communicants. When he left in 1957, it had 89 members and 68 communicants, and had moved from mission to parish status.

On March 24, 1957, Hatchett transferred from the Diocese of Upper South Carolina to the Diocese of South Carolina where he became Rector of St. Peter's Church, Charleston, and chaplain to Episcopal students at the Citadel. He served in these positions until July 1, 1965. When he began his ministry at St. Peter's the church had 575 members and 423 communicants, and when he left in 1965 it had 641 members and 429 communicants, despite flight from that area of the city to the suburbs during this period. While at St. Peter's, Hatchett served in the following diocesan positions: chairman of the College Work Division, 1957–1959, 1962–1965; Board of Examining Chaplains, 1963–1965; and chairman of the Commission on Church Music, 1963–1965. He was also a member of the Commission on Evangelism and the Commission on Christian Education.

On September 1965, Hatchett began his graduate studies at the General Theological Seminary, where he remained in residence until January 1969. In 1967 he received his Master of Sacred Theology (S.T.M.) degree. The title of his thesis was "Thomas Cranmer and the Rites of Christian Initiation." He received his Doctor of Theology (Th.D.) in 1972; the title of his dissertation was "The Making of the First American Prayer Book." He was a Fellow at General and while there assisted at Christ Church, Bay Ridge, Brooklyn, New York. While at the General Seminary, he also studied at New York University, Union Theological Seminary and St. Vladimir's Orthodox Theological Seminary.

Hatchett began his duties at the School of Theology on February 1, 1969, as Assistant Professor of Liturgics and Music. In 1974, he became Associate Professor of Liturgics and Music. In 1981 he became Professor of Liturgics and Music. Hatchett was named the Cleveland Keith Benedict Professor of Pastoral Theology on January 15, 1991. (Benedict was Dean of the School of Theology, November 30, 1910–June 10, 1922).

At the national level, Hatchett was a member of the Standing Commission on Church Music, 1974–1985, the Standing Liturgical Commission, 1977–1982, and the General Board of Examining Chaplains, 1988–1994. He was a member of the Committee on Hymns and the Hymnal of the Standing Commission on Church Music, and was chairman of the Text Committee for *The Hymnal 1982*. He was a member of the Committee on the Eucharist, the Committee on the Use of Scripture, and the Committee on Rubrics of the Standing Liturgical Commission. Hatchett was chairman of the Committee for the *Book of Occasional Services*.

While at the School of Theology, Hatchett has taught the following courses in the Master of Divinity program:

Liturgics, Christian Worship: Theology of Worship; the Jewish background; the origin and development of Christian liturgical forms. Primary emphasis is given to the history, meaning, and use of the liturgies of Holy Baptism and the Eucharist (1968-69, 1969–70);

The Choral Service: Advanced training in the liturgical music for Morning and Evening Prayer, the Litany, and the Holy Communion (1968–69, 1969–70, 1970–71, 1971–72, 1972–73, 1973–74);

Church Music: A survey of the development of church music, with particular emphasis upon the Anglican tradition. Discussion of the pastor's responsibility for congregational and choir music (1968–69, 1969–70, 1970–71, 1971–72);

The Book of Common Prayer: The history, contents, and use of the Book of Common Prayer; practical instruction in the ministration of the services of the church (1969–70, 1972–73);

Christian Initiation: The administration of Catechism, Baptism, Confirmation, and First Communion in successive periods in church history and consideration of some of the problems involved in Christian Initiation today. Particular attention was given to the rites of Holy Week and Easter (1969–70, 1970–71, 1971–72);

The Eucharist in the Early Church: The development of the eucharistic rite up to the time of Alcuin, in terms of its history, and in relation to our contemporary and ecumenical situation (1969–70, 1970–71, 1971-72);

Liturgy and the Parish: A study of contemporary concepts pertaining to the effective ordering of worship and to the relating of worship to the educational, pastoral, and missionary obligations of the Christian community (1969–70, 1970–71, 1971–72);

Guided Studies: Hymnody: The study of an aspect of Hymnody (1970–71, 1971–72);

Prayer Book Studies XVIII-XXIV: Consideration of the rites approved for Trial Use by the 1970 General Convention and comparison of them with other recent revisions and proposals within English-speaking Christendom (1970–71, 1971–72);

Guided Studies: Liturgics: The study of an aspect of liturgics (1971–72);

Special Studies in Liturgics: The study of an aspect of liturgics, the area determined by instructor and students in conversation (1973–74);

Theology of the New Initiatory Rites: The theology and liturgy of the rites of baptism and confirmation in *Prayer Book Studies 26*, and the preparation of the laity for their participation in the rites (1973–74, 1974–75);

Creative Liturgics Worship: The study and creation of two dimensional visual images as vehicles of meaning in the liturgical setting (1973–74);

The Proposed Book of Common Prayer: An examination of the contents and rationale of the book, and guidelines and exercises in its use (1977–78, 1979–80);

Architecture for Christian Worship: A study of the relationship of church architecture to liturgy throughout the ages, with particular attention to new buildings and renovations designed for the new rites which incorporate the insights of the liturgical movement (1978–79, 1980–81); *Guided Study in Liturgics*: History and practice of liturgy (1978–79);

Vestments and Allied Ecclesiastical Arts: A seminar on the history and use of vestments. Students either prepared papers for presentation or design and/or produced vestments or hangings for their own use or for use in the chapel (1979–80, 1981–82, 1984–85, this course was nicknamed "sewing for Jesus");

Theology of the New Prayer Book (1980–81, 1982–83);

Introducing The Hymnal 1982: This course included an examination of the principles upon which the hymnal revision was based, a study of the hymn texts and the hymn and service music, with emphasis on the theology of the hymnal and its liturgical use and on introducing the new hymnal in a congregation (1985–86);

Church Architecture, Furnishings, Vessels, and Vestments: In this course the students studied the development of church architecture, furnishings, vessels, and vestments and their relationship to the liturgy and liturgical theology (1987–88);

Introduction to Liturgics and Church Music: An introduction to the study of liturgy, to the contents of the liturgical books, the principles of religious ceremonial, and the planning and conduct of rites (1988–89, 1989–90, 1990–91);

Historical Development of the Liturgy: A study of the historical development of liturgical texts, ceremonial, music, and liturgical theology (1988–89, 1989–90, 1990–91);

Pastoral Liturgy: A study of the contents and theology of the current liturgical books and their pastoral implications and implementation (1988–89, 1989–90, 1990–91); and conduct of rites (1988–99) theology (1988–99) and implementation (1988–99).

In the Advanced Degrees program, Hatchett has taught the following courses

Christian Initiation: A study of the history of Christian Initiation, with special attention to recent discoveries, and a consideration of problems involved in revision of the rites and preparation for candidates (1972);

The Eucharist in the Early Church: The development of the Eucharistic rite up to the ninth century, in terms of its history and theology, and in relation to our contemporary pastoral and ecumenical situation (1973);

Rites of Ordination: A study of the rites of ordination down through the centuries with a consideration of problems of intercommunion and reunion (1975);

The Rites of Passage: The theological, liturgical, and pastoral aspects of the principal "rites of passage"–initiation, marriage, childbirth, excommunication, and burial–and current trends in the ways in which the crisis points are being met, and revisions in rites associated with them, will be studied against the background of primitive and historic Christian rites (1976);

The Eucharist: The development of the eucharistic rite in terms of its history and theology, and in relation to the contemporary pastoral and ecumenical situation (1976, 1979);

The Daily Office: The development of the daily hours of prayer, the daily office, in terms of history and rationale, with particular attention to the recent revisions of the Episcopal, Roman Catholic, and Lutheran Churches and the new proposed ecumenical daily office (1980);

Christian Initiation and the Development of the Church Year: The development of the rites of Christian Initiation (baptism and confirmation), in terms of history and rationale, with particular attention to their relationships of the church year and to recent revisions of the initiation rites and the church year of various denominations (1982);

Liturgy and Pastoral Care: Theological, liturgical, and pastoral aspects of the principal "pastoral services"–rites related to marriage, childbirth, sickness, reconciliation of a penitent, and death–and revisions of rites associated with them will be studied against the background of primitive and historic Christian rites (1984);

The Hymnal 1982: This course included an examination of the principles upon which the hymnal revision was based and a study of the hymns texts and the hymn and service music, with emphasis on the theology of the hymnal and its liturgical use and on introducing the new hymnal in a congregation (1986);

Christian Initiation and the Pastoral Offices [same description as Liturgy and Pastoral Care] (1988);

The Church Year and the Daily Office: A study of the historical development of the daily office and of the church year with attention to theological, liturgical, musical, and pastoral aspects (1989);

Eucharistic Theology and Practice: A study of eucharistic theology and its liturgical expression (1990);

Christian Initiation, the Catechumenate, and Evangelism: Theological, liturgical, musical, and pastoral aspects of the catechumenate and the rites of Christian Initiation, with their background in primitive and historic

Christian rites, will be studied with particular emphasis on their implications for the Decade of Evangelism (1991);

Liturgical Architecture, Furnishings, Vessels, and Vestments: A study of the historical development of church architecture, furnishings, vessels, and vestments with particular attention to the influence of the Liturgical Movement and to the statements in recent years in the major denominations (1996).

Hatchett was on sabbatical leave for the academic year, 1975–1976, and for the Spring semesters of 1983, 1990, and 1998.

Hatchett has been the outside reader and examiner for two Ph.D. dissertations which have been published with these titles: Byron D. Stuhlman. *Redeeming the Time: An Historical and Theological Study of the Church's Rule of Prayer and the Regular Services of the Church.* New York: Church Hymnal Corporation, 1992. [Ph.D. from Duke University]; and Lesley A. Northup. "The 1892 Book of Common Prayer." *Toronto Studies in Theology,* Volume 65. Lewiston: Edwin Mellen Press, 1993. [Ph.D. from Catholic University]

Bibliography: Books

Music for the Church Year: A Handbook for Clergymen, Organists, and Choir Directors. New York: Seabury Press. 1964. Reprint, 1967.

Lenten Prayers for Everyman. New York: Morehouse-Barlow; London: A. R. Mowbray, 1967.

Sanctifying Life, Time and Space: An Introduction to Liturgical Study. New York: Seabury Press, 1976. Reprinted with updating after the adoption of The Proposed Book of Common Prayer (1976) by Seabury Press. That edition was reprinted by Harper & Row.

A Manual of Ceremonial for the New Prayer Book. Sewanee, TN: St. Luke's Journal of Theology, 1977.

A Manual for Clergy and Church Musicians. New York: Church Hymnal Corporation, 1981.

Commentary on the American Prayer Book. New York: Seabury Press, 1981. Reprinted by HarperSan Francisco (An imprint of Harper Collins), 1995.

Eucharistic Rites of Historic Prayer Books. Sewanee, TN: St. Luke's Journal of Theology, 1981.

The Making of the First American Book of Common Prayer. New York: Seabury Press, 1982.

Hymnal Studies Five: A Liturgical Index to The Hymnal 1982. New York: Church Hymnal Corporation, 1986.

Hymnal Studies Eight: A Scriptural Index to The Hymnal 1982. New York: Church Hymnal Corporation, 1988.

The Altar Guild Handbook (with Anne K. LeCroy). Based on the Book of Common Prayer and the *Book of Occasional Services.* New York: Harper and Row, 1988.

A Guide to the Practice of Church Music. New York: Church Hymnal Corporation, 1989.

Essays in Collections:

"The Layman as a Leader of Worship within the Anglican Tradition with Special Reference to the Armed Forces," in *The Layman as a Leader of Worship.* NAVPERS 15155, Department of the Navy (1968) 27–34.

"The Anglican Liturgical Tradition," in *The Anglican Tradition,* ed. Richard Holloway. Wilton, CT: Morehouse-Barlow (1984) 45–77.

"The Bible in Worship," in *Anglicanism and the Bible,* ed. Frederick Houk Borsch. Wilton, CT: Morehouse-Barlow (1984) 81–115.

"Architectural Implications of the Book of Common Prayer 1979," *Occasional Papers, No. 7* (Standing Liturgical Commission of the Episcopal Church), December 1984 Reprinted in *Open* [the newsletter of Associated Parishes], (August 1985) 11–16, and in *The Occasional Papers of the Standing Liturgical Commission,* Number One. New York: Church Hymnal Corporation (1987) 57–66.

"Prayer Books," in *The Study of Anglicanism,* ed. Stephen Sykes and John E. Booty. London: SPCK; Philadelphia: Fortress Press (1988) 121–133.

"The Eucharistic Rite of the Stowe Missal," in *Time and Community: In Honor of Thomas J. Talley,* ed. J. Neil Alexander. Washington: Pastoral Press (1990) 153–170.

"Benjamin Franklin's Prayer Book," in *This Sacred History: Anglican Reflections for John Booty,* ed. Donald S. Armentrout. Cambridge, MA:Cowley Publications (1990) 89–97.

"Military Prayer Books," in *Creation and Liturgy: In honor of H. Boone Porter,* ed. Ralph N. McMichael, Jr. Washington: Pastoral Press (1997) 69–92.

"The Traditional Anglican Liturgy (1662)," in *The Complete Library of Christian Worship,* ed. Robert E. Webber. Vol. II: *Twenty Centuries of Christian Worship.* Nashville: Star Song Publishing Group (1993–1994) 204–216.

"Unfinished Business in Prayer Book Revision," in *Leaps and Boundaries: The Prayer Book in the 21st Century,* ed. Paul V. Marshall and Lesley A. Northup. Harrisburg, PA: Morehouse Publishing (1997) 3–41.

The Hymnal 1982 Companion, Raymond F. Glover, general editor. 3 Volumes. New York: Church Hymnal Corporation, 1992–1994:

Articles in Volume I (1992): "The Great Vigil of Easter," 116–117; "Holy Baptism," 118–120; "The Holy Eucharist," 121–128.

Biography in Volume II (1994): "J. T. White," 664–665.

Commentary in Volume III (1994): *Texts:* "All hail the power of Jesus' Name!" (450, 451) 846–854; "Come away to the skies" (213) 429–433; "O God, we praise thee, and confess" (364) 672–677; "What wondrous love is this" (439) 825–831; "When Jesus Wept" ((715) 1328–1330.

Tunes: "Birmingham" (437) 820–825; "Bourbon" (146, 675) 293–295; "Charlestown" (571) 1060–1063; "Coronation" (450) 846–854; "Detroit" (674) 1245–1248; "Dunlap's Creek" (276) 533–537; "Foundation (636)," 1162–1165; "Holy Manna (238, 580)," 471–474; "Kedron" (10, 163) 22–25; "Land of Rest" (304, 620) 579–582; "Light" (667) 1226–1229; "Mannheim" (595) 1096–1098; "Middlebury" (213) 429–433; "Morning Song" (9, 583) 14–22; "Nettleton" (686) 1268–1273; "New Britain" (671) 1236–1243; "Pleading Savior" (586) 1082–1085; "Resignation" (664) "Restoration" (550) 1020–1023; "Salvation" (243) 480–482; "Star in the East" (118) 245–248; "Tender Thought" (702)," 1311–1314; "The Church's Desolation" (566) 1045–1052; "Vernon" (638) 1166–1171; "When Jesus Wept" (715) 1328–1330; "Wondrous Love" (439) 825–831.

Articles in *An Episcopal Dictionary of the Church: A User-Friendly Reference for Episcopalians*, Don S. Armentrout and Robert B. Slocum eds. New York: Church Publishing Incorporated, 1999:

"Acolyte," "Alexander, Cecil Frances (Humphreys)," "Baroque," "Black Letter Days," "The Book Annexed," "Bridges, Robert Seymour," "Cantate Domino," "Confiteor," "Confratoria," "Ellerton, John," "Gelesian Sacramentary," "Golden Number," "Gothic," "Hermann von Wied of Cologne," "'Hobart Chancel'" "Hymns Ancient and Modern," "Infant Communion," "Jones, Bayard Hale," "Liturgy of the Table," "Liturgy of the Word," "Lucernaria, Lucernarium," "Metrical Index," "'Mission Services' or 'Third Services,'" "Musical Settings," "Obsecrations," "Olney Hymns," "The Ordinal," "The Ornaments Rubric," "Prayer Book Commentaries," "Prayer Book Preface," "Prayer Book Revisions," "Preparation of the Table," "Proposed Book (1786)," "Proposed Book of Common Prayer (1976)," "Sancta sanctis," "Sarum Rite," "Service Music," "Shape-Note Hymnody," "Southern Harmony," "Stabat Mater," "Stir-up Sunday," "Tucker, Francis Bland," "Upjohn, Richard," "Watts, Isaac," "We Sing of God: A Hymnal for Children," "'Wee Bookies,'" "Willan, Healey," "Winkworth, Catherine," 'Wordsworth, Christopher."

Don S. Armentrout

Articles in Periodicals

"Charles Hartshorne's Critique of Christian Theology." *Anglican Theological Review 48* (July 1966) 264–275.

"Initiation: Baptism or Ordination." *St. Luke's Journal of Theology 12* (September 1969) 17–22. Reprinted in *Open* (the newsletter of Associated Parishes) (January 1979) 11–13.

"Recent Anglican Revisions of the Eucharistic Rite." *American Church Quarterly 6* (Winter 1969–70) 203–211.

"Historic Liturgies in Action." *St. Luke's Journal of Theology 12* (March 1970) 40–45.

"The First American Trial Liturgy." *St. Luke's Journal of Theology 14* (September 1971) 20–27.

"Where Are We Headed in Liturgics?" *St. Luke's Journal of Theology 15* (January 1972) 3–11.

"An Updated Annotated Bibliography in Liturgics." *St. Luke's Journal of Theology 15* (June 1972) 54–72.

"An Introduction to Liturgical Study." *St. Luke's Journal of Theology 15* (September 1972) 19–158. Reprinted separately by *St. Luke's Journal of Theology.*

"Seven Pre-Reformation Eucharistic Rites." *St. Luke's Journal of Theology 16* (June 1973) 13–115. Reprinted separately by *St. Luke's Journal of Theology* and Education for Ministry.

"A Manual of Ceremonial." *St. Luke's Journal of Theology 17* (March 1974) 19–84. Reprinted separately by *St. Luke's Journal of Theology.*

"The Rite of 'Confirmation' in the Book of Common Prayer and in Authorized Services 1973." *Anglican Theological Review 56* (July 1974) 292–310.

With John M. Gessell, Urban T. Holmes and David H. Fisher. "Validity in the Pilgrim Church." *The Virginia Churchman 133* (November 1974) 9.

"Draft Proposed Book." *Worship 50* (May 1976) 213–237.

"101 Reasons Why I Would Have to Vote for the Draft Proposed Book of Common Prayer Rather than for Retention of the 1928 Edition." *St. Luke's Journal of Theology 19* (June 1976) 177–194.

"Celebrating the Eucharist in 1776." *The Living Church 173* (September 26, 1976) 8–10.

"A Sunday Service in 1776 or Thereabouts." *Historical Magazine of the Protestant Episcopal Church 45* (December 1976) 369–385. Reprinted separately by *Historical Magazine.*

"The New Book: A Continuation of or Departure from the Tradition." *Open* (June 1977) 4–11.

"Planning Music for the Holy Eucharist." *Open* (August 1979) 9–16.

"Advent." *St. Luke's Journal of Theology 23* (December 1979) 11–13.

"Lent." *St. Luke's Journal of Theology 23* (March 1980) 87–89.

"Eucharist As Celebration." *National Bulletin on Liturgy 13* (November–December 1980)

"Twenty-five Years of Eucharistic Development." *National Bulletin on Liturgy 15* (January–February 1982) 29–42.

"The Drama of the Eucharist." *College of Preachers Newsletter 29* (Spring 1983) 1–2, 4.

"The Use of 'Amen' after Hymns." *Newsletter of the Association of Anglican Musicians* (May 1983) 8–9.

"Footwashing in Jerusalem." *The Living Church 188* (March 25, 1984) 9–10.

"Epiphany, A Time to be Baptized." *Liturgy: Journal of the Liturgical Conference 4* (Summer 1984) 65–67.

"The Word in Sound and Silence." *Liturgy: Journal of the Liturgical Conference 6* (Spring 1987) 21–25.

"How Long Should a Normal Sunday Service Be?" *Newsletter of the Association of Diocesan Liturgy and Music Commissions* (Holy Cross 1990) 1–3.

"Benjamin Shaw and Charles H. Spilman's *Columbian Harmony*." *The Hymn 42* (January 1991) 20–23.

"Rhythms of Time: Natural and Unnatural." *Reformed Liturgy and Music 25* (Winter 1991) 7–10.

"Teaching about the Holy Eucharist." *Newsletter of the Association of Diocesan Liturgy and Music Commissions* (Pentecost 1991) 3–6.

"Three Little-Known West Tennessee Four-Shape Shape-Note Tunebooks." *The Hymn 42* (July 1991) 10–16.

"Samuel L. Metcalf's *Kentucky Harmonist*." *The Hymn 43* (April 1992) 9–14.

"Early East Tennessee Shape-Note Tunebooks." *The Hymn 46* (July 1995) 28–45.

"Ministry Through the Book of Common Prayer: Legends, Lies, and Cherished Myths about Prayerbook Revision." *Sewanee Theological Review 38* (Pentecost 1995) 267–280.

"Bayard Hale Jones: A Reminiscence." *Sewanee Theological Review 39* (Easter 1996) 105–117.

"Marion Hatchett's Response" [to ADLMC Annual Award (1997)]. *Newsletter of the Association of Diocesan Liturgy and Music Commissions* (Fourth Quarter Issue 1997) 9–11.

Don S. Armentrout

Pamphlet

Hatchett was convener and chair of the ecumenical Committee for a Common Eucharistic Prayer, which published, with an introduction and end notes written by him, *A Common Eucharistic Prayer (1975)*. This prayer has been included in several recent liturgical books, including the Book of Common Prayer of the Episcopal Church [Prayer D], *Word, Bread, Cup* of the Consultation on Church Union [Eucharistic Prayer III], *Supplemental Worship Resources 9: At the Lord's Table: A Communion Service Book for Use by the Minister* [United Methodist, Great Thanksgiving 6], the *Book of Alternative Services of the Anglican Church of Canada* [Prayer 6], the *Book of Common Worship* of the Presbyterian Church (USA), the Cumberland Presbyterian Church [Great Thanksgiving F], and *Eucharistic Worship in Ecumenical Contexts: The Lima Liturgy–and Beyond,* Thomas F. Best and Dagmar Heller, eds. (Geneva: World Council of Churches, 1998.) This prayer, with his introduction and notes is scheduled for publication in *Coena Domini II,* Irmgard Pahl, ed. (forthcoming).

[Note: I would like to thank Shawn Horton, faculty secretary at the School of Theology, for her helpful assistance, and Wendy Watterson, summer intern, 1998, at the School of Theology for her research.DSM]

Contributors

William Seth Adams is the J. Milton Richardson Professor of Liturgics and Anglican Studies at the Episcopal Theological Seminary of the Southwest, Austin, Texas.

J. Neil Alexander is Professor of Liturgics and Homiletics at the School of Theology of the University of the South, Sewanee, Tennessee.

Donald S. Armentrout is Associate Dean for Academic Affairs and Professor of Ecclesiastical History at the School of Theology of the University of the South, Sewanee, Tennessee.

Jill S. Burnett is a doctoral candidate in liturgical studies in the Graduate School of Drew University, Madison, New Jersey.

Joe G. Burnett is Professor of Pastoral Theology at the School of Theology of the University of the South, Sewanee, Tennessee.

Carol Doran is Professor of Worship and Pastoral Music at Bexley Hall Divinity School, Rochester, New York.

Harry Eskew is Professor of Music and Music Librarian at the New Orleans Baptist Theological Seminary, New Orleans, Louisiana.

William H. Hethcock is Professor Emeritus of Homiletics at the School of Theology of the University of the South, Sewanee, Tennessee.

David Holeton is Professor of Liturgics at the Hussite Theological Faculty of the Charles University, Prague, Czechoslovakia.

Paul V. Marshall is the Bishop of the Episcopal Diocese of Bethlehem, Pennsylvania.

Ruth E. Meyers is Associate Professor of Liturgics at the Seabury-Western Theological Seminary, Evanston, Illinois.

Leonel L. Mitchell is Professor Emeritus of Liturgics at the Seabury-Western Theological Seminary, Evanston, Illinois.

Contributors

Linda L.B. Moeller is Associate for Worship and Education at the Parish of Trinity Church (Episcopal), New York, New York.

Joseph E. Monti is Associate Professor of Moral Theology at the School of Theology of the University of the South, Sewanee, Tennessee.

David W. Music is Professor of Church Music at the Southwestern Baptist Theological Seminary, Fort Worth, Texas.

Lesley A. Northup is Associate Professor in the Department of Religious Studies at Florida International University, Miami, Florida.

H. Boone Porter was for many years the editor of *The Living Church* after serving as Professor of Liturgics at both Nashotah House, Nashotah, Wisconsin, and the General Theological Seminary, New York, New York.

Charles P. Price is the William Meade Professor of Systematic Theology Emeritus at the Protestant Episcopal Theological Seminary in Virginia, Alexandria, Virginia.

George Wayne Smith is Rector of St. Andrew's Episcopal Church, Des Moines, Iowa.

Daniel Stevick is Professor Emeritus of Liturgics and Homiletics at the Episcopal Divinity School, Cambridge, Massachusetts.

Byron D. Stuhlman is Rector of Grace Episcopal Church, Waterville, New York.

Thomas J. Talley is Professor Emeritus of Liturgics at the General Theological Seminary, New York, New York.

Louis Weil is the James F. Hodges Professor of Liturgics at the Church Divinity School of the Pacific, Berkeley, California.